A COMPANION TO VERGIL'S AENEID
AND ITS TRADITION

BLACKWELL COMPANIONS TO THE ANCIENT WORLD

This series provides sophisticated and authoritative overviews of periods of ancient history, genres of classical literature, and the most important themes in ancient culture. Each volume comprises approximately twenty-five and forty concise essays written by individual scholars within their area of specialization. The essays are written in a clear, provocative, and lively manner, designed for an international audience of scholars, students, and general readers.

A COMPANION TO VERGIL's *AENEID* AND ITS TRADITION

Edited by

Joseph Farrell and Michael C.J. Putnam

WILEY Blackwell

Registered Office
John Wiley & Sons, Ltd, The Atrium, Southern Gate, Chichester, West Sussex, PO19 8SQ, UK

Editorial Offices
350 Main Street, Malden, MA 02148-5020, USA
9600 Garsington Road, Oxford, OX4 2DQ, UK
The Atrium, Southern Gate, Chichester, West Sussex, PO19 8SQ, UK

For details of our global editorial offices, for customer services, and for information about
how to apply for permission to reuse the copyright material in this book please see our website at
www.wiley.com/wiley-blackwell.

Library of Congress Cataloging-in-Publication Data

A companion to Vergil's Aeneid and its tradition / edited by Joseph Farrell and Michael C.J. Putnam.
      p. cm. – (Blackwell companions to the ancient world)
    Includes bibliographical references and index.
    ISBN 978-1-4051-7577-7 (hardcover: alk. paper) ISBN 978-1-118-78512-6 (pbk. : alk. paper)
1. Vergil. Aeneis.   2. Vergil–Appreciation.   3. Epic poetry, Latin–History and criticism.   4. Aeneas
(Legendary character) in literature.   I. Farrell, Joseph.   II. Putnam, Michael C.J.
    PA6825.C64 2010
    873'.01–dc22

                                   2009027225

A catalogue record for this book is available from the British Library.

Cover image: Angelica Kauffman. *Vergil reading the Aeneid to Augustus and Octavia*, 1788. The State
Hermitage Museum, St. Petersburg. Photograph © The State Hermitage Musuem.
Cover design by Workhaus

Set in 10/12.5pt Galliard by SPi Publisher Services, Pondicherry, India

1   2014

MIX
Paper from
responsible sources
FSC
www.fsc.org   FSC® C013604

Contents

Illustrations

Figures

Plates

(between pages 302 and 303)

Notes on Contributors

Susanna Morton Braund moved to the University of British Columbia in 2007 to take up a Canada Research Chair in Latin Poetry and its Reception after teaching previously at Stanford, Yale, and the Universities of London, Bristol, and Exeter. She has published extensively on Roman satire and Latin epic poetry and has translated Lucan for the Oxford World's Classics series and Persius and Juvenal for the Loeb Classical Library (2004).

Reuben A. Brower (1908–75) was the author and editor of many volumes of criticism, including *The Fields of Light* (1951), *Alexander Pope: The Poetry of Allusion* (1959), *The Poetry of Robert Frost: Constellations of Intention* (1963), and *Hero and Saint: Shakespeare and the Greco-Roman Heroic Tradition* (1971), the Martin Classical Lectures for 1970. A collection of his essays was published in 1974 under the title *Mirror on Mirrors: Translation, Imitation, Parody.*

David Blayney Brown is Curator of Eighteenth- and Nineteenth-Century British Art at Tate Britain, London, where he is responsible for the Turner Collection. He has organized numerous exhibitions and written and lectured widely in Britain, Europe, the United States, and Australia. His books include *Romanticism* (2001).

Sergio Casali is Associate Professor of Latin Language and Literature at the University of Rome "Tor Vergata." He is author of a commentary on one of Ovid's *Heroides* and of numerous articles, notes, and reviews on Ovid, Vergil's *Aeneid*, Vergil's ancient commentators, and the Roman epic tradition. He is currently working on a Cambridge "green and yellow" commentary on *Aeneid* 4, and on a commentary in Italian on *Aeneid* 2 for Carocci, Rome.

Joy Connolly is Associate Professor of Classics at New York University; she has also taught at the University of Washington in Seattle and Stanford University. She is the author of *The State of Speech: Rhetoric and Political Thought in Ancient Rome* and articles about political theory, Latin poetry, education, and cultural identity in antiquity. Her current work includes *Talk About Virtue*, a book about republicanism and its recuperation in contemporary political theory, and articles on Sallust's *Bellum Jugurthinum*, classical rhetoric in eighteenth-century America, and Pliny's *Panegyricus*.

Kristi Eastin is an Assistant Professor in Classics and Humanities at California State University, Fresno. She received her PhD in Comparative Literature from Brown University in 2009. She is currently examining the illustrative tradition of Vergil's *Georgics*.

Joseph Farrell is Professor of Classical Studies at the University of Pennsylvania. He is the author of *Vergil's Georgics and the Traditions of Ancient Epic* (1991) and *Latin Language and Latin Culture from Ancient to Modern Times* (2001), and is working on a book entitled *Juno's Aeneid: Narrative, Metapoetics, Dissent*.

William Fitzgerald is Professor of Latin at King's College London. His most recent book is *Martial: The World of the Epigram*.

Philip Hardie is a Senior Research Fellow of Trinity College and Honorary Professor of Latin at Cambridge University. His books include the Cambridge Companions to Lucretius (ed. with Stuart Gillespie, 2007) and Ovid (ed., 2002), *Ovid's Poetics of Illusion* (2002), a commentary on Vergil, *Aeneid* 9 (1994), *The Epic Successors of Virgil* (1993), and *Virgil's Aeneid: Cosmos and Imperium* (1986). His current research interests include the history of rumor and renown from Homer to Alexander Pope and the reception of ancient literature in the English Renaissance.

Yasmin Haskell is Professor of Latin Humanism at the University of Western Australia. She is author of *Loyola's Bees: Ideology and Industry in Jesuit Latin Didactic Poetry* (2003) and co-editor of several collections, including, with J. Feros Ruys, *Latinity and Alterity in the Early Modern Period* (forthcoming, Medieval and Renaissance Texts and Studies). She is currently writing a book about a cosmopolitan Dutch physician and Latin poet of the eighteenth century: *Prescribing Ovid: The Latin Works and Networks of the Enlightened Doctor Heerkens*.

Kenneth Haynes teaches in the departments of Comparative Literature and Classics at Brown University. He is the author of *English Literature and Ancient Language* (2003), the co-editor (with Peter France) of *The Oxford History of Literary Translation in English, vol. 4: 1790–1900* (2006), and he is currently editing *The Oxford History of the Classical Reception within English Literature, vol. 5: 1880–2000*.

Ralph Hexter is President of Hampshire College. He is the author of *Ovid and Medieval Schooling* (1986) and *A Guide to the Odyssey* (1993) and, with Daniel Selden, co-editor of *Innovations of Antiquity* (1992). His research centers on commentary, reception, and issues of reading and resistance in the classical, medieval, and modern periods.

Rachel Jacoff is Margaret Deffenbaugh and LeRoy Carlson Professor of Comparative Literature and Italian Studies at Wellesley College. She is the editor of *The Cambridge Companion to Dante* and co-editor of *The Poetry of Allusion: Virgil and Ovid in Dante's "Commedia"* and *The Poets' Dante*. Her essays explore Dante's relation to his classical and biblical models and to the visual arts of his time.

Craig Kallendorf is Professor of English and Classics at Texas A&M University. His most recent books are *The Other Virgil: Pessimistic Readings of the Aeneid in Early Modern Culture* (2007), *The Virgilian Tradition: Book History and the History of Reading in Early Modern Europe* (2007), and *A Catalogue of the Junius Spencer Morgan Vergil in the Princeton University Library* (2009).

Karl Kirchwey is the author of five books of poems, including most recently *The Happiness of This World: Poetry and Prose*. His work has appeared in *After Ovid: New Metamorphoses* (ed. James Lasdun and Michael Hofmann, 1994) and in *Poets and Critics Read Vergil* (ed. Sarah Spence, 2001). His verse drama based on the *Alcestis* of Euripides is called *Airdales & Cipher*. Recipient of a Rome Prize in Literature (1994–5), he is Associate Professor of the Arts and Director of the Creative Writing Program at Bryn Mawr College.

Andrew Laird is Professor in Classical Literature at Warwick and is currently a Leverhulme Major Research Fellow. He has held visiting positions in Princeton, the University of Cincinnati, and the Institute for Research in the Humanities at the University of Wisconsin-Madison. His publications include *Powers of Expression, Expressions of Power: Speech Presentation and Latin Literature* (1999), *Ancient Literary Criticism* (2006), and *The Epic of America* (2006). He is editor, with Ahuvia Kahane, of *A Companion to the Prologue of Apuleius' Metamorphoses* (2001) and, with Carlo Caruso, of *Italy and the Classical Tradition: Language, Thought and Poetry 1300–1600* (2009).

Dennis Looney teaches in the Department of French and Italian at the University of Pittsburgh, where he holds a secondary appointment in Classics. His publications include: *Compromising the Classics: Romance Epic Narrative in the Italian Renaissance* (1996); co-editor, *Phaethon's Children: The Este Court and Its Culture in Early Modern Ferrara* (2005); editor and co-translator of Sergio Zatti, *The Quest for Epic: From Ariosto to Tasso* (2006).

Michèle Lowrie is Professor of Classics and the College at the University of Chicago. She is the author of *Writing, Performance, and Authority in Augustan Rome* (Oxford, 2009) and *Horace's Narrative Odes* (Oxford, 1997). She has edited *Oxford Readings in Classical Studies: Horace's Odes and Epodes* (Oxford, 2009) and has co-edited with Sarah Spence *The Aesthetics of Empire and the Reception of Vergil* as a special issue of Literary *Imagination* (2006).

Glenn W. Most is Professor of Greek Philology at the Scuola Normale Superiore di Pisa and also Professor on the Committee on Social Thought at the University of Chicago. He has published widely on ancient Greek and Roman poetry and philosophy, on the reception of antiquity, on art history, and on other subjects. His most recent books are *Doubting Thomas* (2005), an edition and translation of Sebastiano Timpanaro's *Genesis of Lachmann's Method* (2005), and a two-volume edition of the works of Hesiod in the Loeb Classical Library (2006–7). He is also co-editor, with Anthony Grafton and Salvatore Settis, of *The Classical Tradition: A Guide*.

Damien P. Nelis is Professor of Latin at the University of Geneva. He has published widely on Latin poetry and on

Vergil in particular, and is author of *Vergil's Aeneid and the Argonautica of Apollonius Rhodius* (2001) and co-editor (with David Levene) of *Clio and the Poets: Augustan Poetry and the Traditions of Ancient Historiography* (2002).

James J. O'Hara is the George L. Paddison Professor of Latin at the University of North Carolina, Chapel Hill. From 1986 until his 2001 arrival in Chapel Hill, he taught at Wesleyan University in Middletown, Connecticut. His research and teaching interests are in Greek and especially Latin poetry, with special interests in the Augustan period and in epic. He is the author of *Death and the Optimistic Prophecy in Vergil's Aeneid* (1990), *True Names: Vergil and the Alexandrian Tradition of Etymological Wordplay* (1996), and *Inconsistency in Roman Epic: Studies in Catullus, Lucretius, Vergil, Ovid and Lucan* (2007), and is part of a team producing a school commentary on the *Aeneid* for Focus Press.

Vassiliki Panoussi is Associate Professor of Classical Studies at the College of William and Mary. She has published several articles on Roman literature of the late republic and early empire and is the author of a book, *Greek Tragedy in Vergil's Aeneid* (Cambridge 2009). She is currently working on a book project on the representations of women's religious roles in Latin literature.

Henry Power is Lecturer in English at the University of Exeter, and the holder of a Leverhulme Early Career Fellowship. He is the author of articles on Cowley, Denham, and Fielding, and is currently writing a book about the reception of classical epic in the first half of the eighteenth century.

Michael C.J. Putnam is MacMillan Professor of Classics and Professor of Comparative Literature at Brown University. His books are largely concerned with classical Latin poetry. The most recent is *Poetic Interplay: Catullus and Horace* (2006). He is a Trustee of the American Academy in Rome as well as Fellow of the American Academy of Arts and Sciences, and Member of the American Philosophical Society.

J.D. Reed is Professor of Classics at Brown University. His interests lie mainly in Hellenistic and Latin poetry, particularly in the poetic representation of cultural identity. He has recently published *Virgil's Gaze: Nation and Poetry in the Aeneid*, and has a commentary in progress on Ovid, *Metamorphoses* 10–12. He has also published on the ancient cult and myth of Adonis.

Carl J. Richard is Professor of History at the University of Louisiana at Lafayette. His books include *The Founders and the Classics: Greece, Rome, and the American Enlightenment* (1994); *Twelve Greeks and Romans Who Changed the World* (2003); *The Battle for the American Mind: A Brief History of a Nation's Thought* (2004); *Greeks and Romans Bearing Gifts: How the Ancients Inspired the Founding Fathers* (2008); and *The Golden Age of the Classics in America: Greece, Rome, and the Antebellum United States* (2009).

Michele Valerie Ronnick is Professor in the Department of Classical and Modern Languages, Literatures, and Cultures at Wayne State University in Detroit, Michigan. Her books include *Cicero's Paradoxa Stoicorum* (1991); *The Autobiography of William Sanders Scarborough (1852–1926): An American Journey from Slavery to Scholarship*

(2005); and *The Works of William Sanders Scarborough: Black Classicist and Race Leader* (2006). In addition to interests in neo-Latin and in the classical tradition, she has written numerous short articles on the Latin prose of John Milton. She is currently the president of the Classical Association of the Middle West and South.

Ingrid Rowland teaches history of architecture on the Rome campus of the University of Notre Dame School of Architecture. She is working on a book on Athanasius Kircher.

Sarah Spence is Distinguished Research Professor of Classics and Comparative Literature at the University of Georgia. She has published widely on medieval adaptations of ancient literature, including *Rhetorics of Reason and Desire* (1988); *Texts and the Self in the Twelfth Century* (1996); and *Figuratively Speaking* (2007).

Fabio Stok teaches Latin literature at the University of Rome "Tor Vergata." He has published extensively on classical Latin authors and their reception as well as on ancient medicine, ethnography, and lexicography. He is co-editor (with Giorgio Brugnoli) of *Vitae Vergilianae Antiquae,* a critical edition of the ancient Vergilian biography of Suetonius-Donatus and of other medieval and Renaissance lives (Rome 1997). Professor Stok is also one of the editors of Niccolò Perotti's *Cornu copiae* (8 vols., 1989–2001), and is working at present on several other humanist and neo-Latin authors.

Garry Wills is Professor of History Emeritus at Northwestern University. Among his many books are six devoted to Augustine.

Caroline Winterer is Associate Professor in the Department of History at Stanford University. She is the author of *The Mirror of Antiquity: American Women and the Classical Tradition, 1750–1900* (2007) and *The Culture of Classicism: Ancient Greece and Rome in American Intellectual Life, 1780–1910* (2002; pbk. 2004), as well as numerous essays on the subject of American classicism.

Preface

First and foremost the editors would like to thank the contributors to this collection for the enthusiasm that they have brought to the project and for the breadth of interest that has allowed it to offer a wide-ranging prospect over Vergil and his heritage. Alfred Bertrand of Wiley-Blackwell originally proposed a volume on the *Aeneid* and its tradition for its *Companion* series, and his support has continued from the start. Among his helpful colleagues have been Sophie Gibson, Haze Humbert, and Galen Smith, all readily available when assistance was needed. Special thanks to Brigitte Lee Messenger for her expert copy-editing and for her prompt and friendly attention to all queries sent her way. The editors would like also to acknowledge help freely offered by colleagues and staff in their respective departments at Brown University and the University of Pennsylvania. In particular we thank Carrie Mowbray of Penn for the care with which she has organized the bibliography as well as brought order and cohesion to the many practical details that adhere to such a varied enterprise. Additional thanks to Kelcy Sagstetter, Kevin Platt, and Ilya Vinitsky for their timely assistance with matters Slavic and Cyrillic. Finally, a word of gratitude to the libraries, museums, and publishing houses that supplied illustrative material, and granted reprint permissions. Their individual contributions are listed elsewhere.

Joseph Farrell
Michael C.J. Putnam

Acknowledgments

The editors and publisher gratefully acknowledge the permission granted to reproduce the copyright material in this book:

Excerpts from "The Mediterranean" and "Aeneas at Washington" from *Collected Poems 1919–1976* by Allen Tate. Copyright © 1977 by Allen Tate. Reprinted by permission of Farrar, Straus, and Giroux, LLC.

"The Journey," from *Outside History: Selected Poems 1980–1990* by Eavan Boland. Copyright © 1990 by Eavan Boland. Used by permission of W.W. Norton & Company, Inc. and Carcanet Press Limited.

"Poetry Reading," "Turnus," "Bonfires," from *Departure: Poems by Rosanna Warren*. Copyright © 2003 by Rosanna Warren. Used by permission of W. W. Norton & Company, Inc.

Excerpts from "The Queen of Carthage" (101), "The Golden Bough" (121), "Roman Study" (161), from *Vita Nova* by Louise Glück. Copyright © 1999 by Louise Glück. Reprinted by permission of HarperCollins Publishers and Carcanet Press Limited.

"Falling Asleep over the *Aeneid*." Excerpt from *The Mills of the Kavanaughs*, Copyright 1948 and renewed 1976 by Robert Lowell, reprinted by permission of Houghton Mifflin Harcourt Publishing Company.

Excerpts from "Secondary Epic," from *Collected Poems* by W.H. Auden. Copyright © 1976, 1991 by The Estate of W.H. Auden. Reprinted by permission of Faber and Faber Ltd.

"Cento Virgilianus," from *The Continuous Life* by Mark Strand, Copyright © 1990 by Mark Strand. Used by permission of Alfred A. Knopf, a division of Random House, Inc.

"A Poet's Alphabet," from *The Weather of Words: Poetic Invention* by Mark Strand, Copyright © 2000 by Mark Strand. Used by permission of Alfred A. Knopf, a division of Random House, Inc.

Every effort has been made to trace copyright holders and to obtain their permission for the use of copyright material. The publisher apologizes for any errors or omissions in the above list and would be grateful if notified of any corrections that should be incorporated in future reprints or editions of this book.

Note on References

The abbreviations used in this volume are in general those found in *OCD³* (*Oxford Classical Dictionary*, ed. S. Hornblower and A. Spawforth, 3rd ed. 1996, rev. 2003: xxix–liv) and, where those are lacking, in either *OLD* (*Oxford Latin Dictionary*, ed. P.G.W. Glare, 1983: ix–xx) or LSJ (H.G. Liddell, R. Scott, and H. Stuart Jones, *A Greek–English Lexicon*, 9th ed. with a revised supplement 1996: xvi–xlv). Translations of Vergil's works and standard editions of classical texts are cited in the usual form (e.g., *Aen.* 1.203) with the addition of the translator's or the editor's name where relevant (e.g., *Aen.* 1.203, trans. Dryden; schol. Ver. *ad Aen.* 2.717 Baschera). In the case of the ancient lives of Vergil the abbreviations used herein are those of Brugnoli and Stok (1997, 270); Latin quotations from the lives refer to the same edition, and English translations are those found in Ziolkowski and Putnam (2008) unless otherwise noted. Secondary sources are cited by the author's last name and the date of publication, with page numbers where relevant. Abbreviations of journal titles are based on those used in *L'Année philologique*.

Introduction

Joseph Farrell and Michael C.J. Putnam

Companions, handbooks, and other forms of *vade mecum* have for some years been appearing with frequency and on an ever-greater range of subjects. In such circumstances, an author such as Vergil and a poem like the *Aeneid*, both of which hold unshakable positions in any list of canonical authors or "great books," will be well represented. Any additional volume of this sort thus bears a particular burden of self-justification. Our view is that a new *Aeneid* companion could be warranted only if it did not tread well-worn paths, and that, if it succeeded in illuminating unexpected avenues of approach, then it would more than validate its existence. This is the challenge we hope to have met.

Fortunately, the world of Vergilian studies is large and engagement with the *Aeneid* spans many communities. No single book could ever cover all possible topics of interest to all readers. The work that comes closest to doing so is the monumental *Enciclopedia Virgiliana*, but that is a work written mainly for specialists. Other, single-volume handbooks ably cover the main technical, literary, or pedagogical aspects of the poem and its tradition from their different points of view. But in practice, both serious and casual students of the poem are likely to have to consult more than one of the existing handbooks to find the particular kind of guidance that they require. For this reason a new companion presenting approaches to the poem not found in the several that already exist should be welcome. The present volume was designed around this assumption. Our first goal was to address issues that we regarded as likely to interest readers new to the *Aeneid* as well as experts, but ones that we did not find represented in existing handbooks. In a few cases we have commissioned chapters that examine familiar topics from an unexpected angle. But beyond these specific issues, we have attempted to fashion a book of essays that collectively present a coherent, fresh, and distinctive perspective on the *Aeneid* and its reception, one that we hope will prove to be both illuminating for those who consult this book as an introduction to the poem and challenging to those who are themselves in a position to explore new avenues of research in Vergilian studies. What is this perspective?

In the first place, we present this volume as a companion to the *Aeneid* but also to its tradition. Indeed, a glance at the titles of the individual chapters will suggest that this volume is devoted principally to reception studies. By conceiving of the volume in this way, we acknowledge the enormous influence that reception studies have exerted within Classics over the past two decades or so. Many would argue that the different stages of reception are ultimately inseparable from any interpretation; and our own view is that the *Aeneid*, perhaps not more than but certainly as much as any poem, has been defined by the tradition of which it is so central a part. But at the same time, no one interpretation actually *is* the poem, and we have tried to emphasize the rich diversity of the tradition that defines it. This seems to us a necessary intervention. The idea of the monumental *Aeneid*, the imperial epic *par excellence*, successor to the *Iliad* and the *Odyssey*, precursor to the *Divine Comedy* and *Paradise Lost*, keystone of the massive structure that is the Western literary tradition, is very familiar. It is, like the notion of the "Messianic *Eclogue*," a fundamental aspect of the poem's reception, and in that sense it will always be with us. But the notion that Vergil's poetry actually predicted the birth of Jesus Christ belongs to a far distant time. Knowledge of this tradition can inform our sense of what the poem has been thought to mean without playing an intrinsic role in our own interpretation. In contrast to earlier students of the poem, we are just now gaining enough chronological and cultural distance from the middle decades of the twentieth century to understand the extent to which the conception of the imperial *Aeneid* was a product of that time, or, if not actually a product, then an important measure of the extent to which that interpretation of the poem spoke to the needs of mid-century readers. One result of this episode in the poem's reception was that such an interpretation – broadly speaking, the interpretation of Haecker, of Eliot, and in an idiosyncratic way, of Broch – came in the eyes of many to be mistaken for the poem itself. And consequently this interpretation is well represented in many existing guides to the poem.

With these facts in mind, we have attempted to address the situation by emphasizing the highly contingent nature of the *Aeneid*. This contingency reveals itself in the choices that Vergil faced in composing it, so many of which left their imprint upon the finished product. Whether the question has to do with Vergil's sense of his poem as a reinterpretation of Homer, or with its relationship to earlier Greek and Roman literature as a whole, or with the welter of diverse and bewildering Aeneas legends available to him, or with the conflicting roles – roles that are at different times mainly literary, mythic, political, or religious, and sometimes all of these at once – that Vergil's hero is called upon to play, the pivotal fact is that the *Aeneid* is anything but a fixed and stable monument of unitary meaning. In many ways it is much more like the labyrinth of multiplying possibilities that its hero contemplates on the doors of Apollo's temple at Cumae as he concludes his own circuitous wanderings and faces yet another labyrinthine trial in the form of his descent into the world of the dead.

These possibilities have played themselves out in readerly interpretation over centuries and have left their mark on all aspects of the poem's critical reception, both favorable and not. Accordingly, this volume explores the varying fortunes of the *Aeneid* over time and among different groups of readers, emphasizing that the poem dubbed by Eliot "the classic of all Europe" was, perhaps surprisingly, in the Middle Ages held to represent a minority view of the fall of Troy and one that was not very influential on the literature of that time. It presents a poem that has been praised but also blamed as the official epic of conformism, patriarchy, orthodoxy, and complacency, and yet as one that has nevertheless frequently found sympathetic audiences among the disenfranchised and the oppressed. The story of the triumphalist *Aeneid* has been told many times, but the story of this "other" *Aeneid* is no less real or important, and attention to its fortunes repays the effort by immeasurably enlarging one's experience of what already is, for both editors and we dare say for all of the contributors as well, a cherished masterpiece.

The interconnections among all of these essays are many, and no single order of presentation could bring all of them out. Accordingly, we have chosen to arrange them, so far as was possible, in a straightforwardly chronological order.

The essays of Part I deal with the formation of the *Aeneid* and with important aspects of its ancient reception. Damien Nelis leads off by examining the question of Vergil's library, both in the material sense of the books that he owned or to which he might have had access, and in the ideal sense of the poetry as a distillation of the poet's wide and sympathetic reading. The *Aeneid* and its tradition thus signifies here the *anterior* tradition of Latin and (mainly) Greek literature that inspired so much of the form and content of Vergil's masterpiece.

The two essays that follow focus first on Vergil's most important predecessor in epic poetry, and then on the poet's sources for ways taken and not taken regarding the legend of Aeneas. Ralph Hexter considers Vergil's relationship with Homer particularly in light of the scholarly resources available for the interpretation of the *Iliad* and *Odyssey* and suggests how these materials, and the interpretive habits that they encouraged, influenced Vergil's most important intertextual agon. Our knowledge of the ancient scholarship that was available to Vergil has grown significantly in recent years, and with it our sense of how the poet might have used this accumulated learning. The standard view has been that Vergil used Homeric scholarship chiefly as a means of avoiding "mistakes" that Homer's critics felt he had made – those moments when "even Homer nods." Hexter, agreeing here with some very recent work in this field, persuasively argues that the richness of Homeric exegetical scholarship must actually have encouraged the proliferation of interpretive possibilities in the minds of both Vergil and his most sophisticated readers.

In the following chapter, Sergio Casali (who has previously contributed to our understanding of the exegetical traditions that Hexter explores) delves into a different aspect of ancient scholarship in the form of the mythographic and historiographical traditions to sketch in some detail the extraordinary uncertainty and variety that pervaded the Aeneas legend before Vergil gave it (what is often taken for) its definitive form. (We return to this point in discussing Part II below.) What emerges from Casali's survey is a keener awareness both of Vergil's achievement in bringing order to this extremely heterogeneous tradition and his brilliance in allowing elements "excluded" from the main lines of his narrative to make their presence briefly and provocatively felt at crucial junctures.

There follows a trio of chapters that speak to some of the poem's most central Augustan themes, religion, national identity, and exile. In the first, Vassiliki Panoussi examines Vergil's portrayal of Aeneas as a military and a religious leader against the background of the Roman Republican magistrate as one to whom both these roles regularly and necessarily fell, and also in terms of Augustus' program of religious revival. In the following chapter, Joseph Reed considers Vergil's "national epic" with reference to the idea of Roman national identity. He argues that the ethnic identity of the Roman state was open to question, partaking as it did in the characteristics of so many different ethnicities, both cognate and agnate, friend and enemy. These are the ingredients of national identity, the materials and processes of inclusion and absorption that were a fundamental part of Roman character and that, proverbially, enabled a tiny settlement of the banks of the Tiber to grow into one of the largest and most successful world-states in history. Again, the watchword is flexibility and adaptability, not fixity or stability. Then, in the final chapter of this trio, Michael Putnam examines a motif that is the converse of Reed's, that of exclusion in the form of exile as it is found in Vergil and then taken up by the poet who was among the first and certainly among the greatest of Vergil's successors, Ovid. Recent years have seen Ovid make an ever-greater claim on the energy and attention of Latin studies, in some respects because of characteristics that differentiate him from Vergil, especially perhaps his "playfulness" (as opposed to Vergil's "high seriousness"). Here Putnam, following up on previous work, explores a deep sympathy that he perceives between the two poets, one that revolves around a theme that so clearly permeates the poetry of both.

Ovid's Vergil takes us firmly into the area of "reception." But with the two essays that round out this section we move back, in a sense, towards the poem, though with the motive of interrogating the grey area between the poem "itself" and the poem as it is defined by the circumstances of its reception. James O'Hara sounds a theme that will resonate throughout the rest of this volume, just as it does through Vergilian criticism of every stripe: the theme of the unfinished *Aeneid*. O'Hara shows that the idea of the poem's unfinished condition decisively – and, as he argues, excessively – colors the critic's perception of it. The implications of his argument are many. On the one hand, he raises important questions about the validity of certain lines of critical inquiry that are based on (what he shows to be) a much too radical set of assumptions about the "imperfect" state of the poem. On the other hand, he underlines the urgency of those questions that arise not from lack of finish but from authorial design.

Of course, the notion of the "unfinished *Aeneid*" derives only minimally from the condition of the poem itself, and is mainly a creature of the ancient biographical tradition. O'Hara's interrogation thus leads directly into Fabio Stok's reading of the layers of accretion that gradually built up our conception of Vergil's biography. Our information about Vergil's life, and especially his death, rests for the most part on no firm foundation; and yet this information has become inescapably a part of nearly every interpretation of the *Aeneid*, and still more (thanks to the efforts of imaginative writers like Hermann Broch) of the general conception of Vergil that became common in the mid-twentieth century. Stok's chapter reconstructs the stages by which the biographical tradition most likely took shape. In the process, Stok not only comments on the relative proximity to Vergil's own lifetime that is attested for any particular detail within the tradition, but he also shows that each detail, no matter how early it is attested or how plausible it appears, is embedded in its own contexts of production and of reception, and therefore seems anything but disinterested and so all the more likely to have been designed to serve some interpretive purpose.

Part II of the volume deals with the Middle Ages and Renaissance. It begins with Garry Wills' chapter on "Vergil and St. Augustine," which examines Augustine's familiar expression of skepticism about the value of the *Aeneid* in his own education, and proceeds to trace instances in which Augustine returns, almost obsessively, even in spite of himself, to Vergil as an intellectual touchstone throughout his career. Wills thereby offers a trenchant commentary both on Augustine's protestations and on a countervailing tendency (represented, for instance, by Fr. Haecker) to regard Vergil and Augustine as naturally partners in the production of Western Civilization. The next chapter, by Sarah Spence, challenges another myth about the *Aeneid* by reviewing the history of the Trojan legend in the Middle Ages. Spence's contribution on the Aeneas legend *after* Vergil demands to be read in conjunction with Casali's chapter on the legend *before* Vergil. Read together, the two chapters show that Vergil did not succeed, or even aim to succeed, in reducing to order the myriad conflicting sources on his hero once and for all, thus establishing a definitive version that would be followed by all later writers, though he did in a sense construct an official, imperial version of the legend. Nevertheless, as Spence shows, this did not prevent medieval poets from following quite different, earlier traditions that were known to Vergil (as Casali argues) and only quite subtly acknowledged in the *Aeneid* itself, but that survived in prose accounts that travel under the names of Dictys of Crete and Dares of Phrygia. Vergil's importance in the Middle Ages was great, but his Augustan rendition of the Trojan saga was, as Spence makes clear, not the only known version nor, to judge from the vernacular traditions, the most popular. Coming to terms with this fact would obviously involve some qualification of Eliot's idea that the *Aeneid* is "the classic of all Europe."

Eliot's idea certainly does receive support from the treatment of Vergil by Dante, a poet coupled with Vergil as often and in much the same way as Vergil is paired with Homer. As the next chapter by Rachel Jacoff shows, however, Dante's Vergil (and here see again Nelis on Vergil's library together with Hexter on Vergil's Homer) is better understood as just one, even if *primus inter pares*, among many pagan influences on the *Divine Comedy*. As recent research has shown, Horace, Ovid, Statius, and other classical poets mediate and in some sense compete with Vergil's influence on Dante's masterpiece. It is true that, for Dante, Vergil remains important in a way that other poets do not, the imperial poet *par excellence* and, crucially, proto-Christian as well, but proto-Christian only. This is a perspective on Vergil that is consummately well suited to serve Dante's own interests, and perhaps those of Eliot as well, but one that by definition cannot give answer at all precisely to what we know of Vergil's own horizon of expectations nor, we would venture to say, to our own.

From Dante's compelling and yet problematic perspective we move on to the presence of Vergil in Renaissance literature. Like Dante's Vergil, this is a well-worn topic, but the seven essays devoted to it in this volume, like Jacoff's, approach it in fresh and illuminating ways. A standard approach to this theme would involve stressing the powerful connections between the *Aeneid* and the Latin epics of this period, such as Petrarch's *Africa* (1343) and the various continuations of the *Aeneid* itself, of which

Maffeo Vegio's *Aeneidos Liber XIII*, or "Book 13 of the *Aeneid*" (1428), is only the best known example. With this background in mind, one might move on to consider Vergil's influence on the vernacular epics along with the signal departures of those poems in the directions, say, of romance or of the novel.

Instead, this section begins with vernacular romance and moves on to consider later manifestations of neo-Latin epic. In the first chapter, Dennis Looney examines the *Aeneid* as a model for three poets not of Rome but of Ferrara, and not of epic but of romance. The authors and works in question are Matteo Maria Boiardo's *Orlando innamorato* (1486), Ludovico Ariosto's *Orlando furioso* (1532), and Torquato Tasso's *Gerusalemme liberata* (1574). Rather than regarding the element of the fantastic as an indication of how the vernacular epic departs from its classical model by incorporating elements characteristic of romance, Looney brings to bear compelling evidence that all three of these authors worked to find warrant for their departures within the *Aeneid* itself, effectively reinterpreting Vergil's epic as precisely a masterpiece of romance.

The two essays that follow likewise treat of familiar relationships in extraordinary ways. Philip Hardie enriches our understanding of how Spenser incorporated, and varied, the Vergilian career in the span of his own writing, especially of *The Faerie Queen*. Henry Power's essay grounds the reader broadly in the English reception of Vergil in the century ending at the death of Dryden before turning back to view *Paradise Lost* in this same intellectual context. The following two chapters open up powerful new perspectives on Vergil in the Latin culture of the Renaissance. Yasmin Haskell illustrates the deep influence that Vergil's poetic accomplishment, especially the *Aeneid*, exerted on Jesuit educational practice and on the extensive body of Latin poetry that the Order produced in the centuries after its foundation in 1540. The section continues with Andrew Laird's chapter on the Latin epic poetry of colonial Mexico. Here again as in previous essays, especially those of Wills, Jacoff, and Haskell, the theme of Christianity crosses with other central Vergilian topics, particularly those of national identity (Reed) and exile (Putnam), in the process of making known an extraordinary body of literature that is, if anything, more recognizably Vergilian than, say, the vernacular epic romances that Looney shows to be explicitly modeled on the *Aeneid*. This section concludes with Craig Kallendorf's chapter on the history of books about Vergil during the first three centuries of printing. His particular theme is to trace in depth the interplay of "optimistic" and "pessimistic" readings of Vergil's epic as treated in major European editions of the poem.

Kallendorf's treatment of the material book as a factor in Vergilian reception studies affords a direct means of transition to Part III, which focuses particularly on the *Aeneid* and the arts, especially the visual arts, in various forms. With Ingrid Rowland we concentrate on Rome of the seventeenth century. Her essay looks specifically, first, to the propagandistic purposes to which the Pamphili family put the *Aeneid* in the frescoes that Pietro da Cortona created for its Palazzo on the Piazza Navona, then, to the influence of the Jesuit scholar Athanasius Kircher on the invention of Bernini's Fountain of the Four Rivers in the same piazza. The section continues with an essay by the late Reuben Brower, published originally in a venue little frequented by Vergilians and reprinted here in abbreviated form. Its consideration of the influence of the storm scene of *Aeneid* 1, as interpreted through Dryden's powerful translation, on the work of Rubens is prescient of future work on the interplay of the verbal and visual arts fostered by the influence of Vergil. That interplay is the subject of the subsequent three chapters, as well. Kristi Eastin examines in detail one of the great examples of the relationship between text and image in the Vergilian tradition: John Ogilby's first complete translation of the works of the Roman poet into English (1654) and the engravings by the Dutch artist Francis Cleyn that served to illustrate it. With David Brown's essay we turn to nineteenth-century painting and to the particular appeal of Vergil to the Romantic imagination as discovered in English and French painting. We move from a study of Turner across the Channel to Girodet, and then return again to England and a survey of the poet's deep influence on Blake and Palmer. Next Glenn Most examines the Vergilian account of Laocoon as a hinge between earlier and later versions and between verbal and visual representations. In the person of Laocoon, spectacle and pain, prodigy and humanity, intersect at the very limit of what readers are willing to imagine and what viewers are desperate to see. The inevitable result is an aesthetic phenomenon that teeters on the edge of parody and humor, and more often than not falls in. In the last essay in this section William Fitzgerald presents an overview of the Vergilian presence in music from the Renaissance to the modern period, from Josquin Des Prez to Luigi Nono, with Purcell and Berlioz playing appropriately prominent parts. The French composer's devotion to Vergil was lifelong, and Fitzgerald demonstrates how his interpretation of the *Aeneid* as a whole influenced his presentation of the two books of the epic that he chose to dramatize at length and brings out with great clarity the distinctiveness of Berlioz's interpretation. Equally important is the evidence that Fitzgerald gives of how pervasive Vergil's influence has been at so many times in music history, a contribution that we hope will serve as an incentive to future research.

Part IV, which focuses on Vergil in early American culture, we might entitle "American *Aeneids*" for the important strain of pluralism that it suggests. Carl Richard's survey of Vergil's impact on American education identifies peculiarly Vergilian resonances with early American agrarianism and republicanism. At the same time, as he shows, it was possible for skeptical critics to complain that Vergil had served an emperor and so was inimical to democratic ideals, and that his paganism and, especially, laxness in treating of sexual morality made the *Aeneid* an inappropriate object of study within a Christian society. (Here again see Wills, Jacoff, Haskell, and Laird.) But the commitment to Vergil shown by northern elite centers of learning, particularly Yale and Harvard, ensured that Vergil long retained a central place in the college curriculum and so in the habits of mind formed by the alumni of such institutions. It is only to be expected that we find Vergil in this milieu aligned with white male privilege; equally unsurprising is the role that he played among American intellectuals who sought to distance the culture of their new, revolutionary country from that of the specifically European world that they had left behind.

More surprising, perhaps, are Caroline Winterer's essay on the reception of Vergil among nineteenth-century American women and Michele Valerie Ronnick's exploration of Vergil in African American culture and education. "Why," Winterer asks, "did American women read the *Aeneid*?" If there were reasons for American men to find the *Aeneid* objectionable on political and religious grounds, there were still more reasons why it might not have found a receptive audience among women of any nationality. But Winterer, arguing that in fact texts like the *Aeneid* played a key role in American women's efforts to "make themselves modern," goes on to suggest that the bond that these readers formed with this literature "helps us to understand how and why classical antiquity found a new home in the modern world." For Ronnick meanwhile, why African American writers read and imitated the *Aeneid*, why some sympathetic white writers have regarded the experience of African Americans through a Vergilian lens, and why a number of African American intellectuals in the post-Civil War period devoted their careers to Vergilian studies and to Classics more generally, are less important as questions than is the mere fact that they did so. Continuing her earlier research into the reception of Classics by African American culture, Ronnick contributes a rich store of little-known information regarding this fascinating topic, indicating in the process a number of promising avenues for future research.

The section concludes with a pair of more overtly political chapters. Here we reprint, for many of the same reasons as the essay by Reuben Brower, a condensed version of Michèle Lowrie's "Vergil and Founding Violence," which investigates Vergil's depiction of violence against the backdrop of twentieth-century intellectual history, especially the work of Walter Benjamin and Hannah Arendt. The question of violence has of course loomed large in the poem's critical and scholarly reception for decades; and to conclude this section, Joy Connolly addresses this critical legacy by considering the *Aeneid* in relation to Augustus' rise to power. With explicit reference to points raised by Lowrie, Connolly examines the tension between clemency, as the proper finale to the use of violence necessary to establish order, and the exemplification of the hero's personal anti-patriarchal wrath with which the poem ends.

The tenor of the volume thus far will have prepared the reader for the concluding section, which examines various aspects of Vergil's modern role as defined by Haecker, Eliot, and others. To open the section, Kenneth Haynes traces the meaning of the word "classic," especially as applied to the *Aeneid* by comparison to Homer's *Iliad*, over the last two and a half centuries. After looking closely at the work of Heyne and Sainte-Beuve, he ends by asking how, and of what, the *Aeneid* remains representative in the generations subsequent to Eliot and his influential essay, "What is a Classic?" Joseph Farrell discusses the pronounced tradition of anti-Vergilianism that has played a significant role in shaping the Vergilian tradition since even before the *Aeneid* was first made public. In the process, he examines a number of Vergil's modern critics in the light of this ancient tradition, including some who are often taken as the poet's champions.

Vergil's *Aeneid* is probably still the single ancient Greek or Latin text read in the original language, at least in part, by the greatest number of readers. For the majority of modern readers, though, the acquaintance is made even more often in translation. In her essay on translating the *Aeneid*, Susanna Morton Braund first distinguishes between "domesticating" and "foreignizing" renderings, then examines three examples of the latter, Briusov's into Russian (1933), the French version of Klossowski (1964), and Ahl's recent English translation (2007). The variety of approaches represented in this sample is immensely instructive, not only with regard to the meaning of Vergil's text and to the craft of translation itself, but even more for the insight gained into what has been felt to be at stake in translating this poet and this poem. And in the final essay we turn to a very different kind of "translation" as Karl Kirchwey surveys the presence of Vergil in recent poetry in English, from Alan Tate to Rosanna Warren, with a particular bow to Mark Strand whose prose also reflects his deep sympathy with his Roman predecessor.

As editors we feel fortunate to have enlisted such a protean group of collaborators. At the same time, we remain deeply conscious of how much more remains to be done. Our hope is that readers of this volume will put its essays to use, and act on the challenges that they present, individually and collectively, so as further to illuminate important but under-explored aspects of Vergilian scholarship. In addition we hope to have communicated some sense of the abiding affection and admiration we ourselves feel for the poem and for the poet. It is perhaps not usual to speak of such things in academic studies, particularly in a skeptical age when so much scholarly energy is spent in the service of demystifying the aura that traditionally surrounds canonical authors and great books. For that reason it may be all the more important for the editors to say that, over almost a century of combined experience with this poem and this poet, no amount of problematization, complication, contestation, or outright rejection of received wisdom has diminished our enthusiasm, but has only increased it. Vergil's *Aeneid* has been and remains many things to many readers; its tradition is rich and various, not to say complex and contradictory. We hope this volume is a worthy effort at least to suggest something of the power and beauty that we have found in it.

PART ONE

The *Aeneid* in Antiquity

CHAPTER ONE

Vergil's Library

Damien P. Nelis

Throughout the whole of *Aeneid* 3, Aeneas' account of his wanderings after the fall of Troy is modeled on Odysseus' version of his wanderings in *Odyssey* 9–12. Near the end of the book, the Trojans find themselves on Sicily. There, they encounter a Greek left behind by Odysseus at the moment of his flight from the Cyclops (*Aen.* 3.588–654). Despite the fact that this man, who is named Achaemenides, is nowhere mentioned by Homer, the two texts are here operating in strikingly close interaction (Knauer 1964a, 187–96). And so, when the Trojans sail away from Polyphemus and make their way westward around the southern coast of Sicily, Achaemenides is able to act as a guide, since he had only recently sailed in the opposite eastward direction with Odysseus:

> ecce autem Boreas angusta ab sede Pelori
> missus adest: vivo praetervehor ostia saxo
> Pantagiae Megarosque sinus Thapsumque iacentem.
> talia monstrabat **relegens errata retrorsus**   690
> litora Achaemenides, comes infelicis Vlixi.

> … when the North Wind comes blowing from the narrow strait of Pelorus.
> Past Pantagia's mouth with its living rock I voyage – past the Megarian bay
> and low-lying Thapsus. Such were the coasts pointed out by Achaemenides,
> comrade of the luckless Ulysses, **as he retraced his former wanderings**.
> (Trans. Fairclough and Goold)

The verb *relegens* has been translated by "retrace" with remarkable consistency (cf. Day Lewis, Mandelbaum, Fitzgerald, Fagles, Ahl; all are refining Dryden's "tracing"), but it is hard to believe that in this context of remarkably close imitation of Homer Vergil's choice of word (this is the only time he uses it) is unassociated with his reading and rewriting of the *Odyssey*. As we follow Aeneas' westward voyage, we are reading a new version of Homer's narrative of Odysseus' wanderings through the same waters (Barchiesi 1996, 231; Nelis 2001, 22 n.2). Vergil's use of the verb *relego* implies that in order to understand the *Aeneid* we must all be, like the poet himself, readers of the *Odyssey*.

That the composition of the *Aeneid* is based on long and detailed engagement with the Homeric epics is well known, just as it is clear that the *Eclogues* and *Georgics* contain the fruits of prolonged engagement with many texts, both Greek and Latin, from Hesiod and Theocritus to Lucretius, Catullus, and Gallus. But any simple enumeration of the well-known names of authors commonly cited as Vergil's models raises practical questions that are very difficult to answer. What kind of text of Homer did Vergil have? What kind of editions of Theocritus and Hesiod did he work with? Where did he acquire them? And how did he use them? Did he compose with scrolls open on his desk? Did he have a desk? Did he rely on his memory? Or did slaves check up passages for him? Did he dictate to a scribe? How many texts other than the *Iliad* and the *Odyssey* are crucial to the composition of the *Aeneid*? And what kind of editions of these works could Vergil use? Furthermore, when these questions are asked, the tentative answers we are in a position to propose open up a whole series of further questions about Vergil's reading practices, his compositional techniques and their importance for the ways in which his poetry is in turn read and interpreted. A rapid survey of some recent literature on the *Eclogues, Georgics,* and *Aeneid* produces a long list of authors directly imitated by Vergil (see appendix), and even if it is not the result of exhaustive research, it helps make an obvious point concerning assumptions made by modern scholars about the connections between Vergilian allusion, the richness of his library, and the extent of his reading.

Right from the time of its first publication, Vergil's poetry has given rise to a massive amount of scholarship, and a very considerable portion of this has been devoted to elucidating complex relationships between the poet's work and the books he is assumed to have read. Whether thinking in terms of and using the vocabulary of plagiarism, imitation, variation, rewriting, influence and anxiety, allusion or intertextuality, Vergilian scholarship has always seen in this aspect of the poet's technique an essential element of his literary art (see, for example, Horsfall 1991a, 29–53; Farrell 1997; Hinds 1998, 155 index s.v. "Virgil"). Of course, this approach has not been restricted to Vergil, and the very nature of Latin literature's relationship to Greek literature demands a comparative method (e.g., Schiesaro 1998; Farrell 2005b; Feeney 2005; Hunter 2006; essential background in Rawson 1985; Ferrary 1988; Gruen 1992). G. Pasquali's famous and fundamental piece on "Arte allusiva" (1942) emphasized the essentially bookish nature of the process of literary creation in Latin poetry, and R. Thomas (1988, 59), in a review of a book about Latin poets and Roman life that was intended as a criticism of an overtly bookish approach to literary creativity ("it is striking how little the poets have to say about the Library," Griffin 1985, 5 n.30), wrote: "to imagine Ovid writing the *Metamorphoses* at an uncluttered desk is impossible" (for the practicalities implied by this image in terms of handling scrolls and note-taking see Small 1997, 167–9; Dorandi 2000, 27–75). Those interested in biographical criticism, therefore, should be ready to include in their reconstructions images of Roman poets spending long hours reading scrolls. Catullus (68.33–6; cf. Horace, *Satires* 2.3.11–12; Marshall 1976, 252–3) memorably states the inextricable link between access to books and literary composition, when he laments that composition is impossible at Verona because of the lack of books. In fact, his complaint is on one level rather odd, because there is a substantial body of evidence to show that Romans could have considerable private collections in their country villas, and we know also that a lot of borrowing could go on between learned friends. One did not have to be in Rome to find books, and at least in the early first century the most famous collections seem to have been outside the city (Rawson 1985, 41–5). Various sources help us to imagine some aspects of book collection and circulation among the Roman élite (accessible surveys in Marshall 1976; Kenney and Clausen 1982, 15–32; Casson 2001, 61–79; Houston 2009) even if it is necessary to admit that there are vast gaps in our knowledge about Roman libraries in general and, to an even greater extent, about any personal library in particular.

From the beginning, of course, literary creation in Latin is inseparable from questions about access to books. Livius Andronicus seems to have been able to use Homeric scholia while translating the *Odyssey* into Latin (Fränkel 1932). The numerous plays of Plautus and Terence imply relatively easy access to a considerable corpus of Greek comedy (Goldberg 2005, 49), and the impressive education acquired by men like them, and the very existence of a bilingual élite, whatever the actual extent of bilingualism (Adams 2003, 1–15), tend to imply the relatively unproblematic circulation of books, as well as the presence of Greek teachers and men of letters (Feeney 2005, 228f.; and, in general, T. Morgan 1998). Obviously, many Greek books were available in Italy long before Roman conquest in the east is needed to explain the arrival of large and prestigious Greek collections. Aemilius Paullus acquired the royal Macedonian library after the Battle of Pydna in 168 BCE and brought it back home (Plutarch, *Aem. Paull.* 6.5, 28.6), and this collection probably passed to Scipio Aemilianus. Just under a century later, Sulla's taking of Athens led to the acquisition of Aristotle's library, while Lucullus built his collection from the booty won in his campaigns in Asia Minor, and made it accessible to many (Strabo 13.609; Plutarch, *Luc.* 42; see Barnes 1997 on the story of Aristotle in Rome). Cicero visited it regularly, and on one occasion he found Cato deep in books on Stoicism (*De Fin.* 3.2.7–8). By the middle of the first century, therefore, it is clear that considerable collections of books were established in Italy, and not just in Rome (see Casson 2001, 61–79 for an elegant survey). But gradually, Rome would come to assume central importance. Suetonius records Julius Caesar's plans for the establishment of a great library, and Pollio actually opened the city's first public library in 39 BCE (Suetonius, *Iul.* 44; Pliny, *NH* 7.115; Isidore 6.5). There followed Octavian-Augustus' two libraries, one in the Porticus Octaviae, and the other on the Palatine, part of the whole complex including the temple of Apollo. Subsequent emperors follow his example, Trajan's library (together with the scroll of his column) being the most famous, and by the fourth century it has been claimed that there were as many as twenty-eight (Marshall 1976, 261 n.56; in general see Dix and Houston 2006). Ownership of a large collection of books brought with it the onerous tasks of organizing and cataloguing, copying, recopying, correcting and repairing, lending, borrowing, and protecting (Casson 2001, 73–9; Rawson 1985, 39–45; Marshall 1976; on the initial circulation and "publication" of literary works, see Starr 1987; Small 1997, 26–40; and the exchange between Fowler 1995 and White 1996).

Overall, it is remarkable to note (with Rawson 1985, 44) that "we meet no complaints in the surviving literature that a particular book is impossible to track down."

From the archaeological point of view, of course, the identification of libraries is not easy (Hanoune 1997; on Vitruvius' instructions about building one (6.4.1, 5.2) see Small 1997, 160–2; on the layout of the Palatine library and the organization of the two collections, Greek and Latin, see Dix and Houston 2006; Iacopi and Tedone 2005–6; Corbier 2006, 173–4; see also Horsfall 1993). There was no fixed form, and usually only the discovery of the presence of *armaria*, the box-like shelves in which the rolls were stocked, can lead to confident conclusions. By far the most spectacular case is the library of Lucius Calpurnius Piso Caesoninus at Herculaneum, the destruction of which by the eruption of Vesuvius in 79 CE left behind the charred remains of hundreds of texts. Around 1,800 scrolls have been discovered there, and recent developments in computerized imaging mean that previously indecipherable scraps can now be transcribed and interpreted. Much work remains to be done, and it is to be hoped that further excavations will lead to yet more discoveries of lost texts, but the fragments we have are tantalizing. Vergil's name appears in three surviving papyri, along with those of Plotius Tucca, Varius Rufus, and Quintilius Varus. This evidence obviously locates him in the intellectual currents involving Philodemus and Epicureanism (see esp. Gigante in Armstrong et al. 2004, and Armstrong et al. 2004 in general), and it also makes it easy to imagine him actually working in the library itself. Other evidence links Vergil to the Epicurean teacher Siro (*Catal.* 5 and 8; *Vita Focae* 63; cf. Servius *ad Ecl.* 6.13; *Aen.* 6.264; see Armstrong et al. 2004, 1–2, with the skepticism of Horsfall 1995b, 7–8, and Stok's chapter in this volume) and informs us that Vergil spent little time in Rome, preferring the calm of Campania and Sicily (*Vita Donati* 13). Given that all of the library has yet to be excavated, Piso obviously had a very considerable collection of books at his disposal. If Vergil ever went there, what books could he have found? And how would he have worked? The *Life* of Donatus describes Vergil dictating lines to his scribe Eros, completing half-lines and asking for the two additions to be written down (*Vita* 34), and there is no reason to doubt that he could have worked in this way. He no doubt had a fantastic memory, but he will also have had slaves at hand to fetch scrolls and check up particular passages. Certainly, at Herculaneum he would have been able to read many Epicurean texts, much as Cicero saw Cato surrounded by Stoic writings. The remarkable work of scientists and papyrologists over many years enables us to picture in some detail the villa's meticulously organized collection. Its texts were annotated with titles, book numbers, line numbers, column numbers; they were carefully checked and corrected; the average height of the rolls is around 21–2 cm, with many having columns about 18 cm high and 5–6 cm in width. One can go so far as to suggest that when Vergil unrolled a scroll as he read, he would at any given time have visible in front of his eyes around 40 cm of papyrus revealing six columns of text (Delattre 2006, chap. 4; on scroll formats see also W. A. Johnson 2004, 3–13). In something like this form Vergil would almost certainly have been able to consult there all thirty-seven books of Epicurus' *On Nature* and the complete works of Philodemus. One can only try to imagine the interest with which he perused the latter's *De bono rege*, *De pietate*, and *De ira* (see the contributions by Indelli, Fish, Johnston, and Obbink in Armstrong et al. 2004). Latin texts were also present, and writings of Caecilius Statius, Ennius, and Lucretius have been identified. The intensity and complexity of engagement with the writings of others that one senses in all his poetry suggest that a huge amount of direct personal study of the texts went into his writing. To borrow the formulation of R. Thomas, it is impossible to imagine that the *Aeneid* was composed at an uncluttered desk, whether at Herculaneum or elsewhere. But it is necessary also to try to make the connection between attempts at imagining the physical world of Vergil as a reader and the ongoing task of trying to interpret his poetry.

At *Aeneid* 10.24 there is a doubt about the text. Did Vergil write at the end of the line *inundant sanguine fossas* ("they were flooding the ditches with blood") or *inundant sanguine fossae* ("the ditches were flooding with blood")? It is likely (see Conte 2007, 212–18) that we should prefer the latter reading, because Vergil probably had in mind a Homeric formula (*Iliad* 4.451 = 8.65, in each case at the end of the hexameter), "and the earth ran with blood." His *fossae* must be in the nominative case, in correspondence with the Homeric "earth." The parallel between the two texts takes on further importance at *Aeneid* 11.382, when Vergil repeats the same line-ending, thus reproducing Homer's double use of his formula. Obviously, this example illustrates Vergil's remarkably detailed awareness of Homer's repetitive style, and in doing so it raises the question of the ways in which Roman readers may have reacted to this particular aspect of texts which today we are used to interpreting in terms of oral poetics and formulaic composition. How did Vergil interpret verbal and thematic patterns of repetition in Homer? What did he make of them, given that his own epic style, no doubt partially under the influence of the example set by Apollonius Rhodius, eschews formulaic repetition? It seems reasonable to assume that appreciation of the densely intratextual and self-referential nature of the *Aeneid*, those aspects of the text which were so receptive to the application of New Critical readings in the middle of the twentieth century (see Putnam 2001), must begin from full realization of the importance of Vergil's study of and reaction to Homeric technique. In this particular case, use of the Homeric text as evidence for helping to choose the correct reading in Vergilian manuscripts implies acceptance of the fact that Vergil read Homer so closely as to know that he used a particular formula on only two occasions and that this knowledge led him to employ his own version of that formula only twice.

At this point, it is necessary to face up to the objection that modern researchers are too willing to make Vergil one of their own, too ready to see in the scholar-poet of antiquity a subtle postmodernist critic. Such a warning needs to be taken seriously, but certain factors concerning the traditions of scholarship in the ancient world must also be taken into account.

By the Augustan age, Homer had been the subject of study for centuries, and Vergil's debt to the various traditions of Homeric scholarship is very great (as is emphasized by Hexter's chapter in this volume). Behind his meticulous reworking of the formulaic "and the earth ran with blood" stands the work of Aristotle, Zenodotus, Philetas, Aristarchus, and many others, all students of Homer and Homeric language, interested in the collecting and detailed investigation of rare words and their meanings, the exact sense of unusual or outmoded technical terms, and the establishment of reliable editions of the poems. The Hellenistic age was one which saw the systematic collection and study of vast numbers of books, and Roman access to Greek literature came via the labors of scholars working in the great centers of learning that were Alexandria and Pergamum (in general see Pfeiffer 1968). Latin poets were educated in the complexities of Hellenistic poets and were fully aware of the importance of the traditions of Homeric scholarship for their creative efforts (Rengakos 1993). Vergil's library shelves, therefore, may have given pride of place to Homer, but the scrolls containing the *Iliad* and *Odyssey* will not have stood alone. Perhaps the most obvious illustration of this approach is the proposition that Vergil may have read all subsequent Greek and Latin literature as an imitation of or reaction to Homer, the primal Ocean from which all literary streams took their source. Again, a detailed example will give rise to broader considerations.

At the beginning of the second half of the *Odyssey*, the Phaeacians finally bring Odysseus back to Ithaca. Somewhat ironically, Homer, in lines (13.89–92) which recall the prologue of *Odyssey* 1, has Odysseus sleep at this crucial moment in the story, which takes place at dawn (13.93–5). Vergil likewise, at the beginning of the second half of his epic, has Aeneas arrive in the Tiber, at dawn (7.25–30). The two narratives of epic journeys coming to a close are obviously working in parallel. But Vergil was aware of another epic poet who had also structured his narrative of an epic voyage on the Odyssean model. Apollonius' Jason, right in the middle of his epic, arrives at his goal, Colchis. He arrives at night, but Apollonius brings the second book of his four-book poem to a close with a final line describing the arrival of dawn (*Arg.* 2.1285). Apollonius' next line (3.1.) reads, "Come now, Erato, stand beside me...." Vergil, following his account of the arrival in the Tiber, invokes exactly the same Muse, *Nunc age,... Erato...* (7.37). These connections help illustrate something of the care with which Vergil studied the narrative structures of his models. In doing so, of course, he was also studying carefully the use of the book as a unit of composition within a larger whole. One result of these efforts is the extraordinarily complex and polished book structure of the *Aeneid* (Harrison 1980; see more generally Hutchinson 2008, 1–41). But a further essential lesson to be drawn is that Vergil is not only reading Apollonius as a privileged model at the beginning of *Aeneid* 7, he is also reading Apollonius as a preexisting imitation of Homer. This process is in operation throughout the *Aeneid*, as Vergil consistently reads the *Argonautica* against the background of its Homeric models (see Nelis 2001). If more of Ennius' *Annales* had survived, it seems very likely that we would be able to chart the same process in detail. In theory, we could do so for every text (Farrell 2005b, 106–7). Further surviving texts can certainly be brought into the picture. For example, in *Aeneid* 4, the way in which Vergil models Dido on Apollonius' Medea shows that he also has detailed awareness of the importance of Euripides' *Medea* as a key model for Apollonius, and also for the Medea of Ennius, and for the Ariadne of Catullus 64, the latter in turn also being a close imitation of the *Argonautica*. It would of course be nice to know more of how Aeneas left Dido in Naevius, but ultimately, it is Odysseus' departure from Calypso which provides the essential Homeric framework and ensures the coherence of the epic pattern (see Nelis 2001, 159–66). Similarly, throughout the whole of the second half of the *Aeneid* Vergil is reading the cyclic *Nostoi*, Apollonius Rhodius, and numerous Roman historians with an eye to how he can fit the story of Trojans in Italy into a fundamentally

Homeric narrative structure. The most important lesson to be drawn from all this material is that even if Vergil's reading was vast, it was in no way haphazard. He read with an eye for the connections between texts, in doing so establishing patterns and traditions that are reflected in the densely intertextual nature of his poetry. To a remarkable extent, what Vergil does is to trace or create connections which enable him to connect aspects of every text he read all the way back to the *Iliad* and the *Odyssey*, the two poems that provide the basis of the scaffolding for the structure of the *Aeneid*.

A further important aspect of Vergil's relationship to Homer lies in the fact that he was acutely aware of many aspects of the history of the reception of Homer. In recent decades, a considerable body of research has shown that not only did Vergil study the Homeric texts themselves in great detail, he also read commentaries on them. For example, the song of Iopas in Dido's palace at the end of *Aeneid* 1 reworks the songs with which the blind bard Demodocus entertains the guests in Alcinous' palace in *Odyssey* 8. The fact that Iopas sings about natural science suggests that Vergil was aware of the allegorization of Demodocus' song about Ares and Aphrodite in terms of Empedoclean physics, seeing the adulterous divinities as the cosmic forces of Strife and Love. (Nelis 1992, 2001, 96–112 shows that Apollonius had already imitated Homer in the same way in his Empedoclean song of Orpheus in the first book of the *Argonautica*.) Similarly, scientific allegories based on the shield of Achilles in *Iliad* 18 have been shown to form the basis for Vergil's creation of the shield of Aeneas in *Aeneid* 8 (Hardie 1986, 336–76; again, Nelis 2001, 345–59 studies Apollonius' role as intermediary), and the Aristaeus episode in *Georgics* 4 has also been explained in terms of allegorical interpretations (Farrell 1991; Morgan 1999). Moral allegories also influenced Vergil in his adaptations of Homeric models, as he reacts to many of the different ways in which Greek scholars commented on different aspects of the *Iliad* and *Odyssey*. For example, it has been shown how Vergil's characterization of the Trojans and Rutulians in the Nisus and Euryalus episode attests his awareness of the fact that commentators were keenly interested in Homer's characterization of Greeks and Trojans in the Doloneia (Schmit-Neuerburg 1999, 23–65; Casali 2004b). A more detailed example will show the attention Vergil paid to Homeric criticism. Many scholars have noted (e.g., Knauer 1964a, 373 and 436) that the opening simile of the *Aeneid*, in which Neptune's calming of the storm raised by Juno is compared to the calming of a riotous mob by a single man of outstanding *pietas*, is related to the second simile of the *Iliad* 2.144–8, in which a speech by Agamemnon that stirs up the Greeks is likened to the effect of strong winds on waves and fields of grain crops. Given that scholiasts on the Homeric simile commented on it as an image of disorder and noisy confusion, it is striking that Vergil's version highlights just these aspects of the riotous scene, using the strong terms *seditio* and *furor* and thus establishing the latter as a leitmotif for the whole epic (Schmit-Neuerburg 1999, 66–82). Finally, it has been shown that Vergil's whole approach to the combination of both the *Iliad* and the *Odyssey* in the *Aeneid* owes a great deal to ancient discussions about the relationship between the two Homeric poems (Cairns 1989, 177–214). Once again, therefore, it is important to realize that we are not dealing here with a level of complexity which is in some sense beyond control. Vergil works in a highly systematic way, in which he reads the *Odyssey* back onto the *Iliad* and then reads the *Argonautica* of Apollonius back onto both epics, while at the same time consulting scholia on all three works and adopting an approach to reading which then enables him to bring numerous other texts into the picture (as shown above, Euripides, Ennius, Catullus, the Roman historians, etc.). This reconstruction of his creative vision and insistence on his ability to find and imagine transgeneric, thematic patterns suggest that there is validity in a holistic approach to Vergilian *imitatio* in the *Aeneid* which in the end traces every path back to Homer. But in doing so, one must avoid a schematic or procrustean reading that is centered on Homer alone as a consistently primary model, and one must never deny the presence and importance of the traces of many other texts. This point deserves illustration, and there are numerous examples of the way in which Vergil reads books in connecting patterns in order to combine different source texts. We will look at one from each of Vergil's three works, in order to show that this approach has validity for the Vergilian œuvre as a whole and to suggest that the undertaking of systematic work of this kind remains a major desideratum in Vergilian scholarship for the years ahead.

The opening of the *Eclogues* contains a poetic program for Vergilian bucolic, and in the way it reflects Vergil's reading of earlier texts it may be seen as fundamental in establishing the connectedness of his reading process and the resultant patterns of allusion (see Van Sickle 2000). Again, our study and appreciation of the way allusion works cannot be separated from the way Vergil reads texts.

The two opening lines of the *Eclogues* begin with the name of Tityrus and end with *avena*, the reed or pipe which accompanies his song (*Musam*, 2). At line 10, Tityrus explains why he has the leisure to sing, and his words *ludere...calamo* ("play on my rustic pipe") pick up Meliboeus' *meditaris avena* ("practice on your reed"). The scholia on Theocritus 3.2, a poem in which a goatherd leaves his flock in the care of Tityrus and sings his love for Amaryllis, record several etymologies of the name Tityrus, one of them linking it to the word *kalamos*. There can be little doubt that Vergil was reading his Theocritus with scholia and that the learned reader may be expected to pick up on the connections between Tityrus, *avena*, and *calamus* (F. Cairns 1999, 291–2; Hunter 1999, 111; see also on Vergil and Theocritean scholia Courtney 1990, 103; Hunter 2006, 127–8). In fact, he was probably using the edition of the bucolic poets put together by Artemidorus of Tarsus, which included ten *Idylls* ascribed to Theocritus, and probably also the commentary of his son Theon (F. Cairns 1999, 292–3). The procedure may be thought complex enough, but in fact there is much more going on. When a reader pronounces the opening line of the poem (*Tityre tu patulae*) s/he is recreating the sound of *Idyll* 1.1f. (*hadu ti to...hadu de kai tu*; cf. also *fagi/pagaisi*; *Meliboee/poimen...melos*). But even as Vergil engages so closely with Theocritus, there are good reasons for thinking that the name Tityrus comes also from Philetas (F. Cairns 1999, 289 n.1). Furthermore, the opening ten lines also show the impact of Callimachus, Meleager, and Lucretius, and probably also of Ennius, as Vergil draws attention to the "familiar textual world" he is introducing to his readers and creates an interpretive background shaped from earlier poetry about singing and about the countryside in relation to which his own pastoral song must be read (Hunter 2006, 118). It is this integrative aspect of the process that is so vitally important. Vergil's allusive practice is the result of an approach to earlier texts that is based on a keen appreciation of their interrelationships which permits him to focus on associative patterns and thematic connections. As a result, our reading must pay close attention to verbal texture in order to be in a position to trace intertextual links, but it is also vital to develop an instinct for identifying the thematic choices that may lie behind and explain any particular verbal reference to any particular text or texts, in order to be able to appreciate the full complexity of Vergil's technique. Consistently, the intricacies of individual intertextual moments can and must be related to much broader patterns of influence and imitation. The reader learned and alert enough to see that Vergil's second verse, **silvestrem *tenui* Musam *meditaris avena*** ("wooing the woodland Muse on slender reed," trans. Fairclough and Goold), reworks Lucretius, *DRN* 4.589, *fistula* **silvestrem** *ne cesset fundere* **Musam** ("that the panpipes may never slacken in their flood of woodland music," trans. Rouse and Smith), will probably also have recalled its original context, a passage which explains the phenomenon of the echo and the ways in which countryfolk imagine isolated rural places to be inhabited by satyrs, fauns, and Pan, making music with strings and pipe, and so brings us directly into an evocation of rural folk and their songworld. Certainly, Vergil seems to have noticed that a line from this passage, *tibia quas fundit digitis pulsata canentum* (*DRN* 4.585, "which the pipe sends forth touched by the player's fingers," trans. Rouse and Smith), reappears at *DRN* 5.1385, a passage in which Lucretius explains the origins of music and song, *per loca pastorum deserta atque* **otia** *dia* (*DRN* 5.1387, "amid the solitary haunts of shepherds and the peace of the open air," trans. Rouse and Smith). Vergil was no doubt reading both Theocritus and Lucretius in tandem (Breed 2000), since pastoral *otium* is, of course, exactly the context in which we find Tityrus as Vergil originates his own bucolic song: *O Meliboee, deus nobis haec* **otia** *fecit* (*Ecl.* 1.6, "O Meliboeus, it is a god who gave us this peace," trans. Fairclough and Goold).

Moving on to the *Georgics*, a reading of the close of the work will help to highlight further aspects of Vergilian technique.

> Haec super arvorum cultu pecorumque canebam
> et super arboribus, Caesar dum magnus ad altum   560
> fulminat Euphraten bello victorque volentes
> per populos dat iura viamque adfectat Olympo.
> Illo Vergilium me tempore dulcis alebat
> Parthenope studiis florentem ignobilis oti,
> carmina qui lusi pastorum audaxque iuventa,   565
> Tityre, te patulae cecini sub tegmine fagi.

> So much I sang in addition to the care of fields, of cattle, and of trees,
> while great Caesar thundered in war by deep Euphrates and bestowed
> a victor's laws on willing nations, and essayed the path to Heaven. In
> those days I, Virgil, was nursed by sweet Parthenope, and rejoiced in the
> arts of inglorious ease – I who toyed with shepherd's songs, and, in youth's
> boldness, sang of you, Tityrus, under the canopy of a spreading beech.
> (Trans. Fairclough and Goold)

These lines reflect the influence of Ennius, Callimachus, and Rhianus, but most obviously they evoke the reading of the *Eclogues*, as the last line famously echoes the first line of the earlier work, *Tityre, tu patulae recubans sub tegmine fagi* ("You, Tityrus, lie under the canopy of a spreading beech"). Just as Vergil situates the writing of the *Georgics* in Naples, he refers, in contrast to the thundering in war of Caesar, his own rejoicing in the "arts of inglorious ease," *studiis ignobilis oti*. In doing so, he includes a telestich, with the word *oti* running both horizontally and vertically (Schmidt 1983, 317):

> per populos dat iura viamque adfectat Olymp**o**.
> Illo Vergilium me tempore dulcis aleba**t**
> Parthenope studiis florentem ignobilis **oti,**

On the one hand, this kind of wordplay is indeed the fruit of leisured study, but mention of *otium* adds another connection to the opening of *Eclogue* 1, where *deus nobis haec otia fecit* (cf. also *lusi* in line 565 and *ludere* in *Ecl.* 1.10). The thematic importance of *otium* in both passages, when related to the explicit citation of *Eclogues* 1.1 at *Georgics* 4.566, suggests that the telestich is not accidental. Furthermore, its presence helps us to appreciate the fact that seeing it depends on careful study of a written text; such phenomena privilege textuality over orality, and their presence has important implicatons both for the way we should read Vergil and the way he himself read. As is well known, he was so keenly aware of the presence of an acrostic in Aratus that he imitated it with one of his own. At *Phaenomena* 783–7 the worked *lepté* runs both horizontally and vertically in the text, in a passage about weather signs. When Vergil writes about weather signs at *Georgics* 1.424–37, he includes his full name (**Pu**blius **Ver**gilius **Ma**ro) in coded fashion (429, 431, 433):

> Si uero solem ad rapidum lunasque sequentis
> ordine respicies, numquam te crastina fallet   425
> hora, neque insidiis noctis capiere serenae.
> luna reuertentis cum primum colligit ignis,
> si nigrum obscuro comprenderit aera cornu,
> **ma**ximus agricolis pelagoque parabitur imber;
> at si uirgineum suffuderit ore ruborem,   430
> **uer**tus erit: uento semper rubet aurea Phoebe.
> sin ortu quarto (namque is certissimus auctor)
> **pu**ra neque obtunsis per caelum cornibus ibit,
> totus et ille dies et qui nascentur ab illo
> exactum ad mensem pluuia uentisque carebunt,   435
> uotaque seruati soluent in litore nautae
> Glauco et Panopeae et Inoo Melicertae.

In doing so he flags up the acrostic to the reader twice, with the words *sequentis ordine respicies* ("[the moons] that follow in order you will inspect," 424–5) and *is certissimus auctor* ("this is the surest indication," but also "this is quite definitely the author," 432). The practice is neither unique in Vergil (cf. the Mars acrostic at *Aeneid* 7.601–4 signaled by the words *prima movent Martem*) nor particularly uncommon even in sub-literary epigrams (see Feeney and Nelis 2005 for discussion). Related also is the way in which Vergil not infrequently draws attention to the question of literary sources by the use of what has become known as "the Alexandrian footnote." Perhaps even more directly related to actual reading practices and the format of ancient texts available to Vergil is the fact that *Georgics* 4.400 imitates very closely *Odyssey* 4.400, showing that Vergil worked with numbered texts of Homer and illustrating his sense of the importance of structure and placement (see Morgan 1999, 223–9 for full discussion). Perhaps the best example of the latter phenomenon is the striking and much-discussed placing of the name Euphrates six lines from the end of *Georgics* 1 and 4 and *Aeneid* 8, in imitation of a reference to the river six lines from the end of Callimachus' *Hymn to Apollo* (Scodel and Thomas 1984; cf. Wills 1996, 22).

This element of Callimachean allusion at the end of the *Georgics*, when added to the citation of the *Eclogues*, draws attention to a further much-discussed aspect of Vergil's technique, that is, the way in which he constructs the image of a coherently structured poetic career. The sphragis of the *Georgics* unites the poet's career up to this point as a unified whole devoted to the poetry of the countryside. He does so in lines which look back directly to the prologue to *Georgics* 3, a passage in which he had set out his plans for a future epic poem. Discussion of these famous lines (*Geo.* 3.1–48) has tended to center on the question of whether the poem there outlined is in fact the *Aeneid*. Intense scholarly disagreement on this question may best be read as a reflection of the fact that the text can be read as a meditation on the epic tradition and a revelation of Vergil's study of the poetic options open to him as he began planning the composition of a Roman epic. The prologue offers a perspective on the translation of Greek poetic traditions to Italy and the whole process of the creation of a literature in Latin, on Aristotelian and Callimachean criticism of the epic cycle, on generic boundaries, definitions of *epos*, and the choice between writing an historical epic in the Ennian tradition and the construction of a new historical vision based on Homer and the exploitation of Hellenistic etiological narratives (see Nelis 2004). Having completed the *Georgics*, as readers of the *Aeneid*, we do not have to wait very long for confirmation that such considerations are indeed at the center of Vergil's mind:

> hic tibi (fabor enim, quando haec te cura remordet,
> longius et volvens fatorum arcana movebo)
> bellum ingens geret Italia, populosque feroces
> contundet, moresque viris et moenia ponet,

> This your son – for, since this care gnaws at your heart, I will
> speak and, further unrolling the scroll of fate, will disclose its
> secrets – shall wage a great war in Italy, shall crush proud nations
> and for his people shall set up laws and city walls, ...
> (Trans. Fairclough and Goold)

In his note on line 262, R. Austin (1971) notes that "*volvens* is probably a metaphor from the unrolling of a book," providing the image of Jupiter reading either the book of fate or a book of Roman history, depending on one's temporal viewpoint. Certainly, Jupiter's speech has a strongly teleological thrust; it is a narrative of Roman history which owes more to Ennius than we can tell, and it also owes debts to Lucretius in passages where it is easy to imagine Ennius as a direct model. At the same time, the differences between Jupiter's vision and the *Aeneid* are worth pointing out: the latter famously jumps *in medias res* and avoids chronological narrative order; Vergil does not directly relate the founding of Rome and the city's subsequent history (Anchises and Vulcan do that in books 6 and 8 respectively); Vergil does not describe the ultimate caging of *Furor*, as his poem ends with an act based on *furor*. In a strong sense, Jupiter is reading an alternative version of the story, a narrative path Vergil could have taken, one he presented as an option in the prologue to *Georgics* 3, but one he in the end rejected. Of course, as readers of the *Aeneid* we do in fact end up reading about the working out of *fatum*, and Rome's destiny. And it is by no means by accident that the act of reading is once again thematized at what is in many ways the climax of both the scroll Jupiter is reading and of the *Aeneid*, the moment when Aeneas looks at the great shield made by Vulcan, on which the god has depicted the whole history of the city of Rome, from Romulus, Remus, and the wolf to the Augustan triple triumph of 29 BCE. As Aeneas first ponders the shield, we are told that it is a *non enarrabile textum* (*Aen.* 8.625, the shield's ineffable fabric), and as he stops "reading" it and puts it on his shoulder, he admires its beauty but fails to grasp its historical trajectory or comprehend its ideological thrust (*rerumque ignarus imagine gaudet, Aen.* 8.730, "and though he knows not the events, he rejoices in their representation"). Obviously, as readers of the poem we are here implicated in a revealing moment of metapoetic reflection, but perhaps we should also pause to consider the ways in which this scene presents to us Vergil's reflection of his own role as a reader. At the end of *Aeneid* 8, at what is the end of the poem's historical narrative, we are no doubt meant to imagine him reading his own poem, like Aeneas pondering the artwork of the shield. He too is caught up in thinking about the horrible reality of violence and its aesthetical representation in verse, and about the ways in which art can be put to use to make some sense of the tragedy of history or simply to justify what in the short term may be seen as its predetermined end. In a sense, it may be true to say that in terms of our attempts to get a glimpse into Vergil's library, we may imagine that the last book he ever read was his own epic. And maybe, in harmony with the double image of the resentful Araxes and Turnus (cf. *pontem* **indignatus** *Araxes* at 8.728, "Araxes **chafing** at his bridge," and *fugit* **indignata** *sub umbras* at 12.952, "his life fled **resentfully** to the shades below"), we are left at the end with a reflection of a deeply troubled spirit.

APPENDIX

Accius, Aeschylus, Alcaeus, Alcman, Apollonius Rhodius, Aratus, Aristotle, Bacchylides, Bion, Callimachus, Cassius Hemina, Cato, Catullus, Cicero, Calvus, Choerilos of Samos, Cinna, Empedocles, Ennius, Epic Cycle, Epicurus, Eratosthenes Euphorion, Fabius Pictor, Furius Antias, Gallus, Herodotus, Hesiod, Homer, Homeric Hymns, Horace, Laevius, Leonidas of Tarentum, Livius Andronicus, Livy, Lucilius, Lucretius, Lycophron, Meleager, Moschus, Naevius, Nicander, Orphic texts, Pacuvius, Parthenius, Phanocles, Philetas, Philodemus, Pindar, Plato, Plautus, Pollio, Polybius, Propertius, Pindar, Pythagorean texts, Rhianus, Sallust, Sappho, Sophocles, Sophron, Stesichorus, Terence, Thucydides, Theocritus, Theophrastus, Tibullus, Tyrtaeus, Theocritus, Varius, Varro Atacinus, Varro Reatinus.

FURTHER READING

For further information on Roman books and libraries some standard works are Birt (1882), Boyd (1915), and Kleberg (1967). There are useful surveys also in French by Salles (1992) and Valette-Cagnac (1997). On the epic tradition, Foley (2005) offers a rich and wide-ranging collection of studies. On intertextuality, Conte (1986), Pucci (1998), and Edmunds (2001) are central contributions. On Vergil's working methods, Horsfall (1991) is fundamental. Those interested in the format of papyrus scrolls should consult W.A. Johnson (2004).

CHAPTER TWO

On First Looking into Vergil's Homer

Ralph Hexter

The Homeric poems haunt the *Aeneid* and virtually all subsequent Vergilian scholarship. I need not and could not rehearse all the rich and important work that has been done on this, perhaps the most profound of intertextual relations. Uncannily, and in seemingly overdetermined fashion, a literally unknown specter of the *Aeneid* was made to hover about the poem even before the book itself took corporeal shape. Propertius summoned it:

> cedite Romani scriptores, cedite Grai,
> nescio quid maius nascitur Iliade.

> Stand back, Roman writers, stand back, ye Greeks:
> Something greater than the *Iliad* – I know not what – is aborning.
> (Propertius 2.34.65–6; see Schmit-Neuerburg 1999, 2 n.6)

This unknown thing is somehow Homeric, and Vergil's imitative and emulative relationship to Homer, anticipated by Propertius, quickly became an obsession for Vergil's immediate *obtrectatores* (see Stok and Farrell in this volume) and for defenders such as Quintilian, Aulus Gellius, Macrobius, and Servius. It was obscured if not entirely invisible even during the centuries when the inaccessibility of Homer's Greek original stood in the way of Western scholars (Scaffai 2006), but has been constant since the humanists' recovery of Greek, gathering momentum as a scholarly topos over the last century (Knauer 1964b; Cairns 1989; Berres 1993; Dekel 2005). At this late date, is a fresh vision possible?

In the title of this essay I evoke the virginal gaze memorialized in Keats' "On First Looking into Chapman's Homer." The poem describes an experience of revelatory reevaluation. Keats had not, we are to understand, been able to gauge Homer's true greatness, a matter of considerable moment to the Romantics (Simonsuuri 1979; Selden 2006), "Till I heard Chapman speak out loud and bold." George Chapman's translation of Homer, effected in the early years of the seventeenth century (*Iliad*

1611, *Odyssey* 1615), was one that Keats could only have "heard" in his mind's ear. The great eighteenth-century translation of Homer into English was Alexander Pope's, and it would certainly have been bracing for any reader accustomed to Pope's polished rhymed couplets to come upon Chapman's relative roughness and primal vigor. It is this feeling of bracing wonder that Keats conveys in the yet more famous sestet:

> Then felt I like some watcher of the skies
>> When a new planet swims into his ken;
> Or like stout Cortez when with eagle eyes
>> He star'd at the Pacific – and all his men
> Look'd at each other with a wild surmise –
>> Silent, upon a peak in Darien.

This is of course one of the great howlers of English literature – it was Balboa, not Cortez, who first saw the Pacific, as any commentator would note. But the factual error matters not in the least, because what Keats celebrates is the power of speculation, of imagination, an experience one can have perhaps best of all by reading. Chapman's English *Iliad* and *Odyssey* gave Keats an inkling of Homer's "original genius," but clearly an inkling only, just as those men who gazed out at a Pacific for them just hoving into view could hardly imagine what a vast ocean lay before them.

The speculation I propose is rather less grand, but I invoke Keats and "Chapman's Homer" as a constant reminder that mine is also, to a certain extent, an imaginary reading. In addition, I have no wish to traduce Keats by recalling his confusion of Balboa and Cortez. Rather, let the record of this error serve as a parallel to the various criticisms of Homer that we will encounter in this essay: the reader's knowledge of such things in no way diminishes the effect of the poem, and if anything may actually increase it. For Keats, Chapman's Homer is about wonder and proliferating possibility. I argue here that Vergil's Homer was, *mutatis mutandis*, about those same things. And while Keats was describing how Chapman gave him access to Homer, I am not engaged in looking at Homer through Vergil but rather, reversing the optic, will try in a sense to look at Vergil through Homer. Like Keats I will, in my imagination, go back to "a book of Homer," a particular version from an earlier time. The book that permits us to look "into Vergil's Homer" is "Vergil's copy of Homer."

* * *

Can we conjure Vergil's own copy or copies of Homer's poems? Since no work, or rather pair of works, is of more importance for the *Aeneid*, it would be wonderful if we by some miracle could have these particular rolls, just as it would be worth a king's ransom to possess all of Vergil's library, even to know its contents in detail. (See Nelis in this volume.) This idea of Vergil's library, however abstract, is conceptually relevant for what I mean by "Vergil's Homer," for I want to emphasize the importance of thinking about Vergil's Homer historically, i.e., in light of the Homeric scholarship that had accumulated up to Vergil's day, much of which would have been available to him from a variety of sources, including Vergil's own teachers like the Epicurean philosopher Philodemus of Gadara (Cairns 1989, 7, 10, etc.; cf. Schmit-Neuerburg 1999, 8–9; Obbink 1995; Janko 2000). For there is no question but that Vergil's understanding of Homer was shaped by such scholarship.

But coming to grips with this accumulated scholarship is not a simple matter. We cannot, for instance, simply imagine Vergil with a "variorum Homer" on his desk, an edition with notes recording the interpretations of multiple experts, such as one could imagine in many later periods. We can be reasonably certain that such books did not exist until long after Vergil's death. Studies of the genesis of the surviving Homeric scholia, which generally date from the fourth century CE and later, have established that in Vergil's day, Homeric scholarship was by and large not present as marginal commentary in book rolls containing the Homeric poems, or at least not to any significant degree. This qualification refers to the presence of significant Homeric scholarship in the form of marginal marks, such as *obeloi* marking certain verses as "inauthentic" in the opinion of one or more scholar. I will return to these *obeloi* shortly. But our exegetical scholia, which contain explanatory comments of diverse sorts – what one generally calls "commentary" – derive from various individual works that originally circulated independently as monographs (*hypomnêmata*), not as marginalia in the text of Homer. And they circulated abundantly: of that there is no question.

Study of ancient scholarship on Homer, especially in its Hellenistic phases, and of the means by which the earlier *hypomnêmata* and marginal critical marks were selected and layered into the later scholia that have come down to us in the margins of existing witnesses of the *Iliad* and (to a lesser extent) the *Odyssey* comprises a field in itself, advancing with ever greater sophistication as hypotheses and inferences drawn from the collation of extant scholia are controlled with recent papyrus finds. But the process requires great caution: if one wishes to focus on the first century BCE, before the compilation even of the so-called *Viermännerkommentar* (VMK, a "four-man commentary" that drew on the works of Aristonicus, Didymus, Herodian, and Nicander: see Dickey 2007, 19), compiled probably in the fourth century CE, one must be circumspect in one's use of the scholia. It is, however, sufficiently established that many individual scholia that we read in a form that must postdate the first century nonetheless reflect accurately the scholarly opinions and critical views current in Vergil's day.

One of the pioneers in establishing Vergil's knowledge and use of contemporary Homeric scholarship was Robin Schlunk. As Schlunk observed near the outset of his sober but immensely suggestive study of the Homeric scholia and the *Aeneid*, "Vergil assumed a thorough knowledge of the *Iliad* and the *Odyssey* in his readers, but he also assumed that they possessed a general acquaintance of the traditional Homeric literary criticism" (Schlunk 1974, 6; cf. Knauer 1964b, 69 n.1). Indeed, Schlunk argued that not Vergil alone but his readers – his ideal readers at least – shared such erudition. But despite the reference here and occasionally elsewhere to Vergil's readers, Schlunk's analyses of the workings of Homeric scholia function primarily at the level of (or at least are described in terms of) Vergil's own imitative and adaptive processes. To cite an example that he adduces: Aristarchus had expressed criticism of Alcinous' offering his daughter as wife to Odysseus, a complete stranger who had shown up at his hearth in book 7 of the *Odyssey*. Aristarchus' opinion is preserved in the P-scholion on 7.311:

> Aristarchus doubts that these six lines are Homer's…. they might reasonably be removed. For how, when he does not know the man, [can] he espouse his daughter to him – not urging him but beseeching him?

The T-scholia develop this line of thought further, in characteristic fashion:

> The wish ... is unfitting (*atopos*), for neither knowing who he is nor making an attempt, he wishes to take him into his house and make him his son-in-law. (Schlunk 1974, 9; cf. Schmit-Neuerburg 1999, 286–7)

What Schlunk notes, explicitly following Servius' own steps (*ad Aen.* 7.268), is that in his construction of *Aeneid* 7 Vergil is careful to present Latinus as learning exactly who the arriving stranger is before he offers him his daughter Lavinia; indeed, Latinus goes so far as to learn what the prophecies are concerning the new arrival's future in Italy. This is "fitting" paternal behavior. In this manner Schlunk, following some hints by Heinze (1914, as noted by Schmit-Neuerburg 1999, 15), established that a proper evaluation of the expectations with which Vergil's readers approached his text must take as its point of departure Vergil's Homer, that is, the Homer represented by, even produced by, Hellenistic scholarship.

It has taken some time for Schlunk's study, modest in scale if not in its implications, to gain the appreciation it deserves (e.g., Lyne 1987, 227; Cairns 1989, 181). Now, a full generation after Schlunk's work, Tilman Schmit-Neuerburg (1999) carries the work further by systematically presenting a generous set of cases that exemplify how Vergil's response to and adaptation of his Homeric models was filtered through his intimate familiarity with contemporary Homeric scholarship. As he puts it, consideration of Vergil's literary-historical context suggests

> that Vergil had access to the Alexandrian tradition of Homer exegesis. As a "poeta doctus" ["learnèd poet"] who probably adapted whatever struck him as important for his poetry, he was likely aware of Alexandrian commentary and criticism of Homer and its literary-aesthetic categories. Also, his audience's understanding of Homer was in all likelihood strongly influenced by this exegetical tradition. (Schmit-Neuerburg 1999, 14–15)

For my purpose, Schmit-Neuerburg sustains and reconfirms, many times over, the fundamental points that Schlunk had already established: first, that Vergil was familiar with and responsive to contemporary Homeric scholarship, and, second, that while we lack direct witnesses for most of the scholarship to which he had access, extant scholia – if handled carefully – can serve as reasonable proxies for the actual views and opinions Vergil knew.

I propose to take a further step. Building on the work of Schlunk and Schmit-Neuerburg as well as others who have contributed to our enriched and nuanced appreciation of intertextuality, I want to make the claim that in the time of Vergil, reading Homer along with contemporary scholarship on the poem had an impact on readers' conceptions and understanding of the Homeric text and on the process of reading itself, and that it had such an impact on Vergil first and foremost. In making such a claim, I align myself with relatively recent developments in the study of commentary. In previous generations, most scholars of a given tradition have been interested in (later) commentaries only to the extent they might permit them to reconstruct the original of the literary text. For example, they ask if there are textual "readings" preserved in the lemmata or elsewhere in a scholium that are superior to (or at least independent of) the direct tradition of manuscripts. Or, they ask whether a commentary, however late it may be in its present form, reports a fact or an ancient understanding not available in any other source. Perhaps initially only to assess the antiquity of the material transmitted, scholars have sought to reconstruct the critical methods of the ancient critics via material that is excerpted, often at several removes, in the surviving scholia. But now this line of inquiry has developed into a field of study in itself, expanding the investigation of critical and scholarly methods to include explicit and implicit aesthetic and literary views, whether the interest in the latter pair is primary or because such views often undergird critical decisions (Mühmelt 1965; Nickau 1977; Uhl 1998; Scaffai 2006). In the case of Vergil and Homer, both Schlunk and Schmit-Neuerburg similarly conceive of the aesthetic canons of Hellenistic scholarship, for the most part, as a limiting device. By taking note of those passages in Homer with which critics had found fault, Vergil might avoid the same sort of criticism. And there is no doubt that this is a part of the process. But it is not everything.

While obviously dealing with the critic as "reader" of the original text, such traditional studies either remain focused on the original author or shift into a distinct register of "history of scholarship." The two can be linked, of course, and scholars now regularly weigh the impact marginalia or interlinear glosses have on the reception of a particular text. But there is a further, crucial question: what impact does commentary, in its various forms, have on the reading process, a process one must itself understand as a learned habit, or – to employ a usage with some popularity in recent years – as a "technology"? This is easier to trace when one has many roughly datable and localizable extant books, as in the medieval traditions of major Latin classical authors – Vergil, say, or Ovid – where on the basis of accumulating scholarship one can now begin to create a coherent narrative that takes into account modes of textual layout involving commentary that can offer insights into an ongoing reception history (e.g., Baswell 1995).

My focus, then, is on the modes of reading fostered by readers' interaction with scholarly parerga and the institutions of scholarship that this material represents. I am interested here not so much in the way the author of a particular commentary (or scholarly view) read the text on which he comments as in how commentary itself establishes certain expectations which, taken together, call a style or mode of reading into being. And even as I seek to focus on Vergil and his contemporaries as readers of Homer, I will want less to distinguish between the views and tendencies of particular scholars or interpretive schools than to look at the undifferentiated mass, although the fact of difference among views will itself prove important. I will explain this seeming paradox shortly.

First, however, I must address a methodological challenge. However clear it is (thanks to Schlunk and Schmit-Neuerburg) that scholia can serve as proxies for views known to Vergil, there is no evidence whatsoever that variorum editions of commentary circulated in Vergil's time. On the contrary, and as noted above, the individual explanations and criticisms of Homer that made their way into later assemblages of scholia were still in the form of monographic *hypomnēmata*. Marginalia were probably limited to critical markings – *obeloi, diplai*, etc. – whether present in various "editions" of the Homeric poems one could acquire or placed there by scribes and users on the basis of *hypomnêmata* or even oral teaching. What one can assert, however, is that by the first century BCE, Homeric scholarship was a well-established enterprise. Homeric scholars were responding not only to Homer but also to their scholarly predecessors and contemporaries (often rivals), in such a way that the "space" of Homeric reading and study itself constituted a virtual variorum commentary.

The significance of my emphasis on precisely this "variorum" dimension of the space of Homeric scholarship will emerge shortly, but I want to be utterly candid about this step in my argument. Clearly, while the collision of contradictory views may be more obvious in a marginal note that collects two or three competing interpretations for easy comparison, there can be no question that divergent opinions and interpretations circulated and were recognized as clashing. Homeric scholarship was already a notoriously disputatious realm, and not just professional scholars but advanced readers conversant with that world of scholarship – of the sort Vergil surely was, as Schlunk and Schmit-Neuerburg's studies have established – would be aware of a good number of the disagreements, and certainly of the existence of disagreement. For this reason and in this regard, I maintain that the scholia can serve not only as a guide to specific choices that Vergil made in fashioning his imitation of Homer, but also as a proxy, if perhaps only an approximate one, for what I want to call the space of Homeric reading – the universe of interpretive possibilities – as far back as the first century BCE. As I have tried to make clear, however, one need not insist that the scholia themselves play that role, since the disputes existed and were known as such in the scholarly forms that then circulated (cf. Schmit-Neuerburg 1999, 17–18).

To illustrate, let us start with a typical dispute over the reading of a two-foot line-ending word in the *Iliad*. In the text of the verse we describe as *Iliad* 18.485, Zenodotus (born ca. 325 BCE) believed Homer had said that the stars on Achilles' shield "stood fixed," *estêiktai*, while Aristarchus (ca. 216–144) argued that Homer said that they "garland the heavens," *estephanôke* (Porter 1992, 92–3). Now, although each ancient scholar might admit that the passage has its difficulties, neither believes it betrays any ambiguity. A modern reader of the *Iliad* equipped with a variorum commentary cannot help but be confronted with the dispute: we, necessarily, read an ambiguous Homer. Such commentaries, as I have said, did not exist in Vergil's day. But even before the assemblage of such commentaries or even of the full-scale scholia that circulated in later antiquity and the Middle Ages, the advanced reader or student of Homer who had access either to different *hypomnêmata* or to a teacher who summarized the nature of scholarly disagreements for his student, "reads" an ambiguous Homer. And while the example that I have chosen is only one example involving one word, hundreds, possibly even thousands of comparable disagreements confronted a reader traversing the *Iliad* at this point in the exegetical tradition. (For instance, the T-scholion on *Od.* 7.13 quoted above continues with an historical argument to save the disputed moment for the "true Homer," setting up a debate within one and the same note – just one of a hundred such cases.) The tradition teaches the reader that in one and the same passage Homer may mean this or he may mean that. And although each scholar may have wished only to clarify and establish the certainty of one meaning, the accumulative tradition of commentary paradoxically has the opposite effect: it establishes a polyvocal original. This even happens, willy-nilly, when a commentator adduces the view of a predecessor only to refute it, since he thereby inscribes the earlier view within his own commentary. As in the interpretation of dreams, there is no "not" in commentary.

Hellenistic scholarship had a vocabulary for such difficulties: the *aporiai* – difficulties or puzzles – and *zetêmata* – questions to be answered. If the cumulative scholia give any kind of suggestion of what students and readers would have had to go through in learning, for example, about the first line of the *Odyssey* – and I will be satisfied if what we have represents that discussion only approximately – they will have heard about or read of the different senses of man (*anêr*) Homer exhibits and whether "man" necessarily entails bravery (*andreia*) before being confronted with the first major *aporia* (so the scholia describe it) in the poem: how can Odysseus be called *polytropos*? Might that not be bad? When the reader gets to the second verse and comes to the verb *eperse*, s/he must confront the "problem" why Homer mentions Odysseus in this regard and not Achilles. And in the third line, students or serious readers with recourse to secondary literature would have to confront the first textual problem: Zenodotos argued the text should read *nomon egno*, "he knew their custom," not *noon egno*, "he knew their mind." Even as the critics sought to fix the text and make it stable and certain, by the curious, even perverse logic of commentary described above, they actually destabilized it for readers. Indeed, the more attentive and studious the reader, the more unstable the text.

Before I press my argument several steps further, let us pause and take stock. I am claiming that there had emerged by Vergil's day an "aporetic" Homer. This was true mainly for advanced students and readers who proceeded through either Homeric poem with an eye (or ear) to the disputes that had been conducted over several preceding generations by energetic Hellenistic scholars. This Homer is a poet whose inconsistencies and divergences from other mythological traditions were carefully noted, whose every character, in deed and word, was measured against the canon of "the proper" (*to prepon*) or the likely or credible (*to pithanon*), and whose (for that time) indecipherable nonce words were the subject of etymology and fantasy. I do not believe that "aporetic" is too strong a term, for many of the scholia on Homer, and not only those that begin with the words *aporia* or *zêtêma*, suggest that the process of interpreting the Homeric poems was fraught with difficulty at virtually every step. And there are steps that take us beyond Homer the merely vexing wordsmith. We need also to attend to the modes of reading that such a Homer – himself the product of the institutions and technologies of Hellenistic scholarship – in turn produced. It is only with this first sketch of Homer as "aporetic" poet, I would maintain, that we begin to catch sight of "Vergil's Homer."

* * *

Earlier I compared the world of commentary with the psyche as described by modern psychoanalysis: in neither is there a "no." Following the logic of the comparison for a moment, one may note that the commentator, and indeed any reader who has evolved within the tradition, is empowered, like the psychoanalyst, to engage the text in dialogue, to confront it, call its bluffs, resist it. And with critics ready to dispute not only each other but Homer (in the form of the Homeric text), it would not be wrong to term such disputatious readers "resistant." For *aporiai* must be discovered – the rhetorical term "invented" is quite apt – in the text before the interpretive process can proceed to offer solutions. Zoilus (fourth century BCE) is mocked through the ages as the prototype of the unreasonable critic, and there were slews of *Homeromastiges*. These readers were quick to take offense at this or that real or imaginary slight in the text, and it was by being such disagreeable readers that they gained entrance to the interpretive tradition (and, one notes, won long-lasting fame – in however narrow a compass). So Megacleides found it implausible that Achilles, in his fight with Hector at *Iliad* 22.205, could manage to keep his fellow Achaeans from shooting at Hector: "Megacleides says that this single combat is unrealistically constructed, for how could Achilles restrain so many myriads [of warriors]" (Schlunk 1974, 101; Schmit-Neuerburg 1999, 301–2). Again at *Iliad* 4.100, when Pandarus takes aim at Menelaus, someone whose views are preserved in the bT or exegetical scholia is critical: "why does he not [rather] shoot Agamemnon since he is unarmed, or some other one of the nobles, but [chooses] the armored Menelaus?" (Schlunk 1974, 88; Schmit-Neuerburg 1999, 278–9, 324). Whatever we may think of these and other such impertinences, it seems clear at least that such readers are contentious and "resistant" (Fetterley 1978), however modern that term may sound.

* * *

Resistance and independence of judgment may be the literary critic's best tools. With this in mind, let us turn again to the Homeric poems and take account of a yet more radical form of agnosticism that these confident scholars – again paradoxically – imparted to the commentary tradition, which in turn (as I argue) passed it along to readers as a veritable principle of uncertainty. Now in all traditions scholiastic reading of the *Iliad* began with the question – *zêtousi* or *zêteitai* – why the poem begins where and how it does. Why "wrath"? Why at this point in the history of the war? There were many other questions and issues to address, but in line 4, in the very first sentence, students and serious readers were confronted with the issue of athetesis. For while we read that Achilles' wrath "sent many brave souls to Hades," Zenodotus believed that our texts erred in adding that these were the souls of "heroes" whose "bodies became prey for dogs and all birds, as Zeus willed."

Zenodotus' intervention here was a significant one in the history of Homeric scholarship, but its full significance has so far been missed. The great historian of scholarship Rudolf Pfeiffer observes that athetesis was used by Zenodotus and also by Aristophanes of Byzantium (ca. 257–180) and that its use was raised to an art and science by Aristarchus (Pfeiffer 1968, 114, 117, 231, 240; Erbse 1959; van Thiel 1992; Lührs 1992; Nagy 2004). But this focus on issues of priority does not stop to consider what athetesis *does* to the reading process, and why athetesis should be cited as the most radically resistant mode of reading the complex of Hellenistic Homeric scholarship presents – even if, again by that curious logic, it was first created out of a kind of conservatism.

By placing a mark, the *obelos*, opposite a line in the text of Homer, scholars could mark their opinion that it should not be read. In their opinion, and for whatever reason – one of several was usually adduced and eventually memorialized in the scholia – it did not belong to "their" Homer. The basic conservatism of athetesis, which is comparable to modern practices of bracketing rather than actually eliminating certain verses from the printed page, has often been praised. But what was the status of athetized lines in the reading process? Not removed but notionally "not to be read," such athetized lines enter into a peculiarly spectral realm. They have a paradoxical, Cheshire-catlike status, at once there and not there. And, again, can we imagine what the cumulative effect of proceeding through the *Iliad* and traversing alternating patches of verses "under athetesis," signaled by marginal signs, would have been? Even as you follow a particular critic who rejects this line or that, the line(s) remain(s) there as excluded, silenced, as banished, as ghosts. In other words, readers of Homer already in the time of Vergil dealt not only with a text in which lines and words could bear divergent meanings: some portions of the very text might (in some sense) not even be there! This is reading under the sign of athetesis.

At this juncture I propose to stake out one further step in this speculative sequence. Let us consider what effect a text stippled with athetesis, in some cases cumulative and sometimes conflicting atheteses, might have on a reading interpreter's capacities to handle textual evidence. Might one be more than ever inclined to discount bits of textual evidence inconveniently contradictory to one's particular position? Instead of mental reservation, we will have mental athetesis.

* * *

Schlunk and Schmit-Neuerburg both found much in the episode of Nisus and Euryalus (*Aen.* 9.168–449) to exemplify the ways in which Vergil accommodated Homeric scholarship as he "imitated" and "emulated" the Iliadic Doloneia. Although Schmit-Neuerburg's discussion is richer and more detailed, already Schlunk had found in the episode one of the clearest among a number of instances in which Vergil, adapting a passage at which Homeric critics had carped, took care to avoid opening himself to the same criticism. For instance, Homeric critics questioned how Agamemnon could see from behind the Greek walls into the Trojan camp (*Il.* 10.11–12), offering as possible solutions either that the Trojans were on high ground or that this was seeing in his mind (schol. 10.11 [bT] and 10.12 [A], quoted and translated by Schlunk 1974, 60; cf. Schmit-Neuerburg 1999, 30n.101). Accordingly, when Vergil created the corresponding episode of the *Aeneid*, he took care to specify the Trojans' vantage point over the Rutilian camp (*haec super e vallo prospectant Troes*, 9.168). Whether or not Vergil's inclusion of this detail establishes that he thought this specific criticism of the Homeric passage was a reasonable one, it strongly suggests that Vergil shared with Homeric scholars certain canons of coherence, probability, and realism (within the human realm at least). One might even go so far as to say he had internalized them. I wish, though, to shift our perspective away from Vergil as poet to the unintended consequences of an accumulating body of scholarship on Homer that saw again and again myriad problems of diverse nature, perpetuating them for all subsequent readers who accessed their Homer along with accompanying commentary (Lang 1995, 201–2).

Consider in this regard another "problem" of seeing in the Doloneia, namely, how Odysseus could see Dolon in the night. Particularly emblematic, it seems to me, is the

B scholion on *Iliad* 10.399, in which one commentator simply guessed at an answer: "probably because towards dawn the moon arose." As Schlunk reminds us, "there is ... no mention of the 'moon rising ...' in the *Dolonia*, nor ... of the moon at all" (Schlunk 1974, 71). But of course, from Schlunk's point of view it is precisely this moon, which someone inferred *must* have been there even though Homer says nothing about it, that Vergil places in his book 9 and which reflects so disastrously from the helmet Euryalus bears off as the spoils of war. But assuming that Schlunk's inference is right (as I believe it surely is), let us not forget where this moon came from, for it will rise again: it rose out of a reader's imagination.

* * *

I have offered here only the most fleeting of glimpses into Vergil's Homer. One can certainly look beyond and begin to describe – *hoc opus, hic labor est* – what Vergil did with what he saw. My own argument would lead me to the following formulation: Vergil, reading a Homer already rendered problematic by the disputatious discussions that swirled around the text, imitated it by creating a new text that was aporetic from the ground up. In other words, he aimed to recreate the entire structure of the Homeric text itself already rendered polyvalent by the divergent interpretations it inspired.

I believe that this was conscious on Vergil's part, and although I do not actually think that establishing intentionality on this point is the central issue, I do want to make a significant distinction: to claim that it was conscious on Vergil's part does not mean that he would have described it in the same way. The aporetic mode of poetry is certainly continuous with the learned and erudite poetry of the Hellenistic period with which Callimachus (among others) had long been associated, the impact of which on Roman letters can hardly be overestimated (Hunter 2006). Reference to the wider literary culture of the day reminds us that, of course, Vergil's contemporaries – Horace, Ovid, Propertius, not to mention Varius or Manilius – had potentially equal access to Homeric scholarship, and that comparable effects may be found in their works. It would be foolish to deny this. But there is something extraordinary about the degree to which Vergil's poetry – and here I mean all of Vergil's poetry, not only the poem that was his frankest and most ambitious Homeric imitation – is characterized by the effects I have tried to describe here.

Further study could and should test what I have claimed here, namely, that the scholarly context in which the Greek poet was read and received in Vergil's day inspired a particular mode of reading, one which I call aporetic; and, further, that writing in this mode, Vergil recreated a text that is often as problematic as Homer rendered aporetic, a text that as such is treacherous to traverse, requiring wariness, arousing resistance. We readers need to reflect on our tendencies, even susceptibilities, in the presence of such a text. If we bring to the text our own moons that rise and fall, let us at least recognize the true nature of these phenomena.

Not that specters and visions do not appear in earlier literature, described by the poets themselves, Homer included; but now, reading texts of which parts have been rendered spectral by means of athetesis, ghosts themselves may represent aporetic spirits. Following these spirits would be one of the ways to test the impact of aporetic reading on Vergil's program in the *Aeneid*, but one that must be reserved for another occasion.

FURTHER READING

This chapter continues work I have pursued for two decades on commentary not as an abstract form but within distinct historical contexts, in published work more often on the medieval period: Hexter 1986, 1988, 1989, 2002. I have elsewhere offered examples of aporetic interpretations of other episodes from the *Aeneid*: Hexter 1990, 1992, 1997; less provocatively, Hexter 1999. My thanks for encouragement particularly as I have worked on Vergil in recent years to Alessandro Barchiesi, Susan Stephens, Daniel Selden, Daniel Boyarin, Edan Dekel, Curtis Dozier, Tyson Hausdoerffer, and the editors of this volume. I especially appreciate the kind notice that James O'Hara (2007, 24) recently gave to a talk on this general theme that I gave in 1994. I hope to have allayed the concern he (rightly) raises about the argument the published abstract presented. Thanks also to Uwe Vagelpohl for his help at various stages of the preparation of this chapter, and to Joe Farrell in particular, for extraordinary aid in licking, bear-like, my contribution into final and appropriate shape.

Some of the first impulses to broader thinking about the way commentary and commentary traditions work on readers and reading emerged from studies of other traditions, most particularly of scriptures. See, for example, Hartman and Budick (1986), Boyarin (1990), Henderson (1991), Fraade (1991), and Fishbane (1993). There are several very suggestive pieces in both Assmann and Gladigow (1995) and Most (1999), including, in the former, the contributions of Wolfgang Raible, Ithamar Gruenwald, Aharon Agus, Rudolf Wagner, Walter Haug, Hans-Jürgen Lüsebrink, Raimar Zons, and the editors themselves, and, in the latter, the editor's preface and the essays by Daniel Boyarin, Simon Goldhill, Don Fowler, and Hans Ulrich Gumbrecht. There is less of direct interest in this regard in the subsequent collections of Goulet-Cazé (2000) and Geerlings and Schulze (2002), though the recent spate of conferences and volumes testifies to new growth in the field.

For a general overview of the papyri and the history of transmission, see Haslam (1997) (on Homer) and Rengakos (1993, 153–8) (on Hellenistic poets).

On ancient schools of Homeric interpretation: The first volume of Pfeiffer (1968) is still hardly rivaled for detailed information and analysis across the entire field. For a summary and entrée to the vast bibliography, see Kennedy (1989). For further soundings in ancient Homeric scholarship and exegesis (the two are by no means coterminous) see van der Valk (1963–4), Lamberton (1986) (again with further bibliography), Richardson (1980, 265–87), and, on scholia more generally, Wilson (1983). (Yet earlier but still of value, Wilson 1967.) A recent and immensely helpful *vade mecum* to the complex terrain of ancient scholarly texts is provided by Dickey (2007; on Homeric scholia, 18–28).

"Homeric problems" or "puzzles" as a title (and genre) goes back to Aristotle; indeed, in his own *Aporhêmata Homêrika*, now lost, he engaged in debate with the ultimate carping critic Zoilos of Amphipolis. See Pfeiffer (1968, 67–70).

Barchiesi (1984) offers a rich and suggestive account of how Homeric "effects" shape "Vergilian narration." From among the sea of works on the Vergil–Homer complex, I highlight but a few titles: Berres (1993), Cairns (1984), Dekel (2005), Knauer (1964b).

Classicists may well envy scholars of more recent authors the wealth of information preserved, even if modern scholarship now dismisses such genetic library-based studies as John Livingston Lowes' famous 1927 account of Coleridge's "Kubla Khan."

CHAPTER THREE

The Development
of the Aeneas Legend

Sergio Casali

Learning from the Greeks

In the *Aeneid* Aeneas' fleet lands at the mouth of the Tiber, and the Trojans first settle on the site where we can imagine one day will rise the city of Ostia. In the pre-Vergilian tradition things went differently: the Trojans landed slightly to the south in Latium, in the *ager Laurens*, the shore immediately facing the site where Aeneas would settle Lavinium; there was the traditional location of the first Trojan settlement ("Troia"). And it was there, in fact, that the Vergilian reader had been led to believe that the Trojans would land, since in the first words of the proem Vergil had announced his intention of singing of the hero who *Lavinia...venit/litora*, "came to the shores of Lavinium" (2–3) – clearly, and falsely, making the reader anticipate that he would have followed the standard tradition regarding Aeneas' landing in Latium. This is one of the many false tracks that Vergil puts in his poem, and one of the many allusions to versions of the legend that are subsequently discarded by the narration of the *Aeneid*. But why does Vergil decide, for the first time, to make his Trojans land at the mouth of the Tiber?

The answer is obvious. Vergil has a desperate need to bring his Aeneas into strict contact with the river that flows down from the site of the future Rome. And actually, just at the beginning of book 8, the god of the river himself, Tiberinus, appears in a dream to Aeneas (*Aen.* 8.31–65) and communicates to him a prophecy. The point of this prophecy is strategic military advice: before anything else Aeneas must, as chance would have it, go up the river and seek an alliance with the people settled there who had "founded a city upon hills" (*posuere in montibus urbem*, 8.53), a city called Pallanteum from the name of one of their ancestors. These people are Greeks: specifically, Arcadians led by King Evander (8.51–3). They share the same enemies as Aeneas, namely the Latins (8.55). Strangely enough, Aeneas, thanks surely to the great authority of the divine prophet, does not find anything odd in the idea of going to ask Greeks for help (we should recall that at the same time, his enemies, led by

Turnus, have decided, apparently with better sense, to send an embassy to the Greek hero Diomedes, who also had settled in Italy, to ask his support against his old Trojan enemies: 8.9–17).

The presence of the Arcadians on the Palatine is not an original idea of Vergil's (cf. Musti 1984, 271); but an encounter between Aeneas and the Arcadians on the site of the future Rome is an episode that lacks any precedent. Aeneas, then, goes up the Tiber, and arrives before the Palatine hill "by chance" (*forte*, 8.102) on the very day when the Arcadians were celebrating the festival of Hercules – another enemy of the Trojans. (Nobody worries about this, either; and as a matter of fact, in the Homeric model of this entire scene (in *Od.* 3: cf. Eden on *Aen.* 8.97ff.), Telemachus arrives at Pylos during a festival of Poseidon, Odysseus' persecutor.) Evander's son Pallas boldly confronts the newcomers, but Aeneas holds out an olive branch and quietly admits he is a Trojan, but also an enemy of the Latins (8.115–20). Aeneas and Evander exchange speeches which underline their close, unexpected kinship, in the perfect style of the ancient "kinship diplomacy." Then Aeneas has only to listen. A Greek begins to illustrate to the proto-Roman all that is needed to know about the site of the future Rome. To be sure, in the corresponding reception scene in book 7, the Italian King Latinus had also been able to tell Aeneas something about the past; but his memories were appropriately confined to the Italian origin of Dardanus (see below), and above all they were confused, second-hand memories obscured by the years (7.205–11). The Greek Evander, instead, has very clear ideas about everything.

It is, then, a Greek who recounts to Aeneas the story of Hercules and Cacus (8.184–279), transforming what until that moment, in the Latin tradition, was a banal story of cattle-rustling into a sort of clash between Good and Evil. Cacus, in the antecedent tradition, was nothing but a mortal man, a shepherd or a brigand, a vulgar cattle thief, sometimes a servant of Evander, and an Arcadian himself; but here he is magnified, and becomes a fantastic, smoke-belching monster, the son of the god Vulcan. The climax of Cacus' wickedness occurs when he resorts to an unheard-of trick by dragging the cattle that he stole from Hercules backwards into his cave: *at furis Caci, ne quid inausum / aut intractatum scelerisve dolive fuisset…* ("but the cruel mind of the thief Cacus, so as to leave no crime or trick unattempted or undared…," 8.205–6). There is an interesting textual question here: manuscripts and editors are divided between *furis*, "of the thief (Cacus)," and *furiis*, "by the madness (of Cacus)." "*Fur*" is not an epic word ("*vocabulum epica gravitate indignum*," Heyne 1833, 203) and in my view its appearance in Evander's speech is a classic example of the "return of the repressed," namely the traditional version of the story of Cacus (who is called ληστής for example by Dion. Hal. 1.39.2; cf. *Hymn. Hom. Hermes* 14, 292, 446). And the story goes on, with Hercules' triumph and the hymn to the god sung by the Salii. But now Evander brings Aeneas to his citadel: the two men make their way towards the Palatine, and the Greek Evander diffusely recounts to Aeneas his memories about the preceding inhabitants of the site. It is he, a Greek, who teaches the proto-Roman Aeneas the history of ancient Latium and the succession of its former inhabitants (8.313–36). It is again he who accompanies Aeneas on his famous tour of the future Rome (9.337–61). After a night spent in Evander's humble hut, further long speeches await Aeneas the following day: Evander urges the Trojan hero to seek an alliance with the Etruscans (an element never clearly attested in the pre-Vergilian tradition). He relates in detail the wrongdoings of the exiled Etruscan leader Mezentius and offers his son Pallas, with a squadron of Arcadian horsemen, as auxiliaries for Aeneas (8.469–515). After the prodigy of the weapons that appears in the sky and the preparations for leaving, Evander speaks again (8.560–83): his speech should simply be a farewell to his son, but the old Greek does not miss the chance of relating a totally new "Herculean" tale about how he himself, as a young man, had slain the triform monster Erulus (8.560–71).

The Greek Evander is, after Aeneas, the character who speaks the most in the *Aeneid*, more even than Anchises. Evander tells the story of Hercules and Cacus, "which has such a central symbolic role in the *Aeneid*" (L. Morgan 1998, 175); Evander is, surprisingly, called *Romanae conditor arcis* (8.313) as an introduction to his "historiographical" account of the history of ancient Latium. Momigliano (1989, 338–42, esp. 340–1) proposes seeing in the encounter between Aeneas and Evander a symbol of the reconciliation between Greeks and Trojans and between Greeks and Romans. This point of view is certainly valuable. However, at the same time, the talkative and "historiographical" Evander is also a symbol of the way in which the Romans, represented by their ancestor Aeneas, have learned their own past from the Greeks and from a Greek point of view. The process involves two elements. The first is to model Roman or Italian "history" on stories told already by the Greeks about themselves. The second is to claim that the Roman or Italian story is without precedent.

An example: When Evander tells the story of Hercules and Cacus and disparages Cacus for his extraordinary and wicked inventiveness in excogitating the "unheard-of" trick of dragging Hercules' cattle backwards into his cave, we should not forget that, as Aeneas himself says, *vobis* (i.e., to Evander and/or the Arcadians) *Mercurius pater est, quem candida Maia / Cyllenae gelido conceptum vertice fudit*, "your father is Mercury, whom the beautiful Maia brought forth on the icy summit of Mount Cyllene" (8.138–9). For Cacus' trick is after all not so "unattempted or undared" (8.205–6) if, as everybody knows, the first to use it was precisely Evander's "father," Mercury/Hermes. (So, literally, Dion. Hal. 1.31.1 and Paus. 8.43.2; Vergil is vaguer, but Mercury is in any case a direct ancestor of Evander.) The opening line of the *Homeric Hymn to Hermes* describing the birth of Hermes from Maia on Mount Cyllene is furthermore recalled by words spoken by Aeneas himself (8.138–9: cf. *Hymn. Hom. Hermes* 1–7). Evander then does nothing but recall a story that took place a few steps away from his own former home. (Mount Cyllene is located near the Arcadian town of Pheneus, and Evander is precise in indicating that he used to live there (8.165), against the standard traditions which connected him rather with cities like Pallantion or Tegea; cf. Vergil's usual method of alluding to alternative versions at 8.459, where Evander has a *Tegeaeum...ensem*.) If Cacus does nothing but copy a trick performed by Hermes, then we will be less surprised when his terrified flight from Hercules is described with a metaphor which "does not seem found before Virgil" (Fordyce 1977, *ad loc.*): *pedibus timor addidit alas*, "fear had given wings to his feet," 8.224. Winged feet, of course, have always been one of the standard attributes of Hermes.

Evander is the prototype of the Greek historian or erudite who teaches the Trojans/Romans about their own past, even that of the most remote periods. (Cf. 8.355–8, where Evander shows Aeneas that the site of the future Rome, even then, already has the timeworn ruins of the primeval cities Ianiculum and Saturnia.) Aeneas' visit to Evander is a kind of narrative counterpart to the famous article of Bickerman (1952, 65), about the modalities through which "The Greeks dispensed with any imaginative effort respecting the founders of Rome." Their effort was that of explaining the origins and the past of Rome (as well as of the other non-Greek peoples with whom they came in contact) in the light of their own past. The Romans, then, were explained as descendants of Aeneas, of *their* Aeneas, a character from their own national poem. Incorporation, magnification, explanation from a Greco-centric point of view: in the same way Evander incorporates the story of Hercules and Cacus in his own quasi-"familial" history, he magnifies it, transforming the banal and totally human story of cattle-stealing we find in every other source into an epic fight between Hercules and a fire-belching monster; and, for instance, he explains, with careless cultural imperialism, the Lupercal, the vital center of the autochthonous legend of the origins of Rome, not, obviously, through an impossible and anachronistic reference to the story of the she-wolf and the twins, but by tracing it back to the Arcadian tradition of Parrhasian Pan: *et gelida monstrat sub rupe Lupercal / Parrhasio dictum Panos de more Lycaei*, "and he shows him under the icy rock the Lupercal of Pan Lycaeus, dedicated according to the Parrhasian custom" (8.343–4), in neat contradiction to the "Roman" perspective found in the prophecy of Jupiter (1.275) and on the shield of Aeneas elsewhere in book 8 (630–4).

The Prophecy of Poseidon

Everything, in fact, starts with a prophecy of the Homeric Poseidon, without which the Greeks (and then the Romans) would have had to find another founding father for Rome. In *Iliad* 20 Achilles and Aeneas are on the verge of fighting a duel in which Aeneas would surely have died: he is hefting a huge stone in order to throw it at Achilles, but that would have been useless because "from close up the Pelides would have killed him with the sword" (*Il.* 20.290). But the usually anti-Trojan Poseidon notices what is about to happen and addresses the other gods. It is obvious, he says, that Aeneas, (enigmatically) deceived by Apollo (compare with *Il.* 22.212–13 the equally enigmatic *Aen.* 12.405–6, *nihil auctor Apollo / subvenit*; cf. Miller 2009, 179) into entering this uneven duel (*Il.* 20.99–109), is about to die, and the god is worried about the survival of the stock of Dardanus: "Already Cronides has started to hate the stock of Priam; now the strength of Aeneas will rule over the Trojans (Τρώεσσιν), and over the sons of the sons who after him will be born" (*Il.* 20.306–8 (~ *h. Hom. Aphr.* 197–8)). And therefore Poseidon goes on to save Aeneas from Achilles.

Ironically, if we consider its future use in the course of centuries, this prophecy already had an immediate "propagandistic" function: this is the only *post eventum* prophecy found in the *Iliad*, and it was almost certainly intended to please a dynasty of pretended descendants of Aeneas who ruled over the Troad in about the middle of the eighth century BCE. (Smith 1981 denies the historical existence of such Aineiadai in the Troad; but this has no real importance for us because the prophecy was read this way in antiquity: cf. the sources collected by Smith himself.) Ironically again this same passage, which authorizes the Aeneadic origins of Rome, would also become a source of great embarrassment: Aeneas and his descendants, Homer says, are destined to rule "over the Trojans" (Τρώεσσιν, *Il.* 20.307), a limitation that some people might have considered highly inappropriate. Why did Homer not say "over the Romans," or even better "over all the world"? This issue would vex many intellectuals of the Augustan age, who would propose many adjustments, including the possibility that Homer had pronounced a "Roman" prophecy (see Dion. Hal. 1.53.4; Strabo 13.1.53, p. 608). The most interesting, and maybe the funniest, effort involved the direct emendation of Homer's text, with the displacement of Τρώεσσιν by πάντεσσιν ("over everybody"); cf. Strab. cit.; schol. Arn/A *Il.* 20.307–8. (In the exegetical scholia we also found the enlightening explanation that Homer knew about the future of Rome thanks to the Sibylline Oracles: schol. T *Il.* 20.307–308a.)

We can now jump ahead from Homer to the *Aeneid*. In book 3 the Trojans, in their desperate search for prophecies about their future and their goal, land on the island of Delos and are benevolently greeted by the priest and King Anius (a stop attested, with several variants, in the pre-Vergilian legend). However, it is Aeneas himself who interrogates the oracle of Apollo. And Apollo famously replies that they should "look for their ancient mother" ("*antiquam exquirite matrem*," *Aen.* 3.96), namely Italy itself, the motherland of Dardanus in Vergil's extravagant version. It is strange that, immediately afterwards, it is Apollo himself who echoes the words of Homer's Poseidon (who in the *Iliad* had intervened by addressing the other gods in polemic against Apollo's indifference to Aeneas' fate); but in fact it is Apollo who now says: "*antiquam exquirite matrem. / hic domus Aeneae **cunctis dominabitur oris** / et nati natorum et qui nascentur ab illis*" ("look for your ancient mother. Here the house of Aeneas will dominate **all the lands**, and so the sons of their sons, and those who will be born from them," *Aen.* 3.96–8). The Trojans, misguided by Anchises, who brings them to Crete, do not immediately understand what this "ancient mother" is meant to be; but the reader immediately understands that Vergil is performing here a particularly complex operation. In the same moment when he invents (or in any case recuperates from an extremely marginal, even unattested, version) the entirely new myth of Dardanus' *Italian* origin (cf. the elucidations of the Penates in *Aen.* 3.160–71), he comes back to the very point of departure of the very story of the Aeneadic origins of Rome – and he does so, in a splendidly self-reflexive way, by choosing to quote that fundamental Homeric prophecy in the "wrong" way, that is, in the most propagandistically philo-Roman way that was available to him.

From the Promised to the Real Rescue

From the rescue of Aeneas permitted by Poseidon in *Iliad* 20, with the related promise of rule "over the Trojans," to the prophecy of Apollo in *Aeneid* 3 that the house of Aeneas will rule "over the entire world," there is, of course, a long way to run. Not only must Aeneas rescue himself from the sword of Achilles, he must also escape from the destruction of Troy. He must build a fleet and sail towards the west, obviously with some member of his family (for example, an old father, and maybe a son through whom to continue the stock so dear to Jupiter); he must travel a lot, and in the meantime found cities in which he might settle for good – at least until a new stage of the legend uproots him from that place to bring him closer and closer to the fated coasts of Latium. And credit for this entire story, in its infinite variants, goes directly to the Greeks.

Poseidon's words guarantee the rescue of Aeneas from the destruction of Troy. But of course, they were anything but clear regarding his future destiny. The most natural interpretation would seem to be that Aeneas and his progeny (although no son of Aeneas, by the way, is ever mentioned in the *Iliad*) rule in the Troad, maybe after rebuilding Troy. But in the *Iliupersis* ("Sack of Ilion"), according to Proclus' *Chrestomathia* (fifth century CE?), after the Greek fleet has sailed away when the Trojans have gathered around the fatal Horse to celebrate the end of the war, there appear two snakes, which kill Laocoon and one of his sons. "Feeling misgivings at the portent, Aeneas and his party slip away to Ida" (Procl. *Chrest.*, tr. West 2003, 145). This was also Sophocles' version, according to which Aeneas fled towards Ida carrying his father on his shoulders (fr. 373 Radt; see Lloyd-Jones 1996, 198–201 and Most's chapter in this volume). As one can see, these early versions of the flight of Aeneas did little honor to the hero: Aeneas fled from Troy even before the Greeks emerged from the Horse. However, different versions of Aeneas' flight from Troy proliferated: some were more honorable to Aeneas than those of the Iliupersis and Sophocles, while others were even shameful:

1. According to "someone" (*ap.* Dion. Hal. 1.48.4), Aeneas was absent from Troy during the fatal night because he was engaged with a military mission in Phrygia, or for other causes.
2. In various sources, Aeneas escapes from the Greeks thanks to his *pietas*:
    (a) In Xenophon (*Cyn.* 1.15) he gains a reputation of εὐσέβεια ("piety") by saving his ancestral gods and his father.
    (b) In Lycophron (1261–9), when only Aeneas, for some unstated reason, is allowed by the Greeks to take something away from the city, he abandons his wife and children and chooses instead the household gods.
    (c) In Diodorus Siculus (7.4) the Greeks call a truce with Aeneas and some other Trojans who still occupy a part of the city, allowing everybody to leave with whatever objects they could carry with them. While the others choose valuable objects, Aeneas takes his father on his shoulders; the Greeks, impressed, offer him a second chance, and he chooses his ancestral gods.
    (d) According to Aelian (*VH* 3.22), Aeneas can take only one thing: his first choice is the gods, the second his father; then the Greeks decide to let him keep all of his property. In this version, as also in (a) and (c), there is no mention of wife or children.
    (e) A version of this story is attributed to Varro's lost *Antiquitates rerum humanarum* (fr. 9 Mirsch) by Serv. Dan. *ad Aen.* 2.636; cf. schol. Ver. *ad Aen.* 2.717 Baschera 106–7. Lycophron, Diodorus, and Varro may all depend on Timaeus or perhaps Fabius Pictor.

3. The most shameful version of the story involves treason on the part of Aeneas. This is originally a Greek and perhaps specifically anti-Roman version (Gabba 1976, 92–3), but it eventually becomes strangely attractive for Roman authors as well (and extremely popular in the Middle Ages: see Spence in this volume):
    (a) Aeneas betrays his fatherland because he hates Paris: so Menecrates of Xanthos (fourth century BCE?), *FGrHist* 769 F 3 *ap*. Dion. Hal. 1.48.3; cf. *OGR* 9.2; Dares Phryx 37–44; Dictys Cretensis 4–5.
    (b) More or less along this line we should also note Livy 1.1, where Aeneas (along with Antenor) is freed by the Greeks because he had opposed the war and sustained the restitution of Helen (cf. schol. Eur. *Andr*. 14).
4. In Hellanicus' *Troika* (*FGrHist* 4 F 31 *ap*. Dion. Hal. 1.46.2–4) we find the most honorable version of Aeneas' flight. Not surprisingly this is also the version that most resembles *Aeneid* 2: Aeneas, during the sack, orders that women, children, and old people retire to Mt. Ida; then, he strenuously defends the citadel; and only at the very end does he withdraw together with his father, the gods, his wife, his children, and other defenders (see the detailed analysis in Heinze 1993, 55–9; Gantz 1993, 652–3, and especially Horsfall 2008, passim).
5. We should also recall a version attested for the first time by a Roman source, the "miracle" version (schol. Ver. *ad Aen*. 2.177 Baschera 107 = Hemina fr. 5 Peter, fr. 6 Santini): "it is added by L. Cassius [Hemina], ex-censor [the text is uncertain], that it was a prodigious event, rather than his father's nobility, that rendered Aeneas invisible to the eyes of the Greeks, and that allowed him to pass through the enemies without any damage, and to go and sail away with the ships which had been granted to him to sail to Italy." In a similar way, in Quintus of Smyrna (13.326–32) Aphrodite leads the flight of Aeneas' family, the flames divide before them, and the Greek arrows are magically diverted (cf. Vian 1969, 228 n.2; Tryph. 651–5).

The Voyage of the Legend from Troy to Italy

Until now we have seen that Aeneas *had to* be saved from Troy (because of Poseidon's prophecy in Homer), and how in fact he *was* saved (in multiple versions). But Aeneas did not have only to save himself from Troy and take refuge on Mt. Ida. At a certain point he would also have to depart, and depart towards the west. The poems of the epic cycle do not say anything about Aeneas' eventual goal. The twelfth-century Byzantine scholar Johannes Tzetzes (*ad Lyc*. 1268; cf. 1232) quotes a passage that he attributes to the *Parva Ilias* according to which Aeneas was taken away from Troy as a prisoner by Neoptolemus (= frr. 29–30 West): but this is a very dubious piece of information, both because the same lines are elsewhere (schol. Eur. *Andr*. 14) attributed to the Hellenistic poet Simias of Rhodes (ca. 300 BCE) and because Proclus' *Chrestomathia* does not even name Aeneas (see Horsfall 1979b, 378; Gantz 1993, 714).

The *Tabula Iliaca Capitolina* is a stone tablet sculpted as a bas-relief, found near Bovillae, which is part of a series of similar tablets with illustrations of the Trojan War. They contain inscriptions connected to the passages of the poems they illustrate (*Iliad*, *Odyssey*, epic cycle, etc.). The tablet dates to the Augustan period, and in its central panel, which depicts the fall of Troy, Aeneas appears three times. In one scene he receives what appears to be a round box (the Penates?) from another character who is on his knees (Panthus?). In a second, Aeneas appears in a group while he is clearly in the process of leaving Troy (he is depicted as walking through a door): he takes Ascanius by the hand, carries Anchises on his shoulders (who is now holding the box), and is followed by a woman; Hermes leads the group. Finally, we see him boarding a ship together with Ascanius, Anchises, and Misenus (no more woman). This last scene is described with two inscriptions:'Αγχίσης καὶ τὰ ἱερά. ("Anchises with the sacred objects," which the old man is handing to someone on the ship, which is by the way crowded with sailors); and Αἰνείας σὺν τοῖς ἰδίοις ἀπαιρῶν εἰς τὴν 'Εσπερίαν ("Aeneas with his own while leaving for Hesperia"). All of this has been attributed to the *Iliupersis* of Stesichorus (*PMG* 205 Page). The hypothesis that a Sicilian poet of the sixth century BCE might already have known of a connection between Aeneas and the "Hesperia" (a substantive by the way unknown to archaic and classical Greek and in general use only from the Hellenistic period onwards), and maybe also between Aeneas and Cape Misenus (Misenus is not known as a Trojan before Vergil), has given rise to much discussion and a good deal of balanced skepticism (Horsfall 1979a, 1985, 223, with further bibliography). The most we can say is that Stesichorus perhaps knew of a tradition according to which Aeneas sailed towards the west (so Gruen 1992, 14). But even this much is doubtful (cf. Gantz 1993, 714–15).

In fact, the development of the Aeneas legend, especially the way in which the hero is "transferred" from Troy to Italy, remains very difficult to understand. Unlike Horsfall (1985, 223), Gruen (1992, 14–16) tends to believe that the Sicilian Greeks placed great importance on this "transfer." Thucydides (6.2.3), probably following Antiochus of Syracuse, speaks of Trojan refugees who, having arrived in Sicily, took the name of Elymi and founded the cities of Eryx and Segesta. With this tradition we may compare certain details in *Aeneid* 5 (Aeneas founds the new city of Acesta for the companions he leaves in Sicily, as well as the temple of Venus Erycina (746–61); Helymus is a young comrade of King Acestes (5.73); etc.). A certain Alcimus (late fourth century BCE?), author of a work on the antiquities of Sicily and Italy, transmits what is probably the most ancient testimony connecting Aeneas with Romulus and with the foundation of Rome: "Alcimus says that Romulus was a son of Thyrrenia and Aeneas, and that from him (Romulus) was born Alba (!), granddaughter of Aeneas; from the son of Alba was born Rhomus, who founded Rome" (*ap.* Festus 328 L. = *FGrHist* 560 F 4). Another Sicilian, Callias (early third century BCE), the historian of Agathocles, does not seem to know Aeneas, but he speaks about the arrival in Italy of a Trojan woman, Rhome, future wife of Latinus, and mother of Rhomus, Romulus, and Telegonus (?), who founded Rome and named it for their mother (Dion. Hal. 1.72.5 = *FGrHist* 564 F 5; cf. D'Anna 1976, 58; Vanotti 1995, 39–40).

As one can see, the situation is quite complicated. Making it even more complicated is the contribution of Hellanicus of Lesbos (ca. 490–400 BCE). In his *Troika*, as we have seen, Hellanicus had written about the resistance of Aeneas during Troy's fatal night. Our immediate informant, Dionysius of Halicarnassus (1.46.1–48.1 = *FGrHist* 4 F 31 = 77 Ambaglio), closes a narration that he attributes to Hellanicus (but there are many confusions: cf. Horsfall 1985, 222) by discussing Aeneas' final flight, his crossing of the

Hellespont, and his arrival at Pallene in Chalcidica. And this would seem to be Aeneas' final destination. (Chalcidica, by the way, was an area with strong "Aeneadic" associations: suffice it to recall the city of Aineia, which was proud of having been founded by Aeneas.) However, Dionysius himself elsewhere attributes to "Hellanicus" a very different story (Dion. Hal. 1.72.2 = *FGrHist* 4 F 84 = 160 Ambaglio). In this version "the author of the history of the Priestesses of Argo" is supposed to have said that "Aeneas came to Italy from the land of the Molossians [i.e., Epirus] with Odysseus, and became founder of Rome, to which he gave this name because of Rhome, one of the Trojan women." Now, we know that Hellanicus was the author of a treatise entitled *The Priestesses of Argo*. If the story reported here by Dionysius could really be attributed to Hellanicus, then we would certainly have the very first attestation, in the middle of the fifth century BCE, of the foundation of Rome by Aeneas (enigmatically, "with Odysseus"; the variant "after Odysseus" is to be rejected as clearly *facilior*). The attribution of the story to Hellanicus has been strongly contested by Horsfall (1979b, 376–83; 1985, 223), but others are less skeptical (e.g., Solmsen 1986; Galinsky 1992, 94).

Other enigmas, not surprisingly, await us if we turn to a work which is enigmatic by definition, Lycophron's *Alexandra*. Its author can probably be dated to the beginning of the third century BCE (opinions about this differ). But a supplementary problem arises from the so-called "Roman section" of this work (*Alex.* 1226–80), where we find a richness of information about the Roman legend of Aeneas that has no parallel in any other Greek author of the same period. For this reason, many think that this section is in fact an interpolation dating to the Augustan period (so esp. West 1983, 1984; cf. recently Horsfall 2005, who suggests that Lycophron's Roman section is much more pointed if we think of it as post-Vergilian). Doubts about this section, in fact, were already voiced by ancient commentators. Anyway, this is what Alexandra (Cassandra) obscurely prophesies: one day her descendants (the Romans) will rule over the world (1226–30); Aeneas "will leave" two lion cubs (1230–5; evidently Romulus and Remus, but are they sons, grandsons, or more distant descendants? Cf. Cornell 1975, 3; D'Anna 1976, 76); Aeneas will first inhabit Recelos in Macedonia (1236–8); then he will pass to Etruria, where he will make an alliance with a "nanos," a former enemy (Odysseus? Cf. Hellan. (?) *FGrHist* 4 F 84, quoted above), and also with the two brothers Tarchon and Tyrrhenus (1238–49; the only precedent, if it is one, not counting the presence of a "Tyrrhenia" in the genealogy of Alcimus, quoted above, of the alliance between Aeneas and the Etruscans in the *Aeneid*). There follow, in a very peculiar form, the prodigies of foundation which are well known from the *Aeneid* (and other sources): the eating of the tables (1250–2); the foundation in the lands of the Aborigines of thirty towers from the thirty piglets born from a black sow that Aeneas has brought with him from Troy (1253–8; the thirty towers should be identified with cities founded by Aeneas around Lavinium); the sow is "black" instead of being "white" as usual (both in the *Aeneid* and in the rest of the tradition); the difference in color is probably explained by the subsequent lines but, since the original sow must be "white" (*alba*, because she is etymologically linked with Alba Longa), it can clearly be understood only "as a perverse Greek variation upon a Latin original" (Horsfall 2005, 39); Aeneas will consecrate a bronze image of this sow in one of the cities he founds (Lavinium: cf. Varro, *RR* 2.4.18) and he will also erect a temple to Pallas, where he will deposit the Penates

(1259–62). Alexandra then speaks about the honor which Aeneas gave to the Penates, when at Troy he preferred them, together with his old father, to any other object or member of his family (1263–90, quoted above). The section closes with a further prophecy about the power of Rome over the boundaries of Latium (1270–80).

Italian Events: The Fusion with the Twins Story

Whatever the chronology of Lycophron and of his "Roman section," in it we see already developed most of the essential components of what will become the historiographic, and then the poetic vulgate of the legend of Aeneas in Italy. In the *Alexandra* we have seen a direct, genealogical (even if not precisely definable) connection between Aeneas and Romulus and Remus, the "two lion cubs." And we have also seen at least a hint of what will be a not easily explained constant of the legend: Aeneas does not found Rome. The foundation of Rome is to be mediated through that of two other cities, Lavinium and Alba (the latter not mentioned by Lycophron, but already vaguely present in the genealogy of Alcimus: see above). This brings us into a real minefield: the question of what could have been the historical role of Lavinium (to say nothing about Alba) in the transmission of the legend (and the cult) of Aeneas in Latium and at Rome.

   A hypothesis that has had much fortune makes Etruria the main intermediary through which the legend of Aeneas as founder was introduced into Latium and Rome. It is based on archaeological findings of vases and little statues representing Aeneas (see especially Alföldi 1965, 278–87; Galinsky 1969, 12–140; contra, see, e.g., Gruen 1992, 21–2 with bibliography; for the images of Aeneas in Etruria, cf., e.g., F. Canciani, *LIMC* s.v *Aineias* I.1, p. 338, nos. 93a–96). At the moment, in the wake of archaeological research conducted in Latium during the second half of the twenti- eth century, the most widespread idea is that Greek culture introduced itself to Latium directly, and that Lavinium was the intermediary through which the legend of Aeneas penetrated into Rome (Dury-Moyaers 1981; Castagnoli 1972, 1982, 1987a). But reasonable doubts have been expressed (see Gruen 1992, 24–5) about the value of archaeological findings at Lavinium as testimonies of a real and *originary* cult of Aeneas Indiges (or Pater Indiges, or Iuppiter Indiges) corresponding to what is suggested by the literary sources (cf. Liv. 1.2.6; Festus p. 94 L.; *OGR* 14.4; Ver. *Aen.* 12.794–5). It is difficult to demonstrate that the connection of Aeneas with Indiges at Lavinium preceded the Roman adaptation of the Trojan legend (Gruen 1992a, 24). Certainly the Romans did want to see in Lavinium and in Alba their own ancestor cities, but it is almost impossible to evaluate the exact directions of the various influences.

   What is certain is that the historian Timaeus (early third century? late fourth century BCE? cf. Galinsky 1992, 99) considered the Trojan origins of Rome as an indisputable fact, and that he went to Lavinium in search of proof. He was not able to see the sacred objects that were identified with the Penates of Troy and that were supposedly preserved in the innermost part of a temple, but he received information about them from the inhabitants of the place (Dion. Hal. 1.67.4 = *FGrHist* 566 F 59; cf. Dury-Moyaers 1981, 65–72). Varro considered Lavinium as the first settlement of the Roman stock in Latium, and states that there were preserved "our gods the Penates" (*LL* 5.144, *oppidum quod*

primum conditum in Latio stirpis Romanae, Lavinium; nam ibi dii Penates nostri).
The annual festival of the cult of Aeneas took place at Lavinium, not at Rome (Serv. Dan.
ad Aen. 1.260; Asconius, 21C, Val. Fl. Max. 1.6.7). Alba Longa also had its own special
prestige (see Gruen 1992, 25). According to Gruen (1992, 28–9), we can surmise that
the Trojan legend entered and adapted itself to Latium in the late fourth century BCE,
imposing itself definitely at the beginning of the third century. It is not possible to say
whether the legend reached Rome from Latium or vice versa. But, according to Gruen,
it offered advantages to both parties, both for Rome and for the Latin cities. For the
Latins it was prestigious, after the dissolution of the Latin League in 338 BCE, to present
their own cities (even the defunct Alba Longa, which had been destroyed by the Romans
in the seventh century; but the importance of Alba can be easily explained because of its
ineluctable importance in the Romulus story) as ancestors of the new rising power; and
for the Romans these legends gave an analogous benefit: "They lent a cultural legitimacy
to its position of authority in Latium. Rome was now heir to the region's glorious past;
not just conqueror and suzerain but cultural curator" (Gruen 1992, 29). From the
"international" point of view, furthermore, the adoption of a Trojan identity was more
than acceptable to the Romans, who in this way were able to insert themselves in the
cultural complex of the Greek world, but without renouncing a well defined "alterity," a
cultural difference and a specificity of their own (Gruen 1992, 29–31).

Adopting a Trojan origin for Rome meant, however, the necessity of fusing the new
story invented by the Greeks with the autochthonous legend of the twins, Romulus
and Remus, the last descendants of the kings of Alba Longa, who originally had nothing to do with Aeneas or with the Trojans. The various characters named Rhomus,
Romulus, Rhome, and so on which we find in the eponymous fantasies of fourth-
century Greek writers do not have, in all likelihood, anything to do with the autochthonous and folkloric legend of Romulus and Remus, and do not presuppose any
direct knowledge of it. The fusion of the two distinct legends is, this time, the work
of Roman historians – and poets.

The Greek historians who had somehow attempted to connect the names of Aeneas
with those of eponymous founders of Rome (besides those quoted above, we may
recall Hegesianax of Alexandria Troas, who, writing in the second century BCE, made
Rome the foundation of Rhomus, one of the sons of Aeneas, who had three other
sons: Ascanius, Euryleon, and Rhomylos; but the examples could be multiplied: cf.
Plut. *Rom.* 1–2 with Ampolo 1988 *ad loc.*, who counts twenty-five different genealogies) had established very immediate connections between Aeneas and the supposed
eponymous founders, generally making them sons or grandsons of Aeneas. Eratosthenes
himself, if the information is correct, stated that Romulus was son of Ascanius, and so
grandson of Aeneas (Serv. Dan. *ad Aen.* 1.273 = *FGrHist* 241 F 245). At a certain
point, however, there appears in all its clarity an obvious chronological problem: the
date for the fall of Troy is fixed at 1184 BCE (Eratosthenes' date); the date for the
foundation of Rome is established around the middle of the eighth century BCE:
814/13 for Timaeus (synchronism with Carthage); 748/47 for Fabius Pictor; 751/50
for Cato; 753 for Varro, which quickly became the canonical date.

It thus became necessary to fill the chronological gap between the fall of Troy and the
foundation of Rome, and in such a way that the story of Aeneas ties up with the story of

the twins. The canonical version was fixed by Fabius Pictor, unanimously recognized as the first Roman historian (end of the third century; on the date of his work, which is impossible to determine with certitude, see Frier 1979, 227–46), but probably preceded in this by Diocles of Peparethus (cf. Plut. *Rom.* 3.1–3 with Ampolo 1988 *ad loc.*). Fabius Pictor recognizes the gap between the fall of Troy and the foundation of Rome and fills it with a dynasty of Alban kings (as demonstrated by Plut. *Rom.* 3.1–3; and by the Tauromenion inscription published by Manganaro 1974, 394 = Fabius Pictor fr. 1 Chassignet; cf. Casali 2007a, 103 n.2). Aeneas arrives in Latium with Ascanius, and is guided by a white sow to a place where Alba will be founded. The sow gives birth to thirty piglets. Aeneas had received an oracle which had ordered him to found a city in the place where a sow led him; but a dream vision persuades him to wait thirty years before founding the city. Aeneas dies soon after that, and it will be Ascanius who founds Alba. At the death of Ascanius, we have the beginning of the (probably) twelve generations of Alban kings, until the canonical usurpation by Amulius and the foundation of Rome in 748/7 (Fab. Pict. *ap.* Diod. 7.3, ex Syncell. pp. 366–7 Dindorf = *FGrHist* 809 F 2; for the problems of the reconstruction, see Dury-Moyaers 1981, 80–1).

More details, but also major problems of reconstruction, are found in the version contained in Cato's *Origines*. In rough outline, we have the arrival of Aeneas in Italy with Anchises. Aeneas marries Lavinia, daughter of the Aboriginal King Latinus. There follows the foundation of Lavinium. The relationship between Latins and Trojans, however, is broken. There follows a series of wars, during which, one after the other, Latinus, Turnus, and Aeneas himself die. The war is definitely closed by Ascanius, who in single combat kills Mezentius, the last opponent. Lavinia, pregnant with Aeneas' child and thus fearing the menace represented by Ascanius, seeks refuge in the woods (*silvae*) and hides herself in the house of the shepherd Tyrrhus: Silvius Postumus is born. Ascanius leaves Lavinium to his stepmother, and founds Alba for himself. Apparently, he dies without sons. Silvius Postumus succeeds Ascanius as king of Alba: from him, Silvius Postumus, son of Aeneas and Lavinia, descend the Alban kings. The story, then, fuses with the canonical one about the twins.

We should also recall the version of Livy (1.1–3), which begins with the rescue (a bit ambiguous, as we have seen above) of Aeneas and Antenor from Troy. Aeneas arrives in the *ager Laurens*. There is an initial contest with the Aborigines. At this point, Livy registers the existence of a double tradition: according to one version, there is a war before the marriage with Lavinia; according to the other, the war follows the marriage. In any case, we come to the foundation of Lavinium, and to the birth of Ascanius, son of Aeneas and Lavinia. Now there follow two wars: first, Turnus fights against Aeneas, who is allied with the Aborigines; Latinus dies. Then, Turnus, allied with the Etruscans (and with Mezentius) fights against Aeneas, still allied with the Aborigines. Aeneas gives the name of "Latins" to the new people formed by the fusion of Trojans and Aborigines. Aeneas wins the war, but he disappears, to be venerated as Aeneas Indiges. The reign passes to the regency of Lavinia. At this point, Livy raises the not unimportant issue of Ascanius' identity: is he the son of Aeneas and Lavinia, or is he the son of Aeneas and Creusa, namely Iulus (the ancestor of the *gens Iulia*)? Nobody knows. Ascanius, whoever he is, founds Alba thirty years after the foundation of Lavinium. The first of the Alban kings is Silvius, son of Ascanius.

This, however, is not the reconstruction chosen by the two first epic Roman poets. For Naevius and Ennius, Romulus is still a grandson of Aeneas (cf. Casali 2007a, 104–6).

Vergil's Choices

This is a very rough outline of the situation that Vergil had in front of him when he started to write the *Aeneid*. And, of course, one must not forget all the work done in the course of the first century BCE by the Julian propagandists, who were obviously interested in underlining the association between the *gens Iulia* and Aeneas (and Venus, and Jupiter) through the eponymous figure of Iulus-Ascanius. (On the role of L. Julius Caesar (one quotation in Serv. Dan. *ad Aen.* 1.267, nine in *OGR*), see Weinstock 1971, 17 n.6.). Before Vergil there were mainly, on the Roman side, a historiographical tradition (Fabius Pictor, Cato) and an epic one (Naevius, Ennius). The first, necessary Vergilian move is, of course, that of adopting the historiographical version as far as regards the general chronology (cf. already *Aen.* 1.7 *Albani…patres*) and especially Aeneas' offspring: differently from Ennius and (probably) Naevius, for whom Aeneas arrived in Latium with the daughter, Ilia, from whom the twins were born, now Aeneas arrives with the son, Ascanius-Iulus, who is indispensable to the dynastic pretensions of his Augustan patrons (even if, curiously, Vergil omits any reference to the presence of Iulus in the poem until as late as line 1.267: cf. Casali 2007a, 121–4). But the genealogy of Aeneas still remains somehow problematical in the *Aeneid*: who exactly will be the son of Aeneas who is destined to begin the line of the Alban kings? Will it be Ascanius-Iulus, or Silvius Postumus, the son of Aeneas and Lavinia? In the Prophecy of Jupiter it seems that the ancestor of the Alban kings is Iulus (1.267–71); but in the Parade of Heroes in book 6, this ancestor is certainly Silvius (6.760–6): an unresolved contradiction (cf. O'Hara 1990, 145–7 and his chapter in this volume; Horsfall 1991a, 97; Casali 2009a, 318–25).

Vergil's attempt to "conquer the chaos" (cf. Horsfall 1981) of the multiform Aeneas legend leads to a kind of synthesis which, if it recuperates traditional elements on the one hand, introduces unheard-of novelties on the other: In Vergil, Aeneas tries in vain to convince Anchises to leave Troy, succeeding only after the appearance of divine signs. This reverses their roles in Ennius' *Annales*, where it was Aeneas who resisted Anchises' urgings and was convinced only by Venus' intervention (Enn. *Ann.* 15–25 according to Skutsch's reconstruction; cf. Casali 2007a, 116–18). There follows a real *Odyssey* in the Mediterranean, where traditional data (mainly Varronian? Cf. the detailed narration in Dion. Hal. 1.49.3–1.53.3) can either be only slightly modified (e.g., in the traditional stop in Thrace-Macedonia, Aeneas does not found either "Ainos" or "Aineia," but a city called "Aeneadae" (*Aen.* 3.18)) or else dramatically modified (the stopover on Delos is traditional, but certainly not so the interrogation of the Delian Apollo, the Cretan mistake, the revelation of the Penates about the real origin of Dardanus and the nature of the "ancient mother"). They can also be altered either for clearly propagandistic motives (e.g., the stop at "Actium," cf. Casali 2004a) or, for complex metapoetical reasons, either altered (the encounter at Buthrothum in Epirus with Andromache and Helenus and their "little Troy") or even totally invented (as is that "fragment" of the *Odyssey*, the shipwrecked Achaemenides, whom Aeneas rescues from the land of the Homeric Polyphemus; see Nelis' discussion of this episode in this volume). They can introduce extremely relevant variations, like the totally new collocation of the death of Anchises with the Trojans' arrival at Drepanum (in Naevius and Cato Anchises lived to reach Latium). The Carthaginian episode, the broken love with Dido, and probably also her curse, promising eternal hatred between Romans and Carthaginians, might have been present in Naevius' *Bellum Poenicum*, and maybe something on this topic was also present in Varro. The "second" Sicilian stop with the funeral games for Anchises elaborates, with many subtle variations, traditional materials (see above), and then gives life to a real tour-de-force of Iliadic intertextuality (the Games for Patroclus in *Il.* 23). Similarly, some Naevian influence must have been recognizable in the episode of the Sibyl of Cumae – also in this case we know that Vergil introduces essential variations, as well. Eventually, Aeneas arrives in Latium, at the mouth of the Tiber, and this allows the already mentioned encounter with Evander, king of the Palatine. Before meeting Evander, Aeneas witnesses the white sow prodigy, which is "explained" to him by the god Tiberinus: Aeneas will find a white sow that will have given birth to thirty piglets: this means that after thirty years Ascanius will build a city called Alba (*Aen.* 8.42–8); no indication about the place of the foundation, of course, as regards either Lavinium or Alba (we are at the mouth of the Tiber). We have here one of the typical Vergilian "contradictions," which in fact are meant to allude to discarded versions of the myth, since in the prophecy of Helenus the white sow indicated the place where the city of Lavinium should have been founded (3.388–93, as also in Lycophron (1253–62) – part of a section, 1226–80, that may however be by a later hand; Cato, *Orig.* fr. 13b Schröder (= *Origo gentis Romanae* 12.5); and, more or less, Varro, *LL* 5.144 (~ *RR* 2.17–18)). In Fabius Pictor (fr. 4 Peter = 5 Chassignet), as we have seen, the white sow indicated, on the other hand, the place where Alba was to be founded.

The war in Latium is one of the major events that Vergil modifies most deeply. In Ennius and in Naevius there was no war at all. In Cato, instead (as then in Livy), the war between Italians and Trojans went through a series of complex and (in the case of Cato) difficult to reconstruct phases (see especially Stok 2004). Apart from the grandiose exercise in epic "mystification" given by the intervention of Allecto (whose total "uselessness" appears even more clear in the light of the perfectly "human" wars of the preceding tradition), Vergil's main innovations as far as regards the war are: (1) the Trojans are allied with the Etruscans (see above only the case of Alcimus and perhaps Lycophron); (2) the three (?) phases of the Catonian war are condensed into a single war, in which Aeneas does not "die," or "disappear," during one of the battles, but survives until the end of the poem, which famously closes on Aeneas' killing of the disarmed Turnus (but the short earthly life of Aeneas is foretold by Jupiter at 1.261–6). It is Turnus, now, and not Mezentius, who is the main antagonist (Mezentius is killed by Aeneas in book 10), and Ascanius-Iulus does not carry out his duty of putting an end to the conflict: on the contrary, metanarrative intervention by Apollo even forbids him to continue to fight (cf. Casali 2009a). In a way that cannot be paralleled anywhere in the Aeneas legend as Vergil found it, the war closes (?) with a living and furious Aeneas who, in the literary frame of the poem, does not found any city, does not marry Lavinia, does not honor the memory of the fallen.

FURTHER READING

The clearest reconstruction of the development of the Aeneas legend is Gruen (1992). Fundamental also are Horsfall (1974, 1979b, 1985) and Cornell (1975); see also Galinsky (1992) and Vanotti (1995, 1–98).

On the traditions about Evander and the Arcadians on the Palatine, see Musti (1984, 1985). On "kinship diplomacy" in the ancient world, see Jones (1999). On the "transformation" of Cacus, see Small (1982) with the comments of Horsfall (1984). On the figure of Cacus, mainly from a comparative point of view, see most recently Davies (2004).

On Poseidon's prophecy in *Il.* 20.307–8 and the history of its interpretations, see Gabba (1976, 85–6), Smith (1981, 34–43), Gruen (1992, 12–13, 41), and especially Heath (1998); Barbantani (2000, 89–90); and on Vergil's adaptation of the prophecy, in connection with the prophecy of Apollo on the Ptolemies (Call. *Del.* 166–70), see especially Barchiesi (1994, 441–2). On Apollo in the legend of Aeneas, see Miller (2009). On the problems of Dardanus' Italic origins, and the identification of his supposed hometown of Corythus, see especially Buchheit (1963, 151–72), Horsfall (1973, 1987, 2000 (on *Aen.* 7.206–11), Colonna (1980), Bettini (2005), Reed (2006), and Casali (2009b).

On the various versions of Aeneas' flight from Troy, see Heinze (1993, 55–9), Barchiesi (1962, 349–50), Horsfall (2008). For an in-depth discussion of several related problems, see Horsfall (1979b). Dido appears to be fully aware of the version according to which Aeneas betrayed his homeland (*Aen.* 4.596–9), as probably are the authors of the pictures on Juno's temple in Carthage (*Aen.* 1.488): see Casali (1999).

On the *Tabula Iliaca Capitolina*, see Sadurska (1964, 24–37). On the relationship with Vergil, most recently, see Scafoglio (2005) and above all Horsfall (2008, 587–91). On Alcimus, see Manni (1963) and Fraschetti (1981). On the She-Wolf and the Lupercal, see (for the poetic implications) Putnam (1998, 180–8) and (from a historical and topographical point of view) Castagnoli (1987b).

For the fusion between the Greek and the Roman versions of the tales see again Cornell (1975). The pre-Vergilian historiographical tradition obviously is not limited to Fabius Pictor and Cato: on Varro, see Dury-Moyaers (1981, 89–90, who mainly follows Perret 1942, 607–42 in believing that much of Varro can be recuperated, also *ex silentio*, from Dionysius of Halicarnassus) and Vanotti (1995, 68–81). On the other annalistic traditions, see D'Anna (1976, 43–143); Vanotti (1995, 61–8); and the commentaries of D'Anna on the *Origo gentis Romanae* (1992) and of Santini on Cassius Hemina (1995). On the Roman passion for legendary genealogies in the first century BCE, see Wiseman (1974). On Cato's *Origines*, see now Cugusi and Sblendorio Cugusi (2001, 293–305, on book 1, frr. 6–17, with notes); but Schröder (1971, especially 30–7 (text of frr. 2–14), 56–147 (comm. on frr. 4–14)) is still indispensable.

On the Alban kings' list, Brugnoli (1983) is fundamental. On the complicated stories about Ascanius-Iulus, see Bandiera (1986). On Aeneas' voyage in book 3, see now Horsfall (2006a). On some details about Vergil's departures form his sources, see Casali (2007a). On the various foundation prodigies, including the white sow, see Harrison (1985). On the prodigy of eating the *mensae*, see D'Anna (1961, 50–66) and Casali (2007a, 115 n.25) with further references. The best discussion of Naevius' "archaeology," with hypotheses about the roles of Dido and the (Cimmerian) Sibyl in the *Bellum Poenicum*, is still Mariotti (2001³, 29–41); see also Wigodsky (1972, 22–39) and D'Anna (1976, 7–41). On the possible presence of Anna and/ or Dido in Varro, and on Vergil's allusions to Varro's story, see Casali (2008). On the traditional ending of Aeneas' story, see also Hall (1992).

CHAPTER FOUR

Aeneas' Sacral Authority

Vassiliki Panoussi

Religion played an important part in the Augustan political and social order. The new regime launched a rigorous religious and moral reform that was as broad as it was multifaceted. Augustus rebuilt temples and revived defunct priesthoods. He reorganized both public and private worship and gave members of the *plebs* an opportunity to participate in public cults for the first time. The ideological message of restoration of all that was truly Roman with its emphasis on a new sense of unity, peace, and stability found a perfect vehicle in the renewal of Roman religious monuments and institutions.

In ancient Rome, political power was traditionally linked to religious authority. This authority was vested in standing boards or "colleges" (*collegia*) of priests – pontifices, augurs, and so forth – all of whom served for life, as well as in magistrates – consuls, praetors, and others – who were elected to political office on a year-to-year basis. Ritual actions were performed by both priests and magistrates according to the roles prescribed by the state cult. In this sense, it made no difference if, for example, a sacrifice was offered by a pontifex or by the president of a town district (*vicomagister*): in both cases, the sacrificer acted on behalf of the state in an official capacity by virtue of the position that he held. For magistrates, priestly duties were an intrinsic part of the public functions assigned to a given office, along with others that we would consider non-religious. This meant that it was perfectly natural to see a magistrate move between religious and non-religious functions as he carried out his normal duties. For priests, extreme ritual restrictions (as in the case of the *flamen Dialis* or the Vestals) were very rarely an issue. In general they were elected by their peers, did not receive formal training, and were able to perform other civic and social roles and duties, such as holding annual office, on the same basis as any other Roman (Scheid 2003, 130–1); and indeed both priests and the higher magistrates were drawn from the same social class, not to say the same families, generation after generation. During the late Republic, however, the turmoil surrounding Rome's leadership was reflected in the realm of religion especially: several priesthoods were not filled for so many years that they were ultimately rendered defunct. A famous such example is the aforementioned office of the *flamen Dialis,* a priest of Jupiter, which did in fact place extraordinary restrictions on the person who held it and, accordingly, was left vacant for some seventy-six years (87–11 BCE; Broughton 1952, 52; Galinsky 1996, 289).

Deeply aware of the authority and power vested in religious institutions, Augustus assumed a number of priestly offices along with his magistracies and other political powers and even promoted belief in his own divinity as a means to solidify his reign, particularly in the eastern parts of the empire. The cognomen Augustus, conferred on him by the Senate in 27 BCE, has sacral origins and is linked not only to words like *augeo* ("increase") and *auctoritas* ("authority"), but also to the blessings resulting from the worship of the gods (see, e.g., Enn. *Ann.* 155 Skutsch; Cic. *Mil.* 43; Eck 2007, 56–7). Augustus became *pontifex maximus* in 12 BCE and *flamen Dialis* (after eliminating those elements that had previously restricted the *flamen's* activity) the next year. He restored the college of Arval Brothers, became a member himself, and included in it prominent political friends and supporters, such as Valerius Messalla Corvinus. In this way, he transformed an obsolete group into an elite and influential organization. In the *Res Gestae* (7.3), Augustus claims that he was a member of all sodalities and priesthoods, something that was unprecedented, as distinguished Romans rarely belonged to more than one such group. These memberships on the part of the Princeps not only conferred dignity on the sodalities, they undoubtedly enhanced Augustus' own *auctoritas* as well (Galinsky 1996, 292; Grebe 2004, 42, 59).

Sacrifice was the ritual act *par excellence* associated with Augustus, whose monuments throughout the city of Rome showcased a visual program in which sacrifice and its symbolic accouterments signaled the state's restored piety and offered reassurance of the gods' blessings on the city and its people (Zanker 1988, 115–18). A religious connection between Augustus and the hero of the *Aeneid* is reflected in several of these monuments. Aeneas' iconic status as father of the Roman nation can be seen in the Ara Pacis, a monument commissioned by the Senate and dedicated in 9 BCE on which the identification of Augustus with Aeneas is clearly implied. Augustus participates in a procession on the south side of the altar while Aeneas can be seen around the corner in a similar pose performing a sacrifice (Zanker 1988, 203–5; Hardie 1993, 21). Iconography draws the two figures together as well: both Aeneas and Augustus have veiled heads, a detail proper to the performance of a sacrifice in accordance with Roman ritual (*Romano more* or *ritu*) as opposed to Greek ritual, in which the sacrificer's head was left uncovered. The underlying idea had appeared previously in passages like (for example) *Aen.* 3.405, where Horsfall (2006, 306) detects an *aition* for this very practice.

Vergil's ancient commentators, motivated by an antiquarian interest in matters of cult (Starr 1997), rather than by a desire to understand the constitutive elements of leadership, were at pains to pinpoint the extent to which religious elements in the portrayal of Aeneas cast him allegorically as a religious expert or as a particular type of Roman priest. Both Servius and Servius Danielis propound a view of Aeneas as either holding all religious offices or specifically as a *flamen Dialis* (Jones 1961; Starr 1997). Some of the ancient detractors (*obtrectatores*), such as one of the interlocutors in

Macrobius' *Saturnalia* (3.10.3–5), complain about Aeneas' abilities as a priest or as interpreter of omens and portents (see also Rose 1948, 24–5). Modern critics have (rightly) dismissed the validity of such interpretations (Starr 1997, 63 n.1; Bailey 1949, specifically criticizing Rose 1948) and have rather focused on Aeneas' identity as an epic hero, his association with Augustus, or his role as a military leader or as a good king (Cairns 1989; Nisbet 1990).

Undoubtedly, this approach is both important and useful. As the father of the Roman nation, Aeneas resembled Rome's latest *pater*, Augustus, who ushered in a new era, cemented peace and stability, and expanded the boundaries of the empire. At the same time, Aeneas' portrait is partly a product of the poem's Homeric pedigree. He is cast as another Hector, or, at times, as another Achilles, and takes on roles, tasks, and duties appropriate to an archaic Greek *basileus* (Rose 1948, 11). The intersection of these two identities, Roman leader and epic hero, demands a certain caution or flexibility when one examines Aeneas' religious authority. We cannot simply equate Aeneas with specific priestly offices; on the other hand, we cannot dismiss the importance of the depiction of his public religious duties (as does, e.g., Schauer 2007, 224–8). In this chapter, I focus on the ways in which Aeneas' political authority is shaped or intensified by his performance of religious tasks. Most critics today agree that Aeneas experiences a shift of identity in the epic: from a Trojan prince he grows into the father of the Roman nation. He embarks on his journey as a fugitive, unaware of his glorious future. Leadership appears thrust upon him after the fall of Troy, while, during his travels, his father Anchises still makes all the important decisions. Aeneas is repeatedly told of his future, yet seems unable to realize the full importance of his mission until he arrives in Italy.

Even though Aeneas initially appears to fall short of the standards of leadership that a Roman would expect from a founding father, in several key episodes in the *Aeneid* he takes on religious tasks appropriate to a head of state. In what follows, I argue that an examination of Aeneas' performance of rituals throughout the epic reveals a development in his status as a figure of authority. He is established early on in the poem as the legitimate ruler of the fugitive Trojans and his remarkable ability to guide his men through various perils receives emphasis; but his leadership first shows itself in purely secular terms. When the hero attempts to perform religious tasks, at first he appears ignorant or uncertain and he has little success in communicating with the divine. But a pronounced shift takes place when Aeneas becomes *paterfamilias*. At that moment, his family circle extends beyond his son and other relatives to include his people. This shift takes place very clearly in book 5, in which Aeneas executes his private religious duties as a son and sponsors an athletic festival as a community leader. In the ritually controlled environment of the games, Aeneas emerges as a most effective ruler, dutiful to familial tradition and capable of curbing the aggressive behavior of his men. These skills are put to the test in the subsequent episode of the burning of the ships, in which Aeneas' helplessness to diffuse the situation contrasts sharply with his earlier mastery of his boisterous men.

A pivotal stage in the development of Aeneas' ability to lead is reached in his successful performance of public mourning rituals. Such rituals belong primarily to the private realm of the family. But in book 5, Aeneas mourns the loss of his father not as a private matter, but as the public concern of his entire people. Moreover, in book 6, when Aeneas, as instructed by the Sibyl, offers burial to his comrade Misenus, he acts as both a *paterfamilias* (his men are members of his extended family, the Aeneadae) and as a military leader. After the hero has successfully performed his religious duties at this intersection of private and public realms and has embraced these different aspects of leadership, he is more effective in advancing his mission, boldly hazarding a journey to the land of the dead. The fact that his father informs him of his responsibilities as a Roman leader precisely at this juncture is a result of his readiness to fulfill that important aspect of his leadership.

Aeneas' military and political authority over his men is never in question in the epic. Scholars have noted that he bears the marks of the *imperator* (military leader), and that the legitimacy of his *imperium* (military power) is painstakingly established (Nisbet 1990, 379–80). For instance, although Hector's ghost entrusts him with Troy's Penates and urges him to abandon the city (2.293–5), he chooses to stay and fight, and does not leave until, once again, he is explicitly ordered to do so by Venus Genetrix (2.619–20). Nisbet also observes that the flame that appears on Iulus' head (2.682–4) and subsequent celestial portents (2.692–8) represent omens routinely taken by a Republican general at the start of a war.

At these early stages of the poem, examples of Aeneas' proper use of *imperium* abound. The hero is shown instilling hope and courage in his men, as well as dealing effectively with other leaders (such as Helenus and, at first, Dido). So in his famous speech to his comrades in book 1 (198–207), after they had suffered the loss of ships and men, he is able to offer comfort and help his followers think optimistically about the future, even though he himself is as despondent as they are. This is the first time that we are shown Aeneas' leadership abilities, which are both extraordinary and effective, comparable to Neptune's ability earlier to calm the stormy waves (1.142–3) or to that of the statesman who soothes the angry mob (1.148–53). Ritual elements, on the other hand, are conspicuously absent from these passages, as they are from the subsequent episode of the killing and cooking of the stags and the ensuing feast (1.189–93), whereas military language abounds. Even when Aeneas' men remember with great sadness their dead comrades, the word used to describe their action is *sermo* (217), a term devoid of any religious or ritual connotations (*OLD* s.v.).

As we learn from Aeneas in books 2 and 3, in the early stages of Aeneas' voyage it is Anchises who is the Trojans' religious authority. Although, as we have seen, Hector's ghost entrusts Aeneas with the Penates, it is Anchises who actually carries them out of the city (2.717). Anchises is also the main interpreter of omens and prodigies, which dictate the itinerary and goals of the voyage. Nisbet (1990, 380) suggests that at this point Anchises' role is analogous to that of *pontifex maximus* and Aeneas' role to that of *imperator*. He also notes that such a division of responsibilities reflects not the developed practice of the Roman state but rather a more primitive social order. Nisbet is right to attribute this division to the epic's Homeric pedigree: Anchises is a cross between Laertes (who turns all of his power over to his son) and Priam (who remains king even while Hector leads the army). Only when Anchises dies does Aeneas assume the full military and religious powers of a king.

From Family Burial Rites to Public Death Ritual

Aeneas' first attempt at founding a city occurs at the opening of book 3, when the Trojans decide to settle in Thrace. The text is silent about who makes this decision: Anchises is vaguely said to have "bid them spread sails to Fate" (*dare fatis vela iubebat*, 3.9) while Aeneas' words make the operation seem somewhat accidental (*feror huc et litore curvo / moenia prima loco*, "I am borne there and upon the winding shore I place my first city-walls," 3.16–17). But in his first performance of sacrifice as part of a foundation process Aeneas incurs pollution when he unwittingly violates Polydorus' *tumulus* (40). Dyson (2001, 29–38) enumerates in detail all the technical problems with Aeneas' acts, noting in particular that he is glaringly oblivious to the portentous significance of the blood-dripping branches (3.37–8). Aeneas' abortive effort to settle in Thrace displays his lack of expertise and general naïveté regarding his duties, particularly his religious duties, as founder of a city. He receives no specific divine guidance, his technical knowledge is rudimentary and inadequate, and he is forced to abandon his effort in favor of performing burial rites for Polydorus – that is, of fulfilling a private religious duty toward a member of Priam's (and Aeneas') family (3.62–8; cf. Harrison 1985, 153). At the end of this episode, Aeneas is not yet equipped to take on the role of a religious leader in a public setting. Throughout book 3, his ineffectiveness can be explained by the fact that Anchises still retains his authority as *paterfamilias* (even if he too misinterprets divine messages, as the episode of the abortive settlement in Crete reveals: Harrison 1985, 153–4). But after Anchises' death Aeneas, bereft of his father's guidance, faces even more grievous challenges in the episode of the storm in book 1 and in his encounter with Dido in book 4.

Book 5 presents the first instance where Aeneas acts as a capable religious leader. Once returned to Sicily he presides over sacrifices and games commemorating his father. In this way, he plays his new role as head of his family, performing his filial duty to the shades of his father (a rite which, as commentators have pointed out, resembles that of the *parentalia*; Williams 1960, 53). At the same time, in his speech to his people, Aeneas assumes a military and political role, speaking from a mound like a Roman general (see Williams 1960, 49; Nisbet 1990, 382) and stressing the importance of Anchises for the entire community as the father and protector of the new nation (Panoussi 2009, 159–66). Public death ritual, of which the games are the most obvious component, becomes the vehicle through which Aeneas evolves from son of Anchises to father of a new nation. Within the ritual context of the games, where violence and aggression are contained, Aeneas expertly eases tensions and diffuses potential outbreaks of violence among his men.

In the world of the games, Aeneas' authority is indicated by the fact that he is the one both to offer prizes and to recognize the winners (e.g., 5.348–50; 461–72; 485–6). He occupies a seat of conspicuous privilege within the "theater" (5.289–90). In three of the events (the footrace, the boxing match, and the archery contest) there is disagreement about the outcome; each time Aeneas is called on to settle it by choosing a winner. The hero quickly and effectively appeases the heated passions of his men. In the footrace, he uses prizes to console contestants who suffer misfortune, whether their own misfortune or the consequences of another's (5.348–61). He ends the boxing match when it becomes so violent that the life of one contestant is threatened (5.461–4). Finally, in the archery contest, Aeneas correctly interprets the apparition of an omen and assigns prizes accordingly (5.533–8; Cairns 1989, 57–9).

Within the ritual framework of the games, violence can be diffused or altogether avoided. A notable illustration of this fact appears in the boxing match between Dares and Entellus, where the latter offers animal sacrifice in exchange for the life of his opponent (*hanc tibi, Eryx, meliorem animam pro morte Daretis / persolvo*, 5.483–4; see Putnam 1965, 82–3; Hardie 1993, 52). Violence thus takes place in a controlled medium and the communal unity not only remains intact but is reinforced through the performance of ritual (Panoussi 2009, 165–6).

Aeneas is an admirable leader within the ritual context of the games, but he is not as successful when faced with real dissension among his people. Later in book 5 when the Trojan women burn the ships in an attempt to force Aeneas to remain permanently in Sicily, his helplessness at the crisis stands in sharp contrast with his earlier performance during the games (700–4). It takes the intervention of Nautes and of Anchises' ghost before Aeneas is able to reach a solution, which involves fragmenting his community: the old men and women are left behind in Sicily (712–18). As a result, the emphasis in book 5 on Aeneas' brilliant performance as both a religious and political leader within the context of public death ritual showcases his potential as a ruler of the Roman nation while it also reveals serious shortcomings.

In the next book, public funeral rites will provide once again the context within which Aeneas will emerge as father of the Roman nation. The Sibyl instructs the hero to perform funeral rites for his comrade Misenus, whose unburied body is polluting the entire fleet, as a precondition for his entrance to Hades (6.150–5). Aeneas' ritual duty is now explicitly a public one, since the welfare of the whole community is at stake. The subsequent narrative shows all of Aeneas' men hard at work on their ritual duties, while his own participation as *primus inter pares* is emphasized: *nec non Aeneas opera inter talia primus / hortatur socios paribusque accingitur armis*, "no less Aeneas, first among such tasks, urges on his comrades and girds on similar weapons" (6.183–4). As the Sibyl indicated, he is now able to retrieve the golden bough, the key to Hades, the description of which is enclosed within the burial rites (6.190–211). Aeneas' conclusion of the burial (6.232–5) signals his privileged status, while the significance of these events for the community's present and future is confirmed and reinforced in the *aition* that rounds off the narrative. Misenus' name now belongs to the site of his tomb, which will be a perpetual reminder of the trials and toils of Rome's founders.

Crucial as public death ritual is for Aeneas' growth as a religious leader, the bough's famous reluctance to be plucked raises questions about his success. The bough itself has been interpreted as a symbol of liminality, both alive, a growing organism, and inanimate, an inorganic metal. This contradiction is also reflected in the contrast between the luminescence of the bough and its surrounding darkness (*auri*, 208; *opaca / ilice*, 6.208–9). The bough's ambivalent nature reflects Aeneas' own state as both living and dead (Segal 1965, 625–6). The bough's readiness to be possessed is similarly ambivalent: the Sibyl says that if he is meant to have it, it will follow willingly his attempt to pluck it (*ipse volens facilisque sequetur*, 6.146); yet Aeneas needs to exercise a degree of force in order to possess it (*corripit, refringit*, 6.210; D'Arms 1964; Segal 1965).

Consideration of Aeneas as a religious leader may be a helpful way to understand better the famous riddle of the bough. The Sibyl's instructions include a ritual prescription, thus explicitly linking religious practice and Aeneas' action: *rite repertum / carpe manu*, "solemnly find it and pluck it with your hand" (6.145–6). The precise meaning of *rite* in this context was uncertain even for ancient readers, as we see from Servius' note, which indicates that the adverb modifies *carpe* not *repertum*. Austin (1977, 85) takes it as modifying both and thus pointing out that both actions must be performed with due solemnity. Austin's interpretation illuminates the deeply sacral nature of the act and reveals yet another link between the plucking of the bough and Aeneas' religious role. As a result, the bough's hesitation and resistance qualifies Aeneas' success and suggests that the hero, though capable enough of discharging his religious duties at this juncture (i.e., plucking the bough and performing burial rites for Misenus), needs to attain an even higher level of convergence with the divine element.

The connection between death rituals and Aeneas' leadership resurfaces at the opening of book 7 with the announcement of the death and burial of his nurse, Caieta. Her death symbolically severs all bonds with Aeneas' childhood while the etymological *aition* signaling Caieta's permanent association with the site of her demise links Aeneas' Trojan past with his future in Italy. Another link between burial and tomb is indicated by the etymological connection of Caieta's name with the Greek καίω, "to burn," or κοῖλον, "cavity" (Paschalis 1997, 244). As a result, this short vignette underscores the hero's own transitional status from a mere individual to the founder of a new nation.

Successful Foundation

Upon arrival in Italy, Aeneas' ability to interpret prodigies and perform rituals reaches its climax. Two prodigies occur, each of great significance for Aeneas' mission. In book 7, the Trojans consume their plates while feasting, and in book 8, Aeneas spots a sow that has given birth to thirty piglets. The former omen establishes that the wanderers have reached the end of their journey, while the latter marks the location of their new settlement. The two events raise considerably Aeneas' profile as a religious authority, as he correctly interprets both and takes appropriate ritual action. As a result, the prodigies establish not only an important milestone in the progress of his mission but also his readiness to lead fully as both sacral and political/military authority.

These episodes in the second half of the poem also mark a shift in Aeneas' religious role from public mourner to founder of a new community. In the former books, the funeral rituals were a means to forge communal bonds. While they looked to the Trojan past, the present toils, and shared grief for incurred losses, they also helped cement a new, shared identity by simultaneously expressing hope for a prosperous life in a new settlement. In this section, I argue that in Italy Aeneas and his men receive divine aid unmarred by human error and misunderstanding, a common problem earlier in their quest for a new home. Furthermore, I argue that Vergil "purges" this portion of the narrative of potentially troubling elements such as might have arisen from similar events in previous episodes (especially in book 3) or from other traditions on Aeneas' journey (like those of Dionysius of Halicarnassus or Fabius Pictor: see Casali in this volume). Still, Aeneas' sacral identity is revealed to be extremely fragile when the war between Latins and Trojans is at its peak.

The omen of the eating of the tables in book 7 is closely related to Aeneas' identity as a religious leader: the episode's vocabulary is steeped in ritual language and Aeneas is depicted as a reliable religious authority. The narrative opens with a description of a meal rife with ritual connections (7.109–15): *daps* is a term for a sacred or sacrificial feast (*OLD* s.v.), *ador* is a type of spelt used in sacrifice, and *libum* is a sacrificial cake (Fordyce 1977, 81). The use of *augent* also has ritual import, usually connected with sacrifice (Fordyce 1977, 81–2). The same holds for the use of *mensa*, a word at times associated with the altar-table or the act of sacrifice itself (Fordyce 1977, 83–4). This pronounced ritual framework makes the use of *violare* to describe the Trojans' eating their tables all the more emphatic and stresses the sacrilegious nature of their act (*pace* Horsfall 2000, 111–12; cf. Harrison 1985, 157–8). Yet this sacrilege is immediately acknowledged and an attempt at purification and atonement is apparently made later on when the Trojans are said to "renew" the feast (*instaurant epulas*, 7.146; cf. 3.62, 4.63, and 5.94 with Fordyce 1977, 91, and Livy. 2.36.1). Unlike the parallel events in the opening of book 3, where Aeneas was completely unaware of the sacrilege he incurred from the bleeding roots, he now recognizes that this prodigy is a fulfillment of an earlier prophecy (a prophecy Aeneas ascribes to Anchises but which was actually uttered by the Harpy Celaeno, 3.255–7). The speed with which Aeneas acknowledges the omen is conveyed with the expression *eripuit pater* (7.119), which presents a variation on the more usual term *omen accipio* (Fordyce 1977, 84; Horsfall 2000, 120). Similarly, the poet employs the verb *pressit* in the same line, indicating that Aeneas observes the necessary ritual silence so that violation of the omen may be averted (Horsfall 2000, 120).

In addition, the reference to Aeneas as *pater* at this moment (7.119) has a twofold significance. On one level, it denotes Aeneas' position of authority over his son, Iulus, who unwittingly bears witness to the fulfillment of the prophecy (Harrison 1985, 141). The notorious inconsistency in Aeneas' remark that the prophecy came from the mouth of Anchises rather than from that of the Harpy Celaeno has been explained as a plausible consequence of Anchises' role as Jupiter's mediator in the epic and of the importance of Aeneas' family as recipients of divine communication (Harrison 1985, 159, 161–2). I suggest that the mention of Anchises at this juncture and in the prayer that follows (7.134) further marks Aeneas as his true successor in the role of interpreter of omens, and emphasizes his status as father of the new Roman nation, while simultaneously glossing over the vengeful implications in Celaeno's prophecy, which belong to the uncertain and hostile world of book 3.

Immediately following the interpretation of the omen, Aeneas appears yet again to be thinking as a military leader rather than as a religious one. His orders for the next morning (7.130–2) take precedence over the ritual thanksgiving (7.133–4; Horsfall 2000, 125). The subsequent description of his prayer, however, with its attention to ritual form (*ex ordine*, 7.139), followed immediately by the intervention of Jupiter himself through the sound of thunder in a clear sky, the *augurium maximum* (7.141–3), indicates acceptance of Aeneas' prayer by the supreme divine authority, confirms his interpretation of the omen, and sanctions the Trojans' arrival in their new abode (Horsfall 2000, 129).

The importance of Aeneas' sacral role in this instance is also intensified by the possibility that an *aition* is implied in the episode, that of the ritual meal in honor of the Trojan Penates at Lavinium. During this meal, flat wheat-cakes called *mensae* were used. Although the only evidence that connects *mensae* with the Penates is found in Donatus' commentary (on *Aen*. 3.257), modern scholars (Fordyce 1977, 83; Harrison 1985, 158) have found his explanation compelling, as the entire scene of recognition hinges on this word. Aeneas remembers the prophecy and proceeds with a solemn invocation of the Trojan deities: "...*vosque*" *ait* "*o fidi Troiae salvete penates:* / *hic domus, haec patria est*," " '...and hail to you,' he says, 'Penates faithful to Troy: here is our home, here is our country' " (7.121–2: cf. 3.544–5 with Harrison 1985, 158). As a result, the ritual commemoration of the divinities involved in this foundational moment also celebrates Aeneas' perspicacity as a sacral authority.

In the next book, Aeneas' religious identity is solidified as he proceeds with foundational activities. As we have seen, the prodigy of the eating of the tables is followed by the appearance of a white sow. We observe further Aeneas' close connection with the divine as he assumes a priestly role, which is particularly evident in his attention to ritual correctness and form. At the same time, Aeneas (as well as the reader) is presented with a positive model of religious leadership in the figure of Evander. Moreover, religious authority receives a prominent place in book 8, since a host of other Roman leaders appear in formal religious contexts that include a number of altars. Thus Romulus is shown making a treaty (8.639–41), Manlius performing prayers for divine aid (8.652–66), and Augustus offering thanks (8.714–28: Gransden 1976, 92; Miller 2000, 410–4).As a result, Aeneas is first in a line of religious leaders who will dominate Roman public life throughout its history.

The special divine sanction surrounding Aeneas' foundational acts is marked by the appearance of the river-god Tiberinus to Aeneas in a dream, in which he tells him of the portent of the sow, informs him that he has reached the site of his new home, and instructs him to seek the help of the local King Evander and to supplicate Juno. He also promises to offer help himself. When Aeneas wakes up, he performs ceremonial gestures, such as sprinkling his hands with water (*rite*, 8.69), and utters a prayer rife with formulaic elements (Gransden 1976, 90) and archaic touches (Fordyce 1977, 213) that intensify the solemnity of the occasion. The ceremonious nature of these acts spills over to the main narrative: when the sacrifice to Juno is mentioned in indirect speech, similar formulaic language is employed, as the repeated pronoun *tibi* (84), a hymnic feature, attests.

Aeneas thus performs a foundation sacrifice when he beholds the sow with her litter and promptly offers her to Juno. The foundational aspect of this act is emphasized by the striking verbal contact between the description of the sow and that of the she-wolf suckling Romulus and Remus later on in the ekphrasis of the shield (8.630–4: Gransden 1976, 36, 91). Any uncertainty surrounding the correct interpretation of the portent is removed, since Tiberinus himself explains to Aeneas that the white sow and her thirty piglets stand for the foundation of Alba Longa by Ascanius thirty years later. Similarly, Vergil has erased from his version of events the ritually problematic aspects of the sow portent found in other accounts (e.g. Dion. Hal.1.55.4–1.56; Fab. Pict., fr. 5 Peter; see Casali's chapter in this volume). According to these authors, the sow, still pregnant rather than newly delivered of her brood, fled from Aeneas' altar as he was about to perform a sacrifice, so that the hero was forced to chase her down and sacrifice her at a different spot after she had given birth to the thirty piglets. The sources state that the failed sacrifice symbolically represents Aeneas' abortive foundation of Alba Longa (Harrison 1985, 138–9). It appears, then, that in Vergil traditional legend is revised to showcase the extraordinary convergence between the divine element and the Trojan leader in this foundational moment. Topography is similarly adjusted, as is attested by the extraordinary help of the river-god Tiberinus, who changes the course of his waters so that they flow upstream to facilitate Aeneas' arrival at what was, in Vergil's day, the center of Rome (Harrison 1985, 141; cf. Camps 1969, 139). Juno's divine opposition is temporarily erased in these episodes, which seek to connect Aeneas directly with the site of Rome even as the war between Aeneas and the Latins looms ahead (*contra*: O'Hara 1990, 31–5).

The public nature of Aeneas' religious identity receives a further boost from the portrait of King Evander. Evander's religiosity occupies a central place in the narrative, which presents one of the most elaborate descriptions of worship in the epic. Aeneas and his men reach the site of the future Rome, which they find peopled by Arcadian settlers commemorating with great solemnity the foundation of the Ara Maxima and the benefaction of Hercules to their community (8.102–6). Their ruler Evander and his son Pallas attend the rites along with the Senate and noble youths. After the initial introductions have taken place, Evander invites Aeneas to partake of the ritual meal as his guest (8.175–83), and at the conclusion of the tale of Hercules' exploits, the king gives orders for the execution of the rites that are to follow (8.273–5).

Evander's careful observance of ritual solemnity is but one of several qualities he exhibits that are meant to be heeded by Aeneas as he proceeds with the foundation of his new nation. The two heroes share many points of contact: they both have suffered much before they could settle in a permanent home and both contribute significantly to the civilizing of Italy (Papaioannou 2003, 694). Aeneas is thus implicitly called to follow Evander's example and in turn set up religious institutions and customs, and observe sound moral values. The friendship established through hospitality between the two communities is strengthened further as Aeneas makes a tour of a host of present and future historic and religious sites, such as the Asylum, the Argiletum, the rock of Tarpeia, and the Capitol. The links between the two communities are also revealed in the descriptions of the rites at the Ara Maxima, where the sacrificer performs his task following the general rules of the Roman method of sacrifice, even though he has his head unveiled in the Greek custom (Bailey 1935, 54). This blending of Greek, Italian, and Roman institutions in Evander's words and actions offers yet another important lesson to Aeneas, who will be called to become a uniting figure himself at the end of the poem (12.820–40). As a result, ritual, history, and policy emerge as interconnected spheres in the life of a community and its leader.

Sacral Quandaries: Public Death Ritual and Supplication

The motif of public death ritual returns to the fore in the remainder of the poem and raises serious concerns regarding Aeneas' sacral leadership. After the death of Pallas in book 10, the preparations for the young man's burial include the capture of eight Rutulian youths who are to be sacrificed at his pyre. According to Roman funeral rites, eight men could be selected to carry the body upon the bier during the funeral procession (publication of marble relief from Amiternum, Museo Nazionale d'Abruzzo, L'Aquila; Toynbee 1971, 46). If the number of Rutulians captured has any relation to this custom, we see yet another distortion of ritual, namely that the men who would normally carry the dead body now die along with it. In any event, a killing rampage follows during which the hero slays two suppliants and a priest (521–42, 575–601). That is to say, Aeneas, after attaining the status of religious leader in books 5 through 8, then proceeds in book 11 to distort and violate both burial rites and the norms of supplication. He thus appears to abuse his sacral duties and powers, becoming vulnerable to the violent emotions of the battlefield and consumed by his quest for revenge.

To be sure, Aeneas' actions are to some extent a result of the epic's intertextual fabric, which suggests that his response to Pallas' death must be similar to that of Achilles in the *Iliad* after the death of Patroclus (Harrison 1991, 201). And in addition to the literary model, an allusion to an historical event may be implied, namely Augustus' reported sacrifices of 300 hostages at the siege of Perusia in 41 BCE (Suet. *Aug.* 15; D. C. 48.14.4: Tarrant 1997, 179; *contra*, Harrison 1991, 203 with bibliography). Whatever influences or allusion may be at work, though, Vergil transforms this episode to something still more sinister. The narrator refrains from describing the actual sacrifice of humans, yet states twice Aeneas' intention to drain the blood from the slain bodies of the captives and pour it on Pallas' pyre (*inferias quos immolet umbris / captivoque rogi perfundat sanguine flammas*, "so that he might sacrifice them as offerings to the dead and pour the captives' blood on the pyre's flames," 10.519–20; *quos mitteret umbris / inferias, caeso sparsurus sanguine flammas*, "those he would send to the shades as funeral offerings, about to sprinkle the flames with slaughtered blood," 11.81–2). The sacrifice of the eight Rutulians is followed by the offering of *tropaea* – the fitting of a slain warrior's armor onto a tree trunk – to Pallas' funeral pyre (11.83–4; cf. 11.5–11; Nielson 1983, 28; Panoussi 2009, 33–4). Human sacrifice was strictly prohibited in Roman (and Greek) custom; and yet Aeneas commits these acts in the guise of his public persona as both a military and religious leader. The public nature of Pallas' burial is manifest in the entire community's heartfelt participation in the death rites, which include mourning women (11.34–5) and warriors from the entire allied army (11.92–3).

The theme of sacrifice and its importance *vis-à-vis* Aeneas' ability to perform his role as a religious leader is further complicated in the events following Pallas' death, most notably in the killing of the priest Haemonides. The episode's connection with Aeneas' actions before (and after) Pallas' funeral is signaled by the close proximity of the two episodes and the use of *immolare* to describe both the sacrifice of the eight

Rutulian youths (10.519) and the slaying of the priest (10.541). The only other occurrence of this verb in the *Aeneid* is in Aeneas' final words to Turnus (12.949). As a result, the deployment of the theme of sacrifice within a ritual framework (actual in the case of Pallas' burial or metaphorical in the case of Haemonides and Turnus) acquires particular importance for a full appreciation of Aeneas' religious leadership and thus demands that we subject these episodes to further scrutiny.

The verb *immolare* is a sacral term, originally indicating the action of sprinkling a victim with the sacrificial barley-meal (the *mola salsa*) and eventually meaning "to bring as an offering" or "to sacrifice." As we have seen, the killing of Rutulian youths goes against all norms surrounding funerary rites. In the episode of the warrior-priest, the narrative plays with a familiar motif in the *Aeneid*, that of the sacrificer turned sacrificed (*Aen.* 2.220–4; Bandera 1981; Hardie 1993, 19–23, 28–9, 32–5; Panoussi 2009, 13–77). Commentators as early as Servius (on *Aen.* 4.57 and 10.541; see Harrison 1991, 203) have noted the ironic reversal of the roles of victim and priest in this instance. The priestly status of Haemonides is noted (10.537) and his sacerdotal trappings are described in detail: the woolen headband (*infula*, 10.538), worn by both priest and victim to indicate their consecration to the god, and the ribbons (*vitta*, 10.538) that hung on either side of the head. As the killing takes place, the identical accouterments of victim and priest facilitate the latter's transformation from sacrificer to sacrificed. Note also that the episode concludes with the priest's armor being dedicated as a *tropaeum* (10.541–2), a further connection between this "sacrifice" and that of the eight Rutulians that was discussed above. Aeneas thus in this instance violates proper religious custom and law, even as he attempts to discharge his duty of *pietas* toward the slain Pallas. Similarly, the use of *immolare* in the name of Pallas at the end of the poem may very well be interpreted as part of the demands of *pietas* toward a fellow warrior and friend, as some scholars would have it (e.g., Galinsky 1988; Cairns 1989, 78–84). But such an interpretation would also have to account for the incongruity between such a notion of *pietas* and Aeneas' gradual development as a religious authority throughout the epic. As a result, the use of *immolare* here, as in the previous episodes examined, attests to Aeneas' distortion of proper sacrificial custom and law and a gross violation of his sacral duties and functions (Hardie 1993, 19, 28; Panoussi 2009, 73–5).

Aeneas' role as a sacral leader in the final scene of the poem needs to be examined alongside yet another ritual framework, that of supplication. Two episodes involving rejected supplications stand out in book 10: one involves a certain Magus, immediately after the capture of the Rutulian youths (and before the killing of the priest Haemonides); the other concerns two brothers, Lucagus and Liger. In both, Aeneas' response to ritual supplication, much like in the case of public burial previously, clearly defies religious custom.

The killing of suppliants on the battlefield is common in the *Iliad*. In the *Aeneid*, the first instances of such killings appear in book 10, where Aeneas kills suppliants who appeal to his sense of family duty and obligation (Harrison 1991, 204). In both instances, we see numerous elements marking the ceremonial nature of supplication. The killing of Magus, in particular, draws on Achilles' slaying of Lycaon after the death of Patroclus (*Il.* 21.34–135). Magus, like Lycaon, touches Aeneas' knees (*genua amplectens*, 10.523) and makes a formal address, calling upon the hero's dead father and son (*per patrios manis et spes surgentis Iuli / te precor*, 10.524–5). Aeneas' position of authority both as a powerful warrior and as representative of his people is here emphasized by the use of the legal term *sentit* (10.534) during his rejection of Magus' plea. He also displays remarkable cruelty when he repeats the suppliant's own words the moment he delivers the final blow (*hoc patris Anchisae manes, hoc sentit Iulus*, "thus decree the shades of my father Anchises, thus decrees Iulus," 10.534). Similarly, in Liger's case, the young man performs the ceremonial gesture of stretching his hands toward the hero to signify his status as a suppliant (*tendebat inertis / infelix palmas*, 10.595–6).

The appeals of these suppliants in the name of Aeneas' family and of his father in particular illuminate the problems surrounding Aeneas' rejection of Turnus' similar plea at the end of the poem. They are also important in light of Anchises' own treatment of suppliants earlier in the narrative and his bequest of a Roman model of leadership that requires his descendants "to spare the conquered and war down the proud" (*parcere subiectis et debellare superbos*, 6.853). Before we examine the final supplication, let us turn briefly to Anchises' and Evander's exchanges with suppliants earlier in the poem.

In *Aeneid* 3, Anchises, as the religious authority of the Trojans, welcomes into their midst Achaemenides, a Greek suppliant, who warns them of the dangers presented by Polyphemus. Anchises responds to Achaemenides' ceremonial gestures of supplication (*genua amplexus genibusque volutans*, 3.607) by swiftly taking him by the right hand (*haud multa moratus*, 3.610) and offering reassurance in the form of a pledge (*pignore*, 3.611). Similarly in book 8, Evander, who, as we have seen, serves as another model of leadership and religiosity, shows equal compassion and friendship to Aeneas, who came to him in supplication (*cui me Fortuna precari / et vitta comptos volvit praetendere ramos*, "whom Fortune wished me to entreat and offer boughs decorated with ribbons," 8.127–8; *supplex ad limina veni*, "I came as a suppliant to your doors," 8.145). It is thus deeply ironic that Aeneas' rejection of Magus' appeal occurs as his thoughts turn to Pallas, Evander, and their bonds of guest-friendship (10.515–17).

In his rejection of Magus' plea (10.535–6), Aeneas' cruelty is akin to that of Pyrrhus at the moment when he kills Priam (2.552–3; Harrison 1991, 207). In that scene, Priam bitterly remarks that Pyrrhus goes against the example set by his father, Achilles, who eventually honored Priam's supplication and returned Hector's body to his family and people. Moreover, Pyrrhus' killing of Priam at the altar of supplication mobilizes an intertext which sets Aeneas' own disregard of familial duty and religious law in sharp relief. The same intertextual connection confirms that Aeneas does not simply ignore his father's bequest regarding supplication but distorts it with remarkable brutality. In the episode of the second supplication in book 10, the hero declares the importance of the bond of brotherhood only to use it as an argument to kill (*morere et fratrem ne desere frater*, "die and do not let one brother desert the other," 10.600). The employment of *morere* is here particularly poignant, since it is the word Pyrrhus employs as he kills Priam (2.550). Later in book 10 Mezentius, a wicked tyrant and a mass murderer (8.481–8), uses the same verb during his *aristeia* (10.743).

The poem's final supplication is very much in line with those of the passages previously examined. Turnus appeals to Aeneas' sense of duty toward his father and his known adherence to the values of *pietas* (12.932–8). Famously, Aeneas is moved by Turnus' words but, as the flashing baldric causes his thoughts to turn to Pallas, he decides to kill (12.940–9). As in the previous cases, here too Turnus' gestures of supplication observe the ceremonial custom and thus cast Aeneas' action within a sacral context, especially in view of his fully established identity as a religious and military authority (Hardie 1993, 33–4; Panoussi 2009, 73–5). Thus when Aeneas is faced with the conflicting demands of *pietas*, when his identity as a warrior clashes with that of religious figure, he opts to abandon his sacral duty, which prescribes the granting of the suppliant's request and prohibits the sacrifice of humans. Aeneas privileges the identity of vengeful warrior to that of the sacral leader and in doing so abuses religious custom. His championing of a military identity while employing sacral language (as the use of *immolat* at 12.949 makes plain) complicates his own sacrality, which has been painstakingly developed throughout the epic.

In this essay I have argued that Aeneas' religiosity is established through his gradual assumption of public authority in a variety of religious settings. Public death rituals showcase his sacral development, since they provide the context within which Aeneas is able to discharge his ritual duties to his immediate family as a rising *paterfamilias*. Since burial is a rite that is shared by families and community alike, it also facilitates Aeneas' transition from Trojan noble to father of a new nation. Foundation practices also help solidify the hero's religious authority as they present unequivocal divine sanction of his mission. Vergil thus shows Aeneas as an eminently qualified leader, displaying religious, political, and military expertise. Yet, in the last books of the *Aeneid*, he also shows the ultimate fragility of these identities and the impossible quandaries that the various aspects of leadership pose to Aeneas or any human being called on to shoulder the burdens of power.

FURTHER READING

For a work so well studied as the *Aeneid*, there is surprisingly little scholarship on the religious aspects of Aeneas' leadership. A very useful general introduction to priests, priesthoods, and their role and functions in Roman society is Scheid (2003). On ways in which the study of religion and ritual can be applied to Roman literature, see Feeney (1998). The only monograph devoted to Vergil's use of religion is Bailey (1935), which contains valuable information but must be used with caution, since it has much that is out of date. Dyson (2001) offers an interesting argument on Aeneas' portrayal as a priest/king and examines many of the poem's religious and ritual elements. Panoussi (2009) also discusses the use of ritual in the *Aeneid* but considers it through the poem's contact with Greek tragedy. For a most sensitive and influential analysis on the motif of sacrifice in the *Aeneid*, see Hardie (1993). Military and political aspects of Aeneas' leadership are examined by Nisbet (1990) and recently by Schauer (2007) in a monograph. On Augustus' religious program, Zanker (1988) is indispensable, while Liebeschuetz (1979) and Galinsky (1996) are also very valuable. Grebe (2004) examines the relationship between Augustus' religious persona and the *Aeneid*.

CHAPTER FIVE

Vergil's Roman

J.D. Reed

I

Vergil's *Aeneid* is an etiology, a story explaining how something came into being. It is specifically a ktisis, a story of how a nation arose. Its narrative aims at a Roman nation distinct from other nations, particularly from the Trojans with whom it originated, the Greeks whom the Trojans had fought and whom the Romans were to conquer, the Carthaginians who threaten Roman ascendancy, and the Italian peoples among whom Rome arose. Yet as an etiology, and especially as one whose fulfillment is not part of the narrative, the *Aeneid* must speak of Rome proleptically, as a future entity. One effect of this narrative condition is that Rome typically comes into the poem at second or third hand in speeches by its characters, and is subject to the vicissitudes of those discourses. Of the great prophetic tableaux of the poem, the "pageant of heroes" in book 6 is couched within Anchises' tendentious, sharply purposed exposition, and the elaborate designs worked onto the golden shield of Aeneas in book 8 represent Vulcan's interpretation of the events of Roman history, which he has learned from *vates* – "seers" or "inspired poets" (8.626).

Even when the narration itself takes responsibility for speaking about Rome there tends to be a distancing, as when the city is first described (1.19–22):

> progeniem sed enim Troiano a sanguine duci
> audierat, Tyrias olim quae verteret arces;
> hinc populum late regem belloque superbum
> venturum excidio Libyae: sic volvere Parcas.

> Yet [Juno] had heard that a lineage was being drawn forth from Trojan blood to overturn that Tyrian citadel one day; that hence to Libya's destruction would come a people widely sovereign and proud in war: that the goddesses of fate so unwound their tale.

Rome's destiny as a world empire is framed within Juno's anxieties for Carthage and borrows its terms from the way the narrative has characterized Carthage at line 14, "a city rich in material resources and most fierce in zeal for war" (*dives opum studiisque asperrima belli*), reinforced by Juno's own intention that Carthage should "be a kingdom over the nations" (*regnum…gentibus esse*). The narrator's introductory progression from Troy to the promised land at lines 1–7 (through Italian shores, Latium, and the city of Alba Longa) had stopped with a mere glimpse of the "ramparts of high Rome"; when our view is next satisfied, it is through a double scrim of hearsay, grammatically signaled by a series of infinitives dependent on *audierat*, "she had heard" what the fates foretold. Vergil as narrator characterizes Carthage, by contrast, directly (1.12–18). In between, what breaks off his account of Rome's rise is his appeal to the Muse for memory of the causes of Juno's anger (cf. Putnam 2005, 462–3): the etiology, or its trajectory, is diverted from Rome to her hostility toward Rome.

Later in book 1 Jupiter prophesies about the Romans to a worried Venus: "I set them no spatial or temporal limits of power; I have given them empire without end" (*his ego nec metas rerum nec tempora pono, / imperium sine fine dedi*, 1.278–9). And ultimately Juno too, he reassures her, "will cherish and foster the Romans, lords of empire, the nation that wears the toga" (*fovebit / Romanos, rerum dominos gentemque togatam*, 1.281–2). Unexpectedly problematic is Jupiter's characterization of "the nation that wears the toga" – seemingly so clear and distinctive, but one that the rest of the poem ignores. On Aeneas' shield Augustus is seen receiving "the nations" in triumph, "as various in their tongues as in their apparel and armor" (*gentes / quam variae linguis, habitu tam vestis et armis*, 8.722–3): the distinction from the unity of the Romans is plain. But togas are mentioned nowhere else in the *Aeneid*, which clothes its Romans – or at least their forerunners and models, like Aeneas – in everything else, especially the gorgeous purple dye of the Orient, in such forms as *chlamydes* and *leaenae*. According to Suetonius (*Aug.* 40.5), Augustus once quoted Vergil's line on the toga-clad nation in reproach of those he spied in the forum wearing less traditional garb: an earthly Jupiter, enforcing the teleology of the *Aeneid*. But there is a long way to go to reach that *telos* from the national configurations depicted in Vergil's poem, and Jupiter's prophecy offers no clear roadmap.

The ethnopoetics of the *Aeneid* are inextricable from other aspects of its deeper semantics, especially its narratology and intertextuality, and like them are fundamentally based on metaphor. As in Juno's musings, only through a play of likeness to and contrast with other national unities (indicated by the terms *gens* and *populus* or by national names) can the poem give existence to Roman identity. Its basic formula – implied, if not actually compelled, by the myth of Aeneas' foundation – would seem to be Trojan plus Italian: some refugees from the fall of Troy settled in Italy and joined with the Latin people there, and their descendants founded Rome. The *Aeneid*, however, complicates this equation. Often the Roman self is cleanly opposed to an Oriental "other" – suggesting a Carthaginian identity narrowly avoided, an Egyptian identity rejected along with Antony's alliance with Cleopatra, or a Trojan identity left behind. This opposition is implicit, for example, in Anchises' prophecy about Augustus ("the realms of the Caspian Sea and the land of Maeotia already tremble at the oracles of the gods in anticipation of [Augustus'] coming, and the sevenfold mouths of the

Nile are in a turmoil of fear," 6.798–800) or in the Battle of Actium on the shield of Aeneas ("on one side Augustus Caesar leading the Italians into battle…on the other side Antony with a barbaric host and motley arms, a conqueror from the nations of the Dawn and the ruddy shore," 8.678–86), as well as in the triumphal scene quoted above. After being visited by Mercury in Carthage, Aeneas seems to get the message that Troy is finished, and that the future lies with something new (see especially his speech to Dido at 4.340–50); the pathetic simulacrum of Troy contrived by Helenus and Andromache in book 3 furnishes a negative example of his intended restoration.

Yet the *Aeneid* also constantly assimilates Troy to Rome; the separation is never clean. The god of the Tiber, for example, addresses Aeneas as "you who bring back to us the city of Troy from its enemies and preserve its citadel forever" (*Troianam ex hostibus urbem / qui revehis nobis aeternaque Pergama servas*, 8.36–7). Perhaps this is to make the Roman future easier for its human vehicle to understand, as when in his "pageant of heroes" Anchises emphasizes the Roman conquest of Troy's enemy, Greece (6.836–40). But this consideration is no mere solution to a textual problem, an "argument from the *persona* of the speaker" (cf. O'Hara 1990, 93, 123–7) – or from that of the addressee. When Augustus on the shield receives the "gifts of the nations" in triumph and affixes them to the "proud doors" of the temple of Apollo (8.720–2), he emerges like Priam, whose palace doors were "proud with barbarian gold and war-spoils" (2.504). In him recrudesces the Troy that Aeneas sought to preserve; its essence here turns out to be *imperium*, regained in grander form.

The final prophecy of Rome in the *Aeneid* seems to predict an end to Troy once Aeneas' mission is accomplished. At 12.834–40 Jupiter promises Juno, to ensure her acquiescence in the death of Turnus, that

> "sermonem Ausonii patrium moresque tenebunt,
> utque est nomen erit; commixti corpore tantum   835
> subsident Teucri. morem ritusque sacrorum
> adiciam faciamque omnis uno ore Latinos.
> hinc genus Ausonio mixtum quod sanguine surget,
> supra homines, supra ire deos pietate videbis,
> nec gens ulla tuos aeque celebrabit honores."   840

> "The Ausonians will retain their ancestral language and culture, and their
> name will be as it now is; commingling no more than physically, the
> Teucrians will sink away. The custom and rites of religious practice I shall
> add, and I shall make them all Latins with one voice. You will see the
> nation that arises hence, mixed with Ausonian blood, surpass the gods in
> piety, and no people will celebrate your honors as much as they."

"Troy has died; let it be dead together with its name," Juno demanded (*occidit, occideritque sinas cum nomine Troia*, 12.828). Jupiter seems to predict the transition that is fulfilled on Aeneas' shield, when Augustus leads the "Italians" to war against an eastern horde whose very opposition lends them unity. "The Teucrians" are corporeal vessels of ideas that are lost, utterly replaced by "Ausonian." But prophecies in the *Aeneid* are often misleading, or of dubious veracity, customized to the perceived hopes of the addressee (O'Hara 1990). Does Jupiter mean that the Trojans will "sink away" entirely (as I have translated), or "sink in and remain at a lower, hidden level"? Does he mean to add Italian religious rites to Trojan practice, or Trojan to Italian? In any case, the narrative has often etiologized Roman usages from Trojan – for example, the family names in the boat race at 5.116–23:

> velocem Mnestheus agit acri remige Pristim,
> mox Italus Mnestheus, genus a quo nomine Memmi....
> Sergestusque, domus tenet a quo Sergia nomen,
> Centauro invehitur magna, Scyllaque Cloanthus
> caerulea, genus unde tibi, Romane Cluenti.

> Mnestheus steers the swift *Seabeast* with avid crew, soon to be Italian Mnestheus, from whose name comes the *genus* of Memmius.... And Sergestus, from whom the house of the Sergii has its name, rides in the great *Centaur*, and in the blue *Scylla* Cloanthus, from whom your *genus* comes, Roman Cluentius.

That the Trojan spectators of the "Troy Show," which the poem presents as one of the most conspicuous of these survivals, in applauding its youthful participants "take joy as they watch, recognizing the faces of their ancient forebears" (*gaudentque tuentes / Dardanidae, veterumque agnoscunt ora parentum*, 5.575–6), implies a persistence of Trojan looks – perhaps beauty, characteristic expressions, a familiar responding gaze – in their Roman descendants, including especially those of Iulus, the Iulii (another ono-mastic survival). Does this contradict Jupiter's *uno ore Latinos*, which could mean not "Latins with one voice (language)" but "Latins with one unmixed facial appearance"? Or can Jupiter's promise of no more than bodily mixture accommodate that joy?

The poem's "Roman" has an equally fraught relationship with its "Italian." An ancient commentator notifies us that "it is evident from many passages that Vergil was extremely interested in the whole of Italy" (Serv. Dan. *Aen.* 1.44, *totius autem Italiae curiosissimum fuisse Vergilium multifariam apparet*), and this interest indeed takes on multifarious appearances on the antiquarian level of his poem: Italian individuals and nations are repeatedly traced back to origins elsewhere (cf. Zetzel 1997: 190–6). A particularly insistent example comes at 8.600–2, the description of the grove near Caere where Venus gives Aeneas his prophetic shield:

> Silvano fama est veteres sacrasse Pelasgos,
> arvorum pecorisque deo, lucumque diemque,
> qui primi finis aliquando habuere Latinos.

> There is a tale that both the grove and the festal day were consecrated to Silvanus, the god of farmlands and flocks, by the Pelasgians of old, who were once the first occupants of Latin territory.

This tale, *fama*, confects a blatantly artificial unity: Caere is an Etruscan city (and Etruscans in this poem have Asiatic origins); a grove in its vicinity was consecrated by

Pelasgians, or early Greeks; these Greeks were the first to occupy Latium. The cult and its etiology bridge national divisions as Rome must do. Versions of this pattern are widespread in the *Aeneid*: Evander's Arcadian-Italian settlement comes to mind, as well as Turnus' Argive-Italian ancestry. Sometimes divisions are starker: Italians are often oddly Orientalized, as when a simile compares the Rutulian armies to the Ganges and Nile (9.30–2; Reed 2007, 57); the symbolism seems to estrange them from their own land in favor of the formerly Trojan "self." At 12.503–4 the poet's own anguished voice casts the war of the last four books as a proleptic civil war, characterizing its belligerent parties as "nations destined to be everlastingly at peace" (*aeterna gentis in pace futuras*) – but when? That depends on who exactly the anti-Trojan is: if Latin, then upon Aeneas' settlement and – much later – the ascendancy of Rome over Latium; if generally Italian, then not until after the Social Wars of the early first century BCE and the "pan-Italian" Roman ideology that crystallized in the Augustan period. And why "nations at peace," rather than "one single nation," as Jupiter promises? When Augustus' leadership of "the Italians" against Antony and Cleopatra on the shield makes us think of Rome as Italy and Italy as Rome, we must remember that the poem as a whole makes neither a definitive unity. Any element of any compound as easily falls away from the others as coheres with them.

The narrator too is a persona contesting authority for Romanness with the characters (it is significant that the different authorities for the poem's "Roman" present different configurations of sameness and difference: we keep getting different perspectives on the national unity at which it aims). In a prophetic intervention by his own voice into Evander's tour of the future site of Rome, the founding of the city is represented by Romulus' *asylum* (8.342). The term is Greek, meaning a sanctuary, and comes from Greek negative *a-* plus *suláō*, to tear away or strip off (as of armor from a slain enemy). So Romulus' *asylum* is implicitly a place of refuge for people from diverse directions, but also a permanent gathering from which they cannot be removed, a place guaranteed against any further alienation – in contrast to the sequence of impermanent settlements on the site (including, evidently, his own Pallanteum) recounted by Evander. When the narrative finally takes us to Rome, it is a not-yet Rome, a series of gaps between settlements that have little to do with each other. Even Romulus' final settlement on the spot, from different perspectives, is either a vacuum given shape by external forces, or a unity – each idea contains the other within it.

II

The *Aeneid*'s very justification of Aeneas' mission – and ultimately of the existence of Rome – is not only inextricable from prophecies and report, it also both deeply problematizes and is deeply problematized by them. I am thinking in particular of the significance of Corythus and Lavinia, two coinvolved phenomena whose mysteries baffle our complacency with the overt teleology of the poem. Corythus is the Etruscan city where Dardanus, ancestor of Aeneas and the other Trojan rulers, is said to have originated; it is this origin that directs Aeneas to Italy. That the significance of Corythus depends on the authority of words embedded within multiple narrative frames (particularly the Penates' interpretation of the oracles of Apollo at 3.163–71 and the history attributed by Latinus to "Auruncian elders" at 7.205–11) gives a fraught perspective on the place, involving problems with authority and the trustworthiness of all the speakers involved. Though Aeneas' ancestral origin in Corythus wins him a claim to Italian land, it should deny him one to leadership over the Etruscan armies, which according to another oracle (retailed by Evander at 8.499–503) can only be led by a non-Italian. More fundamentally, the divide between origins and historical outcome poses a conundrum: why should an Etruscan city justify the foundation of Rome? Aeneas does not, in fact, settle in this place, but rather in Latium, where Rome will indeed arise. The poem's constant use of the term *Teucri* for the Trojans raises a further puzzle: if they are as much Teucrian, named for their Cretan ancestor Teucer, as Dardanian, named for their Italian ancestor Dardanus, why does fate send them to Italy rather than permit them to remain in Crete? Either land, after all, is their "ancient mother" (3.96 with 164, 131). If origins matter, as they should in a ktisis, the search for Roman identity ends in aporia (Reed 2006).

Aeneas' divinely appointed marriage to Lavinia, the basis for the joint Trojan–Latin heritage of Rome, poses similar riddles. If Turnus' family origin is Greek (7.371–2), he would seem to have less of a claim to Latin land than Aeneas, the descendant of the reportedly Italian Dardanus. On the other hand, if he is Latin, he is not qualified to marry Lavinia, according to the oracle given to King Latinus, which said that he is to find a son-in-law among "foreign bridegrooms," not Latins (7.96–101). Turnus loses either way, and Aeneas wins – but at a price for Roman identity. If origins matter, Aeneas has a right to settle in Italy, but no right to marry Lavinia, which is also necessary for the Roman future. Or else the Etruscan location of his ancestral home makes him eligible to marry Lavinia, leaving the gap between Corythus and Rome, and leaving in doubt his suitability to lead the Etruscans in war. Or else the oracles are wrong – or wrongly reported.

It is worth paying attention to our method here. We provisionally accept some claim as true, and then ask: what else in the text needs to be accepted as true for this to be true? What fictive world does this acceptance entail, and how does it resonate with the other data of the poem – or against them? If Aeneas' destined settlement requires that Latium and Etruria be treated as a unity, how does that comment on the national boundaries that other claims in the poem require? It is easy enough to explain away the poem's conflicting messages as references to Vergil's differing sources (or putative sources), but to stop there, without asking about their meaning within the poem, leaves the *Aeneid* a mere collage. (On this problem in general, see the chapter by Casali in this volume.) Another temptation is to assume that Vergil would have reconciled these inconsistencies in a revision (see O'Hara 2007, 77–8 on this critical refuge). But nothing is gained by bulldozing across the ambages through which Vergilian ethnopoetics uneasily thread; the puzzles we have looked at tend uniformly to problematize Romanness in a way consistent with other aspects of the poem. Feeney, comparing a "pair of binoculars with incompatible lenses," refuses to resolve scenes in the *Aeneid* where irreconcilable interpretations seem equally compelling (Feeney 1991, 168). A similar example is Anchises' adversion to the future Caesar and Pompey, fated to fight a civil war (6.828–31):

> "heu quantum inter se bellum, si lumina vitae
> attigerint, quantas acies stragemque ciebunt,

aggeribus socer Alpinis atque arce Monoeci
descendens, gener adversis instructus Eois!"

"Alas, what a war, what mighty armies and slaughter they will rouse
between themselves should the light of life touch them, the father-in-law
bearing down from Alpine heights and the citadel of Monoecus, the son-
in-law supported on the opposing side by nations of the Dawn!"

What kind of a civil war is this? Pompey is likened to an eastern conqueror threatening
Rome; Caesar, sweeping down upon Italy from the Alps, is likened to Hannibal (Reed
2007, 159–62). No matter which side "we" are opposed to, "we" are constructed as
Roman against a symbolic non-Roman – at the expense of estranging either Caesar or
Pompey, or both.

Is there no touchstone by which we can decide these *problêmata*? It is tempting to
seek an essence of Romanness in *pietas*, the devotion to right principles – here specifically
to Roman destiny – attributed to Aeneas *qua* model Roman. Jupiter predicts to Juno at
12.838–9, "You will see the nation that will arise hence…surpass the gods in piety." And
yet Aeneas' *pietas* boils down to devotion to the *fata* that he knows of through report –
and that thus reduce to their cognate *fama*, retailed (often at second or third hand) by
a variety of seers, storytellers, revenant deceased kinsfolk, and the occasional, usually
doubtfully sincere god. Anchises, too, presents the essential qualities of the future nation
in a peculiarly evasive way: of Marcellus at the climax of his lesson he says (6.875–7),

"nec puer Iliaca quisquam de gente Latinos
in tantum spe tollet avos, nec Romula quondam
ullo se tantum tellus iactabit alumno."

"No boy of the Trojan race will exalt his Latin ancestors so high by his
promise, nor will the land of Romulus ever glory so in any of her
nurslings."

Marcellus, who binds within himself the ethnic components of Romanness ("Trojan"
and "Latin"), will be a model Roman – but only potentially, since he will emphatically
die before realizing any of his exemplary qualities (cf. lines 878–81). Anchises' famous
unfulfilled wish emblematizes this: "Alas, pitiable boy, if only you could somehow
break your harsh destiny!" (*heu, miserande puer, si qua fata aspera rumpas*, 6.885; cf.
Goold 1992, 121). The "ideal Roman" is perpetually deferred.

III

The invocation of Erato at the beginning of book 7 recasts the *Aeneid* as love poetry:
the poet's prayer for memory of the events of the Italian war (*tu vatem, tu, diva,
mone*, 7.41) transfigures the fight for a settlement in Latium into the armed rivalry of
Aeneas and Turnus over the same woman. Yet we do not see any signs that Aeneas

loves Lavinia, or even wants *her* in any way. She emerges as an unmediated object of desire only in the case of the would-be founder, Turnus, especially in his vehement reaction to her famously mysterious blush, which makes him "burn the more with passion for combat" (*ardet in arma magis*, 12.71). Since the end of his affair with Dido, personal satisfaction seems to have become moot for Aeneas: *felicitas* or *fortuna* is implicitly to come some time in the future, if at all, not to Aeneas himself, as he indicates to his son before heading into battle: "My child, learn valor and true toil from me, fortune from others" (*disce, puer, virtutem ex me verumque laborem, / fortunam ex aliis*, 12.435–6). In this regard there is as deep irony as anywhere in the poem's climax when Aeneas, spying Turnus' vulnerable spot, "chances upon *fortuna*" (*sortitus fortunam oculis*, 12.920): *this* is the fortune the poem allots him. Words change meaning to redirect Aeneas' fulfillment, just as his "founding" of Rome (as at 1.33, *Romanam condere gentem*) amounts at 12.950 to his slaying of Turnus, in whom he "buries" his sword: *ferrum...condit* (James 1995). The ultimate ends of his mission are satisfied for Aeneas himself only metaphorically and punningly.

Erato represents a more figurative form of desire, which the *Aeneid* incessantly directs toward national foundation – not inappositely in a story whose presiding deity is Venus and whose goal, *Roma*, is an anciently recognized anagram of *amor* (cf. Reed 2007, 42–3, 149–50). What Aeneas must learn to desire, apparently, is the Roman future. Jupiter tries to ensure this sublimation by sending a warning through Mercury, contriving that Aeneas "burns with passion" to leave Carthage for Italy (*ardet abire*, 4.281); Aeneas suggests that this ktistic passion replaces his love for Dido when he characterizes his Italian destination to her: "this is love, this is home" (*hic amor, haec patria est*, 4.347). Anchises apparently completes the task in his presentation of the Roman future, "igniting" his son's spirit with "love for coming fame" (*incenditque animum famae venientis amore*, 6.889). But in this case, too, desire is always unfulfilled: the poet's wording forbids the tight bond between desire and its object at which Aeneas' metonymy aims. The Golden Age, which Anchises foretells will return under Augustus (6.792–3), is another ungraspable ideal of Romanness, far in the future for Aeneas – and perhaps always just out of reach for Vergil's contemporaries, too (cf. Putnam 1965, xiii–xiv). Even the age of Augustus provides no firmer a *telos* than does *pietas*. The invocation of the Muse of erotic poetry emblematizes the poem's sense of infinite deferral.

In the *Aeneid*, moreover, desire can suggest a figure for imperial subsumption – a gathering-in under a single national identity. Dido, even before she is made to fall in love with Aeneas, speaks of melding their incipient nations into one (1.572–4):

> "vultis et his mecum pariter considere regnis?
> urbem quam statuo vestra est; subducite navis;
> Tros Tyriusque mihi nullo discrimine agetur."

> "Would you, moreover, like to settle with me in these realms on equal
> terms? The city that I am establishing is yours: draw up your ships. Trojan
> and Tyrian will be treated with no distinction between them on my part."

Their love comes to figure this melding, which – as Jupiter indicates to Mercury and
Mercury to Aeneas – threatens Roman destiny. And yet the mirror-quality that obtains
between Rome and Carthage – not least in the surprising image of Carthaginian
coloni, magistracies, consecrated Senate, and so on (1.12, 426) – ends up rather by
conceptually subsuming Carthage into Rome. Empire, the *Aeneid* tells us, is compa-
rability between peoples, places, things: *that* gives control. The characteristic play of
assimilation to and differentiation from other nations can produce a capacious, accommodating sense of nationality that is suitable to an empire, and particularly to the
imperium that the *Aeneid* desiderates. The diverse nature of the opposing armies in
the Italian war, overlapping each other's ethnic boundaries, and the general sense of
a convergence of immigrants in Italy, is a confusion that prepares for empire. The very
oracles that keep prescribing outsiders – as a husband for Lavinia, as a leader for the
Etruscan armies – guarantee the multiethnic reach of Rome even as they confound
the origins of Roman identity.

In defining (etiologically and teleologically) an ethnic identity within a multiethnic
world empire, the ktistic component of the *Aeneid* is different from the Greek *ktiseis*
Vergil could draw on. Its model of a divinely favored nation with a universal mission is
most comparable to Eastern Mediterranean examples – notably the Hebrew Bible, in
which, as in the *Aeneid*, a national hero leads his people back to a former homeland with
much trouble from the indigenes, stimulated by the divine injunction to kindle a light
unto the nations – or at least impose civilized values on a pacified world (cf. Weinfeld
1993, 1–21). A more recent parallel is the universalist program of Cleopatra, who coopted
for Egypt, and as a foil to Rome, Eastern Mediterranean hopes and memories of a world
empire – and whose program was then itself selectively coopted for Rome by Augustus
(cf. Kleiner 2005). The consequence of this program or mission is a syncretistic embrace.
Rome's very status as "widely sovereign" emerges from a contrast with Juno's model of
Carthage as "a kingdom over the nations." Ultimate Romans, like Augustus emulating
and surpassing the Orientalized Antony's patron gods, Hercules and Bacchus, do not so
much defeat their rivals as best them on their own terms (6.801–5):

> "nec vero Alcides tantum telluris obivit,
> fixerit aeripedem cervam licet, aut Erymanthi
> pacarit nemora et Lernam tremefecerit arcu;
> nec qui pampineis victor iuga flectit habenis
> Liber, agens celso Nysae de vertice tigris."

> "Truly, neither Alcides covered so much country, for all that he shot the
> bronze-footed deer or pacified the woods of Erymanthus and made Lerna
> tremble at his bow, nor Liber, who steers his chariot with vine-leaf-
> covered reins, driving tigers down from the high peak of Nysa."

Anchises there is prophesying Augustus' command of East and West, which takes the
form of an appropriation; the acceptance of the other's terms both transforms the self and
absorbs and obliterates the other. If "the Roman" happens only in between other national
definitions, this can be a paradoxically satisfying form of deferral. Centered nowhere, the
Roman can find a center anywhere: Romanness potentially takes in all the world.

This potential is realized again in Anchises' comparison of Rome to the goddess Cybele (6.781–7):

> "en huius, nate, auspiciis illa incluta Roma
> imperium terris, animos aequabit Olympo,
> septemque una sibi muro circumdabit arces,
> felix prole virum: qualis Berecyntia mater
> invehitur curru Phrygias turrita per urbes   785
> laeta deum partu, centum complexa nepotes,
> omnis caelicolas, omnis supera alta tenentis."

> "Look, my son: by [Romulus'] auspices that renowned city, Rome, will make its empire equal to the whole earth, its spirit to heaven, and within its wall it will encircle seven citadels as one city, blessed with manly offspring: like the Berecyntian Mother as she is conveyed in a chariot through the cities of Phrygia, crowned with towers, blessed with the generations of the gods, embracing one hundred grandchildren, all of them heaven-dwellers, all of them possessing the realms above."

The viewpoint is calculatedly Asiatic, again for the sake of Aeneas' still Trojan (or "Phrygian") standpoint, though again it has deeper consequences. Rome is like Cybele because Rome is an ancient Oriental city – insofar as Rome is Troy: that is the identification Anchises urges us to accept in order to accept his analogy (the official worship of Cybele at Rome since 204 BCE helps reinforce this assimilation). Her embrace of offspring bizarrely reverses the reality, in which Rome is the youngest of cities (at least in this poem), the "offspring" of older nations: mainly "ancient Troy" (2.363) and "ancient Italy" (3.164).

Here is a different kind of embrace from that figured by *amor* on the poem's ktistic level, but related to it. Anchises' image of Rome as Cybele has to do with posterity: itself another aspect of desire, especially as concerns the rivalry for Lavinia, which in a sense is a contest for ancestorship. Cybele is *felix prole*, "blessed with offspring": conversely Dido is *infelix* (1.712, 749, etc.) as much for her loss of posterity as for other reasons (O'Hara 2007, 50). At 4.83–5 she seems to sublimate her desire to hear Aeneas' story (already a sublimation of her love for him) into a maternal desire – that is, a ktistic desire (compare her wish for a "little Aeneas," *parvulus Aeneas*, at 4.328–9):

> illum absens absentem auditque videtque
> aut gremio Ascanium genitoris imagine capta
> detinet, infandum si fallere possit amorem.   85

> Apart from him, she sees and hears him apart from her, or detains Ascanius on her lap, captivated by his father's likeness, in the hope that she could fool her unspeakable love.

The hope is vain, of course; the metaphor fails. One recalls her nightmare at 4.465–8, which, in alluding to the prophetic dream of Ilia from Ennius' *Annales* (38–40 Skutsch), replaces the conception of a Roman founder with barren loneliness. At 6.822

Anchises calls Brutus, executor of his own sons, *infelix* – an exchange for the "love of country" and "desire for praise" (*amor patriae, laudum cupido*) that motivated his action. *Felicitas*, deferred by Aeneas on one level, turns out itself necessarily to signify a deferral: a perpetual biological handing-down of self.

IV

Historical epic, both Greek and Latin, is commonly concerned with defining a national self against an Oriental other, making epic poetry a place for establishing or experimenting with national identity. The tradition begins for us with the woefully fragmentary *Persica* of Choerilus of Samos, on the Persian Wars (which he seems to have treated as a self-defining struggle between Greeks and motley easterners), but it may well have a background in the martial foundation-elegies of the archaic period. In its long reception, Homeric poetry was taken this way (Hall 1989); the *Iliad* suggested a template for the "otherness" of the Trojan versus the Greek, and the *Odyssey* is full of cultural antitypes. The age of Hellenistic expansion prompted a fresh wave of *ktiseis* from such poets as Apollonius of Rhodes, and a poetics that often tendentiously maps Greek and "barbarian" onto each other; outside of literature, Macedonian or Greek names are given to places in the newly conquered East, producing suggestive, readily mythopoeic doublets (Stephens 2003, 91–5). This is the poetics out of which Latin epic grew. After Livius Andronicus' translation of the *Odyssey* (itself on different levels a confrontational engagement with a Greek construction of identity), Latin epic is about empire: Naevius' *Bellum Punicum* founded the Roman struggle with Carthage in the ktistic past, and Ennius' *Annales* traced the development of Rome through its wars against, and absorptions of, a widening circle of neighboring peoples. The *Aeneid* adds to a tradition of defining a national self against an other (cf. Quint 1993 on Vergil and Lucan, Hardie 1993 on post-Vergilian epic).

All the interpretive tools developed for (especially) Hellenistic and Latin poetry can serve to articulate a play of identity and alterity, involving all the devices that we have learned to recognize in ancient poets – mythological references, meaningful allusion, significant names of characters, and so on. Lineages, for example, sometimes seem to lead back into nothing, to evaporate, as we have seen with Dardanus and Corythus – or to run into unwelcome or contradictory associations. The narrator at 7.49 calls Saturn the "ultimate founder," *ultimus auctor*, of Latinus' race – but he notoriously had a father (Ennius' Caelus, the Greek Ouranos), whom he deposed: how does Saturn put a halt to the genealogical regression and fix the authenticating moment? In her dying curse upon Aeneas and his posterity, Dido invokes Sol, the all-seeing Sun god, in addition to Juno and various deities of vengeance (4.607): a common motif, as when Aeneas invokes the Sun in his oath at 12.276. But the Sun was evidently an ancestor of Latinus: his daughter Circe was the wife of Latinus' grandfather, Picus (7.189–91), and Latinus is able to give Aeneas horses derived from Circe's own herd, descended from the divine horses of the Sun (7.274–85). Insofar as it is indeed the Sun who fulfills Dido's curse – which envisions something very much like the Punic Wars and especially Hannibal's war on Rome (4.625–9) – does it mean that he, as well as Juno despite her pact with Jupiter (cf. Feeney 1984), remains not wholly reconciled to a Trojan (by now Roman) presence in Italy even at the end of the third century?

> "exoriare aliquis nostris ex ossibus ultor 625
> qui face Dardanios ferroque sequare colonos,
> nunc, olim, quocumque dabunt se tempore vires.
> litora litoribus contraria, fluctibus undas
> imprecor, arma armis: pugnent ipsique nepotesque."

> "Arise from my bones, unknown avenger, to harry the Dardanian settlers
> with torch and sword, now, in the future, whenever strength lends itself! I
> pray for shore to be set against shore, sea against sea, weapons against
> weapons! Let them fight, themselves and their children's children!"

Nationalities depend on these genealogies, which were an important feature of ktistic literature; but as we have seen, national origins tend to disappear into a fog of unknowns. The poem's ekphrases sometimes mirror this art of aporia. Trained to peruse visual representations of origins on objects like Dido's golden dishes at 1.640–2 (engraved with the heroic deeds of her Tyrian ancestors) and Turnus' golden shield at 7.789–92 (depicting his ancestress Io), we are frustrated if we try to peer at Inachus' carven urn as depicted on that shield at 7.792 (Reed 2007, 70), or at the shield dedicated by Aeneas at Actium at 3.287–9, which is theoretically still visible on the door of Apollo's temple there, rendered in minute detail by Vulcan on Aeneas' golden shield at 8.704 (Hannah 2007, 125–6). These teasing *mises-en-abyme manquées* bring to life Hexter's description of the *Aeneid*'s conundrums as highly polished surfaces in which readers see only their own desire for a solution (Hexter 1990, 121–2).

Complications spring out in the poem's announcement of its theme (1.1–7):

> Arma virumque cano, Troiae qui primus ab oris
> Italiam fato profugus Laviniaque venit
> litora, multum ille et terris iactatus et alto
> vi superum, saevae memorem Iunonis ob iram;
> multa quoque et bello passus, dum conderet urbem 5
> inferretque deos Latio, genus unde Latinum
> Albanique patres atque altae moenia Romae.

> I sing of arms and of a man, the first one who came from the shores of
> Troy to Italy and the Lavinian beaches, exiled by fate, much buffeted both
> on land and on the deep by the force of the gods above, because of the
> remembering anger of savage Juno; and enduring much in war as well,
> until he could found a city and introduce his gods to Latium: and from this
> came the Latin race, the elders of Alba, and the ramparts of high Rome.

The sentence leads from Troy to Rome, as Aeneas' mission ultimately will. But the intermediate stages mix things up. Why is it significant that he was the first to come from Troy to Italy? Why are the shores already called "Lavinian," before Aeneas founds Lavinium and names it for his bride? Why is Aeneas' foundation only a stepping-stone to another – itself a stepping-stone? Why will the Trojan gods come generally "to Latium," rather than particularly to Rome? Why is the Latin nation said to spring from Aeneas' settlement, when "the Latins" are evidently on the spot before he arrives? All of these places and peoples are folded into Rome with much straining of geographical and chronological seams. The following twelve books of ktistic poetry will exacerbate these questions rather than resolve them. The "Roman" of the *Aeneid* is a rhetorical entity, founded not on antiquarian certainties, but on tropes that threaten to dissolve and realign under different perspectives – on the variegated lies in which poetic truth reposes.

Ultimately the problem is not just with Roman identity, but is even more radically undecidable: how can the poem fix what "Greek," "Oriental," "Italian," and so on mean? Every definition of the Roman depends on an opposition to another unity, but every other unity too is provisional. The basic problem is how the "Roman" is identifiable with the self – the reader's subject position, which itself is problematically bound up with the poet-narrator's and with any character's (the various personae of earlier literature, too, are intertextually made over into this entity). Any identity is a trope that coheres from some perspectives, not from others. It is hard to go further than to say that the *Aeneid* makes room for a subject that is metaphorical with "the Roman." Yet this indeterminacy is not evidence of weakness or inadequacy to achieve a thorough image of Roman nature, or of a basic meaninglessness; nor may we dismiss the poem's ambiguities as a mere function of poetic language. The *Aeneid* rather exploits the nature of poetic language to win for its readers a compellingly adaptive self.

We are never *there*; we are never done with this poem. The polycentrism of the Vergilian ktisis permits one to read a new *Aeneid* every time – or to become a new subject; Vergil gives his reader no boundaries of place or time. The identity that the poem lends us can be construed as that of an apologist for Roman *imperium* of the subsuming type discussed above. It impersonates conquered peoples; it pretends that the Roman is no one else but his own conquered opponents; it erases boundaries by making every "other" identical with the self. But the poem also lets us analyze that totalization. The incompatibilities and gaps within Anchises' account of metempsychosis on the banks of Lethe (Feeney 1986; Zetzel 1989) encourage us, at least, to inquire into the ontology of those future Romans: who have they forgotten they once were? What identities have they drunk away, like new Roman citizens wiped clean of their former selves (one cannot ignore the curiosity about Italian localities that Vergil insinuated multifariously into his poem)? This question arises most acutely as an antithesis to the climax of Anchises' protreptic, "you, Roman, remember to rule the nations with *imperium*" (*tu regere imperio populos, Romane, memento,* 6.851); his admonition enforces a contrast between "you" (immediately, and proleptically, Aeneas, but metaphorical with any addressee, including the reader) and "others" (*alii*, 6.847), defining each in an imperial hierarchy (Putnam 2005, 459–60). The memory that Anchises' teleology depends on is disturbed by the Lethean subtext of his exposition. And memory is what the poet prays for: empire shares a language with poetry; both have the same terms, the same possibilities, the same problems.

The poetic language that perpetually defers and mediates a Roman identity is, indeed, that same *fama* that is "as faithful a messenger of the invented and the depraved as of the true," as the poem says of personified Fama, and thus of itself (*tam ficti pravique tenax quam nuntia veri*, 4.188), a creature that can motivate dire acts on the strength of fiction. Anchises, after narrating the Roman future, sends Aeneas out through the Gate of False Dreams: whatever the complexities and ambiguities in this image (Zetzel 1989, 275), it is a reminder of what poetry can be, as Servius confidently says in his note on 6.898: "The poetic sense is plain: [the poet] wishes for everything he has said to be understood as deceptive" (*et poetice apertus est sensus: vult autem intellegi falsa esse omnia quae dixit*). The prophetic shield, with its scenes of Roman history, is described as showing Aeneas "the fame and fate of his descendants" (*fama et fata nepotum*, 8.731): as often, the two collapse into each other. And the object of Aeneas' unfulfillable desire, as the poem phrases it, is not exactly Rome or its essential qualities, but rather the glorious rumor of Rome: *famae venientis amore* (6.889).

FURTHER READING

Although many excellent suggestions are to be found in the vast literature on the poem, and detailed information in the relevant articles of the *Enciclopedia Virgiliana*, there is little criticism on the *Aeneid*'s picture of the Roman *per se*. Reed (2007) discusses how the poem constructs a Roman identity out of oppositions to other nationalities. Syed (2005) identifies the self offered by the poem with an image of a Roman male, especially as against Dido and Carthage; for detailed studies of Dido's Carthage as an antitype in the poem see also Hexter (1992) and Starks (1999). On the construction of Roman versus Italian identity in the *Aeneid* see especially Toll (1991, 1997), Henderson (2000), and Johnson (2001). Hardie (1986) and the first two chapters of Quint (1993) connect Vergilian epic with constructions of empire; see also Hardie (1993) for Vergilian influence on later epic constructions of Roman imperial identity. On the way Roman writers, including Vergil, adapted or even created myths of national origins for their own purposes see Bickerman (1952), Malkin (1998), Erskine (2001), Hannah (2004), and Fletcher (2006). The many papers and commentaries of Horsfall trace Vergil's antiquarian sources in detail; on his organization of received ethnography see especially chapter 4 of Thomas (1982). Chapter 5 of Dufallo (2007) contains a discussion of Vergil's construction of a new Roman subject as against late Republican models; see also Feldherr (1995). The bibliography given by these mostly recent treatments will lead back to earlier discussions.

CHAPTER SIX

Vergil, Ovid, and the Poetry of Exile

Michael C.J. Putnam

The theme of exile has engaged writers from the beginning of Western literature to the present. If we look to Roman letters alone, it is a major presence in the works of the prose writers Cicero and Seneca, and of poets like Ovid and Boethius. In their *curricula vitae*, all endured actual banishment, however varied its circumstances, and, especially in the case of the poets, all utilized the experience to craft literature of exceptional richness.

For Ovid, exile came toward the end of his career, but the imagined understanding of the meaning of displacement, whether inner or outer, spiritual or physical, or both, is of significance from near the start of his writings, in the extraordinary *Heroides*, with their varied voices telling of separation and abandonment.[1] And the idea of alienation and isolation, the relentless depiction of selves obliged to mutate but often remaining in essence changeless, the constancy of loss accompanying evolution, are major ideological foci in Ovid's masterpiece, the *Metamorphoses*.

Nevertheless, though the realities of his life and essential aspects of his poetry make Ovid the great Roman expositor of exile, he is abidingly influenced by Vergil, who from start to finish of his œuvre is equally concerned with the horrors that exile actuates. I will probe here this intimacy in one of several areas of overlap, namely the poets' treatment of the act of departure from one's central city for points only vaguely known. It is my hope to spur further examination of this and other spheres of imaginative interaction between the two masters.

The theme of exile from one's native city is important from the beginnings of Latin literature. One of the most moving fragments of Naevius' *Bellum Punicum* tells of wives, presumably of Anchises and Aeneas, departing by night, heads covered, from their native Troy. It is Vergil, however, who, first in the *Eclogues*, then in the *Aeneid*, expands banishment into a major theme of his masterpieces. In fact one unifying factor for his poetry as a whole is the word *fugio*, with its technical meaning of depart into exile. Its iteration takes us from the fourth line of the initial eclogue, where the dispossessed shepherd Meliboeus explains to the lucky Tityrus his own fate and that of his fellows – *nos patriam fugimus* ("we are in enforced flight from our fatherland")[2] – to the final hexameter of the *Aeneid* where the soul of the defeated Turnus is exiled (*fugit*) from his body to the shades below.[3]

Aeneas himself would at first seem to be the spiritual successor of the suffering Meliboeus, dismissed from the land of his birth and destined for foreign parts at first only dimly known. But upon his arrival in Italy he becomes the leader of an invading army that inflicts on Turnus the ultimate banishment, away from the world of the living. In the course of Vergil's epic, then, as its hero turns from passive accepter of fate to its active implementer, he also suffers metamorphosis from exiled to exiler, and Turnus, his victim, by the poem's conclusion has, with no little irony on the poet's part, taken on the role that his conqueror played in the poem's first half.[4]

Ovid is Vergil's extraordinary successor in this regard as in so much else. The sense of loss and of the suffering of separation that is part of the experience of exile pervades the *Heroides*, and the *Metamorphoses*, as we have noted, is the great poem of alienation from one realm to another, of the distance between a former and a transformed self, of life as death.[5] But the Ovidian career brings a dimension to the topic that his predecessor's lacks. Vergil may have deliberately chosen life in Naples over the challenges that the imperial city had to offer. Ovid *in propria persona* endured exile, forced from Rome by Augustus to a life that was no life, on the boundary between civilization and barbarity. In the exilic poetry, in the *Tristia* and the *Epistulae ex Ponto* which chronicle his own ordeal, Ovid therefore adds a dimension of personal involvement that the poetry of Vergil lacked because, if we can trust the early *vitae*, the poet himself apparently suffered no dispossession. Vergilian interiority, the subjectivity of the human condition that he understood and communicated so well, is both absorbed and then dramatically extended by Ovid, the citizen of Rome who also had the poetic genius to transform the horrific details of existence away from Rome into immortal verse.

However dramatic his expansion of the idea of exile, Ovid regularly calls Vergil to mind to communicate the experience of exile. In fact *Tristia* 1.3 deliberately asks its readers to remember the second book of the *Aeneid* as they read, by comparing the speaker's last night in Rome before the metamorphosis of banishment, a night that he appropriately compares to a funeral, with the death of Troy (25–6):

> si licet exemplis in parvis grandibus uti,
>   haec facies Troiae, cum caperetur, erat.

> If I may use an exalted analogy for a lowly case, this was the
> appearance of Troy at its moment of capture.

I would like in the pages that follow to examine the Vergilian influence on Ovid's poem and to suggest, by extension, further ways of treating the interaction between the two poets.[6] *Aeneid* 2, not unexpectedly, will be a focal part of my discussion, but so will other segments of Vergil's epic, especially books 8 and 12. Briefly put, the clear similarities between Ovid's masterpiece and Vergil's tale of Troy's collapse show

Aeneas' narrative as a major source of his inspiration. But the later poet also digests for his readers the experience of exile that unites the whole of Vergil's poetic output, from the opening of his initial pastoral to the concluding line of his epic. Let us begin, however, where we started, with the initial pastoral.

Just as the programmatic aspect of eclogue 1 is important for understanding Vergil's œuvre as a whole, so its dialectic with Ovid is crucial for our comprehension of Ovid's accomplishment. The cast of characters is remarkably parallel. First there is the city of Rome and the ruling *deus* at its heart.[7] In Vergil this center of power can work in two directions. One fortunate shepherd can pay it a visit and gain its young god's assurances that his world, which is at once tangible and spiritual, will remain intact. The other suffers the onslaught of its emissary, "an unholy, barbarous soldier"[8] who both dispossesses and exiles. In Ovid's world the god has grown up to be more fully omnipotent, still capable of exiling not just a figmented shepherd but a real master-poet, departing from Rome itself.

While Vergil makes us empathize specifically with Meliboeus as an exile, it is important to observe that the displaced shepherd also represents the many others who have been dispossessed, to whom exile is now a common, if not a shared, experience. In the case of Ovid the potential participant of his withdrawal from Rome, to whom the poem gives great prominence, is his wife. It is to her that Ovid allots an example of what I would call the "*ibimus*" theme (81–2):

> "non potes avelli: simul hinc, simul ibimus," inquit,
>   "te sequar et coniunx exulis exul ero..."

> "You cannot be torn from me. Together, together we will make our
> way," she says. "I will follow you and I will be the exiled wife of an
> exile..."

She, of course, stays in Rome, but Ovid allots to her, as emotional support for her plea, an echo of Meliboeus' words in *Ecl.* 1.64: "But we others will make our way hence..." (*At nos hinc alii...ibimus*).[9] In between early Vergil and late Ovid we have further variations in Horace and Tibullus on the notions of companionship, departure, separation and the like that *ibimus* implies. But only at the beginning and the end of this arc is exile in particular suggested.[10] It is among the ironies of Latin literary history that one of the places that Meliboeus goes on to mention as a possible site for his relegation, Scythia (65), proves all too proximate to the actual location for Ovid's expatriation.[11]

Ovid thus sets up a challenge between pastoral and elegy, between poetry of idealism ever tested by reality and poetry fully centered on lament for what has been lost. We turn from a dialogue that pits the world of poetry and the imagination's freedom against the sufferings that power in history is prepared to inflict, to a monologue that records the aftermath of such an imposition. There is no addressee in Ovid's poem. Ovid chooses to adopt the stance of a soliloquizer, distant and alone, remembering past conversation on his last night in Rome, but in fact now imagining direct communication only with his reader.

There is one further point of interconnection between the two poems that is perhaps the most poignant of all for its emphasis on the different aspects of temporality that they suggest. As eclogue 1 comes to a conclusion Tityrus, who is allotted the poem's final verses, makes the departing Meliboeus an offer (79):

> Hic tamen hanc mecum poteras requiescere noctem...

> Nevertheless you could have rested here with me this night...

The language leaves it unclear whether Tityrus is extending an invitation that his relegated fellow shepherd can actually accept. What is illuminating for our purposes is the careful juxtaposition that Ovid makes between *hanc noctem*, with which Vergil starts his concluding verses, and *illius noctis* in Ovid's initial hexameter. For Vergil's Tityrus a nightfall is about to commence which for him is but part of a shepherd-singer's quotidian round. For Meliboeus, however, it means the start of exile from dream to actuality. In Ovid's poetry of retrospect, the singular night of horror is long past and we are made to envision it as an *imago* that returns to the speaker's inner vision. Vergil leaves the immediate bitterness of Meliboeus' night ahead for his readers to imagine. Ovid fleshes out the experience for us as a flashback where the evolution of the story over nocturnal time, along with the abundance of detail, makes graphically clear what happens to an exile in the hours after Vergil's brilliant antiphony comes to an end.

The presence of Vergil in Ovid's mind as he recalls the earliest stages of his exile becomes vividly clear when we turn to the opening lines themselves:

> Cum subit illius tristissima noctis imago,
>   quae mihi supremum tempus in urbe fuit,
> cum repeto noctem, qua tot mihi cara reliqui,
>   labitur ex oculis nunc quoque gutta meis.
> iam prope lux aderat, qua me discedere Caesar
>   finibus extremae iusserat Ausoniae.

> When the saddest image of that night recurs which was for me the
> final moment in the city, when I recall the night in which I left behind
> so much dear to me, a tear now also glides from my eyes. Now the
> day was nearly at hand in which Caesar had ordered me to depart
> from the bounds of farthest Ausonia.

Ovid's lines, which center on first-person experience (*mihi, mihi, meis, me*), are built around superlatives connected with inner feeling (*tristissima*), time (*supremum*), and space (*extremae*). These most exaggerated of adjectival forms suggest the outer limits of meaning, lexical ultimates, finalities. But each has a special point. *Tristissima*, which gains special stress by hypallage (if the recollected image is the saddest, imagine what the night must have been like!), announces the theme of the poem and the poetry book. *Supremum tempus* looks specifically to the speaker's last moments in Rome but, since the phrase often refers to death,[12] it suggests that departure is itself a form of demise, of permanent farewell. It thus anticipates a major theme of the poem, as we have seen: Ovid's leave-taking is also his funeral. Finally, *extremae Ausoniae* asks us to view the poet's experience not from a Roman vantage point but from the distance of Tomis, where Italy now seems as far away as possible.

Ovid comments on this pointed moment of space, time, and emotionality from other angles as well. One is the progress from *noctis* and *noctem* to *lux*. In reversing the Catullan progress from *lux* to *nox*,[13] which is to say from light to dark, life to death, Ovid uses irony to vivify his own situation by having night, the dark moment of his metaphorical death and obsequies, be followed by light, which is to say the constancy of living a continuous form of death as an exile. The suggestion of metamorphosis here – of life into death-as-life – is abetted by the words *nunc quoque*. The phrase is one by which Ovid, throughout his *Metamorphoses*, often marks the time after change has occurred.[14] Even then, even after the moment of mutation, aspects of one's old shape or character remain which serve both as a reminder of the past and as a confirmation of present alteration. For Ovid the tears shed during the night of woe are echoed in the drop that still now flows from his eyes. Tears still remain as a sad token of the saddest night.

Vergil permeates these lines, especially the Vergil of *Aeneid* 2, and I will return later to that book's particular influence on Ovid. Here I would like to look only at the earlier poet's appearance in Ovid's opening line, where the writer announces, in a moment of enormous prestige, that interaction with his great predecessor is an important part of his program for what follows. Ovid's *subit illius tristissima noctis imago* looks back to several moments in *Aeneid* 2. We think, for instance, of the picture of Aeneas' wife that occurs to her husband after seeing the headless corpse of Priam: *subiit deserta Creusa* ("abandoned Creusa rose up," 562). Still closer is the hero's vision of the specter of Anchises that immediately precedes: *subiit cari genitoris imago* ("the image of my dear father rose up," 560) where the word *imago* helps make an easy transition from Aeneas' inner vision to Ovid's mental revisualization of past reality.

But one further moment in *Aeneid* 2 is yet more comparable. As the Greek victory begins to become apparent, the poem's hero remarks on the abstractions that now rule events (368–9):

> crudelis ubique
> luctus, ubique pavor et plurima mortis imago.

> Cruel grief is everywhere, everywhere fear and countless
> images of death.

We move easily, in sound and sense, from *plurima mortis imago* to *tristissima noctis imago*. Each phrase, concluding its hexameter, shifts from superlative adjective to the word *imago*, bracketing, in the one case, *mortis*, in the other, *noctis*. But the very distinctions within the reflection, between *plurima* and *tristissima*, and between *mortis* and *noctis*, tug Vergil into Ovid, stressing the sadness of the moment and reminding the reader, as Ovid will do again shortly by means of metaphor, that death inheres in the night he is about to describe.

The context of Vergil's lines, of which 368–9 are the climax, was also on Ovid's mind. Take 360–3, for instance, where Aeneas is making his "way through the city's midst" (*mediae...urbis iter*):

> nox atra cava circumvolat umbra.
> quis cladem illius noctis, quis funera fando
> explicet aut possit lacrimis aequare labores?
> urbs antiqua ruit,…

> Black night sweeps around us with its hollow shadow. Who could
> unfold in words the disaster of that night, who the deaths, or be able to
> match our sufferings with tears? The ancient city falls.

We have the double mention of the city (*urbs*), the double reference to night, "that night." More subtle but perhaps more affective still, we have Vergil's brilliant displacement, at 362, by *lacrimis* of the expected *dictis*. Tears replace words in the rendition of such a tragic tale, and anticipate the *gutta* that still drips from Ovid's eyes as he recalls time past.

Vergil would also have his reader remember the opening lines of *Aeneid* 2, lines which are equally present in Ovid's imagination. Dido's command to Aeneas to "renew" (*renovare*, 3) his former grief becomes Ovid's recollection (*repeto*, 3) of his night of grief. The "greatest sadnesses" (*miserrima*, 5) that Aeneas witnesses become Ovid's *tristissima imago*, and the "last agony" (*supremum laborem*, 11) of the hero's beloved city becomes Ovid's own *supremum tempus*, his own form of inevitable wretchedness as he leaves Rome. Finally we have weeping again, the "tears" (*lacrimis*, 8) from which not even a Greek soldier could refrain upon hearing Aeneas' tale.

The tear-words (362) that could never match the story of Troy's demise or the tears (8) that even a Greek soldier might shed on retelling the tale become Ovid's own manifestation of personal suffering endured. Vergil's imagined Aeneas, now the storyteller, is replaced by the nominally real Ovid, reliving his own suffering in his own language. We will return later to other differences between epic and elegy, but it is well to note here that the downfall of Troy does not herald any literal collapse of Rome by whose chief potentate Ovid has been banished. The demise of Troy is a metaphor for the death of the poet himself, his death above all to the city that inspired him. Troy's death is experienced as his interior woe. For Aeneas, in spite of the hurt brought by the ruin of his homeland, there is a "Rome" in the future to anticipate positively, with an Augustan golden age to come. For the person of Ovid there remains only relegation away from Rome, its glory now fully realized, to a place where the only hope lies in the impossible dream of return.

Let us leave *Aeneid* 2 for the moment and turn to the epic's eighth book, which offers another salient instance of a Vergilian moment that Ovid uses as touchstone in *Tr.* 1.3. At lines 73–6 the poet imagines his situation as parallel to that of Mettus (or Mettius) Fufetius of Alba who promised aid to the Roman King Tullus Hostilius in his war against Fidenae but betrayed the trust:

> dividor haud aliter quam si mea membra relinquam,
>   et pars abrumpi corpore visa suo est.
> sic doluit Mettus tum cum in contraria versos
>   ultores habuit proditionis equos.

> I am torn apart exactly is if I were leaving my limbs behind, and a part
> seemed snatched from its own body. So Mettus suffered at the moment when he
> held the horses avenging his betrayal turned in different directions.

With the word *proditio* Ovid may well be offering us a glimpse into the reasons for his exile that he never explains. But the full context dwells more expansively on the interplay of spiritual and physical hurt that is central to the exile's pain. The word *membra*, for instance, looks back to lines 63–4:

> uxor in aeternum vivo mihi viva negatur,
>   et domus et fidae dulcia membra domus.

> My wife, still alive, is forever denied to me, still living, along with
> my home and the sweet segments of that faithful house.

The "members" of his home are parallel to his own limbs: he is torn from the constituents of his own world, just as his own body appears to be rent in the act of departure.[15]

Ovid is deliberately recalling Vergil's treatment of Mettus during his longest ekphrasis, the description of the shield of Aeneas. Earlier in his elegy, at line 21, the poet has prepared us for allusion to the shield by his use of the word *aspiceres*. This form first appears in surviving Latin letters at *Aen.* 8.650, and has the effect, there as here, of drawing you, the reader, into direct contemplation of events. You are to see the occurrences portrayed on Aeneas' shield just as Aeneas does on first viewing them, and just as Ovid puts forth the *imago* of his last night in Rome for you to visualize through the pictorial brilliance of his imagination.

So the reader is prepared for Ovid's bow to Vergil which occurs a few lines before his initiating use of *aspiceres* (642–5):

> haud procul inde citae Mettum in diversa quadrigae
> distulerant (at tu dictis, Albane, maneres!),
> raptabatque viri mendacis viscera Tullus
> per silvam et sparsi rorabant sanguine vepres.

> Not far from there four-horse chariots, driven in opposite directions,
> had torn Mettus apart (but you, Alban, should have held to your
> words!), and Tullus was dragging through the woods the innards of
> the liar, and the splattered briars dripped bloody dew.

Ovid carries over from Vergil into his description the sheer horror of watching Roman vengeance take a particularly graphic, gruesome form. The exile's state of mind, his emotional suffering as he endures forced departure from the core of his life, can only be imaginatively paralleled in the physical sensation of a body wrenched to pieces. The imagined in Vergil becomes the experiential in Ovid, but realized for us by means of allusion that takes the form of simile, which is to say, by poetic figuration. Ovid is not literally dismembered, though he does undergo the physical hurt of a cruel instance of dislocation, as many of the *Tristia* make vividly clear.

But, as Ovid expands Vergil's *in diversa* into *in contraria versos*, he adds a further dimension to his exposition that we have touched upon before. His phrase looks to his own description of Caeneus, *in contraria versus*, changed from one sex to another (*Met.* 12.179).[16] As such, it is a further reminder, like the phrase *nunc quoque* at the poem's start, that exile is a type of metamorphosis which, here, takes the form of a particularly ghastly death. As we witness Ovid witnessing Vergil but dealing now with his own history, soon to be, and then in the process of being, endured, we are made to behold the dissolution of the speaker's inner self as he, too, suffers the vengeance of Rome's might. The dismemberment of Mettus follows readily on the ruin of Troy as another metaphor, drawn from the *Aeneid*, of the spiritual death that persists for the living Ovid, on the edges of Scythia.

I would like to turn now to the final book of Vergil's masterpiece and to two allusions that allow us still further to observe Ovid absorbing and changing his predecessor's formulations for his own purposes. The first occurs immediately after the Mettus analogy, as one Vergilian moment folds into another. The Morning Star has arisen, and Ovid is torn from his own body (77–8):

> tum vero exoritur clamor gemitusque meorum
> et feriunt maestae pectora nuda manus.

> Then indeed the cries and lamentation of my people rise up
> and sorrowing hands strike naked breasts.

The only other occasion in Latin letters where we find the phrase *tum vero exoritur clamor* is at *Aeneid* 12.756:

> tum vero exoritur clamor ripaeque lacusque
> responsant circa et caelum tonat omne tumultu.

> Then indeed cries rise up, and the banks and pools echo roundabout,
> and the whole heavens thunder with the uproar.

As so often with allusion, context is here all-important in illustrating not only the force exerted by one poetic passage upon another, but also the transformations that occur because of this force. What precedes in Vergil is one of the most extraordinary similes in the epic where Aeneas, envisioned as an animal by himself for the first time in the poem, is compared to an Umbrian hunter hound attacking, and nearly grabbing in his bite, Turnus, imagined as a frightened stag.[17]

Ovid, subject to the exigencies of Roman power, is, by implication, the weaker creature victimized by the stronger, the helpless at the mercy of the all-powerful. The point should be pressed further. In the initial books of his epic, not least during the storm that opens the poem and in the second book where he tells Dido the story of Troy's demise, Aeneas is the prey of circumstances, enduring the hatred of Juno in the first instance and withstanding the destructiveness of the gods in the second. By the time we reach the epic's concluding segment, Aeneas is master of his destiny, fighting an essentially civil war against the inhabitants of Italy which he is fated to win. Vergil makes the point here not only by giving Aeneas the upper hand as far as ability is concerned, but also by calling him *venator canis* ("hunter hound," 751) and, still more à propos, *vividus Umber* ("spirited Umbrian," 753). Aeneas has metaphorically taken control of the Italian landscape and is prepared – so Vergil implies in simile – to brutalize its more helpless denizens.

Ovid therefore, by analogy both with the *Aeneid* and with what we expect from the opening of *Tr.* 1.3, proposes two further examples of mutation to his readers. From the poem's opening we expect the poet to be a figure for Aeneas, like Vergil's hero suffering his own multivalent version of Troy's fall, and then departing from his home city for distant exile. But just as Aeneas, in the course of his epic, changes from vanquished to victor, from the endurer of someone else's wrath to the inflicter of his own furious rage on his defeated foe,[18] so Ovid, by means of allusion, claims kinship through the poem's course not only with Aeneas but also with his victim, Turnus, who experiences his antagonist's omnipotence.

And such parallels raise again the question of banishment and the degrees of its severity. Aeneas is exiled from Troy, as he puts it in his own words,[19] but by the time we reach the end of the poem his exile has in fact come to an end because he has gained control of his promised land. For Ovid exile is a different matter. Through Vergil's language in the last line of his poem, we watch as Aeneas exiles Turnus to the finality of death (*fugit*). And, if Turnus thereby anticipates Ovid, then Vergil helps us also imagine still another metamorphosis for his Aeneas, namely into Augustus, the perpetrator of the decision.

Ovid further urges the parallel upon us by words that he puts into the mouth of his wife (85–6):

> "te iubet e patria discedere Caesaris ira,
>   me pietas: pietas haec mihi Caesar erit."

> "Caesar's anger commands you to depart from your fatherland.
> Loyalty [commands] me. This loyalty will be my Caesar."

Ovid has summarized for his readers perhaps the major ethical paradox that the course of the *Aeneid* raises. At the start of the poem Aeneas' survival is at the mercy of the anger of Juno, which we hear of three times in the opening twenty-five lines.[20] By the poem's conclusion, as we have seen, it is Aeneas' ire that imposes the exile of death on his defeated foe. Since one of the ways Vergil expects his reader to respond to Aeneas is as a precursory allegory for Augustus, Ovid in turn asks from us no great leap of the imagination to visualize Augustus as Aeneas *redivivus,* imposing a more subtle, but perhaps harsher, form of exile in a living-death on the shores of the Pontus.

Let us turn back to the beginning of the poem for one further look at Ovid as Turnus, suggested by lines 7–8:

> nec spatium nec mens fuerat satis apta parandi:
>   torpuerant longa pectora nostra mora.

> There had been neither time nor spirit sufficient for making proper
> preparations. My heart had grown numb from the lengthy delay.

The subsequent four lines contain an equal number of negatives which, in conjunction with the quoted hexameters, develop the picture of someone whose faculties are frozen into inaction by the horror of the situation in which he finds himself. This is how Ovid would have us see his first response to Caesar's dictum: as someone so stunned as to be incapable of response.

The only other line in Latin poetry that begins *nec spatium* is to be found at *Aen.* 12.907 where we are watching the ineffectuality of the boulder that Turnus hurls at Aeneas during the final moments of their duel:

> tum lapis ipse viri vacuum per inane volutus
> nec spatium evasit totum neque pertulit ictus.

> Then the hero's very stone, whirled through the emptiness in-between,
> did not traverse the whole distance nor bring home its blow.

The occasions are, on the surface, very different, as is the syntax of their presentations. Why would Ovid, as he recalls the extent of his own impotence upon receiving the news of his punishment, have us remember Turnus' incapacity as he faces his all-powerful opponent and, in fact, prepares for his possible death? The answer lies, of course, in the very parallelisms that make the episodes complementary. As the epic's concluding duel begins we find Turnus the prey of *torpor* (867) as he confronts the Fury that Jupiter has sent as a warning of his doom. Not long thereafter Aeneas accuses him of "delay" (*mora*, 889) in opposing him face to face. But it is lines 906–7 and those which follow that confirm the essential similarities between the two episodes.

Lines 908–12 contain the final simile of any length in the poem. Its model is in Homer, drawn from the final duel between Achilles and Hector as the one races after the other,[21] but Vergil's alterations to Homer are dramatic:

> ac velut in somnis, oculos ubi languida pressit
> nocte quies, nequiquam avidos extendere cursus
> velle videmur et in mediis conatibus aegri
> succidimus: non lingua valet, non corpore notae
> sufficiunt vires nec vox aut verba sequuntur:...

> As in dreams, when by night drowsy sleep has weighed down the eyes,
> we seem to desire in vain to pursue our eager course and, in the
> midst of the endeavor, fainting we fail; our tongue has no strength, our
> body doesn't provide its usual power, neither voice nor words follow...

The addition of the first person, for instance, has the effect of asking us not so much to sympathize with as in fact to become the enfeebled Turnus. But two further additions help anticipate Ovid in the *Tristia*. First, the dream takes place at night, time of the poet's departure from Rome. Second, more prominent still, is the detailed debilitation, with its reinforcing concatenation of negatives, that afflicts both Turnus and Ovid. We have traced it in Ovid. To Turnus Vergil allots first the three negations within the simile, then the verb *negat* accompanied by three further negatives in the lines that follow (914–18).

Therefore, even at the start of the poem, Ovid suggests to us a parallelism between himself and Turnus that serves as an ironic foil to the more obvious similarity with Aeneas, and gives the poem a further tone of bitterness. Aeneas may leave Troy as despondent exile, but he knows something even then of a glorious future that gradually takes palpable form as he gains formidable strength during the last half of his epic. Meanwhile Vergil allows us to bridge the chronological gap between Aeneas and Augustus, further to confirm that the sorrows of departure from a destroyed homeland have been replaced by a new *patria* and a further, future omnipotence. But just as Aeneas' tale at its conclusion finds its hero forgoing his vaunted *pietas* for an *ira* that kills in violence, so his resplendent successor also has recourse to *ira*, but now to devise the more subtle torture of death-in-life. Ovid's exile corresponds more to Turnus' than to that of Aeneas, with the ugly exception that his death is to be continuously experienced among the living rather than, like Turnus, shared with ghosts, *sub umbras*, among his fellow shades below.

If Aeneas prefigures Ovid, then in essential respects Ovid's wife would represent Creusa, the wife he loses during his departure from Troy whose wraith appears and tells him of what will ultimately be his happy future (*res laetae*, *Aen.* 2.783). Vergil has Aeneas suggest that she may survive as a priestess of Cybele. Ovid by contrast fleshes out the person and the feelings of his *uxor*. Instead of becoming lost in the metaphorical equivalent of Troy's ruin and then reappearing as a larger-than-life *imago*, she shares moment by moment in the hurt of Ovid's farewell in such a way as to serve as his mirror image. If he suffers the death-in-life metamorphosis of the exile, much the same happens to her, with the ironic twist that she is forced to remain in Rome and endure the living death of separation from her husband, in the city of Augustus' anger as well as his glory, a city which to her, as to her husband, is a type of Troy, a site of horror, not splendor.

If we think of Ovid's masterful narrative against the background of the second book of the *Aeneid*, several differences stand out. First, there is no addressee which means, in addition, that there is no Dido figure, no other woman, whether to listen to Aeneas tell his tale or to lure him momentarily from his fated progress. It is we, Ovid's audience of hearers and readers, the we who also share in Turnus' frozen nightmare, who replace the Carthaginian queen as receivers of his tale. We only are the ones who empathize with Ovid. This situation in turn emphasizes the loneliness of Ovid as narrator *vis-à-vis* the setting which Vergil allots Aeneas for the divulging of his story. In the remote bleakness of Tomi, where Ovid writes his story, only those reading his poetry from a geographical distance – his contemporary Romans – or us, still more remote in time, are drawn into the sharing of his suffering.

All of which makes the poem's ending particularly poignant. The last twelve lines of the elegy consist of a summary of what Ovid himself has been told about, and then of how he reacts to, his wife's response to his actual moment of withdrawal. The last part of the story, which frames the dawn of departure into a poetic whole, is something that the storyteller himself did not experience and has learned about only second-hand. Here, too, the speaker's isolation stands out. Even Aeneas can tell the full story of his adventures to a captive audience. Narration of the final events of his tale comes to Ovid from elsewhere. Its reconstruction is due to his imagination, not his experience, and his readers are affected all the more for envisioning as well what distance in space and time from Rome meant to someone of his extraordinary imaginative empathy, and means to us through his words.

Finally, to conclude our suggestions of further ways to read Ovid with Vergil's help, let us turn to the opening lines of the first poem of the *Tristia*. If the initial couplets of *Tr.* 1.3 helped us anticipate many of the themes in the poem to follow, the quartet of verses with which 1.1 begins looks not only specifically to 1.3 but sets the tone for all the poems that follow. Once more Vergil looms large, but so does Horace:

> Parve – nec invideo – sine me, liber, ibis in urbem.
> ei mihi, quod domino non licet ire tuo!
> vade, sed incultus, qualem decet exulis esse;
> infelix habitum temporis huius habe.

> Little book – I am not envious! – you will go without me to the city.
> Alas for me, that your master isn't allowed to go. On your way, but
> uncouth, as befits an exile's work. In your misfortune wear the garb
> of this, my situation.

The most recent occasion in Latin letters that a poet addressed his book, as either the first or last of a collection, is the concluding poem of Horace's first book of epistles:

> Vertumnum Ianumque, liber, spectare videris,…

> You seem, book, to gaze toward Vertumnus and Janus…

Horace's poem is at once an envoi and a sphragis, a farewell to his book and a poetic autobiography. By beginning with an adieu rather than a dedication, say, Ovid prepares us for a series of poems on reaching, and enduring, the topsy-turvy world of which he has now become a part.

But we must be yet more specific. Horace's book is envisioned by its mentor-master as staring, from his master's dwelling, down into the Roman forum with its booksellers. From there its author foresees for it a series of adventures that might take it as far as Utica, in Africa, or Ilerda, in Hispania Tarraconensis. Ovid's bitter setting turns Horace's on its head. The earlier poet's book is imagined heading, under its own foolish volition and against the will of its creator, to parts remote in the Roman world. Ovid's, by contrast, is being sent, from a still more distant spot, back to the mother-city. The self-banishing book is replaced by the volume of an involuntary exile who wishes that he and his invention could be one and the same, and that, instead of going down into the city's center and off from there into faraway lands, it, and he, could return to the core of the city that Ovid so movingly describes in *Tr.* 1.3.

But it is Vergil who also doubly inhabits the opening line. The phrase *nec invideo* is an echo of *non equidem invideo*, the opening words of line 11 in Vergil's first eclogue:

> Non equidem invideo; miror magis...

> In fact I don't envy [you]; rather I stand in awe...

And the phrase *in urbem* also brings to a conclusion the initial line of his ninth eclogue:

> Quo te, Moeri, pedes? an, quo via ducit, in urbem?

> Whither afoot, Moeris? Is it where the road leads, to the city?

In both cases it is the context of which Ovid would have us be reminded.

The first echo is of the words of the shepherd Meliboeus who, as we saw before, is being driven into far-off exile by a barbarous soldier who is an emissary from Rome. He will not, he claims, be jealous of his colleague Tityrus, who has seen the city and been saved by its young *deus*.[22] Ovid's riff here is to have his first book of *Tristia*, the eleven initial laments of an exile, be sent on its way back to the city whence he has been relegated by the anger of the very same god. Just as Meliboeus was not resentful of his fellow-shepherd spared by Rome, so Ovid will not hold rancor toward his surrogate book, returning to the city whence he has been expelled.

The allusion to eclogue 9 serves similar purposes. It picks up and augments both the matter and the manner of the first poem in the collection. Once again exile enters the pastoral haven in the form of a new *possessor agelli* ("holder of our little farm," 3). He is associated with the palpable weapons of Mars, against whom poetry's intangible songs have no avail, and compared to an eagle (*aquila*, 13), the image used as standard in the lead of a Roman army. In this case, though we only hear of one shepherd, Moeris, losing his property, a second, Lycidas, joins him in his journey away from the bucolic landscape, *in urbem*, toward the city. The latter may be just some large nearby entity upon which the shepherds are dependent for selling their goods. But the reader of the first eclogue is schooled to think of Rome when hearing the word *urbs*. But, whether Rome or not, in eclogue 9 the city is an anti-pastoral entity which the reader by necessity associates with dispossession and its concomitant exile.

For Ovid therefore, setting a pattern of remembrance for his reader at the beginning of his *Tristia*, we are made once again, with the help of Vergil, to think of Rome, whence his book is heading, as the source of power. This power can ruthlessly exile Meliboeus, the shepherd, and Ovid the writer, but could also, so the poet hopes, relent and revoke its decree. Ovid could be restored by a god, now no longer young, to the fortunate status of Tityrus.

In conclusion let me turn away from Vergil for two brief moments. I must also mention how the poem's first line initiates for the *Tristia* what I have labeled the "*ibimus*" theme that we have seen Ovid varying at *Tr.* 1.3.81 (and which also there serves as a reminder of the first eclogue). Here in his opening line the poet would have us also recall the initial verses of the third elegy of Tibullus' first book of elegies:

> Ibitis Aegaeas sine me, Messalla, per undas,
>   o utinam memores ipse cohorsque mihi!

> You will go without me, Messalla, through the waves of the
> Aegean. O would that you yourself and the cohort were mindful
> of me!

Here, too, we have a poet in a perilous situation, addressing someone departing from his presence. In this case the protagonist is the elegist Tibullus, deathly ill on the island of Phaeacia (Corcyra) and being left behind by his patron, Messalla Corvinus. By drawing a comparison between Tibullus' situation and his own, Ovid accomplishes several things. He reminds the reader of the extremity, literally and figuratively, of his own situation, not poised between Italy and Greece but abandoned at the farthest edge of the empire. He also turns Tibullus' patron into his *liber*, his own self-extension, who is his metonymic spokesman for making his case to the city of Rome and to its ruler.

Finally in line 4 of *Tr.* 1.1 we have the single word *temporis*, a form of which (*tempora*) also appears in the fourth line of Ovid's masterpiece, the *Metamorphoses*.[23] In the latter poem, through the phrase *ad mea tempora*, the poet suggested an ambiguity in the word which could mean both my contemporary events and my own personal misfortune as the endpoint of the time period his work will survey. The opening of the *Tristia* offers full, direct revelation of what that dire happenstance actually is. The more general history of change that is the subject of the *Metamorphoses* is succeeded by the particular mutation in the life of Ovid of which we have examined some details.

This history is complemented by a series of generic alterations as epic is absorbed into elegy and pastoral is given over fully to lament. Many poets from Ovid's past play roles in this extraordinary poetic drama but Vergil is by far the most salient influence. Allusions to his poetry lead us on an arc of exile, from Meliboeus in the first pastoral to the indignant soul of Turnus at the epic's end. This is what enriched Ovid's fancy, and with good reason. It is my hope that this brief look at his presence will serve to foster further study of Vergilian influence on the sad but brilliant laments with which the last great poet of the Augustan era ended his career.

NOTES

1 For the connection between *Heroides* and *Tristia* see Rosenmeyer (1997), 45–50.
2 Ovid echoes this language directly at *Tr.* 1.2.84 and 1.5.64–6. *Ecl.* 1.3 is paralleled at *Tr.* 1.5.82–3. Ovid uses the adjective *profugus* twice in *Tr.* 1.3 (10, 84), perhaps a reminder of its prominent position at *Aen.* 1.2, describing Aeneas.

3   In the *Aeneid exul* and *exsilium* are used of Aeneas himself at 3.11 and 5.51, of the Trojans in general at 2.638, 780, 798, 3.4, and 7.359.

   Two other characters in the poem are specifically called exile, Saturn (8.320) and Metabus (11.541). The participle *fugiens* is applied to each. Apart from the *Aeneid* we also have Meliboeus *exul* at *Ecl.* 1.61, modern man in exile at *Geo.* 2.511, and the exiled bull at *Geo.* 3.225.

   Even without *exul* or its cognates the notion of exile may be adumbrated in several other Vergilian contexts. In the case of Dido, for instance, the uses of *fugiens* (*Aen.* 1.341) and *fuga* (1.357 and 360) in proximity suggest not only flight but also the exile that they help define.

4   The careful echo of *Aen.* 1.92, where Aeneas shivers in terror at the storm, at 12.951, as Turnus shivers in terror at Aeneas, has long been noted.

5   For exile as living death, see Hardie (2002), 287 and n.9, with reference to Doblhofer (1987), 166–78, Nagle (1980), 22–32, and Claassen (1999), 239–40.

6   The most recent discussion of *Tr.* 1.3, one to which this essay is indebted, is by Huskey (2002), with full bibliography.

7   *Ecl.* 1.6, 7 and, implicitly, in *praesentis divos* (41) and *iuvenem* (42); *Tr.* 1.3.40 (*deo*) and, implicitly, *di relinquendi* (33).

8   *Impius...miles...barbarus* (70–1).

9   At line 81 I accept the reading *hinc*, where Luck (1967) adopts *a(h)*, which is found in three manuscripts (his D, K, and T), not least because it underscores the Vergilian echo.

10 I am thinking expressly of passages where future forms of the verb *eo* are prominent. I do not wish to exclude from the general topic of exile poems such as Horace, *Odes* 1.7, where it is a central theme. Lines 20–2 of Horace's ode (*...seu densa tenebit / Tiburis umbra tui. Teucer Salamina patremque cum fugeret,...*) in fact echo *Ecl.* 1.4 (*nos patriam fugimus; tu, Tityre, lentus in umbra...*). Cf. also *Odes* 2.16.19–20 (*patria quis exul / se quoque fugit?*).

11 See *Ecl.* 1.65, *Tr.* 1.3.6, and some thirty other mentions throughout the exilic corpus. We should note that the word *finibus* (6) also runs through eclogue 1 like a thread (3, 61, 67), as does *patria* (*Ecl.* 1.3–4, 67; *Tr.* 1.3.49).

12 See Lucr. 1.546, 3.595, 6.1192; Catull. 64.151; Hor. *Sat.* 1.1.98; Ov. *Pont.* 2.3.4.

13 Catull. 5.5–6.

14 See, e.g., *Met.* 1.235; 2.706; 3.330; 4.561, 602, 750, 802; 5.328, 677; 7.467, 656; 9.226, 664; 14.73, 289.

15 The word *membra* also looks ahead to 94.

16 Cf. Tiresias who changes sex by giving a blow to serpents, or, as Ovid puts it, "changes the lot of the person who gave the blow into its opposite" (*auctoris sortem in contraria mutet*, *Met.* 3.329).

17 Aeneas is, in simile, one of a group of wolves at *Aen* 2.355, and at 12.715 he and Turnus are, again in simile, compared to two bulls vying over a heifer.

   Could Ovid be thinking here of his depiction of Actaeon, changed into a stag and devoured by his dogs (*Met.* 3.138–252)? He adopts the analogy for himself, in writing to Augustus at *Tr.* 2.105, and curses an enemy with it at *Ib.* 479–80.

18 At *Aen.* 12.946–7 Aeneas is described as *furiis accensus et ira / terribilis.*

19 See *Aen.* 3.4 and 11, and note 2 above.

20 See 1.4 (*iram*), 11 (*irae*), 25 (*irarum*) as well as 130 (*irae*) and 251 (*iram*). In counterpoint to this is the description of Aeneas himself at 1.10 as "a man outstanding for piety" (*insignem pietate virum*).

21   *Il.* 22.199–200: "endless as in a dream…when a man can't catch another fleeing on ahead and he can never escape nor his rival overtake him," trans. Fagles).

22   *Urbs* (19, 24); *Roma* (19, 26); *deus* (6, 7, 18, and cf. 42–5). Already at *Tr.* 1.1.20, we learn that it is a *deus* that causes the speaker's exile.

23   Cf. also *Tr.* 1.7.4 where *temporibus* refers ambiguously to forehead or circumstances. *Tempora* is also the first word of Ovid's *Fasti.*

FURTHER READING

An excellent starting place for studying the presence of the poetry of Vergil in Ovid's *Tristia* is the essay by Bews (1984). For a particular critique of Vergil and *Tr.* 1.3 see Huskey (2002). More general reflections on the presence of the earlier poet in Ovid's exilic work are to be found scattered through Claassen's (1999) excellent survey of the theme of exile in Roman literature (e.g., 178–9, 191–6, 217–22). For *Tristia* 1 in general I have found the work of Kenney (1965), Hardie (2002), Hinds (1985, 1999), and Williams (1994, 2002; Williams and Walker 1997) particularly stimulating, following the distinguished lead of Nagle (1980), Evans (1983), and Videau-Delibes (1991). The edition and commentary by Hinds is eagerly awaited.

CHAPTER SEVEN

The Unfinished *Aeneid*?

James J. O'Hara

Films today live a complicated afterlife: the version released in theaters is later released on disk, followed by expanded versions, versions edited for television, uncensored versions that were too hot for theatrical release, versions with commentary or other "special features" added (much like ancient marginal scholia), including "deleted scenes," and finally the director's cut. For the *Aeneid*, we have basically only one version, although book 2's dubious "Helen episode," preserved only in the late-fourth-century commentator Servius, is allegedly a "deleted scene" that has made it back into most texts, often in brackets that show that the editor thinks the verses are not Vergilian (Goold 1970; Horsfall 2006b, 2008 *ad loc.*). The *Aeneid* was published after Vergil's death in 19 BCE, perhaps as much as two or three years later. It has long been thought to have been given to the world "unfinished," with a number of flawed passages that the poet "would have corrected, if death had not intervened," to quote the words that Aulus Gellius (*NA* 10.16.11), a writer of the second century CE, attributes to Julius Hyginus, a scholarly freedman of Augustus. The poem indeed seems not to have received the poet's final polish – *summa manus* or *ultima lima*, to cite phrases used by the exiled Ovid (Tr. 1.7.28, 30) in discussing his own supposed inability to revise the *Metamorphoses*, and by a Vergilian biography to be discussed below. But for a number of reasons, the extent to which the poem is unfinished has been exaggerated. This chapter will look at some of the major evidence that has suggested to readers that it is unfinished, and also at the way in which the poem, though largely completed by the author, has struck later readers and poets as incomplete or in need of supplement at its close. There are indeed signs that some passages may be lacking final stylistic revision, but often when readers claim that the poem is unfinished they reveal less about the poem's flaws than they do about their own assumptions about life and literature, and the ways in which certain inherent qualities of the poem are incompatible with these assumptions (Thomas 2001; Horsfall 1995b, 2006b; Hardie 1997 on closure). This observation about critics' problems with the poem applies also to the work's sudden ending, with the important distinction that the poem's conclusion actually seems designed to provoke critical discomfort and reaction, especially when compared to other Greek and Roman epics.

Our evidence for Vergil's life comes from biographies written long after his death, and from anecdotes recorded in ancient sources (fuller discussion by Stok in this volume, chapter 8, and Farrell, chapter 30, on Vergil's detractors). The most influential is the life of the fourth-century grammarian Donatus, which is probably taken largely intact from that written in the early second century by Suetonius. For his biographies of the Caesars, Suetonius had access to numerous documents, but for his life of Vergil, which was written over a century after the poet's death, he would have had to rely largely on anecdotes of questionable reliability, along with a few letters and the poet's will. We have little evidence that anyone was terribly interested in Vergil's life (as opposed to his poetry) during his lifetime, and so many scholars in recent years have thought that details in the *Life* were later inventions inspired partly by specific passages of his poetry, in keeping with a practice that was endemic in the usually unreliable biographies of ancient poets (Stok, chapter 8 this volume). For this chapter the most important sections of the *Life* are those (35 and 39–42) that describe the poet's final journey to Greece and subsequent death, and the way in which the poem was posthumously published. The story is that the poet "decided to retire to Greece and Asia [Minor], in order to put the finishing touches on the *Aeneid*" (*inpositurus Aeneidi summam manum statuit in Graeciam et in Asiam secedere*), during three years in which he would "do nothing but revise" (*emendare*). But in Athens he met up with Augustus, who was returning to Rome from the East, and he "decided not to retire" (*destinaretque non absistere*). But at the Greek city of Megara he became ill after spending time under a hot sun, and a few days later died at Brundisium, the first stop in Italy. The *Life* also describes his plans for what should happen to his poem (sections 39–42):

> Before leaving Italy, Vergil had arranged with Varius to burn up the *Aeneid* if anything befell him; but Varius had insisted that he would not do so. For this reason, when his health was failing, Vergil demanded his scroll cases earnestly, intending to burn them himself; but no one brought them, and he gave no precise stipulations in this matter. For the rest, he bequeathed his writings to the aforementioned Varius and Tucca, on the condition that they publish (*ederent*) nothing which he himself had not revised (*quod non a se editum esset*). Nevertheless, Varius published them, on the authority of Augustus, but revised only in a cursory fashion (*summatim emendata*), with the result that he left unfinished verses, if there were any. Many soon endeavored to complete these lines, but they did not succeed, on account of the difficulty, for nearly all of the half lines were freestanding and complete with regard to sense, except this: "Whom Troy to you now…" [*Aen.* 3.340]. Nisus the grammarian used to say that he heard from older men that Varius changed the order of two books, and that which then was second he moved into third place, and also that he smoothed out the beginning of the first book by subtracting these lines:

>> I am he that once tuned my song on a slender reed,
>> then, leaving the woodlands, compelled the neighboring fields
>> to serve the husbandman, however grasping,
>> a work welcome to farmers: but now of Mars's bristling
>> Arms and a man I sing. …
>>> (Trans. Wilson-Okamura, with slight modifications)

Two details from the end of the passage invite simple comment. The two stories passed on by "Nisus the grammarian" are both almost certainly false: Vergil did not begin the *Aeneid* with the words "I am he that once…" (*Ille ego qui quondam…*). Scholars now agree that these four verses are likely to have been invented for an edition of the *Aeneid* produced after Vergil's death, as no competent ancient poet is likely to have begun the all-important first line of an epic with a demonstrative, a pronoun, and a relative pronoun (Ziolkowski and Putnam 2008, 22–5). And book 3 never preceded book 2 (Horsfall 1995b, 24; 2006a, xxxvii–xl; 2006b; *contra* G. Williams 1983, 266). But Nisus' claims are valuable, because like the comment of Hyginus, they show us that at an early date, critics were talking about ways in which the *Aeneid* could or should have been improved, and were maneuvering to create a place for themselves in the reception of the *Aeneid*. If these two stories are false, are any of the other details of the tale correct?

The story that Vergil wanted the *Aeneid* burned (also discussed in chapter 8 by Stok) is not easy to dismiss. It resonates so well for us both with Kafka's death-bed wish for his writings to be burned, and with the image of the anguished, unsatisfied artist presented in Broch's *The Death of Vergil*. Ovid, in the aforementioned poem about the unfinished state of the *Metamorphoses*, claims that he burned that poem (*Tr.* 1.7.15–22), and this passage could suggest that the story of Vergil's request was current in the first decade CE (Stok, chapter 8 this volume; Ziolkowski and Putnam 2008, 420–5). But Ovid's poem also points out flaws in the Vergilian story: the *Metamorphoses* survived, because of course there were many copies (*pluribus exemplis scripta fuisse reor*, *Tr.* 1.7.24; *reor*, "I suppose," is a nice touch of Ovidian humor). In the Vergilian *Life*, "when his health was failing," Vergil "demanded his scroll-cases earnestly, intending to burn them himself." But given the uncertainties of ancient sea travel, can we imagine that Vergil, a man with the resources to ask for a team of slaves to copy any draft at any time, only had one copy of the epic poem he had been working on for ten years, and that he took it on a sea voyage?

So it is unlikely that Vergil could easily have burned all of the copies of the *Aeneid*. Still, the story that he wanted them burned, or that he wanted symbolically to burn the copy with him when he was dying, is not demonstrably false, and constitutes a tiny bit of shaky evidence that Vergil was dissatisfied with the state of the *Aeneid* as he lay dying.

One detail of the story, however, casts doubt on the whole rationale for the trip to Greece as given in the *Life*. In a passage that I have already quoted, it is claimed that Vergil "decided to retire to Greece and Asia [Minor], in order to put the finishing touches on the *Aeneid*. He meant to do nothing but revise (*emendare*) for three straight years." At first glance this is plausible enough, although Horsfall (1995, 21) rightly asks whether, given Vergil's preference for literary rather than accurate depictions of geographical features, three years in Italian libraries might not have been more helpful than three years in Greece. But we also need to look, as Horsfall does, at a later portion of the *Life*, which offers a claim probably to be attributed to Asconius, the first-century CE scholar whose work on some of Cicero's speeches survives, and whom the *Life* has just been quoting. The poet "decided to retire" (*secedere* again) "in order to settle everything to the satisfaction of his ill-wishers" (*ad satietatem malevolorum*). These *malevoli* or ill-wishers sound like those detractors of Vergil discussed elsewhere in this volume by Farrell and by Stok, and indeed, Asconius' story must come from his work "Against the Detractors of Vergil." But although Vergil's detractors had made some complaints about the *Georgics* and especially the *Eclogues*, it is hard to imagine that Vergil's few small public readings of portions of the *Aeneid* could have given them much to complain about in the new poem. These were not test-readings before focus groups, such as film-makers use today ("Could you make the hero a little nicer to Dido as he's leaving?" "Isn't the ending a little abrupt?"). The most sensible and economical explanation of Asconius' position is that it addresses the climate of reception in the first-century CE, when critics began to pick at supposed flaws in the poem, by focusing on the story that Vergil died unexpectedly after a trip to Greece, essentially inventing the idea that on this trip Vergil would have fixed everything in the poem that the *malevoli* would later complain about – a plan tragically thwarted (in this invented story) by the poet's death at the age of 50. Since poets' biographies are often constructed from literal or allegorical readings of their poems, it is not impossible that the whole story of the trip to Greece may have been invented in response to the (possibly allegorical) propempticon to Vergil in Horace *Odes* 1.3 (cf. Thomas 2001, 63–5).

The *Life* also discusses Vergil's *tibicines* or "props" (74). The metaphor is from the construction of a building and concerns bits of verse (*levissimis versis*) supposedly used temporarily to fill out unfinished passages so that Vergil's train of thought (*impetus*) would not be impeded (*Ac ne quid impetum moraretur, quaedam inperfecta transmisit, alia levissimis versis veluti fulsit, quae per iocum pro tibicinibus interponi aiebat ad sustinendum opus, donec solidae columnae advenirent*). This tale could conceivably be true, since most writers of course have better days and worse days. But given that Vergil seems to have written less than a thousand lines a year, his need for "props" should have been less pressing than the story suggests, and it is easy to imagine that it was invented by critics who would delight in the sport of prop-hunting, again to show off their acumen and to create a place of power for themselves in the reception of the poem, not unlike that produced by the Alexandrian critics' athetesis of Homeric lines (and, of course, by many of the things written by all of us Vergilian scholars today). The practice has continued throughout the twentieth century, when any line that a critic finds confusing or inappropriate can be labeled a stopgap.

The *Life* also provides us with a theory of Vergil's famous "half-lines" that deserves longer comment here. The *Life* claims that Vergil asked in his will that Varius and Tucca not publish anything "that he had not revised" (39), and that their response, as we have seen, was to publish the poem lightly revised (*summatim emendata*), with the half-lines left incomplete. There are fifty-eight half-lines in Mynors' Oxford Text; some scholars count slightly more or fewer, because our manuscripts present some doubtful cases. Many of the half-lines occur near the start or finish of speeches or of other discrete sections, and this feature suggests that Vergil worked on many different sections of the poem at once and often had to revise in order to link two passages, the first of which originally ended in mid-verse; this is the important argument of Goold (1970) in a major study of Servius. Some half-lines have seemed to modern readers to work so well that they have been tempted to think Vergil meant to leave them incomplete (e.g., Sparrow 1931, *contra* Goold 1970), perhaps even with a few seconds of silence in a manner suggestive today of work by someone like John Cage or Yoko Ono. One half-line, for example, describes oars made in haste from branches that still have leaves on them (3.400): perhaps an unfinished line for unfinished oars? Aeneas' speech to Dido in which he defends himself from her criticisms ends with the half-line *Italiam non sponte sequor*, "I do not seek Italy by choice" (4.361). Page's Victorian commentary (*ad loc.*) lavishes praise on the hemistich:

> A fine half line. Its powerful terseness is in striking contrast with the wordy rhetoric of the rest of the speech. Whether Virgil, had he revised the *Aeneid*, would have felt it necessary to complete the line is difficult to decide. Nothing at any rate could improve these four words thus left rugged and abrupt.

The one half-line that is not a syntactically complete clause can also be seen as effective and moving. Hector's widow Andromache, whom Aeneas has found living in Greece, asks whether his son Ascanius still lives: *quid puer Ascanius? superatne et vescitur aura? / quem tibi iam Troia* ("What about the boy Ascanius? Does he survive and breathe the air above? Whom to you [*iam?*] Troy (or 'Trojan...')...," 3.339–40). It is easy for us to imagine Andromache being unable to speak Creusa's name, not only because of Aeneas' loss of his wife but especially because Aeneas' son Ascanius must call to mind her own dead son Astyanax. Other half-lines have been found to be equally effective as they stand (see the older sources quoted by Pease 1935 on 4.43).

But though this chapter will go on to suggest that many of the supposed flaws of the "unfinished" *Aeneid* might not be flaws, it will not go so far as to claim that the half-lines are a deliberate literary innovation. For every apparently effective half-line, there are dozens that add nothing to the poetic effect even when looked at from the most experimental modern perspective. Furthermore, Vergil had neither precedent in the use of half-lines (unless we are overly fond of the passage in Catullus 51 where that poet's notoriously flawed manuscripts have a missing short line right where the speaker says his voice breaks off when he looks at Lesbia) nor follower (*pace* Baldwin 1993), save for some centoists, working in close imitation of Vergil (see Sparrow 1931, 26; McGill 2005, 36, 69). This dearth of parallels suggests that no ancient readers operated with a horizon of expectations that would have prepared them to treat half-lines as a deliberate poetic device. (cf. Austin 1977 on 6.94; Harrison 1997 on 10.16; Horsfall 2000 on 7.702 and 2006a on 3.340). One may argue that they are as effective as the fragments of Petronius as viewed by Fellini (or by anyone who notes that the first extant page of the *Satyricon* is a really great opening for a "novel"), or the broken-off ending of Lucan's *Pharsalia*, which has been praised by Masters (1992) and Henderson (1998; brief discussion in O'Hara 1993). Vergil's half-lines are perhaps "deliberate" in that he apparently specified in his will that the poem be published with these lines incomplete rather than let Varius or Tucca try to finish them (the *Lives* also have stories both of the poet finishing half-lines extemporaneously, and of others trying in vain to complete them; Horsfall 2006b is skeptical). If Vergil actually did plan to introduce half-lines as a new poetic technique, his premature death ruined the plan by making the incomplete verses look like an accident of history rather than a deliberate device.

The timing of Vergil's death also has provided a perhaps unfortunate context in which to view other features of the *Aeneid* that might lead readers or scholars to think it is unfinished. The rest of this chapter will discuss (1) flaws or inconsistencies within the text that readers have claimed the poet "would have corrected, if death had not intervened," and (2) the poem's sudden ending and comparative lack of closure.

I open discussion of the former by quoting from a recent book of mine (O'Hara 2007, 77):

> In the *Aeneid* we read that Aeneas will have a son in old age, and that he has only three more years on earth; that Helen both openly helped the Greeks enter Troy, and (if Vergil wrote that passage) that she cowered in hiding in fear of punishment; that Aeneas' Trojan son Ascanius will be the ancestor of the Alban Kings, and that his half-Italian son Silvius will be; that Theseus escaped from the underworld, and that he is still there; that the Italians were peaceful before the arrival of the Trojans and that they were warlike; that Aeneas is fighting on the side of Jupiter, and that he is like a monster fighting against Jupiter; that Palinurus fell from Aeneas' ship the day before Aeneas met him in the underworld, and that he fell three or four days before; that Aeneas will impose customs on the Italians he conquers in Italy, and that the Italians will keep their own customs; that Jupiter both predicted and forbade the war in Italy, and that he both was impartial and gave help to one side; that the golden bough will yield willingly and easily or not at all, but then that it yields only hesitantly to Aeneas.

The argument of my book, which builds on much work by recent scholars, is that many of these inconsistencies can be read as deliberate, or at least as functioning effectively within the poetry; I believe that they can be read in this way more extensively and even "consistently" than can the half-lines. A lightning-quick review of the examples in that paragraph follows in this one; it might not convince anyone that these passages have to be read the way that I read them, but should suggest that they do not have to be read as flawed or as awaiting revision. Anchises in the underworld tells Aeneas he will have a son in old age (6.763–5) even though we have already heard from Jupiter that he has only three more years of life left (1.265–6), as part of a pattern of deceptively optimistic prophecies within the poem. Even if the Helen passage is not genuine, there are significant variations between Aeneas' narration of the Fall of Troy in book 2 and the account in the underworld by Deiphobus, Helen's husband after the death of Paris (6.509–34), which may say more about the uncertainty of "rumor" and the limitations of human knowledge than about the poet's inability to revise the poem. When Vergil blurs the question of whether Ascanius (1.267–71) or Silvius (6.763–6) will be the ancestor of the Alban kings, he is both following the fondness of Alexandrian poets for alluding to variant version of myths, and alluding with characteristic ambiguity to a question of some importance to the Julians and their political foes even before Vergil was born. Theseus' escape from (6.122) and continued presence in (6.617–18) the underworld is one of the problems that Hyginus said Vergil would have fixed had he lived, but the Vergilian underworld is simply packed with details that are inconsistent, both with passages elsewhere in the poem, and with other sections of the underworld. To imagine an *Aeneid* without any of these discrepancies is an irresponsible fantasy, broadly comparable to the practice of idealizing unpainted classical statues, or even removing bits of surviving paint from statues, since we now know that most classical statues were brightly if not even gaudily painted. Viewed in isolation or in small groups, these inconsistencies may look like problems the poet was "planning to fix, had not death intervened." But the sheer number of them and the way that they are woven into the text suggest either that they were deliberate, or that Vergil spent a great deal of time accidentally creating complications for himself to resolve later. To continue: the ambiguous picture of what the Italians were like before the arrival of the Trojans both represents variant versions in the tradition and nicely expresses Vergilian ambivalence about the positive and negative qualities of the Roman/Italian people. The explicit comparison of Aeneas to a gigantic monster fighting against Jupiter (10.565–9) is part of a pattern in which Aeneas is usually associated with Jupiter, and his enemies linked to the Giants and other forces of disorder who fought against Jupiter, but sometimes Aeneas and the Trojans are linked to gigantomachic imagery associated with invading forces repelled by natives. The problems with Palinurus cannot all be easily solved, but may in part reflect imitation of Homeric models, and again the limitations of human knowledge. The passages that say that Aeneas will impose customs on the Italians (1.263–5, Jupiter speaking to Venus) and that the Italians will keep their own customs (12.834–7, Jupiter to Juno) are part of two patterns: that of deceptively optimistic prophecies, and also the complicated way in which simple views of the Romans' Trojan heritage presented early in the poem are replaced as the poem progresses by more complex and ambivalent viewpoints. When Jupiter tells Juno and Venus that he forbade the war in Italy (10.8–9), after we have seen him predict war in Italy (1.263–5, to Venus), and that he will be impartial (10.112) even though he will later make a number of interventions that guarantee the victory of Aeneas, he is probably to be seen as lying, even as he swears by the River Styx, and lying in a way that poses a serious challenge for readings of the poem that depend on a view of Jupiter as a stable source of truth or a "control" to limit readings of the poem. Why the golden bough does not yield easily to Aeneas after the Sibyl says it will, if he is called by fate (*namque ipse volens facilisque sequetur, / si te fata vocant*, 6.146–7), is a problem not easily dealt with, comparable to the question of why Vergil has Aeneas exit the underworld through the Gate of False Dreams (on which see Thomas 2001, 99–100, with further references). But it is only reasonable to say that both are problems of Vergil's invention.

   The argument that inconsistencies within the *Aeneid* might be a part of Vergil's poetic technique rather than a result of his failure to polish the poem before his death is made more plausible by several aspects of his literary context, involving Greek poetry, Roman epic, and his own earlier work. Homeric epic, Greek tragedy, and especially the works of the learned and scholarly Alexandrian poets contain, and arguably make good use of, numerous discordant details, apparently deliberate discrepancies, and allusion or even reference to variant versions of myth (Griffith 1990; Hunter 1993; Thomas 1996; Scodel 1999; O'Hara 2007). A number of Roman poems, particularly epic poems (if we define the term "epic" broadly), contain striking and arguably poetically effective inconsistencies. Lucretius' *De rerum natura* starts with a proem asking Venus for help, and then says the gods do not care about human beings. Catullus 64 starts with the first boat, Jason's Argo, and then in a flashback describes an earlier fleet, that of Theseus. Ovid's *Metamorphoses* starts with a cosmogony directed by a rational philosophical god, but for the rest of the poem the world is in the hands of the impetuous and lustful Olympians; throughout the poem, Ovid plays with variant versions, multiple etiologies, and chronological contradictions. Lucan's *Bellum Civile* starts with praise of the Emperor Nero, then later denounces Caesar and one-man rule; many have seen passages throughout the poem as being on both sides of the struggle between Pompey and Caesar, as part of a kind of poetics of fragmentation. Two of these poems, of course, those by Lucretius and Lucan, are arguably even more obviously unfinished than the *Aeneid*, with Lucretius ending suddenly with a scene from the chaos produced by the plague at Athens (more on this below), and Lucan ending in mid-scene in a tenth book considerably shorter than any of the first nine. And Ovid, as noted above, claims that exile prevented him from adding final polish to his epic.

Closer to home, Vergil's own *Georgics*, which he clearly had an opportunity to polish as fully as he wanted, still contain passages that conflict with one another, as for example on the basic question of whether the farmer's life is easy (*facilis, Geo.* 2.459) or hard (*haud facilis*, 1.122), or on larger questions involved in determining whether the poem is optimistic or pessimistic. Farrell (1991) and with more detail Gale (2000) have suggested that these discrepancies spring at times from Vergil's following different models; the older scholarly model, however, which said that inconsistencies resulting from discordant source material (or any aspect of literary production) are unimportant, and not to be considered in interpretation, has yielded to a model in which we deal with all aspects of the poem as presented to us. Or not: the clearest sign that the *Georgics* are an inconsistent poem is the attempt by one scholar (Cramer 1998; cf. Thomas 2001; O'Hara 2005) to make the poem more consistent by excising 200 lines, or about 10 percent of the text.

Even if largely "finished" by the poet, however, the *Aeneid* certainly ends much more suddenly than any earlier narrative epic. The death of Turnus in the very last two lines of the poem, *Aen.* 12.951–2, corresponds to the death of Hector at the hands of Achilles at *Il.* 22.361–3, but Hector's death in the *Iliad* is followed by over 1,800 verses offering various types of closure and even significant and surprising development (Hammer 2002, 170–98). To a certain extent the *Aeneid* before it ends has already previewed events beyond the end of the poem, as the *Iliad* itself does, when that poem predicts the killing of Achilles by Paris and lets us see in the mourning for Patroclus aspects of the future mourning for Achilles. Vergil has also in earlier books already borrowed material from the last part of the *Iliad*, especially the games for Patroclus in *Iliad* 23 (Knauer 1964b, 73–4). But those factors do little to soften the shock of the sudden ending. In the case of the other Homeric epic, the *Odyssey*, we have evidence that some Alexandrian critics may have thought the poem *should* have ended more abruptly. Ancient sources tell us that some thought that the *telos* ("end") or *peras* ("end," "limit") of the *Odyssey* was at 22.296, when the hero and Penelope go to bed, which could mean simply that this is the culmination or climax of the story, or that everything after it was added by a later poet. Some have seen the casual end of Apollonius' *Argonautica*, as well as a specific Apollonian allusion in *Arg.* 4.1781 to *Od.* 23.296, as showing Apollonius' endorsement of either the moderate or extreme view of this position (Livrea 1973, *ad loc.*; Hardie 1997, 139; skepticism is expressed by Russo et al. 1992, but their concern is to defend the *Odyssey*

rather than explore aspects of the reception of the poem). As was noted above, Lucretius'
De rerum natura ends starkly, with the plague at Athens still raging and people fighting
over the burial of their dead, and is thought to be unfinished both because of some flaws
earlier in the poem and because of the ending. A minor textual transposition (Fowler
1997) makes the ending only somewhat less abrupt, and serious scholars (Sedley 1998,
160–5) still argue, wrongly I think, that the poet meant to add a coda helping us deal
with the problem of the plague. In the *Georgics*, Orpheus dies near, but not right at, the
end of the poem: the end of his story in 4.527 is followed by twenty-one lines on the
successful hero Aristaeus, and an eight-line coda on the poet and Caesar. The *Aeneid*
ends as suddenly as would the *Iliad* if it had stopped after *Il.* 22.363, or the *Odyssey* if it
had stopped at *Od.* 23.296 – or perhaps at *Od.* 22.389, when Odysseus sees that all the
suitors have been killed, or even *Od.* 22.329, when Odysseus is last depicted as dispatching a suitor – in fact one who has begged for his life, like Turnus (cf. Cairns 1989,
212–13). In Aeneas' story the analogue for the reunion with Penelope would have to be
his first meeting with Lavinia, which does not take place in our epic.

Aeneas does meet Lavinia, finally, in the fifteenth century, when the humanist poet
Maffeo Vegio, or Maphaeus Vegius, completed 630 decent hexameters of a thirteenth
book, which was included in fifteenth- and sixteenth-century editions of Vergil, and
even in the first translation of the poem in Britain, by Gawin Douglas (Putnam 2004;
Thomas 2001, 279–84; Kallendorf 1989, 100–28). Vegio's book 13 provides all the
closure that Vergil denies us: eager surrender by the Latins, who blame Turnus (who
was very, very bad) with no one among the Rutulians wanting revenge, the meeting of
Aeneas with Latinus, who blames Turnus (who was very, very bad), and then with
Lavinia, whom he marries in a ceremony followed by a joyful feast. (The Latins' blam-
ing of Turnus and quick embrace of Aeneas in Vegio find close parallels in the behavior
of the witch's soldiers in *The Wizard of Oz* film, as soon as "The Witch is Dead.") The
book uses almost every closural device one could imagine: it has plenty of lamentation,
rejoicing, burials, and finally reward for all his troubles for Aeneas, both in the marriage to Lavinia and in his deification in the poem's final lines. Some readers continue
to share Vegio's dissatisfaction with Vergil's ending and to take even more extreme
views of the poem's "incompleteness." One recent translator (Ruden 2008) refers in
her preface to the "half-finished state of his epic" and claims, bewilderingly, that "only
twelve out of the projected twenty-four books exist." A story about this translation in
the *Chronicle for Higher Education* (Howard 2008) suggests that "It is likely that
Virgil did not intend to end the book with that scene; he probably had in mind a much
longer work, which would have followed Aeneas' evolution from warrior to statesman." Similarly, the Wikipedia article on Vergil, at one point during the writing of this
chapter, said that "many people have felt that the poem is not complete without an
account of Aeneas' marriage to Lavinia and his founding of the Roman race."

But the ending that we have cannot be other than what the poet planned. Although
the poem ends suddenly, there are numerous closural gestures in the scenes leading up
to the end, including the correspondences between the conversations of Jupiter and
Venus in book 1 and Jupiter and Juno in book 12. The book has also played with readers' expectation in such passages as Jupiter's question to Juno in 12.793, *quae iam finis
erit, coniunx?* ("What will the end be, wife?"). And the final few lines of the book allude

and respond to significant passages earlier in the poem: Aeneas' *tune* at the start of his speech, 12.947, corresponds to Juno's *mene* at the start of her first speech (the first speech in the poem) at 1.37 (Tarrant 2004); *indignata* in the final line, 12.952, echoes *indignatus* in the same metrical position in the final line of Vergil's description of the shield at 8.728 (Putnam 1995, 3); and *illi solvuntur frigore membra* at 12.951 reminds us of *extemplo Aeneae solvuntur frigore membra* at 1.92 (Putnam 1965, 200–1; Thomas, 1998, 275–6). Moreover, at 952 lines, book 12 is the longest book in the poem, and it is already the longest before Aeneas aims his weapon at Turnus some twenty lines before the end. Unlike Lucan's undersized book 10 (546 lines; the next shortest is book 1 at 695), then, it is hard to imagine that book 12 could have been longer.

Because the end of the *Aeneid* does not provide the type of gradual closure that we find in the *Iliad* and *Odyssey*, it helps make the poem an open work, and makes discussing the end of the poem a natural result of the way it is constructed. The occasional claims that the ending of the poem is simple and clear do not impress. Do or should Aeneas' actions in killing Turnus fit Anchises' injunction in book 6 that the Roman way would be to spare the conquered, and battle down the proud, or instead do they fit the call for vengeance from another father figure, Evander? The poem perhaps allows both views, although it may be argued that the *pietas* of *clementia* is given a more prominent position in the whole poem, as in Augustan ideology more generally, than is the *pietas* of revenge. Does Turnus deserve to die, and how is this question affected by the poet's manipulation of our view of Turnus in book 12 especially? Is the vengeful ending consistent with the image of himself that Augustus was promoting in the late 20s, or only with that of the youthful avenger of his adopted father's murder? Is the killing a victory for Juno and *Furor*, or even the *Furor impius* of book 1, because Aeneas kills him *furiis accensus et ira / terribilis* (12.946–7), or a victory of order over forces of disorder like Turnus? A less sudden ending could have cleared up some but not all of these questions. Does the killing proleptically represent Augustus' putting an end to civil war, or historically represent the (or an) aetion of the Romans' propensity for violence and civil strife? Does the killing of Turnus show Aeneas yielding to emotion, and ignoring political concerns – the opposite of what he did in leaving Dido in book 4? Is killing Turnus strategically necessary, because an enemy like him needs to be eliminated (as the murder of Caesar by those he had pardoned shows), or a strategic error, because vengeance killings bring only more vengeance – or is this question moot because Aeneas clearly acts out of rage and not calculation? Vegio's supplement makes everything clear; Vergil's poem does not.

Early in Vergil's poetic career, and a decade and a half before the *Aeneid* was started, the debate over the killing of the conspirators in Sallust's *Catiline* can be seen as making a similar or perhaps even more ambivalent comment. Cato argues that execution is necessary, Caesar that one should think about the precedent. Cato is right in a sense, for the execution of the conspirators results in immediate desertions from the Catilinarian cause. But Caesar expresses the fear that the example of killing the conspirators may cause some future consul to use violence unnecessarily, as Sulla did in his proscriptions, and the second triumvirate would do just that, probably right before Sallust's monograph was written and published. This debate can be transferred to the end of the *Aeneid*, without many adjustments.

A longer poem need not, of course, have cleared up everything about the ending. Ursula Le Guin's 2008 novel *Lavinia* focuses much on the events of *Aeneid* 7–12, but then goes far beyond them to cover the rest of Lavinia's life, and a few comments on how this work treats the end of the poem will close this chapter. Besides continuing the story, Le Guin also employs an unusual device that allows her to include additional reflections on the killing of Turnus and the end of the poem. Through incubation, the form of divination by which her father Latinus in the poem is told to marry his daughter to a foreigner and not a Latin (7.81–103), Le Guin is able to have Lavinia speak to the dying Vergil – virtually the dying Vergil from Broch, though with touches of Dante. They discuss the ending and its difficulties. At one point "Vergil" says, "It's all wrong…I will tell them to burn it" (58). Later he says he cannot finish the poem because he is "weak,…so the end will be cruel" (59). It "ends with a murder" (62). At a later meeting, however, Vergil seems more confident, and tells her in short compass the whole story of the war, and the end of the poem: "He will kill Turnus, lying wounded and helpless, just as he killed Mezentius." Lavinia says "he kills like a butcher" – this is before Aeneas has arrived in Latium. But "Vergil" defends him, saying, "he does what he has to do…because that is how empires are founded" (89). Lavinia asks him whether he has finished the poem, and he "seemed to nod, but I could hardly see him, a tall shadow in shadows" (90). Later, Le Guin's Lavinia is able to discuss the killing of Turnus with her husband, who never stops being bothered by what he did, and considers it "murder" and even "*nefas*, unspeakable wrong" (187). Lavinia takes the opposing view, that the killing was necessary, but this argument bothers Aeneas (in Le Guin a very good man) even more (188–90). Three years later Aeneas is killed by a Rutulian, which might suggest that he should have spared Turnus and stopped the cycle of revenge, but it is a Rutulian whose life he has just spared, which suggests that sparing Rutulians who beg for their lives is generally a mistake. Le Guin's continuation of the story is fanciful, but represents one valid response to the end of Vergil's poem.

In a brief afterword, after commenting on the ending's "shocking abruptness," Le Guin says, rightly, "I think the poem ends where Vergil wanted it to end."

FURTHER READING

This chapter owes much to Thomas (2001) as well as to Horsfall (1995b, 2006b). On the Vergilian *Lives* and Vergil's detractors, see the chapters in this volume by Stok and Farrell along with Horsfall (1995b, 1–25), which takes a dimly skeptical view of the historicity of the stories in the biographical tradition. In his commentaries on books 2, 3, 7, and 11, however, Horsfall often comments on passages that he describes as not fully polished. On the composition of the poem, see also Otis (1964, 415–20), Horsfall (2006a, xx–xl), and Günther (1996, in German) with the reviews by Horsfall (1997) and Hardie (1999). The scholarship on the end of the *Aeneid* is of course vast: see Putnam (1995, chs. 1 and 7–10), Horsfall (1995b, 192–216), Hardie (1998, 99–101), Tarrant (2004), Gill (2006, 448–61); Tarrant is writing a commentary on *Aeneid* 12. On closure in general see Hardie (1997) and several influential pieces in Fowler (2000).

CHAPTER EIGHT

The Life of Vergil before Donatus

Fabio Stok

Introduction

The collection of biographical information on famous poets and writers began very early in the Greek world. Lives of Homer, Hesiod, and other authors go back to the fifth century BCE. In general the authors' own works were used as sources, and often the lives of the authors were based on the fictional characters and events of their works. Furthermore, several entirely fictional anecdotes were present in these *Lives*. Variants and developments of these anecdotes can often be reconstructed from the various available versions of a single author's *Life* (Lefkowitz 1981).

Analogous features enter into the Roman biographical tradition from Cornelius Nepos onwards. In the case of Vergil this is well documented: the biographical production on this Latin poet is truly the richest. Vergil's work was immediately success-ful (Horsfall 1995d) and it soon became part of the educational curriculum, beginning with the work of Caecilius Epirota (Suet. *Gramm.* 16). This success supported the collection of notes and anecdotes about Vergil's life, which later nourished a consider-able biographical production that was important in antiquity, the Middle Ages, and the Renaissance. The influence of this tradition on culture, literature, and art has been continually great, and it remains so in modern times.

The oldest biography of Vergil that we have is the one written around the middle of the fourth century by the grammarian Aelius Donatus as a preface to his commentary on Vergil's works. Donatus' biography is believed to be based largely on the one writ-ten at the end of the first century (or the beginning of the second) by Suetonius, who included it in his *De viris illustribus* ("On famous men"). Donatus' version is therefore commonly called *Vita Suetonii vulgo Donatiana* (henceforth *VSD*). However, the presence and quantity of additions and interpolations added by Donatus to the origi-nal of Suetonius have been much debated. In the past, Donatian interpolations were considered many and substantial (cf. Geer 1926; Paratore 2007³, 199–302; Bayer 2002², 330–2; list of proposed interpolations in Brugnoli and Stok 1997, XV–XVIII), but the available thematic and linguistic proofs do not seem conclusive. Today the prevalent belief is that *VSD* coincides largely with the original of Suetonius (Naumann 1981) and that the only addition certainly made by Donatus is *VSD* 37–8 on some of the testamentary provisions made by Vergil regarding the *Aeneid*, together with an epigram by Sulpicius of Carthage about his intention to have the poem burnt. It is possible that *VSD* contains other Donatian interpolations, but there are no sure means of identifying them. It is furthermore unlikely that Donatus omitted large parts of the original Suetonian *Life*: *VSD* is quite long in comparison to other biographies of poets by Suetonius. Our only other witness to the Suetonian *Life* is Jerome's *Chronicle*, which does not quote any part of it that is unknown to *VSD*.

On the basis of this evidence, we will first examine what sources Suetonius may have used, the choices and selections from them that he made in composing his *Life*, and the development of Vergilian biography during the centuries between Suetonius and Donatus. We will then survey some other *Lives* containing further biographical information that might be derived from ancient sources.

Suetonius and his Predecessors

The question of the sources used by Suetonius has been much debated. In spite of the immediate success of Vergil's works, there are no signs that any actual biographies of Vergil existed before Suetonius. Not even the most important biographer of the Augustan age, Hyginus (whom Suetonius includes in the canon of the Latin biographers: cf. Jer. *De viris ill.*, *praef.*), seems to have written one, although he is likely to have written the first commentary on the works of Vergil.

Consequently, it is probable that Suetonius did not use any previous biography, but that he collected and selected from several sources, employing the same procedures that he used in other biographies. Just as in his *Life of Horace*, in *VSD* as well he used letters written to and from Augustus, which were owned at that time by the imperial archives. For instance, in the letter quoted in *VSD* 31, written in 27–24 BCE, Augustus urges Vergil to send him parts of his unfinished poem, or (to employ his own words) "to send me your first sketch of the *Aeneid*, or whatever swatch of it you will" (trans. Wilson-Okamura, in Ziolkowski and Putnam 2008, here and throughout this chapter). Suetonius might also have got information about recitals of the *Georgics* by Vergil at Atella in 29 BCE (*VSD* 27) from Augustus' *Autobiography*. Recitals in about 22 BCE of books 2, 4, and 6 of the *Aeneid* may also have been mentioned there; during this reading, while listening to 6.883 on the death of Marcellus, nephew and heir of Augustus, Marcellus' mother Octavia reportedly fainted (*VSD* 32; also Serv. *ad Aen.* 4.323). Thanks to his governmental position, Suetonius must have had unfettered access to the whole imperial archive, and so to these letters; but he was hardly the only one who knew about them. Their circulation is mentioned by Tacitus in his *Dialogus de oratoribus* (13.2), and even in late antiquity a letter written by Vergil to Augustus on the difficulties that he encountered while composing the *Aeneid* was known to Macrobius (*Sat.* 1.24.11); and another letter by Augustus, on Vergil's coming to Naples to meet him, is quoted by the grammarian Priscian (2: 533.13 Keil).

Besides Augustus, other names from the Augustan age are quoted by Suetonius. They include M. Vipsanius Agrippa, who passed judgment on Vergil's style (the text of *VSD* 44 reads the otherwise unattested *Vipranius*: see Jocelyn 1979), and the poet Propertius, quoted for his remarks at 2.34.65–6 on the *Aeneid* that Vergil was then composing (*VSD* 30). A Melissus is quoted at *VSD* 16 for the opinion that Vergil lacked oratorical skills ("he was very slow in speaking and almost like someone who had not been schooled"). This passage can perhaps be traced to the *Facetiae* of Melissus, a freedman of Maecenas and a grammarian and writer of comedies. If instead the opinion belongs to Aelius Melissus, a grammarian of the second century (Bill 1928, 67), then the passage would have to have been inserted by Donatus. Finally there is Eros, Vergil's own freedman and copyist, whose testimony Suetonius cites to illustrate the way in which Vergil dealt with incomplete verses (*VSD* 34).

All of this supposes an intermediate source: Suetonius could not have spoken with Agrippa, Melissus, or Eros, all of whom lived a century earlier. For the other oral testimonies Suetonius identifies the sources he used: the remarks by Plotia Hieria on Vergil's sexual life are taken from Asconius Pedianus (*VSD* 10), probably from his book *Against Virgil's Detractors* (*liber contra obtrectatores Vergilii*), which is quoted later on in the *Life* (*VSD* 47). A report concerning the opinion of Julius Montanus that Vergil's recitations were unsurpassed (*VSD* 29) is attributed to Seneca (no doubt the Elder; but unfortunately the passage of his work that contained this reference has been lost). According to what the grammarian Nisus heard "from older men" (*VSD* 42), Vergil supposedly changed the order of two books of the *Aeneid* (moving 2 and 3 from the beginning of the poem to their current position) and deleted the original proem (*Ille ego qui quondam*, etc., the so-called "preproemium").

Asconius Pedianus (ca. 9 BCE–76 CE) was at times believed to have been Suetonius' main source, but it is unlikely that he composed a real biography. He certainly defended Vergil against his detractors (*VSD* 43–6) and probably collected anecdotes about him: besides the oral testimony by Plotia Hieria cited above, Asconius recorded (according to Serv. Dan. *ad Ecl.* 4.11) that the son of Asinius Pollio declared to Asconius that he himself was the *puer* celebrated in the fourth eclogue. Asconius was also believed to have heard directly from Vergil that the phrase *spatium coeli* ("space of heaven," *Ecl.* 3.105) alluded to a certain Caelius of Mantua (schol. Bern. *ad Ecl.* 3.105). This same exegesis is known to Servius as well, who adds (*ad loc.*) that Caelius was a wastrel who at his death owned only enough land to be buried in (hence *spatium Coelii*, "space of Caelius"). But the attribution of this statement to Vergil is completely imaginary: Asconius could not have spoken with Vergil himself, as the poet died about ten years before he himself was born. Lastly, Asconius stated that Vergil wrote the *Eclogues* at the age of 28 (ps.-Probus *ad Ecl. praef.*; also ps.-Probus *Vita*; Serv. *ad Ecl.* 1.18 and *ad Geo.* 4.564).

Besides Asconius, Varius Rufus, himself a poet and the first editor of the *Aeneid*, often has been regarded as Suetonius' main source. The only biographical note attributed to Varius regards Vergil's versification: "Varius too tells us that Vergil wrote very few verses in a day" (Quint. *Inst.* 10.3.8, trans. Russell). A similar statement about Vergil's composition was made by the philosopher and sophist Favorinus (ca. 85–155 CE), who is quoted by Gellius: "the friends and intimates of Publius Vergilius, in the accounts that they have left of his talents and his character, say that he used to declare that he produced verses after the manner and fashion of a bear" (*amici – inquit – familiaresque P. Vergilii, in his quae de ingenio moribusque eius memoriae tradiderunt, dicere eum solitum ferunt parere se versus more atque ritu ursino*, Gell. *NA* 17.10.2, trans. Rolfe). The simile between the bear and the poet presupposes the belief by ancient zoographers that bear fetuses were born shapeless and then licked into shape by their mothers (Arist. *Hist. an.* 6.579a). On the basis of the passage in Gellius, it has been suggested that Favorinus might have had access to a *Liber amicorum*, a sort of collection of memories and testimonies by Vergil's friends (Aly 1923). But it is more likely that Favorinus referred to Vergil's best-known friend, namely, Varius himself (Hor. *Serm.* 1.5.40, 1.6.55, 1.10.83; *Epist.* 2.1.247; cf. Hollis 1996). This supposition is confirmed by the words of Quintilian quoted above. The simile of the bear is also attested by *VSD* 22, which refers specifically to the composition of the *Georgics*. In addition, it is quoted by Jerome (*in Zacch.* 3.11 *praef.*) from the original Suetonian *Life*. Naumann (1976, 45–9) believed that Suetonius was the source used by Favorinus, but it seems more likely that both used Varius as a source. It is, however, uncertain where Varius could have mentioned the bear simile. Suggestions have included his edition of the *Aeneid* itself (perhaps in a preface?), a hypothetical work entitled *De Vergili ingenio moribusque* ("On Vergil's talents and character," posited, like the hypothetical *Liber amicorum*, by many scholars on the basis of Gellius' anecdotes), and so forth. But these ideas are very doubtful, and we have in any case no indication that Varius wrote a true biography of Vergil. After his friend's death he worked for a few years on editing the *Aeneid*: Jerome (*Chron. ad Ol.* 190.4) dates its publication to 17–16 BCE. Varius then died himself soon afterwards, in about 15 BCE. He certainly did not write about his editing of the *Aeneid*, because about this matter Suetonius is able to cite only the oral information collected by Nisus.

Varius, Vergil's Will, and the Publication of the *Aeneid*

Already Hyginus (according to Gell. *NA* 10.16.1, 11) pointed out some narrative incongruities in the *Aeneid* and attributed them to the incompleteness of the poem, saying that Vergil would have removed them had he not died without finishing it. The many incomplete hexameters of the poem (about fifty-eight in all) also suggested that the *Aeneid* was unfinished. *VSD* 24 supplies the following explanation on the incomplete verses: "lest anything should impede his *monumentum*, he would let certain things pass unfinished (*imperfecta*); others he propped out, as it were, with light-weight verses, which he jokingly said were placed there as struts, to hold up the edifice until the solid columns arrived" (*quos per iocum pro tibicinibus interponi aiebat, donec solidae columnae advenirent*).

The poem's supposed incompleteness (on which see O'Hara's chapter in this volume) gave rise to the legend that Vergil, before his death, wanted to burn his poem because he could not finish it. This legend was known already to Ovid in the years of his exile (8 CE). Alluding clearly to the *Aeneid*, Ovid affirms that the composition of his *Metamorphoses* was broken off by his banishment (*Tr.* 1.7.22; 2.63–4; 3.14.21–2) and that he consequently wanted to burn his unfinished poem (*Tr.* 1.7.16). The recurring image of the *Metamorphoses* as being snatched from the funeral pyre (*Tr.* 1.1.118; 1.7.38; 3.14.20) strengthens the allusion to the *Aeneid*. Ovid admits, how-ever, somewhat ironically, that copies of the *Metamorphoses* were already in circulation (1.17.24) and that the poem was already being read by the Romans (3.14.23). This irony may involve the *Aeneid* as well, which was known to some extent and even cel-ebrated several years before Vergil's death, at least where those books that were read in the presence of Augustus are concerned.

After Ovid, the legend is mentioned again by Pliny the Elder (77 or 78 CE), who writes that Vergil enjoined in his will that the *Aeneid* be burned: "the divine Augustus overrode the modesty of Vergil's will and forbade the burning of his poems" (*car-mina Vergilii cremari contra testamenti eius verecundiam vetuit*, *NH* 7.11, trans. Rackham). Suetonius seems to reject this version of the legend by leaving it out of his report on Vergil's will: "he bequeathed half of his estate to Valerius Proculus, his brother by another father; a quarter to Augustus; a twelfth to Maecenas; and the rest to Lucius Varius and Plotius Tucca" (*VSD* 37). But Suetonius proposes another ver-sion in which the request to burn the *Aeneid* is connected to Vergil's journey to Greece, where he wanted to go in order to revise (*emendare*) his poem. While on this journey, Vergil met with Augustus at Athens, and returned with him to Italy, landing at Brundisium, where he died (*VSD* 35). Dependable historical data in this story include the information that Vergil died at Brundisium, the usual port of embarcation to or arrival from Greece, and the return of Augustus from the East in October 19 BCE. The idea of the last journey was perhaps suggested either by Vergil's journey to Greece as celebrated by Horace in *Odes* 1.3 or by the sea voyage that Terence under-took to seek new Greek comedies, another voyage that ended with the poet's death (Suet., *Vita Ter.*). In any case, the story of the last journey gave Suetonius a "dra-matic" context in which to place the request to burn the *Aeneid*. The request in this version (*VSD* 39) is made twice by Vergil, first to Varius before leaving, with a sort of premonition of death ("he had arranged with Varius to burn the *Aeneid* if anything befell him"), and then at Brundisium on the point of death ("when his health was failing, he demanded his scroll cases earnestly, intending to burn them himself," *in extrema valetudine assidue scrinia desideravit, crematurus ipse*). The request was rejected, first by Varius (who "had insisted that he would not do so"), then by those who cared for Vergil when he was dying ("but no one brought them").

With the notice that follows ("but he gave no precise stipulations in this matter," *nihil quidem nominatim de ea cavit*), Suetonius seems to deny the version in which the burning of the *Aeneid* was stipulated in Vergil's actual will (Lucarini 2006, 283–5). But this note is somewhat contradicted by the following statement, according to which Vergil left specific instructions in regard to his writings: "For the rest, he bequeathed his writings to the aforementioned Varius and Tucca, on the condition that they pub-lish nothing that he himself had not revised" (*ceterum eidem Vario ac simul Tuccae scripta sub ea conditione legavit, ne quid ederent, quod non a se editum esset, VSD* 40). It is not clear where and when Vergil would have given these instructions: they evidently regard all his works, not just the *Aeneid*, and seem therefore to go back to a previous time. As testamentary provisions, they must have been contained in Vergil's will, but Suetonius reports only that the will bequeathed to Varius and Tucca a part of Vergil's patrimony.

These incongruences suggest that the statement in *VSD* 40 naming Varius and Tucca as literary executors might have been added by Donatus. This is also suggested by the fact that Tucca is mentioned here together with Varius as legatee of Vergilian writings, whereas Suetonius, on the other hand, attributes the revision and publication of the *Aeneid* to Varius alone. This is shown by the next sentence, which concerns Augustus' provisions for editing and publishing the *Aeneid*: "nevertheless, Varius published them on the authority of Augustus, but revised in only a cursory fashion, so that he even left any unfinished verses that there happened to be" (*edidit autem auctore Augusto Varius, sed summatim emendata, ut qui versus etiam imperfectos, si qui erant, reliquerit*, *VSD* 41). This statement is entirely consistent with the earlier one (*VSD* 39) on the absence of "precise stipulations" regarding the publication of the *Aeneid*. The tradition regarding Tucca is therefore post-Suetonian; and the fact that Donatus attributed the edition to both Varius and Tucca shows that his reference to them as "the two who corrected the *Aeneid* at Caesar's behest after Vergil's death" (*VSD* 37) is an interpolation by him.

Jocelyn (1990, 273) does not believe that Suetonius' omission of Tucca's name implies that he excluded him from the role of editor as well. But it is significant that when Suetonius later returns to this theme, he again mentions only the name of Varius ("Nisus the grammarian used to say that he heard from older men that Varius changed the order of two books, and that which now is second he moved into third place, and also that he smoothed out the beginning of the first book," *VSD* 42). Suetonius seems skeptical about the information collected by Nisus, presenting it as gossip transmitted by "older men." Rather, he is convinced that Varius revised the *Aeneid* "only in a cursory fashion" and kept the poem as Vergil wrote it. He adds that incomplete lines, except for 3.340, "were freestanding and complete with regard to sense" (*VSD* 41). It is likely that Suetonius knew also of other interventions that later sources attribute to Varius, such as the omission of the Helen episode (2.566–89) attested by Servius in his preface of other material as specified in his commentary (*ad Aen.* 4.436; 5.871; 7.464; cf. also Serv. Dan. *ad Aen.* 2.566). But Suetonius himself did not pass on this information because, one has to suppose, he regarded it as untrue.

Choices, Selections, and Omissions by Suetonius

Information supplied by *VSD* goes back to different periods and shows a process of stratification that began after Vergil's death. As far as we can see, Suetonius based his choices, selections, and omissions on the material that accumulated during the first century CE.

The first biographical information was collected immediately after Vergil's death. These include his date of birth (October 15, 70 BCE, *VSD* 2; cf. Mart. 12.67.5, Pliny, *Epist.* 3.7.8), date of death (September 21, 19 BCE, *VSD* 35), and the places of his death and burial (Brundisium and Naples, *VSD* 35–6). For his place of birth the poetic tradition (beginning with Ov. *Am.* 3.15.7) indicates the town of Mantua, following Vergil himself in *Ecl.* 9.27 and *Geo.* 3.12. But the earlier passage suggests a village in the countryside, which is identified by *VSD* 2 as Andes. The vagueness of this reference ("a village called Andes, not far from Mantua") suggests that Suetonius was unable to locate this village with precision. Essential biographical data, in addition to information about his works, were incorporated into the epitaph on Vergil's grave near Naples: "Mantua gave birth to me, the Calabrians stole me away, Parthenope now holds me; I sang of pastures, plowlands, and leaders" (*Mantua me genuit, Calabri rapuere, tenet nunc / Parthenope; cecini pascua rura duces*). Vergil's *opera* provided some more information of biographical interest. These include his residence in Naples while composing the *Georgics* (*Geo.* 4.563–4, which were used by the author of the epitaph: Bettini 1976–7); ties with Asinius Pollio, Alfenus Varus, and Cornelius Gallus (all mentioned at various points in the *Eclogues*); ties with Maecenas (the addressee of the *Georgics*). Also the name of Varius is quoted at *Ecl.* 9.35 (and more frequently, together with Vergil, in Horace's works).

Encouraged by the existence of this much reliable information about the poet's life in his own works, Vergilian commentators extrapolated additional, unlikely information as well and created a great number of imaginary anecdotes. The fact that Vergil wrote the *Georgics* encouraged a belief that he came from a family of peasants; but this did not prevent the addition of further, contradictory information. As a result Suetonius was uncertain about two possibilities concerning the occupation of Vergil's father: "some have reported that he was an artisan who was a potter, many that he was at first the employee of a *viator* named Magus, and then a son-in-law on account of his industry, and that he built up a fortune of no mean substance by buying up woodlands and tending bees" (*VSD* 1). The famous *Ecl.* 9.28, where Vergil complains about the consequences of Mantua's nearness to Cremona ("woe to you, Mantua, too close to poor Cremona"), which was punished after the civil war with confiscation of lands, was perhaps the source of the information that connects Vergil to the latter town. According to *Catal.* 8.6 Vergil's father lived in Cremona as well as Mantua; according to *VSD* 6 Vergil studied in this town. The *Eclogues* also gave rise to the idea that Vergil preferred pederastic love: *VSD* 9 names two boys, Cebes and Alexander, who were loved by Vergil and affirms that it is the latter who is serenaded in *Ecl.* 2 under the name of Alexis (cf. Mart. 5.16.12; 6.68.6; 14.12). *VSD* 14 mentions an analogous identification of Daphnis in *Ecl.* 5, in whose name Vergil supposedly laments the death of a brother whose real name was Flaccus.

In addition to information about Vergil's method of composition, which Varius himself may have mentioned, several other elements in *VSD* can be correlated with remarks made about Vergil as early as the Augustan age. Among these are some details concerning Vergil's physical appearance, a usual category in Suetonius' biographies. There was certainly a tradition of Vergil portraits and sculptures: Martial (14.186) knows of manuscripts that featured portraits of Vergil, and *VSD* 8 may refer to them. But some elements may have been suggested by Horace. Ancient commentators identified as Vergil the personage represented at *Serm.* 1.3.31 as wearing his hair "in country style" (*rusticius tonsus*) in the same way as *VSD* 8 describes Vergil as having a "country appearance" (*facies rusticana*). Horace's comment that Vergil was "dyspeptic" (*crudus, Serm.* 1.5.49) correlates with the passage in *VSD* 8 stating that Vergil "suffered very much from pain in his stomach." The "swarthy complexion" (*aquilus color*) that *VSD* 8 mentions when describing Vergil may be traceable, if not to the Augustan period, at least back to the "dark Maro" of Juvenal (*nigro Maroni*, 7.227). It is not certain, however, whether Juvenal refers to a portrait of Vergil or to a darkened manuscript.

Vergil had become an object of hostile criticism already in the Augustan age, as the judgments attributed to Agrippa and Melissus point out, and detractors of Vergil were known already to Ovid (*Rem. am.* 367–8). Anti-Vergilianism increased in the ensuing years of the early principate. Caligula led the initiative to remove the books and images of Vergil from libraries, calling him "a man of no talent and very little learning" (Suet. *Cal.* 34: *nullius ingenii minimaeque doctrinae*). The author of the *Einsiedeln Eclogues* rates Nero ahead of Vergil as poet. On the list of detractors (*obtrectatores*) quoted by *VSD* 43–6 from the aforementioned work of Asconius Pedianus, we find both critics of Vergil and parodists of his works.

Among the issues that occupied the detractors was Vergil's similarity to Homer. The motif was introduced in a positive way by Propertius, who wrote that "something greater than the *Iliad* is being born" (*nescio quid maius nascitur Iliade*, 2.34.66), but afterwards this similarity to Homer was used against Vergil. A certain Q. Octavius Avitus wrote eight books about Vergil's imitations of earlier authors, and particularly of Homer. Melissus' aforementioned judgment on Vergil's oratorical weakness may imply another disadvantageous comparison, namely, with Cicero. This comparison was developed mostly in rhetorical schools. An explicit judgment was given by Cassius Severus, for whom "the felicity of Vergil's touch deserted him in prose" (Seneca, *Contr.* 3 *praef.* 8, trans. Winterbottom).

But anti-Vergilianism in its various forms provoked a reaction that became widespread in the Flavian period. Asconius Pedianus replied succinctly to Octavius Avitus' criticism of Vergil's dependence on Homer, quoting Vergil himself to the effect that "it is easier to steal the club of Hercules than a line from Homer" (*VSD* 46). Vergil's preeminence in poetry gradually extended to eloquence and to various other areas of knowledge. Already Seneca the Younger called Vergil "a very eloquent man" (*De otio* 1.4: *vir disertissimus*); later, in the second century, Florus would debate whether Vergil was greater as a poet or as an orator (this was in fact the title of one of his works: *Vergilius orator an poeta?*). *VSD* 15 credits Vergil with studies in the field of medicine and *mathematica* (i.e., astrology). The ancient tradition of the poet-bard already allowed a sort of "deification" of Vergil in the time of Nero: Calpurnius Siculus spoke of Vergil as an "inspired bard" (*vates sacer*, 4.65). Seneca the Younger called him "the greatest bard inspired with almost godlike utterance" (*maximus vates et velut divino ore instinctus, De brev. vit.* 9.2, trans. Basore).

Many other notes and anecdotes about Vergil go back to this time, such as those that concern the prodigies that supposedly occurred before and after his birth, reproducing patterns well known from the biographies of other famous men (cf. Fairweather 1974). *VSD* 3–5 recites three prodigies, two of which took as their starting point the pseudo-etymology of the name "Vergilius" from *virga*, "twig." Etymologizing is also implicated in another strand of the tradition that appears at this time, the nickname *Parthenias*, but the background here is more complex. During the early principate the *obtrectatores* had attacked not only the poet's work, as we have seen, but evidently his morality as well: we can infer as much from the defense organized by Suetonius regarding Plotia Hieria, Varius' partner or wife (Serv. *ad Ecl.* 3.20), with whom Vergil was believed to have had an affair. Suetonius, in disagreeing with this gossip, quotes Plotia Hieria herself as having denied to Asconius Pedianus that she ever had a relationship with Vergil (*VSD* 10). On the issue of Vergil's pederastic preferences, Suetonius assumes an attitude of "cursory tolerance" (Baldwin 1983, 390). It is against this background that we must understand the nickname "Parthenias" ("little virgin") that was given to Vergil in Naples (*VSD* 11). The name is presented by Suetonius in a positive way as referring to the shyness of the poet, who in Rome "would seek refuge in the nearest house from those who followed him and pointed him out." The nickname was based on the name of the town of Naples ("Parthenope"; cf. *Geo.* 4.564) or on the pseudo-etymology of the name Vergilius from the zodiacal sign Virgo. It refers to the general character of the poet, but maybe also, in reaction against the more salacious anecdotes, to his sexual life. At any rate, Pliny the Elder spoke about Vergil's "modesty" (*verecundia*) in the aforementioned testimony regarding the poet's last will and testament, and by this time modesty must have been a recognized aspect of the poet's image. In fact, some years later, Pliny's nephew spoke about Vergil's "moral integrity" (*sanctitas morum*, *Epist.* 5.3.6).

A third part of the biographical information in *VSD* may have come from the second half of the first century. The earliest quotations from some of the works included in the so-called *Appendix Vergiliana* date to the Flavian period. *Catal.* 2 is cited as Vergilian by Quintilian (*Inst.* 8.3.28), as are *Culex* by Martial (8.55.20; 14.185), Statius (*Silv.* 2.7.74) and eventually Suetonius (in his *Vita Lucani*). *Culex*, remarkably, is the only "juvenile" work for which *VSD* 18 gives a summary, date, and the final couplet; for the others only titles are mentioned. This collection of pseudoepigrapha was likely encouraged by the precedent with Homer. Suetonius was skeptical in the case of Horace: his *Vita Horati* contests the authenticity of certain works (some elegiacs and a prose epistle to Maecenas) that were ascribed to him. In Vergil's case his doubts seem limited to the *Aetna* ("its authorship is still a matter of debate," *VSD* 19). The story about Ballista may also have been produced in this period: Vergil was believed to have written an epigram for this teacher-robber (*VSD* 17), who can be categorized with other strict (not to say violent) teachers attributed to the great poets (for example by Horace himself at *Epist.* 2.1.70–1).

The custom of public recitations began in the Augustan age, and was introduced by Asinius Pollio. It is therefore not impossible that the *Eclogues* were in fact delivered with success on stage, as *VSD* 26 claims. There is also attestation, as we have seen, about Vergil's private recitations in the presence of Augustus. But other anecdotes about Vergilian recitations were certainly created later, when public recitations had become common practice. Thus the story told by Servius (*ad Ecl.* 6.11) in which the sixth eclogue was recited by the famous actress Cytheris in the presence of Cicero seems very unlikely. (Cytheris is mentioned in *Ecl.* 10 under the name "Lycoris," which was given to her by Cornelius Gallus.) The same goes for the anecdote reported by Tacitus (*Dial.* 13) in which Vergil, while attending a theatrical performance at which some of his verses were performed, received an ovation as great as if he were Augustus himself. *VSD* 33 affirms that Vergil "gave recitations to larger audiences, though not often." This refers perhaps to the doubts expressed by Pliny the Younger, Suetonius' friend and correspondent, who declared that he did not know whether Vergil himself recited or not (*Epist.* 5.3.7).

I have already pointed out some selections made by Suetonius in regard to information he presumably must have had, for example about Varius' modifications of the *Aeneid*. In *VSD* evidence about any extensive changes is transmitted under the heading of those rumors collected by Nisus, while in Servius such evidence is treated more extensively and taken more seriously. Suetonius is more skeptical because of the loyalty he attributed to Varius in editing the *Aeneid*, as we have seen previously. Likewise Suetonius must have been aware of information known to Asconius that he himself does not cite. The aforementioned exegesis of *Ecl.* 3.105 about Caelius of Mantua as well as the fact that Vergil composed the *Eclogues* at the age of 28 are two examples. The first omission is not surprising if we consider Suetonius' general skepticism about this type of exegesis. The second detail he omitted because the age it attests does not agree with the time line of *VSD* 25, according to which Vergil spent three years on the *Eclogues*, seven on the *Georgics*, and eleven on the *Aeneid*. If the three works were composed consecutively, Vergil must have begun composing the *Eclogues* at the age of 30. (*VSD* 25 also gives us the age at which Vergil supposedly composed the *Culex*, but the validity of this testimony – regardless of who really wrote the poem – has been debated: the manuscript reading of sixteen years (XVI) should probably be emended to twenty-six (XXVI).)

Suetonius' most striking omission, however, is that of Vergil's adherence to Epicureanism, an adherence confirmed by a Herculaneum papyrus recovered in the 1980s (Gigante and Capasso 1989). It contains the dedication to a treatise *On flattery* in which the Epicurean philosopher Philodemus mentions the names of Plotius (Tucca), Varius, Vergil, and Quintilius (Varus). Three of these names, Varius, Tucca, and Vergil, are found in Horace's account of the journey to Brundisium (*Serm.* 1.5.39–41). The papyrus thus confirms information given by Servius (*ad Ecl.* 6.13; *ad Aen.* 6.264) about Vergil's Epicurean scholarship at the school of the philosopher Siro (who is mentioned in *Catal.* 5 and 8 as well).

VSD 10, however, refers only indirectly to Vergil's Epicureanism, if at all. For instance, Varius' invitation "to share" Plotia Hieria "with him" (*ad communionem sui*) may have been made in accordance with Epicurean custom; but Vergil, as we have seen, refused the offer. Besides underlining Vergil's morality, Suetonius may have wanted to show that Vergil distanced himself from certain Epicurean habits. Moreover, *VSD* 35 affirms that Vergil intended, after the projected trip to Greece and the completion of the *Aeneid*, to devote himself to philosophy; but he does not specify which school of philosophy he wanted to join. By being vague Suetonius may have wanted to imply that Vergil aspired to a philosophy other than the Epicurean that he professed in his youth. Maybe for the same reason, Suetonius omitted Naples from the list of cities where Vergil had studied (*VSD* 6–7: Mantua, Cremona, Milan, and Rome). Naples is, however, found instead of Rome in the list given by Servius – who, unlike Suetonius, made no effort to hide Vergil's Epicureanism.

From Suetonius to Donatus

Suetonius' account of Vergil's last will and testament won general acceptance. Favorinus reproduced it, without significant additions: "when he was laid low by disease and saw that death was near, he begged and earnestly besought his friends to burn the *Aeneid*, which he had not yet sufficiently revised" (Gell. *NA* 17.10.4, trans. Rolfe). The version that was rejected by Suetonius, in which Vergil's will ordered that the *Aeneid* be burnt, seems to reappear eventually in late antiquity, when Macrobius writes that Vergil "**bequeathed (*legavit*)** his poem to the flames" (*Sat.* 1.24.6, trans. Davies). But a new version of Vergil's testament, as we have seen, was added by Donatus, who testifies that Vergil left his writings to Varius and Tucca, "on the condition that they publish nothing that he himself had not revised" (*VSD* 40). This version is attested by the Vita Probiana as well ("Vergil himself had stipulated in his will that nothing which he had not published should exist"); but Servius, in his *Life of Vergil*, refers this instruction to Augustus, who "commanded Tucca and Varius to edit [the *Aeneid*] according to this rule, that they remove superfluous material but add nothing" (*hac lege iussit emendare, ut superflua demerent, nihil adderent tamen*). The addition of the phrase "remove superfluous material" seems intended to justify the testimony concerning Varius' omissions of the "old" proem and of the Helen episode.

Unlike Suetonius, then, ancient scholars of later periods attributed the posthumous edition and publication of the *Aeneid* not to Varius alone, but to the team of Varius and Tucca. This new version was supported by Donatus in his addition to *VSD* 37 and by Jerome in his *Chronicle* (*ad Ol.* 190.4 – the only case in which Jerome follows *VSD* instead of the original *Life* by Suetonius). Servius, too, as we have seen, attributes several editorial modifications on the *Aeneid* to both Varius and Tucca. This version most likely originated in the second century. Donatus provides conformation of this view by quoting the epigram by Sulpicius of Carthage about the burning of the *Aeneid*. This Sulpicius is perhaps identifiable with a homonymous commentator on the *Aeneid* who is quoted in the *scholia Veronensia* for an exegesis on *Aen.* 9.36 (which agrees with an interpretation of Valerius Probus). The identification is validated by the epigram, which might have been composed to appear at the beginning of an edition or commentary of the *Aeneid*: "Vergil had bidden that **these poems** were to be destroyed by flames" (*iusserat haec rapidis aboleri carmina flammis*), where "these poems" (*haec carmina*) seem to refer to the books of the *Aeneid* that were introduced by this epigram. Less certain is the identification of Sulpicius of Carthage with Sulpicius Apollinaris, a grammarian who lived in the second century, a teacher of Gellius and of the Emperor Pertinax (cf. Stok 2008; the epigram was rewritten in late antiquity and accompanied by versified summaries of the twelve books of the *Aeneid*: cf. *Anthologia Latina* 653 Riese; cf. Ziolkowski and Putnam 2008, 422–3). Sulpicius' epigram does not actually address the issue of the editing and publication of the *Aeneid*, but only Vergil's desire to burn the poem, as in Suetonius' *Life*, and the refusal of Varius and Tucca to execute this request ("Tucca and likewise Varius refuse," *Tucca* *vetat Variusque simul*, 3). The epigram could have strengthened the idea that both Varius and Tucca had edited the poem.

Later biographies modified Suetonius' version on another matter as well, namely the question that stems from the *Eclogues* about the confiscation of land that Vergil might have suffered in the triumviral period. In regard to allegorical interpretations of this work, Suetonius seems rather prudent. He speaks only of the identifications of Alexis with Alexander and of Daphnis with Flaccus, but about the confiscations he says that the *Eclogues* were written in honor of Asinius Pollio, Alfenus Varus, and Cornelius Gallus "because they had kept him from being penalized in the distribution of lands after the victory at Philippi, when the lands on the other side of the Po were divided among the veterans by order of the triumvirate" (*VSD* 19). Vergil's land, therefore, in Suetonius' view, was never actually confiscated. Other scholars interpreted *Ecl.* 9.28 ("Mantua, too close to wretched Cremona") differently, namely as an autobiographical statement, and argued that Vergil was indeed victim of the confiscations, but that he was later compensated for this by his patrons. This version is told by Donatus in the preface to his *Eclogues* commentary. In this plot, Vergil trusts his patrons and therefore defends himself against the soldier to whom his land was assigned: "Vergil, relying on the worth of his poems and the friendship of certain powerful men, made bold to stand in the way of Arrius the centurion, who immediately reached for his sword (since he was a soldier); and when the poet rushed out to flee, the pursuit did not end until Vergil had thrown himself into a river and thus swum across to the other bank." Only afterwards, in this version, Vergil recovered his lands "with the help of Maecenas as well as the three officers in charge of land division, Varus, Pollio, and Cornelius Gallus" (*VSD* 63). The name of Arrius is given also by Servius (*ad Ecl.* 1.47; 3.94), but according to Servius Danielis (*ad Ecl.* 9.1) the centurion's name was Clodius.

Donatus says in his preface that Vergil wrote the tragedy *Thyestes*, "which Varius published under his own name" (*VSD* 48). This statement is repeated by Servius (*ad Ecl.* 3.20), who connects it to the story of the relationship between Vergil and Plotia Hieria: she may have had the tragedy written by her lover in her possession, and she may have given it to her husband Varius. This story is likely to be invented on the basis of the supposed affair, which was known to Suetonius (Suerbaum 1983). That Vergil composed the *Thyestes* was perhaps suggested by Martial, in whose imagination Vergil could have really been a dramatist: "he gave place to Varius in the renown of the Roman buskin, though he might have spoken in tragic tone with stronger voice" (8.18.7–8).

Commentators continued, after Suetonius, to deduce biographical information from Vergil's works, on the ground of sometimes entirely imaginary clues: Gellius (6.20.1) read in an unspecified commentary that Vergil, when composing *Geo.* 2.224–5 (*vicina Vesevo / ora iugo*, "the region near Vesuvius's height"), had first written *Nola* instead of *ora*, but that he replaced the name of the town after suffering an offense from its inhabitants: "afterwards Vergil asked the people of Nola to allow him to run their city water into his estate, which was nearby; but that they refused to grant the favor which he asked; that thereupon the offended poet erased the name of their city from his poem, as if consigning it to oblivion" (trans. Rolfe; cf. Barchiesi 1979; Holford-Strevens 1979).

The Other Ancient *Vitae*

Besides Donatus, in late antiquity Vergilian *Lives* were written by Servius (*VS*), by the grammarian Phocas (*VF*), and by an unknown compiler who took the name of Probus (*VP*). The so-called *Vita Bernensis* I ("Life of Bern I") and the two *Lives* attributed to "Philargyrius" are of this period or even later. The Philargyrian *Lives* reused known sources (the first one mostly reproduces *VSD*; the second collects the Vergilian items from Jerome's *Chronicle*); the *Vita Bernensis* I, besides the information from *VSD*, adds that Vergil and the future Augustus together attended the school of the grammarian Epidius. Octavian did attend this school according to Suetonius (*Gramm.* 28.1), but the idea that Vergil, who was seven years older, can have been Augustus' schoolfellow is quite implausible.

The other three ancient *Lives* (*VS*, *VF*, and *VP*) have been generally considered as derivative from *VSD*, and therefore as not having independent documentary value (Naumann 1974). But they also contain material not found in *VSD* and perhaps inherited from traditions that could also be very ancient.

VS appears at the head of Servius' commentary on the works of Vergil. It is likely that the version we have was abridged: Servius himself in another part of his commentary quotes a passage of *VS* that has not otherwise survived (*ad Ecl. praef.*; cf. Murgia 1974, 266). It is based as a whole on *VSD* (not surprisingly, since Servius was a pupil of Donatus), but it also contains the following information: (1) the name of Vergil's mother, Magia; (2) that Naples was among the towns where Vergil studied; (3) that the *Copa* was among Vergil's juvenile works; (4) that Tucca and Varius removed the Helen episode (2.566–89) from the poem as Vergil had left it upon his death. Naples, as we have seen, was perhaps omitted by Suetonius to hide Vergil's Epicureanism. The *Copa* was likely attributed to Vergil after Suetonius; and Servius, unlike Suetonius, did not doubt the authorship of the *Aetna*. The Helen episode was probably known to Suetonius, who nevertheless did not know that Varius significantly modified the *Aeneid* as Vergil had left it.

In addition to these matters of detail, Servius also presents a different image of Vergil's character. He does not mention Vergil's pederastic loves, but presents him as "exceedingly modest" (*verecundissimus*), remarking that he "suffered from only one malady, namely, he was not able to control his lust." In his commentary Servius notes (*ad Ecl.* 2.1) that the character Alexis was intended to represent Alexander, a boy given to Vergil by Asinius Pollio; but he further stipulates that the poet sang about the boy only to please Pollio, presenting his pederastic loves as gossip (*dicitur in pueros habuisse amorem*) and anyway denying that he loved boys "filthily" (*turpiter*).

The versified *Life* by Phocas is dated to the fifth century in consideration of the fact that it appears to rely on *VSD*, but it is not impossible that Phocas used Suetonius directly (cf. most recently Mazhuga 2003, who consequently dates *VF* to the third century). In addition, *VF* contains information that is not found in *VSD*: (1) the name of Vergil's mother, Polla (35), and not Magia as in Servius; (2) the prodigy of bees swarming about the face of the newborn Vergil (52–4); (3) that Vergil was the pupil of Siro (87–8) but apparently in Rome, when in reality Siro taught at Naples); (4) that

Vergil was occupied for nine years in composing the *Georgics* (122; cf. *VSD* 7) and for twelve with the *Aeneid* (125; *VSD* 11).The bee-prodigy is attributed to Vergil also by the *Passion of St. Pansophios of Alexandria* (transmitted in Georgian in a manuscript preserved in Tbilisi), which probably derives from the same source used by Phocas. (The prodigy had been used already for Plato and by Vacca in his *Life of Lucan*). The chronology of the works given by *VF* either aims to reconcile *VSD*'s chronology with the age supplied by Asconius Pedianus for the composition of the *Eclogues* or else simply gives a series 3-9-12, which is more "regular" that the 3-7-11 given by *VSD*.

VP is attributed, together with the commentary that follows it, to the grammarian Valerius Probus (second century CE), but it is certainly a later composition. The author of this *Life*, like the author of *VF*, has also been supposed to have used Suetonius directly (Hurka 2004), but it is more likely that he used *VSD* together with *VS* and *VF*. As Vergil's mother he names Magia Polla, combining the names given by Servius and by Phocas. Regarding the confiscation of lands, he is closer to the version of Donatus and Servius than to Suetonius' version. He connects the confiscations to the civil war between Antony and Octavian and accepts the idea that Vergil actually lost his lands and that he got them back thanks to the intervention of powerful friends. Besides information found in the other sources, *VP* also (1) gives the distance between Mantua and Andes as thirty Roman miles, and (2) notes that Vergil belonged to the Epicurean school together with Varius, Tucca, and Quintilius (Varus). Both notes are probably taken from ancient sources. The distance of Andes from Mantua disagrees with the medieval identification of Andes with Pietole (Grilli 1995), and *VP*'s list of Vergil's Epicurean friends is the only one in any of the *Lives* to be confirmed by the aforementioned fragment of Philodemus' *On flattery* (*PHerc.Paris.* 2; cf. Gigante and Capasso 1989; Brugnoli and Stok 2006, 83n.); the other sources identify only Varius and Tucca as members of this group.

VP is the latest of the *Lives* to give ancient biographical information. All later *Lives* are based exclusively on *VSD*, Jerome, or Servius.

FURTHER READING

The ancient *Lives* and other texts of Vergilian interest are available with English translation in Ziolkowski and Putnam (2008) (only Latin and original texts are provided by Brugnoli and Stok 1991). For critical editions of the ancient *Lives*, see: Hardie (1966²); Brugnoli and Stok (1997); for texts and German commentary of several *Lives*: Bayer (1981⁴). Critical surveys: Suerbaum (1981); Brugnoli and Naumann (1990). On Vergil's epitaph: Frings (1998). On the medieval legend: Spargo 1934; on humanistic *Lives*: Stok (1994); Brown (1998); on Vergilian biography in the nineteenth and twentieth centuries: Ziolkowski (1993, 30–56).

PART TWO

Medieval and Renaissance Receptions

CHAPTER NINE

Vergil and St. Augustine

Garry Wills

As a boy Augustine famously wept for Dido and later regretted it. As an ascetic bishop he deplored his inability to exorcise the memories of "pagan" literature. He says (*De civitate Dei* 1.3) that Vergil above all was instilled in the young, so they could not forget its language, full as it was of Roman gods: "Little boys [are made to] read him, to insure that this great and most famous and best poet of all, drunk into impressionable minds, can never be entirely drained off into forgetfulness. As Horace says, 'A cask's first wine, into it fit, long afterwards will breathe of it' (*quo semel est imbuta recens servabit odorem / testa diu*) [*Epist.* 1.2.69–70]."

Augustine's mind breathed of Vergil all his life. What he learned as a boy he taught as a young man and cited, off and on, ever after. Only in later polemics against the pagan gods did he deplore the effect of Vergil, who clothed the gods in such haunting images and beguiling language. As an instructor of rhetoric, he used Vergil as much as Cicero to illustrate effective language – following his models in the decidedly Vergilian circle he had met in Rome.

Harald Hagendahl, in his two volumes on *Augustine and the Latin Classics* (1967), counts 239 citations from Vergil in the works of Augustine – 186 from the *Aeneid*, 22 from the *Eclogues*, 30 from the *Georgics* – and he does not get them all. Sometimes he misses poetic fragments worked into the flow of Augustine's prose. One such example shows how Vergil could be a vehicle for civilized arguing among educated Christians in late antiquity. Jerome had written an angry letter to Augustine, calling him an uppity young showoff. Augustine humorously defers to the irascible crank of Jerusalem, comparing himself to Dares, Vergil's boastful boxer who is beaten by a veteran hauled out of retirement:

> Iam me arbitror rescriptis tuis, velut Entellinis grandinibus et acribus caestibus, tamquam audacem Daretam coepisse pulsari et versari. (August. *Epist.* 73.1)

> Your letter, like the hailstorm-slashing gloves of Entellus, makes me see myself as the cheeky Dares about to be pummeled, spun about.

The lines he is playing a riff on are *Aen.* 5.458–60:

> quam multa grandine nimbi
> culminibus crepitant, sic densis ictibus heros
> creber utraque manu pulsat versatque Dareta.

> As hail drums on a resonating roof,
> So rapidly with right-hand left-hand blows
> The giant pummeled Dares, spun him about.

Hagendahl was not alone in missing the reference to Vergil. Later copyists, not recognizing the source and wondering what hail had to do with Jerome, changed *grandinibus* to *grandis* or *glandis*. Jerome would have got the reference, since his tutor had been the grammarian Aelius Donatus, a famous Vergil scholar. Since Hagendahl took as his assignment only verbatim quotes, he also missed whole *situations* where Augustine was clearly remembering Vergil. When, for instance, Augustine imagines a personified Lady Self-Control (*Continentia*) beckoning him across a divide he cannot yet cross over, "reaching out holy hands to take and hold me to her" (*extendens ad me suscipiendum et amplectendum pias manus, Conf.* 8.27), a haunting line of Vergil springs to mind, the one describing dead souls unable to cross the River Styx: "Hands yearn out aching for the farther shore" (*Tendebantque manus ripae ulterioris amore, Aen.* 6.314).

We should never underestimate the hold Vergil had on Augustine's imagination, even when he was trying to free himself from that hold. When Augustine is describing the effect vice had on him as he tried to extricate himself from its thrall, he says: "I reviled myself far more intensely than ever, twisting and turning in my trammels...while you [God] pressed hard on my inmost being, your whip redoubling my fear and shame, showing kind severity" (*Conf.* 825). Pierre Courcelles (1968, 192) and others have connected this with Persius' *Satire* 5 (154–5, 158): "Two hooks are tearing you apart...You might claim, 'I have broken the trammel'" (*duplici in diversum scinderis hamo ..."Rupi iam vicula," dicas*). But Augustine is not saying that one whip pulls him one way and another pulls in an opposite direction. He says the twofold whip spins him faster out of control: *Accusans memet ipsum solito acerbius nimis ac volvens et versans me in vinculo, donec...instabas tu in occultis meis, domine, severa misericordia, flagella ingeminans timoris et pudoris* (*Conf.* 8.25). The dizzyingly alliterative phrase *volvens et versans me in vinculo* is closer to Vergil:

> Ceu quondam torto volitans sub verbere turbo
> quem pueri magno in gyro vacua atria circum
> intenti ludo exercent

> A lash will sometime whip a top about
> While boys look hard at its unruly circuit
> Over all the area (*Aen.* 7.378–80)

Here Augustine's whip (*flagella*) is Vergil's spinning lash (*verber*). Vergil is describing Queen Amata's uncontrolled hate, lashed on by Allecto, as boys are intent on their top. Augustine is describing his uncontrollable lust, punished by a God whose intensity is paradoxical, a kind severity (*severa misericordia*).

Dido and Monnica

The Augustinian–Vergilian situation most often recognized is the way Augustine tried to deceive his mother Monnica when he sneaked off from Carthage to Italy, under what he thought was the direction of his (Manichean at the time) gods – exactly what Aeneas had done to Dido, creating the situation that made the boy Augustine weep for her. There are no direct verbal references to Dido in Augustine's account of his escape, but the similarities of the two defections are inescapable, and would have been so to Augustine at the time. "I tricked her as she clung to me with all her might, to detain me or to go with me" (*fefelli eam, violenter me tenentem ut aut revocaret aut mecum pergeret, Conf.* 5.15). And here is Dido:

> ire iterum in lacrimas, iterum temptare precando
> cogitur et supplex animos summittere amori.
>
> She cannot help but launch herself once more
> In tears, once more to plead, love crushing pride. (*Aen.* 4.413–14)

Augustine thought his Manichean gods were summoning him to Rome, but he later attributed this providential guidance to Christian Truth. If he had not gone to Rome, he would not have met the prominent senator Symmachus, who recommended him to the emperor's court in Milan. And if he had not been appointed the imperial orator in Milan, he would not have met the Christian Neoplatonists – Mallius Theodore, Simplician, and Ambrose – who helped free him from philosophical error.

These providences he would equate, on the eve of his baptism, with Aeneas' prayer to Apollo: "God himself will guide us if we follow his lead, by the way he shows to reach our goal, since he gives a sign and merges with our resolve" (*perducet enim ipse, si sequimur quo nos ire iubet atque ubi ponere sedem, qui dat modo augurium nostrisque inlabitur animis, De ord.* 1.20). Here is Aeneas:

> quem sequimur? quove ire iubes? ubi ponere sedes?
> da, pater, augurium atque animis inlabere nostris.
>
> Who is to lead us, what way, and to what goal?
> Father, grant us a sign, and merge with our resolve. (*Aen.* 3.88–9)

So Augustine, though he blamed himself for deceiving his mother, felt under divine guidance when he, like Aeneas, steered for Rome. In fact, Aeneas' response to Dido's tears became his own description of Stoic steadfastness. In a simile, Aeneas is compared to a rooted oak hit by heavy storms:

mens immota manet, lacrimae volvuntur inanes

Immovable his mind. Tears course down useless. (*Aen.* 4.449)

Augustine finally used that line in *The City of God* (9.4), but it came up earlier in a more interesting context. He had three students with him as he prepared for baptism in a villa outside Milan, and he read half a book of the *Aeneid* with them each day before dinner. They undoubtedly read book 4, which had made him weep when he was his students' age. Then, as he discussed wise men with those boys, Licentius, the son of Augustine's millionaire patron back in Africa, said that a wise man must have an immovable mind. It is not surprising that this student, who had Vergil's phrase on his tongue, was an aspiring poet. Augustine's question to Licentius – "how can the mind stay immovable," *quomodo mens immobilis maneat* – clearly echoes Vergil's *mens immota manet* (*De ord.* 2.18). The teacher and his students then talk about the problem of an immovable mind in a movable boat, which calls up, in the context of Aeneas' and Augustine's sailing away from a loved one, the situation in *Aeneid* 4. This is just one of many cases where Vergil haunts whole mental sequences in Augustine's writings. Neither Augustine nor Licentius here expressly refers to Vergil's poem, but it is clear from their conversation that they had already discussed the issue of a *mens immota* when reading their favorite author.

When Augustine describes his own anguish at choosing to follow his divine calling, in the garden in Milan, he says that "A vast storm hit me, loosing great sheets of showering tears" (*Conf.* 8.28). He is like Aeneas in the simile of the oak tree showered on, his mind not shaken. Hagendahl says Augustine is wrong in saying that the tears "coursing useless" in this simile are those of Aeneas himself, when they are really Dido's. But the ancient commentators were not so restrictive. They said: "The tears would be useless for Dido in any case, though some attribute them to Aeneas, some to Dido, some to Anna, and some to all three" (*et utrum inanes quae Didoni nihil prosint – quidam tamen "lacrimas inanes" vel Aeneae, vel Didonis, vel omnium accipiunt*, Serv. *ad Aen.* 4.449). Augustine got Vergil's point.

Teaching Vergil

Augustine not only loved and wept over Vergil. He taught the poet's text in four towns, two in Africa (Thagaste and Carthage) and two in Italy (Rome and Milan). And when he was in Rome, for two stays, he was at the heart of Vergilian scholarship in his time, the circle of the orator Symmachus, who secured Augustine's appointment to the imperial court in Milan. We learn from Macrobius' *Saturnalia* that Romans in the fourth century CE treated Vergil as Athenians in the fifth century BCE had treated Homer – as a font of all wisdom and the basis of all education. They went to these poets for knowledge of religion, law, history, and language. Vergil was especially praised for providing models for every kind of oratory, the very subject Augustine taught as a professor of rhetoric. He is even held to be superior to Cicero for showing what great speeches can do. Cicero has his own great style, but Vergil shows characters using all four possible modes of speech (full, spare, austere, ornate). One of Macrobius' interlocutors, the Greek rhetorician Eusebius, puts the company's view of Vergil this way:

> I believe that Vergil suspected that he would provide models for everyone to follow, and he did so with a skill more divine than human as he deliberately blended different styles. For he followed no guide but nature, the mother of all things, bringing dissonant things into concord as a musician does. Look closely at the universe and you will see how its heavenly creator and our poet work the same way. Vergil's language is appropriate to each character – here full, there spare, here austere, there ornate, and then all combined, whether flowing calm or bursting wild – just as earth itself relaxes in plants and meadows, or bristles in woods and rocks, shrinks to sand or flows out in streams, or widens to a vast sea. Do not blame me for excess if I compare Vergil to the nature of things, since I might say that he combines the skills of all ten Attic orators and still not be overstating the case. (Macrob. *Sat.* 5.1.18–20)

Macrobius places his dialogue in the 380s, just the time when Augustine was in Rome seeing Symmachus, but since Macrobius wrote in the 430s there are anachronisms in his picture of the Vergilian school. (Servius, for instance, would not have joined it yet.) But since the school was already established, in Rome of the 380s, especially by Aelius Donatus, Jerome's teacher, the picture is basically sound (Kaster 1988, 275–8).

That is the view of Vergil that Augustine encountered in Rome and repeated ever after. For him, Vergil is not only "the greatest poet" (*summus poeta*), "the best" (*optimus*) and "most illustrious" (*clarissimus*), but "the most learned" (*doctissimus*) one, who "never made a mistake (*nihil peccasse*), much less wrote anything not praiseworthy" (*Ench.* 17.5; *De civ. Dei* 1.3, 8, 19; *Contra Faustum* 22.25; *De util. cred.* 6.13). He was even "the most socially distinguished poet" (*nobilissimus, De civ. Dei* 7.9, 15.9). In the heady days just before and after his baptism, when Augustine broke a writer's block and produced work after work, he saw no conflict between the gods guiding Aeneas and God guiding him and his pupils and friends. He even applied to the Christian deity Vergil's titles for Jove or Apollo. When he rejoices at a comment by his student Licentius, he imitates Aeneas, crying "So let the father of gods act, and so act lofty Apollo!" (*De ord.* = *Aen.* 10.875). He even invokes his God with Vergil's line for Jove (*De cons. evang.* 1.18; *Aen.* 10.100):

> Tum pater omnipotens, rerum cui summa potestas.

> All powerful Father, supreme above all things.

His and his pupils' joint search for wisdom is compared regularly to the epic labors of the *Aeneid*. When a student falters under Augustine's questioning, he rallies him with Turnus' words to his warriors (*Contra acad.* 2.18; *Aen.* 11.424):

> cur ante tubam tremor occupant artus?

> Why tremble when the trumpet has not blown?

The student, in a bolder moment, compares his search for truth to Venus' command to Aeneas (*Contra acad.* 1.14; *Aen.* 1.401):

> perge modo et, qua te ducit via, dirige gressum.

> Wherever the path leads you, follow it.

Augustine encourages his pupils with a play on the words of Arruns to Apollo: "Let us devotees, relying on ties of faith, tread down the wicked flame of smoky lusts" (*adgrediamur, freti pietate cultores, et vestigiis nostris ignem perniciosum fumosarum cupiditatum opprimamus, De ord.* 1.10). He is referring to *Aen.* 11.787–8:

> et medium freti pietate per ignem
> cultores multa premimus vestigia pruna

> Your devotees rely on ties of faith
> Amidst the fire, treading hot coals down.

There is a kind of fighting excitement in the continual equation of the search for truth with epic struggle. At one point Augustine applies to his students' project Vulcan's cry to his workers: "Make armor for man readying toward war!" (*arma acri facienda viro, Contra acad.* 2.22; *Aen.* 8.441). Elsewhere he equates the Skeptics' errors with the monster Cacus (*Aen.* 8.193), or with Sinon's in pleading for the Trojan horse (*Aen.* 2.152). In another place he describes the elusive truth as shape-shifting like Proteus (*Contra acad.* 3.22, 3.30, 3.11; *Geo.* 4.387); later he would compare the tricky Satan to Proteus (*De civ. Dei* 10.10). In these animated early dialogues with his bright students (including the brightest, his own son), Augustine is not just teaching Vergil but teaching *through* Vergil, making the poet a flexible medium of communication, just as he would use Vergil's boxing match to deal with the grumpy Jerome.

And Vergil is not useful only in the dialogues. At this point in his life, Augustine planned to write an entire cycle of treatises on the liberal arts. He finished only one of these, his *Music*, but in that work he uses examples of metrical musicality from Vergil (*De musica* 2.2, 3.3, 4.31, 5.3, 5.9). If he had finished his project, the whole cycle would no doubt have been crowded with words from his favorite poet. At this point Vergil is "our poet" (*poeta noster, Contra acad.* 3.9). Augustine's view of Vergil was much as Dante's would be, as a type of pagan wisdom leading to even higher things. But that attitude did not last.

Renouncing Vergil

Those who know how Augustine loved and used and taught Vergil may be surprised to learn that he quotes the poet far less frequently than his contemporary churchman Ambrose (Diederich 1931, 124; Hagendahl 1958, 276). But Ambrose and Jerome, though they cite Vergil often, do so casually, without as deep an engagement as

Augustine shows; and besides, Augustine went through a middle period of his life when he developed scruples about citing pagan literature. When he became a bishop, he wanted to devote his and readers' attention to the Bible, and he decided that pagan authors should "be called to witness only on points of style, since these writers serve us only verbally, not for matters of fact or viewpoint" (*Quaest. in Hept.* 1.31). Now Vergil was no longer "our poet," but "their poet" when Augustine wrote to fellow Christians, or "your poet" when he addressed pagans (*poeta illorum, De civ. Dei* 5.12; *Serm.* 105.10, 374.2; *poeta ipsorum, Serm.* 81.9; *auctor ipsorum, Serm.* 241.5; *poeta vestrarum litterarum, Epist.* 91.2). This is the period in which he derided his earlier self for weeping over Dido and for filling his head with "visions of absurdity, a horse of wood cargoed with men, and Troy in flames, and Creusa ghosting by" (*Conf.* 1.21, 22; *Aen.* 2.772):

> infelix simulacrum atque ipsius umbra Creusae

Augustine implicitly blames Dido for resorting to witchcraft against Aeneas (*De civ. Dei* 21.6, 8). He generally mocks Vergil's lines when he recalls them at all, or he uses them satirically, as when he tells Manicheans attacking changes in Jewish law: "We cannot say, can we, that right is a shifty and reversible thing?" (*numquid iustitia varia est et mutabilis? Conf.* 3.13) – a takeoff on *Aen.* 4.569–70 (*varium et mutabile semper / femina,* "woman is always a shifty and reversible thing"). This uneasy and equivocal way with Vergil in Augustine's middle years would lead to a different use of him in 410, when Alaric's army of Visigoths sacked the city of Rome.

Using Vergil

Augustine resumed his frequent quotation from Vergil, but now for apologetic purposes, in response to the fall of Rome. This project would spread out over fourteen years as his propaganda over Alaric's attack turned into his massive book, *The City of God*. Some wealthy refugees from the ravaged capital showed up in Augustine's Africa, and he wrote originally to console, defend, and instruct them. He had to address several issues at once, fighting as it were on multiple fronts. First, there was the task of a *consolatio* to people who had been raped or plundered. He said that raped women were guiltless, and should not imitate the pagan Lucretia, who committed suicide. Her sin was greater than Tarquin's: "He took her body; she took her life. He raped, she murdered" (*De civ. Dei* 1.19). Then there was the charge that the plunderers of Rome were, after all, Christians (though Arian Christians) – should their act be blamed on their religion? Besides, some pagans said that Rome had stood unconquered under its founding gods, and only the Christian God failed to protect it.

Augustine found uses for Vergil on all these fronts. He ridicules the founding gods of Rome – they had been brought to Italy by Aeneas, who took them from Troy, a city they had failed to protect. Vergil himself had called them "conquered gods" and "gods on the run" (*victos penates, Aen.* 1.68; *victos deos,* 2.320; cf. *fugitivos deos, Serm.* 81.9). Aeneas had to take custody of the gods, not they of him (*De civ. Dei* 1.3).

These were "guardians who could not guard" (*De civ. Dei* 1.2). Why should the conquered gods of Troy make Rome unconquerable? Did Aeneas bring with him a blessing or a bane, a *numen* or an *omen* (*Serm.* 81.9)?

As for the religion of Alaric's army, Augustine quotes passage after passage from book 2 of the *Aeneid* to show that the atrocities committed by the pagan Greeks were far worse than what had happened to Rome, where Alaric spared the shrines and priests (*De civ. Dei* 1.1–2). He also mocks the claims to lasting power and happiness in pagan Rome. For him, Jove's promise to Aeneas' descendants is blasphemous (*De civ. Dei* 2.29; *Aen.* 1.278–9):

> his ego nec metas rerum nec tempora pono;
> imperium sine fine dedi.

> No limit I impose of place or time,
> Reign worldwide I bestow without an end.

In a sermon on the fall of Rome, Augustine taunts Vergil with the obvious falsehood of Jove's promise that Rome's empire would never end. Then he imagines Vergil squirming out of the lie:

"What was I to do? I was a phrase salesman to the Romans. How could I flatter them without falsehood? Yet even here I hedged my bet. When I said

> Reign worldwide I bestow without an end,

I brought in their Jove to mouth it. I did not tell the lie in my own voice, but put it in Jove's false voice. As a feigned god, his prophecy was a farce. Do you want assurance that I knew better? Elsewhere [*Geo.* 2.498], when I was not using Jove as an oracle but speaking in my own voice, I forswore

> The Roman state and the realms that die.

See? – I was not hiding that realms do die." (*Serm.* 105.10)

(Servius *ad loc.*, still thinking Rome eternal, limited "realms that die" (*perituraque regna*) to kingdoms *subject to* Rome. But modern commentators of the *Georgics* (e.g., Thomas 1988; Mynors 1990) agree with Augustine.) Hagendahl thinks that this invented speech was a great insult to Vergil, saying that he was a "phrase salesman" (*venditor verborum*). But that is just the term Augustine used of himself when he was an orator to the emperor (*Conf.* 9.13). His job, he said, was to flatter with falsehood, "and the more I lied, the more would my lies be praised by those who knew they were lies" (*Conf.* 7.9).

The ancient Romans, Augustine now sees, claimed prerogatives that belong only to God (*De civ. Dei* 1, *praef.*, quoting *Aen.* 6.852–3):

> hae tibi erunt artes, pacisque imponere morem,
> parcere subiectis, et debellare superbos.

> Your artistry to set the terms of peace,
> Spare those who yield, and beat resisters down.

God's role is properly described in the Bible (Proverbs 3.34): "God rebukes resisters, but sheds his grace on the lowly." The quest of Aeneas, which Augustine once compared to the search for wisdom or the providentially guided path through life, he now dismisses as a mere obsession with power (*libido dominandi*).

From ridiculing the conquered gods of Troy, Augustine moves on to attack the whole polytheistic system of Vergil. Why praise incestuous gods, he asks, quoting the description of Hera as "wife and sister to Jove" (*De civ. Dei* 1.4, 7.3, 4.10; *Aen.* 1.47). Why praise gods who can be overthrown by humans, he asks, quoting Juno, "I am defeated by Aeneas" (*De civ. Dei* 10.21; *Aen.* 7.310). Though Vergil says that "Jove pervades the whole" (*Ecl.* 3.60), there are other deities opposed to him in parts of the universe (*De civ. Dei* 4.9–10, 7.9). Augustine is fiercely satirical in his attack on the divine pettinesses of Vergil's "gang of godlets" (*turba minutorum deorum, De civ. Dei* 4.10).

Remembering Vergil

Though Augustine felt a duty to renounce Vergil, as Aeneas renounced Dido, the memory still haunted him, to the very end of his life. He could not always resist the fascination of the poet. He takes several occasions to praise what he calls "Vergil's finest line" (*nobilissimus Vergilii versus, De civ. Dei* 7.9, 30; *Enchir.* 5.16; *Geo.* 2.490):

> felix qui potuit rerum cognoscere causas.

> Happy the one who knows what makes things be.

Another satirical use of Vergil came in Augustine's late and protracted polemic against Julian of Eclanum. Julian cited Vergil's *Georgics* to show that animal couplings show a sex without original sin. Augustine answers that Julian would reduce humans to the level of animals (*Contra Iul.* 4.38, *opus imperfectum*; for the extensive use of *Geo.* 3 and 4 in this exchange, see Schelkle 1939, 30–7).

Augustine returned again and again (*De civ. Dei* 14.3, 5, 7, 8, 21.3) to Vergil's description of human passions at *Aen.* 6.733:

> hinc metuunt cupiuntque, dolent gaudentque.

> Men fear things or desire, feel sorrow or take joy.

This is a line Jerome admired, too, for its inclusive economy, as describing all human emotion in a single verse (*in Iohel* 1.4). From the same passage, Augustine cites several times the "dread compulsion" (*dira cupido*) that makes people yearn to be reunited to their bodies, according to Anchises' speech in the underworld (*De civ. Dei*

14.3, 22.26; *Aen.* 6.721). Book 6 of the *Aeneid* obviously drew Augustine's thoughts
to the Christian hell. In fact, his longest quotation from Vergil is this (*De civ. Dei*
21.13; *Aen.* 6.733–41):

> Men fear things or desire, feel sorrow or take joy,
> Yet see no sky from their imprisoned clay.
> No, not when they have left the light at last,
> They still have purged not all the body's taints,
> Their soul is still mysteriously immired,
> They must be punished out of their own past –
> Some aerated in the winds, or cleansed
> In rinsing pools, or plunged in caustic fire.

This whole sequence in book 6 impresses Augustine. He calls these verses "dazzling"
(*luculenti, De civ. Dei* 14.3; *Aen.* 6.730–2):

> igneus est ollis vigor et caelestis origo
> seminibus, quantum non corpora noxia tardant
> terrenique hebetant artus moribundaque membra.

> Men's souls are things of fire, from heaven sown,
> When not encumbered by a clogging flesh
> Weighed down toward death in all one's earthy limbs.

There was a fire in Augustine's soul that never quite went out. It was lit by Vergil.

FURTHER READING

For Augustine's use of Vergil, the basic books are by Schelkle (1939) and Hagendahl (1967).
The former usefully establishes Augustine's knowledge of the ancient commentators on Vergil
(mainly Pompeius and Aelius Donatus), but exaggerates his reliance on them. Hagendahl
rightly argues that Augustine's deep love of Vergil, and his years of teaching him, made him
draw more directly on the works by the poet than on those about the poet.

The great biography of Augustine is Peter Brown's (2000). The book in which Augustine
cites Vergil most often is *The City of God*.

CHAPTER TEN

Felix Casus
The Dares and Dictys Legends of Aeneas

Sarah Spence

It all begins with the fall of Troy. The epic tradition that starts with Homer never loses sight of Troy's demise. Whether the authors that follow Homer choose to tell of Troy's antecedents, diaspora, or ruins, the story of the Trojan War creates the beginning of Western epic as we know it. In Apollonius Rhodius' *Argonautica*, for example, the story of Jason and Hercules provides the background to the battle at Troy. In Vergil's *Aeneid*, the focus is placed on the after-effects of the war, especially, but not exclusively, on the losing Trojans. And Lucan's *Bellum Civile*, although ostensibly telling a more contemporary tale of the civil wars of Caesar and Pompey, nevertheless includes a striking description of the ruins of Troy, which Caesar visits in book 9. Moreover, largely because of Vergil, the fall of Troy is linked as well with the origin of the idea of nation, broadly speaking: the story of Aeneas' journey and founding of Rome after the fall of Troy sketches a path for future imperial success and links empire with epic as it identifies the founding of a nation with both the genre of epic and Troy (Quint 1993). The destruction of Troy becomes a founding myth, not so much of Greece as of Rome, and every culture that traces its roots to Rome finds itself responding to Troy in some fashion (Gorra 1887, 69).

Although the main story about Aeneas after the fall is the one told by Vergil, there is a second account, a Rosencrantz-and-Guildenstern-type adaptation of the main myth. In this thread Aeneas is not hero but traitor, and it is his actions, not those of Sinon, that lead to the introduction of the horse into Troy and the subsequent disaster. This version was told by two authors, Dictys Cretensis and Dares Phrygius, one ostensibly Greek and one, surprisingly, Trojan. These tales remain, to classicists at least, largely underplayed and unknown (see, e.g., Rudd 2006). Yet these versions of the story were not unknown in the Middle Ages. On the contrary, as A. Joly notes, "l'auctorité d'Homère [est] ainsi ruinée et celle de Dares bien établie" (Joly 1870, 161). The focus of this chapter will be on just how the stories of Dares and Dictys and their representation of Aeneas as traitor coexist throughout the Middle Ages with the more mainstream account of Vergil's hero. While the *Aeneid* remains the predominant version of the story of Aeneas, known by heart by every student, it appears to be the case that the alternative versions offered by Dares and Dictys were well known and influential. The presence of these anti-*Aeneids* challenged the authority of the Vergilian tale, even as the story of Aeneas as both hero and traitor continued to provide the preeminent foundation myth of nationhood. As we shall see, while certain origin stories clearly stem from the *Aeneid*, others, it would appear, owe their inspiration to the alternative tale of Aeneas as told by Dares and Dictys.

***

Dictys Cretensis writes a prose history of Troy, *Ephemeris belli Troiani*, that covers events from the abduction of Helen to the death of Ulysses in six books. Although the work claims to be written before the time of Homer (since its author was ostensibly a participant in the war), the text is dated to the fourth century CE. All of the extant manuscripts are Latin and are divided into two groups, one introduced by a letter, the other by a preface. The authorial stance of the narrator is that of translator of the original Greek text, narrated by Dictys, a Greek fighter in the war. A complex frame tale introduces the work, describing how the manuscript, written in Phoenician on linden tablets, was buried in a metal box with its author, where it remained until the coffin opened during an earthquake. This frame tale was long thought to be fictitious, but at the turn of the twentieth century a Greek papyrus fragment was discovered that contained, on one side, lines corresponding to the Latin text and, on the other, data dated to 206 CE. Through this, the narrator was shown to be indeed a translator from the Greek, and the frame tale was deemed to be accurate (Frazer 1966; Eisenhut 1973).

The translation is free, with the first five books offering a more or less literal rendering, the last a summary of the stories of the Greeks' activities following the war. It would appear from Byzantine sources that this last book is a condensation of the last four books of the original. Both the letter and the preface set out the circumstances of original composition and discovery of the text, reputedly found in Dictys' tomb and brought by shepherds to a Praxis (or Eupraxides). The preface claims that the work was discovered in the "thirteenth year of Nero's reign," and so can be dated after 66 CE, if we assume that Dictys wrote this as the introduction to the text. Dictys' name would seem to have been chosen to emphasize the Greek, particularly Cretan, bias of the text.

Dares Phrygius, whose work, *De excidio Troiae historia*, is dated to the sixth century CE, offers forty-four short chapters that run from the Argonautic expedition to the destruction of Troy as narrated by a participant in these events. It is known only through a single medieval Latin version, and, like Dictys, is introduced by a letter that claims it to be a Latin translation from the Greek, though no Greek original has been found (Polverini 1984, 1000). Dares thus offers, much like the *Argonautica* of Apollonius Rhodius, the antecedent to the Trojan tale, even as it establishes a context for both his narrative and that of Dictys.

Both authors tell stories that provide, rather than continuations of Homer, refutations of Homer's version of the war. Capitalizing on their purported eyewitness stance, each claims to know the real truth and thus assert an authority that matches the *gravitas* Homer had acquired. Moreover, as R.M. Frazer has pointed out, the two authors work to counter criticisms of Homer, such as his tendency to picture gods as "thieves and adulterers" and have them engage in battle with humans (Frazer 1966, 6). They also suppress details the warriors could not have known, and they rationalize the divine machinery. For example, Dictys writes:

> While we were hastening to sail, Agamemnon…having gone some way from the camp, noticed a she-goat grazing near a grove of Diana and, feeling no awe because of the place, struck it through with his spear. Soon afterward, either because of heavenly wrath or atmospheric contamination, a plague began to attack us. Day after day it raged with greater and greater violence, destroying many thousands as it passed indiscriminately through herds and army, laying waste everything that stood in its way, there being no abatement, no end to death. (1.19)

One could understand the eccentricity of this perspective as a narrative gambit: by late antiquity numerous approaches to the Homeric epics had been played out in the Greek, Hellenistic, and Roman traditions that followed in Homer's wake. With the general questioning of the authority of pagan authors that accompanied the rise of Christian narratives – in the writings of Lactantius, Orosius, and Augustine in particular – the recasting of the prime foundation myth in a form that asserted its own authority while debunking that of the earlier gods would seem believable and expected. As revisions of Homer's Troy, the stories of Dares and Dictys served as well to compete with Vergil's account of the fall.

Yet the role these two texts played in the years that followed is entirely different and unforeseeable. For one thing, as David Benson has lucidly argued, the eyewitness status Dares and Dictys claim to the events of the Trojan War grant them greater authority in the medieval world than the versions of Homer or even Vergil. The fact that Homer's texts were largely unread by the Western medieval audience only served to heighten their questionable status. For a medieval chronicler, "eyewitness testimony is the surest guarantee of truth" (Benson 1980, 10). To a medieval audience, "Dares and Dictys would have appeared to be eyewitness reporters who preserved the truth of their own time just as contemporary clerical chroniclers were preserving the present" (Benson 1980, 11). In contrast to the assumed fictitious accounts of ancient epic (largely because they were reported in the third person), eyewitness accounts are deemed truthful, and the stories of Dares and Dictys surface as the most dependable accounts of this critical event.

As a result, Dares in particular becomes known as the author of the true account of Troy. These references to Dares do not necessarily reflect a choice between the two tales but, rather, suggest that the two late antique tales were often thought of as one and referred to as "Dares," as, for example, in the works of Isidore and Ordericus Vitalis. Both Ordericus Vitalis and Isidore of Seville mention him as the first Gentile historian; Hugh of Saint Victor claims him as the first historian of Troy, with Herodotus named as the second. The anonymous author of the *Itinerarium Peregrinorum* cites Dares as an eyewitness of the battle. Through the popular adaptations by French author Benoît de Saint-Maure (ca. 1160) and the Sicilian judge Guido delle Colonne (ca. 1287), Dares and Dictys offer the primary source for the Trojan War and its aftermath. By this route, the marginal, late antique riff on the battle at Troy becomes canonized as authentic; the variants vie with and in some cases unseat the traditional standardized myths (Faivre d'Arcier 2006, introduction and ch. 4).

The best known example of influence from these texts is the story of Troilus. Troilus, the Trojan hero mentioned once by Homer and named in passing by Vergil (*Aen.* 1: depicted in the murals at Carthage dying at the hands of Achilles), is extrapolated by Benoît de Saint-Maure and fashioned into a more central character. In addition, Benoît creates the possibility for a romantic triangle among Troilus, the Greek Diomedes, and Briseida (the medieval Latin version of Briseis), taking descriptions of all three from Dares, chapters 12 and 13. To these Benoît also adds the fact from Dares that Troilus wounds Diomedes, and then he spins out a romance between Troilus and Briseida. This story of Troilus is retold in the thirteenth century by Guido, who follows Benoît's story closely, especially in terms of these characters, as in the following characteristic passage:

> Troilus, however, after he had learned of his father's intention to go ahead and release Briseida and restore her to the Greeks, was overwhelmed and completely wracked by great grief, and almost entirely consumed by tears, anguished sighs, and laments, because he cherished her with the great fervor of youthful love and had been led by the excessive ardor of love into the intense longing of blazing passion. (19.127–33; trans. Meek, 156)

From Guido's account Boccaccio then expands the romance in his *Filostrato* (ca. 1335) and provides the main source for Chaucer's *Troilus and Criseyde* (1381–6), which, in turn, influences Shakespeare's *Troilus and Cressida* (1602), among other works.

But the accounts of Dares and Dictys do something else as well. While the purpose of Dares' and Dictys' tales may have been to tell an alternative version of the Troy story, what these texts offer to the Middle Ages is a version of the privileged story of Troy that undermines its very authority. Particularly in the case of Vergil's Aeneas, whose story was transmitted to the medieval world with an aura of sanctity that virtually matched that of the Apocrypha, the alternative histories offered by Dares and Dictys showed a character that did not rival and therefore failed to threaten the newer heroes. Gabrielle Spiegel has written that "[t]he prescriptive authority of the past made it a privileged locus for working through the ideological implications of social changes in the present and the repository of contemporary concerns and desires. As a locus of value, a revised past held out for contemporaries the promise of a perfectible present" (Spiegel 1993, 5). Spiegel here is referring to thirteenth-century Franco-Flemish prose: a similar opportunity is offered by Dares and Dictys to the medieval world, starting in the ninth century. Through the texts of Dares and Dictys a window is opened on the story of Troy that enables a dual and seemingly contradictory action: the authority of Troy is retained, even as its iconic perfection is questioned.

Moreover, it is in the story of Aeneas that these two aspects of the Dares and Dictys' tradition – the eyewitness account and the dismantling of authority – are joined. In Benoît, Hecuba (l. 26163) blames both the fall of Troy and the death of Priam on Aeneas, who saw it with his own eyes ("vos oilz veiant"). Aeneas thus is identified as an eyewitness, and the events of Aeneas' character play out on a textual level the stance the authors take in the tradition as a whole; through their own eye-witness accounts Dares and Dictys authorize their renegade status, a status made even more compelling through the actions of the hero-renegade, Aeneas. In both Dares' and Dictys' hands Aeneas is a scoundrel, a turncoat who, with Antenor, colludes with the Greeks to bring about the fall of Troy. This Aeneas clearly runs counter to the hero of Vergil's epic, which has a strong and ongoing medieval presence, from Augustine's *Confessions* through Dante's *Divina Commedia* and beyond. Aeneas as hero and founder of the Roman nation remains the primary Aeneas myth, and Aeneas retains his Vergilian cachet as pious hero, adapting to its new Christian surroundings as *pietas* is replaced by piety. Yet, in addition, the character of Aeneas as recounted in both Dares and Dictys is mentioned explicitly in, for instance, Guido's *Historia*, where Aeneas is a co-conspirator marked by treason and treachery, and in the *Laud Troy Book* (ca. 1400), which describes Aeneas in the most extreme terms:

> 3it was it neuere wonne with fyght,
> With the Gregeis, ne with ther myght;
> Hit was be-trayed falsly – Alas! –
> With Antenor and Eneas. (ll. 4703–6)

Given that Aeneas' role in these later texts is so central, it seems important to get a sense of just how Aeneas is portrayed in Dares and Dictys, in an effort to explore how he might influence other significant medieval texts.

In Dictys' account, Aeneas appears in the first book, where he accompanies Paris in his abduction of Helen. This introduction is crucial for his role later in the work. In the last chapter of the fourth book (4.22) the Trojans, losing, think first of returning Helen in hopes of ending the war. When, however, Deiphobus takes her away, Priam gives in, after Aeneas "heaped insults upon him," and orders Antenor to go to the Greeks and seek an end to the war. The Greeks decide that if Aeneas remains faithful to them he will get part of the booty. Aeneas goes to Priam to propose terms of peace; the king listens and agrees. A long diatribe follows denigrating Priam's collusion in the fall of Troy: as betrayer of the Trojan inheritance he himself is worthy of being betrayed. Throughout the machinations Aeneas is paired with Antenor: Antenor is the first traitor, but Aeneas soon follows suit. In the end Aeneas remains at Troy only to be expelled by the Greeks with Antenor:

> After our departure, Aeneas, who had been left behind at Troy, tried to drive Antenor out of the kingdom....Antenor, who had learned what was happening, refused him admittance. And so Aeneas was forced to set sail. Taking all of his patrimony, he departed from Troy and eventually arrived in the Adriatic Sea...Here he and those who were with him founded a city, which they called Corcyra Melaena. (5.17; trans. Frazer 1966)

In Dares' version, Aeneas is introduced in the twelfth chapter, having been linked with Paris in the ninth. He is described as "auburn-haired, stocky, eloquent, courteous, prudent, pious, and charming. His eyes were black and twinkling." From the thirty-seventh chapter on he plays a large role as he goes to Priam to beg for peace, betrays Troy, hides Polyxena, and, in the last chapter, leaves Troy. In this account, Aeneas and Antenor are both depicted as traitors and, what is worse, they are shown to be indirectly responsible for the death of Priam:

> That night, Antenor and Aeneas were ready at the gate....Neoptolemus, breaking in, slaughtered the Trojans and pursued...Priam. (ch. 41)

The depiction of Aeneas in both of these works is shocking. In both Dares' and Dictys' accounts of the fall of Troy, Aeneas is portrayed not only as scoundrel but also as traitor to the cause. His future successes are of necessity foreshortened and emphasis is placed on his role in the Trojan defeat at Troy.

While the Vergilian tradition of Aeneas as hero persists through the Middle Ages, many of the medieval treatments of Troy rely instead on these versions found in Dares and Dictys. A late-fourteenth- or early-fifteenth-century redaction reads: *Atque datis dextris, loquitur de proditione / Enee mandat subito que res sit agenda* ("Shaking on it, Aeneas speaks of betrayal and orders what must presently be done," Godi 1967, 812–13). In his twelfth-century *roman*, Benoît de Saint-Maure uses plot elements and character descriptions about Aeneas from Dares, while adding his own interpretations. Most strikingly, Benoît identifies Aeneas and Antenor with Christian traitors: Antenor is called Judas, Aeneas Satan. Not only does this contrast strikingly with the cento tradition, in which Aeneas is clearly identified as a Christ figure, but it also opens the door for further exploration of the Aeneas myth in the Middle Ages. Not only are the accounts of Dares and Dictys adapted directly by texts such as those of Benoît and Guido delle Colonne, as we have seen, but also the account of Aeneas as scoundrel is woven into the more mainstream account of Aeneas as national hero, to produce a hybrid figure that proves ultimately very useful to a number of later stories. While the direct adaptation of the Dares and Dictys stories is relatively easy to trace, as in the Troilus story, I would argue that the more indirect influence causes the portrayal of Aeneas to provide material for founding tales including, most notably, the *Chanson de Roland*.

***

The *Chanson de Roland* tells the story of Saracen trickery and Frankish pride that results in slaughter of the French, who are under the rule of the Emperor Charlemagne (manuscripts: Mortier 1940–4; edition: Duggan 2005). Because Charlemagne, the historic figure, saw himself as a second Caesar, an enlightened emperor whose imperial drive is mitigated by his Christian manifest destiny, his adaptation – and that of those who write about him – of the Roman past is particularly complex. Unlike the mythical Brut, founding father of Britain and fictional Trojan who, after the war, reputedly made his way to Great Britain, Charlemagne sees himself as heir to the Roman past and forerunner of the French future. He is the defining force of the nation, the figure who will translate things Roman into what will become France (Beaune 1991, 276–81).

By the twelfth century, the ancient tradition was trifurcated, as noted in the works of Jean Bodel (1165–1210), into the "matters" of Britain, France, and Greece; and the tales were offered as three separate legends: those of Arthur, Charlemagne, and Alexander. The story of Troy was there, but muffled. In the Anglo-Norman tradition of France and Britain though, these three branches take on different roles. Arthur's story is perceived as one concerned with origins, while the transfer of empire to Rome is attributed to Caesar and to the Franks by Charlemagne, thought to have brought the four faculties of humanism from Rome. M. de Troppau argues that the Christianization of Parisian culture and the transfer of learning were due to Charlemagne, and that the two cities of Rome and Paris were differentiated not by what they knew but by what they specialized in: Rome for law and Paris for theology. (Such is the argument of de Troppau as cited in Beaune 1991, 277.) The link with the past is thus provided by a current leader, Charlemagne, whose connection with antiquity is one of renovation and differentiation: he saw his task as one entailing the transfer of learning rather than the handing over of a body of knowledge (Beaune 1991, 277). And yet, as A. Joly points out, Homer was cited by Bede and was a name taken at Charlemagne's court: the ancient past remains important (Joly 1870, 638). Continuity and adaptation of culture were credited entirely to Charlemagne, who was seen as the founder of the French nation.

When we turn, then, to the founding story of the French nation, the *Chanson de Roland*, a story that defines French culture even as it revolves around the figure of Charlemagne, we might well expect to find the Trojan influence explicitly acknowledged. Certainly there is evidence of tying Troy to the founding of France. A Carolingian story specifically links the fall of Troy with the origin of the Frankish nation in the universal history of Frechulf of Lisieux. Here we find an explicit assertion that the Franks are derived from the Trojans. What is striking about this account, however, is that the French line does not stem from Aeneas, who is identified as a traitor and a scoundrel suffering a deservedly bad end: *Qui…saevissimus esset, ac crudelissimus belligerator, et nulli parceret, ob tantam impietatem a Deo ictu fulminis percussus interiit* ("He who was the harshest and cruelest of warriors, sparing nobody, died, on account of such impiety, struck down by a lightning bolt from God"). Rather, the French line derives from "Phrygas" (a reference, perhaps, to Dares Phrygius?) who is identified as Aeneas' twin (*germani fuerunt*). According to this tale, when Aeneas traveled to Latium, Phrygas journeyed to Phrygia. While Aeneas' line died out in Italy, that of Phrygas thrived, as it made its way *per multas regiones* ("through many lands"), finally choosing a king, renowned for his prowess in battle, named Francio, *ex quo Franci vocantur* ("from whom the French are named") (Frechulf, *Historiae* 1.2.26). Frechulf splits the character of Aeneas into two, and assumes the heritage of the good Aeneas, Francio, for the line of the Franks. It is striking that the language he uses of the "bad" Aeneas specifically negates terms Vergil uses to describe his hero: rather than being pious and aiming to spare the suppliant, as Anchises advises his son to do in book 6 of the *Aeneid*, this Aeneas is impious and spares no one. In addition, this Aeneas is described in terms that Vergil often uses for the enemy: *saevus* ("harsh") and *crudelis* ("cruel"). Through his word choice, Frechulf demonizes Aeneas while retaining both the language of the Vergilian account and the connection to the authority of history through the creation of a double, Aeneas' twin, the good seed of the family.

What is particularly interesting about this account is how it blends the two Aeneas figures, that of the Vergilian text and that of the Dares' tradition. In a recent study of the manuscript tradition of Dares' work, Louis Faivre d'Arcier notes that during the Carolingian era the diffusion of the text was limited in number but broad in geographic range (Faivre d'Arcier 2006, 335). Dares is attested in the majority of the important intellectual centers, in particular in the Rhineland, at Lorsch, and at Reichenau; at the last there were not one but two copies of the manuscript. There are copies in the north of Gaul as well: one in Saint-Riquier, where it is listed in the inventory of 831, and one at Saint-Martin de Tours. Dictys, likewise, was available: an extract was discovered at Metz in the last century, which has been dated to the ninth century (Faivre d'Arcier 2006, 336, 338).

Between the tenth and twelfth centuries in France, the interest in Dares seems first to have waned and then to have increased in complexity. The circulation of Dares in France grows even more intense starting in the eleventh century, first by the quotation of several lines in the manuscripts of the *Ilias Latina*, then by four attestations of complete manuscripts, copied in different locations. Of particular interest is MS Pt (= Paris, Bibliothèque nationale de France, lat. 10307 and Bibl. Apostolica del Vaticano, Reg. lat. 1625), dated to the eleventh century, in which the Dares' account was copied as a gloss in the exterior column of a Vergilian manuscript. (There are a total of nine extant manuscripts that contain both the Vergilian and Daretian versions of the Aeneas story; see Faivre d'Arcier 2006, 95–101, 105). Here we have quite literally the two versions of the Aeneas myth side by side, a striking parallel to Frechulf's story of the Franks.

As the founding epic of the French nation, the *Chanson de Roland* could be expected to participate in this enterprise, much as *Brut* drew on the Trojan past to link its populace directly to the Greco-Roman tradition. Frechulf had paved the way through the creation of Francio to do the same for France. Yet nothing, it would seem, could be farther from the truth. The story of the *Chanson* is based on a minor historical moment that took place in 778, in which the rearguard of Charlemagne's retreating army was attacked and destroyed. There is scant mention of the event in the chronicles; not until the eleventh century, and close to the time of the extant manuscripts, do we find repeated mention of "a song of Roland."

The song takes place on the spatial and temporal margins of France but serves a founding role in French identity and literature (Duggan 2005, introduction and bibliography). While the leader of the Franks, Charlemagne, and his army have been fighting for a long time in Spain, the king of the Saracens, Marsilion, agrees to pretend to surrender so that the Franks will withdraw. Charlemagne is persuaded to return home on the promise that Marsilion will soon follow him and convert to Christianity. The Franks, needing to send an ambassador to agree to the terms offered by Marsilion, decide to send Ganelon, Roland's stepfather; Ganelon betrays his side as he collaborates with the Saracens to wreak revenge on Roland, Charlemagne's bravest knight. Roland, with his companion Oliver and the other Twelve Peers, assumes control of the rearguard. In the most famous sequence in the *Chanson*, the Franks see a huge Saracen army approaching and Oliver, who is characterized as wise (*sage*), advises Roland, the brave (*preuz*), to blow his horn, or *olifant*. The battle occurs in two waves, and during the second attack Roland finally blows his horn, too late for rescue, but in the hopes that some dignity will be paid to the dead and that their death will be avenged. Roland's blast is so immense that it bursts his temples; in his near-death state he maims Marsilion, uses his horn as weapon, and dies, with his back to France, holding his sword and horn. Charlemagne returns, arrests Ganelon for treachery, and ultimately kills him at Aix. The widow of Marsilion is baptized and Charlemagne, visited by an angel, is finally able to rest.

The *Roland* is not a Trojan tale, yet its very failure to engage the Trojan past – a failure strikingly out of keeping with Charlemagne's own predilections and efforts – raises the question of the role of Troy in the *Chanson*. That the Troy tradition was available to the author of the *Roland* is made clear in the text:

> Li emperere par sa grant poëstét
> set anz tuz pleins ad en Espaigne estét;
> prent i chastels e alquantes citez.
> Li reis Marsilie s'en purcacet asez:
> al premier an fist ses brefs seieler,
> en Babilonie Baligant ad mandét –
> c'est amiraill, le viel d'antiquitét,
> tut survesquiéet e Virgili e Omer –

The emperor by his great power remained in Spain for seven full years; there he took castles and numerous cities. King Marsilion does what he must. In the first year, he commanded his letters be sealed; he sent a summons to Baligant in Babylon, the old emir, who has outlived both Vergil and Homer. (*laisse* 189, ll. 2609–16)

The thread that is alluded to here, the Troy tradition that begins with Homer and continues through Vergil into the Middle Ages, is clearly not a source for the *Roland*, although it might well have been. Vergil's text, as scholars such as Comparetti (1997) and Ziolkowski and Putnam (2008) have clearly shown, was available without interruption throughout the Middle Ages in Western Europe. In mentioning the Homeric tradition, the way is paved for thinking about the *Roland* in the context of the Greco-Roman tradition, and, given Charlemagne's own predilection, this seems far from unwarranted. By not engaging the Vergilian tradition head on, by discounting the founding of Rome in a story about the man who will found France, and who is credited with the creation of the past in Paris, the story of Troy is nonetheless inscribed – or, at least, its absence felt – in the *Roland*.

The *Roland* offers a foundation story unlike that of the *Aeneid*. Yet the story it tells displays characteristics of other foundation myths. The striking aspect of its narrative style, which doubles back on itself and tells the same event right away again, from a slightly different perspective, functions in this text as ekphrasis does in the Greco-Roman epic: the text stops, stalls, calls attention to itself. So, for example, in a key passage, as Oliver is urging Roland to blow his *olifant* and warn the Franks of the attack of the Saracens, we hear, in the Oxford version of the tale, not once but three times of Oliver's advice, in three successive *laisses* (83–5):

> Oliver: "Paien unt grant esforz;
> de noz Franceis m'i semble aveir mult poi.
> Cumpaign Rollant, kar sunez vostre corn,'
> si l'orrat Carles, si returnerat l'ost."

Oliver says: "The pagans have a huge army; our French, it seems to me, are very small. Friend Roland, sound your horn so Charlemagne will hear, so the forces will return."

> "Cumpainz Rollant, l'olifan car sunez,
> si l'orrat Carles, ferat l'ost returner,
> succurrat nos li reis ad sun barnet."

"Friend Roland, sound the horn, Charlemagne will hear, he'll have the army return; the king will come to aid us with his barons."

> "Cumpainz Rollant, sunez vostre olifan,
> si l'orrat Carles, ki est as porz passant;
> je vos plevis, ja returnerunt Franc."

"Friend Roland, sound your horn so Charlemagne will hear, who is in the pass; I promise you, the French will turn again…"

Defined by the Saracen enemy, featuring characters tormented by guilt and indecision, engaged in events transpiring on the edge of the world, this tale, in its starkest outlines, in fact, shares many qualities with the crusade narratives that were defining the Christian ethos throughout this era. In one such tale, the *Historia destructionis Troiae* mentioned above, the tale of Hercules starts the story (which will end with the capture of Jerusalem) as he marks out the edges of the known world. The *Roland* takes place in a similar setting, though the world is redefined as France, and the edge moves from Gibraltar to Roncevaux.

Yet these Christianized adaptations of the Trojan story are not epic like the *Roland*. In an effort to tie ancient to contemporary history these adaptations focus more on events than on character. The *Roland*, by contrast, is a study of character, and that character is overwhelmingly marked and defined by the presence of treachery. Marsilion, as a Saracen, is by definition a traitor. Ganelon, as turncoat, embodies the ease with which a Christian hero crosses the line. Roland is marked by bravery and then by pride, which is itself a form of treachery, since his actions destroy the Franks: he is, in a sense, the greatest traitor. The cluster of traitors surround and define Charlemagne, who is steadfast, loyal, and trusting: the parallels with the figure of Lucifer and God are clear, and it is Roland more than Ganelon, Roland, the brightest of the angels, the best of the knights, whose actions set everything else in motion.

Roland's treachery, however, is of a particular sort. Lucifer's betrayal is primarily personal. His opposition to God may have long-reaching consequences, but it does not frame itself in national terms. The image of a hero, a shining light, whose rebellious actions cause a disaster that gives rise to a nation, is more like the story of Aeneas as Dares and Dictys tell it. There, as here, the great hero, who is handsome, eloquent, and the best of his kind (and also joined by an accomplice, similar in character, different in degree), backs into a decision, it would appear, that causes, in its disastrous wake, the birth of a nation. Benoît, in causing Hecuba to call Aeneas Satan as she blames the fall of Troy on him, offers a parallel to seeing Roland as a Lucifer figure: the best knight who loses sight of the larger picture and, in the end, creates that picture as he sets the future in motion. In the case of Aeneas his actions lead to the fall of Troy and the death of Priam, out of which the Roman state is born; Roland functions narratively in a similar way, except that Charlemagne remains alive and ultimately reigns triumphant. As the embodiment of the future, Charlemagne absorbs some of the heroic qualities Dares and Dictys ascribe to those who carry the civilization forward.

The fact that the Roland story comes to us from chansons written several centuries after the event at Roncevaux adds weight to this argument (Short 2005, introduction). In the intervening years, as the story was told and retold alongside the various versions of the Troy story, Roncevaux became cast as a kind of medieval Troy which, in turn, caused Troy to be read back through Roncevaux with a consequent heightening of what must have been perceived as *felix culpa* implications and the role of treachery and its Satan-like instigators. It is a striking fact that the first resurgence of the Dares myth occurs, according to Faivre d'Arcier, "dans l'entourage des Pippinides" (Faivre d'Arcier 2006, 426). The complex cycle of influence apparently at work here would seem to be best understood in terms that Michel-André Bossy has suggested: the Roncevaux legend lent confirmation to, even as it was shaped by, the cyclical pattern of *translatio imperii*, where the fall of Troy that led to the rise of Rome is replayed by Charlemagne's revival of the Roman imperial mission, only to fall and be reborn, in the legend, through the victory over the Saracens that leads to an even stronger sense of manifest destiny and crusading zeal.

A thirteenth-century French translation of the Dares' story (MS BN fr. 20125) offers striking proof of this process as it interpolates material from the *Roland*. In the key scene between Aeneas and Priam, in which Aeneas urges Priam to sue for peace and Priam refuses, saying he will fight to the death, echoes of the *Roland* appear (full text in Jung 1996). A comparison with the earlier twelfth-century text of Benoît clarifies the innovations in the later work. In Benoît's text, Aeneas argues:

> Del cumbatre n'i a mes rien –
> Iceste chose sievent bien –
> Ne d'els en bataille sofrir
> Ne des portes contr'els ovrir.
> De vers nos est fete la guerre,
> Autre conseil covient a guerre
> C'est de pes fere, n'en sai plus. (ll. 24611–17)

To fight is sadly useless, and they know that well: we should neither fight them in battle, nor should we open the gates. As far as we're concerned, the war is over. We must find another solution, which is to make peace: I see no other way.

But in the thirteenth-century text: "Eneas parla moult belement et sans ire encontre. Et si dist que ce ne seroit mie raisons ne lor *preus* ne lor biens a ffaire, mes requeïssent pais, si feroient lor honor et que *sage*" (sec. 60, ll. 46–8: "Aeneas spoke eloquently and without any anger. And he said that there was no excuse, neither profit nor gain, but to seek peace: This would bring honor and was the wise thing to do"). The two italicized terms (my emphasis) have been added to the earlier account. Neither of these is found in Benoît's text, and neither is necessary for the meaning of the passage. But the two, *preus* and *sage*, are the two identifying terms for the brave Roland and the wise Oliver. It should be noted that the *preus* in this passage is used as a noun ("profit"), while the one associated with Roland is an adjective ("brave").

Moreover, in the passage that follows, the thirteenth-century version introduces a detail not present in the earlier text. In refusing to cease fighting, Priam argues that Aeneas and Antenor will demonstrate their loyalty to him by calling the Trojans to battle when they have heard "soner les cors et les bucines" (sec. 61, ll. 11–12: "the horns and trumpets sound"). In the lines that follow, it is the failure of these two to respond to the battle trumpets that leads to the downfall of Troy. The silence of Roland's *olifant* reverberates through this translation of Dares.

The renegade quality of the Dares and Dictys tales enables later cultures to use the pagan story without acknowledgment. The mainstream myth, which posits Aeneas as hero of the Trojans, works if allegorized, as in the late antique centos, or if transferred to Arthur's world, as in the twelfth-century *Eneas*, where Aeneas becomes a knight and the romance ends with his marriage to Lavinia. But neither of these approaches offers a structure suitable for a foundation legend. The *Eneas*, in particular, is a story about medieval, not ancient, culture: the use of pagan stories and myths, such as the key role played by the Judgment of Paris, is in the service of medieval values and cultures. By choosing instead the marginal version of the Trojan myth, one that emphasizes the negative aspect of pagan culture, no such allegorization is necessary, nor is the imposition of contemporary values on an inherited plot required. The story has the necessary values already in place: the myth is there, and it is a founding myth to boot. What changes between the Dares' and Dictys' version of Aeneas and the *Roland*'s depiction of a similar story of treachery is the role played by the wise leader. Priam offers an antecedent to Charlemagne. Yet Charlemagne's story in the *Roland* rewrites that part of the inherited myth, causing the leader to rise triumphant from the treachery of his best knight, causing the birth of a nation that is rooted in continuities, not interruptions. The *Roland* is the story of the continuity of tradition, and Charlemagne, as the Priam who lives to tell the tale, drives that point home. In addition to the literary influence noted above, the Digby collection at Oxford does include both the earliest manuscript of the Roland (MS Digby 23) and a complete copy of Dares (MS Digby 166).

The best proof of the fact that the *Roland* comes to replace the Troy story – that the use of the alternate *Aeneid* works to enable France to supplant Rome – comes in its aftermath. As Michel-André Bossy (2006) has recently shown, the *Roland* undergoes a phenomenal afterlife, in which it is read and reread, reproduced as serious, as funny, as lampoon, as history. Roncevaux becomes, in short, the Troy of French literature, the event without which no story about France can be told. It could, of course, have developed in this way without Troy, but the fact that it follows so closely the path taken by the Troy story, and that it, like Troy, tells a tale of success following disaster, suggests strong connections between the two tales. Moreover, the fact that the Dares and Dictys version of the fall includes within it a character that is marked by treachery suggests that the Trojan tradition the Roland apes is the one that sees the story in this way. Treachery was always a part of the Trojan myth: only in the hands of Dares and Dictys, and the context of Lucifer, does it become the central theme of the founding myth, one picked up by the *Roland* and its aftermath.

Dares and Dictys offer a complex retelling of the Aeneas myth. Were it not for resonances within the Biblical tradition in which the version comes to be read and contextualized, coupled with a need of the later cultures to discount the earlier myth while retaining its power, the versions by Dares and Dictys might well have disappeared from view. Instead, this alternate version of Aeneas as renegade hero emerges as central to the medieval appreciation of the ancient world. The tales of Dares and Dictys, and their representation of Aeneas as traitor, complicate the Vergilian tradition in the Middle Ages even as they offer an opportunity to medieval authors. A *felix culpa* that originates as a *felix casus*, the tale of Aeneas as told by Dares and Dictys becomes adapted to inform, among other stories, the founding tale of the French Middle Ages. The fall of Troy via the treachery (rather than the *pietas*) of the national hero affords a mechanism for representing not only the fall of the ancient world, but the rise of a future nation as well.

FURTHER READING

The best introduction to both Dictys and Dares is provided through R.M. Frazer's (1966) translation of the two works. In addition to the texts and notes, Frazer provides a lucid introduction to the works and their histories. The original texts are available in Teubner editions; Dares published in 1873 (ed. Meister), Dictys a century later (ed. Eisenhut). The forthcoming Loeb edition of both texts, edited and translated by Nicholas Horsfall, promises to offer a ready source, strong translation, and invaluable notes. Any further work on the texts of Dares and Dictys must begin with the monumental study of Louis Faivre d'Arcier. His *Histoire et géographie d'un mythe* (2006) offers multiple starting points for rich studies of the Dares and Dictys legacy. Rooted in an exhaustive catalogue of the known manuscripts, both Latin and vernacular, of the legends, Faivre d'Arcier's work offers the means for suggestive and rich studies of the importance of these legends. In addition, recent work by Marc-René Jung and Annamaria Pavano offers an entrée into these fields. Much remains to be done: the story of Troilus has long dominated the scholarship on Dares and Dictys, while studies of Aeneas and Antenor have lagged behind. Moreover, a full study of Priam's character in these texts and its influence on the depiction of medieval leaders could prove fruitful.

I have found the approaches taken by David Benson (1980), David Rollo (1998), and Gabrielle Spiegel (1993) on the relationship between legend and history in the Middle Ages particularly useful, and C. Beaune's (1991) study of the origin of the French nation wonderfully insightful. The Roland bibliography is huge: as noted in the chapter, the new edition of the French manuscripts under the general direction of Joseph Duggan offers a rich introduction to the complexities of this important work.

CHAPTER ELEVEN

Vergil in Dante

Rachel Jacoff

The awakening of Virgil by Dante is an arc of flame which leaps from one great soul to another. The tradition of the European spirit knows no situation of such affecting loftiness, tenderness, fruitfulness.

Ernst Robert Curtius (1953)

One of the best things about being a dantista is the intimacy with Vergil that it fosters. Many in my generation first came to Dante through T.S. Eliot, and Dante then led us back to Vergil and the other classical poets who were important to him. Vergil is present in Dante's *Commedia* both as a text (the *Aeneid*) and as a character. The *Aeneid* is the major non-Biblical subtext of Dante's poem, a source of references and allusions both small and large, serving as both the *Commedia*'s model epic and its foil. Dante thematizes his relationship to Vergil by rewriting the *Aeneid* in ways that suggest its limits as well as its virtues. This doubleness or ambivalence becomes a figure for the larger question of the relationship between Christian and classical culture, a relationship that Dante both vivifies and makes problematic. In his role as guide Vergil is both dignified and tender, "altissimo poeta" (*Inf.* 4.80) and "dolcissimo patre" (*Purg.* 30.50), as Curtius so eloquently affirms. Recent Dante scholarship has, however, been attentive to the way his authority is undercut as well as affirmed. Just as Vergil scholars have long been increasingly sensitive to the ways Vergil rewrites Homer, so Dante scholarship has become more aware of the dialogical nature of many of Dante's Vergilian allusions. Instead of reading these allusions as imitation or homage, we have learned to see them as strategic in Dante's ongoing poetic self-definition. As important as the *Aeneid* is to Dante's project, its "alta tragedìa" (*Inf.* 20.113) is contrasted to and finally appropriated by a Christian "comedìa" (*Inf.* 16.128; 21.2) which sets out to correct and complete the prior text as the New Testament was said to complete Hebrew scripture.

Vergil is famously the poet of *lacrimae rerum*, "the tears of things" (*Aen.* 1.461). Aeneas weeps as he sees the representations of the Trojan War at the temple of Juno in Dido's Carthage, and tears attend many other scenes of loss in the *Aeneid*. Greene (1999, 197–8) writes about the ambivalence that attends much of the weeping in the *Aeneid*. He sees the role of weeping in *Purgatorio* 30–31 as the supreme example of the Christian version of the epic *telos* of tears (Greene 1999, 199–200). St. Augustine, a schoolboy in Dido's Carthage, weeps for Dido, and later is filled with self-reproach for doing so. (See the chapter by Wills in this volume.) It is hard not to think of this moment when Dante, at the climax of the *Commedia*, weeps for Vergil, and is severely reproached by Beatrice who arrives to take Vergil's place as the pilgrim's guide. The reader, like Dante the pilgrim, has known from the beginning that Vergil would not accompany the pilgrim for the whole journey. Nonetheless, Vergil's actual disappearance comes as a shock both to the pilgrim and to the reader. Dante weeps, and we are deeply moved. The character Vergil is the affective heart of the *Commedia*, "the tragedy in the *Comedy*" (Hollander 1983), the source of the poem's purest pathos. Although Vergil is Dante's guide for nearly two-thirds of the poem, he is a pagan who, by the ground rules of Dante's Christian poem, is denied salvation. This is the *donnée* from which Dante creates a complex and provocative drama.

Vergil enters the *Commedia* in its first canto. Dante has left the dark wood and begun to climb upwards towards the rising sun when he is turned back by the appearance of three beasts. In the "gran diserto" (great wilderness) a figure suddenly appears, offering himself ("mi si fu offerto") to the frightened pilgrim in response to Dante's appeal for pity ("Miserere," in the Latin of the Psalms). The figure offers a capsule autobiography, speaking of his region, his historical moment, and his authorship of the *Aeneid*.

> …Not a man, I was formerly a man,
> and my parents were Lombards, Mantuans both by birth.
> I was born *sub Julio* though it was late, and I
> lived in Rome under the good Augustus in the time
> of the false and lying gods.
> I was a poet, and I sang of that just son of
> Anchises, who came from Troy, when proud Ilion
> was destroyed by fire.
>
> (*Inf.* 1.67–75; trans. Durling)

It is a galvanizing moment. Dante responds to Vergil with intense praise as "honor and light of the other poets," as his "master and author," as the source of the "bello stilo che mi ha fatto onore" ("the pleasing style that has won me honor," 1.87). Dante's understanding of Vergil's poem is immediately clear in the way he refers to Aeneas as the "son of Anchises," focusing on the filial piety of Vergil's hero. Dante's awareness of the sympathy Vergil bears both sides in the conflict his poem records is also clear in the way Dante subsequently has him speak of Italy for which "the virgin Camilla died of her wounds, and Euryalus, Turnus, and Nisus," alternating the names of the Trojan and native Italian victims. From the outset, then, it is clear that the Vergil of canto 1 is a historical figure and the poet of the *Aeneid*; he is not, as he was once read, a personification of Reason.

Vergil undertakes to guide Dante through "an eternal place," but he will leave the pilgrim to a "worthier soul" ("anima…più di me degna") to complete the journey.

Speaking, as a Roman would, of God as an "Emperor," he explains that he is forbidden to enter his city "because I was a rebel to his law." This puzzling statement is not borne out by any further glossing in the poem. Rather, the issue of Vergil's non-salvation is repeatedly framed in terms of his having no access to baptism, the gateway to salvation. Vergil explains several times that he, like other pre-Christian worthies, is denied salvation because he never knew Christ and therefore "did not adore God as was needful" (*Inf.* 4.37).

> Because of such defects, not for any other
> wickedness, we are lost, and only so far harmed that
> without hope we live in desire.
> (4.40–2; cf. *Purg.* 7.25–36)

Limbo

Vergil and the other virtuous non-Christians are given, in Dante's heterodox vision, a special place in Limbo, the first circle of Hell that Christianity traditionally allotted only to unbaptized infants (Padoan 1977, 103–24; Ianucci 1998). It is here that Dante stages his legitimization by the great poets of antiquity, the "bella scuola" (Homer, Vergil, Ovid, Lucan, and Horace) who welcome him and make him "sixth among such wisdom" (4.102). This is a key scene for Curtius' reading of Dante's relation to the poets of antiquity. Brownlee (1993) writes succinctly about Dante's relation to the four classical epic poets who are celebrated here. Dante's refigurations of Ovid, especially in *Paradiso*, have been the subject of much recent work (Jacoff and Schnapp 1991; Sowell 1991). As important as Ovid and Lucan, too, are for Dante, neither of them is a character in the poem and thus neither of them generates the powerful affective charge unique to Vergil. Limbo is modeled on Vergil's Elysium, with a hemisphere of light (enclosed, however, in darkness), a noble castle, a fair stream, and a meadow of fresh green. There are no active punishments, but sadness prevails ("grief without torture," 1.28) because the souls live without hope in desire, an endless desire "given them eternally for their grief" (*Purg.* 3.41–2). The absence of hope becomes Dante's critique of classical culture. This becomes clear when one reaches *Paradiso* 25 in which Dante claims for himself precisely that virtue, and says that his greatest hope is for the specifically Christian promise of the Resurrection. Although Dante's Limbo celebrates the achievements of non-Christian poets, artistic, civic, and intellectual figures, it remains a delimited sphere without access to the true "good of the intellect," the beatific vision of God. The word "honor" recurs throughout the canto, but that ultimately secular reward is the best that can be offered.

Inventions

Dante's departure from orthodoxy in his inclusion of classical figures in the Christian space of Limbo intensifies the conflict between the value of classical culture and its ultimate limits in a Christian universe. The same tension is evident in other scenes where Dante departs from tradition, scenes which centrally concern Vergil. For example, Dante makes the guardian figure of his Purgatory a pagan, Cato, whose salvation is thereby implied. Influenced by Lucan's portrayal of Cato's sacrificial suicide in the *Pharsalia* (2.306–13), Dante makes him a martyr for liberty, "one who rejects life for its sake" (1.72). He also reveals the fundamental freedom of his own imagination in such a surprising placement since Cato had been not only a pagan, but a suicide and an enemy of Caesar, categories that are punished with damnation in the *Inferno*. When Vergil asks Cato for aid for the sake of his wife Marcia who is a fellow Limbo dweller, he is abruptly corrected by Cato who dismisses the value of any such ties in the "new law" that obtains in Purgatory. We remember that Cato appears on Aeneas' shield "giving laws" (*Aen.* 8.670), but he speaks for a very different kind of law in Dante's poem (see further Mazzotta 1979, 14–65).

Another remarkable invention is Dante's portrayal of the Silver Latin poet Statius as a secret Christian. Although the fratricidal violence of the *Thebaid* makes Thebes an emblematic site in the *Inferno*, Statius himself is redeemed and given a unique role in Dante's poem because he is the only shade who is shown in the process of being liberated from purgation. Statius describes the way that Vergil was instrumental in his becoming a poet, in his conversion from prodigality, and in his becoming a Christian. Statius' tribute to the *Aeneid* as his mother and his nurse ("mamma fummi e fummi nutrice, poetando," *Purg.* 21.97–8) praises the seminality of the "divine flame" of Vergil's epic, praise that echoes the concluding lines of Statius' *Thebaid* (12.816–17) which place his poem in the footsteps of the "divine *Aeneid*." Dante heightens the power of this praise by having Statius deliver it *before* he realizes that he is in the presence of Vergil.

Later Statius attributes his turn away from the sin of prodigality to the reading of lines in the *Aeneid* that deal with the "hunger for gold" (3.56–7). Statius actually misreads the lines so that a critique of greed becomes a plea for moderation, suggesting that the salvific property of the text operates beyond the intention of its author. Finally, Statius explains that he was drawn to Christianity because of the consonance of the words of the preachers with Vergil's fourth eclogue, a poem read by many Christians as an inadvertent prophecy of Christ. Vergil's centrality in Statius' poetic, moral, and spiritual life is summed up when he says to Vergil, "Through you I was a poet, through you a Christian" (*Purg.* 22.73). Vergil is compared to one who lights the way for those who follow him while remaining in the dark himself. Someone who carries a light for those who follow seems to be a generous rather than an inadvertent enabler, a nuance of the simile that contributes to our sense of the poignancy of the disparity between the two Latin poets' fates. (For a fuller reading of Statius, see Barolini 1984, 256–68.)

Perhaps Dante's most daring invention is the placing of a minor character in the *Aeneid* in the Heaven of Justice in *Paradiso*. Among the outstanding rulers famous for justice in the eye and eyebrow of the eagle of Justice Dante places Ripheus, one of the first to fall in the Trojan War as it is recounted by Aeneas to Dido: *cadit et Ripheus, iustissimus unus / qui fuit in Teucris et servantissimus aequi / (dis aliter visum)* ("Ripheus too falls, foremost in justice among the Trojans, and most zealous for the right – Heaven's will was otherwise," *Aen.* 2.426–8, trans. Fairclough and Goold). Dante implies that the gods did not, after all, think otherwise, and that the *iustissimus unus* receives his due in a Christian heaven. Dante is aware of the audacity of his invention, asking about the presence of Ripheus, "Che cose son queste?" (which has the force of "What is going on here?" 20.82). Dante invents a biography for Ripheus as a proleptic Christian who received a baptism by desire and fought against paganism. Ripheus' startling presence in the Heaven of Justice reminds us that Aeneas, Augustus, and Vergil himself are denied the salvation inscrutably awarded to this minor character. Curtius thought that the salvation of Ripheus was a "touching tribute to Vergil" (1953, 359), but it feels more like another reminder of Vergil's inadequacy and exclusion. It is possible, as some have suggested (Johnson, 1999; Perkell, 1999) that Dante thought of Aeneas' painful sense of the indifference of the gods as characterizing Vergil as well.

Refiguring the *Aeneid*

Dante's attention to the fall of Ripheus also reminds us what a close reader of the *Aeneid* he was. That point is made quite explicitly when Vergil remarks that Dante knows the *Aeneid* "tutta quanta" (all of it) (*Inf.* 20.114). Dante's long and loving study of Vergil's poem is evident in the number of references and allusions to it. Hollander (1993) offers a useful compendium of Vergilian citations. He points out that about a fifth of the citations occur in the first five cantos. The early cantos of *Inferno* are replete with Vergilian figures such as Charon, Minos, Cerberus, the Harpies, and the Furies. Characters and episodes from the *Aeneid* appear in a variety of infernal circles and in the exempla on the terraces of Purgatory. Elements of the geography of Vergil's underworld reappear in Dante, but there are important differences as well. Dante's terrain is much more specific and detailed, and it is rationalized on different terms. The River Lethe functions as one kind of boundary in the *Aeneid*, while for Dante it is moved out of Elysium, placed at the top of the mountain of Purgatory, and paired with the River Eunoe (invented by Dante) in which memory of the good is restored. The forgetfulness of Lethe is a prelude to rebirth on earth for Vergil while in Dante it is a stage in reaching the truly "new life" of beatitude that will follow (cf. Putnam 1991, 110–11).

Refigurations of various important moments in the *Aeneid* keep us aware of the Vergilian original even as we attend to its reworking. Among many examples of such rewriting, we might think of the way Dante's comparison of the multitude of souls waiting to cross the Acheron to autumn leaves (*Inf.* 3.112–17) recalls Vergil's comparison of the unburied souls in *Aen.* 6.309–12 (and cf. *Geo.* 4.473–4); subtle changes shift the emphasis from the sheer number of the souls ("quam multam") to their individual volition ("ad una ad una" (3.116). Vergil's similes rely on natural cycles (falling leaves, migrating birds), while in Dante there is a sense of a decisive "once only" event.

The "umile pianta" (humble plant) with which Dante is girded at the beginning of *Purgatorio* substitutes for the talismanic golden bough of *Aeneid* 6, thereby underlining the centrality of humility to the work of penitence. *Purgatorio* also rewrites the poignant epic topos of the failed embrace by changing its emotional resonance. Aeneas' inability to embrace the shade of his wife (2.792–4) and later of his father (6.700–2) is accompanied by tears that underscore the finality of loss. When Dante encounters his old friend Casella among the first penitents he sees in Purgatory, his threefold attempt to embrace the shade is so Vergilian in its language that we do not expect the response that follows, a *smile* instead of tears. In the context of the promise of salvation, there is no need to weep. A comparably surprising smile attends Manfred's display of his wounds (2.112), so different in tone from Deiphobus' painful display in *Aen.* 6.494–9.

The contrast between the *Aeneid* and the *Commedia* is explicit in *Inferno* 13, the canto of the suicides where the souls are incarnated in thorn bushes. Aeneas' inadvertent wounding of the buried Polydorus in *Aeneid* 3 is reenacted when Vergil urges Dante to break off a branch of a thorn bush, thereby mutilating the shade of Pier della Vigna. The shade's words ("Why do you tear me?") are those of Polydorus, but the dramatic situation is different because Pier della Vigna has undergone an infernal metamorphosis that makes him into a thorn bush, suggesting the superior imaginative "reality" of Dante's version of the event. It is in connection with Ovidian metamorphosis (*Inf.* 25.94–9) that Dante brags of having outdone classical poets ("Let Lucan be silent,…let Ovid be silent"), but a similar competitive move seems to be at work here too.

The rewriting of Vergil is particularly striking in *Inferno* 20 where Dante has Vergil recount the story of the founding of Mantua in a version at odds with that in the *Aeneid*, and then has Vergil insist that this is the only correct version. This is, as it happens, the same canto in which Vergil says that Dante knows the *Aeneid* "tutta quanta," and he does so exactly after giving an account of an event which takes place differently in the *Aeneid*. Canto 20 treats the "diviners," those who claimed to see into the future and are punished by having their bodies turned backwards from their heads. Its four major figures (Amphiaraus, Tiresias, Arruns, and Manto) are drawn from the four epics that are Dante's major classical sources, and in each case the version given of their story is at some variance from the original. This puzzling canto has been read as a critique of the prophetic dimensions of classical texts or as an attempt to separate Vergil from medieval traditions that connected him with magic or sorcery (see further Barolini 1984, 214–22; Hollander 1991, 77–93).

Another specific reference to the text of the *Aeneid* occurs in *Purgatorio* 6. As the souls in Purgatory ask Dante to request others to pray for them, Dante queries Vergil about the Sibyl's reprimand to Palinurus when he begs Aeneas to take him across the Acheron even though he has not yet been buried. Remembering that the Sibyl insists that prayer cannot turn aside the gods' decrees (6.373–6), Dante disingenuously asks Vergil if he has read the text correctly or whether the hopes of the souls he encounters are vain. Vergil responds that Dante has read correctly, but that the real issue is that prayer in his pre-Christian world was "disjoined" from God and therefore without efficacy (6.42). The limits of the *Aeneid* for both its characters and its author are once again identified with the limits of a pre-Christian dispensation.

These quasi-critiques of Vergil's poem are of a piece with the ways his authority as a guide is sometimes called into question. His comprehension of Christian material is incomplete or erroneous, as when he speaks about the Harrowing of Hell (*Inf.* 4.52–61) or the earthquake at the crucifixion (*Inf.* 12.37–43) or marvels at the crucified Caiphas (*Inf.* 23.124–5; see Hawkins 1999, especially 107–19). There is a dramatic crisis at the entrance to the city of Dis where the devils attempt to keep Vergil and Dante from entering. Vergil's hesitation and confusion suggest a lack of faith and an inability to deal directly with evil, a failure that Dante brings up later in the canticle (14.43–5). This is also the episode in which Vergil says that he knows the terrain of Hell because he had been summoned to its depths by Erictho, a disturbing necromantic connection which Dante invents, importing a character from the *Pharsalia*. (Martindale 1993, 69 calls this episode the "most creative use ever made of the *Pharsalia*." He also points out (70) the importance of Lucan's *terribilità* to the "combination of wickedness and violence and horror and black humour and ostentatious verbal paradox" characteristic of *Inferno*.) Vergil and Dante are rescued by the intervention of an angelic figure sent from heaven who is able to easily subdue the devils that are blocking the entrance. In the Malebolge Vergil is taken in by a lying devil (21.111) and then shocked to discover this instance of diabolic evil (23.139–41).

Vergil's authority in Purgatory is delimited by the fact that he has never been there before. Nonetheless Vergil's wisdom and his moral guidance continue to be a powerful presence. Indeed, it is he who gives the great speeches at the center of the canticle that explicate the moral and philosophical underpinnings of Purgatory and he who evaluates Dante's progress through the seven terraces until, just before entering the earthly paradise, he "crowns and miters Dante over himself" (27.142). We think of Vergil even after he has left the narrative when Dante begins his chronicle of Roman history with the death of Pallas (*Par.* 6.36), substituting this sacrificial death for the fratricidal myth of Romulus and Remus as a foundation story. The Cacciaguida episode, as we shall see, is informed by its Vergilian model. Dante's Empyrean, "that Rome where Christ is Roman" (*Purg.* 32.102), is a transfigured Elysium, both city and garden. It is filled with noble "patricians" (32.116), and has a queen who is called "Agusta" (32.119) as well as "Regina caeli." The memory of Vergil returns poignantly in the final canto when Dante compares the evanescence of his vision to the dispersal of the leaves of the Sibyl scattered by light winds (33.65–6; *Aen.* 3.448–50).

The richest example of Dante's transvaluation of Vergil comes in the poem's climax, the arrival of Beatrice and the simultaneous disappearance of Vergil in *Purgatorio* 30. As the character leaves, his text is vividly present, and radically rewritten. In this tour de force of intertextuality, Dante rhymes the Latin of the Vulgate ("Benedictus qui venis," 30.19) with the Latin of the *Aeneid*, as the angels sing "Date, o, manibus lilia plenis" ("give lilies with full hands," 30.21). This line is Anchises' funereal gesture for the early death of Augustus' nephew and heir Marcellus, the painful ending to the presentation of future Roman heroes (6.883). The contrast between the context of the line in each poem could not be greater. Whereas Vergil mourns the defeat of hope and faith by the stark finality of death, Dante transforms Anchises' vain gesture (*inani munere*, 6.885) into a joyous angelic greeting, a sign of the triumph of hope and faith (and love) over death. The contrast invites us to meditate on the differences between the two texts and between the worldviews that subtend them. Although both Marcellus and Beatrice died young, before their promise was fulfilled, Beatrice's promise does not end with death. She speaks of her death not as an end but as a threshold, a "change of life" ("mutai vita," 30.125). For Dante it is the hope and the fact of the Resurrection that authorizes the transfiguration of Vergil's lilies of mourning into lilies of welcome. The hope of the Resurrection is the core of Dante's faith, the great promise of Christian revelation by which he ultimately judges the limits of the classical world.

The other Vergilian allusions in this scene offer comparable contrasts between their original tragic contexts (the death of Dido, then of Eurydice in *Georgics* 4) and the celebratory reunion scene at the top of the mountain of Purgatory (detailed discussion in Hawkins 1991 and Jacoff 1991). As several critics have noted, the allusions constitute a fade-out or effacement of Vergil's voice as they progress from direct quotation, to translation, to allusion. While Vergil's name is given five times in the space of ten lines (30.46–55), Dante's name, Beatrice's first word in this scene, is given for the only time in the whole poem. Vergil's farewell is thus coordinate with Dante's assumption of authorship in this signature canto. So intense is the sense of Vergil's loss at this juncture that it inflects our reading of the whole poem. Looking at the many ways that Dante intensifies the pathos of Vergil's predicament, one could say that Dante's sympathy for him is comparable to Vergil's sympathy for those on the losing side in his own poem. Like those figures, he must be left behind but nonetheless remains indelibly present (Barolini 1984, 144–256; cf. Burrow 1997a, 80–2).

Rome

Although I have spoken of some of the ways Vergil's authority is undermined in Dante's poem, there is one subject on which Vergil's authority is profoundly reaffirmed. Vergil scholars have shown the many ways that the Roman theodicy of the *Aeneid* is open to qualifications and contradictions, but Dante read the claims for the providential history of Rome without ambiguity. (The classic treatment of the subject is Davis 1957.) As early as *Convivio* he attributed the power of Rome to divine providence:

> Furthermore, since we can learn from experience, there never has been, nor will there ever be, a race whose nature it is to rule more gently, uphold more firmly or obtain possession more skillfully than the Italians, and particularly that holy people whose blood is mingled with the noble blood of Troy, namely the Romans, God chose this people for that office. (4.4.10–11; trans. Ryan)

Dante bolsters this claim by citing Jupiter's promise to grant Romans "empire without end" in book 1 of the *Aeneid*. Comparable assertions in *Monarchia* are also glossed by Vergilian "proof texts." Arguing for the necessity of an emperor to bring an end to the factionalism and communal strife of his time, Dante turns to Anchises' speech in *Aen.* 6.851–3 on the virtues of Roman rule to support the idea that the Romans were ordained by nature to rule (*Mon.* 2.6). Dante's idealized view of Roman governance is thoroughly Vergilian in inspiration, although less open to the nuances that Vergil scholars have taught us to see.

There is a telling moment on the terrace of sloth in Purgatory when Dante compares the Hebrews whose backsliding kept them from reaching the promised land to the women of Troy who set fire to Aeneas' ships because they didn't want to continue journeying to the promised land of Italy. The parallelism is a miniature version of the larger parallelism of the Hebrew Bible and the *Aeneid* as sacred scriptures that point towards Christian completion. In *Inferno* 2 Dante speaks of Aeneas as "chosen in the Empyrean heaven...to be the father of mother Rome and her empire" (2.20–1), a reading of the providential terms of Aeneas' mission consonant with the *Aeneid*. But he then adds that Rome was chosen to be the "holy place where the successor of great Peter is enthroned" (2.23–4), something Vergil could never have imagined. Despite this passage, Dante's idea of Rome is actually close to Vergil's version of its idealized role as providential bringer of peace, law, and justice. Dante's exaltation of the idea of empire is coordinate with his critique of the papacy's claims to worldly power. Dante regards the Donation of Constantine, the (forged) document that granted temporal power to the papacy, as nothing short of ruinous (*Par.* 20.58–60). Dante's view of the papacy in his own time is so bitter that St. Peter speaks of the current pope (Boniface VIII) as having made his seat into a cloaca (*Par.* 27.25)!

The three key prophetic episodes in the *Aeneid* that validate the rule of Rome all allude to Augustus and to the recent ending of the civil wars that his ascendancy accomplished. Jupiter's prophecy of the return of "Trojan Caesar" who will bring about the return of the Golden Age (1.286–96), the vision of "Augustus Caesar, son of a god" (6.792) in the parade of future Roman heroes, and the extended concluding sequence on the shield of Aeneas (8.678–728) all speak to the claims and hopes of Augustan achievement. The *Commedia*'s three major prophetic moments are much more ambiguous. These prophetic set pieces are riddles whose meaning commentators are still debating. The Veltro of *Inf.* 1.101, the "DXV" of *Purg.* 33.43, and the enigmatic prophecy of a providential reversal of the current historical situation in *Par.* 27.142–8 lack the historical specificity of the prophecies in the *Aeneid* precisely because it was impossible to see a figure such as Augustus in the historical crisis of Dante's time.

Dante had placed extravagant hope in Henry VII of Luxembourg, who came to Italy to be crowned emperor. Writing to Henry in 1311, Dante addressed him as "King of the Romans and ever Augustus," alluding to the messianic promises of the fourth eclogue and calling him the "Lamb of God who takes away the sins of the world." Henry was opposed by the Florentines, among others, and died in 1314, ending any realistic possibility for an imperial candidate. When Dante enters the Empyrean the first thing he sees is a "great chair" reserved for "great Henry who will come to set Italy straight before she is ready" (30.137–8). By the time he wrote these lines, Henry had been dead for several years. The absence of a historically viable emperor is what allows for Dante's utopian version of the role such a figure might play.

At the same time, one has to think that the poem's repeated harsh critiques of rulers past and present (e.g., *Purg.* 7.88–136 and *Par.* 19.112–48) convey an historical pessimism that cannot be ignored.

Dante shares Vergil's horror of civil war. Contemporary readings point out that the battles of the last half of the *Aeneid* represent a retrospective civil war since the two sides are ultimately to unite and become one, "Latins all, who speak one Latin tongue" (12.835). Dante was himself a victim of the internecine struggles that plagued Florence, "the divided city" (*Inf.* 6.61). The battles between Guelfs and Ghibellines gave way to battles between the two Guelf factions, the Whites and the Blacks. Dante, a White Guelf, was on the losing side of the Black coup that took place in 1301. Aided by Pope Boniface VIII, the Black faction took control of the city and exiled the leading Whites. Dante had been one of the ruling Priors of the city in the summer of 1300, but barely two years later he was forbidden to enter the city. This extraordinary reversal of fortune was traumatic, and it was permanent. Writing in exile Dante returns often to the causes and the key players in the treacherous history of his city and others. Because the fictional date of the *Commedia* is 1300, Dante can include ominous prophecies of his exile and its causes.

Dante's permanent exile made him, like Aeneas, a refugee who needed to find a future that would compensate for profound loss. In book 6 Anchises shows Aeneas the future of his descendants, the historical mission that justifies his coming struggles. In the comparable episode in the *Commedia*, Dante's great-great grandfather, Cacciaguida, tells him clearly about his exile and then gives him the mission to write his poem, making manifest his vision (17.128) and, as we might say, speaking truth to power. The historical dimension of the episode is, however, backward rather than forward looking. Cacciaguida speaks movingly of the "good old days," the idealized Florence of the past whose degeneration he also charts. This episode opens in a Vergilian key as Cacciaguida greets Dante: "with like affection did Anchises stretch forward (if our greatest Muse merits belief) when in Elysium he perceived his son" (*Par.* 15.25–7). Cacciaguida's greeting combines Vergilian and Biblical Latin, converting Anchises' *sanguis meus* (6.835) from his vain call to Caesar to refrain from civil war into an affirmation of genealogical continuity. Once again, Dante's profoundly syncretic imagination presses Vergil's language into a new context that radically alters its meaning (Schnapp 1991 and 1986, 3–69). It is striking that the two Latin citations from the *Aeneid* ("sanguis meus" and "date, o, manibus lilia plenis") that Dante recontextualizes both point to Vergil's awareness of threats that haunt the promise of Rome: civil war and death.

The importance of the father figure in this scene and others reminds us of the centrality of patriarchy in the *Aeneid*, whose emblematic icon is Aeneas fleeing Troy with his father and son. Women in the *Aeneid* are associated with furor and discord or, as Georgia Nugent has shown, they evaporate or disappear from the narrative (Nugent 1999, one among several recent addresses to the question of the women of the *Aeneid*). Women in Dante are often associated with sexuality and transgression, but they are also the vectors of grace. It is the Virgin who initiates Dante's rescue, and she, St. Lucy, and Beatrice are the "tre donne benedette" (three blessed ladies, *Inf.* 2.124) whose female mediation is essential and empowering for the pilgrim. The role of

Beatrice is particularly important since it valorizes the redemptive potential of Eros; it is his love for her that will lead Dante to the love of God. While Vergil's Elysium is all male, women are significant presences both in Limbo and the Empyrean.

As a poem of history and its costs the *Aeneid* has an uncanny relevance in many different historical contexts. I was struck by the way that three modern translations choose to insist on its pertinence. In the postscript to his translation of the *Aeneid*, Robert Fitzgerald recalls first reading the *Aeneid* in 1945 with "more than literary interest" (414) as he was experiencing "the agony and abomination" of the closing months of World War II. Alan Mandelbaum prefaces his translation with thoughts of its intersection with the "personal discontent" generated by the Vietnam War (xi). Bernard Knox, in his introduction to Robert Fagles' new translation, writes of his experience reading Vergil in wartime Italy in 1945. The *Aeneid*, for us as well as for Dante, is a poem of "more than literary interest." While it underwrote Dante's claims for an idealized emperor, it also allows us to call into question idealizations of force and power that have become problematic in our own moment in historical time.

FURTHER READING

This essay expands upon ideas that I treated in the introduction to Jacoff and Schnapp (1991) and in Jacoff (2002). It owes much to the work of other scholars, particularly Robert Hollander, Peter Hawkins, Kevin Brownlee, Jeffrey Schnapp, and Teodolina Barolini.

CHAPTER TWELVE

Marvelous Vergil in the Ferrarese Renaissance

Dennis Looney

Introduction

In this essay I examine the engagement with Vergilian epic by two authors of the Ferrarese Renaissance, Matteo Maria Boiardo (1441–94) and Ludovico Ariosto (1474–1533), to consider Vergil's impact on their understanding and recreation of the marvelous in literature. I argue that these poets, in attempting to perfect versions of vernacular classicism and to produce poems worthy in their own right of print and purchase, identify passages of wonder in Vergilian epic as sources to be transformed and adapted to the developing conventions of their modern literary art. Moreover, the foundation of a tradition of writing in the vernacular that brings together classical and non-classical, Latin and Italian, through the specific genres of classical epic and chivalric romance, sets a precedent for literary theorists in the sixteenth century and seems to influence the way in which they too look at Vergilian epic. That is, the poets reveal aspects of Vergil to the critics that they might not have otherwise seen. Or perhaps it is that the poets whet the critics' appetite for a certain kind of Vergilian epic poetry, which they then seek out and find.

The discussion of the marvelous in Vergil's epic by sixteenth-century commentators, men of letters, and academicians is deeply entangled in the ongoing literary debates over the status of vernacular romance epics like Boiardo's *Orlando innamorato* and Ariosto's *Orlando furioso*, and eventually, after 1581, Torquato Tasso's *Gerusalemme liberata*. While narrative continuity, which will evolve into probing inquiries on the unity of plot as perceived through Aristotelian doctrine, is the primary concern in these debates, the question of verisimilitude in classical epic and the modern equivalents, or the lack thereof, is probably the second most common topic. Perhaps it is not a surprise, then, that the marvelous, *la maraviglia*, will emerge at the end of the century as an aesthetic category in its own right, which later in the eighteenth and nineteenth centuries, I would argue, transmogrifies into the sublime. And it may be that we have some hints of that future transformation from marvelous to sublime even early on in the chivalric romance, at least as the genre is perfected by Boiardo and Ariosto under the influence of Vergil's *Aeneid*.

The general entry on *maraviglia* in the *Vocabolario degli Accademici della Crusca* opens by citing passages from Dante, Petrarch, Boccaccio, and Ariosto that emphasize the role of the onlooker or interpreter of the wondrous thing or event (9: 915). That is, wonder is in the eyes of the beholder, which can be extended to the reader too. The entry gives five additional citations from the *Furioso*, all of which emphasize the act of interpreting a moment of wonder, as well as two citations from Boiardo's *Innamorato* in Berni's Tuscanized version. With the exception of Dante, Ariosto is cited more than twice as much as any other author. The *Furioso* helps the literary theorists and lexicographers at work on the Crusca's dictionary to conceptualize and define the category of the marvelous. The entry also includes a telling passage from Lionardo Salviati's *Lo 'nfarinato secondo*, one of the prime texts in the debate over the literary status of Ariosto's work and chivalric romance in general: "È agevol cosa il compilare un poema di una sola azione; ma difficilissima è poi da poema tale far nascere il diletto, l'utile e la maraviglia" ("To build a poem around a single action is easy enough but it's very difficult to bring forth delight, usefulness, and wonder out of such a poem," 134). Salviati's usage signals the concept's status as an aesthetic category on a par with Horatian delight and utility near the end of the sixteenth century. In what follows we will explore how it came to be thus.

Boiardo and Vergil

Renaissance humanists and their predecessors had been showcasing their knowledge of Vergil in Italian literary culture at least since the early 1300s. It was Dante who famously brought Vergil back to life, as it were, at the opening of the *Commedia* where the Roman poet, identified as a Lombard from Mantua, appears in the nick of time to save the Florentine pilgrim from hellfire and damnation. There Dante, the character in his poem as distinguished from the poet who writes it, envisions Vergil as a figure emerging from a mirage in a vast desert: "Dinanzi agli occhi mi si fu offerto / Chi per lungo silenzio parea fioco" ("Before my eyes a figure was offered up / who appeared faint in the wide silence," *Inf.* 1.62–3). Whatever one makes of the exact language that ushers Vergil into Dante's poem, it seems clear that the modern poet wants to emphasize his role in bringing his primary classical model, previously out of the picture, back into view. Petrarch, for his part, will deliberately imitate the *Aeneid* in his unfinished and imperfect epic poem, *Africa*, in an attempt to recuperate Vergilian epic more authentically than Dante had done. Boccaccio was forging his vernacular classicism even before he met Petrarch in 1350 in the early works of his so-called Neapolitan period, many of which were inspired by Vergilian epic (McGregor 1991). For humanists across Italy in the generations to follow, Vergil remained an important source and focus (Kallendorf 2007). In the second half of the fifteenth century, Boiardo, Ariosto's predecessor at the Estense court in Ferrara, responds to Vergilian epic in the context of his thoroughly romance poem, *Orlando innamorato*, which in turn affects Ariosto's subsequent response to Vergil. In *Innamorato* 1.5,

Boiardo imitates a scene from *Aeneid* 10 in which a phantom Aeneas, fabricated by Juno, lures Turnus from the battlefield. What at first glance appears to be a straightforward example of a chivalric romance poet imitating a classical epic by translating the model into the modern poem turns out to be a much more complex operation. In the move from romance to epic and back, the marvelous is transformed momentarily into something like the sublime (Looney 1996).

In *Epic and Empire*, David Quint has proposed a framework for understanding the juxtaposition of the constituent narrative designs of romance and epic. Quint argues convincingly that within the epic tradition there is a tradition of romance, the *locus classicus* for which is the ekphrasis of Aeneas' shield in *Aeneid* 8 with its detailed description of the Battle of Actium where Octavian's forces overcome those of his rivals, Antony and Cleopatra. The juxtaposition of the winners and losers is based on a series of clearly drawn distinctions between the two sides in battle. The essential difference is between the Romans, who are depicted as unified and ordered,and the barbarians, who are varied and chaotic. In narrative terms, the Romans are on a straight course destined to arrive at the point of victory in a timely fashion, whereas the barbarians are not only deviant but also constantly deviating off course. No wonder they are doomed to lose. But Boiardo's interpretation of the narrative poetics in *Aeneid* 10 suggests that the loss in Turnus' case is a marvel with a glimpse of the sublime.

When Juno whisks Turnus away from the battlefield (*Aen.* 10.606–88), the narrative of killing in this book of combat in the Iliadic half of the *Aeneid* is interrupted, postponing the poem's relentless push toward Turnus' death. We follow Turnus as he chases the phantom Aeneas from the lines of battle to the seashore where they board an empty ship, which sails mysteriously out to sea. For Quint, Vergil draws a deliberate analogy here between Turnus and Cleopatra (1993, 34–5). The phantom vanishes and Turnus finds himself sailing on a boat that has much in common with the typical boat of romance, which carries "knights-errant to whatever adventure may be currently available to give them an opportunity to demonstrate their prowess" (Quint 1993, 248–9). For the character of epic, confinement to such a boat is the narrative equivalent of being caught in the doldrums. The place for the hero to demonstrate his prowess is on the battlefield away from which the boat of romance inevitably transports him: "In epic narrative, which moves toward a predetermined end…the magic ship would signal a dangerous digression from a central plot line, but the boat of romance, in its purest form, has no other destination than the adventure at hand" (Quint 1993, 249). Or so it would seem. For when Turnus enters into what appears to be a romance digression, he has a very un-romance-like glimpse of his death. His chase after the phantom and the subsequent boat ride recreate Aeneas' tracking and dispatching of him at the end of the entire narrative. From the perspective of romance, in other words, the reader has an unexpected vision of the end of the epic. We need to retrace Turnus' steps to the point where he boards the ship to appreciate fully this masterful writing.

When Turnus attacks the phantom as it moves along the battle line, it runs toward the shore and the warrior chases after it:

> instat cui [imagini] Turnus stridentemque eminus hastam
> conicit; illa dato vertit vestigia tergo.

> tum vero Aenean aversum ut cedere Turnus
> credidit atque animo spem turbidus hausit inanem:
> "quo fugis, Aenea? thalamos ne desere pactos;
> hac dabitur dextra tellus quaesita per undas."

> Turnus rushes at it [the phantom], and from afar hurls a hissing spear;
> the phantom wheels round in flight. Then indeed, when Turnus thought
> that Aeneas had turned and yielded, and drank this empty hope into his
> confused mind, he cried: "Where are you fleeing, Aeneas? Forsake not
> your plighted marriage; this hand of mine will give you the land you have
> sought over the seas." (*Aen.* 10.645–50, trans. Fairclough, rev. Goold)

The taunting question "Where are you fleeing, Aeneas?" quickly yields to the more pointed remark: "forsake not your plighted marriage." Turnus tries to arrest "Aeneas" with his veiled reference to his dynastic responsibilities. To leave the marriage bed empty is not the better part of valor. The subsequent claim is also a stinging critique of Aeneas' virility: "this hand of mine will give you the land you have sought over the seas." This macabre allusion to the earth that will make up Aeneas' burial mound suggests that, for Turnus, his adversary is neither a satisfactory dynast nor a competent fighter.

The image of Turnus rushing after a phantom warrior, indeed the scene as a whole, grimly foreshadows his death at the end of the poem when Aeneas rushes upon him (*instat*, 12.887), making him a symbolic victim of the new Troy. In a sense the conquest is complete when the Trojan invader kills the leader of the Rutulians. But Turnus' death does not merely signal the foundation of a new political reality in Italy. Aeneas kills him in a fit of rage brought on by the sight of the baldric of the dead Pallas, which Turnus sports as a medal of conquest. In killing Pallas, the youthful son of one of Aeneas' allies, Turnus had driven Aeneas to swear revenge. Pallas' death scene (10.439–509) occurs, tellingly, not long before the episode in which Juno spirits Turnus away from battle (633–88). The intervening episode of Aeneas' vengeful rampage (510–605) is caused by Pallas' death and is the cause of Juno's attempted intervention with Jupiter on Turnus' behalf (606–32) and of her eventual rescue of the Rutulian hero. Turnus has no control over any of these events, least of all his death, after which in the poem's final lines, in its very last verb, he too becomes nothing more than a phantom in flight (*fugit*, 12.952).

Jupiter grants the temporary reprieve that allows Juno to set in motion the chain of events in book 10 (622–5). That Juno unwittingly provides her charge a glimpse of his death precisely while she is trying to save his life is ironic. The poet, for his part, provides the reader with a glimpse of the end of the narrative in an episode that appears, at first glance, to detour from the path toward the poem's conclusion. What Juno (and many commentators) interpret as a digression is in fact a foreshadowing of the hero's death that takes us to the heart of narrative resolution. What seems like the interpolation of romance into epic is actually the distension of the epic narrative and the exploration of its most appropriate theme: death. A "monstrous marvel to behold" (*visu mirabile monstrum*, 10.637) leads us to a view of the sublime. Boiardo's imitation of the episode at *Innamorato* 1.5.13–56 suggests that he understood this particular detail in the Vergilian passage and that he used it accordingly as an occasion for his own meditation on the generic implications of different narrative structures.

Boiardo's rewriting of the model increases Vergil's 82 lines to 344. To point out only one of the many ways in which he amplifies the original: the wizard Malagise makes a phantom Gradasso to lure Ranaldo away, thus matching Juno's phantom. But Boiardo creates a second phantom from the hand of Malagise, a herald who first reports to one side and then, after a magical Dantesque transformation, to the other. Boiardo trundles out three phantoms to Vergil's one in a crude form of numerical amplification.

Boiardo's version repeats the mechanics of fight and flight, as the phantom Gradasso makes an abrupt about-face and flees (*Aen.* 10.646 + *Innamorato* 1.5.43.2). The vocabulary of such behavior occurs in both texts: *fugis* and words of flight (10.649, 656, 670) have their parallels in the Italian (1.5.43.2, 5, 8); *sequitur* finds its match in the verb "seguire" (*Aen.* 10.651 + *Innamorato* 1.5.43.6). Furthermore, as Turnus believed himself to have overcome Aeneas (*Turnus credidit*, 10.647–8), so Ranaldo believes that he has frightened Gradasso (1.5.43.3). Neither warrior can contain his surprised delight at suddenly winning the battle by default – a delight that both poets express through circumlocutions. Vergil's phrase "and drank this empty hope into his confused mind" (10.648) becomes Boiardo's more simple description of a Ranaldo unable "to contain himself for his happiness" (1.5.43.4). Each warrior addresses the respective phantom with an initial question (10.649 + 1.5.43.7), which then yields to a charge that the warrior in flight is forsaking something he should return to acquire: in the case of Aeneas, his fiancée, Lavinia (10.649); in the case of Gradasso, the prized horse, Baiardo (1.5.43.8). Both speakers imply that flight is unseemly behavior for a groom-to-be, on the one hand, and for a king, on the other, but only Boiardo's text states this explicitly (1.5.44.1).

Each character, once on board ship, realizes that he has deserted his companions and laments accordingly. Turnus presents himself with two options: either he can kill himself or he can jump overboard, swim back to shore, and return to the fight (10.665–81). Ranaldo, however, reduces the choice to a decision between modes of dying: he can kill himself by sword or by drowning (1.5.53). What for Turnus is a moral dilemma in the drama that momentarily reveals the poem's end becomes a brief melodrama in the hands of Boiardo. Imitation verges on parody.

Vergil's episode concludes at lines 687–8, when Turnus circles back to the theater of battle in order to resume fighting against the Trojans. But even here in a seemingly innocuous topographical statement, there is an ominous reference to the end of the poem, to Turnus' death. The warrior is carried back to the city of his birth: *et patris antiquam Dauni defertur ad urbem* (10.688). The text is explicit: "and he is borne home to his father Daunus' ancient city." In another example of a detail from book 10 that illuminates the darkness of the poem's conclusion, the reference to Daunus anticipates ominously the passage in which Turnus refers to his father as he pleads with Aeneas for his life (12.934).

Boiardo diverges from his model at this crucial point in the narrative in a telling way. Ranaldo's ship leads him to yet another adventure, to a garden on an island far out at sea:

> se vede arivare
> Ad un giardin, dove è un palagio adorno;
> Il mare ha quel giardin d'intorno intorno.
>
> Or qui lasciar lo voglio nel giardino,
> Che sentirete poi mirabil cosa,...
>
> he sees he's reached
> a palace in a paradise,
> A garden guarded by the sea.
>
> I'll leave him in that garden now –
> I'll tell about its marvels later.
>   (1.5.55.6–8—56.1–2, trans. Ross)

Ranaldo is about to begin another wondrous adventure when the narrator abruptly breaks off the tale in stanza 56. The episode of Ranaldo on the ship, we discover, is merely one in a sequence of adventures, with little claim to uniqueness in the development of the narrative. But then how does Boiardo respond to the disguised centrality of the Turnus episode at *Aen.* 10.606–88? How does he allude to the stunning revelation of Turnus' death-to-come in his imitation of the scene?

What we see in the episode of Ranaldo is the stuff of romance with not even the slightest intimation of death. The allusion to the central moment of the Vergilian scene comes in the analogy between Turnus and Ranaldo, and their respective relations to death and life. Turnus anticipates the end of his life and, at the same time, the end of the epic narrative; Ranaldo's actions prefigure the fact that he repeatedly escapes death as his life takes on a shape appropriate to the continuous narrative of romance. We learn in the scene from the *Innamorato* that Ranaldo is doomed to reenact one romance adventure after another, sailing off in the boat of romance time and time again. The literary tradition prior to Boiardo represents him in this way and it continues to focus on the character as the embodiment of precisely those romance possibilities that frustrate epic: deviation, adventure, flirtation with everlasting life. Ariosto reprises the scene from Boiardo deep in the *Furioso* (31.91–110) where the character, now called Rinaldo, arranges to fight Gradasso. But their plans for a duel to the death are thwarted at this point and then once again later in the narrative (33.78–95). Orlando will eventually slay Gradasso (42.6), while Rinaldo busies himself with his own adventures in cantos 42–3, extending the narrative of the *Furioso* in a renegade plot for the better part of two cantos before it returns to the epic conclusion in 46 modeled on the end of the *Aeneid*. Tasso, too, has difficulty adapting his traditional character to the epic goal of the *Liberata*'s narrative, but he finally succeeds in harnessing the hero in the last quarter of the poem. In his earlier work, *Rinaldo*, the namesake of the poem plays his hearty romancing self.

The various fortunes of Rinaldo in later literature are consistent with the behavior of Ranaldo in *Innamorato* 1.5 (Sherberg 1993).

The portrayal of Ranaldo in Boiardo's rewriting of *Aeneid* 10 suggests an appreciation of Vergil's poem as a repository of different generic possibilities. But in Boiardo's rewriting of Vergil these modes are not delineated into simply an epic, Iliadic portion and a romance, Odyssean one. The Renaissance poet's interpretation of the *Aeneid* as an epic with a romance interlude whose digression further emphasizes the poem's very epicness enables Boiardo to camouflage the Vergilian source in his poem. That is, Boiardo's apparently slavish adaptation of the passage from *Aeneid* 10, which is followed by a predictable and anticipated "romance-like" diversion from the passage (Ranaldo's adventure in the garden), in actuality masks and covers the subtlety of his reading of the Vergilian epic's romance section, which he reads as, paradoxically, quintessential epic.

It is therefore difficult to argue that the *Innamorato* had a direct impact on critical interpretations of Vergil during the sixteenth century. It is true that Nicolò dell'Abate's striking *Aeneid* fresco cycle (1540–3) in the *studiolo* of the Boiardo castle in Scandiano seems to present Vergil in ways, perhaps not surprisingly, that remind the viewer of Boiardo's poem (Anceschi 2007). But in general Boiardo's entire poetic project was subsumed by Ariosto's in the next generation and eventually forgotten until the nineteenth century. It was through Boiardo's influence on Ariosto's literary sensibilities that he indirectly influenced critical thinking on Vergil and on the question of the relation between the genres of romance and epic. Boiardo used a reading of Vergil to establish one way to respond to the distinction between literary romance and epic in general, a lesson which Ariosto learned well.

Romance and Epic in Ariosto's Prose

I turn now to an early example of Ariosto's writing, a prose piece that recapitulates elements of Boiardo's response to Vergil and anticipates details in the work of the classical poet as seen subsequently by Toscanella and other critics. In a letter of 1512, four years before the first edition of Ariosto's *Orlando furioso*, the budding Ferrarese poet (and sometime diplomat and civil servant) makes a series of striking allusions to the *Aeneid* in what are, I believe, his earliest published references to the Roman epic. The allusions are actually citations of the original Latin text embedded in his letter, which he composed in Italian. What is most striking about this example of Ariosto's recourse to Vergil is the context in which he presents his allusions. Here is the text (with quotations of Vergil's Latin underlined):

> *Ill.ᵐᵒ et ex.ᵐᵒ domino meo obs.ᵐᵒ Ludovico Gonzagae Principi. Mantuae.*
>
> V. S. ex.ᵐᵃ ha certamente de la fada e del negromante, o di che altro più mirando, nel venirmi a ritrovar qui con la sua lettera del *xx augusti*, hor hora che sono uscito de le latebre e de' lustri de le fiere e passato alla conversation de gli homini. De' nostri periculi non posso anchora parlare: <u>*animus meminisse horret, luctuque refugit*</u>, e d'altro lato V. S. ne

havrà odito già: *quis iam locus, quae regio in terris nostri non plena laboris?* Da parte mia non è quieta anchora la paura, trovandomi anchora in caccia, ormato da levrieri, da' quali Domine ne scampi. Ho passata la notte in una casetta da soccorso, vicin di Firenze, col nobile mascherato, l'orecchio all'erta et il cuore in soprassalto. *Quis talia fando etc.* L'illustrissimo signor Duca, con il quale heri ha con ferito longamente il C. Pianelli, parlerà de' duo affari al Cardinale, il quale fra giorni si aspetta da Bologna, et io medesimo per quanto sia bono a poterla servire adoperrò ogne pratica, essendo de l'honore de Vostra Signoria, qual affectionato servitore, bramosissimo. Quello sia da fare e da sperare saprà da m. Rainaldo e fido che ne serà satisfatta, quantunque io non sia troppo gagliardo oratore. Il cielo continua tuttavia molto obscuro, onde non metteremoci in via così sùbeto per non haver anchora ad andar in maschera fuori de stagione e col bordone. Voglia V. S. recarmi alla memoria de la Ill.ma S. Princ.ssa Flisca quanto è permisso a observantissimo e deditissimo servitore, et a quelle in buona gratia mi raccomando.

    Florentiae, 1 octobris MDXII.

        Di V. S. ex.ma

        Humilis et deditus servus Lud. Ariostus.

To my Most Illustrious and Excellent Lord, most worthy of honor, Prince Ludovico Gonzaga. In Mantua.

Your Most Excellent Lordship must have something of the fairy or the magician or of some other being more powerful, with your letter of 20 August coming to find me here as I have just now emerged from the hideouts and dens of wild beasts and returned to the civil society of men. Of our dangers I can not yet speak: *the mind shudders to remember, and it takes refuge from the pain.* On the other hand, your Lordship will have already heard about it: *Which place, which land does not resound with our troubles?* As regards me, my fear has not yet subsided, since I find myself still being hunted, tracked by greyhounds, from whom may the Lord God help us escape. I spent the night in a rural refuge near Florence with the nobleman in disguise, my ears pricked up and my heart thumping. *Who by telling such things, etc.* The Most Illustrious Lord Duke, with whom Count Pianelli conferred at length yesterday, will speak of the two affairs to the Cardinal [Giovanni de' Medici] who is expected to arrive in Bologna in a matter of days. And I myself, inasmuch as it is good to be able to serve you, will be as careful as I can, especially desirous of the honor of being an affectionate servant of your Lordship. From Messer Rainaldo you will learn about what we hope will be done. I trust that you will be satisfied, although I am not a very accomplished diplomat. In any case, the sky remains ominous, wherefore we will not set out on the road immediately so as not to have to disguise ourselves again in masks (out of season) and with pilgrim's walking sticks. May your Lordship please remember me to the Most Illustrious Lady Princess Flisca as much as is permissible for a most observant and dedicated servant. And to you both in gratitude I commend myself.

    Florence, 1 October 1512

        Of your Most Excellent Lordship

        Your humble and most devoted servant, Ludovico Ariosto.

Ariosto drafts this spirited letter to a friend, Ludovico Gonzaga, who is peripherally connected with the ruling lords of Mantua, the town of Vergil's birth. He reports on the outcome of an aborted visit that Alfonso d'Este, duke of Ferrara, made to Rome in the summer of 1512, trying to secure the military support of the papacy in the ongoing political struggles amid shifting alliances across the northern and central parts of the Italian peninsula (Catalano 1930–1, 1: 348–50). Alfonso had arrived in early July but was forced to flee within two weeks, after being threatened with imprisonment by Pope Julius II, a pontiff unwilling to compromise on much of anything. The Este duke escaped in disguise, dressed like a friar, on July 19 and Ariosto, as best we can reconstruct, was sent by his patron, Ippolito d'Este, Alfonso's brother, to meet him at some point later in the summer as the duke made his way back up the peninsula to Ferrara. The months of August and September were spent in hiding and moving carefully across Umbria and Tuscany to arrive finally in Florence at the end of September, where a letter sent by Gonzaga reaches them to which Ariosto responds with the letter that we have.

While the three citations enable us to begin to assess Ariosto's response to Vergil as an epic poet, the context in which they are couched has several of the essential elements of the genre of romance, elements diametrically opposed to epic, or so it would seem. Flight, hiding, and disguise are all constituent features of the literary tradition associated in Ariosto's mind with Franco-Italian and French literature of romance, sometimes based on Carolingian stories but frequently hearkening back to Arthurian legend. Boiardo melded those two bodies of literary sources into an Italian tradition that Ariosto would inherit (Rajna 1975, 22–30). And the opening line of the letter announces the quintessential theme of medieval romance, magic. Gonzaga is nothing less than a wizard (think Merlin) who must have used extraordinary powers to see to it that his letter found Ariosto while our poet was in hiding. Moreover, Ariosto can speculate in amazement that his friend may be a being even more powerful than a mere magician. Carefully, albeit playfully, Ariosto establishes a literary tone of romance in his letter to Gonzaga. Why then turn to the archetypal Roman epic to gloss that experience? Ariosto and Alfonso on the run have some things in common, it turns out, with Aeneas fleeing from fallen Troy. To make sense of their flight and wanderings, the modern poet turns to Vergil's text as a gloss, first calling on a passage from the beginning of book 2 where Dido has prompted Aeneas to speak, which he begins to do despite the painful memories. The Trojan visitor's opening line to his Carthaginian host, *Infandum, regina, iubes renovare dolorem* (2.3), was brilliantly borrowed two centuries earlier by Dante for the beginning of Ugolino's speech in the pit of Hell in one of the grimmest scenes in Italian literature (*Inf.* 33.4–5). But Ariosto turns the seriousness of that reception on its head, forgetting epic and the infernal tragedy of Ugolino to claim that he cannot yet speak of his troubles. It is at this point that he recalls Vergil's Latin from *Aen.* 2.12 for the first of the three citations: "the mind shudders to remember, and it takes refuge from the pain." Despite the genuine hardship Ariosto and his patron have been enduring, the lighthearted tone of the letter gives the lie to the passage cited and its context in the *Aeneid*. If Ariosto is renewing unspeakable sorrow, he doesn't seem too burdened by it. Could it be, rather, that he is casting Alfonso in the role of Aeneas? After all, the duke of Ferrara is the actual leader. If so, then perhaps we should think of Ariosto as representing himself in the role of an uncharacteristically talkative Achates. The subsequent references to Alfonso in disguise, "nobile mascherato" and "andar in maschera fuori de stagione," may be meant to remind the reader that Aeneas first enters Carthage under cover of a magical cloud conjured up by his mother, Venus, who has appeared in disguise earlier in book 1. Ariosto's citation points toward a passage in the *Aeneid* that in fact does have some elements that are analogous to the experience he is trying to illuminate for his reader. That is, the epic source offers up some romance material to Ariosto, which he then works into the text of his letter.

The second citation seems to confirm such a tone in that it undermines the first quote. I can't speak but I don't really need to because: "Which place, which land does not resound with our troubles?" Ariosto borrows from the passage where Aeneas, weeping before the murals of the Trojan War that adorn the temple of Juno in Carthage, commiserates with Achates (*Aen.* 1.459–60). Aeneas arrives in Carthage, a war refugee, and sees the cataclysmic event that brought about the downfall of his civilization depicted in ekphrastic art on the town's main temple. The war hero can reflect with good reason on the spread of his fame, but is it really legitimate for Ariosto to propose an analogous comparison, even if we are meant to associate Alfonso with Aeneas? Have the two moderns really endured anything comparable to the fall of Troy? Is their civilization really at an end? And furthermore, is it the equivalent of Troy in the first place? Again, the tone is a little over the top. But setting aside the context for the comparison Alfonso–Aeneas and the question of whether or not such a comparison is merited, recalling this specific passage from the *Aeneid* sets up a series of weighty parallels within the epic tradition. For Vergil's scene of Aeneas weeping before the depiction of the Trojan War in *Aeneid* 1 recalls Odysseus crying when Demodocus recites the same story in the *Odyssey* (8.521–31; Burrow 1993, 35–6). As is frequently the case, the Renaissance writer alludes to a Roman author who alludes in turn to a Greek text, thus setting up a kind of telescoping of imitation from modern to ancient to even more ancient and thus reaffirming the canon while at the same time placing himself firmly within it. Here Ariosto's citation has the effect of reminding the reader of his engaged attempt to establish Italian culture as a worthy vehicle for the creation of vernacular classics. It is a move in defense of the thinking that underlies his own masterpiece-in-progress, the *Furioso*.

The letter's narrative shifts back to its own plot with the author making another erudite allusion, this time to the initial scene in Dante's *Inferno*: "Allor fu la paura un poco queta" ("Then my fear quieted down a bit," 1.19). Like Dante at the start of his poem, Ariosto pauses momentarily to collect himself, to calm his fear, on the outskirts of Florence in a hut. Finally, we come to the third direct citation, "*Quis talia fando etc.*" ("Who by telling such things etc."), which takes the reader back to Vergil's text with reference to another passage (*Aen.* 2.6) where Aeneas reflects on his inability to recount his unbelievable tale without crying. Alluding to the fall of Troy and to the epic time between the *Iliad* and the *Odyssey*, Vergil has his character ask who among the soldiers accompanying Achilles from Thessaly, *Myrmidonum Dolopumve* ("[who] of the Myrmidons or Dolopians") and among those with Odysseus, *aut duri miles Ulixi* ("or [which] soldier of stern Odysseus") could refrain from crying at having to recount such a tale. The rhetorical question establishes the two poles of Homeric epic as possible examples of conduct. One can write about war, as in the *Iliad*, or one can write about the trip home after the war, with a zig-zagging itinerary full of love and wonder, as in the *Odyssey*. Or one can combine the two generic possibilities of epic and romance into one, as in the *Aeneid*. Ariosto cites passages in the *Aeneid* that emphasize the less heroic underside of war in a context of quintessential romance almost to the point of parodying the epic. Even before the publication of his *Furioso* with its vast array of allusions to Vergilian epic, the poet had established a framework for responding to the *Aeneid* that recognized a romance feature within its epic fabric and in so doing he set a precedent that later critics in the 1500s would have to deal with.

Orazio Toscanella Reading the Marvelous

In a letter dated 1548 (but cf. Weinberg 1961, 2: 957–8), Giovan Battista Pigna reports to Giovambattista Giraldi about neo-Aristotelian critics attacking Ariosto's poem for its many flaws, including the poet's use of supernatural wonders. They criticize him because "he introduces enchanted weapons and those female and male wizards that violate contemporary usage" (Giraldi 1864, 2: 155). Pigna responds to these criticisms, as Daniel Javitch has shown, "by affiliating his [Ariosto's] poem in as many ways as he could to the epics of antiquity. Giraldi, on the other hand, met these same objections by acknowledging the modernity and difference of a *romanzo* like Ariosto's, and by justifying this difference on grounds of historical change" (Javitch 1999, 22). In Pigna's larger critical work on this topic, *I romanzi*, he argues that the presence of the supernatural is made legitimate by Vergil's inclusion of it in his epic (1554, 85). Defending the supernatural in those passages in the *Furioso* where rocks are turned into horses (38.32–4) and leafy branches into ships (39.25–9), he argues that the classical precedent in *Aeneid* 9, where Aeneas' ships are miraculously transformed into nymphs before Turnus is able to burn them up, prepares the reader familiar with the tradition for analogous scenes in Ariosto's poem. Without making claims for direct influence of one passage on another, Pigna implies that the classical marvelous enables the modern. Emilio Bigi, a modern commentator following in this line of thought (1982, 2:1612), goes so far as to claim that Ariosto's "Oh stupendo miracolo" (39.26.7) is a translation of Vergil's *mirabile monstrum* (9.120).

The discussion between Pigna and Giraldi over the generic status of the *Furioso* was a public one, which prompted other commentators to weigh in with their opinions on the subject in the years that followed. Depending on the specific line of argument, as Weinberg and more recently Javitch document, the commentators might invoke the Vergilian marvelous in the context of discussing what Ariosto does in the *Furioso*. Kallendorf (2005, 356) has suggested how Andrea Tordi in marginal notes not meant for public scrutiny may have read the ending of the *Aeneid* in light of his understanding of the way Ariosto responds to the end of Vergil's poem. The two poets were becoming ever more inextricably bound in the reception of each author's work. In *Osservationi…sopra l'opere di Virgilio*, published in Venice in 1567, Orazio Toscanella's presentation of the classical poet is indebted to the image of Vergil that emerges from the rewritings of Boiardo and Ariosto refracted through Giraldi and Pigna. Toscanella was a Venetian schoolmaster who published his *Osservationi* the same year that he moved from a teaching position in the provinces to Venice, where he would become an active member of the teaching, publishing, and editing community (Grendler 1989, 222–3). The *Osservationi* is a commonplace book of passages from Vergil in the original Latin arranged as glosses on topics presented in alphabetical order in Italian. Brief comments in Italian accompany each passage. It was common pedagogical practice in the Renaissance classroom for students to use excerpts from classical texts to create anthologies or working notebooks, which would subsequently provide them with ready access to material for their own writing exercises. Toscanella's *Osservationi* seems to be designed along these lines, but to what end exactly?

Weinberg calls Toscanella one of those Cinquecento "vulgarizers and popularizers" whose responses to literature are conventional and therefore, he implies, of limited interest (1961, 1: 289). But there is another dimension to this work that may give us pause at Weinberg's implicit criticism: the Vergil to which Toscanella turns in creating his commonplace book is noticeably un-epic, decidedly un-Iliadic, and is in fact a Vergil that would be very familiar to Boiardo and Ariosto. Toscanella draws from the *Aeneid*, to be sure, but from a remarkably restricted set of episodes to present his examples of Vergilian art, using passages primarily from books 4, 8, and 9. The Dido and Aeneas story in book 4 had a life of its own in the Renaissance and so perhaps one shouldn't make too much of Toscanella's extensive use of that specific book. His dependence on books 8 and 9 tells a different story. In his citation of passages from them he consistently refers to scenes that move the reader away from battle, passages that challenge the epic nature of the text. Most noticeable is the multitude of references to book 9 (no fewer than forty separate citations), in particular to the scene in which the Trojan ships are transformed miraculously into sea nymphs (9.77–125), the same scene that Pigna and other critics fix on as an example of the presence of the marvelous in ancient epic. Toscanella refers to the scene in book 9 in at least fifteen different contexts to elucidate the following topics: "Nel descrivere stupore" ("In describing awe," 130–1), "Esprimendo effetti" ("Expressing [unusual] effects," 169–70), "Historia" ("History," 204), "Importanza" ("Importance," 207), "Impossibilità" ("Impossibility," 208), "Miracolo" ("Miracle," 261), "Narratione" ("Narration," several citations within pages 269–90), "Narrare cose che eccedano la verisimilitudine" ("Narrating things that exceed the limits of verisimilitude," 287), "Nelle operationi delli dei" ("Concerning the workings of the gods," 307), "Prodigio" ("Wonder," 363), "Promesse" ("Promises," 364), "Promesse di dei" ("When the gods promise," 365), "Come faccia rispondere à dimande" ("How to answer questions," 388), "Nella transformation di corpi come faccia" ("How to handle the metamorphoses of bodies as he does them," 424).

Toscanella cites the transformation of the Trojan ships not only as a straightforward example of wonder but also as a source for a variety of other topics. In the general discussion of "Narratione," for example, he refers to the episode as if it were a case study in how to construct a narrative. The notion of Vergilian epic that emerges if one uses this scene of wonder from book 9 as the primary model for narrative may be distorted. Be that as it may, Toscanella's unusual critical openness to the variety of possibilities in narrative design, even in classical epic, pushes him to formulate an additional insight about Vergilian art. He proposes that awe can be a complementary feature to wonder in the narrative.

Toscanella first makes this connection in the epistolary dedication of the *Osservationi* to the Venetian medical doctor Lorenzo Galupo, whom he calls a miracle worker (for having accomplished "in medicina effetti miracolosi"), by situating the *Aeneid* in a genealogy of poetic work that has its origins in poetry of wonder and – here he adds a new word to the description – awe: "Per la verità i poeti…da un certo spirito divino inspirati, cominciarono à cantar cose d'ogni maraviglia, et d'ogni stupor degne" ("In truth the poets…inspired by a certain divine spirit began to sing about all sorts of things marvelous and worthy of awe," ii verso–iii). Vergil takes his place as an epic poet in a line that descends from Moses and Homer, Toscanella goes on to say, and he is recognized as a poet as much in touch with the divine as these two illustrious predecessors were. The modern critic implies that Vergil's proximity to the divine enables him to transport his audience beyond mere wonder to another level of responsiveness.

An additional detail suggests that Toscanella (if not his printer Giolito) imagined his ideal reader to be especially perceptive along these lines. In the letter to readers that follows the dedication to Galupo, "AI LETTORI ORATIO TOSCANELLA," the figural design surrounding the initial letter "A" is of Abraham on the verge of sacrificing Isaac, with the angel arriving in the nick of time to stop the sacrifice (1r). Although Franca Petrucci Nardelli (1991) instructs us that the images of initial letters need not have a direct connection to the content of the writings that they introduce, here the choice of the particular subject of the miraculous salvation of Isaac appears deliberate. The reader of the *Osservationi* is challenged to connect poetic wonders with scientific medical wonders and awesome divine wonders, that is, to juxtapose the realms of wonder and awe.

The collocation of wonder and awe signals a new way to think about *maraviglia*: not only is it associated with the sort of characteristics located in the romance tradition (e.g., flight, hiding, disguise, and magic, as we saw above in Ariosto's letter, not to mention the wonder of love); it may also be complemented by awe, "stupor," in Toscanella's word, which often depends on the divine. Awe shifts the focus in the interpretation of the wondrous thing or event from the interpreter's amazement to his or her fear. To return to the passage in *Aeneid* 9, which is so crucial to Toscanella's understanding of Vergilian poetics: when the Trojan ships are transformed, Turnus' men are amazed at the wondrous event (*obstipuere*), Messapus is terrified, as are his horses (*conterritus* and *turbatis*), and the Tiber checks itself and pulls back out of fear (123–5). Even nature reacts to the unnatural. Turnus, for his part, attempts to interpret the miracle as merely another example of romance-like wonder. What the narrator describes as *mirabile monstrum* ("wondrous portent," 120), Turnus strips of its adjective to say to his men: *Troianos haec monstra petunt* ("It is the Trojans that these portents are directed against," 128). While Turnus does recognize the event as a legitimate portent, he fully expects to be able to contain it with his epic heroics. For his colleagues, on the other hand, it is a moment of excruciating fear. In passing from Turnus' interpretation to theirs, we move from wonder to awe, from the realm of the marvelous to that of the terrifying sublime. Embedded in *Aeneid* 9 is the same transition that I believe marks Boiardo's reading of the passage in *Aeneid* 10 with its foreshadowing of Turnus' death at the end of the poem. The juxtaposition of romance and epic elements with the obfuscation of the boundaries between the two generic modes we have seen in Boiardo and Ariosto has a precedent in Vergilian epic. And it is this juxtaposition that produces a glimpse of the sublime in Vergil's poem and in the works of the modern imitators.

References to Vergilian poetry also occur in Toscanella's *Bellezze del Furioso* (1574), his extended commentary (nearly 350 pages) on the modern poem's artifice, which we can read as a kind of inverse to the *Osservationi*. In his work on Vergil, we sense the influence of Ariosto, and in the commentary on the *Furioso* we find comments on Vergilian poetry. We know that Venetian schoolmasters were also teaching chivalric romances in the schools alongside the *Aeneid* and other classical texts, and the *Orlando furioso* is one of the vernacular texts singled out, perhaps in response to what the parents wished they could read themselves (Grendler 1989, 289–9). Like the *Osservationi*, *Bellezze* has the feel of a teacher's manual to it and one can imagine the schoolmasters using these pedagogical texts to guide students through the large poems before them in the curriculum, whether in Latin or in Italian.

In one of the most striking notes in *Bellezze*, Toscanella claims that Ariosto overcomes his Latin model in nothing less than the art of narrative closure. The master of romance one-ups the epic model in this gloss on *Furioso* 29.74:

> Il poeta per voler mostrare, che era giunto al fine del canto; si serve dell'allegoria, facendola di più metafore continuate, cioè corde rallentate, canto, suono. Nella quale allegoria mi pare che habbia in un certo modo superato Vergilio, quando disse, volendo significare fine. *Et iam tempus equum fumantia solvere colla* [*Geo.* 2.542]. Perche l'allegoria dell'Ariosto in questo luoco è più conveniente, al canto, & al suono, poi che i Poeti cantano: & il prender metafora di cavalli incantati è del tutto lontano; ò molto lontano effetto. (Toscanella 1574, 227)

> In order to show that he has reached the end of the canto, the poet takes advantage of allegory using a series of continuous metaphors: slackened strings, music, song. With this allegory I believe that he has surpassed Vergil in a certain way, when Vergil said, wanting to indicate an end: "and it is now time to loose the horses' steaming necks" (*Geo.* 2.542). Ariosto's allegory fits better in its setting and it suits the fact that poets sing. Using, on the other hand, the metaphor of magical horses (*cavalli incantati*) is far off the mark or at best creates an effect that is distant.

Toscanella criticizes the classical poet for his faulty ending that depends on "cavalli incantati" ("magical horses"), whereas he praises the modern poet for a sober, serious, and fitting conclusion to the specific canto in question. Of course, one's perception of Vergil's and Ariosto's respective ability to realize narrative closure depends entirely on the work and book/canto one takes as an example. But the point to note here is that for Toscanella, Vergil's ending has been contaminated and accordingly diminished by a feature which the critic interprets as a constituent element of the marvelous: the magical horses that pull the narrative along. He doesn't make the point that the *Georgics* must abide by generic constraints that are different from those that shape the *Aeneid*, as he might, and so one assumes he wants to emphasize a passage where he believes Vergil has nodded. We have come so far in the literary critical history of the reception of the marvelous in the sixteenth century that this quintessential feature of romance, which as we have seen can indeed be found in Vergilian epic, vitiates the ending of a Vergilian narrative in contrast to an Ariostan alternative, which shuns magic and other romance features to come to a conclusion perceived to be more appropriate. In the next generation Torquato Tasso, a fine Vergilian poet and reader of the *Aeneid*, will work hard to associate Ariosto with romance and Vergil with epic, but he too ultimately will not succeed in keeping the two genres and the two poets as separate as he would like. And it would seem that precisely this volatile mix of romance and epic, wonder and awe, creates the context for the literary sublime to come into its own in the centuries that follow.

FURTHER READING

For identification of the Vergilian poetry alluded to by Boiardo and Ariosto, Rajna (1975; originally published 1876, revised 1900) remains fundamental despite its positivist bent. Less well known but good is Romizi (1896). Bigi (1984) and Ragni (1984) update these earlier works in *Enciclopedia Virgiliana*. The most comprehensive modern monograph on Boiardo and the classics is Zampese (1994). There is no book-length equivalent for Ariosto, but see Everson (2001) and Looney (2003). Cavallo (2004) sheds light on Cieco da Ferrara, an important minor figure between Boiardo and Ariosto, whose *Mambriano* alludes extensively to *Aeneid* 4. For the culture of humanism in Ferrara, with discussion of the Vergilian texts available and how the poets studied them, see Bertoni (1919). In a forthcoming piece, Kallendorf similarly considers how students in the sixteenth century read Vergil's *Aeneid* with attention to Toscanella. For a full analysis and bibliography on the Vergilian fresco cycle in Boiardo's ancestral home, see McIver (1998). Many critics consider specific Vergilian episodes in Ariosto. On Ariosto's extensive rewriting of the episode of Nisus and Euryalus, see Cabani (1995), Greene (1963), and Pavlock (1990). Pavlock highlights some of the complexities of Ariosto's intertextuality by showing how the Renaissance poet blends his imitation of Vergil's *Aeneid* with that of the episode of Hopleus and Dymas in Statius' *Thebaid*. On the *Furioso*'s ending, see Sitterson (1992). On Ariosto's representation of the divine influenced by Vergilian poetry, see Gregory (2006) and Greene (1963). For the best attempt to come to some conclusions about Ariosto's overall strategy for engaging with Vergilian sources, see Javitch (1999). For a brief survey that links Ariosto's use of Vergil to poetic adaptations to follow, see Burrow (1997a) and Zatti (2006).

On Ariosto's Vergilian letter of October 1, 1512, Gardner (1906) offers some commentary, as does Bonifazi (1984), who also has interesting comments on the marvelous. Ariosto's letters have largely been neglected but Looney's translation (2010) aims to correct that disregard. Fisher (1998) is provocative on wonder and the sublime.

CHAPTER THIRTEEN

Spenser's Vergil
The Faerie Queene *and the* Aeneid

Philip Hardie

For his early readers Edmund Spenser was the English Vergil. His career, progressing from the pastoral *Shepheardes Calender* to the epic *Faerie Queene*, moves through the *rota Vergilii*. Recent work has both deepened our awareness of Spenser's response to Vergil, and raised questions about the relative importance of Vergil for Spenser's career and works. For example, scholars have had to look hard to find a georgic stage or component in the œuvre (attention has focused *inter alia* on Spenser's own experience as a "planter" in Ireland and on the identification of the Redcross Knight as the "farmer" St. George, *FQ* I, x, 65–6). *The Shepheardes Calender* itself is no straightforward imitation of the *Eclogues*, indebted as much if not more to Renaissance pastoral, Mantuan and Marot in particular, and the extent and nature of its engagement with the Vergilian model is debated.

The Faerie Queene stakes its claim to be the English *Aeneid* in the first stanza of the proem to book 1, as Spenser puts off his "lowly Shepheards weeds," "For trumpets sterne to chaunge mine Oaten reeds," in fulfillment of the Vergilian career change that Cuddye in "October" (55–78) of *The Shepheardes Calender* had despaired of achieving. The first four lines paraphrase the four-line *Ille ego* proem to the *Aeneid*; Spenser swerves from Vergilian epic into Ariostan romance in the fifth line, "And sing of Knights and Ladies gentle deeds," echoing the first two terms of the first line of *Orlando furioso*, "Le donne, i cavalier, l'arme, gli amori," whose last two terms are echoed in the last line of the stanza, "Fierce warres and faithfull loues shall moralize my song" (Cain 1978, 37–40).

This stanza prompts various questions about Spenser's use of Vergil in *The Faerie Queene*. Is Spenser's Vergil the same as ours? Is Vergil the central model, or is the use of the (often imitated) *Ille ego* proem little more than a topos to signal the beginning of a long poem with epic pretensions? What does the move from the Vergilian to the Ariostan model say about Spenser's awareness of the history of epic from antiquity to his own day, and more specifically of the generic difference between epic and romance (a topic discussed by Looney's chapter in this volume)? Recent work on intertextuality in classical authors has explored the self-conscious construction of literary histories through allusive practice. Does Spenser's allusivity reveal a comparable awareness of literary systems and literary history? And in terms of structure and texture, what is the depth and specificity of Spenser's imitation of Vergil?

Spenser's Vergil

At the level of the Vergilian corpus, most modern editions exclude the *Ille ego* proem to the *Aeneid* as inauthentic. In the sixteenth century the Vergilian corpus included much more, substantial parts of the *Appendix Vergiliana* being generally regarded as authentic (Burrow 2008). Spenser translated the *Culex* as "Vergil's Gnat," and the longest single imitation of "Vergil" in *The Faerie Queene* is the episode of Britomart and her nurse Glauce (III, ii, 30–51), which is based on Carme's advice to the lovelorn Scylla in the *Ciris* (206–385). Spenser responds keenly to the eroticism of the *Aeneid* and to Vergil's thematization of the erotic gaze. Belief in the authenticity of the *Ciris* lends additional weight to the perception that these are central Vergilian preoccupations. The Renaissance *Aeneid* came equipped with a supplement as well as an authorial proem, in the shape of Maffeo Vegio's book 13 (1428: edition and translation in Putnam 2004), which extends the story beyond the death of Turnus to the funeral of Turnus, the wedding of Aeneas and Lavinia, and the ultimate apotheosis of Aeneas. Regularly printed in Renaissance editions of Vergil, Vegio's book 13 provides the closural reconciliations and rituals glaringly absent at the end of book 12. The circumstantial narrative of a wedding was also in tune with the greater weight placed by the Renaissance "dynastic epic" on the loving union of the legendary progenitors of a future imperial line (Fichter 1982). Books 1 and 2 of *The Faerie Queene* offer parallel histories of the epic quest of a single hero. But where book 2 ends with the sudden and shocking violence of Guyon's destruction of the Bower of Bliss (~ *Aeneid* 12), the climactic violence of book 1, the killing of the dragon in canto xi, is followed in canto xii by the celebration of the bethrothal of the Redcross Knight and Una (~ *Aeneid* 13).

"Spenser's Vergil" also asks us to consider reading practices in late-sixteenth-century England. In his introductory *Letter to Raleigh* Spenser places himself in a tradition going back to antiquity that defines epic as poetry of praise, encouraging its readers to imitate the virtues of the heroes praised (on the Renaissance tradition see Hardison 1962; Kallendorf 1989; on *The Faerie Queene* see Cain 1978). "To fashion a gentleman or noble person in vertuous and gentle discipline" Spenser will offer in Arthur an example of virtue, following the practice of Homer, Vergil, Ariosto, and Tasso. Servius defined one of the goals of the *Aeneid* as "to praise Augustus through his ancestors." Badius Ascensius, author of the most frequently printed Vergil commentary in the Renaissance, states that in Aeneas Vergil depicted a prince endowed with all the virtues, to be held up to Augustus as an object of imitation (Nelson 1963, 118–19). For Spenser as a "poet historical," the ultimate theme for praise is not his legendary heroes but the contemporary monarch, Elizabeth, shadowed eponymously as glory in the person of Gloriana. The existence of a time-hallowed model of reading epic as praise poetry does not of course close down the possibility of resistance to that model on the part of poet or reader. Predictably perhaps, the political turn of much late-twentieth-century criticism has led to readings of both the *Aeneid* and *The Faerie Queene* that complicate or subvert a superficial panegyrical thrust. Unease is felt at "the tempest of … wrathfulnesse" (compare Aeneas "fearsome in his anger," *ira terribilis*, at the end of the *Aeneid*) in which Guyon, the knight of temperance, destroys the Bower of Bliss; at Artegall's ruthless dealings with those who do not share his conception of justice; at the equivocation over the merciful Mercilla-Elizabeth's assent to the execution of Duessa-Mary Queen of Scots. Increasing attention to the Irish context has produced a Spenser both complicit in Protestant advocacy, to an Elizabeth more inclined to moderation, of the ruthless suppression of Irish rebellion and guiltily aware of the inhumanity of such a policy (McCabe 2002).

In constructing "a continued allegory" (*Letter to Raleigh*) Spenser drew on the tradition of Vergilian allegoresis which interpreted Aeneas' career as a moral progress and, in a Christianizing version, as a journey to a vision of the Christian God. Allegoresis of the *Aeneid* is indebted to the allegoresis of the Homeric epics, and allegoresis of both Homer and Vergil is further mediated to Spenser through allegorical commentary on Ariosto's *Orlando furioso* and Tasso's *Gerusalemme liberata*. Book 1 is the most sustained exercise in writing an allegorical epic of a specifically Vergilian kind. The adventures of the Redcross Knight constitute the complete itinerary of the spiritual epic hero, of which the virtuous exploits of the heroes of the other books are, in a sense, but parts (Warner 2005, 185, 187). Book 1 starts with arms and a man (I, i, 1.1–2, "A gentle Knight…Y cladd in mightie armes"), at the very beginning of his career (5, "Yet armes till that time did he never wield"), and moves towards a vision of the celestial Jerusalem, whose glory transcends that of the earthly Cleopolis, "city of fame," the seat of the Faerie Queene who presides over her knights' epic exploits on earth. In his final encounter as a Vergilian man-at-arms (I, xi, 7.9, "That I this **man** of God his godly **armes** may blaze") the Redcross Knight sends flying the life-breath of the dragon, a figure of Satan (with whom Vegio identified Turnus: Watkins 1995, 108). His earthly betrothal with Una is also a figure for the heavenly marriage of the Lamb. Vergilian too, in a way more easily recognizable to a modern reader, is an ending that is no ending: book 1 ends with a betrothal only, for a wedding that lies beyond canto xii as the wedding of Aeneas and Lavinia lies beyond book 12 of the *Aeneid*; and the conclusive act of violence against the dragon is but a prelude to the greater matter of the wars between the Faerie Queene (Elizabeth) and the Paynim King (Philip II), as we learn from the *recusatio* at I, xi, 7 ("Faire Goddesse lay that furious fit aside, / Till I of warres and bloudy Mars do sing…"), suggesting that the turn to full-scale epic signaled in Spenser's *Ille ego* proem in fact has yet to be realized: in Vergilian terms all the wars that will follow Aeneas' defeat of Turnus down to the *pax Augusta*.

Venuses and Didos

Turning back to the beginning of book 1 we recognize an allegorized version of a number of the inaugural events in books 1 and 4 of the *Aeneid* (for the Redcross

Knight as "a quasi-Aeneas figure" in the opening stanzas of book I see Warner 2005, 188–93). "Arms and the man" is plunged into adventures, *in medias res*, by the sudden rising of a storm. Since he is not at sea like Aeneas, the Redcross Knight takes shelter in a wood, where he encounters a monstrous and foul female creature, Error, half-woman and half-serpent. She shares with the apparition of female beauty that confronts Aeneas "in the middle of a wood" (*Aen.* 1.314, Venus in the disguise of Diana) the feature of hybridity. Error is the first of the series of female epiphanies that punctuate the poem, in her hideous fertility a negative version of the series of Venus-*virgo* apparitions of beauty (the beauty of Una has not yet been revealed, since she enters veiled). Spenser's Error moves closer to the Vergilian Venus through the allegorical lens of Petrarch's reading of the *Aeneid* (*Rerum senilium* 4.5): Venus in the wood of this life is pleasure, wearing the appearance of a fair maiden to delude the ignorant, but if seen as she really is so foul that you would flee in terror. Overlaid on the meeting of Aeneas and Venus is another Vergilian scene in the wilderness: like Aeneas in *Aeneid* 4 the Redcross Knight takes shelter from a storm in the company of a beautiful woman; unlike in *Aeneid* 4 nothing untoward happens. The Aeneas and Dido model continues to play in inverted form when the Redcross Knight is induced to abandon Una through Archimago's machinations: but where Aeneas must leave Dido to return to his true path, the Redcross Knight has been tricked into leaving Truth (Una) (Pugh 2005, 58–66).

The momentary return to the dead Dido in *Aeneid* 6 apart, *Aeneid* 4 marks the end of the hero's involvement with the love of women. Notoriously, his engagement to Lavinia is no love match: by the end of the poem the two have not even set eyes on each other, and the *Aeneid*'s last image of female beauty is Turnus' (and the reader's) disturbing and violating gaze at the roses and lilies of Lavinia's blush, whereby *eros* is converted into Turnus' destructive war-lust (*Aen.* 12.64–71). *The Faerie Queene* channels the disruptive erotic energies of the *Aeneid* to the ends of a dynastic epic, in which fulfillment of private passion coincides with the wedding that will establish *imperium*, and in which desire for Dido is compatible with the love of the fatherland for which Aeneas abandons Dido. The Spenserian equivalent of the Julian *gens* is the line descending from the union of Britomart and Artegall, which as Merlin prophesies, in a reprise of the speech of Anchises in *Aeneid* 6, will issue in the reign of a royal virgin, Elizabeth (III, iii, 21–49). At the beginning of this story Britomart is as confused with blushes as is Lavinia, coloring when the Redcross Knight's question as to the purpose of her quest prompts guilty thoughts of the man, Artegall, with whom she is in love (III, ii, 5). Britomart, like Lavinia, is destined to marry a man whom she has not met, but unlike Lavinia she has been granted, through her father's magic looking glass, a vision of her future husband that arouses a burning passion. The blush is repeated when Merlin sees through her disguise, III, iii, 20:

> The doubtfull Mayd, seeing her selfe descryde,
>   Was all abasht, and her pure yuory
>   Into a cleare Carnation suddeine dyde;
>   As faire Aurora rising hastily,

Doth by her blushing tell, that she did lye
All night in old Tithonus frosen bed,
Whereof she seemes ashamed inwardly.

Britomart has been sleeping with a mental image no more satisfying than the impotent Tithonus, but the confusion of her virginal shame is harbinger to a productive sexual union, no false dawn but an epithalamial image (Britomart's blush as a positive sign: Krier 1986b, 141). In traveling in pursuit of an object of desire she has never seen in the flesh, Britomart is like Paris in pursuit of Helen, whose beauty he knows only by fame. To the Redcross Knight Britomart veils the true reason for her quest, love, under a deviously expressed interest in fame, concluding with an analogy that aligns the desire for fame with sexual procreation, and foreshadows the literal child that she will bear to Artegall, first shoot of a "famous Progenie," III, ii, 11:

The royall Mayd woxe inly wondrous glad,
  To heare her Loue so highly magnifide,
  And ioyd that euer she affixed had,
  Her hart on knight so goodly glorifide,
  How euer finely she it faind to hide:
  The louing mother, that nine monethes did beare,
  In the deare closet of her painefull side,
  Her tender babe, it seeing safe appeare,
Doth not so much reioyce, as she reioyced theare.

The paradoxical figure of an Amazonian warrior in quest of a stable sexual union, in contrast to Vergil's Camilla, for example (one of her literary ancestors), Britomart succeeds in harmonizing two things that in epic are often at odds, fame (or honor) and sexual desire (Burrow 1993, 103). At the beginning of book 4, looking back over the Legend of Chastity which is in truth the Legend of integrated and productive love, Spenser plays a game of fame and blame as he defends himself against the charge, imputed apparently to William Cecil, of "praising love" in "looser rimes," as if he were an Ovid defending his amatory verses before Augustus. By way of answer he boldly states (IV proem ii) that love "of honor and all vertue is / The roote, and brings forth glorious flowres of fame," reversing Ovid's defense in *Tristia* 2 that the sternest epics are as obsessed with irresponsible love as is his own poetry through the claim that love is the motive force for the greatest epic exploits. This accommodation of love and (epic) fame has been seen as a major "correction" of the Vergilian model, a reconciliation of human love and selfhood with the demands of empire, eased by Neoplatonic and Augustinian revaluations of love, and following the romance models of *Orlando furioso* and *Gerusalemme liberata* (e.g., Fichter 1982). There is much truth in this: however, Vergil does not simply substitute self-effacing dedication to public duty for the personal fulfillment of desire, but sublimates erotic desire into a patriotic love. In the Vergilian underworld Aeneas moves on from the pain of his final meeting with an unresponsive Dido to a loving reunion with his father, who, through his own magic looking glass, offers Aeneas a vision of his unborn descendants, inflaming him with a love for the fame to come (*Aen.* 6.889, *famae venientis amore*; Hardie 2004, 144–7). As he tells Dido to justify his departure in search of Italy at *Aen.* 4.347, "this is my love, this is my fatherland."

While Spenser uses Ariostan romance, with its happy ending in the dynastic marriage of Ruggiero and Bradamante, to overgo the catastrophic mismatch of Aeneas and Dido, *The Faerie Queene* is also haunted by specters of Dido (to use the title of Watkins 1995), even as the shade of Dido continues to haunt the *Aeneid* after her death in book 4. Dido reappears negatively as witch, seductress, luxurious queen, Amazon (all roles that she already plays directly or allusively in the *Aeneid*) in the persons of Duessa, Lucifera, Acrasia, Malecasta, Radigund; and positively in the persons of the hospitable and temperate Medina and Alma. In her one person Britomart embodies both positive and negative aspects of the Dido and Aeneas story: she succeeds in her attempt to make it as a woman in a man's world, and although she is the victim of a passion as overpowering as that of Dido, she rejects the temptation to any liaison that could be held dishonorable. She flees from the castle of Malecasta as Aeneas flees from Dido, but the tapestries in Malecasta's castle of Venus and Adonis shadow Britomart's Dido-like passion for Artegall as much as they do Malecasta's own desire for Britomart (Watkins 1995, 151). The passionate and the virginal are cleverly combined in Spenser's use of the *Ciris* in III, ii, where Britomart reenacts the infatuation of Scylla, the girl who conceived a disastrous passion for her country's enemy Minos, but takes her name from Britomartis, who is the daughter of Scylla's nurse Carme who leapt into the sea to escape Minos' lust (Roche 1964, 53–5; Bono 1984, 76).

This doubling of positive and negative Didos reflects the two Didos of tradition, Vergil's fallen queen and the chaste Dido who dies faithful to her first husband, an old division that prompted much discussion in the Renaissance (Watkins 1995, 50–3; Kallendorf 1989, 43–4). It feeds into Spenser's wider obsession with doubles and false images, and is closely related to another Vergilian image of ambivalent and delusive femininity, the apparition to Aeneas in the wood near the shore of Carthage of his mother Venus in the disguise of a huntress-nymph of Diana (*Aen.* 1.314–20). Within the imagistic patterns of the *Aeneid* this virginal *Venus armata* prepares Aeneas, and the reader, for the later appearance of Dido, an object of desire compared in ekphrasis and simile to the Amazon Penthesilea and the goddess Diana. In the commentary tradition on Vergil's Venus-*virgo* that runs from late antiquity to the Renaissance (Wind 1968, 75–80; di Matteo 1989) she becomes a more complex and often darker figure: the wood becomes the dark wood of matter or of the world, and the disguised Venus is either elevated into a celestial Venus, or degraded into a figure of lust, as in Petrarch's reading (see above). This version of the Vergilian Venus-*virgo* is an example of the fair-and-foul female, a recurrent threat in Fairyland.

The most direct Spenserian allusions to Aeneas' vision of Venus-*virgo* and his subsequent response to the vision, *"o quam te memorem, virgo?…o dea certe…"* ("what shall I call you, maiden?…A goddess, to be sure," *Aen.* 1.327–8), occur in the context of epiphanies of innocent female beauty, but which amaze and disturb the beholder. Una in the woods is worshipped by the Fauns and Satyrs "as Goddesse of the wood" (I, vi, 16), and Sylvanus is "In doubt to deeme her borne of earthly brood; / Sometimes Dame Venus selfe he seemes to see, / But Venus neuer had so sober mood; / Sometimes

Diana he her takes to bee, / But misseth bow, and shaftes, and buskins to her knee."
Here the Vergilian Aeneas' uncertainty as to the reality of the *falsa imago* is extended
through an assessment, typically Ovidian in form, of the ways in which the apparition
differs from the chosen standards of comparison. In Spenser's day this apparently
innocent confusion of a mortal with a god carries the more dangerous hint of religious idolatry. Just how dangerous the inability to distinguish between appearance
and reality may be in this world is shown by Duessa, evil rival to Una for the Redcross
Knight's affections, whom Fradubio had unmasked too late as the fair-and-foul
enchantress (I, ii, 40–1), as he tells the Redcross Knight, who is himself unable to see
through Duessa and realize that Fradubio's experience is his own.

Una as Venus-Diana anticipates the more elaborate reworking of the Vergilian scene
in the appearance of Belphoebe to Trompart and Braggadochio, false pretenders to
the heroism of an Aeneas (II, iii, 21–42), followed by minor reprises in Belphoebe's
appearance to Timias at III, v, 35 ("Angell, or Goddesse do I call thee right?"), and
in the witch's reaction to Florimell at III, vii, 11 ("And doubted her to deeme an
earthly wight, / But or some Goddesse, or of Dianes crew"). The Vergilian scene was
earlier the subtext for Colin Clout's lay "of fayre Elisa, Queene of shepheardes all" in
the "Aprill" eclogue in *The Shepheardes Calender*: literally a subtext, since the emblems
of the two shepherds at the end of this fourth eclogue (in which Elisa also takes the
role of the child in Vergil's fourth eclogue: Cullen 1970, 114–16) are taken from
Aeneas' address to Venus, *o quam te memorem virgo?* and *o dea certe.*

According to the *Letter to Raleigh* Belphoebe is the name for one of the two persons of Queen Elizabeth, the "most vertuous and beautifull Lady," corresponding to
the "most royall Queene or Empresse" figured in the Faerie Queene, Gloriana (who
never appears in person in the surviving six books). The relationship between the
alluring but unattainable maiden of the woods Belphoebe and the courtly majesty of
Gloriana, two reflections or "persons" of the same historical individual, comments on
the similarity-in-difference in *Aeneid* 1 between the nymph-like Venus-Diana and
royal Dido. The former wears a mask, a "persona," that the goddess can put aside as
easily as she takes her leave of her mortal son. Dido is destroyed by the conflict
between roles over which she ends up having no control: an Amazon who cannot
dictate her relationship with the opposite sex, a Diana lookalike who must try to function in the more complicated world of court and city, a devotee of chastity who
becomes the victim of sexual passion. For Aeneas, however, she is but a stage on the
journey from Troy to Italy, while for Vergil's contemporary reader she represents the
temporary stumbling-block of a Cleopatra before the final triumph of the Roman
patriarchal order in the person of Augustus. Spenser constructs his epic around a living female monarch, and *The Faerie Queene*'s various hypostatizations of Dido and
Venus-*virgo* dramatize the complex relationships between the English queen and the
predominantly male society within which she must succeed or fail. There is cause for
alarm both in the possibility that the royal virgin will marry (the Protestant fear that
she might wed the Duc d'Alençon) and in the probability that she will not as she
passes child-bearing age, raising anxiety about the succession. The power politics
always inscribed in the male gaze on virginal beauty become more than personal when
behind a Belphoebe hovers the British empress. The couple Britomart and Artegall

embody the ideal of an ultimately harmonious synergy of fame and love; the tangled history of Belphoebe and Arthur's squire Timias (from *time*, "honor") charts the more difficult course of desire and public success at the real court of Elizabeth, with transparent allusion to the historical relations between the queen and Sir Walter Raleigh.

Epic and Romance, Vergil and Ovid

"Ladies gentle deeds" (I proem 1.5) points the reader to Ariostan romance. The first of Spenser's heroes enters accompanied by a virtuous lady, but the Redcross Knight will be led astray by various fallen and deceitful women, before he can reach his goal of marriage to the one true virgin, Una. The labyrinthine Wandering Wood into which the hero and the lady stray is the archetypal locus for the errancies of romance as opposed to the linear quests and conquests of epic. This is the point of entry into the dark woods of the Italian romances of Ariosto and Tasso, behind which lies Dante's *selva oscura* (Nohrnberg 1976, 136–9); Spenser's wood is also a highly Ovidian wood: the elaborate catalogue of trees at I, i, 8–9 has its closest parallel in the catalogue of trees that gather in a shade to listen to the song of Orpheus at Ovid, *Met.* 10.90–105 (Pugh 2005, 45–6). (That there are many other parallels, notably in Vergil (*Georgics* and *Aeneid*) and Chaucer, is itself a sign that Spenser's "Ovidianism" cannot be cordoned off from a larger set of literary relationships.) Is this then the point at which a Vergilian epic plot is diverted into the Renaissance genre of romance, whose classical model is Ovid's *Metamorphoses* rather than Vergil's *Aeneid*? The opposition of epic and romance was central to sixteenth-century debates over the relative merits of Ariosto and Tasso. These in turn have fed fruitfully into recent discussion of the contrasting aesthetics of the *Aeneid* and the *Metamorphoses* (Hardie 2007), and in another turn this work by classicists has been directed back to a renewed reading of *The Faerie Queene* in the light of its Vergilian and Ovidian intertexts: Pugh (2005) argues strongly for an Ovidiocentric as opposed to Vergiliocentric *Faerie Queene*. Yet the dependence of the opening dive into the Wandering Wood on models in *Aeneid* 1 and 4 shows how romance plots may emerge from a certain reading of the Augustan epic: important for medieval and Renaissance dark woods is Servius' identification of the woods at *Aen.* 1.314 and 6.136 as matter or the confusion of this life (Nelson 1963, 158–60). The subdued presence of the story of Dido and Aeneas right at the beginning of *The Faerie Queene* reminds us that with a little pressure the *Aeneid* yields the typical romance plot: the hero Aeneas must extricate himself from the clutches of a woman with a past, Dido, to journey towards marriage with the virgin Lavinia.

The Ovidian model of the poet in exile has also been increasingly applied to Spenser; in book 6 of *The Faerie Queene* the disruptions of the pastoral world into which the poet attempts to retreat are seen as reflecting Spenser's own experiences in an Irish landscape far from the metropolis (Pugh 2005, 217–43). At the same time the last book of the 1596 poem is also a turn back to the pastoral world that is the first stage of the Vergilian *rota*, and to the experience of the exiled Meliboeus in eclogue 1

(McCabe 2002, 233–5), on which, of course, Ovid had already modeled his own exilic experience (Williams 1994, 32–3, and Putnam's chapter in this volume).

The Extent and Depth of Spenser's Vergilianism

The first large-scale study of Vergil and Spenser, by Merritt Hughes (a student of John Livingston Lowes, author of *The Road to Xanadu*, a detailed study of Coleridge's imaginative reprocessing of his insatiable reading), downplays the importance of Vergil. Hughes concludes that "Vergil's influence upon the *Calender* seems to have been slight, indirect, and distorted" (Hughes 1929, 307); in *The Faerie Queene* the story of Fradubio and the bleeding tree (I, ii) is "the only reproduction of a Vergilian legend as an unbroken whole" (Hughes 1929, 368), and even that is closer in detail to Ariosto's imitation of the Vergilian episode in the story of Astolpho changed into a laurel (*Orlando furioso* 6; on reworkings of the Polydorus episode see Scott 1987). A view persists that Spenser practises a magpie-like allusivity that is not interested in intertextual dialogues. In book 5 Artegall rampages Hercules-like through the world as he deals out justice: there are occasional echoes of the exploits of the Vergilian Hercules, as in Malengine's "false footsteps" (V, ix, 6), reminiscent of the trick of the cattle-thief Cacus, but one might not wish to see any larger engagement with Vergil's exploration of a Herculean model of heroism. Artegall's iron policeman Talus "is a fine instance of Spenser's 'curious universal scholarship,' embodying diverse traditions and bringing a unified interpretation out of them" (Nohrnberg 1976, 425). Or perhaps not even unified: a discussion of Spenser's borrowings from political writers of the Renaissance concludes that "Spenser was a *bricoleur*, taking what he needed to fashion a sometimes doubtful 'Allegory, or darke conceit,' from authors who were themselves freely taking from each other" (Baker 2001, 56). Martindale (1996) criticizes Watkins' (1995) study of Spenser's Vergilian allusion for making Spenser "too like a (theoretically informed) modern scholar." In this section I take two examples where Spenser's use of Vergil (at least) appears to be both sharply focused and possessed of a literary-historical awareness.

In III, ix, 33–51, at the dinner-table of Malbecco and Hellenore, Paridell completes the series of histories and prophecies in books 2 and 3 that tell the story of Britain from the Trojan War, via the arrival of Trojans in Britain, to the coming of Elizabeth. He first tells of his own history as the descendant of Parius, son of the liaison of Paris and Oenone long before the rape of Helen. Britomart, who knows of her own Trojan lineage, asks Paridell to tell what happened to Aeneas, as Dido herself asks Aeneas to recount his own adventures at the end of *Aeneid* 1 (III, ix, 40.7, "What to Aeneas fell"; *Aen.* 1.754, *casusque tuorum*). In two stanzas Paridell runs through the contents of, respectively, the first and second halves of the *Aeneid*, with detailed verbal echoes. A third stanza recapitulates material from the prophetic speech of Jupiter in *Aeneid* 1 to take the story down to the foundation of Rome (the second Troy). Britomart then enthusiastically completes the story with the prophecy of a third and "new Troy," Troynovant or London, washed by the waters of the Thames,

"Vpon whose stubborne neck, whereat he raves / With roring rage… / She fastned hath her foot" (III, ix, 45), as the prophetic scenes of Augustan empire on the shield of Aeneas end with an image of the eastern River Araxes "chafing at a bridge" (*Aen.* 8.728). Paridell replies that he "had forgot, that whilome I heard tell / From aged Mnemon ["Remembrancer"]," and now gives a résumé of the history of Brute and his British descendants, repeating material that Arthur has read in the "Briton moniments" in the library of Eumnestes in the House of Alma (II, ix, 59). Paridell is inclined to be unmindful of the post-Vergilian extensions and developments of the *Aeneid*, of which *The Faerie Queene* itself is one of the grandest examples, but has an accurate memory of the Vergilian text itself, as in his own career he faithfully mimics his own antique ancestor Paris, proceeding in the next canto to rape Malbecco's wife Hellenore. This rape of Helen, however, will lead to no great new epic venture: Paridell carelessly casts up Hellenore, once he has "filcht her bels" (III, x, 35.7), and she ends up content to be the sex toy of the Satyrs. Britomart will continue in her quest for her future husband Artegall. An example of Spenser's own creative swerve from over-exact imitation of the classical model is in the framing of Paridell's second narrative, on the history of the Trojans and their descendants: Britomart plays Dido at the banquet in asking for the story (III, ix, 39–40), but at the end the part of Dido entranced and inflamed by Aeneas' narrative is taken over by Hellenore ("Vpon his lips hong faire Dame Hellenore… / Fashioning worlds of fancies evermore," III, ix, 52). Spenser's heroine Britomart will not be trapped in the world of Dido. (For fuller and differently nuanced readings of allusive and narrative strategies in III, ix, see Suzuki 1987; Dubrow 1990).

The second example is from book 2, which taken as a whole is the most epic in the poem, a miniature "moral-allegorical epic of the kind that [Spenser] took Homer and Vergil to have written" (Krier 1986a, 76), "a kind of analytical encyclopedia of the epic tradition" (Quint 2003, 28). The chief models are Homer and Tasso, and the allegorical tradition on both. Pyrochles is a personification of the irascible spirit of Achilles (Nohrnberg 1976, 301–2), but he also displays elements of Achilles' son Pyrrhus and of Vergil's Turnus possessed by *furor*. Spenser recognizes the way in which Vergil resurrects the Homeric Achilles first in Pyrrhus, in *Aeneid* 2, and on a larger scale in Turnus, and further comments on the tradition of Turnus-like opponents in Ariosto and Tasso. Pyrochles also represents the potential for fury within the heroes Guyon and Arthur, a temptation that Aeneas fails to resist at the moment when he most fully embodies the Homeric character of Achilles as he kills Turnus at the end of the *Aeneid*. Spenser allusively pairs Aeneas and Turnus in Atin's rousing to action of Pyrochles' brother Cymochles, personification of the concupiscent part of the soul (II, v, 25–38), whom Atin finds abandoned to sexual pleasure in the Bower of Bliss of Acrasia (one of Spenser's Dido figures). Atin first rouses him by reminding him of his erstwhile fame and glory, "Vp, vp, thou womanish weake knight, / That here in Ladies lap entombed art, / Vnmindful of thy praise and prowest might" (II, v, 36.2–4). This is Mercury's rebuke to the uxorious Aeneas dallying in Carthage: *heu, regni rerumque oblite tuarum!…si te nulla movet tantarum gloria rerum…* (*Aen.* 4.267, 272). Cymochles suddenly awakes out of his dream, to further incitement from Atin, I, v, 37.6–9:

> As one affright
> With hellish feends, or Furies mad vprore,
> He then vprose, inflam'd with fell despight,
> And called for his armes; for he would algates fight.

This is Turnus leaping out of bed infuriated by Allecto and shouting for his arms, *arma amens fremit* (*Aen.* 7.460); but in another city, Troy, Aeneas had also started from a dream with a wild desire to fight, *arma amens capio* (*Aen.* 2.314), *furor iraque mentem / praecipitat* (316–17).

Mirrorings and Repetitions

Spenser has an intimate feel for Vergilian intratextuality, the mirrorings and repetitions that create patterns of likeness and difference, reaching over the whole text and linking images, motifs, and persons. Another example from the first appearance of Belphoebe is the insertion within the rewriting of the encounter of Aeneas with Venus of similes taken from Aeneas' first vision of Dido, II, iii, 31:

> Such as *Diana* by the sandie shore
>   Of swift *Eurotas*, or on *Cynthus* greene,
>   Where all the Nymphes haue her vnwares forlore,
>   Wandreth alone with bow and arrowes keene,
>   To seeke her game: Or as that famous Queene
>   Of *Amazons*, whom *Pyrrhus* did destroy,
>   The day that first of *Priame* she was seene,
>   Did shew her selfe in great triumphant ioy,
> To succour the weake state of sad afflicted *Troy*.

This both recognizes that the Vergilian narrator's comparison of Dido to Diana in the simile at *Aen.* 1.498–502 picks up the character Aeneas' tentative identification of Venus with Diana at 1.329, and that the description of the artistic image of the Amazon Penthesilea at the end of the ekphrasis of the scenes of the Trojan War at 1.490–3 doubles as another *comparans* for the flesh-and-blood Dido, who enters as if on cue. Aeneas will destroy Dido as inevitably as Achilles killed Penthesilea; Spenser's variant of Pyrrhus for his father Achilles is derived from Caxton's *The Recuyeil of the Histories of Troye* (Berger 1957, 113–17). For Martindale (1996: 363) the easy move from Vergil to Caxton is evidence that Spenser's allusivity is casual and opportunistic. One could reply that Spenser uses Caxton to make explicit what remains unstated in the Vergilian ekphrasis, with the further irony that Belphoebe is viewed *not* by the dangerous gaze of an Achilles-like Aeneas, but by the false pretenders to knighthood, Trompart and Braggadochio.

The multiplication of characters and interlacement of plots over the six books of *The Faerie Queene* are very different from the Aristotelian unity of the *Aeneid*. Yet the mirrorings that create multiple connections between different parts of the poem, Spenser's strategy of "continually repeating formulae in differing contexts" (DeNeef

1982, 94), may owe something to Vergilian technique, as does the containment of this proliferating plurality within tightly controlled and intricate architectural structures. For example, the figure of Ate at IV, i, 19–30, a personification of discord and seditious uses of the word who strives to undo the concord to which book 4, the Legend of Friendship, is tending, generates a whole series of figures of strife and slander in the second half of the poem, including Envy, Detraction, Sclaunder, the poet Malfont, and, climactically, the Blatant Beast who ranges unchecked at the end of book 6. At the beginning of the second half of the poem as we have it, the hellish Ate corresponds to the Fury Allecto, who triggers the discord that motivates the second half of the *Aeneid*. In a Vergilian perspective, the Blatant Beast's breaking of his iron chain at the end of book 6 of *The Faerie Queene* echoes the outburst of *furor* in the last lines of the *Aeneid*, as Aeneas kills Turnus. Allecto's eruption in *Aeneid* 7 replays the outburst of the hellish winds in the storm in book 1, and she is related in various ways to other divinities and personifications in the *Aeneid*, not least the *Fama* of *Aeneid* 4, literary ancestor to Spenser's Ate and Blatant Beast, who sows discord in the hitherto concordant relations of Trojan and Carthaginian, and is the ultimate cause of the historical wars between Rome and Carthage.

The underworld is another example of this exfoliating multiplication of a theme in both poets. The literal descent of *Aeneid* 6 is echoed in figurative underworlds in books 2 (the dark night of the Sack of Troy), 3 (the phantom Troy revived at Buthrotum), and 9 (Nisus and Euryalus' entanglement in the dark wood) (Putnam 1965, index s.v. "underworld"). After the vision of cosmic order vouchsafed in the underworld in book 6, Allecto erupts from hell in the next book to play havoc with history, whose final restoration to order will be blazoned on the shield of Aeneas, a pendant to the Parade of Heroes in book 6, and which is manufactured in an underground forge whose infernal energy is directed to the construction of Roman *imperium*. The Spenserian underworld is similarly multifunctional. Archimago sends a spirit down to the House of Morpheus to bring back a false dream (I, i, 37–44), an Ovidian version of the underworld (*Metamorphoses* 11) furnished with the double gates of *Aeneid* 6: for Spenser as, in different ways, for Vergil and Ovid, the underworld is a resource for poetic traditions and makings. In I, v, Duessa rides down to hell in Night's chariot to enlist Aesculapius' services in the healing of Sansfoy's wounds. In II, vii, Guyon descends to the Cave of Mammon, the prison-house for those who pursue the false goods of wealth and immoderate honor, and where the Cyclopes in the Vergilian forge of Vulcan turn into fiends forging gold treasure (II, vii, 36: cf. *Aen.* 8.449–53). Guyon resists the Tartarean temptations, and returns to the world above to learn the positive lessons of the Vergilian underworld in the House of Alma, where a lengthy course in human physiology and psychology (~ the first part of the speech of Anchises on the nature of the soul) is followed by readings in the histories of the British and Elfish races (~ the Parade of Heroes). It is in another version of the Vergilian underworld, the deep delve of Merlin, that Britomart receives a prophecy of her descendants (III, iii). The Garden where Adonis enjoys his afterlife (III, vi) is the place for a cosmic philosophy that takes off from Anchises' doctrine of a thousand-year cycle of reincarnation (III, vi, 33: cf. *Aen.* 6.748–51). This vision of a *concordia discors* is followed in the next book by the discord that emanates from the House of

Ate "hard by the gates of hell" (IV, i, 20.1). In both poets the mythological under-world is a vivid setting for issues of cosmic, psychological, theological, and moral order and disorder.

FURTHER READING

General on Spenser and Vergil: Hughes (1929), Bush (1932, 101–7), Webb (1937), Gentili (1988); much relevant detail is to be found scattered through Nohrnberg (1976). Spenser and the Vergilian career (*rota Vergilii*): Neuse (1978), Helgerson (1983), Cheney (1993), Burrow (2008). Looking for Spenser's "Georgics": Sessions (1980), Ettin (1982), Tylus (1988). Recently on *The Shepheardes Calender* and Vergil's *Eclogues*: Lindheim (1999). On the impor-tance of the *Aeneid* for *The Faerie Queene*'s use of legend to foreshadow history: O'Connell (1977); on the *Aeneid* and the Renaissance "dynastic epic": Fichter (1982). Epic allegoresis and Spenser: di Matteo (1989), Quitslund (2001), Quint (2003). Gaze and ekphrasis: Watkins (1993), Krier (1990). Epic and romance: Burrow (1993), Watkins (1995).

CHAPTER FOURTEEN

The *Aeneid* in the Age of Milton

Henry Power

In a postscript to his translation of the *Aeneid* (1697), John Dryden adopts a mournful tone:

> What *Virgil* wrote in the vigour of his Age, in Plenty and at Ease, I have undertaken to Translate in my Declining Years: struggling with Wants, oppress'd with Sickness, curb'd in my Genius, lyable to be misconstrued in all I write; and my Judges, if they are not very equitable, already prejudic'd against me, by the lying Character which has been given them of my Morals.

There is a curious turning of the tables here. Dryden is concerned not with the extent to which he has given a faithful account of Vergil, but with the possibility that his readers might misunderstand him. Then, as now, *construe* had a grammatical application. To *construe* is to analyze the grammar and syntax "of a foreign and especially a classical language, adding a word for word translation" (*OED* s.v. 3). The business of translation, in other words, does not end with Dryden. What subscribers got for their five guineas was a text which had acquired a new layer of meaning. This might strike us as odd in the present day, when many of us (if not all: cf. Braund's essay in this volume) prefer our translators invisible, but Dryden's version is intended to carry a meaning independent from, if analogous to, Vergil's. Separating the two can be a challenge.

In the eighteenth century, many English readers shied away from the *Aeneid*. Protective of hard-won liberties and a fledgling constitution, they were suspicious of a poem apparently written in support of absolute monarchy. Dryden, a Tory and a Catholic, regarded as "the chief exponent of the seventeenth century's Royalist *Aeneid*" (Harrison 1967, 9), was viewed similarly. The republican writer William Hayley, whose *Life of Milton* was so vehemently anti-monarchist that it had to be toned down for publication, saw Dryden and Vergil in the same light:

> We find that the Roman Bard is supposed to have drawn a flattering portrait of his Emperor in the character of Aeneas, and that the English poet has, with equal ingenuity,

enwrapt the dissolute Charles the Second in the Jewish robes of King David. (Hayley 1782, 125)

Joseph Spence remembers Pope drawing an identical comparison: "The *Aeneid* was evidently a party piece, as much as *Absalom and Achitophel*. Virgil [was] as slavish a writer as any of the gazetteers" (Spence 1966, 229–30). On this basis, Dryden is seen as a second Vergil, politically in tune with the poet he is translating. Not all readers have agreed. In the past few decades, scholars have begun to discover "further voices" in Vergil's epic – opposed to the central, public voice of empire. Dryden has recently been accused of stifling these dissonant voices. Richard Thomas charges him with having "converted Virgil into a flatterer." He has a graver charge still: Dryden "viewed Virgil and Virgilian poetry through the lens of his own times […] and consequently made Virgil's poem something that it had not once been," namely, "a poem depicting and exhorting right action by the prince and urging the obedience of his subjects" (Thomas 2001, 125).

Dryden – worried that readers might misconstrue not Vergil, but him – would hardly disagree that he is making something new from Vergil's poem. But the view of Dryden as a suppressor of Vergilian dissonance or smoother-out of complexity does not stand up to scrutiny. At times, Dryden's remarks on the poem's internal politics are on the threshold of open dissent:

> Æneas, tho' he Married the Heiress of the Crown, yet claim'd no Title to it during the Life of his Father-in-Law. […] As for Augustus, or his Uncle Julius, claiming by descent from Aeneas; that Title is already out of doors. Aeneas succeeded not, but was Elected. (Dryden, *Aeneis*, dedication)

William of Nassau had, through strange coincidence, married the heiress of the English crown in 1677. His father-in-law, James II, was still very much alive when William – lacking Aeneas' patience and good manners – claimed the throne in 1688. Dryden's translation emphasizes Aeneas' mission as one of restoration (see Hammond 1999, 218–82), and this is never clearer than at the poem's start:

> His banish'd Gods restor'd to Rites Divine,
> And setl'd sure Succession in his Line:
> From whence the Race of *Alban* Fathers come,
> And the long Glories of Majestick *Rome*.
> (I.7–10)

There is plenty here unlicensed by the Latin. "Rites Divine" suggests James II's Catholicism, "sure Succession" the hereditary principle violated by William. Even the reference to "*Alban* Fathers," translating *Albanique patres*, points to the title given James during his brother's reign: duke of Albany. All of these phrases recall James' deposition, at a time when there was no realistic prospect of his restitution. If Dryden's *Aeneid* is a royalist epic, it is one whose author identifies with a discarded house.

Dryden, provocatively, refused to dedicate the *Aeneid* to William III, though his publisher Jacob Tonson urged him to do so. Tonson still managed a compliment to the king, though. Dryden complained in a letter to his sons that "in every figure of Eneas, he has caused him to be drawn like K. William, with a hookd Nose" (Dryden 1942, 93). The plates adapted by Tonson were those first used in John Ogilby's sumptuous 1654 *Works of Virgil* (on which see Eastin's chapter in this volume). Ogilby's translation, substantially different from the one he published in 1649, is strongly pro-Stuart. Dedicated to the exiled Charles II, it impressed the king sufficiently for Ogilby to be given a central role in planning the Restoration celebrations six years later. Tonson, to Dryden's evident dismay, was attempting to co-opt a piece of Stuart propaganda for the Williamite cause. Nonetheless, the list of subscribers includes the names of Roman Catholic peers and disgruntled closet Jacobites alongside those of prominent Whigs and Williamites. As John Barnard (2000) shows, this heterogeneity was not simply the result of a tussle between publisher and poet: both of them solicited subscriptions from across the political spectrum. It was appropriate that Dryden's Vergil should have a mixed audience: a sense of dislocation and divided loyalties informs the whole poem.

***

Dryden's *Aeneis* is a complicated response to Vergil's poem. It should be seen as the culmination of a tradition of similarly complicated (though not, for the most part, similarly successful) responses. The second half of the seventeenth century was especially rich in Vergilian translation and imitation, but there is no single ideological thread to unite the fifty or so texts which declare Vergil as a source (Gillespie 1992, 66–7, lists forty-five published between 1660 and 1700). Their one uniting factor is that they were all written during a period of civil war, or its aftermath. This is a factor they have in common with the *Aeneid* itself. Vergil began work on the poem shortly after Octavian had secured victory over Antony at Actium, ending (one might argue) a century of civil war. Dryden gives an account of these struggles in his *Dedication*, and tries to position Vergil in relation to them:

> I say that *Virgil* having maturely weigh'd the Condition of the Times in which he liv'd: that an entire Liberty was not to be retriev'd: that the present Settlement had the prospect of a long continuance in the same Family, or those adopted into it: that he held his Paternal Estate from the Bounty of the Conquerour, by whom he was likewise enrich'd, esteemd and cherish'd: that this Conquerour, though of a bad kind, was the very best of it […] These things, I say, being consider'd by the Poet, he concluded it to be the Interest of his Country to be so Govern'd. To infuse an awful Respect into the People, towards such a Prince: By that respect to confirm their Obedience to him; and by that Obedience to make them Happy. This was the Moral of his Divine Poem. (Dryden 1987, 281)

Dryden regards Vergil's position as being politically compromised, though this in no way lessens his admiration for his poem. After all, he has told his readers at the outset that the primary function of an epic poem is "to form the Mind to Heroick Virtue by Example" (267). Dryden – unloved by William III – is not in so strong a position as his model. Nor (*pace* Thomas) does he have a similar objective: far from inculcating obedience in others, he fails to show it himself. The overwhelming similarity between the two poets is that their relation to their work is determined by the civil wars through which they have lived.

Dryden had a precedent for relating Roman civil wars to English ones. Richard Fanshawe's *Il Pastor Fido* (1648), a miscellany containing a version of *Aeneid* 4 in Spenserian stanzas, concludes with a "short Discourse of the Long Civill Warres of Rome." These troubled times ended happily, Fanshawe tells us, when Rome "being now quite tired out with civill Warres, submitted her selfe to the just and peacefull Scepter of the most Noble Augustus." He goes on to quote and translate (in support of this statement) a passage from *Aeneid* 6. This is the moment during Aeneas' tour of the underworld when Anchises shows him the future *princeps*:

> Hic vir, hic est, tibi quem promitti saepius audis,
> Augustus Caesar, divum genus, aurea condet
> Saecula qui rursus Latio, regnata per arva
> Saturno quondam, super et Garamantas et Indos
> Proferet imperium.
>   (*Aen.* 6.791–5)

> This is that man of men Augustus, hee
> Whom (sprung from Heaven) Heaven oft hath promis'd thee,
> The man that shall to *Italy* restore
> The *Golden Age* which *Saturne* gave before,
> And to the *Parthians* and the *Ind's* extend
> His spacious Empire.
>   (Fanshawe 1997, 139–40)

Written shortly before the execution of Charles I, and addressed to the future Charles II, this is clearly wishful thinking on Fanshawe's part. We might note the particular emphasis given to the word *restore*, not an especially close translation of *condet* (which indicates a new foundation rather than a restoration). The same volume opens with a poem dating from the years of personal rule – a "Pastoral Ode" in which Britain's peaceful detachment from the war-ravaged continent is celebrated in terms recalling the first eclogue:

> Onely the Island which wee sowe,
> (A world without the world) so farre
> From present wounds, it cannot showe
>   An ancient skarre.
>   (Fanshawe 1997, 55–9, ll. 33–6)

In 1630, when the Pastoral Ode was first circulated in manuscript, Vergil's poetry served as a model for panegyric.[1] In the 1648 collection, it provides a means of seeking consolation in the past, and expressing hope for the future. Anchises' words to his son hold out hope of a happy ending beyond civil war.

It is on various late-seventeenth-century interpretations of this passage that I want to concentrate in this essay. It will not, therefore, provide a complete survey of

Vergilian imitation in the period; among the texts excluded are the translations of John Denham, Sidney Godolphin, Robert Howard, and Edmund Waller (on which see Proudfoot 1960), Abraham Cowley's free imitation in *The Civil War* (on which see Power 2007), and Charles Cotton's travesties. The focus should prove, however, a fruitful one. Aeneas' visit to the underworld is of crucial importance in the *Aeneid*. It comes halfway through the poem, at the point when Aeneas and his followers stop being exiles and become invaders; he is forced to confront both his Trojan past and his Roman future. It is here that Vergil's present most obviously intrudes on his narrative (in *Aeneid* 8 it appears in ekphrastic brackets). It is here too that we are given the most direct link between Aeneas and Augustus, with those emphatic words: *hic vir, hic est*. We were told at the outset that Vergil is concerned with a *vir*. Anchises points to Augustus and suggests that this – yes, this – might be the man in question.

Fanshawe's wish came true. Charles II was restored in 1660, and there was no shortage of loyal poets to celebrate the event in terms borrowed from Vergil. Foremost among them was John Boys, a poet whose 1661 translation of *Aeneid* 6 typifies the straightforwardly royalist reading of the poem. He leaves readers in little doubt of his political affiliation, opening the volume with a dedication to Edward Hyde and con-cluding it with an epigram addressed to Charles II:

> Had I, *Great Monarch, Maro*'s divine spirit,
> Or did the Prince of Poets wit inherit,
> You should be my *Æneas*, and what He
> His *Heroe* gave, to you ascrib'd should be.
> (Boys 1661, sig. Gg2^r)

Boys' translation is remarkable only for the fervor of his enthusiasm for his newly restored monarch. Among the paraphernalia at the back of this thick volume is the text of an orotund speech Boys had intended to give on the king's arrival in Dover, "but was prevented therein by reason his Majesty made no stay at all in that town" (sig. Ff4^v). In Boys' version of *Aeneid* 6, as in Fanshawe's, Anchises treats Octavian's reign as a restoration:

> This, this is hee, whom fates to thee commend,
> God-sprung *Augustus*, the golden age again
> He shall restore, as in old *Saturns* reign.
> (Boys 1661, 29)

Less conventionally, in a note on these lines, Boys attributes the incarnation of Christ to the resulting *pax Augusta*:

Wherefore in his *pacifique* reign *Christ* our Saviour, the Prince of peace, vouchsafed to take our nature upon him, to shew that nothing is more acceptable to him then peace, that bond of love and perfect character of his sincere disciples; which (although through the ambition and emulation of Princes it hath been for many years banished Christendome) is now like to return again by the happy & long-desired *redintegration* of amity betwixt

those two great *Luminaries* of this our Western world, *Spain* & *France*: I cannot but add
my prayers for the speedy consummation of so wish'd-for a Good. (150)

Boys' logic is abstruse, but there is no doubt about the connection he is making.
Augustus' reign is not only a restoration of Golden Age values, but also the cause of
man's redemption through Christ. Charles II is cast as a redeemer, as well as a
restorer.

Different in tone, but similar in allegiance, Maurice Atkins published his *Cataplus*,
a travesty of *Aeneid* 6, in 1672. Following the lead of Charles Cotton, in particular,
Atkins offers a poem which stays (for the most part) close to the structure of his
source, but whose style is pointedly base. The principal differences are the use of
jaunty octosyllabic couplets, salty colloquialisms, and contemporary references. No
amount of humorous anachronism, though, can prepare us for the intrusion of the
English Civil War into Anchises' speech. We have already heard about Augustus' reign
("a mighty, high renown'd *Augustus*, / That shall be at least a Justice"), when Anchises
comes in turn to Brutus – in Vergil, in Dryden, and even in Boys, a defender of liberty.
In *Cataplus*, he is blinded by an irrational hatred of kings:

> So that by dealing with them fiercely
> He'l tumble all things arsy versy:
> As when the head submits to tail,
> And State dwindles to Common-weal,
> When Crown is doft in humble rate
> To a Plebeian new-sumpt Hat,
> When crafty roundheads booty share
> Ravisht from local Cavalier.
> (Atkins 1672, 82)

It becomes clear over the course of Anchises' long account of his various depredations
that Brutus has morphed into Oliver Cromwell.

> So *Brutus Tarquin* did out-hector
> That he himself might be Protectour.
> His two sons from the very strummel
> Shall be as loyal as *Dick Cromwel*. (83)

The political histories of Rome and England need to be chopped and changed quite
freely for the comparison to work. Brutus did not make himself Protector; nor did
Richard Cromwell collude in the restoration of Charles II. This is a highly polarized
view of the period which remakes the *Aeneid* as what Pope was to call a "party piece."
In common with most other travesties of the period, Atkins provides quotations from
the original Latin in footnotes, giving the impression of scholarly – if playful – engagement with the text. The lines quoted above are apparently suggested by *Aen.* 6.819–20:
consulis imperium hic primus saevasque securis / accipiet ("He will be the first to receive
the consulship, and the cruel axes"). The presence of Vergil's Latin is more important
than its meaning.

The following year saw the publication of another travesty of *Aeneid* 6. John Phillips was John Milton's nephew and occasional collaborator. He is unlikely to have had his uncle's help with *Maronides, or Virgil Travesty* (1673) – though the title page does identify Phillips as the author of *A Satyr against Hypocrites* (1655), an anti-Presbyterian poem of which one imagines Milton approved (see Hill 1977, 487–91). *Maronides* (the title punning on Charles Cotton's 1664–5 *Scarronides*) is royalist in approach, which is hardly surprising; Phillips wrote for money, and tended to blow with the prevailing wind. He has no great respect for his source material, frankly telling the reader in his preface that "in my opinion this book of *Maro* is but an enthusiastick piece of Drollery it self; so that I have only done him the office of a Commentator" (sig. A3ᵛ). But although he takes the opportunity to picture leading republicans in hell ("There *Bradshaw* lyes in a Symarr / Of burning Canvass, lin'd with Tarr," 99), he is at least consistent in his anti-clericalism. The vision of Augustus is significant, in his view, because his hegemony prepared the ground for a yet more frightening one:

> But hey – my boy, I have him now
> Lyes closer layd the better show:
> With my soules eyes methinks I see
> Great Antichrist, chief of the Three,
> [...]
> *Romes* power shall near and far extend
> *Indus and Garamas* beyond,
> The *Caspian* Seas, *Mæotis* Lake
> Dread *the* fierce noise his bulls there make.
> (Phillips 1673, 151; cf. *Aen.* 6.794, 798–9)

Presenting Octavian as a precursor of the pope is an unlikely twist, and illustrates neatly that even the royalist Vergil supposed to have informed the (Roman Catholic) Dryden is heterogeneous in character.

The foundational text of royalist travesty is Samuel Butler's *Hudibras*, which travesties Vergilian epic in the most general sense possible; specific allusions to Vergil are in fact rare in Butler's poem. Nonetheless, he is adamant that the business of translating Vergil should not be attempted by parliamentarians.

> Thou that with Ale, or viler Liquors
> Didst inspire *Wither, Pryn,* or *Vickars*
> And force them, though it were in spight
> Of nature and their stars, to Write
> (Butler 1967, 1.639–42)

Butler tells us in a note that "this *Vickers* was a Man of as great Interest and Authority in the late Reformation, as *Pryn,* or *Withers,* and as able a Poet; He translated *Virgils Æneides* into as horrible Travesty in earnest, as the French *Scaroon* did in Burlesque, and was only outdone in his way by the Politique Author of *Oceana*" (*ad loc.*) John Vicars' version of the *Aeneid* (the first complete translation of the poem into English heroic couplets) was published in 1632, long before the onset of war. His allegiance to parliament after 1642 prompted Butler retrospectively to politicize his translation. Those who do not understand Vergil risk collapsing into burlesque, or travesty, if they try to translate him. Intentional travesty, then, is the preserve of those with a true sense of the poet. Butler's attitude to parliamentarian translators of Vergil thus exactly mirrors the goings on inside *Hudibras*, where we see plebeian characters making grotesque attempts to act heroically.

Butler's jealous attitude towards Vergil, though, only highlights the fact that many others also laid claim. While Vicars' translation was published long before the war broke out, James Harrington's (also picked out for abuse in the note to *Hudibras*) was explicitly a response to the events of the 1640s and 1650s, and to the isolated position in which he found himself. In 1656, Harrington had published *The Commonwealth of Oceana*, a description of a fictionalized version of England, in which Olphaeus Megaletor (an idealized portrait of Cromwell, or of the man Cromwell might have been) has drawn up a new constitution according to the principles of classical republicanism. The book failed to make waves, and Harrington's first volume of Vergil opens with a crestfallen reflection on the relative usefulness of poetry and political philosophy: "I have reason'd to as much purpose as if I had rimed, and now I think shall rime to as much purpose as if I had reason'd" (Harrington 1658, sig. A2ʳ).

The following year Harrington produced a translation of books 3–6 of the *Aeneid*, along with a new preface explaining his theory of translation in more detail:

> *Virgil*'s poetry is the best in Latine; and he who can bring it to be the best in English, be his liberty for the rest what it will, shall be his truest translator: which granted, the English Reader may sufficiently judge of like translations, without referring himself unto the Originals. (Harrington 1659, sig. A3ʳ)

A poem addressed to Vergil himself makes explicit the connection between poetic freedom and political liberty. It opens with a bold statement of independence:

> *Virgil*, my Soveraign in Poetry,
> I never flatter'd Prince, nor will I thee.

Harrington then goes on to list a number of passages where he has diverged from the Latin text (on rather pedantic grounds of plausibility), before concluding with a courteous expression of dissent:

> Thou never shalt perswade me to inform
> Our Age, *Æneas* in thy greatest storm
> Could raise both palmes, though to the Gods; one hand
> At least had hold, or there he could not stand.
> Nor is it in a Picture to devise
> How *Hector* round his Troy should be dragged thrice.
> [...]
> > Leige Lord,
> In these I may not give thee word for word;

> Nor if my freedom be obtain'd in these,
> Shall I be nice to use it as I please.
>
> (Harrington 1659, sig. A5^{r-v})

Harrington both suggests that Vergil's poetry is peculiarly applicable at a time of civil war, and advertises his republican credentials in having overhauled the meaning, and even the shape, of the text. The notion of Vergil as a monarchical figure also occurs in his *Political Aphorisms*, where he acknowledges the necessity of having preeminent political figures within a democracy: "A parliament of physicians would never have found out the circulation of the blood, nor could a parliament of poets have written Vergil's *Aeneis*; of this kind therefore in the formation of government is the proceeding of a sole legislator" (Harrington 1977, 279).

Though Harrington approaches the *Aeneid* sensitively, his translation is often hard work for the reader; judged by the translator's own chief criterion, it is not a true account of Vergil. It is hard to disagree with John Aubrey, who remarks that "his muse was rough," and recalls that he was eventually persuaded to stop writing poetry by Henry Neville, as he did so "*invitâ Minervâ*." Aubrey also tells us of the close friendship Harrington formed with Charles I in the late 1640s, when appointed a Gentleman of the Bedchamber by parliament; that he was "on the scaffold with the king when he was beheaded"; and that he was severely traumatized by the experience (Aubrey 1898, 1: 288–95). No other evidence places Harrington at Whitehall on January 30, 1649, but the assertion is supported by his extraordinary account of Priam's death in *Aeneid* 2, which he turns into a death by beheading (in Vergil's account decapitation takes place firmly after death): "Which words by unrelenting *Pyrrhus* said, / The other hand strikes off old *Priam*'s head." This is far from a celebration of the regicide, though. Indeed, Aeneas' appalled response to the sight places enormous, and uncomfortable, emphasis on his role as an eyewitness:

> And dire remembrancers, what might befall
> My family, deprived of my aid,
> With horrour to my guilty conscience laid.
> My father in the King, in *Hecuba*
> My undefended wife *Creüsa* lay,
> And of the children that I looked upon
> Me thought *Ascanius* must needs be one.
>
> (Harrington 1658, 38–9)

Although Vergil's Aeneas sees Anchises in his mind's eye, the wholesale substitution of his own relations for those of Priam is Harrington's innovation. It reads like the embellishment of someone brooding on the experience of civil war.

Harrington's Vergil avoids easy political classification, despite our intimate knowledge of its author's politics. In this it is unusual, but it is important to stress that Vergils were not drawn exclusively from the ranks of Stuart apologists. *The Irish Hudibras* is a travesty of *Aeneid* 6, published in 1689 – that is to say, after William had become king, but before his decisive victory over James II at the Battle of the Boyne. It is interesting for a number of reasons: principally because it is a work of Vergilian Travesty, obeying various conventions of the subgenre, written emphatically in support of William. In a preface whose argument is familiar, the anonymous author stresses the peculiar applicability of Vergil's work to the current situation.[2] In particular, he says, the figure of Augustus "appropriated to his present Majesty KING WILLIAM THE THIRD, is as natural and exact a Character, as if Vergil had design'd it for this present Monarch, England's timely Redeemer, whom Heaven long preserve." Aeneas becomes "Nees," a hapless, flatulent Irish Catholic whose thick brogue is rendered phonetically:

> What though of Ready nere a plack,
> Yet many a plugg of good Toback
> It cost me to come to dis Port;
> And not a Turd de better for't:
> Ycome like fool, ygo vidout
> My skeal, vid finger in my mout.
> ("Farewell" 1689, 11)

As with Atkins' travesty, readers are regularly provided with the original Latin. Again the Latin is included not to help readers appreciate the complexities of the relationship between model and imitation – the passage quoted above is apparently derived from *Et tandem Itallia* [*sic*] *fugientis prendimus oras* (*Aen.* 6.61). Rather, it reminds them that the text in hand has its origins in a poem of peculiar relevance at times like these: "And here it is worth observation, to see the Coherence of the Story; which is as exact in the Original, as if *Virgil* had Calculated it for That *Meridian*" ("Farewell" 1689, sig. A4ʳ). There is perhaps a pun intended in *Meridian*, given the author's peculiar transformation of Augustus at the end of the book:

> On a new Sun fix both thine Eyes,
> Exalted in the *British* Skies:
> Who timely through the Tempest broke,
> An *Orange* grafted on the Oke.
> Whose Juice the *English* Hearts shall cheer,
> And shall diffuse it's Vertue here;
> Destroying Popish Priests and Steeple,
> And worst of Vermin here, the People:
> Where ere an *Orange* comes in place,
> Poor *Nees* shall make a sowre Face:
> In's Stomach stick, which to the rest
> Shall be a Cordial to digest.
> This, this is He, the War-like Prince,
> Heaven promis'd long in their Defence;
> *Englands Augustus,* who shall be
> The Subject of Chronology:
> Who, plac'd upon the *British* Throne,
> Shall make poor *Nees* to sing, *O hone!*
> Sent from Above; who shall restore
> The *Dagon* they so much adore.

The identification of Dagon, the heathen deity of the Philistines, with the God of the Roman Catholics is significant. It was the Temple of Dagon that Samson demolished in a final show of strength, as related in the book of Judges and in Milton's *Samson Agonistes* (1671). The author both associates Catholic rites with Philistine idolatry and identifies himself ideologically with Milton. It is an aggressive reading of the *Aeneid*, discovering a triumphalism which translators play down in less troubled times. William is like an orange grafted to an English oak (an image recalling *Georgics* 2), but Catholics and Tories will find his rule bitter-tasting.

   William also takes the place of Augustus in Richard Blackmore's *Prince Arthur* (1695) – an attempt at a post-1688 national epic, of the sort Dryden's *Aeneid* would conspicuously fail to provide. Blackmore restages the parade of heroes from *Aeneid* 6, with Arthur in Aeneas' place and Uter Pendragon taking on the role of Anchises:

> Intently now on that great Monarch gaze,
> So much distinguish'd by his brighter Rays.
> This is the Man, the brave *Nassovian*, whom
> I nam'd, the great Deliverer to come.
> Succeeding Prophets under your great Name,
> This our great Offspring shall aloud proclaim.
>   (Blackmore 1695, 153)

It is no surprise that Blackmore cites Vergil as his major model, nor that he suggests his particular applicability to the times in which he writes.

> In this Work I have endeavour'd mostly to form my self on *Virgil's Model*, which I look on, as the most *just* and *perfect*, and which is most easily accommodated to the present Age, supposing the *Christian Religion* in the place of the *Pagan*. (Blackmore 1695, clv)

Like Boys in 1661, Blackmore finds in the *Aeneid* a useful template for Christian epic, and indeed his William III has something of Milton's Christ about him: "Thy great deliverer, who shall bruise / The serpent's head" (XII.149). His unimaginatively sycophantic lines on William took on a life of their own. John Gay in "A Journey to Exeter" (1716) is prompted by some verses on a tavern-sign to speculate as to Blackmore's true calling:

> How Rhyme would flourish, did each Son of Fame
> Know his own Genius, and direct his Flame!
> Then he, that could not Epic Flights rehearse,
> Might sweetly mourn in Elegaic Verse.
> But were his Muse for Elegy unfit,
> Perhaps a Distich might not strain his wit.
> If Epigram offend, his harmless Lines
> Might in gold Letters swing on Ale-house signs.
> [...]
> Then Maurus in his proper Sphere might shine,

> And these proud numbers grace great William's sign:
> *This is the Man, this the* Nassovian, *whom*
> *I nam'd the brave Deliverer to come.*
>   (Gay 1974, 203–7, ll. 121–44)

Blackmore's recasting of Anchises' prophecy has itself been crudely contextualized, and is now to be found swinging outside a pub called the King William, or the King's Head. The renaming of taverns to celebrate William's arrival in England was common; Gay suggests that Blackmore's literary tribute is no more sophisticated.

By the start of the eighteenth century, Anchises' prophecy of Augustus was perhaps the best known, most bitterly contested passage in the *Aeneid*. Its use by Jacobites is better known: HIC VIR HIC EST was engraved on Jacobite drinking glasses, and the full hexameter is found on a painting of the Old Pretender by a follower of Alexis Simon Belle (Risley 1920, 276). A medal struck to celebrate James' disastrous invasion of Scotland in 1708 also uses the line: *Thule – hic vir hic est quem tibi promitti saepius audis. Iacobus Caesar. Divi genus aurea rursus, secula qui reddet Scotis* ("Scotland, this is he, this is the man whom you have often heard me promise, James Caesar, of divine stock, who will again return a golden age to the Scots." See Brooks-Davies 1985, 129). It is interesting that on the medal the final verb is silently altered, to emphasize the reign of Augustus as a restoration: *condet* becomes *reddet*, as it had in Fanshawe's rendering of *Aen.* 6.792 (discussed above). The line was put to equally vigorous use by those who had displaced the Stuarts. It provided the epigraph for the *Spectator* on November 15, 1714, above a poem by Thomas Tickell on George I's progress through London (Bond 1965, 117). And if we are to believe Tim Thomas, an undergraduate who contributed to a book of elegies on the death of Queen Anne, the last Stuart monarch died with Vergil on her lips, as she endorsed her Hanoverian successor:

> Hic Vir, Hic est, Tibi Quem, ter felix Albion, optas,
> GEORGIUS AUGUSTUS? Nostrum Genus: aurea rursus
> Saecula Qui condet Nobis regnata per arva.
>   (*Pietas…Oxoniensis* 1714, sig. Y2^v)

For Pope, the line had become a joke, and in the *Dunciad Variorum* (1729) he applies it to the hapless Tibbald at the moment Dulness adopts him as her own:

> Now *Bavius* take the poppy from thy brow,
> And place it here! here all ye Heroes bow!
> This, this is He, foretold by ancient rhymes,
> Th'*Augustus* born to bring *Saturnian* times.
>   (Pope 2007, III.315–18)

Pope plays on the double meaning of Saturnian: not only "pertaining to the age of Saturn, or the Golden Age," but also "sluggish and slow-witted." He puns similarly at *Dunciad* I.25–6: "behold her mighty wings out-spread, / To hatch a new Saturnian age of Lead." Pope also merges the line from *Aeneid* 6 with the similar lines from the fourth (and so-called messianic) eclogue. Here, as so often, he engages closely with Dryden's Vergil:

> The last great Age, foretold by sacred Rhymes,
> Renews its finish'd Course, *Saturnian* times
> Rowl round again.
>
> (Dryden, *Ecl.* 4.5–7)

Pope, at the very moment of demolition, points to the suggestion of spiritual redemption in Anchises' words. (We should remember that he had himself already published a free imitation of the fourth eclogue, entitled *Messiah.*) The messianic overtone will be of importance when considering Milton's appropriation of the lines.

***

The question of Vergilian influence on *Paradise Lost* is a difficult one. The *Aeneid* can be found everywhere in Milton's poem – in thousands of local allusions, and in larger structural echoes. Milton's decision to reorganize the poem's book divisons for the second edition of 1674 is widely, and reasonably, seen as programmatic: a shift from a Lucanic ten books to a Vergilian twelve (see Hale 1995). But the *Aeneid* is widely regarded as a royalist poem, and Milton was both a republican and a highly vocal defender of the regicide. This problem has led to a strange tendency to distinguish between Milton the man and Milton the poet.

One solution is to argue that there is no actual contradiction between Milton's politics and his adherence to a Vergilian model. Edward Gibbon, himself a republican, felt that Vergil was similarly inclined, and pointed to the expulsion of the tyrant Mezentius in *Aeneid* 8. In making his case he turns naturally to the example of the most celebrated English republican:

> Milton himself, I mean the Milton of the Commonwealth, could not have asserted with more energy the daring pretensions of the people, to punish as well as to resist a Tyrant. Such opinions, published by a writer, whom we are taught to consider as the creature of Augustus, have a right to surprize us; yet they are strongly expressive of the temper of the times; the Republic was subverted, but the minds of the Romans were still Republican.
> (Gibbon 1770, 13)

Gibbon, it seems, still adheres to a "two Miltons" model, but he can at any rate see how Vergil might appeal to the "Milton of the Commonwealth." Sadly, his views on how Milton's use of a republican model might affect our reading of *Paradise Lost* are unrecorded. Something of this nature, though, is attempted by Kallendorf (2007), who argues that Milton found the *Aeneid* to be "not a straightforwardly Royalist poem, but a source for antimonarchical sentiment" (151), and holds up as evidence Milton's enthusiastic mention of Mezentius' expulsion in the *Pro Populo Anglicano Defensio* (1658).

More usually, the trend has been to play down Vergil's influence and to stress that of the republican poet Lucan. This approach has been influentially taken (in quite different ways) by Martindale (2002), Quint (1993), and Norbrook (1999). Norbrook's

aim is to show that there was a vibrant literary culture associated with English republicanism, and that this has been neglected by later critics. In this he succeeds brilliantly, but his view of the period is (perhaps inevitably) polarized, with Lucan and
Vergil serving as convenient poles. He cedes Vergil to the royalists in a way one suspects Milton would never have done.

Milton appears to reject both Homeric and Vergilian epic in a well-known passage
at the start of book IX, as he prepares to sing of

> sad task, yet argument
> Not less but more heroic than the wrath
> Of stern Achilles on his foe pursued
> Thrice fugitive about Troy wall, or rage
> Of Turnus for Lavinia disespoused,
> Or Neptune's ire, or Juno's, that so long
> Perplexed the Greek and Cytherea's son.
> (Milton 1997, IX.13–19)

As Norbrook points out (1999, 441), there is a curious parallel between one of the
epic motifs rejected by Milton, Hector "thrice fugitive," and one of those rejected by
Harrington: "Nor is it in a Picture to devise / How *Hector* round his Troy should be
dragged thrice." Harrington's particular quarrel is with the possibility of representing
triple movement visually (as suggested at *Aen.* 1.483), but both poets are announcing
their departure from a classical model for important reasons. Harrington (rather
pedantically) asserts his independence from a literary monarch, Milton his dissatisfaction with the models of heroism available – a dissatisfaction stressed by his haphazard
mingling of stories from Homer and from Vergil.

The difficulty of identifying the hero of *Paradise Lost* has often been remarked
upon. Considering Milton's relation to *Aeneid* 6 and the prophecy of Anchises – as
we have seen, a well-known and contested passage in the period – casts some light on
the problem. The lines with which Anchises hails the *princeps – hic vir, hic est* – refer
emphatically to a specific person; he makes sure Aeneas knows exactly which figure he
is talking about. They were, in the later seventeenth century, applied with a wonderful
lack of precision: to Charles II, to William III, to the pope. Even in the *Aeneid* itself,
another figure overlaps with Augustus: it is hard not to associate the *vir* of *Aeneid* 6
with the *virum* of the poem's first line.

Milton, too, opens his poem with a promise to sing – both of man, and of a man:

> Of man's first disobedience, and the fruit
> Of that forbidden tree, whose mortal taste
> Brought death into the world, and all our woe,
> With loss of Eden, till one greater man
> Restore us and regain our blissful seat.
> (I.1–5)

The *man* of the first line refers to all mankind, and to Adam – and possibly also to Eve
(the Hebrew word for woman can be translated as "of man"; see Machacek 1990).

The *greater man* is Christ, described later in the poem (in keeping with Pauline theology) as "our second Adam" (XI.383). Fowler (1997) notes *ad loc.* that the repetition of *man* stresses this point, "besides glancing at Vergil's *virumque*." He adds that "Virgil sings one man, but M. will sing two; adding the supernatural to the natural man, and so departing from pagan epic." In fact, the repetition nods at the appearance of Augustus in *Aeneid* 6, the moment when Aeneas encounters a greater man who can give sense to his wanderings.

Structurally, the strongest echo of *Aeneid* 6 comes in the final two books of *Paradise Lost*, when Michael shows Adam the events which will take place after his expulsion from Eden, culminating in the birth of Christ:

> he shall ascend
> The throne hereditary, and bound his reign
> With earth's wide bounds, his glory with the heavens.
> (XII.369–71)

The lines recall the prophecy of Jupiter at the start of the *Aeneid*: *nascetur pulchra Troianus origine Caesar, / imperium Oceano, famam qui terminet astris* ("From this noble stock a Caesar will be born, who will bound his reign with ocean, his glory with the stars," 1.286–7). This prophecy of Rome's future greatness is revisited, and enlarged upon, in *Aeneid* 6. Milton stresses the parallel by including a condensed version of it in his survey of future civilizations: "On Europe thence, and where Rome was to sway / The world" (XI.405–6). The emphasis on Adam as the ancestor of those he sees strengthens his similarity to Aeneas in the underworld, being shown his *Itala de gente nepotes* ("descendants of Italian stock," *Aen.* 6.757). After Michael has revealed man's future redemption in Christ, Adam exclaims,

> virgin mother, hail,
> High in the love of heaven, yet from my loins
> Thou shalt proceed, and from thy womb the Son
> Of God most high; so God with man unites.
> (XII.379–82)

While Augustus follows Aeneas in being the son of a god, Christ follows Adam in his corporeality – in becoming a man. The revelation is important to Adam because it comes as he and Eve are forced to leave the confines of Paradise, and to search for a "paradise within" (XII.587). Aeneas and his men must likewise forget Troy, which has exerted a strong – and malign – magnetic pull on them in the poem's first half (see Quint 1993, 50–96), and begin the process of building a new civilization. The man with whom Aeneas is confronted in the underworld silently guarantees that this is possible. The man of whom Michael speaks offers Adam salvation.

There was some precedent for this Christian reworking of *Aeneid* 6. As we have seen, various writers and polemicists have found a religious dimension in the lines. John Boys associates the rule of Augustus, the restoration of Charles II, and the birth of Christ. Blackmore, through a Miltonic allusion, was to give a messianic flavor to William III's invasion. Milton may also have known the work of the Dutch neo-Latin poet Caspar van Baerle (often known as Barlaeus), whose work was widely circulated in mid-seventeenth-century Europe. His *Paradisus, sive Nuptiae primorum paren-tum, Adami & Evae* (1643) is a version of the creation story, loosely based on a poem in Dutch by Jacob Cats, *Trou-Ringh*. It is written in florid hexameters, many of them devoted to an account of the marriage of Adam and Eve. As he considers the implica-tions of the match, Barlaeus turns to *Aeneid* 6:

> Hic vir hic est, cuius memorabunt nomina gentes,
> Quae medium adspicient Solem, quae signa Trionum,
> Quas oriens Titan, & quas declivis adibit

> This is the man, this is he whose name all people will mention who see the Sun at its height, and the constellations of the Bears; all those whom Titan will visit when rising, and when setting.

> (Barlaeus 1643, 1–31: ll. 323–5)

The use of the Vergilian tag here stresses the primacy of the poem's subject matter. Barlaeus suggests that Adam's *imperium* (330) surpasses that of Augustus, as he is the common ancestor of mankind. Milton shows that all mankind is descended from one man, and redeemed through another. The connection between the poems has been remarked on before. William Lauder (1750, 111–12) suggested in the mid-eighteenth century that Milton leaned heavily on Barlaeus. He may have had ulte-rior motives for doing so; he falsified a good deal of neo-Latin verse in order to prove that Milton was a plagiarist (apparently in the hope that such a revelation would benefit the Jacobite cause). In this instance, though, his claim seems justified (see Bullough 1964).

The echo of *Aeneid* 6 in the final two books of *Paradise Lost* allows Milton to stress Christ's corporeality. And Milton's use of the passage was informed by the tussle that was taking place over its meaning, and over the meaning of Vergil's poem more gener-ally. Aeneas' vision of Augustus promises hope beyond exile and war, both to Aeneas himself and to the first readers of the *Aeneid*, themselves emerging from a long period of conflict. To Adam and Eve, Michael's promise of salvation in Christ allows them hope as they leave Paradise. And Milton offers his readers, in still more troubled times, a man who transcends faction, and a king whom all parties can tolerate. This is not a rejection of the *Aeneid*. Milton's theme may be greater than Vergil's, but in a poem where we are often required to understand great things through small ones, his Vergilian inheritance is of crucial importance.

NOTES

1   The poem recalls *Ecl.* 1.66: *et penitus toto divisos orbe Britannos.* Abraham Cowley would later return the line to an internecine context in the Lucanic–Virgilian opening to *The Civil War* (1643): "What rage does England from herselfe divide, / More than seas doe from all the world besides?" (Cowley 1973, 1.1–2). Pugh (2008) explores the poem's

various classical sources thoroughly, and argues persuasively that it offers a more troubled vision of the personal rule than is widely agreed. Nonetheless, there is a deliberate contrast between the Vergilian material on display at the start of Fanshawe's collection, and that at the close.

2   The poem is sometimes attributed to a certain "James Farewell," but this is likely to be a mistake; the phrase is commonly used at the close of anti-Jacobite pamphlets (though not this one). See further Carpenter (2005), who also explores the relationship between *The Irish Hudibras* and two manuscript antecedents, dated 1665 and 1686.

FURTHER READING

The fullest account of English translations of Vergil before Dryden remains that of Proudfoot (1960), who has little regard for them, or for Dryden himself. Burrow (1997a, b) provides a useful and provocative survey, which stresses the tendency for translators of Vergil to come from the ranks of the dispossessed. Zwicker (1984) gives an excellent account of resistance to William III in Dryden's translation, Hammond (1999) a wide-ranging and sensitive account of Dryden's relationship with his classical inheritance. There is no general account of Vergilian travesty in the period, though Carpenter (2005) provides some useful background to *The Irish Hudibras*.

Thomas (2001) convicts Dryden of complicity in maintaining a falsely "Augustan" Vergil, but nonetheless gives a penetrating account of the many points at which he diverges from his model. Kallendorf (2007) seeks to build on Thomas' thesis by demonstrating that some early modern authors – Milton included – responded to "pessimistic" elements in Vergil's poem (though Kallendorf is far less dogmatic than Thomas about the extent and function of these elements). Harrison (1967) gives an excellent account of the *Aeneid*'s fortunes in the eighteenth century, though he also sees Dryden as epitomizing a "royalist Vergil" against which later readers reacted.

Lewalski (1985) and Porter (1993) both find evidence for Vergilian influence on Milton, and offer good introductions to the topic. Blessington (1979) is also still useful. Burrow (1993) shows how Vergil's influence on Milton was mediated through earlier English romance. Martindale (2002) argues that Vergil's presence in *Paradise Lost* has been overstated, and suggests Lucan as a major influence. Quint (1993, 301–8) highlights similarities between *Paradise Lost* and the *Pharsalia*, but he has also (2004) demonstrated the extent of Milton's structural debt to Vergil. Norbrook (1999) offers a polarized view of English literary culture in the period, and downplays Milton's interest in Vergil. Wilding (1987) suggests that Milton's version of epic, and especially his account of the war in heaven, is a form of travesty analogous to that of Samuel Butler.

CHAPTER FIFTEEN

Practicing What They Preach?
Vergil and the Jesuits

Yasmin Haskell

Introduction: Vergil Recomposed

The cult of Vergil in the old Society of Jesus has its roots in Renaissance humanism, and perhaps especially in the canonical poetic guides of Marco Girolamo Vida and Julius Caesar Scaliger, widely referenced by Jesuit authors (IJsewijn 1990, 138). In the "Art of Writing Well," a Latin poem in the tradition of Vida's *De arte poetica* (1527) as much as that of Horace's letter to the Pisos, Rainier Carsughi, S.J. (1647–1709) laid down a deceptively simple law for his "Rhetoric" students at the Roman College (Carsughi 1709, §6): "But if perhaps your ardour is more keenly inflamed by Divine Poetry, prostrate yourself and worship your precursor, Vergil, and in your song imitate him to the best of your ability" (*At si forte tuos Divina Poesis amores / Acrius irritat; praeeuntem pronus adora / Virgilium, quantumque vales imitare canendo*). Vergil is to poetry what Cicero is to oratory. Just as we must take care not to stray from the straight and narrow Ciceronian path, so we should resist the temptations of Lucan's "brilliant seriousness" (*gravitas arguta*), of Statius' "noble song" and Claudian's "fluent" one (*nobile Papinii Claudique volubile carmen*). "Praise outstanding poets," Carsughi allows, "but cultivate Vergil: He should be the rule for your Muses" (*claros laudato Poetas, / Virgilium colito: ille tuis sit norma Camaenis*; cf. Vergil, *Geo.* 2.412–13).

Of course, Vergil could never be the model for *all* the genres to which versatile early modern Jesuit poets and their pupils turned their pens. In his very next breath Carsughi exhorts us to "choose the best models, whichever art you choose": Juvenal should be our guide for satire, Horace for lyric, Tibullus and Ovid for elegy, and Seneca for tragedy. In what sense, then, is Vergil the ideal? And what exactly does Carsughi mean by "divine" poetry, given that his own poem is effectively modeled on Horace? The divinely inspired genre of epic, the highest to which we can aspire? Or might he be hinting at a broader category of hexameter verse on Christian themes, embracing eclogue and didactic poetry as well? In the proem to *De arte poetica* Vida had set out to teach the young poet "to sing the deeds of heroes or the praises of the gods." Significantly, his own poetic career culminated in an epic on the life of Christ and "hymns on divine matters." As it happens, the most popular neo-Latin Christian epic in Italy at this time was Tommaso Ceva's *Iesus Puer* (Milan, 1690), on the boyhood of Christ, which took its bearings less from Vergil than from Renaissance poems such as Vida's *Christiad*.

The history of the Jesuits and Vergil is a bit like the history of the Society of Jesus itself – an appearance of codes and rules magisterially dictated and enforced from above, but, in practice, forever adapting organically to local circumstances. In short, it is a natural history. We must look beyond the literal expression of the code to what the Jesuits liked to call their *modus procedendi*, the ideological DNA driving the spectacular profusion of Jesuit Latin verse in the early modern period and manifesting itself in a sometimes bizarre hybridization of classical forms. This genetic code, which replicates itself over two centuries through the myriad literary, intellectual, and cultural productions of the Society's priests and coadjutors, will be mapped in this chapter in a sample of theorists and practitioners of Vergilian imitation. How closely did Jesuit writers capture the likeness of their poster-boy poet in their original hexameter verse? And what light do textbooks and treatises shed on their practice? In what follows I have no illusions about pronouncing the final word on the Jesuits and their Vergil(s). The more modest aim of this chapter is to indicate some pathways into a relatively open field in classical reception studies from the particular perspective of a neo-Latinist.

To begin, as it were, from the top: an obvious departure point for research into Jesuit neo-Latin epic is the massive anthology, "Parnassus of the Society of Jesus" (*Parnassus* 1654), compiled at the height of the Order's cultural powers in the middle of the seventeenth century. The preface to this volume speaks of the phoenix-like resurrection of ancient poetry, "if not more brilliant than the ancient one, then certainly more pure; in which you will know not whether to marvel more at talent or piety; whether to commend learning more, or pleasure." The first and only of the *Parnassus'* seven projected parts, *epica seu heroica*, includes several ambitious poems in a more or less Vergilian mold. However, the reader picking up, say, Francesco Benci's five-book epic on the Jesuit martyrs in Japan (Benci 1509 ≈ *Parnassus* 1654, 1.1: 703–60) and expecting to encounter there a familiar old friend may be disappointed; she may even feel that "her" Vergil has been taken hostage by enemy aliens (and I don't mean the Japanese!). Vergil is transformed almost beyond recognition in Laurent Le Brun's (1608–63) allegorical baroque epic on Ignatius' journey to the Holy Land (Le Brun 1661 see Gaertner 2004), and Jacob Masen's (1606–81) *Sarcotis* of 1654 has attracted critical attention only because of allegations that Milton plagiarized it in *Paradise Lost* (Sommervogel 1890–1909 s.v. "Masen"; Masen 1771, iii–lxxii; cf. Power's chapter in this volume and p. 215 below). And yet both Le Brun and Masen preface their poems with lengthy dissertations on epic/heroic poetry in which Vergil is a touchstone. In no uncertain terms, anticipating those of Carsughi quoted above, Le Brun decrees:

> Vergil distinguished himself in the *Aeneid*, nor indeed should you seek out any other
> Roman author.... The remaining ancient poets are to be considered inferior in rank and

place in competition with Vergil, the leader of the Muses: and I mean even Horace himself, except in certain of the Odes; likewise Catullus, Tibullus and Propertius, although great celebrity has commended them to fame in the art which they professed. Catullus excelled indeed when he wrote about Attis and the wedding of Theseus, but his other works are of so little consequence as not to be worth the price of the oil for the lamp to read them by. (Le Brun 1661, 186)

The doctrinaire tone reveals that Le Brun's treatise was as much a practical manual for aspiring poets in the Jesuit colleges as a *captatio benevolentiae* for his own epic efforts. So also with Masen's *Heroica poesis praeceptionibus et exemplis illustrata* ("Heroic poetry illustrated with precepts and examples"), in which we find a chapter, for example, on how to generate an epic off the Vergilian plan – but also, interestingly, how to move beyond that (Masen 1771, 24ff.). It is not that these Jesuit epic poets didn't know their *Aeneid* well enough, then. They knew it, but also chose to turn it, inside out.

The Vergilian model is certainly closer to the surface in Bartholomaeus Pereira's *Paciecis* (1640), which celebrates the epic voyage and missionary exploits of Portuguese Jesuit Francisco Pacheco ([†]Nagasaki, 1626), and implicitly sanctions Portuguese expansion in East Asia. As Klecker (2002a) observes, Pereira's epic not only recalls Vergil's in the form of its title and the number of its books, it carefully mirrors the structure of the *Aeneid* even down to the distribution of half-verses. (She also shows that his primarily Vergilian orientation did not prevent Pereira from drawing on other models, notably Lucan.) Klecker makes the attractive suggestion that the poet may have aspired to "complete" his Vergilian epic with reference to Maffeo Vegio's Renaissance supplement to the *Aeneid* – it ends with the heavenly reception of its hero by Ignatius, as Vegio's had with Aeneas' death and apotheosis.

Under a broader head of French historical epics written in the years following the siege of La Rochelle, and looking forward to a future French war against the Turks, Braun (1999) includes two Jesuit items: Jean de Bussière's "Scanderberg" (1658) in eight books and Pierre Mambrun's "Constantine, or Idolatry Vanquished" (1658) in twelve. But if in these and many other Jesuit poems we find Christians pitted against non-Christians, pagans, and heretics, it would be a serious mistake to reduce Jesuit epic to military propaganda for modern Catholic monarchs. (See, e.g., Braun 1999, 20 on Jacques Mayre, S.J., author of seven historical epics – each comprising between twelve and twenty-five books! – in which the deeds of Christian heroes past are celebrated more for their own sake than for their military propaganda value.) In spite of, or rather, *through* its imitation of the *Aeneid*, Pereira's poem frankly challenges the very idea of the Vergilian epic hero and the Roman imperial project (Klecker 2002a, 107, 109; cf. Klecker 2003a on the *Ignatias* of António Figueira Durão, sometime student of the Lisbon college, celebrating the empire of Jesuit education and learning). In both the *Paciecis* and the *Saberis* – a juvenile work on the wanderings of St. Francis Xavier by the prodigious Neapolitan Jesuit poet Niccolò Giannettasio (1715–21) – the saintly hero assumes the role of lovesick Dido as much as mission-conscious Aeneas. The wandering and/or wounded deer simile of *Aeneid* 4 is applied to Xavier in the *Saberis* and to the Nagasaki martyrs in the *Paciecis*, merging in both poems with the image of the deer thirsting, as the soul after God, in Psalms 41, 2 (Klecker 2002a, 2002b). In the third part of his dissertation on the epic, the *prolusio* to his own *Ignatiad*, Laurent Le Brun pointedly declares: "the goal of this poem is not the founding of a city or Republic but the Society of Jesus" (225). And in a chapter entitled "whether Ignatius is a hero," Le Brun reminds us that Aeneas himself was hardly a model warrior, while Ignatius combines the Vergilian heroic virtues of piety and prudence – and, for good measure, led a military life until the age of 30!

If any generalization can be made about Jesuit neo-Latin epic it is that it demands a level of reader participation unparalleled in its primary ancient model. The lives of the heroes portrayed in these poems are quite literally exemplary. Klecker observes that the Aeneas-like wanderings of Giannettasio's Xavier serve precisely to point up the reader's own "wrong turnings of sinfulness," and to inspire his own imitation of Christ (2002b, 179). Moreover, by planting their poems with Christian analogues and antidotes to Vergilian characters and situations (the Devil for Juno; an angel for Mercury; the city of Manresa for Carthage) and by giving individual verses an audaciously spiritual "spin," Jesuit poets are not merely inviting us to a game of literary *Quellenforschung*. They are demanding of their readers, who in the first instance will have been Jesuit students and alumni, a continuous meditation on the paradoxical closeness and distance between pagan model and Christian imitation/"improvement." Sometimes the double vision so produced can be disconcerting for the modern reader, as when the pious Isabella Rosa is cast in the role of love-struck Dido near the beginning of the second book of Le Brun's *Ignatiad*. This lady, who befriended Ignatius in Barcelona, attempted to found a female Jesuit order in spite of his opposition. She is described in terms which teasingly hint at her marriageability: "Isabella – herself illustrious in ancestors and not unworthy in the blood of her parents, who, though exceedingly beautiful in form, was more beautiful for the virtues joined thereto – saw rays issuing from his gleaming face: as when the rose, the same color as the purple dawn, shines more beautifully, with the dawn enhancing its native hue" (*Vidit ab ardenti radios absistere vultu / Clara ab avis Isabella, nec ipsa indigna parentum / Sanguine, quam pulchrae florentem lumine formae / Ornabant magis adiunctae virtutis honores: / Ceu matutino fulget rosa concolor ostro / Pulchrius, aurora innatum geminante ruborem*: the broader context here is reminiscent of *Aen.* 1.586–91, but note as well the allusion to Lavinia's blush, 12.67–9). I would go so far as to suggest that there was greater potential for Jesuit poets to exploit this instructive *Verfremdungseffekt* in writing neo-Latin verse than when they ventured into the vernacular (as in Pierre Le Moyne's *Saint Louis* (1653), an attempt at a French national epic). The use of Latin permitted a more comprehensive cannibalization of Vergil's poetry at the verbal and stylistic level, rendering the subsequent consecration (or, dare we say it, transubstantiation) of the original text that much more miraculous.

Outside his natural haunts in neo-Latin pastoral, georgic/didactic, and epic poetry, the Vergil of the Jesuits may be sought in their plays, art, and emblem books (Grant 1965; Ludwig 1982, 151–80; Haskell 2003, *passim*; Monreal 2005). Indeed, several of the epic poets mentioned in this chapter were also playwrights (Benci, Donati, Bidermann, and Masen). Reinhold Glei (2006, 185–6) notes that it was a Jesuit, Jacob Gretser (1562–1625), who attempted the first neo-Latin dramatic recreation of

Aeneid 5 (the "Prologus in Quintum Aeneidos" in Cod. XV 223 of the Studienbibliothek Dillingen, fol. 177ᵛ–183ʳ). The didactic context of such plays must of course be borne in mind; *Aeneid* 5 was one of the easier Vergilian texts (together with *Georgics* 4 and *Aeneid* 7; perhaps also *Georgics* 1 and *Aeneid* 9), to judge from Jouvancy (see below) prescribed for the "Upper Grammar" class, the third of the five ability-graded classes of the lower curriculum in the Jesuits' official code of education, the *Ratio studiorum* of 1599 (Farrell 1938). A book that was not on the curriculum, however, *Aeneid* 4, provided the inspiration for another play (*Pietas in Peregrinos sive Dido Tyriorum Regina Æneam hospitio recipiens...* in Codex Vindobonensis 9813, fol. 150–91; see Adel 1957; Kailuweit 2005, n.0326; Glei 2006, 205–6) by Johann Baptist Adolph, S.J. (1657–1708). In this extraordinary little work, complete with musical interludes, Dido nobly renounces Aeneas for the sake of his historical mission!

The verses in various metres accompanying the emblems of the *Imago Primi Saeculi*, a bumper volume commemorating the first centenary of the Society of Jesus (Antwerp, 1640; trans. Putnam, forthcoming, 2011), contain many erudite Vergilian reminiscences. If the ingenuity and playfulness of those verses and the cherubic cupids of the engravings put us more often in mind of Ovid, it is telling that the emblem celebrating Jesuit humanist education itself (*Scholae humaniorum litterarum*, "Schools of the more humane letters," *Imago* 1640, 471) is inspired by the fourth georgic. The engraving shows bees buzzing around a formal garden in front of a battery of hives sheltered by a homely thatched roof; the caption reads: "youth is let loose to play around the hives" (*Luditque favis immista iuventus*; cf. Vergil, *Geo.* 4.22). The *Imago* as a whole may be read as a sort of graphic epic, and its creators leave nothing to the imagination of the beholder/reader in expounding its allegorical subtext. The preliminary "synopsis of the entire work" draws explicit parallels between the life stages of the Society of Jesus and the birth, youth, teaching, passion, and glory of Christ. This reminds us of the introductory treatises and, as it were, "instructions for use," which prime the reader of the Jesuit epics of Le Brun and Masen, and of the Jesuit practice of providing keyed "captions" to direct interpretation of their emblems and paintings, a practice with its roots in Jeronimo Nadal's *Evangelicae historiae imagines* of 1594 (Bailey 2003, 11). But while all the literature reviewed to this point has been to some extent didactic, in the next section we pursue the Vergil of the Jesuits through the dense forests of their educational literature *stricto sensu*, through curriculum policy documents and teachers' manuals, to school editions and commentaries, academic oratory, poetic dictionaries and handbooks.

Towards a Vergilian "Way of Proceeding"

But where was it written, "Thou shalt follow Vergil"? The *Ratio studiorum* does not in fact prescribe Vergil for poetry in the same global terms as it does Cicero for oratory (*Ratio studiorum* 1616, 112; cf. Farrell 1970, 73). The penultimate class of the lower curriculum, "Humanities" (in effect, the poetry class), was conceived as preparing the soil for eloquence, to receive the pure Ciceronian seed to be sown more liberally in the "Rhetoric." In Humanities, style is perfected and *copia* developed through daily readings in Cicero's moral philosophy, in the historians, and "from the poets, especially Vergil, except the *Eclogues* and the fourth book of the *Aeneid*." Additionally, students will read "select Odes of Horace, elegies, epigrams, and other poems of excellent ancient poets – so long as they are purged of all obscenity."

The most comprehensive guide to what should and should *not* be served up to impressionable youth in the Society's colleges was the "Select Library" of Antonio Possevino (1593). This Jesuit author wore many hats – theologian, historian of Russia, and envoy on His Holiness' secret service to eastern and northern Europe – and his monumental publication, which is part reading list, part *Reader's Digest*, has been aptly described as "a true encyclopedia of the Counter-Reformation" (Balsamo 2001, 55; cf. Biondi 1981). A substantial chapter in the oft-reprinted book 17 on poetry and painting ("De Poesi et Pictura ethnica, humana et sacra") bears the ominous title, "On Vergil, where and how to use him properly" ("De Virgilio, ubi & de recto eius usu," Cap. XXIII). Here Vergil receives the undivided attention of the mature Jesuit diplomat and censor (who had not been averse to a bit of book burning as a young priest). Possevino had already praised the edifying character of the *Eclogues* in his chapter on Theocritus and pastoral: "But Vergil, who has in many respects licked Latin poetry into shape, has shown that eclogues can be seasoned with the salt of wisdom to raise minds to higher and worthier matters – such as those he sang of in the fourth eclogue" (Cap. XVI). While acknowledging the piscatorial eclogues of Jacopo Sannazaro, the pastorals of Giovanni Gioviano Pontano, and the sacred eclogues of Antonio Geraldino, Possevino especially commends the "new and holy kind of eclogue" composed by fellow Jesuit Jacobus Pontanus (Spanmüller) and notes, "But although Vergil is first among the pagan poets, he must cede something in the writing of epic, in which there are quite a few in our age who excel without stain" (Cap. XXV, "On epic proper, and on sacred epic poems"). He had urged his young readers and their instructors not to content themselves merely with a comparison of Theocritus and Vergil, but to read the latter especially in the light of Constantine's speech on the "messianic" eclogue, "as if a friend and guide." To that end, he supplies in the next chapter a translation of Constantine's "Address to the Assembly of the Faithful" (appendix to Eusebius' *Life* of Constantine). In his main Vergil chapter, Possevino undertakes to "talk about the other things, in their order, which pertain to so great a poet as Vergil – so that the best use of him may be made clear." As we shall see, the instrumental force of that word, *usus*, should not be underestimated.

Possevino begins in a relatively conciliatory spirit, observing that obscene and irreligious passages are easier to excise from Vergil than they are from Ovid, Catullus, Propertius, Tibullus, and the like: "Such are the invocation of the gods, profane loves, the lying together of Dido and Aeneas, and the rest – about which the less said the better." Moreover, we are not to be "too anxious in purging or censuring those things which do not pertain to piety." Thus, against the carping of Macrobius, Francesco Campano, and Sebastiano Conradus (= Corrado) are set the vindications of Vergil's style by Julius Caesar Scaliger and Guglielmo Modicio. Under the second head of this chapter Possevino enjoins that "those things [in Vergil] which may be conveniently presented so as to stir souls to virtue and the truth should not be omitted," reminding us of Constantine and now adding a dash of Augustine. But the Augustinian chalice turns out to be a poisoned one. Under his third and final chapter head Possevino warns: "As for those things which offend piety and religion, let us thoroughly refute them using the very firm authority of the Fathers rather than our own. And indeed Augustine himself, a man of the keenest judgment, has paved this road for us also."

Possevino proceeds to quote extensively from the opening chapters of the *City of God*, where Augustine had set the presumption of Vergil's "spare the vanquished and crush the proud" (*parcere subjectis, & debellare superbos*) against the Biblical "God resisteth the proud but giveth grace unto the humble" (James 4:6; 1 Peter 5:5); mocked the irrational piety displayed by the Romans towards their *penates*, the conquered gods of Troy; condemned the sacrilegious looting by the Greeks at Troy of the temples to their shared gods (contrasting this with the Christians' scrupulous donation of objects taken in war to the memorial shrines of the apostles); and, perhaps most pregnantly for our Jesuit's purposes, lamented the pernicious effects on young pagan minds of early exposure to Vergil, quoting from *De civitate Dei* 1.3: "They read Vergil as little boys so that, no doubt, the great poet, the most brilliant and excellent of all, may not easily be forgotten, having been imbibed in the tender years. As the saying of Horace goes: 'The pot retains long the flavour with which it was imbued when fresh' (*Quo semel est imbuta recens servabit odorem / Testa diu* [*Epist.* 1.2.69–70])." (On this passage and on Augustine's attitude towards Vergil in general, see Wills' chapter in this volume.) With Augustine's blessing, as it were, Possevino is emboldened to offer his own opinion:

> And indeed, to speak frankly, if we consider the art, judgment, prosody and diction of Vergil, there are many things which are said elegantly and justly; but those things, to speak most truthfully, are neither appropriate for the use of the Christian state, nor for the sort of poets with whose songs the ears of Christians ought to resound.

The chapter concludes with a handful of *cavenda Virgilii* from Origen, Scaliger again, Celio Rhodigino; some rhetorical fireworks from Lactantius (for which see Klecker 2007, 449); and a final poke at the hellfire of *Aeneid* 6 by the Jesuit author himself:

> But, as we have said of Homer, so we can say of Vergil: a more proper use of him may be made if the obscene parts are removed. And [as for] those things which smack of the cult of the false gods, when it comes to teaching the sixth book of the *Aeneid* – although, to be sure, I would never endorse lecturing [*praelegere*] on that to adolescents – a most solid knowledge should first be imparted to their minds about the truth of Hell, but at the same time there should be a discussion of why Satan has tried to cover and obscure this article of Divine Justice in the veils of myth, viz. lest the fear of God, which is the beginning of wisdom, should occupy the hearts of men. (Possevino 1593, 436).

That Possevino should devote so much space to Vergil's hidden dangers is, of course, a testament to our poet's enormous and enduring cultural influence, not least in the schools of the Society of Jesus. He wastes much less time refuting the errors of, say, Ovid or Lucretius. It may come as a surprise that Possevino expresses reservations about the teaching of *Aeneid* 6, the contents of which strike us today as eminently "reconstructable" in terms of Christian doctrine. And indeed, Ignatius himself in a letter to Andrea Lippomano argues "positively for the ethical content of authors such as Vergil and Terence – they had much that is 'useful for doctrine, and much not unuseful, indeed helpful, for a devout life'" (O'Malley 1993, 256). But Possevino's paranoia bears out my suspicion that Vergil was in general *not* revered by the Jesuits for his moral wisdom, for his "tears in things," much less (*pace* Constantine) for anticipating Christianity. *Aeneid* 6 was perhaps too close for comfort, and the Jesuit teacher had a difficult balancing act to accomplish – to inculcate the beauties of Vergil's style while at the same time insulating his students from the seductions of the pagan worldview.

The more able and adventurous students will always have read beyond the curriculum, and mature Jesuit poets certainly alluded to authors and passages theoretically proscribed (such as Lucretius' hymn to Venus, or the *Ars amatoria*). One of the most frequently printed early modern editions of Vergil's works, by Charles de la Rue, S.J. (1675), gives the unexpurgated text of *Aeneid* 4 and 6. And there is also the rich and relatively uninhibited Vergilian commentary by Juan Luis de la Cerda, S.J. (1608–17; see Laird 2002). But the not-so-glamorous work of cleaning up the classical poets for routine classroom use was carried out by, among others, Father Joseph de Jouvancy (1643–1719), in a famous series of school editions and handbooks. This seasoned pedagogue taught at the colleges of Compiègne, Caen, La Flèche, and Paris and was later the Society's official historian. In his "Method of Learning and Teaching for Masters in the Lower Schools of the Society of Jesus" (1692, rev. 1703: see Dainville 1951; my translations are from Jouvancy 1892), Jouvancy dubs Vergil simply "the prince of Latin poetry" in a list of ancient poets available for imitation. The list gives brief biographical data for each author and a succinct evaluation of his style; the relative brevity of Vergil's entry *vis-à-vis* those on, for example, Horace, Ovid, and Lucan only confirms his position as the standard against which all others are to be measured.

In a separate discussion of the proprieties of epic, Jouvancy holds up the *Aeneid* as an example which "cannot be praised enough." More revealing, though, than his perfunctory demonstration of how that poem fulfills Aristotelian structural criteria is his assertion that all the minor poetic genres are, in fact, subordinate parts of epic. Here are ranged "idyll, satire, ode, eclogue, epigram, elegy...bucolic and georgic poetry.... In all these poems one paints, praises or blames men, their actions, their tastes and the arts or professions in which they are engaged" (Jouvancy 1892, 51). Jouvancy's rhetorical (epideictic) bias is very much in evidence, and it is no surprise that he defines poetry in general as "a liberal art which imitates the actions of men in order to be useful to morals. It differs from rhetoric in that it employs other means of persuasion. In effect, it is through the example of the good to imitate, or the evil to avoid, that it impels us to virtue and wards us away from vice" (Jouvancy 1892, 48).

If Jouvancy's poetics seem at the outset disappointingly simplistic, even prudish, we should not lose sight of the practical rationale of this work. (It would be interesting to compare his *Institutiones poeticae* of 1718, which I have not seen.) In enumerating the various "little poems" from which the epic is comprised, Jouvancy is effectively commissioning Jesuit students *themselves* (through their teachers) to take baby steps towards the perfection of Vergilian verse:

> All these little poems are usually paintings of places, things or morals. The paintings of
> places, for example, are those of the cave of Hunger, the palace of Sleep, the island of

Fortune, the labyrinth of Deceit, the palace of Eloquence, &c. These little poems are, again, paintings of things, such as hunting, sport, a true or fabulous history, a metamorphosis, &c. And they are also paintings of morals, when for example one writes a satire about somebody, when one paints avarice, or the annoying loquacity of a chatterbox... (Jouvancy 1892, 51)

Such compositions were the bread and butter of the Humanities and Rhetoric classes and their associated extracurricular "Academies." The *Ratio studiorum* (1616, §3) provided that the Prefect of Lower Studies might excuse students from verse composition only for very serious reasons. The young Jacques Vanière (1664–1739) found himself unable to wriggle out of this obligation as a student at the college of Béziers – just as well, since he later became one of the Society's most fêted Vergilian poets, author of a sixteen-book georgic on the management of a country estate (Dubois 1979; Soubeille 1982, 1995; Haskell 2003, 38–60). In a work such as Giovanni Battista Ganducci's "Poetic descriptions" (1660) – less a florilegium for recreation than a handbook for *re*-creation – trainee poets could rifle through a handy stock of passages from the ancient and modern (Latin) authors, on everything from Creation to the seasons, cities, rivers, animals, virtues and vices, arts and sciences, sports and games. We are bound to wonder whether the Jesuits' emphasis on assiduous (but circumscribed) imitation, inspired though it may have been for channeling the emulous energies and imaginations of young boys, was ever capable of instilling an appreciation for the "big picture" Vergil – or did it rather dispose students to a bricolage view of Latin verse? Possevino, at least, seems to have favored a policy of divide and conquer. In a supplementary chapter to the one on the "proper use" of Vergil (Possevino 1593, Cap. XXIV, "Another observation on the proper use of Vergil; what a Cento is, and some excellent examples of Latin centos"), he commends the Renaissance centos of Lelio and Giulio Capilupi as examples of how "the Latin treasures of the pagan poets, as once those of the Egyptians, may be transferred for the most proper use of a Christian people and for the worship of God."

In the section of his manual devoted to the *praelectio*, the teacher's introductory lecture on the set text, Jouvancy's Vergil comes into sharper focus (cf. *Ratio studiorum* 1616, §§27–9, "Common Rules for the Teachers of the Lower Classes." Only classical authors were expounded in the prelection). He provides two specimens, no doubt drawn from his own classroom experience, on Cicero and Vergil (cf. *Ratio studiorum* 1616, §8, "Rules of the Teacher of Rhetoric"). The subject of the Vergilian prelection is *Aen.* 12.425–40. The teacher will first briefly set the scene: the injured Aeneas is instantaneously healed thanks to the dittany Venus has secretly added to the water used to wash his wound. The doctor in attendance (Iapyx) is astonished at the miracle. Aeneas arms himself in haste and briefly embraces his son, addressing words to him befitting a father and a hero. In the next part of the prelection the passage is painstakingly glossed, phrase by phrase. This part in fact occupies several pages of Jouvancy's text but a few lines will suffice for the general idea:

Non haec humanis opibus proveniunt ("this doesn't come about through human resources"). This miracle, this healing which occurred against all expectations, should not be attributed to human power or to the ordinary remedies which medicine teaches. *Major agit deus* ("this is the work of a more powerful god"). A greater and stronger deity than human science and nature has effected this, and has restored [Aeneas'] life and health. One should not say which god it is. The master [sc. Vergil] wishes it to be understood that it is perhaps Apollo, god of medicine; or possibly, he implies, Venus, who does not hesitate to look after and protect her son... (Jouvancy 1892, 106)

The third part of the prelection is devoted to "rhetoric," and the teacher might here discuss the effectiveness of the doctor's exhortation to arms; the eagerness with which Aeneas prepares himself for battle as reflected in his speech; and the dignified words he addresses to his son. To better illustrate the excellence of the passage Jouvancy suggests a comparison with the sixth book of the *Iliad*, "where Hector, on his way to battle, plays with his son and talks with him at length, which causes him an unfortunate delay" (Jouvancy 1892, 109; the comparison of Homer and Vergil was a common theme for Jesuit literary theorists, the most famous example being Rapin 1664).

Next comes "erudition," learned observations about ancient history, geography, customs, and culture – for the Jesuits, unlike modern classicists, a relatively minor concern. Jouvancy suggests that *clypeus* might serve as the departure point for a discussion on the various types of ancient shield; *fortunam ex aliis* of the figure of Fortune. Note, however, that his sights remain steadily trained on the text's potential to yield lessons in piety: "*Exempla tuorum* ('follow the example of your ancestors'). What a broad field opens up here for discussion of the examples parents ought to give their children!" We are to direct our charges to the eloquent discussion of this subject in Juvenal's fourteenth satire, and to "instruct them in the use they should make of the good or bad examples of their parents, and how they should be careful not to imitate the latter" (*Ratio studiorum* 1616, 109). Indeed, the positive effect Jesuit students might have *on their parents* was one of the original justifications for the apostolate in education (O'Malley 1993, 213, quoting from Polanco's list of the benefits conferred by the schools). Already in the *Ratio studiorum* Jesuit teachers were warned not to go overboard on erudition: "Let moderate use be made of erudition, so that it may spur and refresh the mind every now and again, but not so that it gets in the way of language study" (*Ratio studiorum* 1616, §1, "Rules of the Teacher of Humanities"; cf. Farrell 1970, 131 n.63). The importance of genre-appropriate diction and style, not for their own sakes but as a training for *practice*, is reflected in the final part of Jouvancy's prelection, "Latinity." If the lesson is primarily for the benefit of the Rhetoric class, the emphasis should be on rhetorical authors and usage; in the Humanities, poetic.

Jesuit teachers were themselves expected to embody models for stylistic (and ethical) emulation, and to this end they performed exhibition orations at annual ceremonies for the conferment of student prizes. Such were the origins of a three-part dialogue comparing Cicero and Vergil (a recurring theme in our chapter!) by a noted professor of Rhetoric at the Roman College, Vincenzo Guiniggi (1558–1653). The *Tursellinus* (originally published in the *Allocutiones gymnasticae*, Rome, 1626; in what follows I refer to the subsequent Venice edition, Guiniggi 1648), named for the Jesuit historian Orazio Torsellino (1545–99), comprises a series of debates between learned and pious friends which take place at sea, in boats off the coast of Ancona (parts one and two), and finally (part three) on dry land, at the house of a local nobleman, Giuliano Cesarini (scil. marquis of Civitanova Marche). Constraints of space preclude a detailed analysis of this charming work, in which contemporary events and the personalities of the interlocutors are conveyed with a deft and light touch: Torsellino is a bit of a pedant, quick to point out his friends' historical errors; Alessandro Maggi a brilliant and plucky youngster, not afraid of showing up his elders; the narrator, Guiniggi, a weary but dedicated teacher, gently reminding us of the ill effects of a heavy teaching workload on his health. The framing conversation of Guiniggi and friends introduces the debates proper, as recounted by one Camillo Andreotti of prodigious memory. As for Cicero and Vergil, they are compared in terms of the relative excellence of the arts they represent, raw talent, judgment, learning, originality, personal charity (e.g., Vergil is criticized for "snubbing" Cicero when giving the palm of oratory to the Greeks, *orabunt causas melius, Aen.* 6.849), even physical appearance – but the modern reader cannot help feeling that much of this discussion, if not the theme of the dialogue itself, is somehow beside the point. A verdict is deferred until the final day and, at Torsellino's behest, it is agreed that this will be decided on the basis of a literary contest. Maggi and Bernardino Stefonio are to compose and deliver original compositions, in the style of Cicero and Vergil respectively, on a miracle wrought by the Virgin of Loreto (Torsellino has just returned from a field trip to Loreto and is about to embark on his history of the cult: cf. Murphy 2002). The palm of victory is awarded to Maggi for his oration on the forbearance displayed by loot-crazed Christian soldiers when confronted by a vision of the Virgin. (One is reminded of the Verrine orations, but also of the Augustinian passage quoted by Possevino above.) Maggi's piece is in fact much more recognizably Ciceronian than Stefonio's poem is Vergilian (on a reformed prostitute on pilgrimage to Loreto, rescued by the Virgin from the jaws of death after being set upon by her traveling companion). But if Cicero is at first declared the winner less on his own merits than those of his gifted young champion, in his summing up Torsellino shares his frank thoughts on why Cicero really is best. The reasons include his wide and deep learning, his role in transmitting Greek philosophy to the reluctant Romans, and, unlike Vergil who only bound one man's soul to himself (i.e., Augustus), Cicero succeeded in taking possession of the Roman people itself, "a beast of many heads to be sure." This, combined with the fact that Vergil sought always to avoid entanglement in public affairs so that he could get on with his writing, renders him less worthy in the eyes of the Jesuit judge. Cicero, we are tempted to add, *is a better Jesuit*, displaying those qualities of rhetorical efficacy and active engagement with the world prized by the Order.

Cursus (and *Recursus*) *Virgilianus*

One Society of Jesus has substituted…many poets for any one that learned antiquity revered and believed divine. One Society has given to the world so many Ovids, Horaces, Senecas, and Martials, that it would be difficult to choose one out of so many to wear the crown, since all deserve it – whereas once it was very easy to award first place in their genre to a single Vergil or Flaccus, who had no runner-up.

Parnassus Societatis Jesu

At least three seventeenth-century Jesuits in France affected to follow Vergil's career path, composing the full gamut of pastoral, georgic/didactic, and epic poems (though not necessarily in that order): René Rapin (1621–87), Pierre Mambrun (1601–61), and Laurent Le Brun (see "Further Reading" below). Did these card-carrying Vergilian poets evince a special feeling for Vergil? As far as Le Brun is concerned, we should bear in mind that the trilogy of poems constituting his *Virgilius Christianus* is followed, in the same volume, by an "Ovidius Christianus." Thus Ovid would seem to serve just as well as template for a Jesuit poetic career – Le Brun provides Christian versions of the *Fasti, Tristia, Ex Ponto*, and *Heroides*, and for "numerous metamorphoses" we are referred back to his poetic textbook *Eloquentia poetica* (Le Brun 1655) – although, interestingly, the Ovidian sequence is not declared on the volume's main title page. Curiously, Le Brun chooses to apply retrospectively to the pastoral and didactic parts of his Vergilian corpus the "perfect" number of books of the *Aeneid*. His didactic poem, "Twelve books of 'Psychurgica,' or the Ecclesiastes of Solomon on the Cultivation of the Soul" (*Psycurgicon sive Ecclesiastes Salomonis De cultura animi capita xii*), is, as its title shows, a Biblical paraphrase. A much more Vergilian poem was the neoclassical georgic on French formal gardens by Rapin, who was perhaps the closest thing the Jesuits had to a high priest of Vergil. But then Tarquinio Galluzzi's effusive panegyric of Vergil (*Parnassus* 1654, 1.2: 526–30) is itself almost a messianic eclogue in praise of the divine poet!

An Italian Jesuit poet and admirer of Rapin's, Niccolò Giannettasio, took the soubriquet "Parthenius," paying homage to the Virgin, his hometown of Naples, and to Vergil himself. We have already noted Giannettasio's epic on the life of St. Francis Xavier; he also wrote piscatory eclogues (Giannettasio 1685, naturally indebted to Sannazaro as well as Vergil: Schindler 2003). But Giannettasio's greatest contribution to Vergilian neo-Latin poetry was a series of long didactic poems on fishing, sailing, warfare, and naval battles (Schindler 2001; Haskell 2003, 70–82). In "down-shifting" from epic and settling into a georgic gear, Giannettasio was by no means alone among his early modern confrères. In the seventeenth and eighteenth centuries a vogue for didactic poetry swept the Society of Jesus, notably in France and Italy, but also, for example, in Latin America (Haskell 2003, 315–20; Laird 2006; Mariano 2010).

Not only did Jesuits write many more "georgic" than epic or pastoral poems, I estimate they were responsible for nearly three quarters of the Latin didactic poetry published in the early modern period. Moreover, while Jesuit poets ranged over every conceivable field of modern intellectual and cultural life, Vergil, strikingly, remained their primary model – even for poems on subjects such as gold-mining, the arts of sculpture and engraving, or the construction and flight of an airship (Bitzel 1997). The Jesuits' forays into Lucretius and Ovid were rarer (Haskell 2003, chs. 4 and 5). One could be forgiven for supposing that Giovanni Maria Mazzolari's "Six books on electricity" (*Electricorum libri sex*, Rome, 1767) would be a Lucretian poem, which in many ways it is, but when that comparison was made by contemporary readers it provoked a surprisingly defensive response from the author – not so much because Mazzolari was ashamed of association with Lucretius' philosophy as because he earnestly aspired to a pure Vergilian style (Haskell 2003, 235–41; cf. 235 for another apparently Lucretian poet, Gregorio Landi Vittori (1767), asserting his Vergilian credentials).

I have argued elsewhere that the roots of this Jesuit predilection for Vergilian didactic lie in a happy correspondence between the thematics of labor in the *Georgics* with the values of Jesuit apostolic spirituality, which sanctified labor and utility (Haskell 2003, 12–16; cf. Harris 1989). Unlike their contributions to pastoral and epic, however, the Jesuits' georgic remained, with very few exceptions, resolutely secular in orientation, and served to demonstrate the compatibility of their Latin humanist education less with Catholic piety than with modern culture and science. The *Georgics*, as a nonnarrative poem, seems to have been more amenable to modular recombination than the *Aeneid* or *Eclogues*. It provided Jesuit poets with a fund of *topoi* they proved endlessly capable of refilling: Vergil's description of the plow becomes the template for so many technical ekphrases of modern inventions; the bees for a model society of native Americans; the Cyclopes for plantation slaves; the cattle plague for an epidemic of hypochondria (to say nothing of the ingenious changes rung on the Corycian gardener and Aristaeus epyllion). Here, at last, the Jesuits had found a Vergilian model which needed no introduction, which justified itself as a product of learning, as an exhibition of unusual poetic industry, and as an unmediated source of useful instruction.

Why Vergil? Tradition, the received wisdom of the Church Fathers and Renaissance humanists, a paradigmatic poetic career – but also, I suspect, Vergil came to represent for the Jesuits in poetry, as Cicero did in oratory, a *via media*, a discreet elegance and neutrality of style that resonated with their *modus procedendi* in spiritual matters. Jacob Masen asks the "benevolent reader" of his *Sarcotis* not to expect in his work the "perfect body of a heroic poem," and to indulge his rather liberal use of descriptions (designed to appeal to adolescent readers). He has, all the same, "aspired to the modesty and candour of Vergil's style, as he was almost the only one to unite discrimination with majesty of speech in a most fitting bond, and, whenever necessary, he is humble without being abject, great without pride, refined and learned without obscurity, melodious without straining for effect" (1771, 81–2). He is, in short, the model Jesuit teacher, preacher, and confessor – dignified but unassuming, prudent, tactful, and consoling. If the Vergil of the Jesuits is not one we readily recognize today, much less appreciate, we have seen in this chapter that he was very much a living presence in the early modern Society of Jesus. He was also almost always a didactic one – and not only when he was teaching agriculture.

FURTHER READING

On neo-Latin epic, in addition to the literature cited above, see Hofmann (1994, 2001); IJsewijn and Sacré (1998). Several full-blown epics in the *Parnassus Societatis Iesu* (1654) would repay proper exploration: Franciscus Vavasseur, *Theurgicon, sive de Miraculis Christi* (four books); Carolus Werpaeus, *Raptus Manresanus S. Ignatii Lojolae Fundatoris Soc. Jesu* (four books); Iacobus Bidermann, *Herodiados* (three books); Ludovicus Gellotius, *Mauritiados Andegavens* (three books); Jacobus Damianus, *Bellum Germanicum* (ten books); Joannes Henricus Auberius, *Leucata triumphans* (two books); Alexander Donatus, *Constantinus Romae Liberator* (twelve books). Note, however, that even this ambitious anthology could never contain the *mare magnum* of Jesuit heroic verse, which flows into the eighteenth century.

Like Le Brun and Masen, Donatus wrote an influential poetic textbook (1633), as did Jacobus Pontanus (or Jakob Spanmüller), the author of the sacred eclogues praised by Possevino (Pontanus 1594). In addition to his panegyric of Vergil (in *Parnassus* 1654), Tarquinio Galluzzi wrote *Virgilianae vindicationes* (1621). Le Brun compiled a *Novus apparatus Virgilii poeticus* (1667). Rapin's reverence for Vergil is evident in his *Comparaison* of Homer and Vergil (1664), in the preface to his *Horti* (1665), and in his *Les Réflexions sur la poétique de ce temps* (ed. Dubois, 1970).

As for Rapin's Vergilian poems – *Eclogae sacrae* (1659), *Horti* (1665), *Christus patiens* (1674) – the perennially popular "Gardens" has received the most scholarly attention (Dubois 1979; Effe 1975; Ludwig 1982; Bitzel 1997; Haskell 2003; Monreal 2005; cf. Dubois 1955 on the eclogues). Mambrun's *Eclogae*, *De cultura animi*, and *Idolatria debellata* are collected in his *Opera poetica* (1661); see Haskell (2003) on the "georgic" poem. Mambrun was not an uncritical admirer of Vergil; comments in the preface to his *Idolatria* provoked the anonymous counterblast, *Virgilius defensus, sive defensio Virgiliani Certaminis Aeneae cum Turno* (1685). Mambrun also criticized the French epic of fellow Jesuit Le Moyne, but Rubidge (1998) finds that the treatises on epic by Mambrun *and* Le Moyne, as well as Rapin and Le Brun, evince a common (Jesuit) ideology predicated on admiration, emulation, and aristocratic audience.

The Jesuit *Ratio studiorum* is available online in an English translation of the 1599 edition (Farrell 1970: www.bc.edu/bc_org/avp/ulib/digi/ratio/ratiohome.html) or in the original Latin of the 1616 edition (www.uni-mannheim.de/mateo/camenaref/societasjesu.html#sj3).

Klecker (2007, 449) finds the influence of Lactantius' critique of Vergilian "piety" in the *Crispus* (1620) by Roman Jesuit playwright Bernardino Stefonio (1560–1620) – a play about Constantine, Fausta, and Crispus, modeled on Seneca's *Phaedra* but also deeply indebted to the *Aeneid* (Stefonio 1998).

CHAPTER SIXTEEN

The *Aeneid* from the Aztecs to the Dark Virgin

Vergil, Native Tradition and Latin Poetry in Colonial Mexico from Sahagún's Memoriales *(1563) to Villerías'* Guadalupe *(1724)*

Andrew Laird

Vocabula, ut Fatum, Fortuna, Dii, Iupiter, Mars, & huiusmodi alia, cum constet primum fuisse Autoris ethnici, & a nobis accipi per Allegoriam aliter atque ipsa sonant, reprehendi non debent.

Terms like "Fate," "Fortune," "the Gods," "Jupiter," "Mars," and others like them ought not to be reproached, since it is understood that they were first the property of a pagan author and that through allegory we endow the sound of them with a different sense.
Bernardino de Llanos, *Poeticae Institutiones* (Mexico City, 1605, fol. 442)

I know of many in our land who see the image of their own fortune in the fortunes of the hero who goes from tomb to tomb, preserving the sacred Penates, and I doubt anyone capable of reading the Aeneid *without being moved is someone we could call a good Mexican.*
Alfonso Reyes, *Discurso Por Virgilio* (Mexico City, 1931, 395)

In his essay *Mexico in a Nutshell*, the poet and thinker Alfonso Reyes (1889–1959) suggested that the history of the Spanish conquest followed a classical epic design:

Cortés…took advantage of the superstition that made him appear as emissary of the Sons of the Sun (the true lords of Mexican soil, who according to the oracles, would one day return to reclaim their own), and protected by the fortunate apparition of the comet, he triumphed without a struggle over the startled mind of the Emperor Moctezuma, who behaved toward him like King Latinus in the *Aeneid* on the arrival of Aeneas, the man of destiny…. Did a few hundred men and a few dozen horses achieve victory on such a scale? Oh, no: as in the *Iliad*, all the forces of heaven and earth were taking part in the conflict. (Reyes 1930, 45)

Alfonso Reyes noted further parallels with the *Aeneid* in his *Appendix on Vergil and America* (1937): the Trojan Aeneas united with the Etruscans and Arcadians in Italy, just as the Spaniard Cortés (1485–1547) formed alliances with the peoples of Tlaxcala and Texcoco against the Aztecs in Anahuac; while Cortés' brutal killing of Cuauhtémoc (1499–1524), the young chieftain of Tlatelolco, was no more necessary to secure victory than Aeneas' slaughter of Turnus, the prince of the Rutulians. There are some important differences, of course – Aeneas' marriage with Lavinia led to the formation of a new race that would adopt the local Latin tongue, whilst Cortés did not marry his indigenous mistress and the invader's language of Spanish would prevail in the Americas (Brading 2005, 23). Still, the overriding parallels led Reyes to "look through the *Aeneid*...at the spectacle of Mexico" (Reyes 1937, 178).

Vergil did not really create Mexican history, but Mexican history has played a part in recreating Vergil. The poet had a role in the earliest accounts of Aztec traditions compiled by Sahagún and his native collaborators, as well as in the culture of classical learning that had begun to develop in New Spain (as colonial Mexico was known) during the 1520s. From the mid-seventeenth century onwards, the reading and literary imitation of Vergil in Latin became closely involved with poetic panegyrics of the "Dark Virgin," the Lady of Guadalupe, who appeared to an indigenous Mexican in 1531. Those baroque texts paved the way for José Antonio de Villerías y Roelas' *Guadalupe* (1724), a neoclassical Latin epic, to which most of this discussion will be devoted. The *Aeneid* is the matrix for Villerías' remarkable work, a unique poem of historical theology for the Americas, accommodating the pagan myths of both pre-Hispanic Mexico and the European Mediterranean.

As well as highlighting the richness and complexity of Mexican Latin writing, this selective account of Vergil's presence in New Spain may also help to show that familiarity with the poet's corpus is of some heuristic use in the study of colonial cultural history.

I

Knowledge of Vergil's *Aeneid* reached the shores of New Spain soon after the conquest. This is effectively illustrated by the work of Bernardino de Sahagún (1499–1590), the celebrated Franciscan missionary and ethnographer, on whom historians now depend for so much of their knowledge of Aztec culture. It may well be significant that Sahagún, unlike Cortés, had actually completed his classical education in the renowned University of Salamanca. From 1563 until 1577 he supervised the production of the bilingual *Historia General de las Cosas de la Nueva España* (1563–77; Nahuatl text in Sahagún 1950–82; Spanish text in Sahagún 1990), based on oral testmonies in Nahuatl, the language of the Aztecs, or the Mexica as they are more properly called. The first book of the *Historia General* introduces the major Mexican gods by comparing them to Roman divinities: "Huitzilopochtli was another Hercules as he was the most robust indeed, of great strength and very warlike, a great destroyer of towns and killer of peoples"; "Tezcatlipoca is another Jupiter"; "the goddess of things carnal which they call Tlazoteotl is another Venus"; "Xiuhtecutli is another Vulcan" (*Historia General* (*HG*) 1). The attributes of those Greco-Roman deities are too pervasive to be credited to the *Aeneid* alone, but Sahagún's characterization of the Mexican goddess Chalchiutlicue is revealing:

> She is another Juno, goddess of water. They used to depict her as a woman and they said that she was one of the rain goddesses that they call *Tlaloques*. She has power over the water of the sea and rivers to drown those who go on the waters, and to make storms and whirlwinds in the water and to sink ships and boats. (*HG* 1.11)

One might have expected Sahagún to compare a deity with these faculties to Neptune – and he *had* done so in the original five-book version of his history produced in 1563–5 (the *Memoriales* or "Tlatelolco manuscripts"). Control over water was not a customary attribute of Juno in the Roman tradition (Roscher 1897–8), but in the 1565–8 revision of the *Memoriales*, Juno was substituted for Neptune and that substitution was retained in the definitive 1577 version of the *Historia General* (Nicolau d'Olwer 1952, 139–40). Sahagún's change makes sense only in terms of *Aeneid* 1: there Juno instigated Aeolus to stir up a sea storm in order to prevent the Trojans from safely reaching the coast of Italy, while Neptune had the role of pacifying the tempest (*Aen.* 1.124–56). The parallels Sahagún drew between the profoundly divergent Aztec and Roman pantheons were, after all, meant only to orient his Spanish readership and they do not appear in the Nahuatl version of his text.

There is another hint of the *Aeneid*'s influence in book 8 of the *Historia General* when the tales of two ancient Mexican cities are told. Both long predated the foundation of the Aztecs' capital of Tenochtitlan: the city of Tula was destroyed, leading to Quetzalcóatl's flight to the mythical realm of Tlapallan; and the city of Cholula, which the Spaniards called "Rome" on account of its grandeur and splendid buildings. "It appears that both cities went the way of Troy and Rome," Sahagún comments drily (*HG* 8 pref. 3–7; cf. i: book 1 pref.). The connection of Tula to Troy and Quetzalcóatl to the refugee Aeneas, though anecdotal, could be the first evocation of the Roman hero's fortunes in the context of Mesoamerican history.

Bernardino de Sahagún conducted his research for nearly forty years as a lector at the Imperial College of Santa Cruz de Tlatelolco. The College had been founded in 1536 to teach children of the indigenous aristocracies to speak and write in Latin (Laird 2010a). The language of Rome was the conventional medium of education in the Catholic world of the sixteenth century, and training of the *indios latinos* or "Latinate Indians" had begun in Texcoco in the early 1520s. The native students read Vergil in order to compose their own Latin poetry: the poet's works and those of many other classical authors were in the library at Tlatelolco. Although no verse compositions have yet come to light, the prose texts written by the indigenous scholars of the 1500s infused an enduring multiculturalism into the Latin "humanism" of Mexico which soon acquired, and retained, a distinctive identity. Hispanisms, Nahuatl words, and American themes became commonplace in the majority of Latin authors from New Spain who were *criollos* or "creoles," born in the New World but of Spanish ancestry.

By 1600, systematic instruction of indigenous Mexicans had come to an end. The foundation of the Royal University in Mexico City and the restriction of study in colleges and seminaries to Spaniards and creoles also reduced interest in native questions: the polemics about the status and rights of the Indians (which had been prominent in the Latin writing of the earlier sixteenth century) rapidly petered out. Instead the educational ethos of the Jesuits, who came to Mexico in 1572, laid emphasis on the practical imitation of classical authors, among whom Vergil was preeminent. (Cf. the preceding chapter by Haskell in this volume.) Initially, the *Eclogues* rather than the *Aeneid* or the *Georgics* provided the model for poetic composition in Latin: verse dialogues (*éclogas*) were a more manageable exercise for students than the production of heroic or didactic epic poetry.

Literary activity in both Latin and Spanish would remain confined to the colonial elite, but it was reinvigorated from the mid-1600s by the creole fascination with the cult of the Virgin of Guadalupe. The narrative of the Virgin's apparition in Mexico, now recognized as a creole myth, and not indigenous in origin, is well known. In December 1531, the Virgin Mary appeared and spoke to the Indian Juan Diego, on the hill of Tepeyac, north of Mexico City, instructing him to seek an audience with the first bishop of Mexico, Juan de Zumárraga. The bishop at first did not believe him, but when Juan Diego returned and unfastened his cloak in which the Virgin had told him to gather flowers from the hill, the bishop saw the image of the Virgin imprinted on the cloak. Significantly her face, as it was depicted, was "courtly but somewhat dark" (*tecpiliti achi yayactic*: Laso de la Vega 1998, 88; Karttunen 1992). The Virgin accomplished further miracles, including the alleviation of a plague (*cocoliztli* – this Nahuatl word will be significant in what follows). The bishop ordered a church to be built at Tepeyac where she had first appeared – the very site where human sacrifices had once been offered to the goddess Tonantzin.

Accounts of the apparitions in Nahuatl, spuriously attributed to Antonio Valeriano (?–1605), a celebrated indigenous Latinist at Tlatelolco, via the *mestizo* historian Fernando de Alva Ixtlilxochiltl (1570s–1648), were published in the *Huei Tlamahuiçoltica* (Great Miracle) by the vicar of Guadalupe, Luis Laso de la Vega, in 1649. Vega's Nahuatl text is often regarded as the first printed source for the miracle, although Miguel Sánchez's Spanish narrative had appeared earlier in 1648 (Brading 2001; Poole 1995). Various poetic works prior to these "historical" versions allude to the myth. These include seventy surviving Latin hexameters from Mateo de Castroverde's 1645 *Panegyric of the Conception of Mary celebrated in America* that were incorporated into a vernacular poem, *El triunfo parténico* (The Triumph of the Virgin), by Carlos de Sigüenza y Góngora in 1683. Sigüenza also wrote two Guadalupan poems in Spanish: *Primavera indiana* (1668) and *Glorias de Querétaro* (1680).

The first Latin work directly to honor the Virgin of Guadalupe was the *Poeticum viridarium...* by José López de Abilés (1669). Those words ("Poetic pleasure garden") may allude to the role of flowers in the original myth. The text, though it consists of only 210 elegiac couplets, is daunting: only a few lines of the poem appear in the center of each folio, as a lemma surrounded by a forest of annotations citing patristic and classical authors. This bombardment of baroque learning shows how far the creole elite had made this supposedly Indian myth their own: López de Abilés' version of it would have presented a challenge to the devotees of the cult who could read Latin. But line 125 of this elaborate poem:

VIRGINIS OS, habitumque gerens, et VIRGINIS arma
Bearing the VIRGIN'S FACE, and her demeanor, and the VIRGIN's emblems

is easily recognizable as a transplantation of *Aen.* 1.315 where Aeneas catches sight of Venus disguised as a huntress. This Vergilian verse had already been purloined a century before, by the Italian centonist Giulio Capilupi for the proem of his *Ad Mariam* – and that particular Marian cento had been widely disseminated in Mexico by Bernardino de Llanos' 1605 manual on Latin prosody, the *Institutionum poeticarum liber* (Book of Poetic Principles). López's further recontextualization of this and other verses from the *Aeneid* could well be responsible for making Vergilian themes and expressions an enduring constituent of all the Latin poetry in the Guadalupan tradition.

As a votive extravaganza, the *Poeticum viridarium* was more of an artifact than a work that is practically readable. That quality, together with the initial prominence López gave to Vergil in this text, helps to explain the curious title of the next volume of Guadalupan Latin poetry that appeared in 1680: the *Centonicum Virgilianum Monimentum* (Vergilian Centonic Monument). The principal composition in this volume is a cento, by Bernardo Ceinos de Riofrío, recounting the Virgin of Guadalupe's miracles at Tepeyac in 365 hexameters. The literal meaning of *cento* in Latin is "patchwork cloth" or "cloak." Riofrío's preface affirms in his prose preface that this poetic form is especially appropriate given the role of Juan Diego's cloak in the story, and of the Virgin herself as "cloak of protection" for the people of Mexico – an image drawn from the Church Father Tertullian (Laird 2007a, 211–15). The opening line of the cento is a verse from Vergil's fourth "messianic" eclogue, followed by verses from the *Eclogues, Georgics*, and *Aeneid*:

Iam redit et Virgo redeunt Saturnia regna	= *Ecl.* 4.6
Iamque novum terrae stupeant lucescere solem	= *Ecl.* 6.37
Hinc canere incipiam vos o clarissima mundi	= *Geo.* 1.5
Lumina, labentem Coelo quae ducitis annum	= *Geo.* 1.6
Et vos o coetum Tyrii celebrate faventes	= *Aen.* 1.735

Now the Virgin returns, now the kingdoms of Saturn return, and now the lands are agape at the shining of a new sun. Now I will begin to sing of you, o brightest lights of the firmament, that guide through Heaven the gliding year. And you, o Tyrians, graciously celebrate…

(Riofrío 1680, 1–5)

The appearance of the Tyrians is as incongruous as the later intrusion of Trojans, Greeks, Romans, Olympian gods, and individual agents like Dido, Turnus, and even Maecenas into this Vergilian rendering of the Mexican miracle. The Guadalupan theme is conveyed most effectively when longer continuous excerpts from Vergil are grafted into this text. Riofrío develops the connection first drawn in the *Poeticum viridarium* between the epiphany of the divine Mother to Juan Diego and Aeneas' encounter with his mother, Venus, by attributing to Juan Diego almost all of Aeneas' speech at *Aen.* 1.326–34. In a similar fashion Riofrío conveys the bishop's astonished reaction to the Virgin's image on the cloak, first by means of *Aen.* 8.730 (Aeneas' amazement at receiving his divinely depicted shield from Venus) and then *Aen.* 4.282–6 (the hero's consternation at Mercury's apparition in Carthage). The cento conjures up a zone somewhere between Vergil's poetic realm and the purportedly historical world of Mexico – perfectly reflecting Isidore of Seville's influential definition of a cento as "material arranged according to the verses, and verses arranged according to the material," which is quoted in Riofrío's preface.

An original Latin poem in the same 1680 volume, a *silva* of 200 hexameters by Bartolomé Rosales, specially composed to herald Riofrío's Vergilian cento, is no less important: the *Aulica Musarum Synodus Crisis Apollinea in Laudem Authoris* (The Courtly Synod of Muses – an Apolline Judgment in Praise of the Author). This epyllion stages the god Mercury reporting an apparition to a tribunal of Muses, chaired by Apollo:

> praesens cito sistit Imago
> Fatidici somni reserans secreta: referre
> Incipit…

A present Image swiftly approached, unlocking the secrets of a prophetic dream and began to speak…

Aulica Musarum Synodus 81–3

Contrary to what might be expected, the "Image" is not that of the Virgin:

> …accipias modo quae mihi verba loqutus:
> "En **ego, qui quondam** Latio monumenta reliqui,
> Quique **duces cecini**, diri Phrygia agmina belli,
> Tempora cui cinxit circum Parnasica laurus,
> Quem totus miris extollit laudibus Orbis,
> Quem decus ipsa suum veneratur Roma Maronem…

May you now hear the words he spoke to me: "Lo, **I am he who once** left monuments for Latium, and who **sang** of the **leaders**, of the Phrygian columns in grim war, I am he whose brow was crowned with the laurel of Parnassus, whom the whole World extols with wondrous praises, Maro, whom Rome itself reveres as its own glory…

Aulica Musarum Synodus 83–8

The speaker is none other than Vergil himself: his first words, recalling the apocryphal incipit to the *Aeneid* (*Ille ego qui quondam gracili modulatus avena*: "I am he who once composed poetry in a pastoral strain"), are followed by an evocation, in *duces cecini*, of the poet's reputed epitaph: (*cecini pascua rura duces*: "I sang of pastures, farms, leaders"). But while both those ancient verses allude to all his works, in Rosales' poem Vergil calls attention to the *Aeneid* alone before he explains that he has been reborn in the New World:

> Nunc iterum toto celebrandus in orbe poeta
> pulchrior exurgo, faciesque reficta refulget.
> Nunc et in orbe novo resonat romana Thalia
> Quae redimita rosis Indis caput extulit undis.

O vos Pyerides vobis nova gloria surgit:
Nunc meus in *Rosea* vultus *Imagine* maior
Noscitur, auctus honos eludet tempora vivax.

Now I rise again, more beautiful still, as a poet to be celebrated all over the world and my features, refashioned, shine once more. Now Roman Thalia sounds again in the New World as she raises her head from the waters, garlanded with Indian roses. O you Pierides, your glory is rising, now my countenance is greater in the image of the roses and my honor, enhanced and alive, makes mockery of time…

Aulica Musarum Synodus 108–13

This prompts a joyful response. The reappearance of "Roman" Thalia proclaims Rome's renaissance in Mexico, just as Claudian (*Getic War*, pref. 1–2) Thalia, really a Greek Muse, heralded a cultural renewal in late Roman antiquity. Rosales again is presenting Vergil's achievement exclusively in terms of the *Aeneid*: a "cold river" – the meaning of Riofrío's name in Spanish – has quenched the flames that had threatened the survival of the poem Vergil had ordered to be burnt (Ziolkowski and Putnam 2008, 420–5).

The real marvel of the volume containing the *Centonicum Virgilianum Monimentum* is its legacy: the flowering of original Latin epic in New Spain, pioneered only a generation later by Villerías y Roelas. The Vergilian tradition of European late antiquity might provide a literary-historical parallel for this remarkable development, as the Biblical epics of Juvencus, Sedulius, and Arator probably evolved from Vergilian centos on Christian themes (Green 2006). Although those late antique poets had been taught in the Indian colleges, broader religious and political factors, more pressing than artistic considerations, were inclining creole Latin poets to celebrate their devotion to the Virgin of Guadalupe.

II

By the late seventeenth-century the creoles in New Spain were in a disadvantaged position. The Crown had long regarded its interests as best served if economic and political control in the colony remained in the hands of native Spaniards. Thus the creoles, deprived of the prosperity that their own labor had secured, could no longer identify themselves with *peninsulares* for all that they shared the same ancestry. Nor could they see themselves as direct inheritors of Mexico's pre-Hispanic past because that would threaten their claim of privileges to which the conquest should have entitled them – a conquest that had always been justified ideologically by the triumph of Christianity over a diabolicial paganism. Appropriation of the Guadalupan myth usefully offered the creoles a sense of "manifest destiny." The apparition of the Virgin demonstrated that the greatness of pre-Hispanic Mexico had been the prelude to New Spain's special election for future greatness: *Non fecit taliter omni nationi*. That Latin tag from Psalm 147 which began to be subscribed under visual representations of the Virgin of Guadalupe from the 1600s onwards was thus laden with a kind of political significance: "God did not act in such a way for every nation" (Brading 2001, 99). That special privilege of New Spain as a dominion of the Virgin Mary is the central message of the full-blown epic account of the myth in Villerías y Roelas' *Guadalupe.*

What little is known of José Antonio de Villerías y Roelas' life exemplifies the hardships faced by the creoles in his time (Beristáin y Souza 1821, 329–31). Born in Mexico City in 1695, he was probably educated by Jesuits before entering the University in 1714 to study jurisprudence. In the decade before he graduated, Villerías took part in the literary contests or *certámenes* that were a feature of cultural life in Spanish America (Leonard 1959, 130–44). His Latin epigrams name those whose patronage he sought – few opportunities were open to creoles who did not follow an ecclesiastical career, and Villerías had married in 1722. After failing to secure a position as a chronicler for the University, he found work in the Royal Audiencia (the colonial court). Villerías' poor health, exacerbated by chronic poverty, may account for his early death in 1728 at the age of 33 years.

Villerías was a prolific and adventurous author – of epigrams in classical Greek, as well as of longer works in Spanish and Latin (Osorio Romero 1991, 376–407). The Spanish works all went to press, but most of Villerías' output is still in manuscript. There are Latin hymns, elegies and a hundred epigrams (many translating Greek poems in the *Palatine Anthology*), the 300 hexameters of *Victor* (1721–3), and a versification of the Vulgate Song of Songs (1725), subtitled "The *Eclogues* of Solomon King of Jerusalem." The prose works in Latin comprise a letter to a physician named Jacobo Stevenson (1724), some short essays and the *De dialectis linguae Graecae* ("On dialects of the Greek language"), a translation of a Greek treatise by the twelfthto thirteenth-century grammarian Gregory of Corinth or "Corinthus," first edited by Aldo Manuzio in the 1500s (Schaefer 1811).

However, the *Guadalupe* was Villerías y Roelas' greatest achievement. In 1,755 hexameters it was the longest Latin poem that had yet been produced in New Spain, showing that the innovative kind of epyllion that had been attempted by Bartolomé Rosales could be attempted on a larger scale. A transition from panegyric to narrative poetry and from baroque to neoclassical style is fully effected in the *Guadalupe*. At the same time vernacular epic romances like Alonso de Ercilla's *Araucana* (1589), Camoens' *Lusiads* (1572), and Juan Rufo's *Austriada* – a 1584 poem on the Moorish uprising crushed by John of Austria – were popular in New Spain (Quint 1993; Leonard 1967, 119). Such works, which contained burlesque elements, were still modeled in different ways on the *Aeneid*, and they evidently influenced Villerías' project.

The *Guadalupe*'s direct debt to the *Aeneid* will be clear from the synopsis of the poem to follow. The central theme, however, is indicated at the opening (1.1–4):

> Indigenam, dic, Musa, Deam, quam Mexica quondam
> conspexit tellus, patriis emergere pulchram
> floribus, et sese (Veneris miracula contra)
> purpureo nitidam decorare cruore rosarum.

> Tell of the Indigenous Goddess, Muse, whom the land of Mexico once beheld emerging in her beauty from her native flowers and (in contrast to Venus' miracles) adorned herself with the purple blood of roses.

The first verse recalls the translation of the opening of Homer's *Odyssey* in Horace's *Ars poetica* ("Art of Poetry"):

> **dic** mihi, **Musa**, virum captae post tempora Troiae.

> Tell me, Muse, of the man after the time of Troy's fall.
> *Ars poetica* 141

But it also echoes the invocation of the eponymous Urania (Heaven) in the cosmological epic by Giovanni Pontano (1429–1503):

> **Dic,** dea, quae nomen coelo deducis ab ipso,
> Uranie, **dic Musa**, Iovis clarissima proles

> Tell, goddess, as you derive your name from the sky itself, Urania, tell Muse, most renowned offspring of Jove
> (Pontano 1902: *Urania* 9–10)

This suggests a parallel between Urania as the daughter of the supreme deity and the cosmogony in the *Guadalupe*. Villerías next sets the "indigenous" goddess's apparition in implicit contrast to the birth of Venus: the Virgin emerges, not from sea foam (like Venus in Ovid *Met.* 4.537 and the late antique *Vigil of Venus*, 9–14), but from the "native" or "paternal" flowers accompanying her Mexican epiphany. The more explicit opposition to "Venus' miracles" can be interpreted in terms of Catholic theology: the Virgin's Immaculate Conception meant her own birth was free from sin. But the Virgin is also said to have produced her own image from the roses on the cloak, while Venus' role in producing a miraculous depiction was far more indirect: her sexual allure prompted Vulcan to forge Aeneas' Shield (*Aen.* 8.370–452).

Book 1 of the *Guadalupe* begins by explaining the terrestrial origins of the conquest: the Holy Roman Emperor Charles V seeks to advance his rule beyond the ocean, and the rich human and material resources of the Western world are described (16–40). The infernal god Pluto, expelled from the Christian East, had taken over this region and corrupted it with a bloodthirsty cult of human sacrifice (1.41–62), requiring the evangelization of Mexico (1.63–112). Pluto enlists the help of the grim native goddess Tonantzin, his daughter by Night, to incite the Mexican peoples against this development; while Mary, who is in heaven, obtains the permission of her Son and Lord to give Mexico her protection (112–239). She makes her first apparition to the pious Indian Juan Diego and bids him seek an audience with Bishop Zumárraga in order to propose the construction of her temple (240–371). However, Pluto and Tonantzin sow doubts in the bishop's mind about the Indian's word. When Juan Diego explains to the Virgin that the bishop did not believe him, she enjoins him to try again (372–521).

In book 2, Pluto and Tonantzin make a nocturnal visit to the god Atlas, who is now exiled from Europe and dwells in a secret part of the lake of Mexico. He prophesies that the Virgin will reign in Mexico and that she will provide protection against floods and Cocoliztli, a personification of the plague (2.62–100, 222–59). A description of the murals in his home provides a detailed overview of the history of Mexico's dynasties from the foundation of Tenochtitlan until the death of Moctezuma (2.101–221). Tonantzin asks Atlas to reveal current events to enable her to thwart the divine plan. She and Pluto are granted a vision of Juan Diego's second suit in Zumárraga's palace: the bishop seeks a sign to confirm the truth of what he has heard and also sends his servants to follow the Indian in secret. Tonantzin and Pluto leave Atlas' cave, all the more determined on their designs. Disguised as Indians, they bump into Zumárraga's servants and tell them that Juan Diego is well known as a black magician – this news is relayed to the bishop. Mary then appears with her glorious train for the third time to Juan Diego, who explains that the bishop seeks a sign. She promises this on the following day and the Indian returns home.

At the beginning of book 3, Pluto, still intent on opposing the divine plan, goes to a poisonous grove, the location of the noxious abyss inhabited by Cocoliztli or *Cocolistus* (an episode modeled on the visits to Hunger and Sleep in Ov. *Met.* 8.777–813 and 11.583–709). Pluto asks the pestilential god to kill Juan Diego with a lethal disease. Cocoliztli explains that the laws of nature prohibit this but that he can infect Juan's uncle, Bernardino. Juan Diego is thus compelled to nurse him and misses his appointment with the Virgin – but meets her again as he searches for a priest to administer the last sacraments to his uncle. The Virgin assures Juan that Bernardino will be cured and instructs him to gather in his cloak the flowers that will serve as a sign for the bishop.

Book 4 opens in Zumárraga's palace where Pluto and Tonantzin, having made themselves invisible, prompt the bishop's creole (*coloni*) servants to snatch the flowers from Juan Diego. The flowers are transformed into a woven pattern on his cloak until he can present them to the bishop. The poet invokes Apollo, the Muses of Helicon, the Roman Camena, and the Nymphs, before relating the miracle which next occurs: the bishop, who was expecting only flowers to fall from Juan Diego's cloak, sees imprinted upon it the image of Mary made by God, finer than any likeness Zeuxis or Apelles could have produced. The bishop falls to his knees in tears as he recognizes the Virgin's miracle and declares his readiness to obey the Virgin's commands. Hearing this, Tonantzin and Pluto flee to their caves. Zumárraga has the image, in which Juan Diego recognizes the Virgin's face, placed in his chapel for all to venerate. *Fama* spreads the news through the city, and the learned among those who behold the picture associate it with the revelation that inspired Saint John in Patmos (Book of Revelation 12; Sánchez 1648; Brading 2001). The poet invokes the Muses again, before calling on God and the Virgin herself to assist in his greatest endeavor yet: a long interpretative ekphrasis of her image, which closes the work.

III

In common with the *Aeneid*, the narrative of the *Guadalupe* offers *mises en abyme*, predictions, and flashbacks that point to a bigger historical, mythological, and cosmological picture beyond the story directly presented (Hardie 1986; Feeney 1991). Another important ancient model, Claudian's *De raptu Proserpinae* ("On the Rape of Proserpina"), had portrayed Pluto's infernal disruptions, possibly a reflection of Rome's uneasy rapport with the Germans and other peoples in late antiquity – a historical scenario not wholly dissimilar to the one addressed by the present poem. Villerías also knew Pontano's *De hortis Hesperidum* ("On the Gardens of the Hesperides") as well as the *Urania*, and he annotated a Delphine edition of the *Astronomica* by the Roman poet Manilius (Osorio Romero 1991, 407).

Atlas in particular, is associated with cosmic knowledge and a new world beyond the Hesperides in Vergil (*Aen.* 1.741, 6.795–6), and he appropriately becomes a seer in the *Guadalupe*, assuming the role Faunus had in *Aen.* 7.81–106. But the character in Villerías is not drawn from Vergil alone: in Ov. *Met.* 4.628–45, Atlas rules over the far west and is linked to the art of prophecy; and the explanation for his expulsion from Tartessus in *Guadalupe* 2.28–9 – for prophesying to his father Oceanus "that it would be through Ocean that the New World would be sought by Hesperian fleets" – recalls a prediction from the chorus in Sen. *Med.* 375–9, made famous in the age of discovery (Clay 1992). The Titan's relegation to the Lake of Mexico allows Villerías y Roelas to confirm an association between Atlas and Gabriel which had already been made in López de Abilés' *Poeticum viridarium* 152:

> Coeli fortis Atlas iste mihi Gabriel.

> Heaven's strong Atlas is my Gabriel.

In Guadalapan iconography it is the angel Gabriel who is depicted bearing the Virgin on his shoulders, while in Villerías' epic, it is Atlas' speech (2.62–1001) which heralds the new age and new progeny (cf. *Eclogue* 4) brought by Mary to New Spain.

The pictures in Atlas' home in the Lake of Mexico have their immediate precedent in the Latin epic of 1526 by the Neapolitan poet Iacopo Sannazaro, *De partu Virginis* ("On the Virgin Birth") 3.305–17. There, an urn in the underwater cavern inhabited by the god of the River Jordan depicted a single "king and lord of the gods" being washed in a stream by a young man in animal skins (Gospel of Matthew 3:4). But here the illustrations of the Aztec monarchs, in common with the images of the future on Aeneas' shield, enhance the poem in which they appear with a broader historical panorama. And this monumentalization of indigenous tradition in the *Guadalupe*, no less than the role of Atlas himself, is actually serving as a vehicle of creole pride. For example, we are told that Moctezuma II's predecessor Ahuitzotl built the Great Temple of Tenochtitlán on a scale that "neither Egypt could construct it, nor mendacious Greece, nor Ammon on the shores of Libya" (*Guadalupe* 2.199–200). Yet this recollection of Martial's claim that Vespasian's Colosseum had surpassed the architectural accomplishments of previous imperial powers (*On Spectacles* 1) prompts comparison of New Spain's ancient past with that of Rome.

That comparison is certainly encouraged by the setting of the first speech in the *Guadalupe*. Juno's antipathy to the Trojans and her response to the imminence of the future ordained for Rome (*Aen.* 1.34–8) are echoed in Pluto's unhappy reaction to the growth of Christian faith in Mexico:

> Iam delubra Iovis certatim plurima veri
> surgebant, totaque Dei regione vigebat
> cultus; cum Pluton amisso excedere regno

deflens, atque imo ducens suspiria corde
haec secum: "mene incaepto desistere victum?
Mene cavernosis vitam tolerare latentem
rupibus?"

Already a great number of shrines to the True Jove were rising up to compete with each
other, and the worship of God was flourishing all over the region, when Pluto, lamenting
his departure from his lost realm and drawing the sighs from deep in his heart said to
himself: "So am I to abandon my enterprise in defeat? Am I to tolerate a life of lying low
in rocky caverns?"

Guadalupe 1.110–16

The transformation of this famous utterance into a soliloquy by Pluto, the god of the
underworld, indicates Villerías' recognition of Juno's own internal associations in
Aen. 7.312–40. At the same time this Pluto is a distinctive figure: the names of the
Mesoamerican peoples incorporated into the hexameters of his speech show how far
he has become naturalized in Mexico:

Namque habeo indociles Otomites, more ferarum
sub Jove degentes, et terrae gramine pastos;
Guastecos graveis, cultos sermone Tarascos,
atque Matlalzincas et pictos corpora Mecos...

I have at my disposal the indocile Otomi, who subsist under heaven like beasts and live
on the grass of the ground; the grave Guastecos, the Tarascans of refined speech; and the
Matlalzincas and the Chichimecs with their tattooed bodies...

Guadalupe 1.126–30

In fact Pluto had already been aligned with the evil forces of indigenous religion some fifty
years before Villerías was writing: octave 24 of the *Primavera indiana* ("Indian Spring"),
one of the vernacular poems on the Virgin of Guadalupe, published in 1668 by the creole
polymath Carlos de Sigüenza y Góngora (1645–1700), had presented Tepeyac – the location of the Virgin's apparitions – as the original domain of *Pluto*, not Tonantzin.

The goddess Tonantzin, who really had been worshipped in Tepeyac (Nicholson
1971), is genuinely autochthonous, but she too recalls a specific figure in the *Aeneid*
– an autochthonous divinity who sought in vain to oppose fate's designs for her country, but who ended up being forced to recognize the futility of her position as a result
of direct intervention from heaven. Vergil's Juturna is of course a completely different
character: her pathos is endearing and demands sympathy, while the rage of Villerías's
Tonantzin only renders her more hideous. And the joyous epiphany of the Mother of
God to Juan Diego could not be more unlike the terrifying apparition of the *Dira* to
Juturna – yet the Italian nymph's final words to Turnus (*Aen.* 12.872–3) are clearly
echoed in the speech from Tonantzin to Pluto that is prompted by Mary's apparition:

"Quid nunc? quid talia cernens
praestolare, pater?" (Primum est sic orsa frementi
voci furens, spiransque incendia saeva Tonanthis)
"Quid superest nobis? Quo Iupiter amplius optat
mittere?"

"What now? What hope do you have after witnessing this, father?" (Tonantzin was first to begin speaking in a roaring voice, as she breathed cruel fire). "What remains for us? To what further destination is Jupiter choosing to send us?"

Guadalupe 1.393–7

In this speech Tonantzin goes on to reveal that she was once known in ancient Italy as the *Mater Deum* ("Mother of the Gods," i.e., Cybele), Berecintia, and Vesta (1.410). In pre-Hispanic Mexico, Tonantzin was historically identified with the mother goddess Cihuacóatl or "Woman-snake," as Bernardino de Sahagún had explained in the 1500s:

[The Mexicans] used to say that this goddess brought adverse things like poverty, misery, toils. She often appeared, so they say, in garments like those worn in the palace.... They said that at night she used to shout and roar in the air. This god was called *Cihuacóatl* which means "woman of the serpent" and they also called her *Tonantzin* which means "our mother." (*HG* 1.6)

Sahagún also reported that during the reign of Moctezuma II, Cihuacóatl was frequently heard weeping at night, a grim harbinger of the Spanish conquest:

She cried out loudly; she went about saying: "O my beloved sons, now we are at the point of going!" Sometimes she said "My beloved sons, whither shall I take you?" (*HG* 8.1)

Thus the goddess's words to Pluto at *Guadalupe* 1.393–7 quoted above ("What remains for us? To what further destination...?") may not only echo Juturna's lament, they could also be a recollection of that ominous utterance, which was recorded on at least three separate occasions in the *Historia General* alone (8.1, 8.6, 12.1; Mendieta 1870, 3.2: 180).

According to Villerías' carefully constructed mythical system, Tonantzin is the daughter of Pluto and Night. Many of the children of Erebus and Night, listed by Cicero in *On the Nature of the Gods* 3.17, exhibit an obvious family resemblance to Cihuacóatl-Tonantzin: Guile, Fear, Toil, Resentment, Fate, Old Age, Death, Darkness, Misery, Complaint, Deceit, Obstinacy, the Parcae, the Hesperides – especially pertinent to the *Guadalupe* – and Dreams. But for Villerías y Roelas, the meaning of Tonantzin's name is even more disconcerting than her parentage:

nataque quam patria lingua dixere Tonanthin,
nostra, quod (infandum!) Mater sonat ore latino.

His daughter whom in their native tongue they called Tonantzin which – unspeakably!
– means "Our Mother" in the Latin Language.

Guadalupe 1.147–8

Modern speakers of Nahuatl still refer to the Virgin Mary as "Tonantzin." That association, combined with the association of Tepeyac with Cihuacóatl's worship as Tonantzin, had exasperated Sahagún:

In this place [Tepeyac] they used to have a temple dedicated to the mother of the gods whom they called Tonantzin, which means "our mother."... Now the church of Our Lady of Guadalupe has been built there, they also call her Tonantzin, taking their cue from the preachers who call Our Lady, the Mother of God, Tonantzin. What may be the basis for this use for Tonantzin is not clear. However we know for certain that the ancient use of the word means that ancient Tonantzin. It is something that should be remedied because the proper name for the Mother of God, Our Lady, is not Tonantzin but *Dios inantzin.* (*HG* 11.12)

These circumstances explain why Tonantzin was chosen to be a protagonist in Villerías' poem, when other Aztec gods like Quetzalcoatl and Huitzilopochtli loomed larger in the creole imagination. Tonantzin's key role in this epic composition is not in spite of her potentially sacriligeous association with Mary, but because of it. The poet's consistent portrayal of this ugly, rabid goddess in the *Guadalupe* as the direct adversary of the Christian Virgin precludes any equation of the two figures. The opposition is a neat move – not because any of Villerías' potential readers would ever really have needed the distinction between the two to be clarified, but because it ensures a decisive *creolization* of the Guadalupan myth by ensuring that the Virgin is completely purged of her association with the indigenous figure of Tonantzin.

   The manipulation of different historical and mythical traditions is familiar from the *Aeneid*: the connection of Juno to the Carthaginian goddess Tanit and of Dido to Cleopatra, or the opposition of Aeneas to Turnus and of Hercules to Cacus, along with other Gigantomachic elements of the poem can enhance our understanding of the fusions and divisions constructed by Villerías (Feeney 1991, 116–17, 130–1; Horsfall 1973–4; Hardie 1986, 33–156). But though much attention in the *Guadalupe* is given to Pluto and Tonantzin, the resolution achieved at the end of the poem is far less equivocal than the ending of the *Aeneid*. Readers can feel little sympathy for the villainous pagan gods who receive their just deserts. And while there may be genuine native sources for the poetic figure of Tonantzin, she and Pluto are crafted as inimical caricatures: no authentic or subversive indigenous "further voice" can really be heard in Villerías' epic. An emerging "creole patriotism" (Brading 1991) is what lies behind the syncretic conception of the *Guadalupe*: Cortés is praised at the same time that the courage of his indigenous adversaries is affirmed – and the achievements and marvels of pre-Hispanic Mexican history are really serving to contribute to the glorification of New Spain.

   The *Aeneid* has provided a framework for Villerías' epic – but as well as Vergil's successors in antiquity such as Ovid and Claudian, Renaissance imitators were crucial too. In addition to the Latin poems of Pontano, Sannazaro, and Capilupi, Villerías would have known the Latin epics on Marian themes by another Italian humanist poet: Battista Spagnoli, or "Mantovano." Spagnoli's *De sacris diebus* (1513), for example, had presented the pagan Roman gods devising some aggressive but futile plans to delay the triumph of Christianity, after Mercury had informed them of Gabriel's Annunciation to the Virgin Mary (Marrone 2004). The incorporation of Greco-Roman myth, Mexican indigenous legacies, and Christian tradition into Villerías' epic of cosmology, theology, and history thus reflects a rich fusion of sources from Europe – classical literature, humanist poetry, and vernacular romance – as well as a wide range of earlier Latin and Castilian writing from New Spain. The *Guadalupe* usefully exposes the cultural cosmopolitanism and ideological complexity that characterizes the extensive corpus of Mexican Latin writing from the colonial period.

Villerías' own impact on later authors in this tradition also serves as a reminder that the influence of the *Aeneid* on the later Latin literature of New Spain is rarely uncomplicated. For example, the beginning of the *Rusticatio Mexicana*, a didactic epic on Mesoamerican nature and culture first published in Italy in 1781 by the Guatemalan Rafael Landívar, contains the following verses on the early history of Mexico City:

> **Urbs** erat occiduis procul hinc notissima terris
> **Mexicus**, ampla, frequensque, viris, **opibusque** superba.

> There was a city far from here in the western lands, the very famous
> city of Mexico: large, populous, and distinguished for its men and resources.
>   *Rusticatio Mexicana* 1.32–3

They clearly recall Vergil's first presentation of Carthage in *Aen.* 1.12–14:

> **Urbs** antiqua fuit, Tyrii tenuere coloni,
> **Karthago**, Italiam contra Tiberinaque longe
> ostia, **dives opum** studiisque asperrima belli.

> There was an ancient city possessed by Tyrian settlers, Carthage, opposite Italy and the
> distant mouth of the Tiber, rich in resources and most ruthless in the pursuit of war.

However, Landívar's hexameters also exhibit a *stichometric* correspondence with Villerías' lines on Mexico City – which had themselves echoed the very same Vergilian description of Carthage in a different way:

> **Dives opum**, dives pictai vestis et auro
> dives et armenti.

> Rich in resources, rich in dyed textiles, and rich in gold and cattle.
>   *Guadalupe* 1.32–3

The *Guadalupe* was known to the Latin authors of Landívar's generation (Laird 2006, 21, 80, 261) – even though it was forgotten for the next two centuries. It is astonishing that the poem remained in manuscript form until it was edited by Ignacio Osorio Romero in 1991.

IV

The Mexica, originally a nomadic tribe, were supposed to have been instructed by the war god Huitzilopochtli to establish their city of Tenochtitlan ("Place of the Nopal") when they came upon an eagle perched on top of a nopal cactus with a writhing serpent trapped in its beak. The resemblance of this motif to a simile in *Aen.* 11.751–8 – which compares Tarchon's killing of Venulus to an eagle carrying off a snake – provided Alfonso Reyes with a coda to his demonstration of the uncanny convergences between Vergil's epic and the history of Mexico (Reyes 1937, 181).

Reyes, however, did not know that this fortuitous resemblance had been acknowledged by more than one Latin poet of the eighteenth century. In Villerías' *Guadalupe*, the scenes from Mesoamerican history in Atlas' cave include that Aztec omen, providing a reprise of that simile in the *Aeneid*, along with the "hissing swollen neck" of the viper in *Geo.* 3.421:

> alituum princeps volucrum (mirabile visu)
> quae tortum spiris, et **sibila colla tumentem**,
> ardua discerpit, rostroque, atque **unguibus** anguem.

The queen of winged birds (a wonder to behold!) proudly rips apart the twisted coils and swollen hissing neck of the snake with her beak and her claws.

Guadalupe 2.143–5

And, following Villerías, Rafael Landívar uses this vignette to link Vergil's poetry to ethnohistory in another way, as he describes a *cenchris* or hawk, in his book on birds:

> aut colubrum campis cernit fera **colla tumentem**…
> …sin vero pedibus serpentem sustulit uncis,
> **unguibus**, et rostro discerpit corda furentis,
> dum rabiem vita ponat, fugiatque sub umbras.

Or the hawk sees a snake in the fields, fiercely swelling its neck…If with his clawed feet he has carried off the serpent, with his talons and beak he also plucks out the heart of the raging creature, until it lays aside its rage along with its life and flees down to the shades.

Rusticatio Mexicana 13.353–5

The hawk kills his victim by ripping out his heart – the standard practice of Aztec sacrifice. At the same time Landívar's language in 355 recalls the killing of Turnus in the closing verse of the *Aeneid*: Aeneas' own "sacrifice" (*immolat*) of the conquered Turnus had long had positive associations in the ideology of Spanish imperialism (Laird 2003). But while Landívar's poem merely implicates Vergil in the history of New Spain, Villerías' *Guadalupe* illustrates – far more directly than the *Aeneid* ever could – Alfonso Reyes' own pronouncement that "all the forces of heaven and earth took part in the conflict" triggered by the Spanish invasion of Mexico.

Even if the Latin poets of the colonial era had been more widely known in the first decades of the twentieth century, the sense of creole hegemony and the unwavering Guadalupan devotion which united and inspired them would have had little appeal to the anti-clerical nationalists of Reyes' generation. But in spite of their considerable differences, the literary theorists of the 1910 Revolution and the creole patriots of the seventeenth to eighteenth centuries alike succeeded in endowing Vergil with fluidity and contemporary relevance – qualities that have sometimes eluded the poet in his more rigidly traditional role as the Classic of all Europe. Vergil's rebirth in the New World enabled – as Bernardino de Llanos put it in 1605 – "the sound of his words to be endowed with a different sense."

FURTHER READING

A short overview of the classical traditions in Latin America, with further bibliography, is in Laird (2006). Lupher (2003) is an outstanding historical study of the uses of Classics in Spanish America in the 1500s; Laird (2010a) examines Latin writings by indigenous Mexicans. Quint (1993, 131–85) and Kallendorf (2007) detect "Vergilian pessimism" in the poetry of Alonso de Ercilla and Sor Juana Inés de la Cruz. The unity of cosmic and political forces in the *Aeneid* explored in Hardie (1986) offers the best model for understanding Vergil's Latin successors in New Spain. Brading (2001) examines the religious and political significance of the Virgin of Guadalupe for Mexican history and nationalism.

On Individual Authors: León-Portilla (2002) is an introduction to Sahagún. López de Abilés' *Poeticum viridarium* and Riofrío's cento are edited and translated into Spanish in Peñalosa (1987), although further prose and verse texts in these volumes (including Rosales' *Aulica Musarum Synodus*) can only be read in seventeenth-century editions. Laird (2007a) attempts to rehabilitate Riofrío. Osorio Romero (1991) is a magisterial exposition of Villerías y Roelas in the literary tradition of New Spain. Of all the Latin poets from New Spain, Rafael Landívar is most frequently identified with Vergil: Laird (2006) is a complete collection of Landívar's works with accompanying essay studies. Alfonso Reyes' "Discurso Por Virgilio" ("Discourse on Vergil") is surveyed in Laird (2010b) – an account of the role of classical culture in Mexico from independence until the post-revolutionary period; see further Conn (2002). Cabrera (2004) is a collection of Latin hexameter poems on Mexican historical themes by the contemporary poet Francisco Cabrera.

CHAPTER SEVENTEEN

Vergil and Printed Books, 1500–1800

Craig Kallendorf

I

No one knows exactly, or even approximately, how many times the works of Vergil were printed in the early modern period. Giuliano Mambelli (1954) listed 1,637 editions published between 1469 and 1850, but the real total may well be double Mambelli's, perhaps even more. Yet even if we cannot determine how many editions of Vergil were printed between 1500 and 1800, the ones that are known and accessible merit closer attention than they often receive today, for they provide unique insight into the succession of post-classical cultures in which they were produced. Reading Vergil's poetry in the enormous, three-volume edition of Juan Luis de la Cerda (1608–17), in which the text often disappears almost completely into the mass of notes, is a completely different experience from reading it in the modern Oxford Classical Text of Sir Roger Mynors, and anyone with a serious interest in unraveling the intertextual relationship between the *Aeneid* and *Paradise Lost*, for example, should use the edition that Milton (probably) used, La Cerda's (Martindale 2002, 3, 108–9), and not its modern successor. What is more, these early editions retain their value because the roots of our modern understanding of Vergil are found there. As Charles Martindale (1993, 7) put it, "our current interpretations of ancient texts, whether or not we are aware of it, are, in complex ways, constructed by the chain of receptions through which their continued readability has been effected" – in other words, how we read Vergil's poetry now cannot be extricated from how it was read in the past. The most direct access to these past readings comes via the books that earlier readers used. Accordingly in this essay, I shall examine a series of older Vergilian editions from this double perspective, with one eye on what they show us about how Vergil's poetry was read in the past and the other on how these past readings can help to clarify issues of importance in Vergilian criticism at the beginning of the twenty-first century.

II

At the end of the twentieth century, interpretations of Vergil's *Aeneid* tended to begin from one of two basic perspectives. In the first, Aeneas is seen to articulate more and more successfully the values that would come to be associated with imperial Rome, until in the final scene of the poem he slays Turnus, the enemy leader, and removes the last obstacle to Roman power and glory. By this point he has overcome the forces of *furor* ("rage") and *ira* ("anger"), both within himself and as represented by the people who oppose him, so that he successfully embodies *pietas*, that particularly Roman virtue that embraces one's duties to God, country, and family. This approach is fundamentally optimistic, with Aeneas serving as the ideal hero of ancient Rome, the *Aeneid* celebrating the achievements of Augustus and his age, and the poem enduring as a monument to the values of order and civilization.

After World War II, however, a group of English-speaking scholars began listening more carefully to what have come to be called the "other voices" in the *Aeneid* – not the voice of Aeneas as the prototype of Roman imperialism, but the voices of those who stood in opposition to him: Dido, the Carthaginian queen whose love is sacrificed to Aeneas' higher mission; Turnus, the Italian prince who falls before Aeneas while trying to defend his country against the Trojan invaders; and so forth. Within the narrative structure of the poem, these "other voices" also project worthy values, and this new school of criticism has helped us see what was sacrificed in pursuit of Rome and the civilization it engendered. This group of scholars has also pointed out that Aeneas himself is often inconsistent in the set of values he articulates, especially in the last scene of the poem, which has been reinterpreted as a key failure in which Aeneas surrenders to the very voices of barbarism and fury within himself that he had struggled throughout the poem to suppress.

In the last decades of the twentieth century, the adherents of this first approach came to be called "optimists" and those of the second approach "pessimists." Scholars have been pointing out for some time now that there are dangers to dichotomies like this, which can easily become reductionist if applied insensitively, but in the end there is a difference in emphasis between the two approaches, even if the difference is more a matter of shades of grey than black versus white (Kallendorf 2007, v–viii).

The "optimistic" reading of the *Aeneid* was the one adopted by a succession of established political and cultural powers throughout the early modern period, who simply traced the roots of their kingdoms and empires back to Augustan Rome and presented themselves as the successors of Aeneas and the values they felt he represented (Tanner 1993). This becomes clear in the dedication of Pierre Perrin's seventeenth-century translation to Cardinal Mazarin, the influential cleric and diplomat who played an important role in shaping the foreign policy of several French monarchs:

> In effect, sir, the famous century of this grand author, does it not seem to have come around again in the present? Is Paris not now a Rome triumphant, like her enormous in population and territory, like her queen of cities, mistress of nations, capital of the world?

And your eminence, sir, are you not a faithful Maecenas, like him a Roman, like him the most grand and the most cherished minister, and the sacred depository of his secrets and his power? To complete these illustrious connections, does not Heaven require for France a French Vergil? (Perrin 1664, fol. 31r–31v; Schneider 1982, 180–1)

Perrin, of course, is presenting himself as the French Vergil, but in doing so he transfers the entire ideological framework of Vergil's Rome to seventeenth-century France. This transferral is straightforward and unproblematic: as Vergil had served and supported Augustus, so the new Vergil will serve and support his ideological successor.

This "optimistic" Vergil provided the model for the imperial expansion that projected the power of Europe onto every continent of the newly expanded world (Waswo 1997). Thus the first Brazilian edition of the *Aeneid*, for example, contains the translation of José de Lima Leitão, which was presented to King João VI as a "monument to the elevation of the colony of Brazil to kingdom, and the establishment of the triple Portuguese empire." As the dedicatory letter notes, "your majesty will point out a never-before-seen number of moral and political points of contact with the hero of this story, who has laid the foundations of the most perfect nation on the globe, and who in filial piety and in royal virtues will always be held as a model" (Lima Leitão 1818–19, fols. A2r, A3r). The Portuguese empire, in other words, is connected to the Roman one, and the Portuguese king should model his behavior, both public and private, on that of Aeneas.

This story has been told many times before, since the "optimistic" interpretation of the poem has dominated among most, if not all, its generations of readers (Thomas 2001). Less well known is the fact that the "pessimistic" interpretation of the *Aeneid* also has a history, and that this history can also be traced through the early editions of the poem. As an example, let us turn to a little-known work of Victor Alexandre Chrétien Le Plat du Temple, *Virgile en France*, a parody of the first six books of the *Aeneid* that makes the events of the poem into an allegory of the French Revolution.

Although Vergil's Augustus traced his roots to Aeneas, Le Plat's Aeneas is not an imperialist but a republican, for throughout the poem Aeneas aligns himself with "the good republicans" of revolutionary France (Le Plat 1807–8, 1.123, 1.128). Unfortunately for Le Plat, at the time *Virgile en France* was published, France was no longer a republic but an empire under the control of Napoleon Bonaparte. In describing how he came to be emperor, however, Le Plat presents him as the winner of an election, which suggests that authority rests in the will of the people, who could, one would think, also remove Napoleon at will. This suggestion is amplified in a note to book 5, in which Le Plat explains that an emperor who abuses "common law" must be replaced, the idea seeming to be that the citizens of a republic can choose temporarily to transfer some of their power to an executive, but that they can also take it back again when they want it. Le Plat's *Aeneid* thus remains a pro-republican poem, not the support for the establishment of the new Roman empire on the Seine that Napoleon would undoubtedly have preferred. This makes it a thoroughly subversive document, one that challenges the traditional association of Vergil's poem with the new Augustuses of the early modern era. Napoleon responded by seizing and destroying all the copies he could find and by trying to prevent the author from finishing the poem. Only a few copies escaped the hands of the censors, making *Virgile en France* a rare book indeed today.

Like other "pessimistic" readers of the *Aeneid*, Le Plat linked his challenge to Vergil's imperial ideology with a pronounced sympathy for those who suffer at the hands of Vergil's hero. His retelling of the love story between Dido and Aeneas, for example, contains some significant changes which seem to have been designed to exculpate Dido and make Aeneas' behavior look even worse than in the *Aeneid*. Dido's sister Anna, for example, is replaced by her confessor (2.1ff.), so that when she tries to decide how to handle the passions rising up inside her, she does so not with the aid and support of a sympathetic sister but with the guidance of the church. Juno in turn proposes that a priest be present at the scene in the cave where Dido and Aeneas are joined together (see Fig. 17.1), thereby giving the union greater legitimacy than it had in Vergil's poem (2.11). Le Plat's sympathy for Dido is part of a broader sympathy for women in general that appears elsewhere in his poem. In his retelling of the revolt of the Trojan women in book 5 of the *Aeneid*, for example, Le Plat adds a note that explains that religion and politics have conspired throughout history to oppress women (2.244–5). Here, and elsewhere, Le Plat responds to and strengthens the "other voices" in the poem (Kallendorf 2007, 196–212).

As one would expect, modern "optimists" and "pessimists" part company in their analysis of the character of Aeneas, and as the early printed editions show, their early modern counterparts did so as well. Beginning at the end of the fifteenth century, many of the earliest editions of Vergil's poetry carried the commentary of Tiberius Claudius Donatus (1905–6), a fourth-century CE writer who exercised considerable ingenuity in making Aeneas the morally perfect model for monarchs like Portugal's King João VI. Thus Vergil's goal is to show Aeneas as "free of all guilt and one most worthy to be presented publicly with great commendation" (1.2–5), and Donatus is convinced that Vergil praises Aeneas' virtues on every possible occasion: he is a good leader (*Aen.* 1.159–79), pious toward the gods (*Aen.* 1.379), handsome and brave (*Aen.* 1.594–5), and so on. It might appear that Aeneas is culpable now and again, but Donatus takes pains to show that this is not so. Abandoning Dido, for example, might look like a fault, but to Donatus, Aeneas emerges from his stay at Carthage with his reputation intact: Dido, after all, was deceived by Cupid, "so that even in this respect the poet might preserve the good name not only of Dido herself but even of Aeneas" (*Aen.* 1.720).

Then as now, however, not everyone read the *Aeneid* in this way. In 1741, for example, Thomas Cooke published a commentary to the *Aeneid* that would fully satisfy a twenty-first-century "pessimist" but which has not been reprinted since the middle of the eighteenth century. The first indication of this comes at *Aen.* 3.10, where Aeneas' tears as he sets out on his journey lead to this scholarly outburst: "Our hero is wimpering and sighing so often that our compassion is worn out for him: I really believe, if *Virgil* had lived to have corrected his *Aeneis* more than he did, he would have wiped away some of *Aeneas*'s tears." Aeneas' behavior in *Aen.* 4.318 is also roundly criticized: "Unhappy Dido uses sufficient arguments in this speech for the exercise of her hero's humanity, if his love is fled: he ought, from the consideration of the dangers which surrounded her, to have made her more the object of his care than he did."

Figure 17.1   Le Plat (1807–8, 2.11), *Wedding of Dido and Aeneas.*

Along with the objections to Aeneas' character goes a reevaluation of Turnus'. At *Aen.* 10.825 we get the first explicit praise of Turnus: "Turnus appears in the unexceptionable character of an intrepid gallant soldier…he is not a savage fighter void of reflection, but appears in the true dignity of a hero." This is not an isolated observation, with Turnus being praised at *Aen.* 10.261 for appearing "with an air of heroic gallantry, not only void of fear, but pleased with the opportunity of entering into action and acquiring glory." Cooke's comments on the final scene of the poem (*Aen.* 12.952) mark his final assault on the "optimistic" reading of the poem:

> We have been thro' a poem that is one of the noblest monuments of the genius of the antients: it is a diamond, but not without flaws…. *Aeneas* asserted his claim to the *Italian* dominions as promised him by the gods, and fixed by fate: *Turnus* disputed his

title very justly, for the other is a claim that any man might make. *Turnus* was guilty of no disobedience to the divine will; for unless *Jupiter*, or some other good-natured god, had acquainted *Turnus* with the will of heaven in regard to *Aeneas*, how could *Turnus* distinguish *Aeneas* from any other invader?… [T]hey who read the *Aeneis* with taste and reason send their wishes along with *Turnus*, because he was right in his opposition, and because *Aeneas*'s title from heaven was not half so good as *Turnus*'s right of inheritance from his father *Daunus*.

This is a remarkable passage. Most "pessimistic" critics of the early twenty-first century acknowledge that characters like Dido and Turnus represent worthwhile values that must be sacrificed on the altar of Aeneas' greater achievement. Cooke goes even farther than this, declaring Turnus to be morally superior to Aeneas, making the end of the poem even more tragic than modern readings of it.

III

Modern scholarship has been insisting with greater and greater force that reading has a history, and that we should not simply assume that past readers processed texts in the same way that we do. For example, the prologue to Fernando de Rojas' *Celestina* (printed in the 1507 Saragossa edition) offers a remarkably clear and self-conscious description of the ways in which a book could be read in the early modern period. There were three possibilities. First, a reader could focus not on the story as a whole, but on certain detached episodes. Second, the text could be used as a source for easily memorized formulas, proverbs, maxims, and ready-made expressions. And finally, a reader could work to grasp a text in its totality without reducing it to episodes or maxims, to develop a plural reading that recognizes diversity of interpretation and adapts whatever lessons the book contains to individual needs (Kallendorf 1999, 68; see also Cavallo and Chartier 1999; Baron 2001). As we shall see, it is the books themselves that provide the best evidence for the reading practices of the past. Let us take up each of these three possibilities in turn, with a focus on the second one, which is most alien to contemporary reading practices.

Then as now, certain parts of the *Aeneid* received greater attention than others. A quick survey of the *British Museum General Catalogue of Printed Books* and the *National Union Catalogue*, both of which separate out and record editions of individual books of the *Aeneid*, shows that as we might expect, books 1, 2, 4, and 6 were most often printed (and presumably read) separately. Even here, however, there are some surprises. Book 4, for example, is often given special attention by modern readers, but it was seldom printed alone in Latin until late in the nineteenth century, although separate editions in the vernacular languages are common. Another way to see what was being read, and how, is to look at the handwritten marginalia in early printed books, many of which come from a school environment. Even a cursory examination of the records of teaching activity left in the margins of student texts shows that it was unusual for a teacher to read a long poem like the *Aeneid* straight through from beginning to end (Kallendorf 1999, 68–71). More common by far was to dip in at certain key episodes, with the descent to the underworld in book 6, for example, being a favorite. Finally, one can look at the imitations and travesties of the *Aeneid* that were produced during this period, on the assumption that material was recast more or less in proportion to the attention given to it in the original. Here, again, as Vladimiro Zabughin pointed out almost a hundred years ago, book 6 is the source of the most interesting and courageous imitative work in this period, with the Dido story being used only rarely (1921–3, 1.302). It would thus appear that schoolmasters in the early modern period found themselves more uncomfortable with Aeneas' behavior at Carthage than their modern counterparts.

Handwritten notes left in the margins of early printed books can also shed light on the second style of reading in the early modern period. A copy of Vergil's works printed by Nicolaus Hoffmannus in Frankfurt in 1616 (Meyen 1616) and now in a private collection records the marginal annotations of one Rector Hesse, a German schoolmaster (see Fig. 17.2). Herr Hesse marked parallel passages from a variety of ancient authors along with variant readings and cross-references to other Vergilian commentators. But what interests us is his habit of underlining passages he wanted to be able to find again. In some cases his comments have a decidedly moral cast. Two underlined passages in book 2, which recounts the fall of Troy, provide advice on what to do in hopeless situations: "The lost have only / this one deliverance: to hope for none" (*Aen.* 2.354), and "at times / new courage comes to beaten hearts" (*Aen.* 2.367). Another passage reminds the reader of the lesson to be drawn from seeing the Great Sinners in the underworld – "Be warned, learn justice, do not scorn the gods" (*Aen.* 6.620) – signaled in the margin with an "NB" (*nota bene*, "note well"). Other passages, however, are obviously underlined because they are phrased in a memorable way: *Aen.* 2.255, "beneath / the friendly silence of the tranquil moon," carries the marginal reminder *Nox quieta* ("a peaceful night"), and the marginal note *Simile de subito pavore* ("simile concerning sudden fear") directs the reader back to the simile in *Aen.* 2.379–81. The passages underlined in Hesse's Vergil, in other words, illustrate moral topics (what to do in hopeless situations) or stylistic flourishes (a memorable simile), often with marginal annotations that serve as "indexing notes" to allow the reader to find them again and remember what they illustrate.

Sometimes these marginal annotations themselves were published. As an example, let us turn to another early printed edition, the text and commentary of Juan Luis de la Cerda (1608–17) that was mentioned earlier. La Cerda's commentary to *Ecl.* 3.14, for example, bears the marginal note *Dolor in affectu invidiae*, with the accompanying commentary directing the reader to note that grief is found within the passion of envy (*Nota in affectu invidiae dolorem*) and listing parallel passages from elsewhere in Vergil on the same topic. La Cerda's marginal notes to this same eclogue draw attention again and again to an adage, a pithy saying that encapsulates one of life's lessons: *Ecl.* 3.91, *mulgeat hircos*, is identified as an adage, *Hircos mulgere* ("to milk a he-goat," that is, to do something impossible). The phrase *amores…dulces…amaros* at the end of the eclogue (ll. 109–10) gets La Cerda to note that Erasmus discusses this proverb as a reference to something that is at the same time both happy and sad. Stylistic features are noted, too, as we saw in Hesse's marginal notes: on *Ecl.* 5.30, for example, La Cerda notes that to indicate that a man is great, one describes the scattering of flowers in his path, and at 5.56, we are

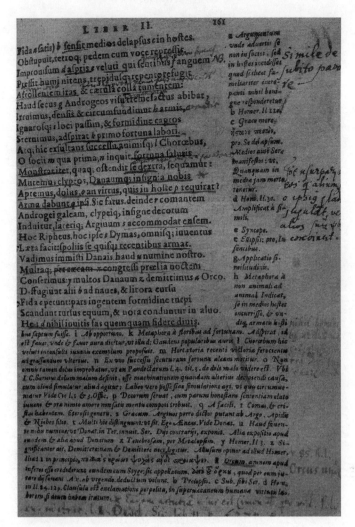

Figure 17.2 Meyen (1616, 161), with marginalia of Rector Hesse.

reminded that if one wants to describe a god, *candidus* ("white") is the appropriate color. In other contexts these proverbs were sometimes illustrated, either in the emblem books that were so popular during this period, or on the title pages of books like Perrin's French translation, discussed above (see Fig. 17.3).

Then, in a third step, books like the *Osservationi…sopra l'opere di Virgilio* by Orazio Toscanella (1567) made their way into print. Toscanella's book consists of headings like "rebuke" and "love," "nation" and "nature of things," "amplification" and "comparison," with passages from Vergil's poetry copied out underneath the relevant heading. In *Ammonitione* ("rebuke" or "warning"), for example, Toscanella considers how to rebuke a young man who has done something good but also made a mistake. Toscanella instructs his reader first to praise the young man for the good he has done, because praising virtue makes it grow and because praise makes one more disposed to

Figure 17.3   Perrin (1664), title page.

accept correction. Doing it the other way around (that is, beginning with the rebuke) hardens the heart and alienates it from the good, or at least makes the heart grow cold, he explains. Then comes the example, from *Aeneid* 9, where Apollo warns Ascanius not to put himself at such great risk in battle. First comes the praise: continue as you have been and you will become immortal (*Aen.* 9.641–4). Then comes the rebuke: "but after this, my boy, enough of war" (*Aen.* 9.656) (16–17). For a modern reader, this is a puzzling book, but it would not have been so for her early modern prede-cessor: Toscanella has simply taken the handwritten indexing notes left in the margin of an early printed book, or their printed counterparts in editions like that of La Cerda, and made them the headings. He then shattered Vergil's poetry into shards of several lines each and rearranged the shards under the appropriate headings.

So, to recapitulate: we have here a three-step process. Teachers like Hesse would buy an early printed edition of a poet like Vergil and read it with an eye on the moral wisdom it contains and on phrases that were expressed well, often signaling key phrases with "indexing notes" in the margin. In the next step, the marginal signals themselves could be printed, as in La Cerda, as a guide to other readers who would not in turn have to do all the thinking themselves. Then, finally, the whole business could be reformatted, as Toscanella did in step three, with the marginal notes becoming the headings and with Vergil's text broken up and rearranged under those headings, some focused on content and some on style. The result is a way of reading in which Vergil's poetry is seen as a repository of maxims and proverbs, of moralizing sayings and stylistic ornaments. This procedure, which was the dominant way of reading Vergil's poetry in the early modern period, has largely receded into the background today, although a quick look at the passages listed under "Vergil" in the *Oxford Dictionary of Quotations* suggests that it has not disappeared completely.

The third possibility is for a reader to work to grasp a text in its totality without reducing it to episodes or maxims, to develop a plural reading that recognizes diversity of interpretation and adapts whatever lessons the book contains to individual needs. This is the most common way of approaching the text today, but as we have seen, it was hardly unknown during the early modern period. Cooke's commentary, for instance, offers the basis for a "pessimistic" reading of the text into which the key episodes were incorporated in turn, while Donatus presents an "optimistic" approach to the text that embraces literally every relevant detail.

IV

As Charles Martindale has shrewdly observed, period labels have no greater claim to universal validity than do the interpretations of art and literature fashioned within them; both are cultural constructs, created at a particular point in time and subject to recreation at any time in the future (1993, 9). Nevertheless, I believe that there is at present some basic agreement among art historians about how early modern Europe might be divided into periods and about how successive responses to the artifacts of Greece and Rome might provide a rhythm to that periodization. Medieval painters and sculptors tended to see everything in terms of their own culture, to appropriate the "other" and make it their own – hence the late Gothic statues of Jupiter as a monk and Mars as a knight from the bell tower next to the Florentine cathedral. Under the influence of humanist historians, Renaissance artists sought to envision antiquity on its own terms, to preserve its "otherness," so that artists of the period attempted to remove themselves and their values from their works. Baroque artists in turn sought to focus attention on themselves, using classical subject matter as a means to show off their ability to solve technical challenges in a flurry of motion and activity; we might think, for example, of Bernini's *Apollo and Daphne* or his *Rape of Persephone*. It seems that in art, as in physics, actions provoke reactions, so that neoclassical artists responded by shifting attention away from themselves to their subject matter, again attempting to let the grandeur and nobility of the classical past shine forth in the pure vision of, say, David's *Oath of the Horatii*. The romantic vision shifted from public to private, from the mind to the heart – another version of action and reaction – so that classical subject matter now serves as a source for pathos, which must be felt by the artist and communicated to the viewer. In other words, the way in which

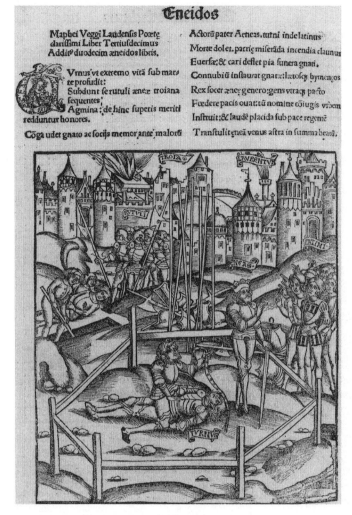

Figure 17.4 Brant (1502, 407v), *Death of Turnus*. Photo: Junius Spencer Morgan Collection of Vergil. Rare Books Division. Department of Rare Books and Special Collections. Princeton University Library.

classical subject matter is appropriated provides a sort of rhythm to this periodization. First the emphasis is on the artist and on how he or she might manipulate the past to meet the needs of the present in a way that might be labeled "mannerist." Then the emphasis is on the subject matter, as the artist attempts to suppress the present to see the past on its own terms, which we might label "neoclassical." Next the artist returns to center stage, then the classical subject matter, then the artist.

The illustrated editions of Vergil show how this works (Suerbaum 1992). The most famous of the early illustrated editions is the one edited by Sebastian Brant and printed by Johannes Grüninger in Strasbourg in 1502 (Schneider 1982, 66–7; 1983; Leach 1982, 175–210). In the scene illustrating the final battle between Turnus and Aeneas (Brant 1502, fol. 407v; see Fig. 17.4), for example, the characters are dressed in costumes from

Figure 17.5 [Vergil] (1586, 221v), beginning of *Aen.* 11. Photo: Junius Spencer Morgan Collection of Vergil. Rare Books Division. Department of Rare Books and Special Collections. Princeton University Library.

the late Middle Ages, not from ancient Rome, and the wooden ring in the foreground, along with the helmets and pikes stacked behind it, suggest that Aeneas and Turnus have just finished fighting according to late medieval conventions. The cities in the background look like the northern European cities that Brant and Grüninger knew, and the perspective (or rather, lack of perspective) is typically medieval as well (Kallendorf 2001, 124–5).

The blocks from the 1502 Strasbourg edition were copied in Italy and France and remained very popular for several decades, but after mid-century several other series of woodcuts began to compete successfully with them. One of these competing series appeared in an Italian translation published in Venice near the end of the century. The battle scene depicted here ([Vergil] 1586, fol. 221v; see Fig. 17.5) clearly reflects the

Figure 17.6   Dryden (1716, vol. 2, following p. 454), *Death of Dido* (*Aen*. 4). Photo: Junius Spencer Morgan Collection of Vergil. Rare Books Division. Department of Rare Books and Special Collections. Princeton University Library.

norms of Italian Renaissance art: it represents one and only one point of action within book 11, and it is rendered in reasonable perspective and a pleasingly balanced composition. The towers of the town in the background still look like what a Renaissance reader would have seen in an Italian city of his day, but the effect is totally different from that of the Strasbourg edition (Kallendorf 2001, 124–7).

At the end of the following century, John Dryden's monumental English translation appeared, first with the baroque engravings of Franz Cleyn (Leach 1982, 211–30; cf. chapter 20 by Eastin in this volume), then with another series published by the same printer in 1716. The scene depicted here (Dryden 1716, vol. 2, following p. 454; see Fig. 17.6), the moment of Dido's death, was obviously selected to allow the

Figure 17.7 Bartoli (1780–2, nr. 37), *Laocoon.* Junius Spencer Morgan Collection of Vergil. Rare Books Division. Department of Rare Books and Special Collections. Princeton University Library.

flurry of movement so favored by baroque artists. It is dominated not by Dido but by Iris, who is depicted at the very moment of descent, which requires the greatest technical skill to render, encouraging the viewer to admire the artist's ability in controlling a difficult composition. The building behind the pyre is typically baroque as well, showing the dissociation of form from function that characterizes, for example, Il Gesù in Rome. In this case, the artist clearly sees the *Aeneid* through the filter of the baroque aesthetic that dominated his culture (Kallendorf 2001, 127–8).

In the history of Vergilian illustration, the reaction to this engraving may be found in the *Picturae antiquissimi Virgiliani codicis Bibliothecae Vaticanae...*, which reproduces scenes from two very old manuscripts, the Codex Vaticanus and the Codex Romanus, along with other scenes from gems, monuments, mosaics, and other artifacts of ancient Rome (Odermann 1931, 18). The depiction of Laocoon (Bartoli 1780–2, nr. 37; see Fig. 17.7) comes from the Codex Vaticanus, but it ends up suiting a neoclassical temperament quite well. The composition, for example, shows signs of symmetricality, with one child on either side of Laocoon, who has his arms upraised in perfect balance and the two snakes draped across his body in perfect parallelism. What is more, the figures maintain their dignity and restraint, even in an agonizing death. It is impossible not to think of this scene as a contrast to the famous Hellenistic statue of Laocoon, which was widely known at this time and

Dear pledges of my love, while heaven so pleased
Receive a soul, of mortal anguish eased:

Œn.4.r937.

Figure 17.8   Dryden (1803, vol. 1, following p. 160), *Death of Dido*. Junius Spencer Morgan Collection of Vergil. Rare Books Division. Department of Rare Books and Special Collections. Princeton University Library.

which represents a mannerist aesthetic completely foreign to what we see here (Kallendorf 2001, 129–30; cf. the chapter by Most in this volume).

Dryden's translation remained popular for several generations, eventually picking up another set of illustrations that was published right at the turn of the nineteenth century. These illustrations show signs of an emerging romantic sensibility. For example, in this depiction of Dido giving her dying speech (Dryden, 1803, vol. 1, following p. 160; see Fig. 17.8), the artist is trying primarily to convey the emotion of the moment. The woman in the foreground rushes toward the collapsed queen, while the one in the background throws up her arms in grief. This is the point in the story with the greatest emotional force, and the illustrator was clearly drawn to it as a vehicle for communicating the emotional content he valued in the story (Kallendorf 2001, 130–3).

These woodcuts and engravings are obviously valuable for the insight they offer into how Vergil's poetry was envisioned during the successive periods of early modern culture. But they can also serve to enrich our current understanding of this poetry. For centuries Vergil has stood as the incarnation of classical restraint and order. Yet there is another Vergil as well. Donatus quoted a contemporary of the poet as saying that he had developed a new *cacozelia*, "a mannerism that was elusive, neither swollen, nor thin, but made up of ordinary words" (Thomas 2001, 12). And in one of the most influential of all works of literary criticism in the period immediately after World War II, Ernst Robert Curtius anchors his discussion of mannerism in Vergil as well. If, as he explains, classicism (and by extension neoclassicism in its various manifestations) can be defined as "Nature raised to the Ideal" and mannerism as whatever runs counter to it, then Vergil's poetry is certainly suffused with much that is classical. But Roman classicism falls between two mannerist periods, the Alexandrian and the late imperial, and as Curtius develops his discussion of mannerism as the indiscriminate piling on of rhetorical embellishment, he turns to Vergil's poetry again and again for examples (Curtius 1967, 273–301; Clausen 1987; Thomas 2001, 15–19). In other words, the Renaissance artist and his baroque successor were dealing with the same poem; they were simply responding to different aspects of it, just as we do today.

V

There are, then, two reasons to spend time with the earlier editions of Vergil's poetry. The first is so that we can better understand the central place of this poetry in the development of early modern culture. The prefaces and commentaries in the early printed editions capture the complexities of power in this period, with those at the center (like Perrin) and those on the margins (like Le Plat) focalizing their attitudes through the *Aeneid*. The early printed editions also carry the evidence of reading practices during this period, some of which, like the tendency to see Vergil's poetry as a series of stylistic examples or moralizing proverbs, are quite different from ours. And the succession of illustrations offers clear evidence of how the *Aeneid* was envisioned from one period to the next.

Yet if "our current interpretations of ancient texts, whether or not we are aware of it, are, in complex ways, constructed by the chain of receptions through which their continued readability has been effected," then what we do with Vergil's text today has its roots in what our predecessors did with it. The roots of both the "optimistic" and the "pessimistic" interpretations of the poem that remain influential today extend deeply into the commentaries and prefatory matter of the early printed editions. Modern readers, like those who went before them, focus on some parts of the *Aeneid* at the expense of others, and they develop readings of the poem as a whole that are not so different from those of the past. And the oscillation between mannerist and neoclassical aesthetics that is seen in the early illustrated editions provides the foundation for a modern discussion of similar elements in

Vergil's poetry. Past meets present, then, in the pages of these books, which offer considerably more than antiquarian interest for those who are willing to invest time and effort in understanding them.

FURTHER READING

There is no reliable bibliographical guide to the early printed editions of Vergil: Mambelli (1954) is seriously deficient, although a replacement by Kallendorf is in progress. One of the largest discrete Vergil collections in the world is the one at Princeton University; the catalogue of Kallendorf (2009) has just been published. Much useful information is available in the exhibition catalogues that appeared to mark the bimillennium of Vergil's death in 1981–2; especially good are Fagiolo (1981) and Schneider (1982). On the "optimistic" and "pessimistic" interpretive schools, see Kallendorf (2007, v–viii, with bibliography); on the historical roots of this division, see Tanner (1993), Thomas (2001), and Kallendorf (2007). From the growing literature on reading and its history, Cavallo and Chartier (1999) and Baron (2001) provide a useful orientation. The standard work on marginalia is Jackson (2001), with Rosenthal (1997) providing a roadmap for what remains to be done. Of the topics treated in this chapter, the illustrated editions of Vergil have received the most discussion; see Odermann (1931), Mortimer (1982), Suerbaum (2008), and Pasquier (1992) for an overview. Suerbaum has recently completed an extensive catalogue of the illustrated editions in the Bayerische Staatsbibliothek, Munich. The other topics treated here have been touched on in several works of Kallendorf (1999, 2001, 2002, 2007, 2008b).

PART THREE

The *Aeneid* in Music and the Visual Arts

CHAPTER EIGHTEEN

Vergil and the Pamphili Family in Piazza Navona, Rome

Ingrid Rowland

Shortly after his uncle Giovanni Battista's election as Pope Innocent X in 1644, Camillo Pamphili (1622–66) found himself a cardinal. One writer described this promotion as "his happiness," and indeed it was; it got Camillo out of the marriage that had been arranged for him by his formidable mother, Donna Olimpia Maidalchini. Rather than marry the previous pope's homely niece, Lucrezia Barberini, Camillo therefore prepared himself to enter the "Sacred Senate." For once his will was as implacable as his mother's.

Normally, the first sons of Italian aristocrats, or only sons like Camillo Pamphili, were the ones who married and carried on the family name. It was only second sons, and any subsequent sons, who went into the church, where they could earn a sumptuous living by collecting clerical offices and, at the same time, stand conveniently outside the line of inheritance (just as superfluous daughters were usually dowered as nuns to a convent). This, in fact, had been the case for Camillo's father and his paternal uncle, the two Pamphili brothers, Pamphilio and Giovanni Battista. Pamphilio, the elder brother, had married Donna Olimpia, then a wealthy widow thirty years his junior, whereas Giovanni Battista, the younger sibling, had become a priest. Although members of the Pamphili family had worked in the Vatican since the 1470s, none had achieved any particular prominence until Giovanni Battista, whose promotions, piloted, allegedly, by his sister-in-law, began to determine the family fortunes. When he was appointed papal nuncio to the Kingdom of Naples, Pamphilio and Donna Olimpia moved together with him, and there, above the splendid bay beneath the slopes of Mount Vesuvius, they had borne their son Camillo. Thanks to his uncle's position, Camillo Pamphili learned to move in the highest circles of the Neapolitan aristocracy, a social rank that only improved when Giovanni Battista moved on to Madrid as ambassador to the Spanish court, and then returned to Rome as a cardinal – not, as would be the case for Camillo, because of family connections, but for his diplomatic abilities. Roman gossip (and not only Roman) also suggested that Donna Olimpia's relationship with her brother-in-law, even before she was widowed, seemed suspiciously close.

At the time of his own elevation to the purple, Camillo Pamphili was a good-looking, personable young man, with an immaculately trimmed goatee, stylishly upturned moustaches, and carefully barbered curls. A contemporary writer notes that the young Pamphili still retained a certain Neapolitan flair after moving to Rome:

> Nacque in Napoli a tempo [che] detto suo zio era nuntio in quella città, però non può dirsi questo Cardinale esser romano per esser nativo Napolitano.... Questo Signore è di buoni costumi, amabile e spiritoso e quanto è giovane d'anni, tanto è canuto di senno.... È grato con gli suoi amici e servitori et in particolare con quelli che lo conoscevano avanti la sua felicità e però se ne spera da lui buoni successi. È giovane vago nell'aspetto e di colore olivastro, né si diletta d'andare su le grandezze e pompe, né è inclinato a vitii di sorte veruna, ma le commodità sono quelle che possono far trascorrere per così dire qualsivoglia persona per santa che sia.

* * *

> He was born in Naples at the time that his uncle was nuncio in that city, and hence this cardinal cannot be called a Roman because he is a Neapolitan native.... This Lord is well-mannered, amiable and lively, and however young he may be in years, he has the good sense of a graybeard.... He is pleasant to his friends and servants, and particularly with those who knew him before his present happiness, and for that reason good things can be expected of him. He is a handsome young man, with an olive complexion, and he takes no delight in going about in grandeur and pomp, nor is he inclined to vices of any sort. (Paris, Bibliothèque Mazarine, MS. 1659 cc. 7v–10v; Claudio Costantini 1888–2008)

Other reports were less enthusiastic: the new cardinal was allegedly so lazy that he sometimes rose from bed to start his day at 7 p.m.

Camillo's mother was another matter altogether. Grasping, imperious, iron-willed, and penetratingly intelligent, Donna Olimpia Maidalchini (1591–1657) terrorized every level of society in Baroque Rome. Unlike her frivolous Neapolitan son, Donna Olimpia sprang from the Etruscan stock of Viterbo, just north of the Eternal City, and fit in perfectly with the Etruscan tradition of emancipated women. As a young woman, she had been attractive; as she grew older she grew plump, but the resolution of her character showed nonetheless through her small gimlet eyes and the set of her jowly jaw. Romans liked to call her "la Pimpaccia," a pejorative form of her name.

Donna Olimpia's personal fortune, based on extensive landholdings north of Rome, only increased as her brother-in-law grew ever more powerful. Her machinations within the city itself, oiled by money, were rumored to have procured the very offices that bolstered Cardinal Giovanni Battista Pamphili in his bid for the papacy, long before her son Camillo's promotion to the purple. Her eyes may have been small and beady, but they missed nothing, including the opportunity to turn special occasions into grand artistic plans. For Donna Olimpia was more than a political plotter of rare ability; she was also one of seventeenth-century Rome's most discerning patrons of art, and beyond doubt the city's most rapacious collector. She would enter artists' studios and demand whatever painting struck her eye, no matter who might have commissioned it in the first place. If she could not have an Old Master, she ordered a copy. The Pamphili collection swelled with works by Raphael, Caravaggio, Titian, and modern masters, including a stunning portrait of Innocent X by the chief painter to the Spanish court, Diego Velázquez, a startlingly vivid likeness in oil that lets the man's commanding intelligence triumph over his legendary ugliness.

It was Donna Olimpia who guided the transformation of the Pamphili palazzo in Piazza Navona into a residence worthy of a cardinal nephew, having decided that she and Camillo should continue to live together in the family stronghold rather than having him take up residence in the Vatican. The former site of the Stadium of Domitian had long been a Spanish outpost in Rome, dominated since the later fifteenth century by the palazzo of the Neapolitan Cardinal Oliviero Carafa, which rose over the site of Domitian's ancient starting line. (Another Carafa, Don Tiberio, Prince of Bisignano, had held baby Camillo Pamphili at the baptismal font.) Nearby, Antonio, the first member of the Pamphili family to move from the rugged hills of Umbria to work in the Vatican, established his own palazzo in 1471. As a cardinal, Giovanni Battista Pamphili had already begun to embellish the old family property, but in 1644, when he moved on to the Apostolic Palace as Innocent X, it was Donna Olimpia who took the project in hand on her son's behalf. Within a decade she would transform both the cardinal's palace and the ancient piazza.

As cardinal, the future Innocent X had already enlarged the building in 1639. Now Donna Olimpia entrusted the remodeling of Palazzo Pamphili to the father and son team of Girolamo and Carlo Rainaldi, under the supervision of the secretive, cerebral Lombard, Francesco Borromini, whose architecture was far more idiosyncratic, but far more exciting. Her plans for Palazzo Pamphili posed one outstanding challenge, for, like several other prominent cardinals' palazzi in Rome (Palazzo Venezia, Palazzo della Cancelleria), the new residence was to incorporate an entire early Christian church in its fabric: Sant' Agnese in Agone, the church of "Saint Agnes in the Circus." The first shrine on the site had been erected in the seventh century, on the spot where local legend held that St. Agnes, a Roman maiden converted to Christianity, had been condemned to being stripped naked and exposed in Domitian's stadium for all Rome to behold. Miraculously, the virtuous Agnes had been protected from shame when her long hair suddenly grew so long and thick that it covered her in dignity.

Borromini responded to the challenge of the site by creating a building that cleverly combined the functions of church and palazzo, private life and religion. To emphasize Cardinal Camillo's responsibilities to both spheres, the architect set the prelate's bedroom inside the body of the church, beneath one of its massive bell towers (an expedient that would also have allowed this notorious late riser to hear mass without leaving his bed). Aristocratic bedrooms in the seventeenth century were highly public spaces, used to receive guests and to do work as well as for sleeping. Typically, therefore, Camillo Pamphili's bedroom opened directly onto a spacious, sunlit gallery (see Plate 1), a reception hall that ran the full breadth of the palazzo and stood as the glorious endpoint of a long suite of seven rooms. This was the climax and the focal point of the building's interior.

There was only one problem with Donna Olimpia's carefully laid plans: her son. On the very day of his uncle's elevation, an attractive, capable, fabulously wealthy woman arrived at the palazzo to pay her respects, and the cardinal-to-be began to fall passionately in love.

Olimpia Aldobrandini, Princess of Rossano (1623–81), was the great niece and sole heir of Pope Clement VIII Aldobrandini (r. 1592–1605). Married young to Prince Paolo Borghese (another papal nephew), she had already borne three children, but this did not keep her from dressing in the most modish fashions of mid-seventeenth-century Rome, a cinched bodice accentuating her narrow waist, corkscrew curls framing her head, large earrings dangling from her delicate ears. She ranked, by universal acclaim, as one of the city's most beautiful women, as gentle as that other Olimpia, the cardinal's mother, was steely. Painted portraits in those days emphasized her large eyes, her flawless complexion, and the graceful figure beneath her stiff, stylish dresses. No wonder Camillo was smitten, accustomed as he was to an Olimpia of an entirely different mettle.

In June of 1646, Olimpia Aldobrandini was suddenly widowed; Paolo Borghese was only 24. Her late uncle's will demanded that Olimpia's second son carry on the Aldobrandini name (the first son had taken the name of his father, Borghese), but Olimpia Aldobrandini had no second son, as yet. Clearly she would want to marry again, and quickly. Before the funeral was over, let alone the eight months of mourning she would be required to observe, rumor already had it that Olimpia Aldobrandini would be marrying Cardinal Pamphili. He had proposed almost straightaway.

The strength of his passion drove the normally indolent Camillo Pamphili to an act of extraordinary initiative. He asked his uncle for a dispensation from his priestly vows, and Pope Innocent, after some months of indecision, resolved that in the end, he, too, would weather the blasts of Donna Olimpia's wrath. From the pope's personal standpoint, the loss of Camillo Pamphili to the purple was not a matter of any great significance. There were other nephews to take up the role (in fact his nephew Camillo Astalli was rechristened Camillo Pamphili when he donned his own cardinal's hat). Furthermore, Innocent was wise enough to entrust the real work of his papacy to people of proven ability, like his nuncio in Münster, Fabio Chigi, whom he named in 1651 as secretary of state.

With only a token protest, then, the pontiff released his nephew from holy orders, and on January 21, 1647, Camillo Pamphili officially resigned his position as cardinal. As autumn set in, on October 2, 1647, the man now known as Prince Camillo Pamphili married his beloved Olimpia Aldobrandini. The wrath of his mother, when it exploded, must have rivaled the *memorem iram* of Vergil's Juno. She banished the couple from Rome, and wielded the power to make their exile stick.

Initially, Camillo and the woman Rome called "little Olimpia," *Olimpiuccia*, took up residence in the Villa Farnese outside the village of Caprarola. Fortunately, the bride's Aldobrandini fortune ensured that the couple and their growing family (the first of their five children, Giovanni Battista, was born in 1648) would never go homeless. So long as Donna Olimpia Maidalchini lived – that is, for the first decade of their marriage – they were compelled to live in small towns rather than Rome itself, but they made the best of that intimacy, enjoying the Aldobrandini villa on the hill of Frascati, with its view of Rome, and remodeling two sumptuous palazzi, one in Valmontone, near Frascati in the volcanic hills to the northeast of the city known as the Castelli Romani, and one along the coast south of Rome at Nettuno.

Donna Olimpia, meanwhile, carried on with the decoration of Palazzo Pamphili, the home she no longer shared with her wayward son Camillo. In 1651, as a crowning flourish, she commissioned a series of fresco decorations for the palazzo's gallery and master bedroom from the Tuscan artist Pietro Berrettini da Cortona, whose frescoes celebrating the previous pope, Urban VIII, had quickly gained a reputation as one of the chief glories of seventeenth-century Rome. Now Pietro concentrated on two rooms, both of them designed by the great Borromini: the gallery that linked Palazzo Pamphili to the church of Sant'Agnese, and the adjoining bedroom that had been meant for Cardinal Camillo. Their theme, directed, of course, by Donna Olimpia, was Vergil's *Aeneid*, its grand outlines unfolding along the walls and ceiling of the gallery, from the windstorm that begins book 1 to the slaying of Turnus that ends book 12. Only one book of the epic was missing from the gallery's spacious hall: the romantic Carthaginian interlude of book 4. Pietro reserved the romance of Dido and Aeneas for the bedroom, beginning with their meeting in Carthage, and ending with the hero's eventual departure for Latium, accompanied by Dido's suicide.

Pietro's decorative scheme, as we shall see, was cleverly tailored to the specific realities of the Pamphili family, but its choice of themes remained far more appropriate to a cardinal than a family man, especially one in ignominious exile from Rome. Evidently Donna Olimpia could not quite face the reality of her son's choices in life. Hence the frescoes of the gallery are, in a sense, a grand monument to Donna Olimpia's obstinate powers of denial, although it was hardly the great painter's job to bring the commission's surreal qualities to the attention of his patroness. He simply painted, as beautifully as he knew how, and she rewarded him with the lavish sum of 3,000 scudi.

Like most works of Baroque art, especially art in public places, Pietro da Cortona's frescoes present plain ideas in sumptuous visual form. The symbolism of the *Aeneid* for the Christians of papal Rome, and especially for a cardinal, a member of the "Sacred Senate," was meant to be clear, not elusive, and clear it is: Rome, the ancient *caput mundi*, now ruled a spiritual rather than a temporal empire, and this spiritual mission was in fact the true fulfillment of the ancient empire's political mission. If the *pietas* of Aeneas was best translated in ancient times as "duty," the *pietas* of the new Rome added Christian piety to the range of duties for which a modern Aeneas must assume responsibility. This Christian awareness is already evident in the two identical inscriptions that bridge the gallery's two windows: *Sub umbra alarum tuarum*. The line comes from Psalm 17:8, "Hide me *under the shadow of thy wings*." Hence when Cortona's frescoes show an Aeneas guided by Venus and Jupiter, that picture of divine protection must always be understood, in characteristic Baroque fashion, as a foreshadowing, or an image, of the protection that the God of Abraham offers to those who keep his commandments.

The idea that ancient Greek and Roman gods might provide an image of Christian salvation gathered its greatest momentum in the fifteenth and sixteenth centuries, together with the idea that Rome was an Eternal City, forever destined to fulfill – but in a Christian sense – the civilizing mission that Vergil describes in the *Aeneid*. In the Middle Ages the capital's precipitous decline from a population of one million to twenty or thirty thousand had seemed only to tell a tale of humbled pride. The Renaissance papacy changed that message of decline and fall into one of rebirth, through which the visual elegance of ancient art, the persuasive power of ancient literature, and the technological achievements of ancient architecture, infused with Christian faith, would be harnessed to spread the Gospel with renewed conviction. The city's ruins, and standing monuments like the Pantheon, presented both a challenge and an inspiration to everyone who set foot in the city, whether as a longtime resident or as a temporary visitor. Latin literature provided an unbroken connection to the minds of the ancients, with Vergil heading the list of indispensable writers from antiquity; his fourth eclogue's homage to the birth of a miraculous child was taken as proof that he had anticipated the birth of Jesus and was hence an *anima naturaliter christiana*, a "naturally Christian soul."

Over the course of the fifteenth and sixteenth centuries, Rome's population grew as steadily as its cultural importance within Europe; the city's urban development began to fill the long-vacant terrain enclosed within its third-century Aurelian Walls. By the seventeenth century, despite the spiritual, military, and economic setbacks posed by the Protestant Reformation, Rome had turned into a magnificent modern capital, whose single most important industry was the building trade. The rise of ancient Rome from the smoldering ruins of Troy therefore foreshadowed the rise of modern Rome from the ashes of barbarian attacks that ranged from Alaric's Visigoths in 410 to the *Landesknechte* of Charles V in 1527. Hence Pietro da Cortona's fresco cycle for the Palazzo Pamphili was only one of many renditions of the *Aeneid* to appear on Roman walls from the fifteenth century onward, all of them pointedly emphasizing the modern Christian fulfillment of the city's ancient destiny.

Within these broad outlines, however, the Vergilian scheme in Palazzo Pamphili also makes specific connections to the family and to its historical situation in the mid-seventeenth century. The Pamphili coat of arms bore a dove with an olive branch in its beak above three fleurs di lis. It is not surprising, then, that Venus, as mother of Aeneas, should feature prominently in several scenes, always accompanied by her doves. As the divine ancestress of Rome, and more specifically of the Julian *gens*, her place in the city's history, and in the *Aeneid*, is fundamental, but here she is shown in direct connection with the Pamphili family, not only because of the dove on their coat of arms, but also through their Greek-derived name, *pam-philos*, which might be translated as "entirely lovable," or "friends to all," or any number of similarly loving, friendly meanings. The *imperium* that once belonged to the Caesars has passed here, then, to the papacy, and, by extension, to the papal family. Typically for Roman Renaissance and Baroque art, this Venus should be understood as an entirely Christian figure of Vergil's "naturally Christian" imagination; she is the fulfillment of ancient eros in Christian *agape*, just as the College of Cardinals was called the "Sacred Senate," and the pope, the Christian *pontifex maximus*, right up to Benedict XVI, still wears the red shoes proper to Roman patricians.

Pietro da Cortona's images of Venus for the Palazzo Pamphili also pay visual tribute to a famous Renaissance fresco, again an apparently pagan theme that more truly represents Christian salvation: Raphael's image of Venus in a dove-drawn chariot from a loggia devoted to the legend of Cupid and Psyche, painted in Rome in 1518 for the Sienese banker Agostino Chigi, and itself inspired visually by a now lost ancient Roman painting and philosophically by Apuleius' *Golden Ass*. One of Agostino Chigi's descendants, Fabio Chigi, was already a rising star in Pope Innocent's diplomatic corps, and would be named secretary of state at about the same time that Cortona began to paint the Pamphili gallery. Chigi himself was destined to become a great patron of art, including Pietro da Cortona's, in his own right.

In the Rome of 1651, however, the dove of peace had an immediate political significance that would have occurred immediately to any visitor. Throughout most of the 1640s, through his nuncio in Münster, Fabio Chigi, Pope Innocent X was working to conclude the negotiations that would bring an end to thirty years of terrible,

Figure 18.1   Pietro da Cortona, *The Council of the Gods* (*Aen.* 10). Galleria, Palazzo Pamphili, Rome. 1651–4. Fresco. Courtesy Istituto Nazionale Centrale per il Catalogo e la Documentazione, Rome.

bloody conflict with French, German, and Swedish Protestants – the Thirty Years' War. When the delegates in Münster came to drafting the settlement known as the Peace of Westphalia in 1648, its terms were so detrimental to the papacy that Chigi refused to sign the final document; Innocent himself would decry the peace as "null, void, invalid, iniquitous, unjust, damnable, reprobate, inane, empty of meaning and effect for all time." Yet it was a peace treaty all the same, a peace long sought for, and binding on an international scale. Appropriately, then, the main event in Pietro da Cortona's Pamphili gallery, portrayed within a gold-framed panel that dominates the very center of the ceiling (Fig. 18.1), is the Council of the Gods from *Aeneid* 10,

Figure 18.2   Pietro da Cortona, *Aeolus Unleashes the Winds* (*Aen.* 1). Galleria, Palazzo Pamphili, Rome. 1651–4. Fresco. Courtesy Istituto Nazionale Centrale per il Catalogo e la Documentazione, Rome.

which will eventually bring peace at last to Latium. A majestic Jupiter stretches out his arm to Venus and Cupid to declare, as John Dryden's translation puts it:

> Why this protracted war, when my commands
> Pronounc'd a peace, and gave the Latian lands?
> What fear or hope on either part divides
> Our heav'ns, and arms our powers on diff'rent sides?
> [...]
> Let now your immature dissension cease;
> Sit quiet, and compose your souls to peace. (*Aen.* 10.9–15)

Dramatically, Justice flies in with balance in hand and Mercury trumpets the news. The Great Mother Cybele features prominently in her lion-drawn chariot because her temple was one of the important landmarks on the Palatine Hill, and because Pietro da Cortona obviously delighted in painting his magnificent lions. The silvery yellow color of the heavens derives from the vision of Ezekiel 1:4, where the color of deep space is likened to electrum, the alloy of gold and silver.

This large central scene is flanked by two scenes set, for the sake of variety, within fictive oval frames: one of these shows Juno prevailing on Aeolus to release his winds (Fig. 18.2), a prelude to the two scenes that flank one another on the end of the vault that faces Piazza Navona.

Figure 18.3 Pietro da Cortona, *The Landing of Aeneas.* Galleria, Palazzo Pamphili, Rome. 1651–4. Fresco. Courtesy Istituto Nazionale Centrale per il Catalogo e la Documentazione, Rome.

The travails of the Thirty Years' War probably lie behind the prominence that Pietro da Cortona gives to the earliest episode on the ceiling: the tempest in book 1 that occurs after Aeolus unleashes his unruly winds. Not only do we see Juno appealing to Aeolus, but we also see the tempest itself, dominated by Neptune riding over the troubled sea (Fig. 18.2). The "winds of war" were an old, evocative image, and one that Peter Paul Rubens had recently used with a painterly effectiveness equal to Pietro's to decry the ravages of the Thirty Years' War in Flanders. That same war may be symbolized here, especially because Neptune bears the features of Pope Innocent, albeit a very handsome version of Pope Innocent. Pietro also populates the roiling seas with nymphs and Tritons who look back to another fresco that Raphael executed for the banker Agostino Chigi, the *Triumph of Galatea.* Neptune's sea-chariot has the same curious paddle wheel as Raphael's Galatea, who scuds along in a dolphin-drawn conveyance. Unlike the paddle wheels of nineteenth-century steamboats, these wheels do not produce motion: they are hodometers, the devices for measuring distance mentioned in book 10 of Vitruvius, Vergil's contemporary. The most charming part of the fresco, especially for viewers who stand in the room itself, is the sturdy little *putto* in the center of the ceiling who spreads his maroon cloak to the tempest and rides it with jaunty aplomb.

On the opposite part of this same vault, the seas have calmed, and Aeneas leaps eagerly out of his ship as he and his crew first catch sight of the River Tiber (book 7; Fig. 18.3); like Neptune's sea-chariot, his vessel is outfitted with a hodometer.

262   Ingrid Rowland

Figure 18.4 Pietro da Cortona, *Venus Receives the Arms of Aeneas from Vulcan*. Galleria, Palazzo Pamphili, Rome. 1651–4. Fresco. Courtesy Istituto Nazionale Centrale per il Catalogo e la Documentazione, Rome.

The gallery's other scenes continue to read Vergil's epic with a strong local as well as personal and historical resonance.

The window overlooking Piazza Navona, appropriately, shows the descent into the underworld of book 6. Pietro calls attention to the fact that the golden bough is an olive branch, just like the branch in the Pamphili coat of arms, and the two doves who guide Aeneas and the Cumaean Sibyl on their way are carefully juxtaposed with the dove on prominent Pamphili coat of arms.

The opposite side of the gallery begins with the oval scene showing Venus receiving the arms of Aeneas from Vulcan (Fig. 18.4). The lame blacksmith god is still dazzled by the sight of his glamorous wife, as are the young Cyclopes who peer from behind

Figure 18.5 Pietro da Cortona, *The Slaying of Turnus*. Galleria, Palazzo Pamphili, Rome. 1651–4. Fresco. Courtesy Istituto Nazionale Centrale per il Catalogo e la Documentazione, Rome.

their clouds, tools in hand. This is the side of the room devoted, like the second half of the *Aeneid* itself, to *bella, horrida bella*.

One side of the gallery's long vault shows the most troubling scene of the *Aeneid*, Aeneas' slaying of Turnus in book 12; we can be certain that the conspicuous blonde Lavinia who surveys the scene is not a portrait of another young bride, Olimpia Aldobrandini (Fig. 18.5). Like Vergil's hero, Pope Innocent X had made one violent decision in his papacy, one that virtually coincided with the peace negotiations in Westphalia. In 1641, his predecessor Urban VIII had declared war on the Farnese family, the clan of feudal barons who had produced one of the sixteenth century's most influential popes, Paul III. For three years, papal troops had battled mercenaries in Farnese pay in a disastrous campaign known as the War of Castro after the name of the family's feudal stronghold north of Rome. It would remain for Innocent X to bring the Farnese under papal control. He did so in the first few years of his reign (this was why Camillo Pamphili and Olimpia Aldobrandini retired to the Farnese stronghold of Caprarola just after their marriage – in effect, as they lived out their exile, they were also performing a holding action for the pope). In 1649, with the ink barely dry on the Peace of Westphalia, he performed an action as violent in its way as the slaying of Turnus: he confiscated a chain of Farnese feudal properties and razed the town of Castro to the ground. The site of that onetime Renaissance city is still open countryside today.

Only one book is clearly missing from the gallery: book 4, the romance of Dido and Aeneas. But Pietro (presumably under Donna Olimpia Maidalchini's explicit guidance) has reserved that subject for the master bedroom, where it was destined to have a more private, personal significance than the public gallery. It was not hard to fathom that the scenes ranged around the cornice have been placed there as a reminder that duty, *pietas*, should come first – the bedchamber is inside a church, and it was supposed to belong to a cardinal. In the ideal world of his mother Donna Olimpia, Cardinal Camillo might have looked upon Pietro da Cortona's paintings of the manifest destiny that had guided both his own story and that of Rome, and remember, in the privacy of his nighttime ruminations, that attractive widows were ultimately a distraction from his divinely ordained mission: as Aeneas had said to Dido of Rome, *hic amor, haec patria est*. But Prince Camillo, from his exile, had clearly conceived a different interpretation of *pietas*. The room now serves as the bedroom of the Brazilian ambassador to Italy, and because the embassy considers it part of the ambassador's private sphere, it cannot be photographed.

However disappointed she may have been by her son's defection, Donna Olimpia Maidalchini continued with her plans for developing the rest of Piazza Navona, taking advantage of Camillo's exile to move into the Palazzo Pamphili herself. As she looked out the windows of the palazzo in the late 1640s, once again Vergil came into the picture as a significant inspiration. No matter what Camillo Pamphili chose to do with his life, the piazza's panoramic open space, its palazzo and its church still stood as conspicuous symbols of the pope and his family.

The greatest immediate impact of the Peace of Westphalia on the Rome of Innocent X (and Donna Olimpia) was not its effect on the decoration of Pietro da Cortona's glorious gallery, but rather its effect on planning for the great Jubilee of 1650, when pilgrims who came to Rome would be granted special pardon for their sins. Set along one of the city's main roads to the Vatican, Piazza Navona would be guaranteed a stream of visitors; the pope therefore decided to transform a rough-and-ready watering-trough in its center into a glorious fountain, topped by an obelisk that lay in pieces alongside the Appian Way in the ruins of the circus, or chariot-racing stadium, built in the early fourth century by the Emperor Maxentius. Francesco Borromini, already busy with the church of Sant'Agnese and Palazzo Pamphili, was awarded the fountain commission as well, and produced an elegant design; his drawing for the project is still preserved in the Vatican Library.

Events, however, would take an unexpected turn. Borromini's rivalry with the sculptor Gian Lorenzo Bernini was already the stuff of Roman legend; the two had worked together at St. Peter's Basilica and at Palazzo Barberini before Borromini's dramatic defection from the St. Peter's project in the late 1620s. A favorite of the previous pope, Urban VIII, Bernini had fallen from favor under Innocent; indeed, several of his commissions had passed to Borromini. But Bernini was a resourceful courtier as well as a brilliant sculptor; he made a model in silver for what he would do with the fountain in Piazza Navona, and invited Donna Olimpia to drop by his studio. Donna Olimpia left with the model, and shortly thereafter Bernini walked off with the project.

For once, the clever sculptor would not be given an entirely free hand; in the first place, the pope and his sister-in-law provided constant input. Secondly, Innocent's decision to include the ancient Egyptian obelisk imposed a collaborator of another sort, for seventeenth-century Rome boasted a resident expert in the interpretation of Egyptian hieroglyphs, a figure as flamboyant in his own way as Bernini himself: the German Jesuit Athanasius Kircher. Kircher had come to Rome in 1634, a refugee from the Thirty Years' War with expertise in mathematics and languages, already convinced (correctly) that Coptic, the liturgical language of Egyptian Christians, would provide the key to reading ancient Egyptian hieroglyphs. In the meantime, Kircher taught mathematics at the Jesuits' Roman College and began to amass a collection of strange and marvelous objects that was given official status as a museum in 1651. If his claims to read ancient Egyptian outstripped his real abilities, none of his contemporaries yet had the tools to prove him right or wrong, and his attention to the script itself was impeccable – the restorations he proposed to Bernini for the obelisk's missing hieroglyphs were confirmed when modern excavations at the Circus of Maxentius turned up additional fragments.

Initially Kircher was simply charged to help Bernini restore the missing or damaged hieroglyphs on the shattered obelisk, but soon, with his fervid imagination and his infectious enthusiasm, he had taken a pivotal role in the design of the whole fountain; perhaps this is why Bernini always declared afterwards that his best-loved work was the one that "pleased him least."

The *Fountain of the Four Rivers*, as it was finally unveiled in 1651 – Bernini missed his deadline of 1650 – lofted its Egyptian obelisk above a hollow travertine rock that serves as a perch for four colossal figures representing four great rivers from four continents of the world (Fig. 18.6). Beneath the veiled figure of the Nile, representing Africa, a thirsty lion laps up water from the fountain's basin; a horse prances through the waters under the Danube (Europe); a sea monster gambols before the River Ganges (Asia), and a giant armadillo shelters below the rock on which the Rio de la Plata (America) cringes back from Borromini's façade of Sant'Agnese – the Roman legend has a grain of truth in it. The stuffed armadillo that acted as Bernini's model still exists; once part of Athanasius Kircher's collection, it now belongs to the Biology Faculty of the University of Rome. Its lips are curled back in the process of desiccation; hence Bernini, who had never seen a living armadillo, gave his sculpted creature the same remarkable curling smile.

To explain the meaning of it all to pope and public, Father Kircher published a book called *Obeliscus Pamphilius* in October of 1650, just in time to catch the last crowds for the Great Jubilee. In its lavishly illustrated folio pages, five hundred of them, he provided a history of the obelisk, his own translation of its hieroglyphic inscriptions, and a summary of the profound lessons this ancient artifact preserved for humanity. Never a man to shrink from self-promotion, he also included tantalizing descriptions of two forthcoming books, *The Egyptian Oedipus* (*Oedipus Aegyptiacus*), whose three massive volumes would be issued between 1652 and 1655, and the two-volume *The Subterranean World*, published at last in 1665. All three works document Kircher's longstanding obsession with the Egyptians on the one hand and with geology on the other, and so, indeed, does the *Fountain of the Four Rivers*. But the real

Figure 18.6 Gian Lorenzo Bernini, with help from Athanasius Kircher, S.J., *The Fountain of the Four Rivers*. 1651. Piazza Navona, Rome. Image courtesy of Scala/Art Resource, NY.

key to the *Fountain of the Four Rivers*, as to the gallery that overlooks it from Palazzo Pamphili, is a passage from *Aeneid* 6 (724–30), in which the shade of Anchises, with the second sight of the underworld, provides his son with an account of the universe and its structure. As John Dryden rendered the passage in 1697:

> "Know, first, that heav'n, and earth's compacted frame,
> And flowing waters, and the starry flame,
> And both the radiant lights, one common soul
> Inspires and feeds, and animates the whole.
> This active mind, infus'd thro' all the space,
> Unites and mingles with the mighty mass.
> Hence men and beasts the breath of life obtain,
> And birds of air, and monsters of the main.
> Th' ethereal vigor is in all the same,
> And every soul is fill'd with equal flame…"

In this passage, Vergil shows his own acute awareness of the philosophical currents in Augustan Rome (as well as a substantial poetic and philosophical debt to Lucretius): Anchises will go on to tell his son about reincarnation. For Kircher, however, as for many sixteenth- and seventeenth-century readers of Vergil, the passage proved something quite different: namely, how the poet's naturally Christian soul had grasped the way in which God had imparted the breath of life to matter in the act of Creation, and the imminent fulfillment of that first action in the incarnation of Christ. In Kircher's view, both the physical structure of the universe and the deepest truths of ancient Egyptian religion had pointed the way to Christian revelation from the very beginning, and he proclaimed his convictions tirelessly in an endlessly inventive, endlessly lengthy series of books, tens of thousands of printed pages produced over four decades of activity.

Bernini must have been captivated by Kircher's yarns, for the fountain of Piazza Navona, as we have it now, proclaims the same triumphant Christian revelation in its ancient granite obelisk, rising above a sculpted miniature of the world, with its mountains, rivers, animals, plants – and the live weeds that nest every spring in the pockmarked surface of its travertine (and that surely belong there as definitely as their sculpted counterparts). A paragraph from *The Subterranean World* provides a good summary of what Kircher had already proclaimed, at a more leisurely pace, in the five hundred pages of *Obeliscus Pamphilius* – although Kircher, like any good Baroque orator, never said anything important without its proper complement of flowery speech:

> This world's most wise architect, God Supreme and Almighty, in setting up this worldly machinery, because he saw that it could neither remain stable nor function in the generation of things, first fixed this admirable Vessel in which we all live, move and have our being, an image, as it were, of His Divinity, a true work of the Most High; he created the Sun, I say, as a Heart and spirit, or a kind of Mind and principal guide of Nature, if one can call it that; a divinity, a vicar of the True Divinity, so that the Universe could be governed by it, and the hidden sacraments of God's Wisdom, snatched from chaos and the dark abyss, might be made plain, and from that visible and material divinity, the invisible majesty of that Supernal Godhead might be made known to mortals. And endowing it with various kinds of motion, *This active mind, infus'd thro' all the space, Unites and mingles with the mighty mass*...so that He might make the universe, by its fecund motion, pregnant with His power. (Kircher 1655, 1: 58)

As the source of this glorious fertility of imagination, Kircher's *Obeliscus Pamphilius* diplomatically pointed neither to his own ideas nor to Bernini's, but to the pope himself – the pope, and not his overbearing sister-in-law. By all accounts, Athanasius Kircher was an unusually brave man, the veteran of hairbreadth escapes during the Thirty Years' War, the explorer of the craters of Etna and Vesuvius, a man who expressed radical opinions about the cosmos and religion beneath the nose of the Roman Inquisition. Equally bold was his decision to publish *Obeliscus Pamphilius* without making a single nod in its text to Donna Olimpia Maidalchini, but so he did, and lived to tell the tale:

> It pleased His Beatitude to raise the Obelisk above a fountain in the form of a hollow crag. Furthermore, on the four sides of the crag he wanted to insert as many colossal statues, equipped with various symbols as decoration, which would display the four-sided face of the World graphically in their symbols. And from vessels or libation-cups, which

they clutch in their arms, a four-part surge of water would cascade as if down the water-falls of precipitous cliffs with a joyous murmur and commotion into a huge basin beneath the rocks. (Kircher 1655, c recto–c verso)

Above all the "joyous murmur and commotion" stands the obelisk, whose message, as Kircher deciphers it, has to do with the eternal truths of religion, sensed by the ancient Egyptians, passed to Moses, Pythagoras, Plato, Vergil, and the rabbis before reaching fulfillment in Jesus. As he declares in *Obeliscus Pamphilius*:

> The ancients used symbols in two ways…one expressed in words, one not. The Egyptians used both, especially in expressing the mysteries of Religion and the science of Theology, regarding it as unbecoming to the majesty of such mysteries were they to be understood by any common person. Therefore their priests indicated the divine mysteries under the cryptic and shadowy guise of allegorical figures, and no one but priests, sages, and phi-losophers were trained in this discipline. Among the Greeks, Pythagoras, a true student of Egyptian wisdom, particularly tried to emulate them…and the great Moses…hence the Rabbis showed that all of Holy Scripture was nothing other than an extended Symbol of the most sublime matters and mysteries, properly known only by Teachers who had been instructed long and thoroughly in the Law. Indeed, what we read in the Gospel Writers often confirms that Our Savior Christ used this way of speaking in parables [to convey] this same eternal Wisdom. For the hidden substance of GOD does not know how to enter into a profane and polluted ear through naked speech. Hence Julian the Apostate, impious though he may be, speaks correctly when he says "Nature loves to stay remote and hidden." (Kircher 1655, 115–16)

For Athanasius Kircher, in other words, the discovery of Nature's mysteries is itself a part of religion. That process of discovery, he asserts in *The Subterranean World*, will lead invariably to the same conclusion: the physical world is one of perpetual flux. Only God's truth is stable and unchanging. As he writes:

> But the Conversions of the Terrestrial Globe are so large and so horrible that they lay bare both the infinite power of GOD and the uncertainty of human fortune, and warn the human inhabitants of this Earth to recognize that nothing is perpetual and stable, but that all things are fallible, subject to the varying fates of fortune and mortality, and that they should raise their thoughts, studies, soul and mind, which can be satisfied by no tangible object, toward the sublime and eternal Good, and long for GOD alone, in whose hands are all the laws of Kingdoms, and the boundaries of universal Nature. (Kircher 1665, 1: 83)

In Piazza Navona, Bernini has set up a graphic contrast between the pocked traver-tine mountain of the *Fountain of the Four Rivers*, where weeds grow happily in among the sculpted foliage, and the smooth ancient granite of the Pamphili obelisk. The eternal truths of Egypt stand still and stable, far above the four corners of a world made up of hollow rock and gushing water. At the obelisk's peak flies a gilded bronze dove with an olive branch in its beak. The dove symbolizes the Pamphili family, but in the immediate wake of the Peace of Westphalia, it would be hard not to think about the dove in its usual role as a symbol of peace, even as a Christian hieroglyph of that idea. The fountain's design, however, celebrates not so much the temporal peace of 1648 as peace of another kind: the partnership of natural philosophy – science – and religion. Only profound knowledge of nature's laws could pump water into the middle of a city square in this profusion, or carve graceful texts into the surface of granite. But only faith could inspire the effort of carving granite in the first place. Mastery of physics keeps the obelisk standing above a hollow shell of travertine, but neither Kircher nor Bernini doubted that what guided them to create that hollow shell was divine inspiration. The *Fountain of the Four Rivers* simply could not exist if its makers did not believe that science and religion belonged together – and miraculously Vergil, in *Aeneid* 6, had foreseen it all.

Pope Innocent lived to enjoy his fountain for four years. When he died in 1655, he was replaced by his former nuncio Fabio Chigi, elected as Alexander VII. Donna Olimpia died in 1659. With her death, the ban was lifted from Camillo Pamphili and his wife Olimpia, who were able at last to return to Rome with their five children to see Palazzo Pamphili and the *Fountain of the Four Rivers* for themselves. To our own good fortune, three and a half centuries later, we can see them still.

FURTHER READING

Comparatively little has been written in English on the papacy of Innocent X, surrounded as he is by two great patrons of art and architecture, Urban VIII Barberini and Alexander VII Chigi. As a result, the best general introduction to the period remains Magnuson (1982). For the fountain of Piazza Navona and its connection with Athanasius Kircher, see also Rowland (2001). A new biography of Donna Olimpia has recently been published in English: Herman (2008).

CHAPTER NINETEEN

Visual and Verbal Translation of Myth

Neptune in Vergil, Rubens, and Dryden

Reuben A. Brower

Although we commonly speak of "the Oedipus myth" or "the Hercules myth," and though anthropologists refer to mythical "archetypes" or "structures," it can be said that there are no myths, only versions. To put it another way, there are only texts for interpretation, whether the text is written or oral, a piece of behavior – a dance or a cockfight – a drawing or painting, a sculptured stone, or a terracotta pot. The principal texts I have chosen for exploration here are two of them verbal, the third a painting. My primary concerns in exploring each text will be with how the "same" myth is transformed when rendered in words or in line and color, and what parallels and contrasts can be observed between these different events in expression.

While making some comparisons between Dryden's *Aeneid* and Vergil's, I remembered the beautiful picture by Rubens in the Fogg Museum, *Quos ego –*, or *Neptune Calming the Tempest*, which is based on a well-known scene in the first book of the *Aeneid*. From that encounter, and later visions and revisions, comes this venture into the notoriously beguiling study of a "Parallel Betwixt Poetry and Painting."

In Vergil's poem Neptune rises from the sea to calm the storm in which Aeneas was shipwrecked on his voyage from Troy. Aeolus, king of the winds, acting on Juno's orders, had loosed violent gales from the south, east, and west. Neptune breaks off his denunciation of the winds, "*quos ego –*," "whom I –," in order to smooth the waves, scatter the clouds, and bring back the sun. He then rides off driving his horses and chariot beneath a cloudless sky. A glance at Rubens' picture (Plate 2) will show that the painting is strikingly like and unlike the narrative. Dryden's translation, though reasonably true to the speech and actions of the original, has revised the myth in ways that can be better understood once we are more familiar with Rubens' painting and the transformation that has taken place there. The painting, which I refer to henceforth as the "sketch," is a beautifully executed modello for a large work, a sketch in no pejorative sense (van Puyvelde 1940, 57). Many questions besides the primary one concerning the transformation of a myth will arise as we explore our various texts. What is the mythical action "like" in each version? What does each version tell us about the mythical thinking or imagination of the author? What does it tell us about the world in which the translation grew? And since all three artists are rendering an event in nature, what is the experience of nature that comes through to us in the Vergilian narrative, the translation, and the picture?

Translations, in whatever medium, can be best understood not only in relation to an original text but in light of the "conditions of expression" within which they were created. Dryden's version is in rhymed pentameters because that was held to be the proper measure for heroic poetry. Rubens' sketch has a pictorial rhythm common to many baroque paintings of mythological and religious subjects. Two conditions that affected Dryden and Rubens with almost equal force are the Renaissance and seventeenth-century doctrine and practice of "imitation" and the complex of literary and pictorial traditions variously referred to as "heroic" or "historical." The most important sense of imitation for the present study is not the exact copying of classical vocabulary or motifs, but that dynamic process of "assimilation," as Gombrich calls it (1963, 2.31; cf. Pinto 1970, 52–3), by which a Renaissance artist remakes in his own terms what he has lovingly learned in active commerce with masterpieces of the past. Though Dryden spoke scornfully of modernizing imitation in contrast with translation, he indicates in "The Dedication of the *Aeneis*" that his aim has been imitation in a sense common to many of his contemporaries: "Yet I may presume to say…that taking all the Materials of this divine Author, I have endeavour'd to make Virgil speak such English, as he wou'd himself have spoken, if he had been born in *England*, and in this present Age." Earlier in the same essay he shows that he recognized the close parallel between creative imitation in poetry and in painting:

> By reading *Homer, Virgil* was taught to imitate his Invention: That is, to imitate like him; which is no more, than if a Painter studied *Raphael*, that he might learn to design after his manner. And thus I might imitate *Virgil*, if I were capable of writing an Heroick Poem, and yet the Invention be my own: But I shou'd endeavour to avoid a servile Copying.

We can sharpen our perception of what Dryden and Rubens "saw" in Vergil by considering briefly how the Greek Neptune, Poseidon, was presented in Homer and in one or two examples from the Greek arts of a later period. As Cedric Whitman has noted (1958, 95), we have no certain illustrations of Homer's text from the Geometric vases more or less contemporary with the *Iliad* and the *Odyssey*, though there are paintings of episodes from the Trojan story not included in the Homeric poems. The contrast drawn by Whitman between Minoan and Geometric art is most helpful for understanding Homer's representation of his gods, and of Poseidon in particular:

> For the one, reality lies in the actual appearance; for the other, it lies in action and inner nature, and there can be no question as to which view is nearer to Homer's. Homer almost never describes anyone's actual appearance. His method is strictly dramatic, emphasizing always deed, motive, and consequence. (Whitman 1958, 89–90)

To all who are familiar with the vivid images of Greek vase painting and sculpture it may be surprising to discover how little we are made to *see* the gods of Homer. We have, it is true, impressions of Athena's dazzling brightness and of the shining eyes of Zeus. But though we are told how Poseidon took three giant strides from Samos to Aigai, the point is not the visual image it may suggest to the modern reader, but the action as testimony of things not seen, of *numen*, divine power. In general, we see the Homeric gods doing and suffering, not "looking." For if the heroes of the *Iliad* are "godlike," the gods are like heroes. While Zeus sleeps, Poseidon defends the Danai, leading them to battle with the usual heroic cry, *iomen*, "let us go forward!" (13.374). He comes to the rescue of one warrior, Antilochus; he is angry because of the death of another, Amphimachus, and enters the battle to avenge him: "A god, he strode through mortals' struggle" (13.238). We hear in prophecy how he will lead the way "with trident in hand" (12.27) in destroying the Greek Wall. This is the sole mention of the trident in the *Iliad*, the phrase implying that Poseidon is using it as an instrument, as he does later in the *Odyssey*, when angered at Ajax, son of Oïleus, "taking the trident in his mighty hands, he struck the rock on Gyrai, and split it off" (4.506–7). But if the actions and emotions are manlike, the scale is gigantic. Poseidon speaks with the voice of "nine or ten thousand men" (*Il.* 14.135). The epithets commonly used of Poseidon similarly imply action on a huge scale: He is *gaioxos ennosigaios*, one "who encircles the earth and shakes it." He is not grey-haired, no old man of the sea. Zeus is in fact older and more powerful. But though Poseidon acknowledges Zeus' superior strength, he reminds him that they are both equal in honor, and that as the lot gave Hades the underworld, and Zeus the heavens, so his share was the "grey sea." He adds that the earth and "broad Olympus" are common property of all three, thus emphasizing both his Olympian character and his role as earth-god (15.190–5). He is the great earth-shaker when he steps down to Aigai, an episode that anticipates in part the scene in Vergil:

> He took three long strides forward, and in the fourth came to his goal,
> Aigai, where his glorious house was built in the waters'
> depth, glittering with gold, imperishable forever.
> Going there he harnessed under his chariot his bronze-shod horses,
> flying-footed, with long manes streaming of gold; and he put on
> clothing of gold about his own body, and took up the golden
> lash, carefully compacted, and climbed up into his chariot
> and drove it across the waves. And about him the sea beasts came up
> from their deep places and played in his path, and acknowledged their master,
> and the sea stood apart before him, rejoicing. The horses winged on
> delicately, and the bronze axle beneath was not wetted.
>
> (13.20–30, trans. Lattimore)

There is visual splendor in these lines, but gold, it should be remembered, is not merely something beautiful to the eye, but a sign of kingliness and divinity, of the "unperishing." Equally notable is the matter-of-fact character of the narrative. The horses are "bronze-shod," as elsewhere in Homer; the lash is "well-made," and the language of harnessing, mounting, and driving is standard and formulaic; the chariot, *diphros*, is no different from those used by Homeric warriors. Miracle enters with: "[Poseidon] drove it across the waves" and "the bronze axle beneath was not wetted." But "miracle" as I have used it is a term of the Enlightenment, of a world governed by laws of nature, whereas in Homer the marvelous "occurs as it occurs," and it is recorded in the same tone in which "real" events are recorded. As there is no distinctly physical world, so there is no distinctly spiritual one. The "will of Zeus" is not *la sua volontade*, but what Zeus quite simply wants and intends. Magic is present often in other actions of Poseidon. He takes the form of many persons; he strikes a man with his staff and it fills him with courage; he bewitches one hero with his eyes and makes the spear stroke of another useless. These and similar actions of many gods are "just the things gods do," and the resultant effects on mortals might well have taken place without divine intervention. To say that a god caused or occasioned the behavior is not to rationalize it away, but to make the commonplace mysteriously wonderful. (As it is: How does a man suddenly become brave? Why does the spear miss its mark?)

It may be said that when the Greeks represented their gods definitively in painted and sculpted images, they ran the risk of making the wonderful commonplace. The unnamable god of the Hebrews rightly forbade graven images: he was a *spiritual* divinity in a sense that Christians and Platonists well understand. It is the human that is glorified in Greek sculpture as in the Homeric poems. None of Homer's gods can compare in heroic dignity with Achilles and Hector. The well-known bronze in Athens, whether of Poseidon (Richter 1959, 89) or of Zeus, is majestic in stance and noble in facial expression. The impression of contained, arrested motion, as often in Greek sculpture, is the "thing" – the effortless ease of the athlete, of a *man*, not of a divinity in the Judeo-Christian sense. (A "god" yes, but not God.) The heroic character of the figure comes out if it is compared with a Hellenistic counterpart (Richter 1959, 190) – in the overripe, sensuous handling of muscles, the melodramatic pose, the turbulent locks of hair, the absence of an implied inner life.

We can see what happens when the heroic vagueness of Homer is translated into clearly outlined figures by looking at the Poseidon of the Amphitrite Painter in the Boston Museum (Caskey and Beazley 1963, pt. III, no. 152.98.932, 52–3, pl. LXXXV.2). Here Poseidon is shown as a slender young man in the act of attacking Polybotes, whom he has already wounded. The god, bearded, his long hair crowned with a wreath, seems about to run his trident into the giant's side (as he actually does in another version: see Ridder 1902, 2.429 no. 573). Over Poseidon's left arm a "small wrap" falls in elegant motionless folds from beneath a pillowy mass, "the island of Nisyros (which he snapped off with his trident from the Island of Cos)," and which he is about to "bring down on his opponent" (Caskey and Beazley 1963, 53 no. 10). "What man, what god is this?" His glance is alert and amused, and his slight figure – David to Polybotes' Goliath – looks more like the quick-devising Odysseus than the great god of the *Iliad*. If Homer's Poseidon were accurately rendered, he would be of Brobdignagian proportions. A more serious version of the same scene, by the Troilus Painter, shows the god going after the giant with a more violent if less well-aimed forward thrust (Beazley 1963, 1643, 10 bis; images in Emmerich Gallery 1964, no. 24). Both these figures, like many representations of gods on Greek vases, are barely distinguishable in size or type from the heroes or the young men leaving for wars. Their divinity is marked principally by their icons, the trident, the club of Hercules, the helmet of Athena, the drinking cup of Dionysos.

To jump from these fifth-century forms to Vergil's scene is to have a curious sensation of moving both backward and forward in time – a characteristic response to a poem that is at once a recall of the Homeric world and a prophecy of Rome's Augustan age. Postponing consideration of this mixture of impulses and motifs, let us concentrate first on picture, on scene and gesture in Vergil's account of how Neptune calmed the storm:

> Interea magno misceri murmure pontum
> emissamque hiemem sensit Neptunus et imis   125
> stagna refusa vadis, graviter commotus; et alto
> prospiciens summa placidum caput extulit unda.
> disiectam Aeneae toto videt aequore classem,
> fluctibus oppressos Troas caelique ruina.
> nec latuere doli fratrem Iunonis et irae.   130
> Eurum ad se Zephyrumque vocat, dehinc talia fatur:
> "Tantane vos generis tenuit fiducia vestri?
> iam caelum terramque meo sine numine, venti,
> miscere et tantas audetis tollere moles?
> quos ego – ! sed motos praestat componere fluctus.   135
> post mihi non simili poena commissa luetis.
> maturate fugam regique haec dicite vestro:
> non illi imperium pelagi saevumque tridentem,
> sed mihi sorte datum. tenet ille immania saxa,
> vestras, Eure, domos; illa se iactet in aula   140
> Aeolus et clauso ventorum carcere regnet."
> Sic ait et dicto citius tumida aequora placat
> collectasque fugat nubes solemque reducit.
> Cymothoe simul et Triton adnixus acuto
> detrudunt navis scopulo; levat ipse tridenti   145
> et vastas aperit syrtis et temperat aequor
> atque rotis summas levibus perlabitur undas.
> ac veluti magno in populo cum saepe coorta est
> seditio saevitque animis ignobile vulgus;
> iamque faces et saxa volant, furor arma ministrat;   150
> tum, pietate gravem ac meritis si forte virum quem
> conspexere, silent arrectisque auribus astant;
> ille regit dictis animos et pectora mulcet:
> sic cunctus pelagi cecidit fragor, aequora postquam
> prospiciens genitor caeloque invectus aperto   155
> flectit equos curruque volans dat lora secundo.
>
> (*Aen.* 1.124–56)

To read this narrative properly demands, in Henry James' phrase, "a sharper survey of the elements of Appearance" than any similar episode in Homer – Poseidon's journey in the *Iliad*, or the shipwreck of Odysseus. Vergil asks us much more often to attend to the seen thing, the picture in words, as in the memorable lines just before this passage:

> apparent rari nantes in gurgite vasto,
> arma virum tabulaeque et Troia gaza per undas.
> Here and there are seen swimmers in the vast gulf,
> arms of men, and planks, and Troy's wealth on the waves.
>
> (*Aen.* 1.118–19)

The first impression in the Neptune narrative is of the sea's confusion, *magno misceri murmure pontum*, the storm that the god "sees," *sensit*. Next, the waters sucked up from the lowest depths, *imis / stagna refusa vadis*, the phrase neatly placed between *Neptunus* and *graviter commotus*, "mightily stirred," so that we take the participle as describing the sea's "wild commotion" and the god's anger. (Note here and throughout the importance of descriptive adjectives – aural, visual, emotive.) Then follows the unforgettable contrast: the god "looking forth," *prospiciens*, raises his "calm head," *placidum caput*, from the sea's surface. "He sees," and we see, "the scattered, broken fleet," *disiectam classem*. We hear of his "divine power," *numine*, and glimpse again the confusion of earth, sky, and masses of water (133–4). "Sooner done than said," the god "calms the swollen waters," *tumida aequora placat*; "he chases the clouds away and brings back the sun" (143). "The nymph Cymothoe and Triton, working together, *adnixus*, shove, *detrudunt*, the ships from the sharp rock, *acuto scopulo*." In a series of swift action verbs – like Homer's in describing Poseidon's destruction of the wall – the god "himself with his trident lifts the ships, lays open the vast sandbanks, soothes the water, and on light wheels goes gliding over the very top of the waves" (145–7). At the end Neptune is seen guiding horses and chariot with the reins, moving away against a clear sky, *caeloque invectus aperto* – one final brilliant image of light, reviving by contrast the clouds and "the black night brooding on the sea," *ponto nox incubat atra* (89), when the storm struck.

The increased emphasis in Vergil on appearance and scene, as compared with similar passages in the *Iliad*, is proof of an interest in the natural setting for its own sake rare in Greek poetry. Yet if we think of the phrase Wordsworth once used of Vergil in a disparaging contrast with Dryden, "his *eye* upon his object" (de Selincourt 1935, 541; cf. Proudfoot 1960, 196), we must feel that Vergil had his eye on much more than the event in nature. The storm is being "done up," given scenic value in a kind of mythological drama. It is surprising that so much of the simple anthropomorphism of Homer has survived: down-to-earth human actions and feelings – using the trident as a lever to heave up ships, the passionate anger of the god. But there is also some loss of the immediately magical and the divinely mysterious, some imminent separation between icon and intended religious significance. The presence of the looming Roman *fatum* is more felt, as everywhere on the *Aeneid*, than the imported Olympians. As often happens in translations, a retraction in one area is matched by a gain in another area of experience slighted or vaguely implied in the original. The Neptune of the *Aeneid*, this scene notwithstanding, is much less of a dramatic character than Poseidon in the *Iliad*. In nearly every episode in which Poseidon appears, he is vigorously carrying out his role as ally of the Greeks in the long drama of the Trojan War, and his will be the final act, when with Apollo he destroys the wall of the Achaeans. The gain in Vergil comes through dynamic assimilation: Vergil turns Poseidon into something new, a literary symbol, which bears a part in the imaginative order of the whole poem. The order is not Homer's, but the creation of a different kind of poet, a poet of symbolic and lyric narration.

Before considering how Vergil's form of "proceeding" is reflected in his transformation of the Poseidon myth, let us look briefly at Neptune's speech to the winds and the related simile of the man whose wise words put a stop to an incipient uprising, *seditio* (148–53). Even when Neptune sounds most like the Greek god – as when Poseidon reminds Zeus that the three brothers born of Kronos and Rhea each got an equal share of honor "when the lots were shaken" (15.190) – the rhetoric, the accent, and the implications are very different. Poseidon's rhetoric is familial, though saved from vulgarity by the formulaic style, but Neptune has been through a course in Roman forensics, and the tone is reminiscent of Cicero to the followers of Catiline – shrewd, but senatorial. The aposiopesis, "*quos ego* –," is the master stroke of an accomplished orator: the terrors of the incomplete sentence are more fearsome than anything he might merely *say*. Instead of a "lot," we hear of *imperium* (almost "sphere of influence"), a term reeking of Roman power and law, of the Augustan world constitution, the peculiar political achievement that Vergil's poem is celebrating. In an admirable passage, Viktor Pöschl reminds us of the surprising force and extension of meaning and of the links with a larger imaginative design through Vergil's use of a political simile for "the subjection of the storm." In so doing, Vergil was "highlighting a very important sphere of the poem (namely that of the historical world)." "The connecting symbol becomes an expression of the symbolic relation between nature and politics, myth and history, which is at the heart of the *Aeneid*." In speaking of Vergil, we may refer rightly to an "order of Nature" under divine law, implying a sophisticated notion, an *idea*, of which there are only faint hints in the poetry of Homer. But we also feel that the Neptune–Aeolus myth has a new function in Vergil as a poetic symbol for the storm, locally for the actual storm, and in the larger economy of the poem for the "wave breaking against Roman destiny" (so Pöschl 1962, 22–4). Or, as Brooks Otis points out in his analysis of *Aeneid* 1 (1964, 230), "the contrast [in the simile] between the *vir pietate gravis ac meritis* [the man revered for 'piety' and his services], and the *ignobile vulgus* [the common herd] armed by *furor* reveals at a stroke the human meaning of the storm." In Otis' view, the storm and its calming becomes an instance of the dominant moral and thematic pattern of the *Aeneid*, the opposition of *pietas* and *furor*, enacted in countless events throughout the poem. A use of myth so easily open to thematic interpretation comes close to allegory. Though many readers will agree that Vergil does not quite cross the line between the two modes, they may at the same time feel that we are too often distracted from men or gods in action, from drama, to something beyond, to large values and concerns – the history and destiny of Rome, the moral and religious ideal of "piety," the dream of a harmony attainable among personal, political, divine, and natural realms of experience.

If we turn to Rubens' sketch, what strikes the viewer above all is violent motion – in the waves, the horses, and the wind-tossed clouds – seen against the mellow golden light at the horizon and opening in the distant sky. The center and director of this movement is Neptune, who is stepping forward and upward in his chariot-shell, his piercing look following the line of that marvelous gesture of command toward the departing winds and the returning light. The streaming hair and beard, the twisting torso, the whole body "works" with the emotion implied in glance and gesture. The mighty right arm and the trident-thrust (exactly on the line of the forward-bending knee), symbolize, like the outstretched left arm and pointing finger, power and intention – no question here of anything so practical as raising ships or splitting rocks or wounding a giant adversary. Yet the trident is no mere identifying icon or stage prop as in its decorative use by many artists, including Rubens himself on occasion. The grandly serious look, the body's total gesture, are alone sufficient: no further evidence of things seen or unseen is necessary, as in Homer and in Vergil. We are nearer to something like the imagined gesture of *Fiat lux*.

As we should expect, the pictorial element has been much enhanced. The buxom nymphs, in lighter tones of brown and pink, with faint sea-blue touches on the hair, blend below into sea-green waves, as if to blend mythical figure and its origin. The winds appear as half-seen faces and forms emerging from cloud-wind streaks, figures and clouds alike done in a range of fused colors from grey and slate blue to brownish and pinkish tones. The chariot-shell – no literal Homeric or Roman war chariot – has produced a kind of wheel with incomplete spokes sprouting "naturally" from the shell whorl. No wheels as in Vergil move lightly over the water: this wheel is involved in the hazy watery motion. The horses are sea horses, hippocampi, legs entangled in panic violence, vivid expressions of the sea's turbulence. These creatures could hardly be driven, nor does this god think of driving, though one nymph pulls – ineffectually – on a "pink bridle" (Rosenberg 1943, i, 14). Rubens' scene is not least pictorial in overall composition, in the manner in which violent motion is ordered and contained: the central and echoing diagonal thrusts, of which Jacob Rosenberg speaks so eloquently, the balancing of light and dark in human and animal figures, in ship and sail forms, in areas of sea and sky, the posing of definite and less definite outlines – color, line, and light so harmonized that all actors, animate and inanimate, seem to be caught up in the total natural and supernatural event.

How composition works in the two media of picture and poetry is particularly significant for defining the different reinterpretations of the Poseidon myth. "Words move in time only." In Vergil the action-picture is enmeshed in other narrative and non-narrative contexts of metaphor, theme, and history. The painter has only one instant, at the most the brief time while the eye moves, as in viewing Rubens' sketch, from left to right, upward and downward within the frame. The shift from poem to painting is all the more striking when the artist has chosen for his moment a speech, an effective piece of rhetoric compared to another piece of rhetoric.

What happens, then, in Rubens' translation? No "calm head" rises from the water; Vergil's anticipation of the calm to come is rendered here immediately in the outstretched hand pointing toward the smoother sea and the brighter light. What was storm and darkness *before* in Vergil is in the picture storm and coming brightness here and now. Vergil's contrasts are compressed with a much more shocking effect. The overwhelming violence of the horses and waves in the foreground is countered directly above by the lovely arc of sails as the favoring breeze fills them. At one point the compactness of poetry is equaled or surpassed in picture: Vergil's *graviter commotus*, simultaneously the sea's and the god's disturbance, is rendered in Rubens' sketch by Neptune's figure moving in harmony with waves, horses, clouds, and other deities. "Consider," Burckhardt says of Rubens' rare lapses into theatricality, "how seldom his figures are shown in loud, emotional speech, how they never rant, how his hands, with all their abundance of beautiful gesture, never gesticulate" (1950, 73). In *Quos ego* – the whole body speaks, language is gesture, drama compressed to the uttermost. And with what result? – an increase in the sense of miracle, of spiritual power. Vergil's speech, noble as it is, makes the god himself proclaim his power, *meo numine*; and his invective is uncomfortably like scolding, as it is in Homer. To compare the marvelous act to the feat of an orator is to run the risk of bringing miracle down to political real-ity (a risk Vergil willingly embraced).

In Rubens we are brought closer to the unexplained wonders of Homer, but with the matter-of-fact "doings" left out. Hence Rubens' drama and his god are more deeply serious, splendidly and ineffably godlike. The compression and the immediacy enforce the implication of a purely spiritual power, paradoxically "out of the blood" of this warmly living god. But he is not the dark-haired youthful god of Homer or of the "Landing of Marie de Médicis" who puts his hand to the great ship, bringing it against the pier (illustrated in Rosenberg 1905, 239). The head of the *Quos ego* – Neptune, white-haired and bearded, with his intent eye, can scarcely be disassociated from images of God himself. We find much the same head and expression in many religious pictures by Rubens, of God in the coronation of the Virgin and in the Trinity, of saints and Old Testament patriarchs. The contemporary audience, well educated in religious art, would have seen and felt this association more instinctively than we do. The ease and frequency with which Rubens transforms pagan figures and motifs into Christian ones, and occasionally, Christian into pagan, has often been noted (Stechow 1968, 47 and 58, with further examples from ch. 3).

It is commonly assumed that Rubens had seen the *Quos ego* – of Marcantonio Raimondi (ca. 1480–1527/37), based on a drawing by Raphael (Fig. 19.1; cf. Bartsch 1803–21, 14.264–9; Delaborde 1888, 146). A look at the engraving will reinforce what I have been saying about the spiritual in Rubens' sketch and show the difference between more or less literal illustration or visual translation and live reworking of a poetic text. Marcantonio has chosen the exact moment when the god, rising from the sea, launches his verbal attack on the winds. His lips are parted in speech, and he pulls hard on the horses' rein. Ships are seen wrecked or sinking, and a slightly earlier event is introduced – Aeneas "stretching his palms to the stars," *duplicis tendens ad sidera palmas* (1.93). The figure as a whole is less dramatically expressive than Rubens': for example, the right arm thrusting the elegant trident downward (not forward) seems comparatively weak. The hippocampi, with their oddly elongated necks and snouts, comically equine expressions, and inextricably entangled fish-tails, seem to belong to a more prehistoric age than Rubens'. The all-too human faces of the slightly sullen wind-cherubs may have given Rubens a hint for his beautifully vague cloud beings, but they are curious substitutes for Vergil's revolutionary "mob," as Michael Putnam calls them (1965, 11). Though well composed, the engraving has little of Rubens' composition in emotional and imaginative depth, or in subtle echoings and blendings of line and color.

Figure 19.1 Marcantonio Raimondi, *Neptune Quelling the Storm*. ca. 1515–16. Engraving. Harvard University Art Museums, Fogg Art Museum, Gift of William Gray from the collection of Francis Calley Gray, G2513. Photo: Imaging Department © President and Fellows of Harvard College.

But, as readers familiar with Rubens' sketch must be saying, the painter had other and more complex intentions than the engraver. The sketch was a model for a huge painting on an architectural stage erected to welcome Ferdinand Cardinal Infante of Spain on his entrance into Antwerp, April 17, 1635. Ferdinand, brother of Philip IV, had journeyed from Barcelona to serve as governor of the Netherlands in succession to Isabella, Rubens' patron and friend. Antwerp had commissioned Rubens to design a series of magnificent triumphal arches and stages to adorn Ferdinand's progress through the city (Rooses 1886–92, 3.292–3). Though assistants executed most of the paintings, Rubens gave the finishing touches to the large *Quos ego* –, if he did not do the whole picture (as some accounts suggest). Before the painting (now in Dresden) was turned over to the cardinal in 1637, Rubens "again repainted" it along with the companion piece on the meeting at Nordlingen between Ferdinand of Spain and Ferdinand of Hungary (Rooses 1886–92, 3.298; Rosenberg 1943, 14). The event that lay behind sketch and picture was, according to a contemporary narrative, somewhat less disastrous than the shipwreck of Aeneas. Ferdinand's fleet, having sailed from Barcelona, arrived safely at Caduquès. "Après le temps se changea, avec des tramontanes et vents contraires," and it proved impossible to continue the voyage for "thirteen whole days": Then came the morning when "the sea grew calm, and with the wind [from the south] in the stern, they parted at mid-day, and the weather was so constant and favorable, that on the next morning they began to make out the coast of France" (Aedo y Gallart 1635, 19–20). At a distance of three years and many miles, this princely contretemps became to the eye of imagination the glorious event of Rubens' sketch, in which Vergil's simile was in effect reversed, the historical reality now being compared to the storm and calm of myth. In Rubens' adaptation of the Vergilian moment, the ships are seen quite unharmed, the dark-hued clouds moving through and above them, and the spectral wind-face to the far right, Boreas (the wind unfavorable for sailing toward France), is pursued by southern and western winds that fill the sails of the splendid vessels now getting under way. In Vergil, it will be remembered, all the winds are loosed by Aeolus, and Neptune directs his wrath especially against the Southeast and West, Eurus and Zephyrus.

We are beginning to see meanings in Rubens' work that would not be apparent apart from three "translations" that his sketch underwent: the large painting by the master and his pupils, the engraving (Fig. 19.2) by a colleague, T. van Thulden, and the verbal explanation by Gevaerts (Gevartius 1641, 19–20), which accompanied the engraving in the *Pompa introitus...Ferdinandi*, a splendid folio memorializing and interpreting all the works of art and the various celebrations of the Cardinal Infante's entrance into Antwerp. The first shock comes when we see the Dresden version, inferior in nearly every respect to the sketch, though less obvious in its outlines and less abrupt in its transitions than the engraving. Since the commentary is based on the engraving, we may consider a few changes from the sketch, along with Gevaerts' interpretations. In general, we may say that everything has become terribly definite, with a loss in the effect of a hazy and mysterious mythical-natural sea change. The wind-faces have taken on the solidity of Marcantonio's cherubs, and Boreas is now an aged swimmer with fin-like wings and hands and legs like twisted forms of half-baked pastry, *brachiis in pennas desinentibus & serpentinis pedibus*, Gevaerts says. The whorl of the shell blending easily into the wheel has disappeared, and one nymph hangs heavily on a spoke, turning it, we are told, with the help of her sisters. The suggestion of rationalizing in Rubens is crudely exposed: *Qua re vortex marinus denotatur, qui in gyrum actus ipsam promovet. NYMPHAS autem quasi LYMPHAS, notum est* ("By [their turning of the wheel) is signified the sea's whirlpool, which being driven in a circle, carries it [the shell] forward. It is well known that we speak of 'Nymphas' as it were for 'Lymphas' [waters]," Gevaerts 1641, 16). In Rubens' sketch all three nymphs are caught up in the dramatic and visual movement, one looking forward with arm outstretched, the second pointing ahead and glancing back to engage the attention of her

Figure 19.2   Theodoor van Thulden (after Peter Paul Rubens), in Jean Gaspard Gevaerts (Gevartius), *Pompa introitus honori Serenissimi Principis Ferdinandi Austriaci Hispaniarum Infantis...* (Antwerp, 1641). Typ 630.41.422 P, Department of Printing and Graphic Arts, Houghton Library, Harvard College Library. Plate between pages 14–15.

sister, who is also looking toward the god. In the engraving, the inert turner faces forward, the next nymph turns away, and the third looks coyly out at the viewer. The god's gesture has lost its full effect, since as Jacob Rosenberg notes, his hand comes uncomfortably close to the serpentine legs of Boreas. (Neptune's hair and beard no longer stream in the wind.) Parts, including the too accurately equipped "triremes," shatter the blended life of the whole.

Gevaerts' commentary brings some interesting support and some surprising increments to our earlier reading of the sketch. The inscription on the title page of the *Pompa introitus* is a bald adaptation of the Vergilian prophecy, *Aen.* 6.851, 853:

> Tu regere imperio Belgas, Germane, memento:
> Parcere subjectis et debellare superbos.

Later in the commentary, the great triumphal arch for Ferdinand is compared with the "Arch of Titus Augustus" (plate before p. 109). In another scene, the temple of Janus is adorned with sculptures of Peace and War, and Gevaerts offers an appropriate quotation (7.601–5) that echoes Jupiter's words in *Aen.* 1.291–6, on the closing of the temple and the binding of Furor (a thematic echo of Neptune's action in the storm scene according to Otis 1964, 230). In the whirl of quotations from Latin and Greek authors, it is curious that Gevaerts never cites or refers to the "*quos ego –* " passage. When describing a Neptune on another stage, Gevaerts quotes in Greek the Homeric epithets for Poseidon and comments on them with appreciation of the god's role as earth-shaker. Neptune "bears the trident, since he strikes and lashes the earth with his waves" (1641, 149). Gevaerts' interest in historical evidence, *historica fide*, helps us appreciate what he and the people of Antwerp saw most vividly in Rubens' scene. An inscription below the engraving begins with *Neptuno sternente fretum*, "Neptune calming the sea," but most of the five lines are spent in praising the "noble cargo" and the ship that brought it safely over "the Tyrrhenian waters." One suspects that Rubens or his associates reread his sketch in a way to fit this more obvious emphasis, one more to the taste of a seaport town.

What then was Rubens doing in the sketch as compared with the engraved version? Something much more complexly organized, and more subtly related to local history, to contemporary and older artistic, literary, and religious traditions. Both versions are very much of their time, but the sketch is more profoundly baroque than the painting in many features we have noted – the focus on the "moment," the strong contrasts and violent movement, the diagonal thrust, and above all in the dramatic expressiveness of Neptune's form and gesture. The effect of spontaneity in the whole is characteristic of Rubens' better sketches: "La forme surgit du pinceau en même temps qu'elle naît avec la pensée artistique dans l'esprit de l'artiste" (van Puyvelde 1940, 28). Behind the sketch lies a powerful mythical vision, Vergilian and Homeric and peculiarly Rubensian. If Rubens renews for us the moment of anger in the *Aeneid* and the change that followed, and if he suppresses some of the humbler actions of the god in both ancient versions, he also revives the religious mystery of divine action in Homer. He goes still further along the road toward a purely spiritual interpretation of mythical action and toward a more immediate and impressionistic expression of an event in nature, while not forgetting the human actor – a combination that allies him with Homer of the storm similes and the landscape painters of the later seventeenth and even the nineteenth centuries. There is in Rubens' sketch the oddest blend of precise observation, of rationalizing (as in the treatment of the chariot-shell), and of primitive mythical vision (as in the wind-faces): "The wheel survives the myths."

But as Svetlana Alpers reminds us in her splendid introduction to the Torre de la Parada series (1971, 166–73), Rubens' alliances with the past and the future are not easily defined. His treatment of the human body as dramatically expressive is at once in line with contemporary theory and related to practices of Hellenistic sculptors, whose work Rubens had closely studied. If like Homer and "unlike Ovid, Rubens commanded a heroic style, which he could inform with a sense of real life without puncturing its ideality" (Alpers 1971, 167–8), he was also capable of entering into the Ovidian world of irreverence and comedy, as he did in creating the paintings for the Torre de la Parada. Here too he was working in an earlier tradition, that of the sixteenth-century illustrators of the *Metamorphoses* (Alpers 1971, 80–100). Looking through some of the volumes to which Mrs. Alpers refers, we come on plates that may account for some of the departures from Vergil's text in Marcantonio and in Rubens or his colleagues. In *La Métamorphose d'Ovide figurée* (1557), a "Fin du déluge" pictures Neptune in a shell driving two hippocampi. The verses below, based on *Met.* 1.324–44, tell how the clouds give way to "Aquilon, leur ennemi contraire." In "Vénus et Pluton," Pluto comes from the underworld in a shell-like chariot drawn by horses. In the *Metamorphoseon Libri XV* (1582), a very animated Neptune rides on a lively and amusing hippocampus (Alpers 1971, 52) – a version also illustrated by Gevaerts from ancient coins. This continental Ovidian tradition appears in England in Franz Cleyn's "engravings for Sandys's Ovid [1632], which…represent a parallel effort to Rubens' works" for the Torre de la Parada. "They share with Rubens an interest in the mythological narratives as human dramas" (Alpers 1971, 92–3).

Cleyn also illustrated the Ogilby translation of Vergil (1654; see chapter 20 by Eastin in this volume), a volume well known to Dryden, who spoke scornfully of the translator, though on occasion borrowing from his fairly accurate if inept version. With an eye to costs, Dryden and his publisher took over Cleyn's illustrations for the *Virgil* of 1697. Dryden's visualization of figures from Greco-Roman mythology was almost certainly influenced by these Rubensian baroque engravings. Though Cleyn did not illustrate the *Quos ego* – episode, Ogilby's rationalizing notes on the passage – of a kind we have encountered in Gevaerts – are worth noting. Aeolus is referred to as the "king of the Aeolian Islands," who, famed for his ability to foretell "the change of Winds,…therefore was thought to have power over" the stormy weather. On the same page we are told that "the physical ground of all, is this: Tempests are begotten by the Clouds, over which *Juno* presides, they being agitated by the Winds, of which Aeolus is Lord" (Ogilby 1654, 168). The note on Neptune's horses is even more illuminating: "Turnebus, and others understand here, *Hippocampi*, Sea-Horses." Ogilby then quotes Statius (*Theb.* 12.47, *postremi solvuntur in aequora pisces*) as evidence that hippocampi have hooves in front but "trail off behind in the form of fish" (1654, 171). While this fits Rubens' steeds, it does not fit Cleyn's illustration for the Neptune scene of book 5 (Fig. 19.3), where the god assures Venus that the Trojan ships may pass safely on, though "one [Palinurus] must give his life for many" (815). This plate, also used in Dryden's volume, gives a much lighter-hearted impression than the *Quos ego* – illustrations, in part since Neptune is here shown in a milder mood, soothing the fears of the goddess. His erect figure and gesture dominate the scene as in Rubens, and he strides forward with dignity and strength (in spite of an awkward twist of the right flank). Neptune is not pointing with his trident, but in the act of launching it (at what?), and he is holding the reins of four spirited and capering horses (?), with fin-like forefeet, though without fish tails.[1] He is snub-nosed and crowned, his somewhat protrusive eye fixed on the goddess above. This Neptune is beneficent-looking, and seems to have the beginnings of a smile on his lips, parted perhaps in speech. From her triumphal car, Venus answers with a tender glance and a charmingly deferential gesture. The upper sky opens for her epiphany, as in Vergil, *fugiunt vasto aethere nimbi* (5.821). The god's shell (ending in a cheerful dolphin's head) has the most cunning and convincing wheel-whorl we have yet encountered. It apparently works as a paddle-wheel, something like the vortex in Gevaerts' note. (It may be of course that both Rubens' and Cleyn's chariots derive from a common original in illustrations of Ovid.) The lighter tone of Cleyn's scene is

Figure 19.3 Franz Cleyn, *Neptune and Venus*, in *The Works of Publius Virgilius Maro*, translated by John Ogilby (London, 1654). Typ 605.54.868 (A) F, Department of Printing and Graphic Arts, Houghton Library, Harvard College Library. Plate facing p. 321.

picked up – perhaps with a glance at Vergil's nereid band (825–6) – in three decorative mermaids gaily swimming, one with "locks blown forward in the gleam of eyes"; another with a comic-book smile of flirtatious satisfaction. Not far off, a male swimmer (Palinurus?) half-emerges from the waves.

One slightly unsettling question before we turn to Dryden: was Rubens' sketch surely based on Vergil's *Quos ego* – ? Not solely, as we have seen, but as the focal mythical image in a complex of historical allusions and many sorts of visual impressions. To strains noted earlier, we may now add one of Ovidian lightness – in the eager nymphs (for Vergil's lone Cymothoe) and in the lusty Triton blowing the way for the sea lord. This is Triton's usual function in both Vergil and Ovid, but not in *Aeneid* 1, where with Cymothoe he is a vigorous helper in freeing ships from the rock. He is prominent in the scene from *Metamorphoses* 1 (above), where Neptune "the wild waves calmes, his *trident laid aside*" (Sandys' translation). There is also that pink bridle held by the smiling nereid. A glint of Ovidian comedy – of Homeric and Shakespearean "relief" – enters the Renaissance *Fiat lux* of Rubens.

Dryden had access to Rubens' Olympian imagery through other channels than Cleyn's engravings, as Jean Hagstrum suggests in his interesting account of baroque pictorial elements in Dryden's odes (1958, 197–208). He could hardly have avoided seeing Rubens' apotheosis of James I on the ceiling of Whitehall, although "by 1687, humidity had already been fatal to it" (van Puyvelde 1940, 287). (It is appropriate that James II "authorized a complete restoration.") The passage on Rubens in the supplement to Dryden's translation of Dufresnoy's *De arte graphica* shows some acquaintance with criticism of Rubens, if not surely direct knowledge of the paintings (Scott and Saintsbury 1892, 503–4). More to the point is the remark in Dryden's own *Parallel of Poetry and Painting*, cited by Hagstrum (1958, 318–19), on the close correspondence between pictorial posture and epic description: "The posture of a poetic figure is…the description of [the] heroes in the performance of such or such an action." Dryden follows this with a highly pictorial account of Aeneas' "posture" before killing Lausus. It should be noted that Dryden had interrupted his *Aeneis* to do the translation of Dufresnoy, and that these notions of pictorial rendering of heroic gestures were in his mind at the time he was translating Vergil.

How does Dryden's *Quos ego* – appear in the context of the literary and pictorial traditions we have been observing in Rubens and in various writers and artists, ancient and modern? It is still the most readable and energetic version in English:

> Mean time Imperial *Neptune* heard the Sound
> Of raging Billows breaking on the Ground:
> Displeas'd and fearing for his Wat'ry Reign,
> He reard his awful Head above the Main:
> Serene in Majesty, then rowl'd his Eyes   180
> Around the Space of Earth, and Seas, and Skies.
> He saw the *Trojan* fleet dispers'd, distress'd
> By stormy Winds and wintry Heav'n oppress'd.
> Full well the God his Sister's envy knew,
> And what her Aims, and what her Arts pursue: 185
> He summon'd *Eurus* and the western Blast,
> And first an angry glance on both he cast:
> Then thus rebuk'd; Audacious Winds! from whence
> This bold Attempt, this Rebel Insolence?
> Is it for you to ravage Seas and Land,   190
> Unauthoriz'd by my supream Command?
> To raise such Mountains on the troubl'd Main?
> Whom I – But first 'tis fit, the Billows to restrain,
> And then you shall be taught obedience to my Reign.
> Hence, to your Lord my Royal Mandate bear,   195
> The Realms of Ocean and the Fields of Air
> Are mine, not his; by fatal Lot to me

> The liquid Empire fell, and Trident of the Sea.
> His Pow'r to hollow Caverns is confin'd,
> There let him reign, the Jailor of the Wind: 200
> With hoarse Commands his breathing Subjects call,
> And boast and bluster in his empty Hall.
> He spoke: and while he spoke, he smooth'd the Sea,
> Dispell'd the Darkness, and restor'd the Day:
> *Cymothoe, Triton,* and the Sea-green Train   205
> Of beauteous Nymphs, the Daughters of the Main,
> Clear from the Rocks the Vessels with their hands;
> The God himself with ready Trident stands,
> And opes the Deep, and spreads the moving sands;
> Then heaves them off the sholes: where e're he guides   210
> His finny Coursers, and in Triumph rides,
> The Waves unruffle and the Sea subsides.
> As when in Tumults rise th' ignoble Crowd,
> Mad are their Motions, and their Tongues are loud;
> And Stones and Brands in ratling Vollies fly,   215
> And all the Rustick Arms that Fury can supply:
> If then some grave and Pious Man appear,
> They hush their Noise, and lend a list'ning Ear;
> He sooths with sober Words their angry Mood,
> And quenches their innate Desire of Blood: 220
> So when the Father of the Flood appears,
> And o're the Seas his Sov'raign Trident rears,
> Their Fury falls: He skims the liquid Plains,
> High on his Chariot, and with loosen'd Reins,
> Majestick moves along, and awful Peace maintains.   225

   The large contrasts of Vergil's and Rubens' scene are there, though the analogy between god and orator is less salient in this much expanded version. The rhetorical tone, which has a counterpart in Vergil, is louder and more insistent throughout. Other stresses, emotive and visual, also have some basis in the original, but their character can be best understood in relation to sixteenth- and seventeenth-century pictorial styles. As in Rubens and the engravers, there is much violent movement and feeling, sharply contrasted with their opposites. There is also the continual emphasis on *seeing* Neptune in various poses and with various looks and implied emotions. "He *reared* his *awful* Head" ("awful" is Dryden's addition), yet he is also "Serene in Majesty" (180). "The god himself *with ready Trident stands*" (208). Attention is directed first to the pose, then to the action. Again, "the Father of the flood *appears*…and…his *Sov'raign Trident rears*" – sight and gesture without words are sufficient: "Their Fury falls" (221–3). Neptune is seen "High on his Chariot" (224) (as in all the pictorial versions; cf. Milton's "High on a Throne of Royal State," *PL* 2.2). He moves "with loosen'd Reins" (224–5), which is reasonably close to Vergil's text (note, however, the descriptive "with" and the participle for an active verb). But the final picture, "Majestick moves along," is nearer to Rubens: this god is no mere charioteer. One line, "And first an angry glance on both he cast" (187), though not in Vergil, is quite comparable to the strong look of Rubens'

Neptune. The line and a half added by Dryden, "then rowl'd his Eyes / Around the Space of Earth, and Seas, and Skies" (180–1) suggests something of the scale of Rubens' scene; but the "rowling" eyes are baroque with a vengeance, more grotesque than those of Cleyn's engraving. Other pictorial elements not in Vergil are added: "and the Sea-green Train / Of beauteous Nymphs, the Daughters of the Main" (205–6) – which has the effect of dimming the precise if "low" acts that follow. Dryden does mention the "Chariot," but like the painters he brushes over the awkward business of a chariot race on the water. The wheels are not mentioned, and the "finny Coursers" recall the pictorial style and the rationalizing tendency of the seventeenth-century versions and their commentators. Stock poetic diction – note also "Wat'ry Reign" and "the liquid Plains" – elevated and vaguely visual, is the verbal equivalent of the heroic descriptive style in painting. The writer makes a gesture toward picture, without giving much evidence of having *seen* anything in particular.

What probably most strikes twentieth-century readers of Dryden's lines is the heightening of the imperial and the political themes, although there are analogies in the arbitrary gesture of Rubens' god and in the many references to the historical occasion, more blatant in the painting than in the sketch. As often, Dryden adopts a note in Vergil, heightens it, and loads it with local applications. The underlining of the imperial and royal character of Neptune appears from beginning to end of the passage: "Imperial *Neptune*," "Wat'ry Reign" and "obedience to my Reign," "Majesty" and "Majestick," "my supream Command," "your Lord," "my Royal Mandate," "sov'raign." Finally, the god is the ruler who "awful Peace maintains" – language that might suit the Supreme Deity of the next century. In the grand generalizing force of this phrase and in the insistent "my" emphasizing the royal prerogative, Dryden reflects Charles II's serio-comic obsession with the image of an absolute monarch, ruling by divine right (Ogg 1963 [1956], 2.450–4). The scornful references to "th' Ignoble Crowd" are more vulgar than Vergil's, and we hear the Tories' fear and mockery of "Rebel Insolence" and "Rustick Arms." The dignity and wisdom of Vergil's "grave and Pious Man," though the translation is literal to a fault, is brought down by the context to English political realities. "The subtle adaptation of the mythological scene" in Rubens, says Rosenberg, "to the actual life of the prince shows how earnestly the Baroque humanists and artists undertook to prove the Divine support of the sovereigns" (Rosenberg 1943, 9). Rubens is doing more than this, as we have seen, in the commanding presence of a Godlike figure who reminds us of a spiritual order perceptible in Nature and superior to kings, though the allusion confers honor on them. In Dryden's version, as in his royal odes, the strain of the royal-divine rhetoric is all too evident.

What finally can we say about Dryden's translation of myth in relation to Vergil, Rubens, and the other texts, verbal or visual, that we have surveyed? We can hardly suppose or expect that Dryden's mythological event will reveal the complex poetic, historical, and moral ordering of Vergil's poem. That cannot be if Vergil is to "speak such English, as he would himself have spoken, if he had been born in England, and in the present Age." Resonances are lost on which larger connections depend: "pious" is not *pius* and "Fury" is not *furor*. But it should be said that in spite of these inevitable losses, Dryden's *Aeneis* as a whole carries over much of Vergil's sense of history and "destiny." The political and rhetorical accent of Dryden's lines, which has some justification in

Vergil, unfortunately also inclines his version toward the values and mores of the rising Tory party in the reigns of Charles II and his brother. That Dryden attempted to *picture* the action again starts from a Vergilian quality, though the style of his verbal "painting" derives from the baroque manner of Cleyn and more generally from the Rubens tradition. Although the "postures" of Dryden's Neptune remind us of Rubens' god, they also remind us that Dryden did not take either his visual apparatus or the divine machinery very seriously. The tendency to emphasize the pose, not the act or the *numen*, to rationalize miracle by omission or soften it by veiled poetic diction, will find a point of arrival in the picturesque gods and goddesses of decorative painters and landscapers of the eighteenth century in Italy and in England. Pope, who looked on Nature with more reverence and with a keener eye as painter and mythmaker, and who loved mythological allusions in landscape and garden, also saw their possible triviality and abuse:

> Here Amphitrite sails thro' myrtle bowers;
> There Gladiators fight, or die, in flowers;
> Un-water'd see the drooping sea-horse mourn,
> And swallows roost in Nilus' dusty Urn.

But if Ovidian irreverence, which anticipated the death of the gods, had its effect on the tradition that touched Dryden in the Cleyn engravings, if it also affected Rubens even in the noble mood of the *Quos ego* –, it did not prevent him from embracing other mythical modes and ways of seeing, even contradictory in impulse. He, too, quietly omits the more humble operations of Homer's Poseidon and Vergil's Neptune, and he subdues the literalism of "wind-men and -women," and of war chariots at sea and their human drivers. How Vergil regarded Neptune's "shovings" and "liftings" we cannot know, though some see a "rough humor" in this and similar narratives in the *Aeneid*. What is most remarkable about Rubens is that he harmonizes both the deeper Vergilian and the Homeric visions. His *Quos ego* – bears a weight – perhaps too great a one – of historical and ideological reference: the heavens themselves, God and Nature, further the purposes of the king of Spain and his emissary. But if we return to the visual "thing," we see that without literalism, Rubens renews the Homeric vision of human figures and gestures dramatically expressing events both natural and supernatural (Alpers 1971, 173; cf. Burckhardt 1950, 157). In the way in which rushing lines, subtle harmonies of color and light, work to give a sense of how Powers are "begotten" from our sensations of the physical world, he takes us beyond Homer to where all myths begin.

NOTE

1 John Pinto has suggested a possible connection with Bernini's "Neptune and Triton," ca. 1620, where Neptune thrusts his trident downward, with great vigor, apparently toward the water of the fountain in which it was originally placed. See Hibbard (1965, 39–43; note, in relation to Cleyn's shell, "the trailing cloak that suddenly becomes a dolphin," 40). Cleyn's triton bears some resemblance to the rear view of the triton in Bernini's group, and possibly to the triton of Piazza Barberini.

FURTHER READING

The most recent critical edition of Dryden's translation of Vergil's *Aeneid* is in *The Works of John Dryden*, vols. 5 and 6, ed. W. Frost (1987). In addition, the following studies, which have appeared since this essay was first published, speak to many of the issues raised herein:

Burrow, C. (1997). "Virgil in English Translation," in *The Cambridge Companion to Virgil*, ed. C. Martindale. Cambridge: 21–37.

Davis, P. (2001). " 'But slaves we are': Dryden and Virgil. Translation and the 'Gyant Race,' " *Translation and Literature* 10: 110–27.

Frost, W. (1988). *John Dryden: Dramatist, Satirist, Translator*. New York, chs. 7–8 ("Dryden's Virgil"), 182–216.

Hammond, P. (1991). *John Dryden: A Literary Life*. New York. The translations are discussed on 142–68.

Hammond, P. (1998). "Classical Texts: Translations and Transformations," in *The Cambridge Companion to English Literature*, ed. S. Zwicker: 143–61.

Hammond, P. (1999). *Dryden and the Traces of Classical Rome*. Oxford, in particular 218–82.

Haynes, K. (2001). "Dryden: Classical or Neoclassical?," *Translation and Literature* 10: 67–77.

Hopkins, D. (1986). *John Dryden*. Cambridge, ch. 5 (" 'Studying Nature's Laws': The *Juvenal* and *Virgil*"), 134–67.

Thomas, R.F. (2001). *Virgil and the Augustan Reception*. Cambridge, ch. 4 ("Dryden's Virgil and the Politics of Translation"), 122–53.

Tomlinson, C. (2001). "Why Dryden's Translations Matter," *Translation and Literature* 10: 3–20.

Winn, J. (1987). *John Dryden and his World*. New Haven.

Zwicker, S.N. (1984). *Politics and Language in Dryden's Poetry: The Arts of Disguise*. Princeton.

CHAPTER TWENTY

The *Æneas* of Vergil
A Dramatic Performance Presented in the Original Latin by John Ogilby

Kristi Eastin

In the dedication to his translation of Vergil's *Aeneid*, John Dryden addressed the relationship between epic and tragic poetry. According to Dryden, tragedy originates from epic: "For the Original of the Stage was from the Epick poem. Narration, doubtless, preceded Acting, and gave Laws to it: What at first was told Artfully, was, in process of time, represented gracefully to the sight, and hearing" (1987, 269).[1] Tragedy, of course, is a performance by definition, yet by this analysis epic too is inherently theatrical. Dryden understands both genres to be essentially performative: the "greatness of action" that is the hallmark of epic and tragic poetry is characterized by a "Dignity of Actours," by which he refers to the characters of both epos and play (1987, 272). Dryden's extensive career as a dramatist informs his theory, but the theatricality of Vergil's *Aeneid* had already been explored by an earlier English translator of Vergil's *Aeneid* (1654). This essay examines how Dryden's predecessor, John Ogilby, expressed this theatricality with the set of illustrations that accompanied his English translation of the *Aeneid*; it shows how word and image are combined in these illustrations to create short, dramatic performances of Vergil's poem and how, when the images are considered as a series, they work together as a kind of play.

Image and Text: The Significance of the Latin Captions

Studies of seventeenth-century print illustrations of Vergil's *Aeneid* almost always address a set of images drawn by the Dutch artist Francis Cleyn. The engravings and etchings are a high point in seventeenth-century book illustration in England: seventy-one full-page royal folio plates provide abundant examples of artistic and technical virtuosity. Moreover, the Cleyn images are the only set of illustrations for Vergil's *Aeneid* published in Britain in the seventeenth century. The plates were created to accompany the first English translation of Vergil's complete *Works*, translated by John Ogilby and published "for the author" in London in 1654 (Ogilby 1654).[2] The volume was a grand production. Ogilby chose the largest size volume available, a royal folio (42 cm), and he had it bound in dark red morocco with gold tooling and with 586 leaves of high-quality paper. His translation was set off in a single column of verse lines in a large font, and it was accompanied by extensive technical and erudite annotations (all translated into English) that fill the wide margin of nearly every page.[3] The poems were preceded by Donatus' *Life* of *Vergil*, also translated into English for the first time. Elaborate head- and end-pieces and ornately illustrated capital letters decorate the whole of the volume, but most striking are the illustrations. Ogilby commissioned one hundred and three full-page illustrations from some of the leading artists then working in England: Francis Cleyn, Wenceslaus Hollar, Pierre Lombart, Ludwig Richer, and William Faithorne, all men previously associated with the Stuart court and in high demand in its circles.[4] To finance this edition, Ogilby sold subscriptions to his book, soliciting advance payment from wealthy patrons. In return, each patron's name, title, and coat of arms was inscribed on the bottom of a single plate, centered amid a Latin quotation from Vergil's poem (Clapp 1932–3, 366–7).

Ogilby's volume was very popular in the mid-seventeenth century: he would issue two Latin editions (1658 and 1663), both illustrated imperial folios, but without the marginal annotations, and a second English edition in 1668. Yet the illustrations might have been relegated to relative obscurity were it not for their inclusion in the second complete English translation of Vergil's works, the much-anticipated translation by England's former poet laureate, John Dryden. This edition, published in 1697, was also an elegant folio volume; it was sold by subscription; and it contained all but two of the same illustrations. Dryden's publisher, Jacob Tonson, had acquired the plates from Ogilby's son, and he and Dryden each worked to solicit subscribers, whose names and coats of arms would then replace the sponsors of the final Ogilby edition (in Dryden 1987, 1180–1). A comparison between the original illustrations and those reprinted by Tonson reveals only a few modifications. Most famously, Tonson had the nose of Aeneas, formerly donning the courtly mustache worn by Charles II, reworked to resemble the nose of William III. Less conspicuous but equally important are the newly inscribed patrons' names. Ogilby's patrons had been almost exclusively Stuart royalists, and the names of the patrons inscribed on the plates of the Dryden edition are partisans of both the old and new regimes (Barnard 2000).

One change that has been little addressed – and the subject of this chapter – is Tonson's removal of the Latin inscription. Each illustration in the Ogilby edition was inscribed with a Latin quotation from Vergil's poem, which corresponds to the image above. In the Dryden edition, the Latin inscription has been replaced with a line number that refers the reader to Dryden's translation. The literary prominence of Dryden has somewhat overshadowed the absence of the original Latin inscriptions, and this has important implications for how the illustrations have been viewed. Though scholars note the inscriptions in Ogilby's edition (and their absence in Dryden's translation), the Latin captions are understood to provide a "key" to the

Figure 20.1   *Aeneas in the Storm* (*Aen.* 1); Francis Cleyn, in J. Ogilby, trans., *The Works of Publius Virgilius Maro* (London, 1654). Brown University Library.

illustration, directing a reader to the relevant text of the poem – just as the inscribed line number in the Dryden edition. Yet a more thorough investigation of the illustrations shows that the Latin inscriptions, as conceived by Ogilby, are an integral part of the illustrations, working in conjunction with – and essential to – the picture above. That is, each plate contains an image and an inscription, and without the accompanying words, the illustration is incomplete. Further still, when considered in their original format, the illustrations reveal an overarching, sophisticated illustrative program, conceived and executed by a theatrical mind.

Let us look at the first illustration to book 1, considering it first without acknowledging the Latin caption (as it appeared in the Dryden edition). The illustration shows the episode of the great tempest that wrecks Aeneas' fleet and forces his ships to Carthaginian shores (Fig. 20.1). In the center of the scene, personified winds blow visible air to create a raging sea, and desperate men scramble to save their floundering ships. Juno and Aeolus, the gods responsible for the mayhem, converse in the sky above; and in the bottom right corner is Neptune, entering as if he has just arrived upon the scene, and with trident raised is about to take control. In the center of the chaos we see Aeneas, lifting his arms to the sky. The illustration reads as a series of vignettes from the episode of the storm, and a reader familiar with the *Aeneid* will recognize all the components of the scene. Analyzing the Cleyn illustrations from a Dryden edition (i.e., without the Latin inscriptions), E. W. Leach describes this image as follows: "Cleyn's first engraving...plunges the reader *in medias res* with the storm that drives Aeneas's fleet off course from the Sicilian coast to Carthage. Swelling waves and pitching vessels make a stirring, if conventional, composition. In this first appearance the hero himself is recognizable by no pronounced physical distinction but only by the posture of appeal that accompanies his desperate outcry to the gods" (1982, 192).

Leach's description makes it clear that to identify Aeneas and correctly interpret the focal point of the illustration, the viewer must recall the moment in the story when Aeneas raises his arms to the sky in a plea to the gods. This recollection is not difficult, as it is our first encounter with the hero, as well as a striking scene. But the chaos of the action and the more easily recognizable figures of Juno, Aeolus, and Neptune distract the viewer's attention from the pathos of the scene. Moreover, in the Dryden edition, the line number inscribed on the plate directs the reader to the first line of Dryden's translation (see Frost in Dryden 1987, vi–vii), which begins,

> Arms, and the Man I sing, who, forc'd by Fate,
> And haughty *Juno's* unrelenting Hate,
> Expell'd and exil'd, left the *Trojan* Shoar:
> Long Labours, both by Sea and Land he bore. (trans. Dryden)

Although there is some correspondence between the illustration and the opening lines of the poem – the central figure of "the Man," Juno's presence, and "Long Labours by Sea" – a description of the illustration actually comes before the first line of the poem, in the opening lines of Dryden's argument:

> *The* Trojans, *after a seven Years Voyage, set sail for* Italy, *but are overtaken by a dreadful Storm, which* Æolus *raises at* Juno's *Request. The Tempest sinks one, and scatters the rest:* Neptune *drives off the Winds and calms the Sea.* (343)

The layout of the volume (picture, argument, poem) is such that Dryden's argument serves as a quick and ready description of the illustration, and the proximity of Dryden's description of the storm reinforces a narrative reading of the plate.[5] The importance of the hero (emphasized by his centrality within the composition) is perhaps even negated by the argument, as Dryden's description of the storm does not mention Aeneas at all.

Consider now the same illustration with the Latin inscription, as it was originally designed and published by John Ogilby. The caption is a direct quotation from Vergil's poem, taken not from the first lines of the poem (as the inscribed line number in Dryden's edition might suggest), but from a passage almost one hundred lines into the poem:

> ingemit et duplicis tendens ad sidera palmas
> talia voce refert: "o terque quaterque beati

quis ante ora patrum Troiae sub moenibus altis
contigit oppetere:"

(*Aen.* 1.93–6)

Who sighing, up to Heaven his hands did hold:
Then said, "O happy, more than happy, you,
Who near Troy's wall dy'd in your parents view!"   (131)[6]

When the Latin inscription is present, the experience of extracting meaning from the illustration changes remarkably. Now the viewer must attend to both word and image, and there is an interaction that takes place between the two. Instead of moving through a series of vignettes, the quotation directs the viewer to the plight of the central figure, narrowing the subject of the illustration to a depiction of the episode at its greatest pitch of intensity. A general illustration of the tempest becomes the precise moment when Aeneas throws up his hands in despair. For a reader well acquainted with the poem, the stance of the hero likely recalls this same moment, but even so, the experience is not the same. The direct quotation, containing, as it does, the actual cry of Aeneas, adds an aural element to the illustration, and the interplay between word and image is such that we see the hero and also "hear" his groan and pitiful cry for help. By placing the words of the poem on the page, Ogilby has provided the viewer with the means to infuse the image with action and sound – effectively to animate the scene.

The suggestion of dramatic action is present, of course, even without the Latin. Leach notes that Cleyn's "style and taste show the influence of Rubens's baroque heroics and [his] compositions eschew narrative for the dramatic concept of the frozen moment or tableau" (1982, 179). Even so, when the illustration is considered together with the Latin quotation, the frozen moment is animated. The words introduce a delineating or temporal element, vivifying the scene for the duration of the time it takes to fulfill the action or speech contained in the text below. Additionally, the caption precisely directs our visual experience, as the words hone the subject of the illustration to a precise moment in a dynamic scene.

Let us briefly consider two additional illustrations. The first image to book 4 depicts Dido in her bedroom, confessing her passion for Aeneas to her sister Anna (Fig. 20.2). A close inspection of the details of this picture reveals that Cleyn has artfully captured the tensions of this scene. The queen's chastity is emphasized by the empty bed and curiously sculpted bedpost (with its symbolically placed hand), but Dido herself – with her hair down and her regalia, crown, and scepter set off to the side – is an exceptionally vulnerable woman, not a powerful queen. She holds her hand over her heart to further emphasize her pain, and Anna's gesture suggests that a conversation is taking place. In the Dryden edition, the line number inscribed again directs the reader to the first line of this book. In this instance there is a greater correspondence between the opening lines of Dryden's translation and the image: "But anxious Cares already seiz'd the Queen: She fed within her Veins a Flame unseen" (451). As before, however, a reader would first encounter Dryden's argument, which again provides a succinct description for the illustration: "Dido *discovers to her Sister her Passion for Æneas, and her thoughts of marrying him*" (451). The essence of the conversation between the sisters is easy to recall, but the experience of the illustration changes markedly when it is considered with the Latin verse, which supplies the precise (and pitiable) words of the queen:

> agnosco veteris vestigia flammae.
> sed mihi vel tellus optem prius ima dehiscat
> vel pater omnipotens adigat me fulmine ad umbras,
> pallentis umbras Erebo noctemque profundam,
> ante, pudor, quam te violo aut tua iura resolvo.
> (*Aen.* 4.23–7)

> I feel the Sparks of my old Flame revive.
> But may the Earth first swallow me alive,
> Or *Jove's* dire Thunder sink me down to Hell,
> Where Shades, pale Shades, of Night eternal dwell,
> E're I with Shame, and those dear Ties dispense: (262)

The integration of the Latin quotation greatly enhances the pathos of this scene. The image of two sisters conversing becomes an actual conversation, and we "hear" the words of Dido, whose confession of "*her Passion for Æneas*" is actually subordinated to a fervent expression of the personal sanctity of her vow. Through interaction of word and image, the vulnerability of the queen expressed in the picture belies the strong resolve of her speech, and the tragic irony of her words is poignantly excerpted and placed upon a stage.

In both of these illustrations, the caption intensifies our viewing experience, transforming what is a descriptive relationship in the Dryden edition into an emotive one, wherein the anguished words of the characters evoke the moment of greatest pathos from the scene. Elsewhere, the effect of the Latin quotation is pure spectacle. Book 6 opens with an image of Aeneas' encounter with the Cumaean Sibyl (Fig. 20.3). Dryden's argument again provides a ready description of the illustration: "*The Sibyl foretells* Aeneas *the Adventures he should meet with in* Italy" (527); but in this instance the force of the scene is almost entirely lost without the inscription. The caption focuses our attention not on the prophecy of the Sibyl, but on her astonishing transformation:

> ventum erat ad limen, cum virgo "poscere fata
> tempus" ait: "deus ecce deus!" cui talia fanti
> ante fores subito non vultus, non color unus,
> non comptae mansere comae, sed pectus anhelum,
> et rabie fera corda tument, maiorque videri
> nec mortale sonans, adflata est numine quando
> iam propiore dei.
> (*Aen.* 6.45–51)

> As he drew neer, the Virgin calls, Be bold
> To ask thy Fate, the God, the God behold!
> This said, her colour straight did change, her Face,
> And flowing Tresses lost their former Grace;
> A growing Passion swells her troubled Breast,

Figure 20.2 *Dido and Anna* (*Aen.* 4); Francis Cleyn, in J. Ogilby, trans., *The Works of Publius Virgilius Maro* (London, 1654). Brown University Library.

> And Fury her distracted Soul possest;
> Greater she seems, nor like a Mortal spake,
> As the God nearer did approaches make. (321)

In the previous examples, the words gave voice to the plight of the characters. Here the experience of image and text is one of pure spectacle: we witness, with Aeneas, the metamorphoses taking place as the young priestess becomes possessed by the god. Even with the Latin, the illustration is not entirely successful; the two-dimensional medium scarcely conveys the action of the words. Nevertheless, the incorporation of Vergil's poetry supplies dynamism to an otherwise static scene.

As these few examples demonstrate, the caption is an integral part of each of the Cleyn illustrations, working with the picture above to create the illusion of an animated scene. Whether or not Ogilby could explain the complex semiotic process that produces such an illusion, his sophisticated understanding of this hybrid medium is clear. Within the vibrant visual culture of the seventeenth century, we need not look

Figure 20.3   *Aeneas and the Cumaean Sibyl* (*Aen.* 6); Francis Cleyn, in J. Ogilby, trans., *The Works of Publius Virgilius Maro* (London, 1654). Brown University Library.

far to account for such insight, as many fashionable media integrated image and word. In print culture, even apart from book illustration, emblem books were much in vogue, combining picture and caption to create a "speaking picture" that espouses a moral, religious, or literary conceit (Bath 1994; see also Daly 1998, esp. 158–86).[7] On the other end of the social spectrum, the genre of comics – to which the experience of these plates is ironically akin – traces its origins to the integration of word and image in the European illustrated broadsheet. This medium was rapidly gaining popularity in England during the seventeenth century (Kunzle 1973, 122–5), and these plates might well be considered sophisticated early explorations of that modern art form, though directed at an elite audience. Ogilby was, of course, influenced by and active within this powerful cultural milieu, but to understand his inspiration and the genius of these illustrations, we must turn from print culture to the theatrical arts: masques, plays, and even triumphal processions – word joined with spectacle for dramatic performance.

Until events in the civil war forced him to pursue a new career, Ogilby had spent his life absorbing and mastering the art of the stage. He had come to England from Scotland with his father in the train of James I (VI) in 1603. As a young man, Ogilby apprenticed with a dancing master and danced in at least one masque (possibly more) at the court of James I, before an injury on stage lamed him for life. By the favor of the Duke of Buckingham, he was allowed to remain associated with the court theatre, and by the 1620s Ogilby had become a well-known theatrical manager and producer, moving in the same circles as popular writers and actors, and maintaining his close connections with the court (van Eerde 1976, 15–25). In 1633 he traveled to Dublin with Charles' first minister, Thomas Wentworth, Earl of Strafford, who attempted to create a royal court in Dublin that would emulate the one at Whitehall, and Ogilby soon found himself charged with the building and management of a court theatre. Using his extensive connections within the theatrical circles in London – and aided by the closure of the theatres there due to plague – Ogilby flourished in his task. He was appointed the first Master of Revels of Ireland, and when his playhouse opened in 1637, it had as its chief dramatist the prestigious playwright, James Shirley. These two men worked closely together for the next four years, developing a lifelong friendship. It is speculated that they may have collaborated in the writing of one or two plays, but Ogilby's primary role was that of producer (Morash 2002, 2–6; Stockwell 1968, 1–11).

His theatre was a great success until 1641, when the trial and execution of Thomas Wentworth effectively disbanded England's Irish court. The execution of his patron left Ogilby penniless. He remained in Ireland for a few years but eventually made his way back to England, where his prospects were no less bleak. Puritan sentiment now condemned the theatres, and by 1642 they had been officially banned. It was during this period that Ogilby began to promote himself as a translator and publisher of the classics, and his first endeavor was Vergil. His first translation of Vergil's *Works* was published in 1649. The volume was a plain unillustrated octavo, dedicated to his new patron, William Seymour. From the dedicatory epistle we learn that Ogilby had been translating Vergil for quite some time: "this translation," he states, was "bred in the phlegmatick Regions" – presumably Ireland. Shirley's residence in Dublin lends credence to this claim, as it was under the tutelage of Shirley that Ogilby took up his translation efforts in earnest upon his return to England (van Eerde 1976, 29–30). Yet the more significant aspect to this dedication is that it reveals that Ogilby's translation enterprises were still informed by his long theatrical career. Of this first volume, he writes:

> I call it but the shadow, and cold resemblance of Virgil...
> Yet if your Lordship shall be pleas'd to smile upon the dress she now wears, it may live to be receiv'd (when time shall ripen more ornament of Sculpture and Annotations) with none of the meanest attempts of this nature. (Ogilby 1649, A2v)

Whether the humble reference to his work is genuine or rhetorical, what is clear from this passage is that the translation by itself is insufficient. A complete English *Works* of Vergil is but one aspect of the former impresario's vision of a grand, spectacular production – the largest volume, the best artists, the most images, and the finest scholars all adorning the only complete *Works* of Vergil translated into English – a production he brought to fruition five years later in the royal folio of 1654.

When we consider the 1654 illustrations in their original format (with the Latin inscription), we discover that this same theatrical instinct motivates Ogilby's illustrative program and explains the Latin captions beneath each scene. Ogilby could understand the integration of word and image to function similarly to that of dramatic performance: taken together, picture and caption render the acting of a short scene. Even without the Latin there is a performative element to the pictures. Leach addressed this briefly with respect to Dryden, stating that such a presentation would be in accord with the poet's "long career of writing for the stage" (1982, 179). Yet when the image is viewed with the caption, it becomes clear that the illustrations would appeal to a connoisseur of the stage precisely because they were designed to mimic it. Ogilby had spent his life assimilating the visual intricacies that were part of dramatic performance, and he transposed his life's work onto the art of illustration, synthesizing word and image on the printed page.

Ogilby's cognizance of this integration is best demonstrated by a comparison of illustrations. The 1654 Vergil was clearly influenced by a French prose translation by Michel de Marolles, published in Paris in 1649. The French volume – a luxury folio edition, embellished with commentaries, extensive notes, a short *Life* of Vergil, and twenty-four full-page illustrations – served as a model for Ogilby's 1654 edition (Griffiths 1998, 184). The illustrations were designed and engraved by France's famed print maker, François Chauveau. Almost all of the twenty-four images were imitated in some fashion by Cleyn. In some instances Cleyn's illustrations are virtual copies of Chauveau, rendered so closely that at first blush it appears that the artists were one and the same (a confusion unfortunately perpetuated by the fact that Francis Cleyn signed his plates with only his initials, "F.C."). In other cases, such as the example considered here, the topic of illustration is the same, but Cleyn departs significantly from Chauveau's presentation. In this illustration, Chauveau has captured the moment in book 3 when Aeneas and his men, about to consume the cattle they have recently slaughtered, are assaulted by a flock of Harpies, who harry the men and despoil their fare (Fig. 20.4). The image itself is a flurry of motion, as grotesque, half-human Harpies swoop down from the sky and the Trojan men either recoil or boldly advance in response.

Cleyn's illustration of this same episode is strikingly different (Fig. 20.5). The acute action which is the subject of Chauveau's image has been relegated to the background, and the viewer is somewhat distanced from the panic and chaos of the scene. Here the focal point of the image is devoid of motion, as a stationary Aeneas looks up at Celaeno, the leader of the Harpies, as she sits perched upon a high rock. While the experience of the frenetic action in the French illustration is immediate, deducing the narrative from the Cleyn illustration requires a greater effort on the part of the viewer. This is not the case, however, when the image is considered with the Latin. The words belong to Celaeno, who chastises Aeneas for waging war against her brood:

> bellum etiam pro caede boum stratisque iuvencis,
> Laomedontiadae, bellumne inferre paratis
> et patrio Harpyias insontis pellere regno?
> (*Aen.* 3.247–9)

Des Oyseaux jnconnus, les gourmandes Harpies,
Infectent de leur bec les mets delicieux,
On les bat, on les chasse, ils s'enuolent aux Cieux
Et retournent soudain sur les Tables seruies,

Figure 20.4 *Encounter with the Harpies* (*Aen.* 3); François Chauveau, in M. Marolles, trans., *Les Œuvres de Virgile traduites en prose* (Paris, 1649). Beinecke Rare Book and Manuscript Library. Yale University.

> Raise you *Laomedontians* a War,
> For Slaughter'd Cattle: and by Force prepare
> Innocent Harpies from their Realms t'expell: (241)

With the inscription, the experience of the image changes significantly. "Listening" to the harsh accusations of the Harpy, the background and foreground of the image become an integrated scene: the pile of slaughtered cattle and the now-despoiled tables recall the hero's hubristic act, and the skirmish taking place in the background underscores the justice of Celaeno's charge. Aeneas, with his sword lowered and shield aside, stands motionless in his response, receiving her harsh words but unable to defend his actions.

The French poem beneath Chauveau's illustration reveals that the notion of a corresponding inscription was not original to Ogilby; each of the French illustrations is accompanied by a few lines of corresponding verse. Yet the French inscription is inert compared

Figure 20.5 *Aeneas and Celaeno* (*Aen.* 3); Francis Cleyn, in J. Ogilby, trans., *The Works of Publius Virgilius Maro* (London, 1654). Brown University Library.

to the caption chosen by Ogilby. Like Dryden's arguments, the poem beneath Chauveau's illustration is merely descriptive; it explains the picture that we see on the page:

> Des Oysaux inconnus, les gourmandes Harpies,
> Infectent de leur bec les mets delicieux
> On les bat, on les chasse, ils s'enuolent aux Cieux
> Et retournent soudain sur les Tables seruies.

> Some strange birds, the gluttonous Harpies
> Despoil the delicacies by pecking on them.
> Those dining beat them, shoo them off; and they circle into the sky
> And suddenly dive again onto the laden tables.

The descriptive poem effects little interaction between word and image; the words reflect back on the picture, but they do not interact with it. In contrast, in the Ogilby edition, the Latin inscription becomes part of the visual experience.

Comparing the plates from the Marolles and Ogilby editions, the eminent French engraver and print collector Pierre Mariette (1654–1742) wrote: "Les desseins d'après quoi il a gravé sont fort mauvais" ("The drawings after which [Hollar] engraved are quite bad") (as quoted in Griffiths 1998, 186). His opinion was supported by modern scholar Antony Griffiths, who notes that Chauveau's plates "were indeed much finer than Clein's" (ibid.). Such criticism fails to account for the dramatic vision of the editor, and so evaluates the Cleyn illustrations on insufficient criteria. To fully appreciate the artistic and editorial decisions of Cleyn and Ogilby, one must consider the Latin.

A Unified Performance

The Latin inscriptions are also important for understanding (and appreciating) Ogilby's dramatic vision as it applies to the set of illustrations as a whole. The captions suggest that Ogilby was attempting to create – out of the highlights, pathos, and spectacle of the story – an integrated series of images. Celaeno's speech, for example, does not end with her admonishment of Aeneas. The inscription skips four lines of Vergil's verse and then continues with the Harpy's foreboding prophecy:

> ibitis Italiam portusque intrare licebit.
> sed non ante datam cingetis moenibus urbem
> quam vos dira fames nostraeque iniuria caedis
> ambesas subigat malis absumere mensas.
> (*Aen.* 3.254–7)

> That *Latium* which you seek for, you shall find,
> And the Port enter with a favouring wind:
> But e're your City is with Bulwarks fenc'd,
> You for these Slaughters shall be recompenc'd
> With Famine, which shall make you Trenchers eat. (242)

This part of Celaeno's speech is, strictly speaking, extraneous to the illustration; but it is important in terms of plot. The prediction of the Harpy introduces an element of suspense that must be reconciled later in the poem. Ogilby's decision to include this portion of the speech allows him not only to highlight the foreboding suspense of the scene, but also to link the illustrations together, creating interconnected scenes.

We see the realization of Celaeno's prophecy in book 7 (Fig. 20.6). Having finally reached their destined shore, Aeneas and his men rest on the river's banks and enjoy a sparse meal. In the picture Aeneas and his son are not especially highlighted, but the Latin caption directs our attention to these two central figures. After several lines of verse explaining the lack of food and the need to consume the flat bread that had served as their plates, we hear Ascanius exclaim: *heus, etiam mensas consumimus?* ("We eat our Trenchers too," 7.116). The image is comparatively banal (especially in light of Baroque aesthetics) and, assessed independently, might support Mariette's unfavorable

Plate 1 Pietro da Cortona and Francesco Borromini, Galleria, Palazzo Pamphili, Rome. 1651–4. Courtesy of Brazilian Embassy, Rome.

Plate 2 Peter Paul Rubens, *Neptune Calming the Tempest.* 1635. Harvard University Art Museums, Fogg Art Museum, Alpheus Hyatt Purchasing Fund, 1942.174. Photo: Imaging Department © President and Fellows of Harvard College.

Plate 3 Joseph Mallord William Turner (1775–1851), *Aeneas and the Sibyl, Lake Avernus* (ca. 1798). Oil on canvas 76.5 × 98.5 cm.

Plate 4 Joseph Mallord William Turner (1775–1851), *Dido and Aeneas* (1814). Oil on canvas, 146 × 237 cm.

Plate 5 William Blake (1757–1827), *The Inscription over Hell Gate* (1824–7). Chalk, pencil, ink, and watercolor on paper 52.7 × 37.4 cm.

Plate 6 El Greco, *Laocoön* (1610). Samuel H. Kress Collection. Image courtesy of the Board of Trustees, National Gallery of Art, Washington, ca. 1610/1614.

Plate 7 Angelika Kauffmann, *Vergil Reading the "Aeneid" to Augustus and Octavia* (1788). The State Hermitage Museum, St. Petersburg, Russia. Photograph © The State Hermitage Museum.

Plate 8 Jean-Auguste-Dominique Ingres, *Auguste écoutant la lecture de l'Enéide/Tu Marcellus eris*, ca. 1810 (Inv. 1836). Musée royaux des Beaux-Arts de Belgique, Brussels.

Figure 20.6   *"We have eaten our tables!"* (*Aen.* 7); Francis Cleyn, in J. Ogilby, trans., *The Works of Publius Virgilius Maro* (London, 1654). Brown University Library.

judgment. Yet if one subordinates an exclusively aesthetic program to a more inclusive dramatic one, the decision to include this rather mundane illustration makes sense. It provides the requisite reconciliation of the Harpy's grim prediction (which is necessary to sustain the story's plot), and it creates a connection to a previously illustrated scene.

Not all of the Latin inscriptions include speeches, but the majority do: of the seventy illustrations, forty-two contain some aspect of direct speech – ranging from the short exclamation of Ascanius to a lengthy declamation by Juno. Even in the images that lack a "spoken" component, the inscription remains integral to the illustration. Compare again illustrations by Chauveau and Cleyn (Figs. 20.7 and 20.8). The episode depicted is the final stand of Nisus, which takes place in the middle of book 9. Euryalus has just been killed by Volscens, and Nisus, distraught at the death of his young friend, makes a crazed but successful attack on his killer. The similarity in composition demonstrates Chauveau's strong influence on Cleyn. In this instance, however, Cleyn's depiction is less accurate in terms of the poem: Nisus is too apprehensive (as well as much too young), and the weapons of the opposing soldiers do not convey

Figure 20.7 *Nisus' Last Stand* (*Aen.* 9); François Chauveau, in M. Marolles, trans., *Les Œuvres de Virgile traduites en prose* (Paris, 1649). Beinecke Rare Book and Manuscript Library. Yale University.

as vividly the Trojan's impending doom. Consider, however, the different experience of each inscription. As before, the French poem provides a description of the scene:

> Euryale est tué par la main de Volscens,
> Nise uange sa mort: et son amour fidelle
> Contrainte de ceder a l'effort de trios cents
> Le Joint a son Amy par une mort cruelle

> Euryalus is killed by Volscens himself.
> Nisus avenges his death, and his deep loyalty,
> Destined to lose to the force of three hundred,
> Unites him with his friend by a cruel death.

Figure 20.8   *Nisus' Last Stand* (*Aen.* 9); Francis Cleyn, in J. Ogilby, trans., *The Works of Publius Virgilius Maro* (London, 1654). Brown University Library.

The poem evokes little interaction between word and image: the words only tell us what we see. This can be contrasted with the experience of the verse quotation from Vergil:

> quem circum glomerati hostes hinc comminus atque hinc
> proturbant. instat non setius ac rotat ensem
> fulmineum, donec Rutuli clamantis in ore
> condidit adverso et moriens animam abstulit hosti.
>
> (*Aen.* 9.440–3)

> Wheeling his glittering Sword, on bravely goes,
> Till in his Mouth the deadly Stuck he threw,
> And thus his Enemy in dying slew. (419)

In this quotation the characters have no speaking parts; the poet, as narrator, tells us what is taking place in the scene. Yet there is an important distinction between the

Figure 20.9 "Aeneae Troiani Navigatio," frontispiece for the *Aeneas*, Wenceslaus Hollar, in J. Ogilby, trans., *The Works of Publius Virgilius Maro* (London, 1654). This item is reproduced by permission of The Huntington Library, San Marino, California.

two inscriptions: whereas the French poem describes the image, the direct quotation from the *Aeneid* supplies the image with a dramatic narrative, and we "hear" the omniscient voice of the poet. Once again the words dramatize the frozen moment, honing the illustrated passage to its greatest pitch of intensity and effectually animating the scene. Indeed, to clarify this difference, consider the Chauveau illustration together with Vergil's words.

Ogilby's intimacy with the theatre provided him with a sophisticated understanding of the interaction between word and image, and it is this same dramatic sophistication that defines his illustrative program. So successful is his careful selection of passages and pairing of quotation with illustration that when viewed in their original format – with the Latin inscription – the illustrations to Ogilby's *Aeneis* become dramatic performances, animated vignettes of the poem's central scenes.

One final illustration is important for exploring how Ogilby conceived of his illustrations as a sort of play. In the 1654 edition, a map charting the journey of Aeneas' fleet for the first six books preceded the *Aeneid*, separating it from the *Georgics* and serving as a grand frontispiece for the epic poem (Fig. 20.9). The map, drawn and etched by Wenceslaus Hollar, was inspired by a similar frontispiece in a French translation of the *Aeneid*, published in 1648 and illustrated by Chauveau's colleague, Abraham Bosse (trans. P. Moreau). Bosse's map was entitled *Voyage d'Enée*, and it charted the progress of Aeneas' fleet by a simple dotted line. In Hollar's version, the artist has enhanced the visual narrative of the voyage by actually depicting the Trojan fleet. Following the journey along the dotted line, one encounters Aeneas' ships at various moments in the story: setting sail northward from Antandros (with full sails), approaching the island of Crete (again with sails full), or moored in the harbor there (now with sails furled and tents pitched on the island). Though Hollar occasionally provides commentary corresponding to the story (e.g., at Antandros: *unde Aeneae classis solvit*, "whence the fleet of Aeneas set sail"), in most cases the location and illustrated action of the fleet speaks for itself.

Commenting on the illustrations that correspond to Aeneas' travels in book 3, Leach observes that Cleyn's illustrations do not convey a sense of journey: "Cleyn's more narrowly focused compositions rarely provide a sense of wandering through distance" (1982, 201). This is likely because the detailed map of the "Voyage of the Trojan Aeneas" – which was not included in the Dryden edition – was meant to serve as a guide to the reader, to be used in conjunction with the individually illustrated scenes. Yet as with all of Cleyn's pictures, the principal role of this particular illustration cannot be ascertained without a consideration of the two Latin passages. The foremost passage, set off in an elaborate frame, is a quotation from book 1, when Aeneas introduces himself to his disguised mother and explains his plight:

> Sum pius Aeneas, raptos qui ex hoste Penates
> classe veho mecum, fama super aethera notus.
> […]
> Bis denis Phrygium conscendi navibus aequor,
> […]

vix septem convolsae undis Euroque supersunt.
[...]
Europa atque Asia pulsus.
                                             (*Aen.* 1.378–85)

I am *Æneas* who from Enemies bore
My Gods with me aboard; my Fame above
The Stars is known;
[...]
I twenty Ships launch'd to the *Phrygian* Sea
[...]
                        scarce seven remain
By Waves and Tempests craz'd...
Driven from *Europe*, and the *Asian* Shore (181)

Though the actual narration of the poem plunges directly *in medias res* (as does the first illustration to book 1, depicting Aeneas in the throes of the storm), this quotation supplies the story's background. Ogilby has condensed the Latin passage to capture the essence of what has taken place, and it is in Aeneas' own "voice" that we are given an introduction to the forthcoming tale. When considered in theatrical terms, the principal role of this frontispiece is that of a prologue: an actor steps forth and explains the context of the play. Hollar's map reduces the geographic complexity of the poem, and it serves as a backdrop to the words of the prologue – depicting the actual ships, storms, and seas as well as Europe and Asia. The second quotation, set adjacent the fleet in the midst of a storm, provides additional context to the setting and introducing the story to come:

septima post Troiae excidium iam vertitur aestas,
cum freta, cum terras omnis, tot inhospita saxa
sideraque emensae ferimur, dum per mare magnum
Italiam sequimur fugientem et volvimur undis.
                                             (*Aen.* 5.626–9)

Since *Troy's* sad ruine, now seven years are gone,
Whil'st we so many Shores, and dire Rocks shun,
Guided by Stars, whil'st *Latium's* flying Coast
Through troubled Waves we seek   (309)

The specific function or role of this passage as a "prologue" is made clear when one considers its actual context. The passage is from book 5, and the speech belongs to Beroë, the old Trojan woman who, possessed by Iris, laments their wretched pilgrimage and incites her female companions to burn the Trojan ships. Though Ogilby would never presume to alter the poet's "script," he was not afraid to excerpt a short speech in order to properly set the stage. Those most intimate with the *Aeneid* will "hear" the voice of the old woman and recall the pathos associated with this particular scene. Like a prologue, the two passages are preparatory, providing the storyline and setting the tone.

John Ogilby's 1654 edition of Vergil's *Works* was a seventeenth-century "multi-media" production, a production so creative in its vision that it found new life in the subsequent generation. But the reuse of the illustrations in the Dryden edition was not the same. The focal point of Dryden's *Works of Virgil* was the translation, and the illustrative program was subordinated to the long-awaited translation by the former poet laureate. For Ogilby, the focus was never on himself. No one anxiously awaited his translation, and his version of Vergil's poetry was only one component of his grand edition. The effectiveness of the illustrations stems from Ogilby's theatrical vision: with the verse quotations, the illustrations come alive, creating the illusion of animated scenes. Without the inscription, the vitality of the illustrations cannot be sustained. Why did Ogilby not place his own translation of Vergil beneath each image? Would not an English translation similarly animate each scene? Knowing that most of his clientele read Latin, perhaps he gave prominence to the hallowed verses of Vergil. Yet it is enticing to think that even this decision may have been motivated by his stagecraft. Even if his English words could reproduce the sense of the Latin, they could never reproduce the sound: the dramatic rhythms of Vergil's powerful language produce a music, a background music, if you will – music to the senses, for a novel play, presented by John Ogilby, Master of Revels.

NOTES

1   All citations of Dryden's *Works of Virgil* are from the "California Dryden," ed. W. Frost and V.A. Dearing (Dryden 1987).
2   *The Works of Publius Vergilius Maro. Translated, Adorn'd with Sculpture, and Illustrated with Annotations by John Ogilby.* London, Printed by T. Warren for the author, 1654.
3   Ogilby's main reference was the work of the Spanish Jesuit Juan Luis de la Cerda (1560–1643), whose commentary on the *Aeneid* was first published at Lyon in 1612–17.
4   Francis Cleyn [Clein] (1582–1658) is the artist who conceived and drafted the majority of original images, which the other artists copied and executed as prints (Griffiths 1998, 186); there is one image for each eclogue, five for each book of the *Georgics*, and four to eight for each book of the *Aeneid*; the volume opens with a portrait of Ogilby, and a frontispiece image of Vergil reading his poems to Augustus.
5   Dryden's arguments include descriptions of, or references to, the illustrations with enough frequency to suggest that the poet often wrote his arguments to coincide with the illustrations of each book, a discussion that is beyond the scope of this essay.
6   Except where noted, all translations of Vergil are Ogilby's, taken from the 1654 edition.
7   The idea of "speaking pictures" is drawn from the title of M. Bath's work, *Speaking Pictures: English Emblem Books and Renaissance Culture* (1994); see also Daly (1998, especially 158–86).

FURTHER READING

Three excellent diachronic studies of illustrations of Vergil include: Kallendorf (2001); Pasquier (1992); and Rabb (1960). Leach's comparative study (1982) is the most comprehensive on the

Cleyn illustrations. The only full-length biography of John Ogilby is van Eerde (1976). Frost's commentary in the California Dryden (1987) is the most comprehensive discussion of the Tonson/Dryden relationship, though Barnard (2000) explores the subscription enterprise and patron list in greater detail. Visual culture in the seventeenth century is a broad field. Two very useful studies of the Renaissance emblem are: Bath (1994); and Daly (1998). For the European broadsheet and the history of comics see Kunzle (1973). On book illustration one should begin with Harthan (1997), which contains a discussion of Cleyn, Hollar, Ogilby, and other contemporaries and is a useful introduction as well; and Griffiths (1998), who has a chapter devoted to Ogilby and his contemporary, William Dugdale. Benesch (1943) remains an insightful introduction to book illustration from the seventeenth century.

CHAPTER TWENTY ONE

Empire and Exile
Vergil in Romantic Art

David Blayney Brown

In 1779 the English painter Joseph Wright of Derby exhibited the first of six versions of one of his most popular pictures, *Virgil's Tomb, with the Figure of Silius Italicus* (private collection). As the painter's educated audience knew, often from personal experience, the poet's supposed tomb on a hillside above Posillipo was one of the most venerated sites of the Grand Tour (Trapp 1986a, b); and even if they were unable to read Vergil in the original Latin, most would have known John Dryden's translation of the epitaph that Vergil, according to tradition, had written for himself which so aptly summed up his literary career and its enduring appeal: "I sing Flocks, Tillage, Heroes." In this particular version of his composition, Wright included one of Vergil's early admirers, Silius Italicus, himself an epic poet who had also been consul under Nero before retiring to the country near Naples; he is shown reciting his idol's verses, as he did each year on the poet's birthday. Wright's is a neoclassical vision, secure in its assumption of classical values and prototypes, but it hints also at Romantic hero-worship, the mysteries of creative inspiration (though Silius proved a poor imitator: Radice 1963, 3, 7: 91) and, by its moonlight and clouds, the otherworldly realms into which Vergil took his readers.

A decade later, the French Revolution would unleash events that cut off Italy at least from British travelers for more than fifteen years, leaving them only vicarious experience of the actual places associated with Vergil's poetry or the man himself; J.M.W. Turner, for example, was unable to pay homage at the tomb at Posillipo until 1819. But for a generation imbued with the value of historical associations this proved to matter less than might have been expected. It simply transferred its attention to home territory, finding Vergilian or post-Vergilian associations there instead. This resulted in a revival of interest in the pastoral that flowed alongside the Romantic passion for nature. Meanwhile the Napoleonic occupation of Italy had encouraged a fresh outbreak of Vergilianism in France – a cultural appropriation reminiscent of that of Greece by ancient Rome, and by Vergil himself of Homer. For history painters, Vergil remained an iconic source, recommended by Jacques-Louis David to his French students in Rome or Paris and Joshua Reynolds and Henry Fuseli to the young men of

London's Royal Academy. When Reynolds and Fuseli painted the death of Dido from book 4 of the *Aeneid*, they offered emblematic examples of academic history but also exploded them by their intense depiction of anguish and suffering. If there was a risk here to Vergil's canonical position, it was one of subversion, experienced more strongly still when Fuseli turned another famous passage, describing the underworld's ivory gates through which Aeneas passes under the delusion of false dreams, into an excuse for an obscene fantasy of female masturbation. And this was not long after Thomas Wharton, in a history of English poetry, had reprimanded even Dante for obtruding "Gothic and extravagant innovations" and "grotesque and fantastic circumstances" on Vergil's vision of Hell (Toynbee 1909, 1: 283–96). So fast were the times and taste changing and darkening that it might be wondered how Vergil could hold his place, yet in fact he proved peculiarly suggestive to the Romantic mind and relevant to contemporary historical trends.

The key to this lay in Vergil's variety. On the one hand was the historian-poet of the *Aeneid*, the supreme patriotic narrative of empire and nation-building that nevertheless contained within itself the story of fallen Troy and the foreboding of Rome's destruction of Carthage. At the time of the collapse of the *ancien régime*, Britain's loss of the American colonies and the coming of independence, the wars with revolutionary France and the rise and later the fall of Napoleon and ensuing century of British hegemony, Vergil's epic was rich in parallels. They were such as to ensure that the story of artistic responses to him during this period is largely a French and British one, as it is in this essay. But of course the *Aeneid* is not only about public affairs; it is also a very human story of penetrating psychological insight, reaching into the heart and the unconscious mind. Its superhero is made vulnerable by his passions and prone to dreams and visitations. Then on the other hand were the pastorals, the *Georgics* and the *Eclogues*. Vergil's bucolic world of produce and plenty had given its classic authority to ideas of rural life and good husbandry for centuries. In the seventeenth it had inspired the landscape paintings of Claude Lorrain, in the eighteenth it had helped feed concepts of the picturesque and inspire theorists like William Gilpin (Roethlisberger 1961). But in the war-torn beginnings of the nineteenth it took on a more practical edge, as land was put to new uses to feed armies and the home front (Payne 1993). And then again there was Vergil the man, active in public life but also withdrawn, who lost his precious country estates in civil war and mourned them in pastorals written back in the city. Above all, Vergil struck the Romantics for his powers of imagination. He was reinvented as a prototype of the ideal artist at the very time that the artist was reinvented as the perfect human type. In this light, he survives and transcends what is perhaps the more familiar narrative, driven mainly by German critics, that has elevated Greek over Roman, the primitive above the sophisticated and thus brought Homer to the fore among ancient poets.

Most if not all the ingredients of this rich mixture are to be found through the long career of J.M.W. Turner, who first painted a Vergilian subject in 1798 and chose the *Aeneid* for his last exhibits at the Academy in 1850. The 1798 picture, *Aeneas and the Sibyl, Lake Avernus* (Tate, London; Plate 3) holds a mirror to Turner's hard-won classical education and to the restrictions and opportunities of the time. It was intended for a patron, Richard Colt Hoare, whose estate at Stourhead in Wiltshire had been laid out by his father as a Vergilian landscape, in the style of Claude, picturing Aeneas' journey to found Rome as a parallel to his own establishment of a great banking dynasty (Woodbridge 1970). Colt Hoare was of a more literal mind than his father, interested in local topography and antiquarianism, and he had brought Turner to Stourhead to draw the grounds. But their effect on the young painter can easily be imagined. Hoare lent Turner a drawing of Lake Avernus that he had made on the spot during his Grand Tour before the war, and Turner adopted it as the background for Aeneas' fateful meeting with the Cumaean Sibyl, Deiphobë, in book 6 of the *Aeneid*; the Sibyl's words, *Procul, o procul este, profani*, were inscribed on Stourhead's Temple of Flora. Whether Turner was tutored in this pictorial scheme by Colt Hoare, or devised it himself to display the exponential leap in his education inspired by the patron is unknown; what can be guessed is that he now saw himself, like Aeneas and the Hoare family in his legendary footsteps, setting out on a great creative adventure – this was his first classical subject in the manner of Claude and (as the more immediate stimulus) his British imitator, Richard Wilson.

For Turner, Vergil proved a fertile source of themes for historic landscape, and a link to Claude who had painted many Vergilian pictures (Nicholson 1990, 277–94; Finley 1999, 63–81). The artist owed nothing to what were currently the most famous illustrations of a classical text, John Flaxman's outlines of Homer. But Turner had a real appreciation of the poetry too, which he read in translation. In another version of this early composition, painted in 1815 (Yale Center for British Art, New Haven), the narrative and attributes are made more emphatic, following a closer reading of Vergil's text; the Sibyl holds aloft the branch from a sacred tree that Aeneas must offer to Proserpine, and near him worshippers sacrifice at an altar as he himself will do before starting out on his quest. When we survey Turner's career, we see that a sacrifice to tradition was necessary before he could emerge fully himself. By now Turner had developed a broad and deep love of poetry and had written a good deal of his own, so was accustomed to the layering of poetic imagery and suggestion. In the spirit of poetry, he was an interpreter, not an illustrator, and in keeping with Vergil's role as guide to the imagination, he subsumed his experience of Vergil into that of the wider classical world and then into his own. In a complex work of 1806, *The Goddess of Discord choosing the Apple of Contention in the Garden of the Hesperides* (Tate, London), he sublimated his concerns about the current war with Napoleonic France and professional rivalries within the Royal Academy (as well as between the Academy and the newly formed British Institution where he exhibited the picture) into a fantasia on the origins of the Trojan Wars. Insofar as there was a classical source for this picture, it was Homer, but Vergil is invoked too by its forebodings of the coming wars, the falls of Troy and Carthage. For John Ruskin it was to suggest even more, beginning a great cycle of pictures whose real theme was the fall of modern England.

Turner's artistic model was a picture by Nicolas Poussin, *Landscape with Polyphemus*, then as now in Russia but accessible in an engraving. But his vision of the Hesperidean garden was Alpine, based on memories of a visit to Switzerland during the peace of Amiens in 1802, and it was dreamt up by the Thames, where he had several out-of-town retreats from early in the century. Two sketchbooks used there around 1805 (Tate, London) were given the name "Hesperides" (not necessarily by Turner himself) because they include drawings for this and other pictures and many in which he looked at the river and its banks and turned them into an antique world peopled by gods and heroes. Studies from nature from this time are full of beauty. But perhaps it was the war, the danger that the Thames valley could be overrun by French troops at any moment, or even Turner's own complicated emotional life, that lent his drawings a melancholy tinge. He brooded on losses and partings of lovers, fathers and sons. In another sketchbook used by the Thames he explored related themes from book 8 of the *Aeneid*, Aeneas' idyllic interlude with the aged Evander in his new city on the Palatine and Evander's gift of his son Pallas to join Aeneas and fight for him in his place; Pallas will be killed and returned to his father wrapped in materials embroidered by Dido (*Aen.* 11.72–5). Also from this time dates Turner's long preoccupation with the romance of Dido and Aeneas themselves, from book 4, and his early studies for the picture exhibited at the Royal Academy in 1814 (Tate, London); he chose the dawn hunting party laid on by Dido for her visitor, outside her city of Carthage, before the storm that drives them to shelter and consummate their passion (*Aen.* 4.129–59, 160–72).

Turner's *Dido and Aeneas* (Tate, London; Plate 4) appeared before the London public in the same year as Wordsworth composed his Vergilian imitation *Laodamia*, in which the bereaved heroine is shown a vision of her slain husband, the Thessalian commander Protesilaus, the first Greek to die on the beach at Troy. Like Wordsworth's poem, the picture was a historical project, invoking the history of its own art by imitation of Claude and Vergil through his British admirers. Turner probably already owned the folio Vergil recorded in his library, but although he copied lines from the *Eclogues* in Latin in a sketchbook about 1809 he hardly knew the language and read Vergil instead in Robert Anderson's thirteen-volume *Works of the British Poets* (London, 1795), the last two volumes of which contained translations by British poets of the major classical writers including Dryden's versions of the *Aeneid*, *Eclogues*, and *Georgics*. With *Dido and Aeneas* he quoted Dryden's lines:

> When next the sun his rising light displays
> And gilds the world below with purple rays,
> The Queen, Aeneas, and the Tyrian Court
> Shall to the shady woods for sylvan games resort
> (*Aen.* 4.164–7)

If Turner's rustic Thames became a Vergilian world from his delvings into Anderson, it was for the same reason an Ovidian and Homeric one; but it was also Augustan, and not only heroic and epic but pastoral, mediated through his readings of Alexander Pope and James Thomson. The Augustan pastoral, with its rhyming couplets and benign view of nature at the service of man, was what he aspired to when he came to write poetry himself. There is a great deal of it in his notebooks and sketchbooks from this time, and not only the Augustans but also Vergilian characters like the shepherd Menalcas have walk-on parts in it (Wilton and Mallord Turner 1990). This too was a historical exercise, like his adaptations from Claude or Poussin, and on first reading it sits oddly with his painted dramas of awesome nature, which seem so modern. But it was one mode of many, just as, when determining the categories of landscape art itself for a series of didactic prints, the *Liber Studiorum*, he distinguished the pastoral from its epic or elevated class, and from the historic, mountainous, and other categories too. He seems to have felt that this eighteenth-century value system, which reached back to antiquity, was under threat and ought to be preserved. It was because Turner regarded Pope as the "British Maro" that he made such a fuss about the demolition of the poet's famous villa and garden at Twickenham by the philistine Baroness Howe, painting a picture and composing many angry verses on the subject.

Turner's first ideas for the seaport setting of *Dido building Carthage: or the Rise of the Carthaginian Empire* exhibited at the Royal Academy in 1815 (National Gallery, London), and his grandest classical picture thus far, belong to the same time as his plans for *Dido and Aeneas*. This picture too was given a reference to the *Aeneid*, to book 1. It depicts the queen presiding over the construction of her new city (494–519), but Turner also inscribed the picture with the name of her murdered husband Sychaeus, a reminder of the crime that had forced her to flee Tyre for Libya and a portent of retribution to come – her own betrayal by Aeneas. Turner wanted the picture to be his shroud, thinking perhaps of Dido's fateful wrappings for the slain Pallas. In 1817 he followed it with *The Decline of the Carthaginian Empire* (Tate, London), showing the city brought low by its enemy, Rome, and forced to surrender its children and weapons. Although not treated or discussed as a pair at the time, the pictures chimed with contemporary moralizing on the rise and fall of empires that had been revived by the collapse of Napoleon, though it is arguable which side, France or the Allies, might be identified with Rome or Carthage; the pictures could be as much a warning to the victors against complacency as an allegory of a just defeat. They suggest that such historical cycles are inevitable and forever repeated – as in Dido's dying curse of perpetual war between Rome and Carthage – rooted as they are in human frailty.

In these two pictures, Turner moved from the Vergilian Carthage of Dido to consider its later history in the light of her prophecy. He had already painted the Carthaginian Hannibal, crossing the Alps on his way to invade Italy, and in Rome in 1828 he painted the captive general Regulus, blinded by the sun as punishment for deliberately failing to negotiate an exchange of prisoners with the Carthaginians. Around the same time he paid an oblique tribute to Vergil by painting the hill town of Praeneste, mentioned in book 7 of the *Aeneid*. *Palestrina – Composition* (Tate, London) is an image of ruined beauty, a ghost, as if ancient Rome and the flames of passion and war described by Vergil have burned low and left only embers imprinted on the landscape of Italy. It is built around a double perspective, on the left the town with its ruined Temple of Fortune, on the right an avenue of trees and shady pasture evoking both the Vergil of the pastorals and the agriculture on which the region now depended. In an epigraph of his own, Turner wrote of Hannibal looking down, "with eagle-eye," on "Rome as his victim," moving the Carthaginian's vantage-point here from the Alban Hills. In 1834, Turner reworked his earlier compositions of Lake Avernus and the Sibyl yet again in *The Golden Bough* (Tate, London). In this third version, sparkling mist hovers over the lake, giving it a magical air, and Turner added the dancing figures of the Fates. The title now came from Christopher Pitt's translation of the *Aeneid* (London, 1790). Turner had by now assimilated Vergil, but his primacy among his poetic models, along with Claude among painters, was shown by his four last exhibits at the Royal Academy in 1850, a suite on the theme of Aeneas' stay at Carthage, affair with Dido, and abandonment of her to fulfill his destiny in Italy. In the three surviving pictures (Tate, London) the story, from book 4 of the *Aeneid*, is almost dissolved in fog and light and Turner's shivering paint, while the epigraphs are no longer from Vergil or his translators but by Turner himself: extracts from his own would-be epic, *The Fallacies of Hope*. He had been working on this, and quoting it, for years, but it never existed as a complete entity; rather, it reflected the fragmentary, aphoristic tendency in Romantic writing as much as the historical epics to which he aspired – a contradiction he was never to reconcile.

In France, the conceptual and stylistic transformations in Turner's treatment of Vergil and his works are better seen across a range of artists than within a single outstanding painter. The exception is Anne-Louis Girodet, whose approach reflected first his devotion and then his rejection of his teacher David. Unlike Turner, Girodet read Vergil in Latin, and was to translate his works. But like Turner, he went on to write poetry himself, in imitation of the antique – poetry whose overly respectful historicism has tended to obscure or negate the important ideas it expresses, notably of his creative identity as an artist in *Le Peintre*, and contrasts with the innovations he made as an artist. For this painter-poet, illustrating Vergil, along with Anacreon and other ancient poets, became almost an obsession (Fumaroli 2005, 53–79). His first sustained work on Vergil, with his fellow student in David's studio, François Gérard, was a set of illustrations for a luxury edition that David agreed to supervise for the publisher Pierre Didot, who advertised it in 1797 as "a monument worthy of the glory of the Prince of Poets." Illustrated editions of the classics, whether of antiquity or French literature, were new to France, where there was nothing comparable to, for example, the illustrations to Shakespeare published by Boydell or Flaxman's illustrations to Homer.

David may well have hoped their work on Didot's Vergil might sustain the *esprit de corps* of his *atelier* of young followers. It might also have played some part in establishing Davidian classicism as the official style of the new France arising from the Revolution. But Girodet's genuine passion for ancient poetry can be explained as a symptom of alienation, a refuge or retreat from a fallen society that no longer deserved the vocation of the true painter or poet of history. In the designs for Didot and his many later Vergil subjects undertaken on his own account and published after his death, notably for the *Aeneid* but also for the *Georgics*, he could leave the world of "events" for that of the imagination, or pursue the chimera of a golden age. He was particularly susceptible to Vergil's evocations of dream. One of his first designs, of Aeneas' household gods appearing to him in his sleep, was an occult nocturne, with mysterious vapors encircling the hero. Later, he depicted another of Aeneas' night visions, the ghost of Hector. Most vivid of all is his rendering of the "false dreams" conjured up to Aeneas by the demons of the underworld as he is led from the ivory gates of sleep by the Sibyl Deiphobë – grotesques worthy of Fuseli. So vivid and effective are Girodet's realizations that they have been compared to comic strips. He was deeply versed in the text and prepared to interpret it freely or combine incidents to draw out its meaning. But he was also highly subjective, exploring an inner world, probing the psyche, as far as the irrational or extreme, and his Aeneas is a creature of Romantic melancholy. Even his technical approach to Vergil underwent a transformation, his later drawings losing the tight control of the Didot designs and displaying instead a febrile, nervous energy.

In a particularly frenzied drawing (Louvre, Paris), which perhaps defeated the lithographers who translated his designs after his death, Girodet conflated several passages in book 2 of the *Aeneid* to show the arrival of the Trojan horse outside Troy, that doomed city now "buried in wine and sleep" (*Aen.* 2.265). In a gloss on Vergil's text, he added the name of the horse's builder, Epeos, to its wooden withers. The Greeks' arrival is viewed from the perspective of the Trojans, through the columns of Priam's palace, its guards slumped in despair. If this vision of the last days of an empire suggests a contemporary parallel (in fact it is undated), Girodet had perhaps already drawn another from Gérard, his collaborator on the Didot project. The memory of Gérard's image of Aeneas carrying his father and son from the embers of Troy lies behind the similar rescue motif in Girodet's *Scene from a Deluge* of 1806 (Louvre, Paris). Girodet distanced his subject from the Bible, claiming instead that it depicted a "convulsion of nature" and comparing it to one that occurred later in 1806 at Goldau in Switzerland. This was disingenuous, for its portrayal of victims of forces greater than themselves struggling in a wasted land could hardly fail to evoke traumas closer to home in France. Girodet's evidently jaundiced view of these makes it unlikely that he would have endorsed another translation of Vergilian imagery, the reappearance of his Vergil crowned by the Muses from his Didot frontispiece as Napoleon on his Imperial Throne, in a portrait by Jean-Auguste-Dominique Ingres (Musée de l'Armée, Paris).

Vergil himself was coopted into Napoleonic propaganda in 1812, when Ingres painted the poet reading the *Aeneid* before Augustus and Livia as part of a decorative scheme for the bedroom of General François de Miollis, the French lieutenant-governor of Napoleonic Rome, in his official residence in the Villa Aldobrandini. As governor of Mantua, near Vergil's birthplace, the general had already drained a swamp to create a piazza and erected a column in the poet's honor (Auréas 1961). The program for his Roman apartment, which Ingres reworked for the Paris Salon, exploited the parallels between Roman and Napoleonic history, but unequivocally from the point of view of the conqueror and the inheritor of empire; France was then the new Rome, not the future Troy. Within a few years, such bombast would look absurd. When Pierre-Narcisse Guérin painted *Aeneas recounting the Misfortunes of Troy to Dido* (Louvre, Paris) for the Salon of 1817, he produced a charming boudoir scene, softly and hazily lit. Aeneas lounges at ease, an elegant androgyne, his muscles grown flabby, emasculated by passion. Davidian classicism, along with the state that supported it, seems to be mutating before our eyes, but it would be several years before its rejection was complete. In 1822 the young Eugène Delacroix showed the way with his Salon sensation *The Barque of Dante* (Louvre, Paris), an early manifesto for the Romanticism of color, feeling, and creative heroism. On a fragile vessel tossed by waters churning with the writhing figures of the damned, borrowed from Théodore Géricault's *Raft of the Medusa* (Louvre, Paris) shown three years earlier, Vergil and Dante cross the Styx, poet guiding poet, while a city burns on the distant shore (*Inferno*, canto 8). Critics wondered if in post-Napoleonic, Restoration Paris, Delacroix had found it impossible to paint his own times. But his picture offered them a lesson, that in a world of turmoil art and imagination survive and inspire. On the advice of the painter Baron Gros, it was bought for the nation and put on display in the Luxembourg palace.

While at work on the picture, Delacroix had been "electrified" by passages from the *Divine Comedy* read by a friend in the original Italian. Two years after it was exhibited in Paris William Blake, in totally different circumstances in London, began his great project to illustrate Dante's *Divine Comedy*. The aging Blake was now a withdrawn and neglected figure, and a younger admirer, the artist John Linnell, gave him the task to revive him. Working on it until 1827, Blake made this the culmination of his career. It too required a vision of Vergil as artistic paradigm, guide and soulmate to Dante, but more complex, nuanced, and sustained over a series of tableaux as the poets move through Hell and Purgatory. Vergil is Imagination, the inspiration for Dante's Feeling. He wears blue, the color associated with Los, the ideal type of the artist in Blake's mythology. Both poets are graceful, sinuous figures whose elegant forms are contrasted to the visions of error and evil that they witness as they pass through Hell in the first designs for the *Inferno*. Their journey is realized through recognizable pictures of landscape and the seasons – pictures unique for Blake who otherwise avoided nature but convincing precisely because he regarded it as part of our fallen world, and that Coleridge described as "Topographical REALITY...Nature worse than CHAOS, a thousand delusive forms having reality *only* for the Passions, they excite" (Coleridge in Coburn and Harding 1973, 1: 450). At the outset (canto 3), Vergil leads Dante into an elemental world beyond the River Acheron, through the gates of a Hell whose circles are like continents, layered with mountains and filled with fire and ice (Tate, London; Plate 5). He has proposed a terrifying pilgrimage, but with the prospect of salvation. Throughout, Vergil points and explains. In a wintry wasteland, Arctic or Alpine, looming pillars that Dante sees as frozen towers are in fact primeval giants, imprisoned in ice (canto 31). Homer and his fellow Ancient Poets, on the other hand, are encountered in a lush valley, beneath trees in summer leaf (canto 4). But rather than shelter, the trees symbolize the poets' error and, like the rolling clouds above, divide them from the realm of the imagination. In another valley, Negligent Rulers are similarly huddled, but Dante and Vergil, and the poet Sordello who has brought them there, are set apart in a privileged space and can see angels hovering above the tree-tops (*Purgatorio*, canto 7).

Blake's imagery and narrative are, as always, self-interrogating. He was critical of all the ancient poets, whom he saw as compromised by their warlike age. In a rare print made separately about 1822, perhaps for circulation to friends, titled *On Homer's Poetry and on Virgil*, he declared that "It is the Classics...that desolate Europe with wars" and claimed that Vergil "says Let others study Art: Rome has somewhat better to do, namely War & Dominion." In reaction, we should "reverence The Word of God," but this too had been corrupted by its worldly followers. Blake was equally disgusted by the revenge and punishment implicit in Dante's text, and by Dante himself whom he thought complicit with the Roman church yet also dismissed as an atheist and "mere politician busied ab[ou]t this world." As a historical figure, Vergil speaks with experience even as he appeals to the imagination, and the great statue of the "Course of Human History" in Mount Ida that he describes to Dante is one of tyranny, flawed and tragic, made of potter's clay as well as precious metals and rent with tears (*Inferno*, canto 14). As Blake well knew, Vergil's life and work exemplified both the epic and the bucolic, the active and the contemplative. Thus Vergil remains awake and on watch as, having passed through the flames of Purgatory, Dante and the Roman poet Statius rest asleep on a rocky stair, and Dante dreams of Leah and Rachel, the active and contemplative types of the Old Testament (*Purgatorio*, canto 27). Vergil may have been absolved from some of Blake's skepticism because Blake prized pastoral as the highest form of poetry. But how Blake truly saw the Roman poet, and whether Vergil is really qualified to lead Dante to a full redemption, is left ambiguous. It is inevitable in the *Divine Comedy* that the poets must part, provoking the disciple to a bout of desperate loneliness. At the River Lethe they bid farewell, leaving Dante poised between Vergil and Statius and the prospect of an Earthly Paradise in which Beatrice approaches in a dazzling procession (*Purgatorio*, canto 30). She will now take over from Vergil the project of Dante's salvation that she has hitherto entrusted to the older poet.

Blake had entered Vergil's pastoral world a few years earlier, when he made a set of woodcuts for Ambrose Philips' "imitation" of the first eclogue for Dr. Robert Thornton's edition of the *Pastorals*. Vergil's original touches the poet's experience closely, for it was born of his wistfulness at the loss of his country estates in civil war and enforced return to the city, and sublimated it in the dialogue between the herdsmen Meliboeus and Tityrus, the one driven off his lands, the other, having appealed to the authorities in Rome, being allowed to stay. Philips' version simplified the text with differently named characters. Thornton aimed to attract new schoolboy readers to these classics, but Blake's approach was typically personal and layered with equivocation, emphasizing the contrasting psychological states of Philips' two shepherds, Thenot and Colinet, whose resigned contentment born of long experience, and youthful restlessness and wanderlust undermine the myth that the rural life is necessarily a happy one. Colinet is full of teenage angst, unhappy in the fields, a rolling stone drawn away to Cambridge and London, alienated and mocked; he is born in a "hapless hour of time." Blake shows him as a drooping, listless figure, cut off from flocks and fields. Wise Thenot takes him in, feeds him, and invites him to share the tending of his sheep, but somehow it is Colinet's condition that sticks in the modern mind. It was typical of Blake to empathize with this rather than rely on a more obvious comparison with the older man, and paradoxically, the young shepherd's detachment may have echoed his own in old age, a kind of absence from the world forced upon him by the pursuit of his art. The notion of Vergil's political exile, which returned him to town against his will, stirred the Romantic mind because it chimed with ideas of the artist as a creature apart, proud but persecuted. When Turner painted the ups and downs of life and reputation, it was Vergil's fellow Romans, Ovid and Cicero, that he presented instead, the one banished from Rome in a picture of 1838 (private collection) and the other at his villa at the zenith of his career in a work of the following year (Rothschild Collection, Ascott). But the message to be drawn from these reversals of fate is the same; fame, like empire, is fickle, and the inner life is our salvation. Exile and withdrawal were thus the proper condition of the creative artist.

No artist of the period was more self-consciously withdrawn than the young Samuel Palmer, who retreated in the decade after 1824/5 to the Kentish village of Shoreham, surrounded by his friends and fellow "Ancients" under the motto "Poetry and Sentiment." His mentor and "Interpreter" was none other than Blake, whom he saw as Blake saw Dante and Delacroix painted Dante and Vergil, as the creative spur. At first at least, he may not have entirely understood his idol, whose messages he was inclined to simplify. He loved Blake's Dante illustrations and especially the Vergil woodcuts, which he called "the most intense gems of bucolic sentiment in the whole range of art." As he described: "I happened first to think of their sentiment. They are visions of little dells, and nooks, and corners of paradise; models of the exquisitest pitch of intense poetry.... There is in all such a mystic and dreamy glimmer as penetrates and kindles the inmost soul, and gives complete and unreserved delight, unlike the gaudy daylight of this world. They are like all that wonderful artist's works the drawing aside of the fleshy curtain, and the glimpse which all the most holy, studious saints and sages have enjoyed, that rest which remaineth to the people of God" (from a lost sketchbook of 1823/4, quoted by Palmer 1892, 15–16). This missed Blake's little psychodrama between the shepherds altogether, and turned the series into a Christian allegory. The visual impact of its archaic simplicity and chiaroscuro can be seen in Palmer's youthful masterpiece, a set of sepia landscapes executed in 1825 (Ashmolean Museum, Oxford). Palmer was a great reader and the sepias also acknowledged his favorite writers, with epigraphs from Vergil, the Bible, Shakespeare, and what he thought was Chaucer (but was in fact John Lydgate). He inscribed the mount of *A Rustic Scene* (Fig. 21.1), depicting a plowman at work in the early morning, with Vergil's lines on plowing and sowing at the autumn equinox (*Geo.* 1.208–11). It is a vision of harmony between man and nature, recreating Vergil's message of good husbandry. Palmer gave this too a religious aspect and, unsurprisingly, was among those who believed that Vergil's fourth "messianic" eclogue had been a prophecy of the birth of Christ. Unsurprisingly again, Palmer missed the ambivalence underlying Blake's rendering of the natural world. Adopting the tree that shelters Blake's Ancient Poets from Imagination in his Dante design for another sepia from the 1825 set, *The Skirts of a Wood*, Palmer turned it into the inspiration for the music of a piping shepherd – itself the source of the life of the soul.

Was Palmer naïve, or were these inversions of Blake's complicated messages entirely knowing and deliberate? We should not discount Palmer's own convictions; different, but no less passionate. Of the *Georgics* he told his younger son in 1866 that they "teach the wisdom of all life and the mysteries of intellectual discipline under the veil of agriculture…so that the veil itself is glorious…the diamond is set in gold" (letter to A.H. Palmer, October 14, 1866, in Lister 1974, 2: 749–50). As an artist he aimed to express enduring truths rather than contemporary realities, and did not consider that painting nature need mean naturalism or engaging with the lives of Victorian agricultural workers. He was a nostalgic, appalled by the spread of suburbia (though he spent many years living within its sights), and could ask in 1862, "Ah where is the Vergilian muse? At the railway whistle she fled forever" (letter to William Linnell, January 29, 1862, in Lister 1974, 2: 636). Yet, responding to Vergil's promise of a returning Golden Age, he aimed to recover her by his own efforts of imagination and memory, and as translator and illustrator. Inspired by his son Thomas More's promise as a classical scholar and then after his death as a memorial, he made his own translation of the

Figure 21.1 Samuel Palmer (1805–81), *A Rustic Scene* (1825). Ink and sepia with gum, varnished, on paper 17.9 x 23.5 cm.

Eclogues and illustrations for them that he planned to reproduce as etchings; only one was completed at his death in 1881, and the rest were finished by his surviving son Alfred Herbert and published with *An English Version of the Eclogues of Vergil* posthumously in 1883. With another series illustrating Milton's pastorals this was the climax of his career, summing up his feelings for the literature he loved and his memories of Shoreham and of Blake, whom he would ideally have chosen as his illustrator. While indulging himself he was also altruistic, intending that "those who do not read them [the *Eclogues*] in the original should have some version from which the pastoral essence has not quite evaporated" (letter to P.G. Hamerton, January 26, 1872, in Lister 1974, 2: 835).

It was the critic P.G. Hamerton who encouraged Palmer to illustrate the *Eclogues*, believing that his translation was unpublishable by itself. Hamerton's verdict has found echoes in a tendency to belittle Palmer's "English Version," which was in fact an immense undertaking on which he staked his reputation. Like Turner and Girodet, he believed in the natural affinity of art and letters. Like both these artists, he was in awe of earlier writers. He was more critical than Turner of the Augustans and their own versions of pastoral – the "Strephons and Chloes of the coffee house poets" – preferring the originals and his own translations of them, as Girodet did (Palmer was helped by another keen classical scholar, his friend and fellow artist Edward Calvert). But like Turner and Girodet again, his own writing tended to be old-fashioned, if not archaic in style. He rendered the *Eclogues* in rhyming couplets. At the same time, he tidied up any features of Vergil's original that might offend Victorian readers, such as the love between male shepherds in the second eclogue and in the third (8–9). Vergil did *not* write:

> 'Tis gentle Phillis I love best of all,
> For when I left, some tears began to fall;
> "Adieu!" She said, while her sweet tresses fell,
> About me, "Charming boy, a long farewell!"

Yet when Palmer was able most closely to empathize with Vergil's experience and sentiment, and bring together text and image, the results are moving. His own lost youth and the rapture of rural discovery that he had felt at Shoreham are recovered as Meliboeus finds Tityrus beneath his beech tree surveying his patrimony and cries out (*Ecl.* 1.46–7):

> O fortunate old man!
> Then those ancestral fields are yours again;
> And wide enough for you.

Also from the first eclogue (80–1), Palmer chose to illustrate his version of the description of a traveler's simple meal that must have recalled his Shoreham fare:

> Ripe apples are our supper, cream unstirr'd,
> Boil'd chestnuts, plenty of the sweeten'd curd.

Other passages and their illustrations are agricultural, others pagan-classical, as when in the sixth eclogue (13.4):

> The young Mnasylus came
> With Chromis to a cave, and chanced to find,
> In a deep sleep Silenus there reclined

or the tenth (26.7):

> Pan came,
> Arcadian tetrarch ever good;
> I myself saw him, glowing as he stood,
> With wall-wort berries, crimson'd like the West.

Rendering the "messianic" fourth (23), Palmer's imagery and words merge beautifully in a vision of all nature exploding into life; cows are milked and watered, bees swarm at the hive, fruit dangles from the trees, and

> Thy very cradle quickens, osiers loose
> To tendrils turn, with flowery shoots diffuse.

Palmer's translation and illustrations were published with an essay he had been mulling over for years – "Some Observations on the Country and on Rural Poetry"

(Palmer 1883; rpt. Abley 1985, 151–66). This was doubtless intended to be a ringing defense of the arts, his own especially, but is more notable for its resignation. It was never written to introduce the *Eclogues* but matches their sophisticated urban nostalgia perfectly. Beginning by recalling a friend mocked for sitting down under a tree and reciting them aloud, Palmer pities city-dwellers who have no time for poetry and are immersed in a world of "facts he believed and mutton" and the morning papers. Nevertheless, he goes on to admit that their urban condition is now inevitable for the majority and might drive them back to rural poetry that "presents to fancy what is lost to sight." He now spoke from experience, just as he believed Vergil did in the *Eclogues*, where great themes emerge while recalling the country rather than by describing the activity of "camps and courts." Summarizing the poet's experience, Palmer concludes, "Nay, in Virgil's hands, the theme itself, the subject of a pastoral too, rises above the old heroic argument and leaves it far below: the fourth and sixth Eclogues indicate events – the creation of the universe and the final restitution, compared with which, the fall of Troy, nay, even the founding of Rome, are but an interlude." And in a final gloss, "Virgil sang of arms, but of arms and the man; the pious and all-enduring man Aeneas; and of much besides.... In the sixth Eclogue, when Cynthius touches his ear, he apprehends the inner sense of the admonition not to exchange the crook for the falchion; on this he prunes his wing for a loftier flight, and leaves the battle fields to the dogs and vultures."

FURTHER READING

Abley, M. (1985). *The Parting Light: Selected Writings of Samuel Palmer*. London.

Aurias, H. (1961). *Général de Napoléon: Miollis*. Paris.

Bain, I, Chambers, D., and Wilton, A. (1977). *The Wood Engravings of William Blake for Thornton's "Virgil."* London.

Bellenger, S., ed. (2005). *Girodet 1767–1824*. Paris.

Brown, D.B. (2001). *Romanticism*. London.

Brown, D.B. (2005). "'To fancy what is lost to sight': Palmer and Literature," in W. Vaughan, E.E. Barker, and C. Harrison, *Samuel Palmer 1805–1881: Vision and Landscape*. London.

Coburn, K. and Harding, A.H., eds. (1973). *Notebooks of Samuel Taylor Coleridge*. Princeton.

Finley, G. (1999). *Angel in the Sun: Turner's Vision of History*. Ithaca.

Honour, H. (1991). *Romanticism*. London.

Klonsky, M. (1980). *Blake's Dante: The Complete Illustrations to the "Divine Comedy."* London.

Lightbown, R. (1978). *Samuel Palmer: A Vision Recaptured: The Complete Etchings and the Paintings for Milton and for Virgil*. London.

Lister, R., ed. (1974). *The Letters of Samuel Palmer*. Oxford.

Nicholson, K. (1990). *Turner's Classical Landscapes: Myth and Meaning*. Princeton.

Palmer, A.H., ed. (1892). *The Life and Letters of Samuel Palmer*. London.

Payne, C. (1993). *Toil and Plenty: Images of Agricultural Landscape in England 1781–1890*. New Haven.

Radice, B. (1963). *The Letters of the Younger Pliny*. London.

Roe, A.S. (1953). *Blake's Illustrations to the Divine Comedy*. Princeton.

Roethlisberger, M. (1961). *Claude Lorrain: The Paintings.* New Haven.

Toynbee, P. (1909). *Dante in English Literature, from Chaucer to Cary.* London.

Trapp, J.B. (1986a). "The Grave of Virgil," *Journal of the Warburg and Courtauld Institutes* 47: 1–31.

Trapp, J.B. (1986b). "Virgil and the Monuments," *PVS* 18: 1–17.

Vaughan, W. (1991). *Romantic Art.* London.

Wilton, A. and Mallord Turner, R. (1990). *Painting and Poetry: Turner's "Verse Book" and his Work of 1804–1812.* London.

Woodbridge, K. (1970). *Landscape and Antiquity: Aspects of English Culture at Stourhead.* Oxford.

CHAPTER TWENTY TWO

Laocoons

Glenn W. Most

Vergil's Laocoon

The queen has asked the wanderer to speak the unspeakable, to recount the fall of Troy that has become celebrated in world literature. All fall silent and stare up at Aeneas in expectation. The whole episode of Laocoon, at the beginning of book 2 of the *Aeneid*, is constructed around the oppositions of silence and sound, sight and concealment, height and depth, expectation and surprise, curiosity and pity, enigmas and their interpretation and misinterpretation.

Aeneas must explain to his listeners, and to himself, how it is that the Trojans could possibly have chosen to bring their destruction upon themselves by breaching the impregnable circle of their walls and conveying into the center of their city the Wooden Horse constructed by the Greeks; his story interweaves the limited viewpoint of an immediate participant in the events with the omniscient perspective of an impersonal narrator possessing information that Aeneas himself could only have obtained much later, if at all, thereby creating a deep narratorial pathos that reflects and enhances the profoundly dramatic pathos of the contents of the story he tells.

He begins reluctantly, thereby inflaming all the more his listeners' curiosity to hear his pitiable tale, but then consents to reveal its beginning: a visible island, Tenedos, concealing the Greek fleet; the Trojans who can finally burst forth from the town to gaze like tourists, in silent astonishment, upon the monuments of the long Greek siege which seem almost to have become a *lieu de mémoire* already for themselves; and, focusing all their attention, the hugely looming enigma of the Wooden Horse. What does it mean? How is it to be interpreted? And what in consequence is to be done with it? The Trojans are divided – when suddenly Laocoon appears, rushing down blazing with fury from the still unburning citadel, to warn them against accepting any Greek gifts and to suggest that this one conceals Greek warriors in its hidden depths or has been devised to spy upon their houses from above. He climaxes his tirade by hurling a spear at the Horse, causing an echo from its hollow interior. But Laocoon's intervention, far from resolving the interpretive difficulties, only exacerbates them: is his forcefully stated view correct and will the Trojans understand the echoing reverberation as proof that the Horse conceals something potentially dangerous within it, or is he launching a hubristic attack upon a dedicatory offering that is holy to the gods? Breathless, we await the answer.

Instead, suddenly, at this moment of the greatest perplexity and intensity, a single, initially nameless Greek appears, Sinon, bound and surrounded by Trojans. We, outside Aeneas' story, together with the Aeneas who is telling it, can recognize in Sinon a figure for the other treacherous Greek warriors, outnumbered and constricted in the Horse but nonetheless, and indeed all the more, lethal; but the Trojans, within his story, presumably together with the Aeneas about whom it is being told, see in him an emblem of pathos, an epitome of their own sufferings at the hands of the Greeks. Sinon's narration is the negative projection and foil for Aeneas' own, which incorporates and enlarges it: both tales appeal for pity, recount sufferings, invoke the gods, and rail at Greek duplicity – with the small but essential difference that Sinon is himself a duplicitous Greek while Aeneas is a pious Trojan. Sinon's brilliant eloquence, by telling the Trojans exactly what they want to hear, grants him the same full mastery over his compassionate audience within Aeneas' tale as Aeneas' own artistry accords him over his listeners ancient and modern (who perhaps do not wonder enough about the dangers of pity and of self-pity): on the purely human level of fallacious rhetoric, Sinon secures full assent, the Horse is accepted, and the Trojans' doom is sealed.

The episode could perfectly well have ended here – if Vergil had jumped from line 198 directly to line 234, no one would ever have noticed. Instead he chooses to astonish us with a third *coup de théâtre*: suddenly, while Laocoon, chosen by lot to be priest of Neptune, is sacrificing a bull to the god, two huge snakes appear, swimming across the water from Tenedos (where the Greek ships are hiding); first they kill Laocoon's two young sons and then they slay him while he roars hideously like a sacrificial bull that has escaped a misaimed axe; their work done, they slip away to conceal themselves beneath the feet of the cult statue of Athena. To us, the meaning is clear: the gods have decided that Troy must fall, and the sacrifice they require is not a bull of gratitude for Neptune but human victims of expiation for Athena; the snakes that come from Tenedos to kill Laocoon and his sons prefigure precisely the Greek boats that all too soon will make the very same voyage with results even more terrifyingly catastrophic. But the Trojans read the sign differently: they see it as a divine punishment for Laocoon's sacrilegious spearthrow, and they hasten to bring the Horse into the city before the gods' anger can aim at them too. So Laocoon's fate does not convince the Trojans to accept the Horse – Sinon has already seen to this – but instead provides, after the scene of human seduction, a larger theological context, and, after the subtle display of insidious eloquence, a spectacularly gruesome finale – and prelude, to the carnage that can now begin.

Laocoon before Vergil

The West's Laocoon is ultimately Vergil's – not only because Vergil's version of the story is so memorable in its language and construction, but also because his was, surprisingly, one of the very few treatments of the subject in ancient literature (Zintzen 1979; cf. Kleinknecht 1944). We know of only two significant versions preceding Vergil's; and we know very little even about these, as neither one has survived except in a few fragments and testimonies.

Laocoon is not mentioned anywhere by Homer, but he plays a key role in the narrative structure of the heroic legends of Troy. For a fateful symmetry requires that horrific events at the beginning of the Trojan War are echoed no less disturbingly at its end: just as the sacrifice of Iphigenia at Aulis before the Greek fleet can sail to Troy finds its counterpart in the sacrifice of Polyxena that the ghost of Achilles demands if the Greek ships are to be able to sail home again, so too the snake that devours the mother sparrow and her eight nestlings at Aulis, which Calchas interprets as a portent foretelling the capture of Troy after nine years of siege (*Il.* 2.301–29; Argument *Cypria* 6 West) has its gruesome complement in the two snakes that kill Laocoon and his children just before the city is captured. This structural function explains Laocoon's prominent appearance at the very opening of the Cyclic Epic called the *Iliupersis* (*The Sack of Troy*), assigned to the poet Arctinus: as we know from the prose summary in Proclus' *Chrestomathy* (246 Severyns), supplemented from the mythographer Pseudo-Apollodorus' *Library* (5.16), that poem began with a scene in which the Trojans hesitated about whether to accept the Wooden Horse or not. Cassandra and Laocoon warned that it contained soldiers and some wanted to destroy it, but others thought that it was sacred to Athena and should be dedicated to her, and it was the view of these latter that won the day. The Trojans then celebrated the end of the war, but the festivities were interrupted by a gruesome portent: two serpents appeared, sent by Apollo, swimming across the sea from a nearby island, and killed Laocoon and one of his two sons. Aeneas, apprehensive at this divine sign, slipped away together with his followers to Mount Ida (Argument *Sack of Ilion* 1 West).

Vergil's homage to the *Iliupersis* is evident in his decision to place an account of Laocoon at the beginning of his own tale of the sack of Troy, and the outline of his story is not very different from that in Arctinus; yet, characteristically, the Roman poet has transformed his Greek model, subtly but profoundly. There are some changes of detail: Vergil's Laocoon is no longer a priest of Apollo but is assigned by lot to Neptune, and the snakes seem to be associated with Athena – in the *Aeneid* Apollo is always a fervent supporter of Aeneas' cause, as one would expect of a god closely associated with Augustus, and can therefore not, as in the *Iliupersis*, slay his own priest. Moreover, Vergil's snakes heighten the macabre effect of the scene by killing both of Laocoon's sons together with their father: indeed, by killing the sons first they ensure that he will suffer not only physically but also psychologically. But the crucial difference involves the specific function of the episode within the immediate narrative context. In the Greek epic, what happens to Laocoon has nothing at all to do with the question of whether the Trojans should accept the Wooden Horse into their city or not: it is introduced in order to motivate Aeneas' decision to leave Troy together with his followers and thereby, alone of all the Trojan heroes, to survive the fall of his city. In Vergil, of course, Aeneas must stay on beyond the death of Laocoon in order to fight at the fall of Troy as a proper epic warrior must, even if to no avail (indeed, to motivate Aeneas to flee Troy, Vergil must first introduce a spectral dream of the dead

Hector and then, when this is not enough, add various supernatural omens); so in Vergil he too, like the other Trojans, must misinterpret what happens to Laocoon. And yet in Vergil it is not an impersonal omniscient narrator but Aeneas himself who tells the story, and his account is colored by hindsight, by experiences and knowledge that he could not possibly have had at the time of the events but that inevitably inform his narrative. The result is a thoroughly subjective tale, typically Vergilian, full of layers of ambiguity, irony, and self-deception. No doubt these qualities contribute in large measure to its success.

Laocoon's significant role in the Trojan cycle meant that various ancient poets and mythographers, both Greek and Latin, mentioned him when they recounted the fall of Troy and told details of his story, often diverging from one another. Thus Servius (*ad Aen.* 2.201) summarizes versions of the story he attributes to Bacchylides (fr. 9 Snell-Maehler) and Euphorion (fr. 70 Powell). But whether these represented full poems or only passing allusions, and to what extent we may rely upon Servius' accounts, are very uncertain.

What we can be sure of is that Sophocles wrote a tragedy called *Laocoon*, now lost, of which we have seven fragments (frs. 370–7 Radt), the largest of which (fr. 373 Radt) is only six lines long. In basic plot Sophocles seems to have followed Arctinus: one fragment (fr. 370) tells of the festive city, and may well have come from the prologue; another (fr. 373) comes from a messenger speech and recounts Aeneas' withdrawal from Troy together with his father and his household. Other fragments (frs. 374–5) tell of the psychological effects of hard labors now past: though gnomic in character and hence difficult to assign to specific dramatic situations, they may well refer to the Trojans' relief after ten years of warfare. But in other regards Sophocles seems to have innovated. A lyric prayer to Poseidon (fr. 371) might suggest that Laocoon was identified as a priest not of Apollo but of Poseidon, anticipating Vergil's version. More remarkably, according to Servius (fr. 372), Sophocles told the names of the two dragons; whether they had been assigned individual names because they had formerly been humans or would later be transformed into humans (the question is debated and unsolvable), it is hard to imagine how this information could possibly have been conveyed dramatically except by a *deus ex machina* at the conclusion of the play; to the same scene might belong another, one-word fragment about an eagle (fr. 377). But Sophocles' most striking novelty is that his snakes seem to have killed Laocoon's two sons but spared the priest himself (so too Pseudo-Apollodorus, *Library* 5.17–18).

These scarce textual indications might perhaps be supplemented by two fragmentary south Italian vases of the late fifth to early fourth centuries BCE (LIMC, Laokoon 1 [Basel, Antikenmuseum Lu 70] and 2 [formerly Ruvo, Museo Jatta, now lost]): both show Apollo as a cult statue, entwined by a pair of snakes, and also as the living god (this doubling may serve here to indicate on the one hand the locale of the god's sanctuary, and on the other his own responsibility for the attack); a woman rushes at the statue and is about to attack it with an axe (the weapon is missing on the less completely surviving of the two vases); between her and it lies the motive for her assault, pieces of dismembered children's bodies; on the better conserved vase a man rushes behind her, holding his head in helpless despair. Though the question of the relation between vase paintings and specific Greek tragedies is always highly problematic, in this case it seems very tempting to interpret these images as representations of a tragic Laocoon whose wife tries to attack the shrine of Apollo in her rage at the loss of her children, who have been killed by the god's snakes; and then we may well incline to connect them with Sophocles' play, since it is the only fifth-century tragedy we know of on this subject.

If so, then we may suppose that Sophocles concentrated his tragedy on the person of Laocoon himself, as already the title suggests: Laocoon's survival makes him the locus of tragic loss and grief, particularly if at the end he was deprived not only of his two innocent sons but also of his hubristic wife. But Sophocles enriched this individual focus with other elements, partly divine ones – maybe the named snakes, maybe a *deus ex machina* – partly conjugal ones – the wife, who plays an important role in other versions (Bacchylides, Euphorion, Hyginus, *Fabulae* 135), sometimes providing by illicit sexual activity with Laocoon a justification for his death. In comparison, Vergil maintains the tragic pathos and heightening, especially in the narrative of the snakes' arrival; but he resolutely excludes both any hint of the marvelous, beyond what Aeneas himself could have seen and reported, and any reference to the wife. Vergil's version is obstinately heroic, masculine, human – and no less tragic than Sophocles' could possibly have been.

And that is all we can be sure of: a lost archaic Greek epic and a lost tragedy by Sophocles, a few passages in surviving poets and mythographers, and perhaps also a few lost poems by Bacchylides, Euphorion, and others. All other references earlier than Vergil's, like that in Lycophron's *Alexandria* (347), are no more than passing allusions. All Latin versions later than Vergil's, like that by Petronius (*Sat.* 89), are deeply influenced by Vergil's own account. Without Vergil, no Laocoon.

Laocoon on the Esquiline

But if the ultimate source of the West's Laocoon is Vergil, its proximate source is a single statue (Fig. 22.1) that was discovered on January 14, 1506 on the Esquiline Hill in Rome. Perhaps the most extraordinary feature of this extraordinary artwork is that, while Vergil's poetic account of Laocoon is only a rarity within ancient literature, this statue is apparently a complete singularity within ancient art (Simon 1992; cf. Simon 1984).

Astonishingly well preserved – the only important elements missing, besides large segments of the serpents, are the raised right arm of the younger son, the right hand of the older one, and Laocoon's raised right hand (the arm to which it belonged was not discovered until 1905 and was not restored to its proper place until 1959, cf. Magi 1960) – the sculpture shows three humans interlaced with two serpents. The younger son, on our left, is already dying or has just died; with its coils, a snake ironically binds his leg and arm to the leg of his father, to whom the son was casting an imploring glance in his last moments; his figure is shadowed by his father's mighty arm and thorax, but Laocoon is now no longer in a position to be able to help him. On our right, the other, older son has his right arm loosely coiled by the other serpent

Figure 22.1   Laocoon sculpture group from the Esquiline (40–20 BCE).

and is in the process of slipping off another coil from his left ankle; he stares in fascinated horror and compassion at what is happening to his father and younger brother – within the sculpture he is the figure of the spectator and represents us – but the torsion of his whole body is springing away energetically from the direction of his father's: will he succeed in saving himself (as in the *Iliupersis*) or will he be drawn back by the serpents' strength or by his own pity so that he too dies (as in most other versions)? In the center, collapsed onto an altar, majestic in his sublime but futile strength, straining every muscle and sinew of his monumental frame, Laocoon still struggles – or rather, his body still combats against the snakes and tries in vain to rise from the altar onto which he has fallen, his legs no longer able to bear him, while his head has just now subsided backwards in defeat (its torsion establishes a striking contrast with the arc of his own body and a parallel with the head of his dead younger son): the father has already succumbed to his own grief at his inability to save his son and to the serpents' deadly venom, his eyes have only now stopped seeking heavenly assistance in vain, and his mouth is half-open in a dreadful grimace – not so much to express a groan, and certainly not to restrain one (as Winckelmann mistakenly thought), but rather because he has already screamed his heart out for the very last time and is now collapsing into the silence of death. The dynamic spatial symmetry of Laocoon and his sons not only establishes a series of parallel and counterpoint relations fraught with psychological and aesthetic meaning, but can also be read temporally, as three successive moments in the victims' progressive defeat: caught, then struggling, finally dead. Coiled around all three figures are two long, sinuous snakes, which unify them into a single composition and lead the viewer's eyes incessantly through and around them.

As soon as the sculpture was discovered it was connected with a well-known passage in Pliny's *Natural History*:

> And that is why the fame of many more [*scil.* sculptors in marble] is non-existent, for the celebrity of certain ones, even in works of the highest quality, is impeded by the plurality of artists involved, since neither can one of them claim for himself the full glory nor can more than one be named equally: just as in the *Laocoon* which is in the house of the Emperor Titus, a work to be preferred to all others, both of painting and of bronze sculpture. The greatest artists – Hagesander, Polydorus, and Athenodorus, all of them from Rhodes – made him and his sons and the marvelous coils of the serpents from a single block of marble (*ex uno lapide*), by common consent (*de consilii sententia*). (36.37)

The location on the Esquiline where the statue was found has long been identified with the house of Titus; and Pliny's description, which is already cited in the earliest documents telling of the discovery of the statue (Settis 1999, 16–17, 101–3, 110–11), fits it like a glove – with one exception: the statue we possess is not really carved from a single block, but only gives the appearance of having been made in this way, by virtue of the sculptors' cunning interlocking of its various component pieces. Pliny's point is precisely that the impression the sculpture gives of perfect unity, despite the number and variety of the figures it represents, corresponds to the identity of intention of the three great artists who worked on it together and were willing to subordinate their own individual personalities to their common project – a decision that has impaired the fame of many other artists who worked in collaboration with one another, but seems not to have had that effect in this case. Some earlier scholars supposed that our Laocoon is not the monolithic one Pliny mentions but only a later copy of it, made out of several pieces of marble; but the location and quality of the sculpture argue for its identification with the one Pliny describes, and most experts now interpret Pliny's reference to a single block as hyperbolic, or as intended to describe the statue's appearance to the viewer, or as simply erroneous.

So there is now general agreement that the statue discussed in Pliny's text is to be identified with our *Laocoon*; but the dating and interpretation of the latter have remained controversial, and are likely to continue to do so. For many years the dominant view was that our *Laocoon* was sculpted sometime during the first century CE, either as an original composition or else as a Roman marble copy of a Hellenistic

Greek bronze original (so, for example, Andreae 1988, 1991; Simon 1992, 199–201); but recently that idea has come in for strong criticism, without however its having been replaced by a new consensus. Thus the interpretation sketched here, which takes its starting point from the recent monograph by Settis (1999), cannot claim to be more than one plausible suggestion among others – though it is the one that seems to me to make the best sense of the available evidence.

Starting on the one hand from the observations (1) that a relatively large number of inscriptions indicate that two of the three sculptors of the *Laocoon* were active in Rhodes during the decade 50–40 BCE, (2) that the very same three Rhodian sculptors to whom Pliny assigned the Laocoon also "signed" some of the statues illustrating episodes from the *Odyssey* and the Cyclical Epics (and revealing a style very close to that of our *Laocoon*) that were discovered some decades ago in a grotto, adapted to the functions of a triclinium, in a Roman villa at Sperlonga associated with the Emperor Tiberius (but not necessarily belonging to him), and (3) that the phase of the construction of that villa to which these latter statues most likely belong can be dated on architectural grounds fairly precisely to the decade 30–20 BCE, and on the other hand from the historical fact (4) that the flourishing cultural activity of Rhodes was brought to an abrupt end by Cassius' siege and looting of the city in 43/42 BCE, Settis concludes that these three sculptors, like other Rhodian artists, fled to Rome after the destruction of their city and continued their professional activity there. If so, then the *Laocoon* can be dated with some degree of probability to ca. 40–20 BCE (Settis 1999, 27–39, 50, 56). To be sure, its style, with its baroque pathos and dynamic asymmetry, is at variance with the calmer Apollonian sculptures we are accustomed to associate with Augustus' cultural politics (Zanker 1974, 1988); but Settis' dating on the basis of external criteria seems secure enough that it is surely preferable to accept the coexistence of different sculptural styles, especially during the first decade of Augustus' principate, rather than to discard that date for the sake of a presumed but unattested and improbable thorough-going stylistic homogeneity in the culture of the time.

Dating the *Laocoon* to ca. 40–20 BCE renders the question of its exact relation to Vergil's treatment of the story in his *Aeneid* urgent, indeed inescapable: for Vergil began work on his epic poem about 29 BCE after publishing his *Georgics*, and continued to compose and revise it until he died in 19 BCE, his manuscript still unfinished. During that decade, he is known to have given a number of more or less public recitations of parts of his poem, and contemporary references show that Romans were well aware of what he was working on and expected great things from him. Given these facts and dates, only three possible connections between the sculpture and the poem can be envisioned:

1. Hagesander, Polydorus, and Athenodorus made their sculpture, and Vergil his episode, in complete ignorance of one another (in this case the temporal relation between the two artworks is indifferent). But why should the three Rhodians have been given the commission to portray so monumentally this minor mythological episode? As we shall see shortly, there was no tradition of sculptures of Laocoon, hence no evident artistic reason for the Rhodians to have made one.

Moreover, the celebrity of the sculptors and the fact that, at this level of society (the commission certainly came from the very highest echelons), Rome was not a very large town, makes it quite unlikely that Vergil and they could have been operating more or less simultaneously but entirely unaware of one another.

2. Hagesander, Polydorus, and Athenodorus made their sculpture first, and Vergil wrote his episode afterwards, precisely because of the sculpture: the statue gave rise to this section of the poem. But again, this leaves unexplained why the sculpture should have been made in the first place; and it remains thoroughly obscure why Vergil should have chosen to pay such lavish homage to a contemporary statue by inserting this story so prominently into his poem.

3. Vergil wrote his episode first, and Hagesander, Polydorus, and Athenodorus made their sculpture afterwards, precisely because of the epic: the poem gave rise to this statue. This is surely the most likely explanation (and it is the conclusion to which Lessing arrived after a very careful examination of the evidence). Vergil's decision to begin his own *Sack of Troy* with Laocoon was motivated not by a contemporary statue but by an ancient epic, Arctinus' *Iliupersis*. But, on this view, once it had become generally known what he was up to in his new poem, someone was inspired to pay homage to him (and, no doubt, especially to his powerful patron, Augustus) by commissioning a monumental statue of the Laocoon with whom Vergil's own account of the fall of Troy was known to have begun. If we wish to, we might imagine that the three Greek artists, probably refugees from a town that the Romans had destroyed, could have derived some degree of private satisfaction from depicting a Trojan defeat, the horrific death of close relatives of the Aeneas who was the ultimate founder of the Roman race; but even were that so, it did not prevent them from glorifying Laocoon and endowing him with a heroic, indeed, with a superhuman pathos.

If this suggestion can be regarded as plausible (it is of course very far from being certain), then it will mean that our *Laocoon* is quite likely the very earliest surviving artistic response to the *Aeneid* – indeed, it may well even predate the poem's publication. But on balance it does not seem as though the statue can be construed satisfactorily in any simple sense as a direct illustration of the Vergilian text as we know it – to name only the most striking difference between the two versions, in the epic the snakes kill the two sons before turning upon their father. While it is not perhaps entirely impossible to attempt to explain, as Lessing did, the discrepancies between the sculptural treatment and the poetic one by reference exclusively to the differences between the two media involved, the number, variety, and extent of the differences in treatment between sculpture and poem render such an attempt not fully convincing; if so, then we may wish to suppose that the sculptors did not themselves have an intimate and precise knowledge of the details of Vergil's version – perhaps it had not circulated widely at this point and they had not heard it themselves, and in any case it may well have been revised somewhat before Vergil composed the version that he left at his death and that we know. If so, then the statue is not so much a specific response to this episode of the poem as we have it as a general tribute to Rome's great poet (and, doubtless, to his great patron too).

Astonishingly, as far as we can tell, no other statue of Laocoon was ever produced in antiquity: our *Laocoon* is entirely without exact precedents in ancient art, and indeed was never even copied, depicted in any way, described, or even mentioned by any other ancient artist or author later, except by Pliny in the one passage quoted above. There was, to be sure, a tradition of paintings of the subject, as evinced by a series of works all later than the *Aeneid*: two wall frescoes from Pompeii, dating from the first century CE (LIMC, Laokoon 4 [Pompeii, Casa del Menandro] and 5 [Naples, Museo Nazionale 111210]); a number of contorniate medallions from the end of the fourth or the beginning of the fifth century CE (LIMC, Laokoon 8); and a miniature in an early-fifth-century manuscript of Vergil (LIMC, Laokoon 6 [Vat. lat. 3225, f. 18v]); I leave out of account here what some scholars have identified as an Etruscan engraved gem dating to ca. 300 BCE and representing Laocoon and his two sons (LIMC, Laokoon 9 [London, British Museum 673]), as its authenticity and even antiquity are disputed. That there was a tradition of such paintings is also strongly suggested by the passage from Petronius' *Satyricon* (89) mentioned earlier, in which the character Eumolpus describes a painting showing the sack of Troy and culminating in a detailed representation of the death of Laocoon and his sons. This painting tradition (which need not be construed as deriving from some single Hellenistic masterpiece, but could go back to various pictorial versions of the story) is different in several crucial details from our *Laocoon* statue: in the paintings, the priest always holds his hands up in prayerful protest to the heavens rather than struggling with contorted downward-bent arms against the serpents' coils, and he is always kneeling with one knee upon the altar rather than collapsing downwards onto it; and the painted children are usually tiny, are already dead, and are well removed from the scene of their father's death. Thus the paintings emphasize Laocoon as a pious and innocent priest and focus our attention upon him, whereas the statue emphasizes Laocoon as a heroically struggling father and focuses our attention upon the interrelations between his sons and himself.

So, although the extant paintings are later than our statue, they do not arise from it nor do they represent it: instead, they go back to an earlier convention for representing Laocoon, one that was, though apparently quite rare, nonetheless quite consistent. Our *Laocoon*, too, might possibly go back to such a painting tradition, for it is in fact far more two-dimensional in its impact than fully three-dimensional. Despite the contortions of the human and reptile bodies, almost the entire mass of the sculpture is distributed along a single vertical plane; only Laocoon's right knee (on our left) thrusts somewhat into our own space. Surely the statue was intended to be seen only from in front, not from the sides or back; presumably it was set in a niche in a garden, following a taste for sculptures distributed throughout pleasure gardens that we know to have been popular among cultivated Romans in this very period. We might perhaps think of it as the one surviving element of a complex Augustan theme park that was devoted to episodes from the sack of Troy sculpted by the same artists who carved a similar theme park in Sperlonga (perhaps, indeed, commissioned by the very same wealthy patron). Its extraordinary pathos was evidently calculated carefully to provoke extreme emotions in the spectator who encountered it suddenly while promenading through the garden. The son on our right, gazing like us upon this terrifying scene with the tragic emotions of pity and horror, transports us from our quotidian real world into the sublime mythic domain of the statue: will he succeed in freeing himself from the snakes' coils and manage to join us in the garden, or will he draw us together with him into the aesthetic elation of ineluctable destruction?

But just as our *Laocoon* is not completely dependent upon the earlier iconography of this theme, so too it had absolutely no effect whatsoever upon its later iconography; except for Pliny, who was closely connected to the Emperor Titus in whose house it was installed, we have no record that anyone in antiquity ever noticed or even saw this statue. Its location in an emperor's house may provide part, but surely not all, of the explanation; other artworks in imperial households exerted a much broader artistic influence. Perhaps we may hypothesize that the contradiction between the Rhodian artists' baroque taste and the classicism that went on to become dominant in the later years of Augustan culture could have led to the statue's being neglected: to be sure, it remained available for some private viewers, at least a few of whom, like Pliny, greatly appreciated it (but is not his hyperbolic praise to be understood as homage to Titus' personal tastes?); but otherwise it seems to have entirely vanished from public awareness – for just over a millennium and a half.

Laocoon's Renaissance

But ever since its discovery in January 1506, the Rhodians' *Laocoon*, neglected, indeed almost unknown in antiquity, has gone on to achieve an extraordinary success in modern culture, becoming one of the most frequently copied, studied, described, represented, and parodied of all ancient works of sculpture. Over the past half millennium, the fame of the *Laocoon* has far outstripped that of the Vergilian poetic episode which probably gave rise to it: today, when people think of Laocoon – and it is astonishing how often they do so – they are most likely to think not of a narrative, but of a statue: or indeed, of an image.

The result is at least doubly paradoxical. First, when the Laocoon statue was rediscovered, Vergil's fortunes were as high as they ever had been since his lifetime, or even higher; but in the centuries that followed, they declined precipitously, whereas the fame of a sculpture that had most likely been fashioned in response to his *Aeneid* grew steadily. Without Vergil, no *Laocoon*; and yet the statue came to eclipse his epic. And second, we can easily identify in the Western tradition of Laocoon both a literary reception centered on Vergil's *Aeneid* and an artistic reception centered on the Rhodians' sculpture, and we can assert with some confidence that it is likely that the sculpture depends in some way upon the epic – and yet it is impossible to determine to what degree, if at all, the sculptors actually had a detailed familiarity with the Vergilian episode as we know it and were not simply responding vaguely and generally to the existence of such an episode in the epic. Of course, as time went on, and fewer and fewer people knew Vergil's text by heart, this second paradox diminished in force (was this one of the reasons the statue could become so famous?). And yet the discrepancy remains odd. So without Vergil, no *Laocoon*; yet the precise relation between the two remains evanescent and ungraspable, like the shade of Creusa.

The unearthing of the *Laocoon* caused an immediate sensation that spread rapidly throughout Italy and soon reached the rest of learned Europe. In one of the
defining moments of the Italian Renaissance, a celebrated passage of the greatest
ancient Latin epic suddenly took on concrete materiality and a lost ancient statue
that Pliny himself had declared to be greater than all other works of painting or
bronze sculpture unexpectedly came to light: the Rhodians' marble provided a
bridge from one ancient text to another ancient text and from both of them to the
visible reality of the contemporary world – this, if anything, was a true rebirth of
the glory of antiquity.

We can trace the expanding wave of the *Laocoon*'s growing celebrity in letters,
poems, guidebooks, and woodcuts starting already within the month of its discovery (conveniently collected by Sonia Maffei in Settis 1999, 99–230). Artists, including Michelangelo, rushed to study and learn from their ancient predecessors – but
it was not until our very own time that an American archaeologist went so far as to
propose that the statue, so far from being a genuine antiquity, had actually been
sculpted by Michelangelo himself (Catterson 2005). Rich and powerful collectors
jostled with one another to acquire the statue for their private collections (it was
also proposed, briefly, that it be set up at the civic heart of Rome, in the Campidoglio);
in the end it was the richest and most powerful collector of all, Pope Julius II, who
won, purchasing the statue from the man on whose land it had been discovered and
assigning it to a special niche in the Cortile del Belvedere of the Vatican Palace
(Brummer 1970), where, by and large, it has remained (though not always easily or
fully visible) ever since – with the exception of a brief sojourn in France, from the
spring of 1798, when Napoleon's victorious troops transported it to Paris together
with other precious cultural artifacts, until its return to Rome at the end of 1815
after his defeat.

Julius' monopolization of the statue itself did nothing to impede its steadily increasing celebrity. Visitors to the papal palace viewed and marveled at it in the sixteenth
century just as millions of tourists do now. More or less exact copies of the *Laocoon*
ornamented public, and later private, spaces throughout Europe. Primaticcio made a
bronze cast for the palace of Fontainebleau and François Girardon made one at
Houghton Hall, Baccio Bandinelli sculpted a marble copy for Florence and Jean
Baptiste Tuby made another, life-sized one for Versailles; plaster casts adorned private
and academic collections throughout Italy and the rest of Europe; bronze miniatures,
beginning as early as the sixteenth century, brought domesticated versions of the
Laocoon's terrible grandeur into the bourgeois serenity of private households. By contrast, fewer sculptors dared to compete with the three Rhodians by proposing their
own, differing versions of the theme: around 1625, Adriaen de Vries brilliantly
restored the subject to genuine three-dimensionality with a heroically nude Laocoon
rising up column-like above the bodies of his two writhing sons (Stockholm, National
Museum); in 1837, Luigi Ferrari sought originality by symmetrically reversing the
positions of the three figures and varying their postures (Brescia, Pinacoteca Tosio-
Martinengo) – but only succeeded thereby in reminding us all the more forcefully of
the superiority of his ancient model; by contrast, the recent *Laocoon* by Eva Hesse
(Fig. 22.2: Oberlin, Allen Memorial Art Museum) provides a strikingly inventive

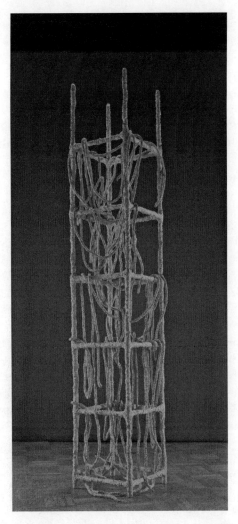

Figure 22.2 Eva Hesse, *Laocoon*, 1966. Acrylic, wire, rope, papier-mâché, cloth, plastic 130 × 23 1/4 × 23 1/4 inches. Allen Memorial Art Museum, Oberlin College, OH, The Fund for Contemporary Art and gift from the artist and Fischbach Gallery, 1970 © The Estate of Eva Hesse. Hauser & Wirth Zürich London.

meditation on the formal properties of the ancient statue in its refined interplay between linear elements and sinuous ones, and a hint at an even more archaic pathos in its rough, primitive surface modeling.

Common as these sculptural versions of the *Laocoon* have been over the past five centuries, it cannot be doubted that it has been above all two-dimensional pictorial media that have made the most significant contribution to broadcasting its fame. Nor is this surprising: for the ancient statue itself, as we have seen, certainly does not take full advantage of the possibilities offered by sculptural three-dimensionality but instead presents itself to the viewer frontally, almost like a relief – this sculpture has in fact far less to lose by being illustrated pictorially than most other ones do. Within a very short time after its discovery, artists began making drawings, paintings, woodcuts, and etchings of the sculpture, occasionally as mere historical documentation, more often as professional training, most frequently in order to satisfy an ever-growing public hunger for such illustrations. As is only natural, many artists, rather than taking the trouble to examine the sculpture with their own eyes, preferred to copy from one another; the result was the widespread diffusion of tralaticious portrayals that diverged ever further from the original and that filled the imagination of generations of European intellectuals with images whose details and general tonality were adapted ever more thoroughly to contemporary tastes and needs. Rare indeed were the painters who ventured successfully to create their own versions of the theme – perhaps most remarkably of all, El Greco, who around 1610 transformed the suffering priest and his sons into what look more like three isolated, meditative gymnasts, set before their city and its fateful Horse and viewed by dismayed but impotent spectators (Plate 6: Washington, National Gallery). By contrast, Francesco Hayez's version of 1810 merely places a slightly varied (but respectably clothed) version of the sculpture within a dramatic context of horrified Trojans at an altar before the gate of their city, thereby producing not so much verisimilitude as rather kitsch (Milan, Pinacoteca di Brera).

The *Laocoon* has played no less important a role in aesthetic theory than it has in art history, through the immediate and long-lasting impact of Johann Joachim Winckelmann's various enthusiastic accounts of the statue in his "Thoughts on the Imitation of Greek Works in Painting and Sculpture," first published in 1755 (Winckelmann 1913, 61–113) and *History of the Art of Antiquity*, first published in 1764 (Winckelmann 1972; see especially Giuliani 1999). In his early essay, Winckelmann, who at that time had not yet ever seen the statue and relied upon printed illustrations, thoroughly misunderstood the priest's grimace as a magnanimous attempt to restrain the vocal expression of his suffering, as was noted above, and he went so far as to praise the sculpture, astonishingly, as a supreme example of "noble simplicity and tranquil grandeur" (Winckelmann 1913, 85–6); even his later discussion, which is evidently based upon his detailed, intensive, and repeated examination of the original sculpture in Rome, does not quite succeed in correcting this mistake (Winckelmann 1972, 167, 324–6). Gotthold Ephraim Lessing attacked Winckelmann's interpretation in his *Laocoon: An Essay upon the Limits of Painting and Poetry*, first published in 1766 (Lessing 1957) – but not his Stoicizing account of Laocoon's heroic self-restraint. Instead, taking issue with Winckelmann, Joseph Spence, the Comte de Caylus, and other eighteenth-century art critics who had maintained that what was beautiful in one artistic medium must likewise be beautiful in any other one, Lessing undertook an extended and detailed comparison of the differences between the representations of Laocoon in Vergil and in the Vatican statue (which he too had never seen in the original). If Vergil could highlight Laocoon's screams while the Rhodian sculptors (at least according to Lessing) had done all they could to repress them, this could only be due, Lessing argued, to the differences in the nature of the two artistic media employed: language uses signs successive in time and hence can represent actions and passions, while the visual media use signs coexistent in space and must therefore limit themselves to portraying simultaneous positions of bodies. Lessing's distinctions between the mode of existence of the various arts, like the conclusions he drew from them for the kinds of subjects allowable in the different media, were highly influential but deeply erroneous; more important historically were his emphasis on the impact upon the viewer or reader of the representation of intense human passions and his attempt to deduce aesthetic norms, not from abstract canons of reason but from the concrete reality of the artist's materials.

One of the most interesting phenomena in the reception of *Laocoon*, finally, has been the large number of (pictorial, never sculptural) parodies of the statue that have been produced in the last five hundred years. These parodies have been of many kinds. Already in the sixteenth century Titian provided the design for a woodcut in which the three humans have been replaced by three apes battling serpents in a forest setting, and, centuries later, Goethe's friend Johann Heinrich Wilhelm Tischbein created an etching in which instead it is lions that struggle with giant snakes: the overwhelmingly, indeed almost embarrassingly robust corporeality of Laocoon's mighty frame is thereby reduced from human to animal status, the scandal of human beings defeated by snakes is domesticated by its simplification into a purely bestial conflict. From the mid-sixteenth century too dates a violently anti-Catholic German medallion in which a naked Pope Paul III rides a snake which coils around him, while one figure relieves himself into the papal tiara and another vomits onto his head: here the extensive Vatican art collection is reinterpreted polemically as a symbol of pagan immorality and irreligious avarice and is turned as a weapon of Protestant propaganda against the pope himself. More recently, images of Laocoon have lent themselves above all for use in political caricature – Daumier showing Britannia wrestling in vain against the serpent of Fenianism, or Richard Nixon struggling futilely with the Watergate tapes that coil around his unheroic body. But one of the funniest parodies is not at all political: Charles Addams' unforgettable cartoon of a butcher and his two young assistants grappling desperately with serpentine sausage links while a passer-by gazes at them through the window in astonishment (Fig. 22.3).

It is worth speculating about just why the *Laocoon* has shown itself to be so appropriate for the purposes of parody and caricature. Part of the reason may reside in the very painfulness of the human suffering that this sculpture brings so memorably to expression: in the text but, even more, in the statue, spectacle and pain, prodigy and humanity, intersect at the very limit of what readers are willing to imagine and what viewers are desperate to see; the inevitable result is an aesthetic phenomenon that, by reason of its very intolerability, teeters on the edge of parody and humor, and at least sometimes falls in. But another part of the reason, undoubtedly, resides in the statue's very celebrity: its unique visual form and its universal dissemination make it instantly recognizable not only as an illustration of a particular myth but also as an emblem of antiquity itself – as a symbol of sublime artistic values that may be thought to have been more at home in a different, ancient world, and that may well be somewhat out of place in our prosaic modern one. No rebirth, after all, can ever be fully intact: *Laocoon*, rediscovered, tells us not only about cultural continuities but also, and even more, about historical discontinuities, reminding us not merely of how much we owe the ancients, but also of how irreducibly different we are from them.

Figure 22.3   *Laocoon Sausage.* © Charles Addams (1975). With permission Tee and Charles Addams Foundation.

FURTHER READING

Vergil's Laocoon: the standard commentary in English is Austin (1964, 44–51, 94–108). There is still much to learn from Plüss (1884, 57–104), Heinze (1914, 12–20, 67–71), and Knight (1932, 83–91). See also more recently Klingner (1967, 410–15), Putnam (1965, 4–26), and Maurach (1992).

The Esquiline sculpture group: see especially Settis (1999); also Gombrich (1957), Sichtermann (1957), von Blanckenhagen (1969), Hampe (1972, 70–9), Hiller (1979), Himmelmann (1991), Maurach (1992), Kunze (1996), Winckelmann (2006, 222–4), and now in general Gall and Wolkenhauer (2008).

Modern reception of Laocoon: see in general Bieber (1942); also Ettlinger (1961), Hertl and Hertl (1968), Oechslin (1974), Pigler (1974, 330–1), Winner (1974), Nisbet (1979), Preiss (1992), Richter (1992), Reid (1993, 1.624–6), Barkan (1999, esp. 2–17), Giuliani (1999), and Hinz (2001).

Lessing's *Laocoon*: see in general Fischer (1887), Frey (1905), Nolte (1940), Bialostocka (1964), and more recently especially Wellbery (1984).

CHAPTER TWENTY THREE

Vergil in Music

William Fitzgerald

What kind of a subject is "Vergil in music"? A story, perhaps, starting with reports that the *Eclogues* were sung in antiquity (*VSD* 26: see Stok's chapter in this volume), continuing with the musically annotated (or "neumed") passages in some medieval Vergil manuscripts and leading to the modernism of Luigi Nono (1924–90), with high points and fallow periods in between? This is how the subject has been framed in the past and it is the approach that the reader of a *Companion to Vergil* will expect. The topic might also imply that Vergil has a distinctive presence in the history of music; that there are Vergilian passages, episodes, or characters that have acquired their own tradition within the history of Western art music. Another approach to the topic would be to examine how the medium of music itself provides a distinctive perspective on Vergil's works. At the simplest level, music can supply what Vergil's text occasionally calls for but cannot contain. On the fly-leaf of his libretto to *Orfeo ed Euridice*, Calzabigi quoted the lines *Te, dulcis coniunx, te solo in litore secum, / te veniente die, te decedente canebat* ("It was you, sweet wife, you he would sing on the lonely shore to himself, you as the day approached, you as it fell away," *Geo.* 4.465–6). When in 1726 Gluck set the libretto, with its famous lament "Che faro senza Euridice," he supplied the music to which Vergil's verses gesture. But composers do not simply supply incidental music to Vergil's text. Part of the life of Vergil's texts is their transposition into different media, with attendant shifts of emphasis and different relations between background and foreground, between what can be represented and what cannot, and this is an important aspect of the topic "Vergil in music." Finally, in our own times, the best rationale for a chapter on Vergil in music is the fact that, for the late twentieth and early twenty-first century, Vergil's *Aeneid* has become opera. It is a fair bet that, at least in the English-speaking world, more people know Purcell's *Dido and Aeneas* than have read book 4 of the *Aeneid*, even in translation, and it is arguable that the single most exciting development in the reception of the *Aeneid* over the last half century has been the gradual entry of Berlioz's *Les Troyens* into the operatic repertoire. In a very real sense, the *Aeneid* lives on in opera. At the same time, both of these works are eccentric to the core operatic repertoire and have contributed to its expansion in the twentieth century, an expansion that has helped to keep the form growing in the absence of contemporary accessions. Purcell's *Dido and Aeneas*, which received its first performance at a girl's school, is distinctively unoperatic in scale and economy of means, if we measure opera by the central repertoire of Verdi and Puccini. Berlioz's massive opera was long considered unperformable because of its length (five hours when performed *in toto*) and its demands on resources. In scale and ambition it invites comparison with Wagner's contemporary *Ring* cycle. But Berlioz is the unWagner, the summation of a French tradition that includes Rameau and Gluck; the clarity, light, swiftness, and variety of *Les Troyens* are as French as Wagner is German and yet this, too, is epic opera. So, while Vergil speaks to our time in large part through a medium that is distinctly unVergilian, within the contemporary repertoire of opera Vergil picks out some works that provide eccentric perspectives on the genre. I will come back to a more detailed look at Berlioz and Purcell at the end of this chapter, after I have surveyed some of the other Vergilian moments in the history of Western art music.

Berlioz's attempt to represent something like the *Aeneid* as a whole makes it unique, for the history of the *Aeneid* in music is overwhelmingly dominated by Dido. There is evidence that book 4 was already adapted into ballet and *tragoedia cantata* in antiquity (Macrob. *Sat.* 5.17.5) and the majority of the neumed passages in medieval texts of Vergil are speeches of Dido. It is hardly surprising that Dido dominates the operatic scene, given the genre's penchant for abandoned heroines who lament and die in the last act. Purcell's *Dido and Aeneas* represents in its starkest form a story pattern that will become increasingly central to the medium: the woman who transgresses and then pays for her transgression with death. In fact, we might say that *Aeneid* 4 aspires to the state of opera, reversing our usual backward-looking concern with the congeries of different genres that feed in to *Aeneid* 4 (Alexandrian epic, tragedy, Catullan lyric).

Purcell's Dido, noble in her death ("Remember me but, ah, forget my fate") is a figure that has a musical life before the advent of opera. Dido's last words, *Dulces exuviae…* (4.651–4), provided a favored text for the Renaissance motet, and eight settings from around 1500 have been identified, including settings by Josquin des Pres and Jean Mouton. These settings tend to focus on the final words *et nunc magna mei sub terras ibit imago* ("and now a glorious ghost of me will go beneath the earth"). Josquin's motet, perhaps the finest of this group, ends with the upper voice ascending a major third on the word *imago* for a strikingly open ending that belies the words *sub terras* ("beneath the earth"). Dido enters classical music as the stoic Roman who vindicates her life in submission to *Fortuna* and offers up her soul, turning transient breath into persisting *imago* as she expires.

Osthoff (1954, 99–101) speculates that some of these motet settings may have been prompted by Isabella d'Este of Mantua, a lover and scholar of Vergil who commissioned a Vergil memorial from Mantegna in 1499. Castiglione's Latin poem "De Elisabella Gonzaga canente" describes Isabella singing "Dulces exuviae" to her own keyboard accompaniment and it compares her to Orpheus, charming beasts and nature. The form of her name that Castiglione uses, Elisabella, indicates that she was identified with Dido (Elissa) by her courtiers and that she encouraged the connection by singing a version of Dido's last words (Prizer 1999, 30–4). It is not only women in high positions who were drawn to ventriloquize Dido's last words; Martin Luther, too, liked to participate in a three-part setting of these words that was published in the *Symphoniae iucundae* (!) of Georg Rhaw (1538). A (mistaken) tradition that Luther himself composed a setting of these words and that lines 653–4 were his last words had some influence in the nineteenth century (see Draheim 1993, 323–4). At the end of the sixteenth century, the Bohemian Handl (otherwise known as Gallus) set lines 651–4 in his second collection of *Moralia*, partsongs set to Latin texts, moralistic and proverbial. Clearly Dido's last words were favored as much for their edifying moral force as for their dramatic quality. In this connection it is significant that the other Vergilian text that was occasionally set as a motet (by Josquin des Pres, for instance), also comes from book 4 (174–7); it is the decidedly moralistic allegory decrying *Fama* as *malum qua non aliud velocius ullum* ("an evil than which none is swifter," 174).

Several hundred years later, the tradition of polyphonic versions of Dido's last words was both recalled and challenged by the Darmstadt modernism of Luigi Nono's *Cori di Didone* (1958), settings of a section from Giuseppe Ungaretti's *La Terra Promessa* titled "Cori descrittivi di stati d'animo di Didone." Nono's version of the polyphonic motets of the Renaissance dissolves the rhetoric of Dido into layered cries that rise out of and fade into the resonating percussion that accompanies them. Ungaretti's texts represent the elements of nature as sharing the grief of Dido, making her death the occasion for a universal protest rather than an intimation of further self-destruction (Carthage's disastrous wars with Rome). For the reader of Vergil the wild music that accompanies Dido's death is made meaningful by the simile comparing the lamentation to the destruction of a city (*non aliter quam...*, 4.669–71). Nono's notes accompanying these settings take Dido's fate as exemplary of the creative sensibility that tragically explodes, as represented by the suicide of certain politically engaged artists (Nono was himself a committed Marxist).

Josquin and Nono stand at either end of a tradition of polyphonic treatments of Dido's suicide. In the case of the Renaissance motets, Dido's last words become a meditative, devotional text by association with the genre itself, which more commonly sets religious texts in Latin: the soul rises from the (all too) sweet "leavings" of the body (*dulces exuviae*). By its very nature, the motet *dwells on* the text, with the voices repeating words, imitating each other, and suggesting the meditation of a community on this exemplary figure and on Vergil's treasured words. Nono's setting, by contrast, reminds us of the inarticulateness to which Vergil's work sometimes gestures – the chorus is the responsiveness of a universe that is permeated at every level by *furor*.

Dido was an important figure in opera from the genre's birth as a court entertainment, with composition and performances tied to the celebration of festive dynastic events. Monteverdi, the father of opera, wrote a (now lost) *Didone*, an intermezzo in honor of the marriage of Odoardo Farnese and Margherita Medici, in 1628 (librettist unknown). The first public opera house opened in Venice in 1637 and many of the operas produced in the early years had a Trojan connection, for Republican Venice saw itself as the reincarnation of Republican Rome. Monteverdi's *Le Nozze d'Enea con Lavinia* of 1641 ends with a prophecy of the greatness of Rome and of the auspicious birth of Venice at the moment when Rome was overwhelmed by the barbarians. Another Venetian Dido opera, Cavalli's *La Didone* of 1641 (with libretto by Busenello), sets Aeneas and Dido in an imperial context by beginning with *Aeneid* 2 (anticipating Berlioz's *Les Troyens*). Towards the end of the century (1686), Franceschi's *La Didone Delirante* was performed in Venice (libretto by Pallavicino) and Bologna saw *La Didone* of Mascardini (libretto by Mattioli) in 1656.

Eighteenth-century operatic Didos are almost exclusively settings of the *Didone abbandonata* of Metastasio (1698–1782), the preeminent librettist of *opera seria* whose texts were set by every important composer of the period, including Mozart (*La Clemenza di Tito*). Metastasio's *Didone abbandonata* was set over eighty times in the period between 1724 and 1824. In their own time these operas would have been considered ephemeral settings of Metastasio's enduring libretto, which led a separate existence as a published text. None of these operas retains a foothold in the modern operatic repertoire, though there is an available recording of Nicolo Jommelli's version (first performed in 1748). The librettos of *opera seria* concentrated on the conflict of human passions in an action that was usually based on a story from an ancient author. A complicated intrigue and a varied succession of affects were essential. *Didone abbandonata* begins with Aeneas resolved to sacrifice love and follow duty. As Selene (Dido's sister and confidante) puts it: "contrastano in quel core, ne so chi vincera, gloria ed amore" (glory and love are opposed in this heart, nor do I know which will prevail). Metastasio's libretto affords the composer ample opportunity to trace the fluctuating emotions and wavering resolution of both Dido and Aeneas as the latter gradually moves to make good on his original decision; *Didone abbandonata* is at the opposite pole to the headlong rush of Nahum Tate's libretto for Purcell. *Opera seria* requires at least two interlocking love stories and Metastasio brings on Iarbas as a (swaggering) suitor for Dido and has her sister (Selene) secretly in love with Aeneas as well. To deepen the intrigue still further, Iarbas' confidant, Araspe, is in love with Selene. Alignments are created and dissolved; enemies act magnanimously and friends treacherously; anger gives way to love and vice versa; impossible choices are presented (Dido asks Aeneas whether she should marry Iarbas or kill herself). Finally, after Aeneas has departed and Dido reneged on her promise to marry Iarbas, Iarbas fires Carthage and Dido throws herself into the flames. The drama ends with an epilogue spoken by Neptune, after he has extinguished the flames with a storm in a modified version of his role in *Aeneid* 1 (142–56). Vergilian material finds its way into the confrontations between Dido and Aeneas, but it is the potential for hesitation, delay, and emotional fluctuation in Vergil's text that Metastasio realizes (cf. *Aen.* 4.285–7, 413–14, 432, 436–7). *Opera seria* produced at least one non-Metastasian Dido opera in the *Didon* of Piccinni/Marmontel, first performed in 1783 in Paris, and significant as a work that Berlioz would have known.

Metastasio's libretto was so well known that it migrated into other genres. Both Schubert and Loewe set passages as *Lieder* and Clementi published a sonata for solo piano under the title "Didone abbandonata" in 1821. Clementi's intense and tragic late sonata makes no attempt to tell a story but seems rather to enter the subjectivity of Dido, where anger, regret and self-dramatization, inwardness and protest melt into one another. The requirement that a sonata end with a fast movement leaves us with a Dido driven across the tragic stage like Orestes (*scaenis agitatus Orestes, Aen.* 4.471). Clementi's sonata bridges the classical and Romantic styles, and our next exhibit takes us to late Romanticism and away from Dido. Liszt's *Sunt lacrymae rerum* was composed in 1872, late in his career, and published as part of the third of his *Années de pèlerinage*. The collection, which is rarely played, contains some of Liszt's darkest and most enigmatic piano music; it interweaves pieces of religious inspiration with threnodies, including *Sunt lacrymae rerum*. Aeneas' words on seeing the fall of Troy depicted on Dido's temple have been taken as the quintessence of the pity and pathos that characterize the *Aeneid*, but Liszt has turned them into something much more bitter. The work begins in the lower register of the piano with a repeated four-note descending motif that emphasizes the dotted second note. We inevitably hear it as *sunt LACrymae*, with the word *lacrymae* becoming something like a cretic. The cretic is then truncated into an obsessively repeated iamb until the opening *sunt lacrymae* returns in a complete transformation: the opening four-note motif becomes four descending chords of equal value in the left hand, the first three repeated once, while the missing short note of the *sunt lacrymae* motif appears in the obsessive iamb of the right hand, now linking the pairs of crunching chords to give them extra weight. The effect is to turn the speaking lament of the *sunt lacrymae* motif into a pitilessly percussive and repetitive assault. Liszt's *Sunt lacrymae rerum* does not so much set Vergil's words as brood on them, obsess over them, and, above all, test them. The musical processes destroy the rhetorical gesture, truncating it, atomizing it, rearranging it and allowing it to wander, as though Liszt were questioning the adequacy of Aeneas' comforting words and finding them wanting. Very different was Berlioz's response to the famous Vergilian phrase. After composing an aria for Dido in *Les Troyens* which paraphrases her *non ignara mali miseris succurrere disco* ("not unacquainted with grief myself I have learned to aid the unfortunate," 1.630), Berlioz reports in a letter that he said out loud, as though Vergil were there, "that's it, isn't it, dear master? *Sunt lacrimae rerum.*"

Liszt's treatment of the quintessentially Vergilian tag represents one way in which the procedures of instrumental music may afford a new perspective on a literary text. Another is by a change of scale. In the twentieth century it is, surprisingly, a text from the *Eclogues* that has received the most significant attention. The second half of the eighth eclogue, in which an enchantress draws her beloved Daphnis to her with a magical incantation, has inspired works of a scale and power that burst the delicate frame of Vergil's pastoral. The title of Charles Martin Loeffler's symphonic *Poème païen* (1902) says much about what has made this tale of magic and love attractive to composers of the twentieth century. Scored for full modern orchestra with an important piano part, and running for over twenty minutes, the work conjures up sinister forces and lush pastoral landscapes in equal measure. The drama is enhanced by three offstage trumpets, which seem to represent the pull of magic on the absent Daphnis and appear triumphantly onstage at the climax of the work. Krzysztof Penderecki's *Ecloga VIII* (1972) for six male voices focuses on magical speech itself; few of Vergil's words are audible through the impressive display of extended vocal techniques, but *carmina* is one of them. One is reminded of the medieval tradition of Vergil the wizard, as Kenneth Elliott suggests in the liner notes to the recording of the dedicatees, the King's Singers. The setting of the same passage by the Czech composer Jan Novak, who composed for Latin texts throughout his life, calls for the appropriately slender forces of piano, clarinet, and soprano. Novak's delicious *Mimus magicus* (1969) captures the amused detachment of the *Eclogues* from their personae and stands at the opposite pole to Loeffler's *Poème païen*.

If we exclude the Orpheus and Eurydice story, the *Georgics*, perhaps not surprisingly, have inspired no significant compositions. But David Cairns suggests that we can hear Berlioz's response to the *Georgics* in the entrance of the farm workers in the third act of *Les Troyens* (no. 22). Cairns (1969, 603) argues that the "strange antique sadness" of this music recalls a passage in Berlioz's *Memoirs* which describes a visit to the *soi-disant* villa of Maecenas in Tivoli: Berlioz imagines "Virgil's melancholy voice reciting, at a feast presided over by the minister of Augustus, some splendid fragment of the Georgics." In the grave circularity of this dance we can imagine the farmer's year *actus in orbem* (2.401) and we may catch the internal incidental music that accompanied one man's reading of Vergil.

I turn finally to a closer look at the two best-known musical versions of Vergil, both of which hold a secure place in the contemporary operatic repertoire, Purcell's *Dido and Aeneas* (probably first performed in 1689) and Berlioz's *Les Troyens* (composed 1856–9; first performed complete in 1968). The two operas could hardly be more different, though they both follow tradition in giving pride of place to Dido. Tate's libretto for Purcell is condensed to the point of obscurity, and it focuses on the swift trajectory from Dido's confession of her love to her dying lament. Berlioz's massive work has a libretto written by the composer himself, a lover of Vergil since childhood. It falls into two parts, *La Prise de Troie* and *Les Troyens à Carthage*, drawing on material in books 1, 2, and 4 of the *Aeneid* in which the Trojans are driven both from Troy and Carthage towards the fated Italy.

Berlioz's time was ripe for such a project: the age of empire was the age of Grand Opera, with its historical subjects, spectacular scenes of public life, plots focusing on the conflict between the public and the private, and its emphasis on local color. But the subjects of later Grand Opera tended to be orientalizing, or medieval, rather than classical. Berlioz was going against the grain in choosing a classical subject, but to that classical subject he brought the interest of Grand Opera in the exotic, archaic, and orientalizing elements that are notably missing from Vergil's epic.

In the case of Purcell, the fourth book of the *Aeneid* inspired a much more focused dramatic work than he had yet produced, so that *Dido and Aeneas* has come to be known as the first English opera. But the masque tradition to which much of Purcell's dramatic work belonged is absorbed into the drama to give us a Dido who stands at the center of a court. If Purcell and Tate are not interested in the broader historical context of the story of Dido and Aeneas within the epic of Rome, they have nevertheless given us a Dido who is more embedded in a social context than is Vergil's. *Dido and Aeneas* gives a prominent role to the chorus, a component of the genre that decisively affects Tate and Purcell's treatment of the material, as it does that of Berlioz. Purcell's choruses of courtiers and witches represent the social environment in which courtiers both depend on Dido for their "sport" and envy her for her status. They are in some respects dramatic versions of Vergil's *Fama*.

A common reference point for the two operas and their Vergilian model is the hunt around which the action of *Aeneid* 4 pivots. A crucial element in Vergil's fourth book, the hunt is also a musical topos that has its own conventions and it features in both operas. For a long time Berlioz's "Royal Hunt and Storm" was the only part of *Les Troyens* that was played, and it appeared with some frequency as a separate item in the concert hall. In the opera house, Berlioz's stage directions call for an elaborate scenario in which an idyllic natural world with sporting Naiads and so forth is interrupted by the royal hunt. The sounds of the hunt mingle with those of the elements as a storm is unleashed on the countryside; Aeneas and Dido enter and take shelter in a cave; nymphs with disheveled hair run wild; cries of "*Italie*" are heard; streams become rivers and an oak is struck by lightning. The Trojan destiny, which intrudes throughout the opera in the form of the cry "*Italie*," appears here as a Bacchic drive mingling with the *furor* of nature and disrupting the countryside through which it passes. Are the Trojans the intruding hunters who throw a peaceful countryside into confusion (as they will in the *Aeneid* when they reach Italy), or are they the prey, hounded by the cries of "*Italie*" that drive them from their promising new alliance? This section is the place in the opera where Berlioz most spectacularly addresses Vergilian *furor*, but it is present from the opening chorus of Trojans delirious with relief at the departure of the Greeks to the final Carthaginian chorus of vengeance.

Tate and Purcell's hunt is central to their scenario on several levels but it leads us in quite different directions. The hunt is a court ritual, rooting the fate of the protagonists in the world of the court. Belinda (Dido's sister), echoed by the courtiers, sings voluptuously of the pleasures of the hunt, which we might easily mistake for pleasures of a different sort. It is the chorus, rather than Dido, that is the locus of eroticism in this opera:

> Thanks to these lovesome vales,
> These desert hills and dales,
> So fair the game, so rich the sport,
> Diana's self might to these woods resort.

A famous Vergilian simile compares Dido to a deer whom a shepherd has shot unknowingly (4.69–73), and in Purcell's opera Dido is hunted from the start, when her courtiers urge her to succumb to what will prove a fatal love. Vergil's narrator introduces his wounded queen with the ominous adversative "But" (*At regina gravi iamdudum saucia cura*, 4.1). Purcell's Belinda begins the opera with a more encouraging kind of adversative ("Shake the cloud from off your brow, / Fate your wishes does allow") and is echoed by the chorus ("Banish sorrow, banish care / Grief should ne'er approach the fair"). Dido's blithe entourage draws her out into an open confession of her love, and once the first step has been made Belinda sounds the hunting motif with her song "Pursue thy conquest, Love; her eyes / Confess the flame her tongue denies."

The ensuing trajectory of the opera is as clear as that of *Aeneid* 4, in which the "hidden fire" that consumes Dido from the second line burns itself out as the warmth of life leaves her in the last line of the book. Purcell and Tate imitate the clarity of this trajectory, but with a different emphasis: the swiftness of the opera is the shortest distance between Dido's opening confession "I languish till my grief is known, / Yet would not have it guessed" and her final prayer "Remember me, but ah! forget my fate." Dido does and does not want Belinda and her court to intrude on her interiority, and she does and does not want to be remembered. A contradictory desire finds its denouement in an impossible demand, for we remember Dido *because* of her fate. Does Purcell point us to a person behind the drama, struggling to escape the forms in which she has been trapped, the endless repetition of her story in version after version?

Tate's libretto gives us an *Aeneid* without deities. Instead, a scene that transpires at the same time as the hunt introduces us to a coven of witches who conspire to destroy Dido. It is they who send a false image of Mercury to order Aeneas to leave Carthage. The witches help to streamline the plot by eliminating long-range influences on this focused little drama. But the witches also make a very effective incarnation of Vergil's *Fama*, for they are motivated by spite ("The Queen of Carthage, whom we hate, / As we do all in prosp'rous state..."). They conjure up the storm, not to bring the lovers together but "to mar their hunting sport," and their laughing chorus nicely represents the countless tongues of Vergil's rumor to which Purcell's music gives a concrete sound: instead of Vergil's terrifying monster representing the uncontrollable spread of news, true or false, Purcell gives us the timbre of spiteful jealousy. Purcell's witches, then, are not substitutes for the Vergilian gods, but uncanny agents of the malevolent speech allegorized by Vergil's *Fama*. They are also the counterparts of Belinda and the courtiers, who encourage Dido's love in order to indulge their own pleasures. Dido is hedged about by parasites on one side and jealous spoilers on the other, and, like the courtiers, the witches have their own particular pleasures:

> Destruction's our delight,
> Delight our greatest sorrow!
> Elissa dies tonight,
> And Carthage flames tomorrow.

Are these not the pleasures of tragedy and of the satisfying swiftness of events on the dramatic stage? Purcell's doomed Dido is trapped in a ritual that has been endlessly repeated for our tragic pleasure. By contrast, Berlioz's reception of Vergil involves the rescuing and refiguring of Vergilian characters and episodes, and it subjects the *Aeneid* to a thorough reorientation. Berlioz intervenes in a work that has been his lifelong companion to realize fully what has caught his imagination and affection. When Vergil's Anchises acknowledges (*Aen.* 3.183–7) that Cassandra had told him about Italy, he asks, "but who then would have believed her?" Berlioz, the misunderstood artist out of step with fashion, identified both himself and his opera with the unheeded prophet. When he realized that he would never see his opera performed in its entirety, he lamented in his *Memoirs* (Cairns 1969, 603): "O my noble Cassandra, my heroic virgin, I must then resign myself: I shall never hear you." Much of the pathos of the *Aeneid* resonates in Berlioz's accounts of the enormous labor of producing this work, which he knew stood little chance of success with the public. If Coroebus fails to rescue Cassandra (2.402–8), Berlioz succeeds, putting Cassandra at the center of *La Prise*. He makes a full-blown love story out of the relationship between Coroebus and Cassandra that is only glimpsed in the *Aeneid*, and in the process he reverses the relative importance of the lovers: Cassandra tells the disappointed and confused Coroebus that their love is doomed and, in the final act, leads the Trojan Vestals in an act of mass suicide, dying with the cry of "*Italie*." Cassandra's sense of impending disaster colors the musical texture as does Aeneas' narrative in the *Aeneid*. Her voice replaces the sound of Aeneas' guilt-ridden sorrow with a tragic power that absorbs the authority of the male prophets in the *Aeneid* (Jupiter, Helenus, Anchises).

Carthage, too, is rescued from its Vergilian role as foil to Rome. In some respects, the glorious city that Vergil anticipates is deflected to Dido's Carthage and certainly there is a strong feeling of relief when the curtain goes up on the scene at Carthage at the beginning of *Les Troyens à Carthage* (Act 3). A grateful and admiring people is singing a national anthem, addressed to Dido. The anthem marches along with a confident swing, a sure-footedness that tells us that we have arrived – but not in the "*Italie*" to which the dying Cassandra has pointed us in the final bars of Part 1. It is here in Carthage, if anywhere in the opera, that political ideals are voiced. Dido is acclaimed by her loving people; she greets and rewards delegations of builders, sailors, and farm workers, representing the arts of peace, and urges her people to provide an example to the earth: great in peace, let the Carthaginians become heroes in war. This is a city with a project, and the whole act reflects the Saint-Simonian utopianism to which Berlioz had at one time been attracted. When Berlioz has Ascanius address Dido as "**auguste** reine," it is as though the promise of Vergil's Augustan Rome has been diverted to Carthage, where it will be cut short by the arrival of the Trojans. David Cairns (1988, 86) is surely right when he suggests that Berlioz's Carthage owes something to Vergil's picture of Latium as a kingdom of Saturn, still enjoying the blessings of the Golden Age.

Berlioz's scenario is based on books from the first half of the *Aeneid*, but his opera, like the *Aeneid*, is divided into two parts, each of which is distinguished by locale, musical color, and dramatic style. *Prise* is tragic, swift, and teleological; *Carthage* is expansive, and its generic affinities are with pastoral and romance. Though the final pages of the opera anticipate the coming of Rome, there is nothing to mark the distinctive presence of a third entity, which permeates the very texture of Vergil's Roman epic. Berlioz's two panels juxtapose the destruction of an ancient city with the hopeful beginnings of a utopia, overshadowed by the arrival of the Trojans. It moves from what is about to pass away (archaic Troy) to what will never come to be (utopian Carthage) in a radical reinterpretation of Vergil's bipartite *Aeneid*. The cries of "*Italie*" that punctuate the action hurry the protagonists on without crystallizing into a vision of the Roman future so that the dynamism of history turns into the Bacchic revel of the royal hunt and storm. Berlioz's contrast between the two tragic cities is underlined by the effects of local color characteristic of Grand Opera. Vergil makes little attempt to supply the Trojans with any cultural specificity, and it comes as a shock when Iarbas describes Aeneas' effeminate headgear and toilette (4.216–17). Moments like this (compare similar remarks in the speech of Numanus Remulus, 9.598–620) remind us of the exotic eastern provenance of these proto-Romans and leave us wondering how (or whether) to imagine them. True to his genre, Berlioz uses a panoply of exotic and obsolete instruments as well as harmonic features to characterize the archaic or the oriental aspects of his locales.

Vergil, of course, has musical moments of his own. The onomatopoeic verb *ululare* ("to wail"), for instance, occurs once in book 2 (488) and once in book 4, at the wedding of Dido and Aeneas in the cave (168). Vergil also uses its cognate noun, *ululatus*, at the suicide of Dido (*femineo ululatu*, 4.667, with an onomatopoeic hiatus). It is the latter occasion that contains Vergil's most complex musical effects, as the sound of the destruction of a city (prophetic of the Punic Wars) is layered onto the lamentation at Dido's death in an elemental uproar. Berlioz displaces these effects to the royal hunt and storm where the ululation of the nymphs is accompanied by cries of "*Italie,*" which supply the historical dimension of this elemental riot. It is the birth of Rome, not the destruction of Carthage, that is imagined in this uproar, and the *moles* of history's burden in the *Aeneid* (1.33) becomes a much more immediate, and equivocal, energy in Berlioz.

One of the most striking musical effects in Vergil is the passage in book 2 where the sounds of mingled grief (*diverso interea miscentur moenia luctu*, 2.298) are transformed into the distinct and terrifying sound of weapons (*clarescunt sonitus armorumque ingruit horror*, 301). Berlioz reverses this progression, producing an eerie transition from Aeneas' cry "Le salut des vaincus est de n'en plus attendre" (*una salus victis nullam sperare salutem*, 354), accompanied by brass fanfares, to the low wailing of the Vestals in the following, final scene at Troy. The Vestals, whose suicide before the wondering eyes of the victorious Greeks brings *La Prise* to a climactic end, are Berlioz's invention. When Vergil's Greeks break into the palace of Priam the interior resounds with the wailing of women (*ululant*, 488). But the panicked mothers quickly give way to the business of men. Not so in Berlioz, whose opera feminizes heroism. The irony of "Troy falling, Rome arising" is enacted in the triumphant suicide of the Vestals as Cassandra cries "*Italie, Italie.*"

One of Berlioz's greatest challenges was to find an appropriate ending to his opera. Opera is the most closural of forms, but Vergil's ending to the *Aeneid* is one of the most puzzling in ancient literature. Berlioz managed, after an interesting false start, to settle on a scenario that had all the necessary ingredients of a Grand Opera finale: the death of the heroine, a chorus, spectacular scenic effects, and a vision of the future. Nonetheless, Berlioz's finale is curiously unsatisfying and it has even been suggested that his rejected first thoughts are preferable. The original ending, quite different from the final version we see today, is more straightforwardly triumphalist, comprising a vision of the Roman future inspired by *Aeneid* 6 as well as a prophecy of French rule in North Africa. Berlioz later eliminated the latter reference as "pure childish chauvinism." His final ending is more complex than his first effort, insofar as the vision of the Roman future is not separated from the action at Carthage. Dido stabs herself after prophesying the coming of Hannibal, but as she dies she has a vision of the triumph of Rome. The Carthaginian people, who do not share this vision, then curse the Trojans and vow a hatred that will encompass the destruction of the Romans to the astonishment of the whole world. Unseen by the chorus, a tableau appears in the distance representing legions marching past the Capitol and an emperor surrounded by a court of poets and artists. The word *ROMA* looms ironically over the Carthaginians as they prophesy the destruction of the Trojans. The clash between the two simulta-neous scenes is brutal, and Berlioz's stage directions underline the irony with a point that cannot be represented in performance: "*on entend au loin la marche troyenne transmise aux romains par la tradition et devenue leur chant de triomphe*" (at a dis-tance is heard the Trojan march that was handed down to the Romans and became their triumphal song).

But there are deeper ironies in the relation between words and music. The Roman tableau is accompanied in the orchestra by the final triumphant statement of the Trojan March from Part 1 as the Carthaginians on stage utter their curse. Berlioz comments in his stage directions that the people of Carthage "*lance son imprécation, premier cri de guerre punique, contrastant par sa fureur avec la solennité de la marche triomphale*" (hurl their curse, the first shout of the Punic War, contrasting in its fury with the solemnity of the triumphal march). But Berlioz's description of this scene is strangely misleading. We are led to expect that the music of the choral imprecation will clash with the March, but, disturbingly, it does not. The chorus' vision of a vengeance that will make the world sit up and take notice is sung *to*, not against, the Trojan March. Its fanfares seem to *support* the bloodthirsty vow of the Carthaginian chorus, so that the vengeful fury of the Carthaginians inhabits the Trojan March. This complicates the triumph of the final apotheosis considerably. The vengeful Carthaginians might repre-sent the continued resistance of the vanquished to the empire that has crushed them. But there is another sense in which the vengeful Carthaginians might inhabit the Trojan March/Roman anthem, one in which the Carthaginians represent an aspect of the triumphant Romans themselves. The combination of triumphalism with revenge must remind us of the similarly truncated, and hotly disputed, ending of the *Aeneid*, where Aeneas plunges his sword into the defeated Turnus as revenge for the latter's killing of Pallas. It may be that here, as elsewhere, Berlioz managed to include ele-ments of the second half of the *Aeneid* into his scenario from books 1, 2, and 4.

Berlioz's ending may accord with the norms of Grand Opera, but it is emotionally very unsatisfying. Even without the ironies I have described, the recovery of the defeated Trojans in the final triumphant vision of *Rome immortelle* is focalized through Dido, now the center of our emotional investment, and the abstract form of this tri-umph as Berlioz represents it must compete with the very distinctive Carthaginian utopia that Berlioz has staged in the third act. It is hard to know what we are meant to feel as the curtain comes down, and that is a very unusual experience for the audi-ence of a nineteenth-century opera. As Berlioz rewrites the *Aeneid* he exerts in turn a Vergilian pressure on the norms of opera.

FURTHER READING

Study of the reception of antiquity in music lags behind reception studies in the other arts, but McDonald (2001) points the way, with chapters on both Purcell and Berlioz. Strunk (1930) and Draheim (1993) provide good surveys of Vergil in music. The neumed medieval manuscripts of

Vergil are discussed by Ziolkowski (2004). Osthoff (1954) deals with the Renaissance motets. Cavalli's *La Didone* and its context are the subject of Heller (1998), which comes in a valuable collection of essays on Dido's reception (Burden 1998, with an essay on Purcell by Burden). Harris (1987) is the most convenient treatment of Purcell's *Dido and Aeneas* from a variety of perspectives, and Kemp (1988) is an excellent introduction to Berlioz's *Les Troyens* (with essays on Berlioz and Grand Opera and on the performance history of *Troyens*). Fitzgerald (2004) and Cairns (1988, in Kemp) deal specifically with Vergil and Berlioz. Robinson (1985) is a provocative treatment of *Les Troyens* from the perspective of cultural history.

PART FOUR

The American *Aeneid*

CHAPTER TWENTY FOUR

Vergil and the Early American Republic

Carl J. Richard

From the colonial period until the late nineteenth century, the poems of Vergil occupied a central position in the education of American youth. During this formative period of the United States, the pastoral strain in Vergil's poetry played a crucial role in inculcating a widespread belief in the moral superiority of the rural, agricultural lifestyle, a belief that undergirded the shift from the classical mixed government established by the United States Constitution to a more democratic system in which the nation's agricultural majority possessed the predominant power. Although Vergil and the other classical authors continued to receive the same political, moral, religious, and utilitarian criticisms they had for centuries, antebellum critics of the classics were no more successful than previous generations of critics at ending their dominance of the educational system.

Early Americans derived their grammar school and college curricula from the English educational system, which, like the other European systems, had originated in the Middle Ages. The medieval "trivium" (rhetoric, logic, and grammar) and "quadrivium" (arithmetic, music, geometry, and astronomy) continued to dominate Western curricula through most of the nineteenth century in both Catholic and Protestant nations. Latin retained its primacy over Greek even during the Philhellenic movement of the antebellum period, and Vergil remained one of the principal Latin authors studied (Cohen 1974, 11, 22–4; Jones 1974, 121–2).

American grammar school students commonly read the Greek and Latin classics every morning from eight to eleven and every afternoon from one until dark. The learning process generally began with the memorization of the grammatical rules contained in Ezekiel Cheever's *Short Introduction to the Latin Tongue*. The pupil then translated the Latin dialogues in Marthurius Corderius' *Colloquies*, which contained both Latin and English columns. At more advanced stages he translated Cicero's *Epistles* or *Orations*, followed by Vergil's *Aeneid*. The first day the student translated a given passage aloud, the second he wrote out his translation, and the third he converted his own English translation back into Latin in a different tense. Only then did he take up Greek, converting Greek passages into Latin as well as English. Not until after the Revolution did students begin to study their mother tongue in grammar schools. Even then, many educators and laymen considered the study of English grammar a mere matter for the home, unworthy of formal academic attention. The "grammar" in grammar school referred largely to Latin (Middlekauff 1963, 80–4, 164; Gummere 1963, 58; Richard 1994, 13).

Vergil was a staple of grammar school education. In the 1760s Donald Robertson's boarding school near Dunkirk, Virginia, provided James Madison, John Taylor of Caroline, John Tyler (father of the future president), and George Rogers Clark with a rigorous classical training that included selections from Vergil's works (Brant 1941–61, 1: 64–5). Madison later testified regarding Robertson, "All that I have been in life I owe to that man" (Davis 1964, 36). Similarly, as an instructor in Lebanon, Connecticut for most of the second half of the eighteenth century, Nathan Tisdale taught the poems of Vergil to children from every North American colony and the British West Indies. His students praised his kindness and his ability to transform their ignorance of the classics into competence within two years (Cremin 1970, 506–9). At his various boarding schools in Georgia and South Carolina, which were said to have resounded with the echoes of Homer, Vergil, and Horace, the Reverend Moses Waddel taught such luminaries as William H. Crawford, a future secretary of the treasury, and his own brother-in-law John C. Calhoun (Berrigan 1968–9, 18–19). Calhoun's biographer Charles M. Wiltse noted, "So great was the emphasis on the works of the ancient world that to construe a mere 150 lines of Vergil or Horace as a day's assignment was considered next thing to failing altogether." The record at one of Waddel's schools was set at 1,212 lines of Vergil in a single day (Wiltse 1944–51, 1: 29).

In the antebellum period a plethora of female academies (and a few coeducational academies) introduced the classics to girls for the first time. (On this topic see the following chapter by Winterer in this volume.) Catharine and Mary Beecher's Hartford Female Seminary was fairly typical in touting its offerings in Greek and Roman history, Euclid, and Vergil in 1824 (Tolley 1996, 132 n.9, 135). When she was only 6, the Transcendentalist Margaret Fuller received a pile of books from her father, including some written in Greek and Latin (Cleary 2000, 65). Vergil and several other Roman authors were her daily companions, lessons from whose works she recited each evening. She then studied Greek at Cambridgeport Private Grammar School with the boys (Conrad 1976, 52, 54).

One reason that Vergil was so widely taught in grammar schools was that most colleges required the ability to translate passages from his works as part of their entrance examination. When John Winthrop's nephew, George Downing, applied to Harvard in the mid-seventeenth century, he was required to "understand Tully [i.e., Cicero], Virgil, or any such classical authors, and readily to speak or write true Latin in prose and have skill in making Latin verse, and be completely grounded in the Greek language." When John Adams entered Harvard a century later, in the 1750s, Harvard demanded that he be able "extempore to read, construe, and parse Tully, Vergil, or such like common classical authors, and to write Latin in prose, and to be skilled in making Latin verse, or at least in the rules of the Prosodia, and to read, construe, and parse ordinary Greek, as in the New Testament, Isocrates, or such like, and decline the paradigms of Greek nouns and verbs" (Chinard 1933, 11–12). In 1760, when John Jay entered King's College (now Columbia), he was obliged to give a "rational account of the Greek and Latin grammars, read three orations of Cicero and three books of Vergil's *Aeneid*, and translate the first ten chapters of John into Latin" (Hofstadter and Smith 1961, 1: 117). In 1774, when Alexander Hamilton chose King's College over the College of New Jersey, the Princeton entrance examination required "the ability to write Latin prose, translate Vergil, Cicero, and the Greek gospels, and a commensurate knowledge of Latin and Greek grammar" (McDonald 1979, 12). In 1816, when Horace Mann applied for entrance to Brown University, he faced requirements with which Downing would have been completely comfortable almost two centuries earlier: the ability "to read accurately, construe, and parse Tully and the Greek Testament and Vergil…to write true Latin in prose, and [to know] the rules of Prosody." Colleges were interested in a candidate's ability to read Latin and Greek and little else (Gummere 1963, 56–7).

These entrance requirements were not restricted to the prestigious universities of what is now the Ivy League. In the antebellum period Davidson College in North Carolina, Emory and Henry College in Virginia, Sharon College in Mississippi, the University of North Carolina, South Carolina College (now the University of South Carolina), and numerous other colleges throughout the nation continued to demand the ability to translate Vergil as an entrance requirement (Knight 1949–53, 3: 297; 4: 308–9, 323, 331; O'Brien 1985, 14).

Nor did an American boy's study of Vergil cease with his entrance into college. Indeed, until 1763, classical reading at Harvard was confined almost exclusively to Vergil, Cicero, and the New Testament (Chinard 1933, 14). Students at the University of North Carolina studied Vergil their freshman year (Knight 1949–53, 3: 297). Even at the new colleges on the northwestern frontier the classics were king. During the antebellum period, a number of colleges were established there, to serve as symbols of civic pride, as magnets to attract settlers, and as bastions of civilization against the feared barbarism of the wilderness. The classics suited each of these goals perfectly. Therefore, Allegheny College embedded some mortar from Vergil's tomb, along with a piece of Plymouth Rock, in its cornerstone, and introduced the customary Latin orations at its first commencement. Ohio University, the University of Michigan, and the University of Wisconsin all emphasized classical instruction, including the study of Vergil (Agard 1955, 106–9).

If the correspondence between Brown students in the year 1789–90 is any indication, pupils obsessed over Vergil even during breaks. One student complained that he had managed to read only six books of the *Aeneid* and one oration of Cicero during a break, while yet another confided his embarrassment at having read only seven books of Vergil and having "looked at Greek grammer [*sic*], mind, looked at it." One student informed his roommate, "Your chum studies Latin like a Trojan," an obvious reference to Vergil's myth that Aeneas' Trojans had formed the Roman people by intermarrying with the local Latins (Pomfret 1932, 138–40, 145).

The study of Vergil had a profound impact on the founders of the United States. Although Thomas Jefferson, one of the few Americans whose proficiency in Greek equaled his command of Latin, was partial to Homer, he considered Vergil the second greatest poet of all time (Bergh and Lipscomb 1903, 18: 448). John Adams claimed that even John Milton's *Paradise Lost* fell short of Vergil's *Aeneid*. He added: "The Aeneid is a well ordered Garden, where it is impossible to find a single Spot that does not produce some beautiful Plant or Flower" (Reinhold 1984, 232). Even Benjamin Rush, who advocated the abolition of the requirement of the classical languages in the schools, loved Vergil. Rush wrote: "In painting, as well as poetry, the attention should always be directed to some object, to which every other part of the work should be subservient; Vergil's Aenead [*sic*] would cease to please us unless our eyes were kept constantly fixed upon the illustrious hero of the poem" (Runes 1947, 375). Rush and his friend Ebenezer Hazard always exchanged a hand clasp originally described by Vergil at *Aen.* 1.408–9 (Gummere 1967, 69).

The founders often quoted Vergil. As a marginal note to a poem from the *American Magazine* that described a field, a young James Madison copied a line from Vergil's *Eclogues* (1.69) into his commonplace book: "And marvel as I gaze at the ears of corn, my realm of old" (Rutland et al. 1962–77, 1: 17–18). In a 1758 diary entry John Adams quoted a line from Vergil, which he himself translated as, "He nurses a Wound in his Veins and is consumed by a blind, hidden fire" (*Aen.*4.2, where Dido is the subject). Adams followed this line with the names of five young men who were in love (Reinhold 1984, 233). Writing for the Boston Sons of Liberty a decade later, he embedded a line from Vergil's *Eclogues* (1.45) in a statement addressed to the British Whig John Wilkes: "'Tis from your endeavors we hope for a Royal 'Pascite, ut ante, boves'" (Taylor 1977–, 1: 215–16). The Latin, meaning "put your cows out to pasture as you did before," no doubt confused Wilkes, who was not known for his classical prowess. In 1767 Benjamin Rush exulted over John Witherspoon's appointment as president of the College of New Jersey with a line from Vergil's *Eclogues* (4.6): "The reign of Saturn returns." In 1792 Rush called his firstborn son, John, the *spes gregis* ("the hope of the flock," *Ecl.* 1.15). In 1809, envious of his son James' sojourn in Edinburgh, Rush quoted the *Aeneid* (8.560): "O! If Jupiter would but restore to me the years that are gone!" Lamenting the United States' defeats in the War of 1812, he quoted the *Georgics* (1.199–200): "Everything is rushing to deterioration" (Butterfield 1951, 1: 48, 616; 2: 1016, 1189). In the last year of his life, decrying "a nation debased by love of money," Rush again quoted Vergil (*Aen.* 1.462): "Hence are there tears for things" (Adair and Schutz 1966, 277). In 1802 Alexander Hamilton borrowed Vergil's description of the Cyclops (*Aen.* 3.658), "shapeless, huge, [and] blind," to describe the masses (Syrett 1961–79, 26: 13). Even Benjamin Franklin, who had no formal classical education and who supported the abolition of the requirement of the classical languages, quoted Vergil. In 1775, he lambasted Britain, writing, "When I consider the extream Corruption prevalent among all Orders of Men in this old rotten State, and the glorious publick Virtue so predominant in our rising Country, I cannot but apprehend more Mischief than Benefit from a closer Union…. To unite us will only be to corrupt and poison us also. It seems like Mezentius [an Etruscan king] coupling and binding together the dead and the living." Franklin then quotes *Aen.* 8.487–8: "Truly torture: as they floated in the poisonous, putrid blood in vile embrace, he slew them with a lingering death" (Wilcox et al. 1978, 509).

Vergil's influence held steady during the antebellum period. Hugh Swinton Legaré, one of the leading intellectuals of the antebellum South, marveled at the combination of elegance and instruction in the *Georgics*, writing, "The wonder is how the poet was able to reconcile his genius to his subject – how he could describe a plough, for instance, without ever sinking down into prose or elevating his style so far above the matter, and how he has contrived to throw a sort of Epic dignity and animation without any air of the Burlesque, into his pictures of the Beehive…. The perfection of the *Georgics* is unapproachable in Didactic poetry, and were it not that we have that work and Lucretius' *De Rerum Natura* before our eyes, we should even doubt whether the very phrase 'Didactic poetry' were not somewhat of a contradiction in terms." Legaré admired the literature of Augustan Rome because in it the Romans allowed their traditional pragmatism to be moderated by Greek elegance. In 1832, when the Catholic bishop John English addressed his fellow members of the Literary and Philosophical Society of Charleston, he recommended Vergil as a stylistic model. In fact, English went on to publish an essay on Vergil ("The Descent of Aeneas to the Shades") in the *Southern Literary Journal* a few years later. Widely exhibited paintings, such as Joshua Shaw's *Dido and Aeneas Going to the Hunt*, dealt with Vergilian themes. Thomas Bulfinch, a bank clerk who wrote in his spare time, used Vergil as one of his principal sources for *The Age of Fable* (1855), a compendium of Greco-Roman myths. Popularly known as "Bulfinch's Mythology," the volume became one of the most popular books ever published in the United States and the standard work on classical mythology for nearly a century (O'Brien 1985, 106; Fox-Genovese and Genovese 2005, 262; O'Brien 2004, 1090–1; Winterer 2002, 66–7; Cleary 1990, 1, 20, 48, 76).

Steeped in Vergil, early Americans were anxious that their sons (and sometimes their daughters) receive the same benefit. Patrick Henry's father, John, considered his son's classical education so vital that he refused to surrender him to a tutor, teaching the boy Latin himself. Patrick not only studied Vergil, he also carried out the family tradition of demanding detailed knowledge of the classics in their progeny. Patrick Henry's grandson claimed that he dreaded his grandfather's quizzes far more than any recitation before a professor (Henry 1969, 1: 4, 8; Meade 1957–69, 1: 57). John Adams secured a rigorous classical education for his son, John Quincy, in Europe. He wrote letters to the boy, then studying at the University of Leyden (now Leiden) in the Netherlands, demanding that he discard simple authors like Phaedrus and Cornelius Nepos for the grand masters of Latin, Vergil and Cicero. Four years later he proudly noted that John Quincy had translated all of the *Aeneid* (Butterfield 1963–73, 3: 309; 4: 48, 144; Koch and Peden 1946, 72). In the antebellum period, when classical education became more common for girls, Ralph Waldo Emerson encouraged his daughter Ellen to read Vergil in the original Latin (Rusk 1939, 4: 333, 422).

The Adams family's successful transmission of the love of Vergil across several generations illustrates the power of the classics over the heart as well as the head. John Quincy called the *Georgics* "the most perfect composition that ever issued from the mind of man." Praising its "transcendent excellence," he noted that some passages had been "the special delight of twenty centuries" and would "enchant the ear of harmony and transport the soul of fancy as long as sentiment shall last among mankind"

(Reinhold 1984, 239). One of his prize possessions was a bust of Vergil, which he bequeathed to his own son Charles Francis, who later served as the US ambassador to Great Britain during the Civil War. The product of classical conditioning from his own father and grandfather, Charles Francis grew to love Vergil as well. Of the *Eclogues* he wrote: "They are fine specimens of the highest polish of which verse is susceptible. Vigorous yet smooth." To Charles Francis, the *Georgics* were "models for that specimen of composition, a sign of which is that all subsequent times have only imitated them." He added regarding this "exquisite" work: "There is an amazing sweetness in these Poems. They present agreeable images. Country scenery, quiet innocence, and peace…. The high polish, the ease and familiarity with which the versification is conducted, and the beauty of it throughout are now and must remain unequalled monuments of ancient mental exertion." At the end of the *Georgics*, Charles Francis wrote in his copy, "These books have never been equaled." According to Charles Francis, the *Aeneid* was "an honor to the human intellect for imagination, for pathos, for perfect harmony, for beauty." He added: "The pictures are graphic, the versification smooth and the language elegant. In short, about as good as one can imagine a thing of the kind." Of Homer and Vergil he wrote, "Perhaps it is one of the most curious of occurrences that perfection in this kind of style should have been reached so early" (Donald et al. 1964–, 4: vii, 247, 252–5, 279).

The most important influence of Vergil on the early American republic was his central role in the use of classical pastoralism to promote representative democracy. Democratic Republicans like Thomas Jefferson and James Madison comforted themselves with the notion that the United States could safely adopt a democracy, however vilified by classical political theorists, because the abundance of land in the United States would allow a citizenry of Vergilian farmers.

No theme was more ubiquitous in classical literature than that of the superiority of the rural, agricultural existence, a lifestyle wedged comfortably between the extremes of "savage" and "sophisticated." A motif of some Greek poets, like Hesiod and Theocritus, pastoralism became the central theme of the leading poets of Rome's Augustan Age, Vergil and Horace. Convinced that farmers were the backbone of Rome, Vergil's *Georgics* (2.458–74) exhorted his fellow Romans to regenerate the community after a century of civil war by returning to the plow:

> How lucky the farmers are – I wish they knew!
> The Earth herself, most just, pours forth for them
> An easy living from the soil, far off
> From clashing weapons. Though the farmer has
> No mansion with proud portals which spits out
> A monster wave of morning visitors
> From every room, nor do his callers gasp
> At inlaid columns, bright with tortoiseshell,
> Or gold-embroidered clothes or bronzes from
> Ephyre, nor in his house is plain white wool
> Dyed with Assyrian poison, nor does he
> Corrupt his olive oil with foreign spice,
> He has untroubled sleep and honest life.

> Rich in all sorts of riches, with a vast
> Estate, he has all the leisure to enjoy
> A cave, a natural pond, a valley where
> The air is cool – the mooing of the cows
> Is ever present, and to sleep beneath
> A tree is sweet. Wild animals abound
> For hunting, and young people grow up strong,
> Hardworking, satisfied with poverty:
> Their gods are holy; parents are revered.
> Surely, when Justice left the earth she stayed
> Last with these folk, and left some tokens here. (trans. Wender)

The farmer's lifestyle was the source of republican virtue. Vergil's conclusion was supported by classical political theorists like Aristotle and by most ancient historians, who credited the triumph of Sparta and Rome over their vice-ridden commercial adversaries, Athens and Carthage, as much to their pastoral virtues as to their government forms (Rahe 1992, 414).

Thomas Jefferson cherished the pastoral tradition, especially as found in the poetry of Vergil and Horace. He read Roman agricultural treatises, designed his estate to resemble the Roman villas Pliny and Varro had described, and planned the inscription of a passage from Horace's *Epodes* concerning the joys of the agricultural life near a small temple that he hoped to build on his burial ground. In a famous passage in *Notes on the State of Virginia*, Jefferson glorified agriculture in a manner strikingly reminiscent of the *Georgics*:

> Those who labor in the earth are the chosen people of God, if ever he had a chosen people, whose breasts He has made His peculiar deposit for genuine and substantial virtue. He keeps alive that sacred fire, which otherwise might escape from the face of the earth. Corruption of morals in the mass of cultivators is a phenomenon of which no age nor nation has furnished an example. It is the mark set on those, who, not looking up to heaven and to their own soil and industry as does the husbandman, for their subsistence, depend for it on casualties and caprices of customers. Dependence begets subservience and venality suffocates the germ of virtue and prepares fit tools for the designs of ambition.

The secret of the ancient republics' success was their pastoral virtues. Jefferson later wrote: "Cultivators of the earth are the most valuable citizens. They are the most vigorous, the most independent, the most virtuous, and they are tied to their country, and wedded to its liberty by the most lasting bonds.... I consider the class of artificers as the panders of vice, and the instruments by which the liberties of a country are overturned." Hence Jefferson predicted: "I think our governments will remain virtuous for many centuries; as long as they are chiefly agricultural; and this will be as long as there shall be vacant lands in any part of America" (Wilson 1981, 347–54; Lehmann 1965, 181–2; Chinard 1928, 32; Griswold 1971, 46–7).

Jefferson's passionate embrace of the pastoral tradition colored his perceptions of the world. So determined was he to perpetuate the agricultural character of the United States that he was willing to violate one of his core principles, the strict construction of the Constitution, in order to purchase Louisiana. When the absence of a constitutional provision allowing Jefferson to buy foreign territory threatened the future of the republic's agricultural base, and hence its virtue and longevity, Jefferson reluctantly sacrificed constitutional scruples in order to extend the life of the republic. The Virginian frequently compared the British commercialism he detested with that of the Carthaginians, implying an analogy between the United States and the frugal Roman Republic (Bergh and Lipscomb 1903, 12: 375, 433; 13: 361; 14: 271, 365).

The ancient and august tradition of classical pastoralism provided the essential service of legitimating the shift from the mixed government established by the United States Constitution – in which the representatives of the one, the few, and the many (the president, the senators, and the representatives) were balanced against each other – to a more democratic system. The near-unanimous judgment of ancient political theorists and historians against democracy could be overcome only by resorting to an equally revered tradition. Only by arguing that the liberty of the ancient republics had been founded on their agricultural lifestyle, rather than on their mixed governments, could Democratic Republicans like Jefferson and Madison succeed in persuading both themselves and others that a new and unprecedented system of government might be safely adopted. Democratic reforms, such as the linkage of the selection of the Electoral College with the popular vote and the elimination of property qualifications for voting, accomplished by the 1820s, were predicated on this optimism regarding the virtue of the agricultural majority.

Nevertheless, despite Vergil's usefulness in bolstering the transition to a more democratic system, some Jacksonian democrats charged the poet with treason against not just democracy but republicanism in general for glorifying Augustus in the *Aeneid*. When assaulting the European dogma that works of literary genius required royal patronage, a doctrine based largely on the glorious literature of Augustan Rome, Thomas R. Dew, president of the College of William and Mary, could not decide whether to denigrate Augustan literature or to characterize it as constituting the last vestiges of the Roman Republican spirit; so he did both. After praising the masterpieces of democratic Athens, he wrote:

> Under the great patronage of the first of the Roman Emperors we find, it is true, the arts and light literature rising to a pitch which perhaps they had not reached under the republic. After the death of Brutus the world of letters experienced a revolution almost as great as that of the political world. The literature of the Augustan age is distinguished by the tone and spirit which mark the downfall of liberty, and the consequent thraldom of the mind. The bold and manly voice of eloquence was hushed. The high and lofty spirit of the republic was tamed down to a sickly and disgusting servility. The age of poetry came when that of eloquence and philosophy was past; and Vergil and Horace and Propertius, flattered, courted and enriched by an artful prince and an elegant courtier, could consent to sing the sycophantic praises of the monarch who had signed the proscriptions of the triumvirate and riveted a despotism on his country.

Following this harsh indictment of Augustan literature, Dew then took a new tack, ascribing its better qualities to the lingering effects of republicanism: "But the men who most adorned the various departments of learning during the long reign of

Augustus were born in the last days of the republic. They saw what the glorious commonwealth had been – they beheld with their own eyes the greatness of their country, and they had inhaled in their youth the breath of freedom." Ovid, who was born too late to appreciate the republic, was an inferior poet, "too fanciful and effeminate." Similarly, George Bancroft, one of the first historians of the United States, as well as a leading Jacksonian Democrat, contrasted the sycophantic Roman literature of the Augustan Age with the more manly and democratic writing of Athens. Bancroft wrote: "In Roman literature we have sometimes cause to be disgusted with servile adulation. We could wish that Horace had not employed his genius in celebrating the victories of Augustus, and should cherish Vergil the more if something of the rustic republicanism of the elder days were discoverable in his verse" (Dew 1992, 130; Winterer 2006, 50).

Some early Americans criticized Vergil on religious and moral grounds as well. A few Christians assaulted the polytheism and vices featured in classical mythology, including the poems of Vergil. As early as 1769, John Wilson had resigned as Latin master at the Friends' Latin School in Philadelphia partly on moral grounds. His resignation letter contained the tirade:

> Is it not surprising? Is it not monstrous? That Christian Children intended to believe and relish the Truths of the Gospel should have their earliest and most retentive years imbued with the shocking Legends and abominable Romances of the worst of Heathens and should be obliged to be the Pimps of the detestable Lusts of Jupiter & Mars, attend the thefts & Villainy of Mercury, or follow Aeneas on his Murdering Progress, while the Actions and Sufferings of the great and worthy Propagators of the Holy Religion that Succeeded the Apostles are totally hid from their Eyes. Is Bacchus preferable to Ignatius, Apollo to Origen or will Helena and Clytemnestra yield an affecting Instruction or warm our Hearts with the Love of Virtue like the Virgin Martyrs & Heroines of the Christian Story? (Straub 1967, 453)

During the antebellum period, at the height of the Second Great Awakening, Christian criticism of Vergil increased. Thomas Grimké of South Carolina, one of the most vocal critics of classical education, made such criticism the centerpiece of his *Oration on the Comparative Elements and Dutys of Grecian and American Eloquence* (1834), a comprehensive assault on classical civilization and its influence in America. Claiming that "the virtues of Jesus Christ [are]…the very reverse of what are called the heroic virtues of classical antiquity," Grimké denounced the militarism, paganism, and immorality inherent in the classics. Grimké declared, "I am strangely mistaken if there be not more power, fidelity, and beauty in Walter Scott than in a dozen Homers and Vergils." He bewailed "the degrading, polluting, deforming influence of the classics over modern poetry." His criticism was tinged with guilt, since he confessed concerning the classics, "It has been my misfortune to have spent so much time upon them that my stock deriv'd from other sources is comparatively small." He found the morality of Homer and Vergil particularly disturbing, writing, "As for their morals, who would be willing to have a brother like…the mean and treacherous Aeneas, the hero of the Aeneid, if it indeed has a hero?" Grimké claimed that Aeneas acted with ingratitude and perfidy in abandoning Dido and with violence in killing Turnus.

Grimké added: "The beauties of Shakespeare are worth all the beauties of Homer and Vergil.... I do not doubt that Paradise Lost is worth the Iliad, Odyssey, and the Aeneid all together; there is more sublime, rich, and beautiful poetry in Childe Harold than half a dozen Georgics." Grimké believed that American students should read the Gospels, the early Church Fathers, and the Protestant reformers in place of the classics for moral instruction (Miles 1971, 261; Lounsbury 1986, 346, 362; Reinhold 1984, 238; Winterer 2002, 48). Even Senator Charles Sumner of Massachusetts, who had been applauded for his accurate recall of large passages from Vergil and other Latin authors while a Harvard student, later wrote: "No Roman ever wrote from the elevation of the Second Commandment, 'Love thy neighbor as thyself.' [Even] the gentle nature of Vergil, formed for the reception of such a truth, was unconscious of it" (Pierce 1878, 1: 58–9; 2: 267).

But most critics opposed Vergil and the classics on utilitarian grounds. In 1853 James H. Thornwell, the president of South Carolina College, wrote to the state's governor complaining of the dominance of classical studies at the university. Thornwell wrote that some students "do not want Latin, Greek, and philosophy, and it is hard that they cannot be permitted to get a little chemistry, a little engineering, or a little natural philosophy, without going through Homer and Vergil, Aristotle and Locke." He claimed that many graduates lost their classical knowledge within a few years, retaining only a smug sense of superiority over ordinary citizens (Knight 1949–53, 5: 153). Similarly, California journalist John S. Hittel spoke for many when he claimed, "The superiority of our time over antiquity is due...to the possession of machinery." Hittel was so romantic about materialism that he declared: "If I were a poet and felt myself capable of maintaining the epic flight, I think I would find in the great Californian gold discovery and its results a subject more congenial to the taste of this age, richer in impressive suggestions, in strange and romantic incidents, and generally in material for a great poem than the conquest of Troy or Jerusalem, the adventures of Ulysses or Aeneas" (Wright 1955, 165).

But defenders of the classics roundly defeated their utilitarian critics, just as their forebears in each generation had defeated essentially the same religious, moral, and utilitarian arguments for centuries (Schmidt 1936, 53, 57–8, 65). The Yale Report of 1828, which vigorously defended the classical educational system against its detractors, received almost universal praise and, in the words of Meyer Reinhold, "assured the entrenchment of the classics, not only at Yale, but throughout the country, until after the Civil War" (1984, 194). Yale's status as the largest and most diverse college of the time, boasting students from a greater number of states than any other college, contributed to this effect. College speakers throughout the 1830s paraphrased the report, and Yale was applauded throughout the nation for defending the classics. Yale became the northern school of choice for southerners and its graduates played a leading role in establishing schools and colleges on the frontier. Thirty-six of the nation's seventy-five college presidents in 1840 were Yale alumni (Rudolph 1977, 73; Urofsky 1965: 55, 62–3). Yale's chief rival, Harvard, demonstrated its full agreement with Yale's defense of the classics by dramatically increasing its classical admission requirements in the 1830s and 1840s; by 1850, the Harvard qualifying examination lasted eight hours (Story 1975, 285). Harvard president Josiah Quincy responded to William Ellery Channing's appeal to make Harvard more "popular" through the reduction of its classical requirements by declaring, "Let there be at least one institution in the country the criterion of whose worth and merit shall be measured by something other than the number of its polls" (McCaughey 1974, 147–8, 167–8). Efforts at introducing elective systems and non-classical degrees in order to reduce the role of the classics failed miserably nearly everywhere they were attempted due to public disapproval. In short, Vergil continued to thrive in spite of his detractors. It was not until the late nineteenth century that the utilitarians finally succeeded in weakening the hold of Vergil and the other classical authors on education and, hence, on the public mind.

By then, Vergil had played a crucial role in inculcating the pastoralism that undergirded the nation's transition to a more democratic system. That the Augustan poet was no democrat, and could hardly have imagined such a role for himself, is one of the many ironies of history.

FURTHER READING

There are many excellent books concerning the influence of the classics, including that of Vergil, on early Americans. The pioneering works in this field were Gummere (1963, 1967) and Reinhold (1984). Subsequent books that are worthy of note include Benario and Briggs (1986); Cleary (1990); Rahe (1992); Wiltshire (1992); Richard (1994); Roberts (1994); Sellers (1994); Gregg (1999); Shalev (2009); Shields (2001); and Winterer (2002, 2007).

CHAPTER TWENTY FIVE

Why Did American Women Read the *Aeneid*?

Caroline Winterer

Everyone knows about Helen Keller, who was left blind and deaf by a disease in early childhood. We know that with the help of her teacher Annie Sullivan, Keller grew up to be a cultured and internationally renowned champion of Americans with disabilities. We know that she could sign with her fingers, and that she could read Braille. But what literature exactly did she read and sign, as an educated American woman at the turn of the twentieth century? As it turns out, one of her favorite books was Vergil's *Aeneid*: in Latin, in Braille, which she learned with her tutor to prepare for her entrance examinations to Radcliffe College, at a time when Harvard still did not admit women. "Virgil is serene and lovely like a marble Apollo in the moonlight," Keller wrote of the *Aeneid* (Keller 1903, 111). Her tutor marveled at her achievement. "I believe Miss Keller is capable of giving the world, at some future time, in rhythmical prose, a new version of Virgil, which would possess high and peculiar merit," he wrote (Keith 1899, 53).

Helen Keller never did give the world a new version of the *Aeneid*. In fact, of the roughly one hundred major English translations of the complete text that have been published in England and the United States, only one is by a woman, and that very recent (Ruden 2008). Yet Helen Keller's homemade Braille, Latin *Aeneid* draws our attention to the shadow world of the *Aeneid* that flourished underneath the vast canopy of male translations and scholarly editions stretching from antiquity to the present. The question that heads this essay – "Why did American women read the *Aeneid*?" – is one that is appropriate to ask for the period before the twentieth century because women and men did not have equal access to this work before that time. Until the late nineteenth century, American women were largely barred from higher education and politics. Classical history and literature – and especially epic literature – were thought to be masculinizing and therefore unsuitable for and even dangerous to women. Yet Helen Keller's Braille *Aeneid* suggests that many women found Vergil's epic deeply meaningful to their own lives. Tracing their responses to the *Aeneid* uncovers the curious paradox of how women used this ancient text to make themselves modern.

More than this, though, Helen Keller's Braille *Aeneid* can help us to understand how classicism as a whole successfully made the transition to modernity – why even two thousand years after it was written the *Aeneid* could find publishers, translators, and readers galore. Much more than a trivial niche market, female readers of the *Aeneid* and other classical works were a key element in classicism's survival into the twentieth century. Traditionally denied knowledge of Greek and Latin, women by the eighteenth century were courted by publishers with English translations and illustrated editions of Vergil's epic. Charged after the American Revolution with educating the children of the young republic, women bought children's and "family" editions of the *Aeneid*, simplified, streamlined, and studded with illustrations. Women decorated their parlors with plaster busts of Vergil; they visited his tomb in Italy and composed poems on the experience of seeing it. This nineteenth-century mania for the *Aeneid* persisted because of skyrocketing literacy rates, the massive dissemination of print through inexpensive translations, and the successful transport of these works to distant markets by ships and railroads. Like so many other classical texts, Vergil's *Aeneid* rode to the twentieth century on the very symbols of modernity that also threatened to make it irrelevant. Women's growing access to the *Aeneid* helps us to understand how and why classical antiquity found a new home in the modern world.

The best way to appreciate the shadow world of women who read the *Aeneid* is to map the rather more conspicuous world of male readers of the *Aeneid*. From the seventeenth century to the late nineteenth, as Richard documents in the preceding chapter, the *Aeneid* loomed like Goliath for American boys, a text to be feared, read, reread, recited, hated, conquered, and finally, perhaps, loved. It ranked among the most commonly found classical texts in elite family libraries, both in Latin and in English translations. In a number of well-stocked private libraries at this time, classical texts ranked second only to religious works, sometimes numbering in the hundreds (Winterer 2005a, 1269). The most popular English translation of the *Aeneid* was John Dryden's, but many others also circulated (Reinhold 1975, 134). The Latin *Aeneid* was read by boys in grammar schools or studied with a tutor at home; it was not unheard of for boys as young as 6 to be able to read passages of the *Aeneid* (although what they understood is another question). For college-bound boys such preparation was necessary, since the *Aeneid* (among other classical texts) was required for admission in the late eighteenth century to Columbia, Brown, Williams, Harvard, Yale, and Princeton (Broome 1903, 39). Students also continued to study the *Aeneid* in the first year in college. At South Carolina College in 1801 freshmen read from the Greek Testament, the *Aeneid*, some of Cicero's political orations, and Xenophon's *Cyropaedia* (Durrill 1999, 472). These requirements make clear that the *Aeneid*, like much Latin and Greek learning at this time, was viewed in a vocational way, as though the *Aeneid* were a giant Latin grammar and Roman oratory lesson, useful for boys aspiring to the ministry, the bar, or any career that required public speaking, where classical allusions were basically required (Winterer 2002, 13–22).

Some boys took to the *Aeneid* like fish to water. The Adams family of Massachusetts supplies us with a treasure trove of revealing examples from an elite, educated family that over the generations continued to read the *Aeneid* as though by genetic compulsion. John Adams loved classical literature, and he was one of the few founders who could read and write in both Latin and Greek. His library contained over 100 books by ancient authors, in Latin, Greek, and modern vernaculars. His diary from 1755, when he was 20 years old, records him rising day after day to read thirty or forty lines of Vergil. With the help of a tutor and his erudite wife, Abigail Adams (who could not read Latin or Greek but who helped to educate their four children in classical history during his long absences), John Adams made sure his eldest son, John Quincy, also learned the *Aeneid* early and often. John Adams bragged about his young son's grasp of Latin. "It is rare to find a youth possessed of so much knowledge," he wrote in 1785 to a friend. "He has translated Virgil's Æneid, Suetonius,..." (John Adams to Benjamin Waterhouse, April 24, 1785, in Koch and Peden 1946, 72). We get a sense of how the family prized the *Aeneid* from the two bookplates – one with the name of John Adams, the second with the name of John Quincy Adams – that adorn Alexander Strahan's English translation of the *Aeneid* that is now kept in the John Adams Library at the Boston Public Library (Strahan 1753). Of the six bronze busts ("household Gods") adorning John Quincy Adams' study in the White House, one was of Vergil (Friedlaender and Butterfield 1968, vii).

For other boys, the struggle was long and fruitless, bringing tears, anger, despair, even violence. In his diary John Adams recorded the story of a boy who bruised his uncle's lip by hurling the *Aeneid* at him. There are dismal recollections of failed memorization. "*Arma*, – arms; *virumque*, – and a man; *cano*, and a dog," sputtered one young boy in the mid-nineteenth century when asked to translate the opening lines of the poem (White 1905, 13). The poem was also served up as retribution. Discovered shooting their guns in town, two South Carolina College students in 1824 were punished by being forced to recite fifty lines of the *Aeneid* to the faculty (Winterer 2002, 36).

The *Aeneid* also offered boys lessons about heroism, imperial expansion, quasi-Christian virtue, and the stoic acceptance of fate. Although the lessons of the *Aeneid* were not inherently more applicable to republicanism than to monarchism, Americans during and after the revolutionary era applied its themes to their project of creating a republican, Christian nation. Aeneas was taken to represent the republican quality of *pietas* (selfless duty toward the state); Dido became the embodiment of the unruly, selfish passion that undermined republics, a fear usually embodied in the phrase "luxury and effeminacy," suggesting its association with women and Oriental despotism (Winterer 2007, 5). Works like Philip Freneau and Hugh Henry Brackenridge's dramatic dialogue, "The Rising Glory of America," which was first performed in 1771 at the College of New Jersey (later Princeton), tacked Vergilian imperialism onto an American canvas. In a Vergilian *translatio imperii* it foretold an America that would span the continent from the Atlantic Ocean to the Pacific. Others mined the work for its moral sentiments and tried to knit the *Aeneid* to a Christian frame of reference. Charles Francis Adams (son of John Quincy Adams) distilled a century of sentiment when he praised the *Aeneid*, which he read almost daily in the spring of 1832, a feat he records in his diary: "The thing seems to me to be an honour to the human intellect for imagination, for pathos, for perfect harmony, for beauty. And there is moral in it so far as the Ancients allowed themselves to have moral" (Charles Francis Adams, diary entry for April 15, 1832, in Friedlaender and Butterfield 1968, 279).

A rite of passage into adulthood for boys and a lifelong symbol of masculine achievement for men, the *Aeneid* was much more problematic for women. First, the core values of the *Aeneid* – war, heroism, and imperial destiny – were more immediately relevant to the lives of young men than young women, who were barred from politics and careers like law and the military where one might conceivably apply such knowledge. Second, classical learning beyond the most rudimentary kind was thought unsuitable for women. In private conversation, excessive classical knowledge was thought to make women into intimidating pedants. Eighteenth-century moralists advised young brides to "Shun learned Clacks, and Females talking Greek" (Anon. 1744, 699). The traces of women's intellectual lives – which were largely non-institutional, up until the late eighteenth century – are much more sparse and nebulous than those for men, and so it is often impossible to tell which work by an ancient author women were reading. Learnedness was not prized in women; educated women tended to conceal rather than display their virtuosity. Sometimes we know of extensive reading of Vergil, but not which work of Vergil. The South Carolinian Eliza Lucas Pinckney (ca. 1722–93) knew Latin, taught it to her daughter, and ran her father's several large plantations in South Carolina, pioneering the cultivation of indigo. She sometimes rose at 5 a.m. to have time to read classical literature. But though she alludes several times in her letters and diaries to her reading of Vergil, she seldom specifies which work (Winterer 2007, 12, 18–20).

Despite all these barriers, a few women in the most elite colonial households clearly knew the *Aeneid*. The case of Anne Bradstreet (1612?–1672), known as "the tenth muse," shows how even at the dawn of American colonization the text reached educated women. Her arrival in 1630 puts her among the first group of English Puritans to reach the Massachusetts Bay Colony. Her relatively high social status was typical of those few women who knew the *Aeneid*: her father, Thomas Dudley, and her husband, Simon Bradstreet, both served as governors of the colony. Like most girls she did not receive a formal education, but during her childhood in England she lived in the cultivated household of the Earl of Lincoln, whom her father served as steward, and later had access to the erudite men in her husband's intellectual circle. Her classically infused poems display knowledge of the characters and themes of the *Aeneid*. These poems were published in London as *The Tenth Muse* (1650) as an example of the finest the New World could offer. (One admirer claimed rather hyperbolically that if Vergil could hear her poems he would toss his own works into the flames.) One poem, "In honour of…Queen Elizabeth" (1643), compares Dido to Queen Elizabeth I, showing that Elizabeth's glories endure while Dido's have vanished, like Carthage itself. "*Dido* first Foundresse of proud *Carthage* walls, / (Who living consummates her Funerals) / A great *Eliza*, but compar'd with ours, / How vanisheth her glory, wealth and powers" (McElrath and Robb 1981, 157).

By the late eighteenth century, the proliferation of print culture exposed more young women to the *Aeneid*. Many more books and magazines were now published in both the United States and England; these in turn fed the ever-richer networks and institutions of intellectual life in America. The growing popularity for women's reading of the work is suggested by the renewed popularity in painting of an old story: Vergil reading to the Emperor Augustus and his sister Octavia a passage from book 6 of the *Aeneid*, in praise of Octavia's dead son, Marcellus; Octavia faints in grief. In the late eighteenth and early nineteenth centuries, neoclassical painters such as Angelika Kauffmann, Jean-Joseph Taillasson, and Jean-Auguste-Dominique Ingres each tackled the theme (Plates 7 and 8).

A measure of the dispersion of this text is the extraordinary case of Phillis Wheatley (1753?–1784), the young Massachusetts slave whose master made sure she was given a classical education that rivaled that of many elite white men. "She had a great Inclination to learn the Latin Tongue, and has made some Progress in it," wrote her master, John Wheatley (Mason 1989, 47). When her collection of poems was published in London in 1773, she included one entitled "To Mæcenas" to thank her patrons. The Maecenas of the title referred to the Roman patron of Vergil, and the poem itself announced Wheatley's wish to rival Vergil: "O could I rival thine and *Virgil's* page, / Or claim the *Muses* with the *Mantuan* Sage" (Mason 1989, 50).

Wheatley was exceptional: most American girls in the colonial period encountered the *Aeneid* not *in toto* but in translated scraps scattered in conduct manuals, women's magazines, and books of mythology. These books and magazines attracted a wide audience of women because they were written in English and French and so were accessible to people unschooled in the classical languages. They also offered practical advice for how to navigate difficult social situations, like tea-time conversation with mixed company where a bit of classical learning was fetching and a lot was a recipe for spinsterhood. The books also linked pagan learning to the Christian piety prized for women in eighteenth-century polite society. Madeleine de Scudéry's *The Female Orators* (1714) typifies the genre. Scudéry heaped praise on "*Virgil's* divine *Eneids*," a book "worthy to be envy'd by all the Monarchs of the World." She especially liked that the *Aeneid* was a poem, since poetry was a genre more conducive to female piety than history or philosophy. "Every time I consider the Advantages and Charms of Poesy, I am the more in love with it; and if the Decency of my Sex would permit me, I would say that *Dido's* Chastity pleases me less in History, than her Weakness and Despair in the *Eneids*" (Scudéry 1714, 156). Women also found reference to the *Aeneid* in mythology books made just for girls, like Mary Monsigny's *Mythology* (1794). Such works attempted to distill the essence of classical mythology in a way that was suitable for women's refined yet easily corruptible natures. Remarking that Aeneas' story was so well known that it was pointless to repeat it, Monsigny then did just that and summed up the moral lesson of the *Aeneid* in a tidy package that could be easily digested by young girls: "Æneas is represented as remarkable for his piety and submission to the will of the Gods" (Monsigny 1794, 309).

The American Revolution caused some American women and men to revisit the *Aeneid* in light of their political opposition to Britain. What lessons did this story hold for revolutionaries and for builders of the new nation? While poems written by men, such as Freneau and Brackenridge's "The Rising Glory of America" and Joel Barlow's *The Vision of Columbus* (1787) and *Columbiad* (1807), praised the new nation in Vergilian terms, educated women sought parallels between the epic poem and their own experiences as women. The American Revolution was difficult for women. The long war, fought on American soil, was devastating to displaced American families, who saw their crops destroyed and homes burned. Many women lost husbands, brothers, and sons; a few even served in battle.

The poet Ann Eliza Bleecker (1752–83) of upstate New York captured her revolutionary tragedies in terms familiar to readers of the *Aeneid*. In 1777, British troops under the command of General John Burgoyne swept down from Canada and forced her to flee southward with her mother and two young daughters while her husband joined the New York state militia. In one year Bleecker endured the death of her infant daughter, her mother, and her sister. Poetically gifted from childhood, she expressed her sorrow in her poems. As was typical in the eighteenth century, she did not publish them: this was considered unseemly for women, a trespass onto the male terrain of public visibility. Instead she circulated her poems among her friends. Eventually her surviving daughter, Margaretta Bleecker Faugeres, published these poems in the 1790s. In her poem "On Reading DRYDEN'S VIRGIL," Bleecker imagines that she is Aeneas. As Aeneas mourns Creusa, Bleecker mourns her baby daughter. "Like him I lost my fair one in my flight, / From cruel foes – and in the dead of night" (Faugeres 1793, 230).

American women's access to the *Aeneid* began to change in the 1790s with the increasing acceptance of women's learning. Many historians have observed that the American Revolution had not been much of a social revolution. As before the Revolution, women afterward could not vote, hold elective office, bear arms in defense of the nation, or serve on juries, and their property and custodial rights to their children after marriage remained precarious. Yet the Revolution did popularize the Enlightenment idea that moderately educated women made the best mothers and wives of virtuous male citizens, the pillars of the republic. It was increasingly accepted that women should be educated not so much for their own good as for the good of the republic, as they could help to teach sons and to provide sound companionship for husbands.

These attitudes encouraged the spread of female academies. Serving young women roughly between the ages of 12 and 16, they began to be founded in the 1790s and flourished well into the late nineteenth century, when women's and coeducational colleges started displacing them. The historian Mary Kelley has recently charted the impressive increase in the number of female academies after the Revolution: between 1790 and 1830, 182 academies were established just for young women in the North and South; at least 158 more were opened between 1830 and 1860 (Kelley 2006, 67). By the 1820s their curricula increasingly moved away from "ornamental" activities like embroidery and music and toward more academic subjects, like botany, literature, and mathematics. The most progressive of them taught not just classical history and mythology but Greek and Latin (often for a surcharge). However, as was noted before with regard to women's classical reading in the eighteenth century, the general listing often seems more important than the specific text, so the academy curricula often list "Latin" or in the most specific cases "Virgil," making it difficult to tell which work of Vergil or how many of them this meant. Another historian's survey of fifty female academies in twelve states found that of the thirty-eight that offered Latin, "Virgil" was listed as a subject by eight (Cleary 2002, 228). It is often difficult to tell whether girls read the *Aeneid* in Latin in these academies; the syllabi are often vague, and many inexpensive English translations were available. The new Harper's Classical Library series, for example, which included an English translation of the *Aeneid*, was marketed specifically toward women and families.

Whether in academies or at home, young women of the nineteenth century clearly read more Vergil than had previous generations of women. They also were more likely to read it in the original Latin. Here is the granddaughter of Thomas Jefferson, Ellen Wayles Randolph (1796–1876), telling her classically learned mother in 1819 how Dryden's English translation pales next to the *Aeneid* in Latin: "I am reading Virgil in latin & reading with as much difficulty as I do, I find that I shall never again tolerate a translation. Dryden whom I admired so much; there is as much difference between his Ænead & Virgil's as there is between a glass of rich, old, high flavored wine, and the same wine thrown into a quart of duck-water –even the passages which I admired the most I can now criticise without mercy" (Ellen W. Randolph (Coolidge) to Martha Jefferson Randolph, 11 August 1819, Papers of Thomas Jefferson, Retirement Series, Digital Library).

Another diligent recorder was Ellen Tucker Emerson (1839–1909), daughter of Ralph Waldo Emerson. She typifies the profile of the early nineteenth-century American woman who read the *Aeneid*: she was elite and raised in a family that supported women's education, even if that education was not intended to fit the young woman for any adult career beyond becoming a wife and mother. Ralph Waldo Emerson was himself a careful reader of ancient literature; he had studied at Harvard during the career of the Hellenist Edward Everett (Winterer 2002, 53). Young Ellen was exposed to a rich world of classical literature and reading. When away from home, she kept her classically erudite father abreast of her progress through the *Aeneid*. "We are getting 120 lines a day in Virgil now and if necessary we shall take still longer lessons that we may finish the Aeneid this term for we don't want to leave it unfinished," she informed her father in one letter from school (Ellen Tucker Emerson to Ralph Waldo Emerson, June 18, 1854, in Gregg 1982, 65). In 1855 she enrolled at the Agassiz School in Cambridge, Massachusetts. Typical of the informality of many women's academies, this one was held in the home of the Harvard scientist Louis Agassiz, and the Greek and Latin lessons were handled by the moonlighting Harvard Greek scholar Cornelius Conway Felton (Gregg 1982, xxiii; Winterer 2007, 151).

The American Transcendentalist Margaret Fuller (1810–50) was another early nineteenth-century reader of the *Aeneid*. Like Ellen Emerson, she was born into an elite New England family and early on received the intellectual attentions of her father, Timothy Fuller. Inspired by Enlightenment ideals of female learning, Timothy Fuller tutored his eldest child himself, giving her a mastery of Latin and Greek that was more typically reserved for well-schooled boys. Timothy Fuller himself was well steeped in classical literature, so not just any edition of Vergil would do for his children. In the Stanford University Special Collections researchers will find the Vergil schoolbook owned by Timothy Fuller, with his name carefully inscribed in the front. It is an 1811 Latin edition of Vergil's *Aeneid*, *Georgics*, and *Eclogues* whose title page announces that it is "for the use of schools." The introduction – directed toward the "gentlemen" who would teach the book in schools – explained Vergil's utility in the education of children whose moral faculties needed careful tending; the advice is clearly applicable as much to boys as to girls. "But it must be owned," it explains, "to the immortal honour of Virgil, that his style is so strictly pure and chaste, that the most raw and inexperienced might be left to steer their course through the whole of his works, without meeting with those rocks and quicksands on which unpractised virtue runs no small hazard of being shipwrecked" ([Vergil] 1811, iii). Yet Timothy Fuller's 1811 edition also gives us a tantalizing glimpse into the persistent gender inequities in classical learning. Underneath Timothy Fuller's signature on the inside of the front cover are two other ones of Fuller men – but no signatures of Fuller women, suggesting that the father had bequeathed the book preferentially to a son rather than a daughter, much as John Adams had also passed on his *Aeneid* to his own son.

Whatever the meaning of the men's signatures in the Fuller family Vergil, it is clear that Timothy Fuller delighted in Margaret's intelligence and classical flair. The father of many children, he also liked that Margaret's command of classical literature meant that she could tutor her young siblings, since he had little time to spare. Seeing her walk with her young sister, he called out to Margaret a line from the *Aeneid* (1.46), about Jupiter's sister-wife, Juno: *Ast ego quae divum incedo regina!* ("But I who walk a queen of the gods") (Capper 1992, 37).

Regal she may have been, but Margaret found the *Aeneid* tough going. At work each day until early evening, Timothy kept Margaret awake after he got home, teaching her Latin and Greek well into the night. The routine gave her insomnia, anxiety, and nightmares. As an adult she recalled reading of "trees that dripped with blood" in the *Aeneid* (Emerson et al. 1852, 16). She was not a particularly patient Latin teacher to her siblings, either. Her younger brother Richard remembered her being annoyed "inexpressibly" when the children fidgeted as they "were drowning in the deep places of Virgil"(Capper 1992, 135).

But with her mastery of Greek and Latin, Margaret was allowed to attend the rigorous coeducational Cambridgeport Private Grammar School. Established to compete with Boston Latin as a preparatory school for Harvard, the Port School (as it was called) admitted girls, and there young Margaret attended classes in Latin and Greek along with the boys of the future Brahmin literati, such as the young Oliver Wendell Holmes. Like the boys, she recited her *Aeneid* in Latin. This intensive background left Margaret with a lifelong love of what she called "my Romans," and her Transcendentalist philosophy was rooted to some degree on this intensive classical preparation (Winterer 2007, 150–1).

In addition to this world of words, the nineteenth century also brought American women a Vergilian world of things. Few Americans in the eighteenth century participated in the Grand Tour, but by the nineteenth century rising wealth and better education meant that middling and elite American women could count a journey through Europe's major cultural monuments as a must. "We…are going to Europe; only think, to Europe!" exclaimed Anne Everett in 1840. "Oh! I feel so pleased with the idea…. So I shall at last see beautiful Italy; the land where Cicero and Virgil lived and wrote; the land of poets, painters, sculptors" (Bush 1857, 68). Once there, Everett visited the tomb of Vergil: "It is a very pretty, rural spot, but difficult of access, and it is very doubtful if he was buried there," she wrote (Bush 1857, 169). She also popped in at the Vatican library, where she saw a Vergil manuscript dating from the fifth century locked in a cabinet (Bush 1857, 187). The world of Vergilian relics also lay closer to home. Catherine Elizabeth Havens in 1849 fondly recalled the clock in the family library – memorable because it was topped by an enormous gilt head of Vergil (Havens 1920, 13–14).

By the mid-nineteenth century, as a few women ascended into more public roles as social activists and cultural reformers, reading Vergil in the original Latin increasingly loomed as a symbolic marker of women's ascent into the masculine realms of erudition and public oratory. The 1830s and 1840s marked a revolutionary era in American political life. The franchise had expanded to include all adult white men regardless of property holding. Despite their inability to vote, women and free blacks joined this democratizing civic life to lobby for social reforms like abolitionism, women's property and voting rights, and temperance. Still, vestiges of eighteenth-century elitism remained; classical learning still stood as a *de facto* prerequisite for entry into public life in the antebellum period, and some of the greatest orators of the age – Daniel Webster, for example – strived to emulate the delivery of Demosthenes and Cicero. Middle-class and lower-class women who sought to be heard in this forum desperately felt the need to acquire some knowledge of classical history and mythology; at the bare minimum it would give them some credibility in public life.

An example of these increasingly political reasons for non-elite women to learn the *Aeneid* in Latin is Lydia Maria Child (1802–80), one of the first American women to use her hard-won knowledge of classical history and literature in the service of social and moral reform. Today most Americans remember her (if they remember her at all) from her children's ditty ("Over the river, and through the wood"), but in her day Child was lauded by her admirers as the "first woman in the republic." Child was among the first Americans to criticize black slavery by reference to classical antiquity. In a series of publications in the 1830s, Child connected the enslavement of blacks to the oppressions of women both in the modern United States and in the classical past (Winterer 2007, 169). But before this career as a feminist and abolitionist, Child first had to overcome the typical girl's exclusion from classical learning. She was denied the Harvard education in classics given to her older brother Convers Francis. The exclusion irked her, as she explained in a letter to Convers in 1819, when she was 18 years old. "I have long indulged the hope of reading Virgil in his own tongue. I have not yet relinquished it. I look forward to a certain time when I expect that hope, with many others, will be realized" (Child 1883, 4).

Even late in the nineteenth century, when the first women's colleges were opening and classicism was quickly fading from public discourse, ambitious, politically minded women turned to the *Aeneid* as a way to engage the male world of politics. This was the case with Elizabeth Cady Stanton (1815–1902), one of the leading feminists of the nineteenth century, who lobbied tirelessly during her long, active life for numerous women's rights, from custody law to the franchise. Her early education in classical literature was a calculated endeavor on her part to do what boys were doing. She was one of eleven children in a prosperous family in which all six sons died young. Her father was heartbroken. "Oh, my daughter, I wish you were a boy!" her father cried after the death of the last son (Stanton 1993, 20–1). Determined, as she put it to him, to "try to be all my brother was," Stanton decided to learn the two things she thought defined manhood: ancient Greek and horseback riding. She sought lessons in Greek from the family's minister and went on to become a star in ancient languages at her local academy, where she earned one of two prizes in Greek. At his death, her teacher bequeathed to her his Greek New Testament, lexicon, and grammar (Stanton 1993, 21–4). One result of this superb classical education was that as an adult she felt qualified to judge the merits of classical literature. Stanton recorded in her diary that on her way to the annual meeting of National Woman Suffrage Association she read the recent translation of the *Aeneid* made by Massachusetts governor John Davis Long, a supporter of women's suffrage. "'On my way from New York to Boston the other day,' I said to him, 'I bought and read your volume and never did time pass more quickly'; which was quite true, for when I get absorbed in a book I am oblivious to everything else" (Elizabeth Cady Stanton, diary entry for May 29, 1881, in Stanton and Blatch 1922, 184).

By the early twentieth century it no longer made sense to ask why American women (specifically) read the *Aeneid* because the older, distinctively female world of classicism had begun to vanish. The best education for women was no longer in the female academies but in the women's and coeducational colleges and universities founded after the Civil War, which offered not just an undergraduate education equal to that of men, but also the first doctoral degrees in classics. Still, change comes slowly. In 2008 Sarah Ruden became the first woman to publish an English translation of the whole of the *Aeneid*. (Though note also the unpublished, partial translation of 1934 by the poet Gwendolyn Brooks, which is discussed by Ronnick in the next chapter of this volume.) In an interview with the *Chronicle of Higher Education* (May 16, 2008), Ruden remarked on how women continue to shy away from the *Aeneid* even after a century of educational equity in classics. "Several generations of women have been trained in classical languages and literature just the same as men. But you still see many, many women working on love poetry – a tiny portion of the works that survive – and talking and writing endlessly about 'gender' in prescribed terms. It's like a seraglio."

FURTHER READING

The only book-length study of American women and classicism is Winterer (2007). The classic study of the virilizing intent of classicism is Ong (1959). For women's place in this masculine Renaissance classical culture see Grafton and Jardine (1986, 29–57). American women engaged with classicism both as a literary activity and as an artistic practice. The scope of educated colonial women's reading is presented in Hayes (1996). Neoclassical objects prized by American women appear in Cooper (1993) and Ring (1993). The importance of neoclassicism in American portrait painting is also clear in John Singleton Copley and Gilbert Stuart's portraits of American women. See Rebora et al. (1995) and Barratt and Miles (2004). In addition to the American women mentioned in this essay who were classically erudite, there are also others from the period mostly before 1900, such as Theodosia Burr Alston (who knew ancient Greek) and M. Carey Thomas, president of Bryn Mawr College. For Alston see Pidgin (1907) and Van Doren (1929). On M. Carey Thomas see Horowitz (1994).

CHAPTER TWENTY SIX

Vergil in the Black American Experience

Michele Valerie Ronnick

Virgil is a pretty fancy name for a black boy.

John Ball, In the Heat of the Night (1965)

O, Queen of Carthage, wert thou ugly, black,
Aeneas could not choose but to hold thee dear.

Christopher Marlowe, Dido, Queen of Carthage (1594)

Introduction

This essay is necessarily inchoate. Focusing on facts, it is more descriptive than analytic, and it offers a point of departure rather than a summative plateau. This is because scholars of history and literature, both modern and ancient, have only just begun to examine the reception of classical literature among people of African descent using the evidence provided by people of African descent. The classical tradition has been ever present in the cultural life of African Americans, even if this fact was hardly ever noticed by the academy. But even our sports culture reveals it. Take, for example, the case of football player Aeneas Williams (b. 1968), who retired from the National Football League St. Louis Rams in 2005. Williams is an African American, and his heroic, classical, Vergilian name might seem an aberration. But it is not; he also has an older brother named Achilles. In fact the Williams brothers are not alone among black, male athletes who bear classical names. In the US we have Mercury Morris (b. 1947), Mercury Hayes (b. 1973), Titus Ivory (b. 1977), Orpheus Roy (b. 1973), and Julius Pepper (b. 1980). In Africa we have the Liberian football player Dionysius Sebwe (b. 1972) and Aeneas Chigwedere (b. 1939), Zimbabwe's minister of education, sports, and culture. There is also the black linebacker Quintus MacDonald selected by the Indianapolis Colts in the 1989 NFL draft. (MacDonald first played at Penn State under football coach Joe Paterno who, while not black, described his own admiration for Aeneas in his 1990 narrative, *By the Book*.) Thus a certain preference for classical names in the Williams family and others like them seems more deliberate than accidental. Until recently, scholars might have explained Aeneas Williams' Vergilian name with reference to articles concerning the amusing, but often derisive, use of slave names like Cato, Pompey, Cupid, Caesar, or Eneas. Once slavery came to an end, such names often survived in surprising forms, sometimes being changed to suit the ear of perceptive but illiterate people: thus "Pericles Smith" became "Perry Clees Smith," for instance – an apparent transformation of the slave owner's classicizing nomenclature into something more homely. But, conversely, the aural culture of African Americans was also capable of reimagining the informal "Polly's Jim" as "Mr. Appollos James" (Inscoe 1983, 552–3), classicizing what must have been a perfectly familiar, colloquial form. So these names are more than just vestiges of the plantation and colonialism: they are part of a culture that has taken over the language of its former masters and made that language its own. Important too is the twentieth-century phenomenon of black people who have rejected their slave names, as the boxer, Cassius Marcellus Clay, Jr., did on March 6, 1964 when he renamed himself Muhammad Ali. Such evidence suggests that this dynamic, i.e., accepting, adapting, or rejecting classicized names, is quite complex, and further study is needed before we can claim a real understanding.

Names and other classical symbols can have very different meanings in different cultural milieux. This fact was not always appreciated. Until recently, one could easily find studies about the appropriation and use of classical symbols by white slave owners, such as the cap of liberty, the soft, felt hat worn by freed slaves in Rome, whose image later appeared on badges worn by slaves in nineteenth-century Charleston – an appeal to classical precedent as an argument to justify the place of slavery in society. But no less a figure than Jefferson Davis – who, while Secretary of War in the Pierce administration, oversaw the construction of the Capitol Extension between 1853 and 1857 – understood the potential of this symbol to take on unwelcome meanings, and he would not allow the statue of Freedom on the dome of the Capitol building in Washington, DC, to wear it (Korshak 1987, 52–69; Greene et al. 2004, Plate B; Wiesen 1980, 3–16; Wiltshire 1977b).

The effect of earlier scholarship has been "insidiously and consistently" to deny "both historicity and cultural integrity to the artistic and cultural fruits of black life" (Gilroy 1993, 188). Just twenty years ago, the rancorous debate between Martin Bernal and Mary Lefkowitz threatened an even deeper division between disciplines of classical and African studies (Moses 1998, 8–9; DuBois 2001, 44–53). But the situation has begun to change. The first panel on black classicism sponsored under the aegis of the American Philological Association meeting in 1996 was a notable turning point. Since that time, a new area of scholarly inquiry, black classicism, Classica Africana, a distinct subdiscipline within the burgeoning field of reception studies, has come into its own. My own study of the life of William Sanders Scarborough (1852–1926), our nation's first professional classicist of African descent, has now been joined by other book-length studies, such as Patrice D. Rankine's investigation of the Ulysses motif in Ralph Ellison's *Invisible Man* and Tracey Walters' monograph on classical themes in the work of black women writers (Ronnick 2005, 2006; Rankine 2006;

Walters 2007). In regard to Aeneas himself we have John C. Shields' well-received study, *The American Aeneas: Classical Origins of the American Self*, which interprets Aeneas' American reception in terms of the interplay of Biblical, classical, and racial heritages (Shields 2001). The result is that it is now possible to address the reception of Vergil's *Aeneid* in African American culture alongside such topics as the medieval Aeneas legend, Dante's use of the *Aeneid*, Spenser and Vergil, and so forth.

The field that I address in this chapter is large and since the work of coming to terms with it has just begun, I can only survey some of the major highlights both in African American literature and in the work of African American classicists who were involved with Vergilian studies in order to stimulate further work. The first part of the chapter deals with a Vergilianizing narrative of homecoming set in the years of Reconstruction, with a black hero and a white author. The second part turns to the experience of black people as students and teachers of the classics and of Vergil and the *Aeneid* in particular. The third and final part summarizes one of the most challenging but relatively unacknowledged poetic engagements with Vergil's poem written in the twentieth century, the product of a black woman. These are, to repeat, just some of the high points in a story that is very rich and still largely unexplored by scholars.

Harry Stillwell Edwards' *Eneas Africanus*

Themes from the *Aeneid* have long appealed to writers of many different backgrounds. An enormously popular story published in 1919 was *Eneas Africanus* by Harry Stillwell Edwards (1855–1938). Edwards was a son of the South, a white man whose family was disenfranchised after the Civil War. He went to Washington, DC, as a youth and pulled himself up by his bootstraps. "At night young Edwards haunted the halls of the Library of Congress where he literally 'read' his education…He sought out the classics and translations from the Greek and Latin, French, Spanish and Russian" (Smith 1969, 4–5). He returned to Macon where William McKinley appointed him to be the postmaster, a job he held for fourteen years. He then began a career in the newspapers and eventually become the owner of the *Macon Telegraph*. Friends and acquaintances included James Whitcomb Riley, Chase S. Osborne, governor of Michigan (1911–13), Jefferson and Varina Davis, Henry Ford (who gave him a car), and Theodore Roosevelt, whose presidential nomination in 1904 he seconded with a speech. Edwards was also an accomplished writer of fiction, which earned him a place in the American Academy of Arts and Letters in 1912.

Edwards had an abiding interest in liberal arts education, as he made clear in "The Tenth Generation" (1928), but he was a man of his time and a separatist. He thought that the "South was immensely friendly to the good negro," and that "side by side, each in his own sphere, the two races could abide mutually" (Edwards 1906, 215). His *Eneas Africanus* was first published in the *Macon News* on Sunday, March 19, 1919. The story consisted of a series of imaginary letters sent in October 1872 by a Major George E. Tommey to newspapers all over the South in search of information about his slave Eneas, who had been ordered to go away in 1864 and hide the family silver. Tommey's letters and his correspondents' replies to them found an immediate audience, and the work stayed in print for many years.

During 1938–9 Kurt Weill and Maxwell Anderson attempted to turn Edwards' story into a musical. For reasons unexplained they changed the name to *Ulysses Africanus* and tried first to interest Paul Robeson and then Bill "Bojangles" Robinson to take the part of Eneas. But neither man wanted the role and *Ulysses Africanus* was never finished. Instead portions of it were adapted for reuse in *Lost in the Stars*, a musical the two men wrote in 1949 based on Alan Paton's *Cry the Beloved Country*.

The most recent study of *Ulysses Africanus* places no value on Edwards' original. "Its only virtue" was its "brevity" and "certain trivial associations" with the *Aeneid* (Rabel 2007, 553, 555). A closer look shows us that this is not the case. Edwards' account of the eight-year journey made by Eneas in search of his former master in fact takes place in a fictionalized landscape that merges Edwards' own world, that of Macon and of the southerners displaced by the Civil War, with the postbellum world of the Trojan prince Aeneas who was both a hero and a war refugee carrying his people's gods out of the ruins of Troy.

A look at the geography of Georgia helps us see what Edwards saw. His hometown of Macon had its very own section called Troy. It was platted around 1822 and was the first subdivision made in Bibb county. Toward the north of the state is the city of Rome, the scene of much fighting during the Civil War. It was founded in 1838 and so named because of its seven hills. In 1906, like Major Tommey, Edwards himself carried on a search for a lost servant named Lummie Long, who had served his family faithfully. Long had been convicted of murder and Edwards had "possession of some facts" which he believed would exonerate her. But Edwards could not find Lummie. She had disappeared in the penal system of Georgia, listed in the Prison Commission records as a man.

Eneas himself acts with the piety of Aeneas and remains devoted to his mission amid trouble and temptation. He is also as loyal as Achates. With the family silver (Edwards' equivalent to Vergil's *penates*) in tow, he arrives back at the plantation in time for Major Tommey's daughter and her bridegroom to make the traditional wedding toast with the family's silver loving cup. Eneas' task is then complete. By bringing the sacred cup home, he has helped to refound his people, a new generation of Tommeys in the South of the Reconstruction.

The Context: African Americans and American Classicism

Edwards' narrative has a long history behind it. Our evidence concerning black people's relationship with classical studies in the New World dates back to the eighteenth century. It opens with Francis Williams in Jamaica and Phillis Wheatley in Boston, two poets who struggled to prove their authenticity as human beings through their literary work (Ronnick 1998b, 19–29; Shields 1980, 97–111). The nature of their struggle is summed up by a famous declaration attributed to John C. Calhoun by Alexander Crummell, who himself as a youth was a student of Greek at Cambridge University (1846–53). Calhoun is reported to have said: "If he could find a Negro who knew the Greek syntax, he would then believe that the Negro was a human being and should be treated as a man" (Ronnick 2005, 7, 334).

This comment and variants of it echoed as a challenge through black America for decades. Black educator and missionary Fanny Jackson Coppin (1837–1913) quoted it. William Sanders Scarborough did as well; and so did Charles S. Spivey, dean of Payne Theological School, in an essay published in 1941 entitled "What's in a Boy – A Black Boy?" (Coppin 1913, 19; Ronnick 2005, 44; Spivey 1942, 210). Twenty-six years later the statement, redirected toward the study of Latin, found renewed energy in William Styron's Pulitzer Prize-winning novel *The Confessions of Nat Turner* (Styron 1967, 165): "If you show me a little darky whom you've taught to read the complete works of Julius Caesar forward and backward in the original Latin language, I will show you a darky who is still an animal with the brain of a human child that will never get wise, not learn honesty, nor acquire an human ethics though that darky live to a ripe old age."

In an ironic twist, Calhoun's challenge proved to be a catalyst rather than a deterrent, and the new schools that opened in postbellum America offered many opportunities for the newly freed population to study classics. This is because "black leaders and educators adopted the New England classical liberal curriculum" with the goal of developing a well-trained intellectual class (Anderson 1988, 28). Classical elements soon pervaded the world of the black intelligentsia and classical references began to appear everywhere in nineteenth-century African American rhetoric. We find them for example tucked into the eulogies made in honor of Frederick Douglass in 1895. P.B.S. Pinchback (1837–1921), the first black governor of Louisiana, declared that Douglass "never faltered, and for over half a century, with more than Spartan courage, he performed…inestimable service for his downtrodden and helpless people." Richard Theodore Greener (1844–1922), the first black member of the American Philological Association (1875) and the first black to earn a BA at Harvard University, praised William Scarborough's *First Lessons in Greek* with the archaic Latin phrase *macte virtute* in a review Greener published in the *Christian Recorder* (September 29, 1881). Scarborough himself used the phrase in closing a letter dated March 14, 1907 congratulating the black philosopher Alain Locke for winning a Rhodes scholarship (Ronnick 2005, 77–8).

These references were not made to make black people white. Black educators "did not view their adoption of the classical liberal curriculum or its philosophical foundations as mere imitation of white schooling. Indeed, they knew many whites who had no education at all. Rather, they saw this curriculum as providing access to the best intellectual traditions of their era and the best means to understanding their own historical development and sociological uniqueness" (Anderson 1988, 29). However, the success of the Hampton-Tuskegee model of practical learning that was promulgated by means of a "well-organized campaign" and operated by a coalition of white philanthropists and educators, both black and white, has led us to believe that the Hampton-Tuskegee model was the model advocated by the mainstream of those involved in black education (Anderson 1988, 78). In reality, "a careful analysis of the curriculum reveals that most black colleges relegated industrial education to a subordinate role" (Anderson 1988, 66–7). Nevertheless, the Hampton-Tuskegee model, with its emphasis on manual and industrial training, is the one that has prevailed. Part of the reason for this is that it remained an "immense shock to one's sense of propriety" to see a "former chattel whose expected role was that of a field-hand or house-boy seriously engaged in the study of Quintilian" – or, for that matter, of Vergil (Bond 1966, 364).

Thus developed, to use Stanley Crouch's phrase, "the politics of perpetual alienation," and the idea that "Negro Americans" weren't "supposed to identify with the ideals of the country at large." In regard to high culture, educated blacks had been taught that "great significance was not the franchise of any singular group…we were supposed to identify with the best from whomever and wherever in the world it happened to come." But a misleading "fus[ion of] genetics and cultural vision" has led to the belief "that race transcends place," and the idea that classical studies were not suitable subjects for black folks (Crouch 1995, xiv, 43, 24).

To be sure, blacks argued over the position of classical studies in their curricula (Ronnick 1996, 60–1); whites did the same in the eighteenth century. Reverend A.A. Whitman warned in a lecture, "An Educational Sermon on the Needs of the Negro," delivered in Sherman, Texas that:

> The man who reads Greek and Latin while he sits in idleness waiting for something to do is an inferior man; while he who tills the soil is a sovereign, though he knows little of books…Cincinnatus, Washington, Lincoln, Grant, mightiest of earth, dignified their lives by tilling the soil.

(Mention of Cincinnatus is, of course, somewhat ironic in such a context.) On the other hand, Reverend George C. Rowe used the mastery of ancient languages as proof of Negro uplift. The seventh stanza of his nine-stanza poem, "We Are Rising," reads:

> Within the class-room in his place,
> Greek, Latin, criticism,
> To raise the youthful of his race,
> And show the world we're rising!
> (Haley 1895, 453, 552)

With this background in mind, we can take a closer look and see what happened in the case of Vergil.

Vergil and African American Education

Vergil was both admired and despised, but was continually read by early Americans (Reinhold 1984, 221–44; cf. the preceding chapters by Richard and Winterer in this volume). Many eighteenth-century American writers took the *Aeneid* as their model. Joel Barlow's (1754–1812) epic poem *The Vision of Columbus* (1787) and its revised version *The Columbiad* (1807) were explicitly based on it. Many other writers were simply steeped in Vergil's work. Vergil came quickly to the minds of educated whites who held different perspectives on the question of race and on the display of their own learning. Thus some of their classical references were not always very serious in their intent. A modification of Vergil's phrase *sic itur ad astra* (*Aen.* 9.641) placed over the fireplace mantle in the ballroom of Drayton Hall, an eighteenth-century Anglo-Palladian plantation house near Charleston, South Carolina, reveals the Drayton family's educated and droll sense of humor: the smoke from the fireplace will rise to the stars as quickly as Vergilian fame (Ronnick 1993). At times a jeering spirit was also in evidence. The Reverend Thomas Craddock (1718–70) wrote parodies of Vergil's *Bucolics*, one of them concerning the affection between two black slaves, Pompey and Daphne, who were also subjected to their owners' sexual advances (Reinhold 1984, 226, 243; Davis 1978, 3: 1394). But the heroic element played its part as well. In a stirring episode from African American history, ex-president John Quincy Adams in 1841 quoted from the *Aeneid* (*hic…caestus artemque repono* 5.484) to draw a parallel between himself and the aged boxer Entellus and drive home the point of his speech for the Amistad Africans, namely, that they were human beings who deserved to be treated justly and that he, an old warrior, would fight for them (Ronnick 1998a, 477).

It was not only whites who had the educational background to view African Americans through a Vergilian lens. A sample of school catalogues from historically black colleges and universities shows that the *Aeneid* was taught there on a regular basis for decades.

Wilberforce University in Wilberforce, Ohio, is the oldest private African American university in the United States. In its Biennial Catalogue for 1883–4 and 1884–5 it lists as faculty M.D.M. Roberts, teacher of Latin and arithmetic; William Anderson, teacher of Greek; and William Sanders Scarborough, professor of ancient languages. During those years, the Academic Department of the University offered for the second and third terms of the senior year "Virgil, *Aeneid*, Chase & Stuart." In the Wilberforce University Catalogue for 1895–6, W.E.B. Du Bois is listed as professor of Latin and Greek, and the College Preparatory Program offered for the first, second, and third terms of the senior year specifies "Virgil, *Aeneid*, Greenough." Similar conditions prevailed elsewhere. At Tillotson College in Austin, Texas, the Catalogue for 1912–13 notes that the Foreign Language division offered "Virgil and Ovid, Six books of the *Aeneid* of Virgil with selections from Ovid, 4 periods, one year." The Catalogue for 1916–17 specifies Miss Aurel Ellsworth Jones as the faculty, and notes that the Collegiate Department offered "Virgil and Ovid, Six books of the *Aeneid*, 3 periods, one year," while the Secondary Department offered "Virgil, Six Books of the *Aeneid*, prosody, mythology, sight reading, 5 periods, one year." In 1918–19 the curriculum remained unchanged, but the teaching staff was augmented as Miss Jones was joined by Caroline Whitman Hurd. Up until this time, Vergil was a mandatory subject at Tillotson. By 1924–5, however, Latin is listed as "optional alternating with Spanish": a student might take "Virgil, Six books of the *Aeneid*, prosody, mythology, sight reading 5 periods, one year," but was no longer required to do so. By then classics had begun to suffer the same sort of pressure at historically black colleges as it was encountering in traditionally

white schools. Nevertheless, generations of African American students had the opportunity to study the *Aeneid* in African American colleges with African American teachers.
Here are profiles of three of them.

Henry Alexander Saturnin Hartley (1861–ca. 1935), pharmacist, physician, and
licensed preacher in the British Methodist Episcopal Church and the African Methodist
Episcopal Church, was born in Port of Spain, Trinidad. Hartley attended Queen's
Royal College, the leading secondary school in Trinidad, whose education was
founded upon an acquaintance with ancient Greek and Latin. He put that training to
work compiling a group of his own translations from various Latin and Greek authors
for his first book, *Classical Translations* (1889). In his second book, a personal memoir entitled *Ta Tou Pragma Emou Biou* [*sic*], *or Some Concerns of My Life* (1890), he
described a morning he spent with his family on the feast of Epiphany:

> Mother and self and our Fides [*sic*] Achates, our devoted servant, my respected nurse and
> friend, Mrs. Penelope Bailey, having just returned from the Cathedral…had alighted
> from our carriage and betook ourselves to the several apartments of the house, awaiting
> the summons of a breakfast bell…. [We were] [s]itting then in our study and just then
> we were reading "Aeneas' Descent to Hell" in Virgil's *Aeneid*, when the sound of the
> parlor bell drew our attention. (Hartley 1890, 129)

Hartley says nothing more about his family's reading habits, but we may assume from
his casual manner that he felt it was not out of the ordinary for his family to read
Vergil together after church services – or, at the very least, that this was the way he
chose to represent his family in his memoir.

Another classically trained man is William Pickens (1881–1954), whose life began in
straightened circumstances on January 15, 1881 near Pendleton, South Carolina. Amid
endless financial struggle, he developed a keen desire to learn and he "learned so readily" that his older sisters let him tag along with them to the local school. When he was
7 years old, the family moved to Little Rock, Arkansas. Although Pickens still worked
in the fields, "for the next 7 years," he never missed a day of school (Pickens 2005, 13).
In 1899 during his senior year at Little Rock's colored high school, a local reporter
heard Pickens scanning the *Aeneid* aloud in class and described him in a subsequent
newspaper article as "a Negro boy that possessed the language of the Romans, although
he had the color of Erebus." A local attorney who wanted to "convince his law partner
that a Negro could learn Latin" invited the youth to his office (Pickens 2005, 33).
Pickens graduated as class valedictorian, but hard times continued and he says that he
comforted himself by "the truth of Virgil's line that 'perchance some day it will be
pleasant to remember even these things' [*forsan et haec olim meminisse iuvabit, Aen.*
1.203]" (Pickens 2005, 32–3). In the fall of 1889 his luck changed and he set out for
Talladega College in Alabama. Upon arrival he breezed through oral exams in Cicero,
Vergil, and math and was admitted as a sophomore, skipping his freshman year.

After graduation from Talledega in 1902, Pickens decided that "he wanted to go
to Yale or Harvard" (Pickens 2005, 35). His college mentor Dr. Andrews had written to the Latinist Henry P. Wright. Wright in his capacity as dean at Yale admitted
Pickens to the junior class. The school was almost entirely white and Pickens recalled

in his memoirs that "the Negro students numbered less than one-half of one percent of the three thousand men" (Pickens 2005, 39). Pickens studied Latin with Wright and began to distinguish himself in oratory. A fellow student jealously dubbed him "the Black Demosthenes" (Pickens 2005, 40). He graduated with a BA degree in classics in 1904. He was the first black at Yale to win the Ten Eyck Prize for oratory and the second black member of its chapter of Phi Beta Kappa. After teaching classical languages for eleven years – ten at Talladega and one at Wiley College – he became the first black dean at Morgan State before giving himself over completely to the National Association for the Advancement of Colored People (NAACP) in 1920. Between the world wars, Pickens was "one of the most popular platform orators in America" (Avery 1989, 9). Unfortunately, until his speeches are collected, we will not be able to see how his classical training influenced his oratory. But we may form an opinion from one well-received speech he gave on Abraham Lincoln. It survives in an abridgement that he published in 1930, and it opens with a Vergilian blast: "We are here today in praise of 'arms and a man.' And in praising the wisdom of the man or recounting the success of the arms it is no part of our purpose to deride those who disagreed with that man nor to taunt them who were vanquished by those arms" (Pickens 1930, 3).

Our last example is Paul Robeson (1898–1976), whose father Reverend William Drew Robeson (1844–1918) personally attended to Paul's classical education. "So for me in high school there would be four years of Latin and Greek. Closely my father watched my studies, and was with me page by page through Virgil and Homer and the other classics in which he was well grounded" (Robeson 1971, 18). Later on Robeson, who was the third black person admitted to Rutgers, put his study of Latin to good use by tutoring the son of his football coach, G. Foster Sanford. Sanford, Sr. "helped pay [for Robeson's] law school tuition in return for Paul's traveling to New Jersey every Saturday morning to tutor Sanford, Jr., in Latin" (Duberman 1988, 34). Had Kurt Weill and Maxwell Anderson persuaded Robeson to appear in either of their plays, *Ulysses Africanus* or *Lost in the Stars*, Robeson's study of the language of both Vergil and Homer would have brought into his stage performance a fascinating and personal interpretation.

Educators: Scarborough and Lightfoot

Students like Hartley and Pickens were instructed by a vanguard of deeply committed and fair-minded teachers of both races. Among the black professoriate who spent their careers teaching Greek and Latin were William Sanders Scarborough and George Morton Lightfoot.

Born in slavery on February 16, 1852 in Macon, Georgia, Scarborough achieved iconic status as the exemplary black scholar in the liberal arts. His response to Calhoun's aggressive challenge to "find a Negro who knew the Greek syntax" was the publication of *First Lessons in Greek* in February of 1881, which made him famous. Its publication was a thrilling and long remembered vindication of himself and black people everywhere. When Scarborough died forty-five years later the obituary writer for the *New York Times* (September 12, 1926) noted the feat. Scarborough "was the first member of his race to prepare a Greek textbook suitable for university use."

The philologist Scarborough blazed a unique path in the world of American letters. As the first black member of the Modern Language Association and the third black member of the American Philological Association, his career paved the way for future generations. Today those African American academics who study language on a professional basis are in his debt. He was the "consummate academic," and if "W.E.B. Du Bois, the antecedent of today's black public intellectuals himself has an antecedent, it is W.S. Scarborough, the black scholar's scholar" (Gates, in Ronnick 2006, xviii).

To stay abreast of his field and carry on his own research Scarborough built up an impressive collection of books. A hand list from Wilberforce University ("W.S. Scarborough Library Manuscript" from the Rembert E. Stokes Library, Wilberforce University, Wilberforce, Ohio) indicates that he had about 1,600 items in his personal library, about 400 of which dealt with classical studies. The hand list does not provide complete bibliographic information. Book titles and names of authors are often abbreviated and the publication dates are not given. Since most of these titles went through multiple editions and reprints, one can only guess, but I have supplied as much missing data as possible. Among the Vergilian titles in Scarborough's library were the following:

1. Edward Searing, *The First Six Books of Virgil's Aeneid* (New York: A.S. Barnes).
2. Thomas Chase, *Six Books of the Aeneid of Virgil* (Philadelphia: Eldredge & Brother).
3. William Rainey Harper and Frank Justus Miller, *The Aeneid (Six Books) and Bucolics of Vergil* (New York: American Book Company).
4. James Bradstreet Greenough, *The Bucolics, Aeneid, and Georgics* (Boston: Ginn and Company).
5. Thomas Leslie Papillon, *Virgil*, 2 vols. (Oxford: Clarendon Press).
6. J. G. Cooper, *The Works of Virgil* (New York: N. & J. White).
7. Harold Whetstone Johnston, *A Collection of Examples Illustrating the Metrical Licenses of Vergil* (Chicago: Scott Foresman).
8. Henry S. Frieze, *The Twelve Books of the Aeneid* (New York: American Book Co.).
9. C.S. Jerram, *Bucolics* (Oxford: Clarendon Press).

(One title pertaining to Vergil has been omitted because I cannot verify it. This is the cryptic entry, "new Virgil.") To better understand what these books meant to him we should never forget that in his time, black people had limited access to libraries. With these books Scarborough must have prepared some, if not all, of the papers he produced concerning Vergil. Spanning a period of twenty-two years, these include the last paper he gave at the American Philological Association (in which he made a passing reference to Dido). Sad to say, few of his books have survived along with any additional evidence they might have given us. Among his Vergilian papers are the following titles:

1. "Fatalism in Homer and Virgil," *TAPA* 16 (1885): xxxvi–xxxvii [summary].
2. "On Fatalism in Homer and Virgil," *AME Review* 2 (1886): 132–8.

3. "Observations on the Fourth Eclogue of Vergil," *TAPA* 19 (1888): xxxvi–xxxviii [summary].
4. "The Teaching of the Classical Languages V., On the Accent and Meaning of *Arbutus*," *Education* 9 (February 1889): 396–8.
5. "The Teaching of the Classical Languages VI., Observations on the Fourth *Eclogue* of Virgil," *Education* 10 (September 1889): 28–33.
6. "The Greeks and Suicide," *TAPA* 38 (1907): xxii–xxiii [summary].

In contrast to Scarborough, George Morton Lightfoot spent most of his career in the classroom. He was born on Christmas Day, 1868 in Culpeper, Virginia. In the fall of 1888, having completed one year of college work at Howard University, he entered Williams College in Williamstown, Massachusetts as a sophomore (Ronnick 2002, 22). He earned an excellent record in classics at Williams and was hired by the Preparatory Department at Howard University. In 1912 he was appointed professor of Latin, a post he held until his retirement in 1939. During these years he immersed himself in his work. He organized the school's Classical Club, and was a member of both the American Classical League (ACL) and the Classical Association of the Atlantic States. He also earned an MA in 1921 from Catholic University with a thesis on Roman satire.

In 1930, Lightfoot was part of the ACL's national committee to mark the bimillennium of Vergil's birth and in this capacity organized a special celebration that was held at Howard University on April 23, 1930 (Fig. 26.1). The address that he gave for the occasion, "*Bimillennium Vergilianum:* Vergil Through the Ages," was published by Howard University in 1932 as a twenty-two-page pamphlet.

The careers of Professors Lightfoot and Scarborough provide a window into black university life. We need as well to gather materials concerning black students' secondary school education in classics. This work was carried out more often than not by women. It lacked the same level of prestige, is less well documented, and will be harder to assemble.

Gwendolyn Brooks' *Anniad*

Let us conclude with an outstanding example of Vergil's presence in African American *belles lettres*. In 1950 Gwendolyn Brooks became the first black writer to win a Pulitzer Prize. Her poem *Annie Allen*, published in 1949, was one of the reasons she won. With this honor came racially and sexually charged indictments, as if the poet were of the wrong gender or the wrong race, or had written the wrong poem, and won the wrong prize. Brooks' use of classical imagery – or her "Euro-American definition," as the black poet Don L. Lee (a.k.a. Madhubuti) described it – became contested ground. Lee declared that the work, although important, "seems to have been written for whites." It was therefore, according to him, not "read by blacks" (Lee 1972, 17). The selection of Brooks for the Pulitzer award shocked some, such as the noted poet Wallace Stevens, who asked, "Why did they let the coon into Pulitzerland?" (Perry 1992, 106).

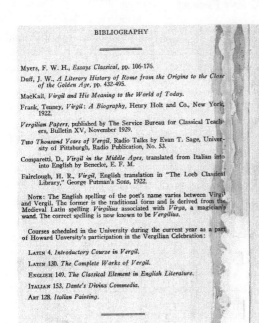
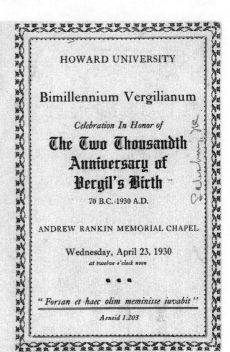

BIBLIOGRAPHY

Myers, F. W. H., *Essays Classical*, pp. 106-176.

Duff, J. W., *A Literary History of Rome from the Origins to the Close of the Golden Age*, pp. 432-495.

MacKail, *Virgil and His Meaning to the World of Today*.

Frank, Tenney, *Virgil: A Biography*, Henry Holt and Co., New York, 1922.

Vergilian Papers, published by The Service Bureau for Classical Teachers, Bulletin XV, November 1929.

Two Thousand Years of Vergil, Radio Talks by Evan T. Sage, University of Pittsburgh, Radio Publication, No. 53.

Comparetti, D., *Virgil in the Middle Ages*, translated from Italian into into English by Benecke, E. F. M.

Fairclough, H. R., *Virgil*, English translation in "The Loeb Classical Library," George Putman's Sons, 1922.

Note: The English spelling of the poet's name varies between Virgil and Vergil. The former is the traditional form and is derived from the Medieval Latin spelling *Virgilius* associated with *Virga*, a magician's wand. The correct spelling is now known to be *Vergilius*.

Courses scheduled in the University during the current year as a part of Howard Unversity's participation in the Vergilian Celebration:

LATIN 4. *Introductory Course in Vergil*.

LATIN 130. *The Complete Works of Vergil*.

ENGLISH 149. *The Classical Element in English Literature*.

ITALIAN 153. *Dante's Divina Commedia*.

ART 128. *Italian Painting*.

EXHIBITS

Vergilian Library Exhibit ....Howard University, Carnegie Library

Vergilian Art Exhibit ....New Art Museum

HOWARD UNIVERSITY

Bimillennium Vergilianum

Celebration In Honor of

The Two Thousandth Anniversary of Vergil's Birth

70 B.C.-1930 A.D.

ANDREW RANKIN MEMORIAL CHAPEL

Wednesday, April 23, 1930

at twelve o'clock noon

● ● ●

" *Forsan et haec olim meminisse iuvabit* "

Aeneid 1.203

... PROGRAMME ...

ADDRESS - - - - George M. Lightfoot, A.M.,
Professor of Latin, Howard University

VERGIL THROUGH THE AGES

1. THE LIFE OF VERGIL

2. VERGIL'S ROME

3. THE WORKS OF VERGIL

4. VERGIL, AS A PROPHET OF CHRISTIANITY

5. VERGIL, AS A MAGICIAN

6. VERGIL AND THE EARLY RENAISSANCE

7. VERGIL'S INFLUENCE ON ENGLISH LITERATURE

8. VERGIL IN THE TWENTIETH CENTURY

MUSIC

TENNYSON'S POEM FOR THE NINETEENTH CENTENARY
OF VERGIL'S DEATH

Roman Virgil, thou that singest
Ilion's lofty temples robed in fire,
Ilion falling, Rome arising,
wars, and filial faith, and Dido's pyre;

Landscape-lover, lord of language
more than he that sang the Works and Days,
All the chosen coin of fancy
flashing out from many a golden phrase;

Thou that singest wheat and woodland,
tilth and vineyard, hive and horse and herd;
All the charm of all the Muses
often flowering in a lonely word;

Poet of the happy Tityrus
piping underneath his beechen bowers;
Poet of the poet-satyr
whom the laughing shepherd bound with flowers;

Chanter of the Pollio, glorying
in the blissful years again to be,
Summers of the snakeless meadow,
unlaborious earth and oarless sea;

Thou that seest Universal
Nature moved by Universal Mind;
Thou majestic in thy sadness
at the doubtful doom of human kind;

Light among the vanish'd ages;
star that gildest yet this phantom shore;
Golden branch amid the shadows,
kings and realms that pass to rise no more;

Now thy Forum roars no longer,
fallen every purple Caesar's dome—
Tho' thine ocean-roll of rhythm
sound for ever of Imperial Rome—

Now the Rome of slaves hath perish'd,
and the Rome of freemen holds her place,
I, from out the Northern Island
sunder'd once from all the human race,

I salute thee, Mantovano,
I that loved thee since my day began,
Wielder of the stateliest measure
ever moulded by the lips of man.

Figure 26.1a and b Howard University program, "The *Bimillennium Vergilianum* Celebration In Honor of the Two Thousandth Anniversary of Vergil's Birth, April 23, 1930." Courtesy of the Moorland-Spingarn Research Center, Howard University Archives.

The central portion of the poem is called the *Anniad* and it is the heroine's own *Aeneid*. Carl Phillips, a noted African American poet who is himself well trained in classical languages, says that the poem is a "not-so-subtle argument, via punning, that Annie's is no less of an epic journey than was that of Aeneas as told in Vergil's *Aeneid*" (Phillips 2004, 221). For Phillips and other critics the poem is a mock epic, and a means for Brooks to use "seminal Greek and Latin poetic texts from the ancient Western tradition," to place "the poem within the dominant [i.e., white] culture of the United States" (Jimoh 1988, 169).

The classical roots of Brooks' epic extend back to her youth. Fascinated by language from her earliest days, at age 11 she began to keep a notebook of poetry (Kent 1990, 6). She studied Latin in school, and among "her surviving apprentice work for 1934" is a mock lament entitled "To Publius Vergilius Maro" dated February 26, 1934 (Kent 1990, 28). This was the year she graduated from Englewood High School. It reads:

> Oh, Virgil, dust and ashes in thy grave
> Wherever that grave sepulchered may be,
> Forgive me this small speech, wherein I rave
> That thou didst ever live to harass me.
> Oh, not that I do not appreciate
> The mild, concordant beauty of your lines –
> But I am puzzled by them; I translate,
> And every word seems but a set of signs.
> (Kent 1990, 31)

In March 1934, Brooks made a rhymed and a prose translation of *Aeneid* 3.1–444 (i.e., up to the point at which Aeneas goes to Crete, meets the Harpies, and is told about the Sibyl) and a prose and lyric translation of lines 472–7 (when Anchises gives the order to set sail from Buthrotum and is saluted by Helenus; Kent 1990, 29).

The poem *Annie Allen* was dedicated to the memory of a fellow poet named Edward Bland who was killed in Germany in March of 1945. Like the epics of Vergil and Homer, the poem is a narrative of love and loss set against the background of war. Its original working title was the *Hesteriad*. About the heroine, Brooks says "at first, interestingly enough, I called her Hester Allen, and I wanted then to say The Hesteriad." She herself says she first "thought of the *Iliad* and said I'll call this the 'Anniad,'" blending the titles *Iliad* and *Aeneid* with Annie's name (Lee 1972, 158).

The *Anniad* begins *in mediis rebus*. It turns on the destructive influence of war contrasted with feminine idealization of romantic love. The first stanza plays on the classic invocation of the (pagan) gods:

> Think of sweet and chocolate
> Left to folly or to fate,
> Whom the higher gods forgot,
> Whom the lower gods berate.
> (Stanza 1.1–4)

The heroine clings valiantly to a dream of marriage as endless romance. The bivalent language of the poem tells us from the start that happiness is not to be. Beauty will turn to blight:

> Pretty tatters blue and red
> Buxom berries beyond rot.
> (Stanza 2.2–3)

When the heroine and hero consummate their affection, the reader recalls Dido and Aeneas' ill-fated affair. She sees him godlike, fertile, even dangerous, and is attracted:

> Printing bastard roses there;
> (Stanza 5.2)
> And the godhead glitters now
> Cavalierly on his brow.
> (Stanza 7.2–3)
> Doomer, though, crescendo-comes
> prophesying hecatombs.
> (Stanza 12.1–2)
> [He is]
> Unfamiliar to be sure with celestial furniture.
> (Stanza 8.2–3)
> [And] like a nun of crimson ruses
> She advances. Sovereign
> leaves the heaven she put him in
> for the path his pocket chooses;
> leads her to a lowly room.
> (Stanza 9.3–7)
> Which she makes a chapel of
> where she genuflects to love.
> (Stanza 10.1–2)

After "[w]aiting for the paladin" (Stanza 3.4) and "[w]atching for the paladin" (Stanza 4.1), who is "a man of tan" (Stanza 6.1), Annie's husband becomes a soldier and leaves to fight:

> Where he makes the rifles cough
> (Stanza 13.3)
> Then to marches. Then to know
> The hunched hells across the sea.
> (Stanza 13.6–7)

But unlike Aeneas, he returns a changed and unfaithful man, and their marriage is doomed. At once full of adventure and romance like Helen, but naïve as Dido, Annie is caught in a web of fate. As her husband consorts with other women, she looks to other men. She turns to dead authors like Plato, Aeschylus, Pliny, and Seneca to find "kisses pressed in books" (Stanza 30.7) and suffers an emotional death as certain as Dido's suicide.

Conclusion

Although much remains to be done through further philological study and continued archival research, it is clear that the study of the classics played a central role in the acquisition of literacy and the establishment of a literary culture by black Americans. It is not surprising that the *Aeneid* was at the center of this movement: as was the case in the education of whites as well, Vergil held a central place within the black classical curriculum. Nor is it surprising, then, that African American students became devoted to the *Aeneid*, and that this devotion would bear fruit in the form of scholarship and imaginative literature. It is, unfortunately, equally unsurprising that the accomplishments of these people are not as well known as they deserve to be. The black reception of Vergil together with the white perception of this dynamic pervade and inform our national literature at every point. I hope that this essay will encourage further investigation of this fascinating tradition.

FURTHER READING

On the American reception of classical culture in general see Reinhold (1984) and the contributions of Richard and Winterer in this volume. On African American popular culture see Moses (1998). On African American education in general see Anderson (1988), Anderson and Moss (1999), and Walters (2007). On classical nomenclature in African American culture, see Brucia (2001). On classicism in African American literature, see Rankine (2006). On African American classicists, see Ronnick (2005, 2006) and the website: 12blackclassicists.com.

CHAPTER TWENTY SEVEN

Vergil and Founding Violence

Michèle Lowrie

In the first half of the twentieth century, there was an assumption that ancient Rome stood as an exemplum for Europe, though ever since the Founding Fathers framed the American Constitution in partial imitation of Rome's, there has been a competing assumption that Rome is an exemplum for the United States. What exactly this exemplum means was and is still contested. The Roman Republic has been exemplary for the American Constitution, the Roman Empire for fascism, for the American Empire, and possibly for the European Union. Not one of these exemplary acts misinterprets Rome, and yet they cannot be valid in all respects at the same time. I will focus on the particular formulation of violence in that paradigmatically Roman work, Vergil's *Aeneid*, and ask whether that understanding of violence was still around in the twentieth century.

The *Aeneid* culminates with a double act of violence, one human (Aeneas kills Turnus) and one divine (Juno eliminates Trojan culture). Turnus' death and Juno's reconciliation are both acts of foundation, and are multivalent. Many different kinds of violence come together in the poem's final scenes and establish legitimacy for what emerged as Rome (Feeney 1991, 150; Morgan 1998, 185; Farrell 2001, 19). Vergil's commentary on violence pertains to the immediate concerns of his age: the transformation of Rome from a period of civil war, in which the future emperor Augustus played a signally bloody role, and the transformation under Augustus to a period of peace. Walter Benjamin's essay "Critique of Violence" (1921/1978) provides the frame for my analysis for two reasons. He establishes a number of categories of violence that will help elucidate the *Aeneid*, and the time of the essay's composition corresponds to the period between the wars when Vergil held a preeminent role in defining European unity (see "Vergil and the Roman Exemplum" below). In his critique of Benjamin's essay, Jacques Derrida (2002, 233–4) asks a question that essentially sums up the central interpretive problem that has dogged the *Aeneid*: "What difference is there between, *on the one hand*, the force that can be just, or in any case judged legitimate…, and, *on the other hand*, the violence that one always judges unjust?" Derrida parts company with Benjamin in disavowing any notion of revolutionary violence justified by God. He furthermore makes a division between Greek and Jewish violence, although he is tentative about the distinction. Vergil's treatment of violence in the *Aeneid* demonstrates that Rome must be brought into the picture, and Rome comes up again and again, however latently, in the critical tradition's attempts to come to terms with Benjamin. Arendt famously avoids confronting Benjamin's conception of divine violence directly, though her *On Violence* (1970) is clearly a response to Benjamin and she treats the *Aeneid* extensively in *On Revolution* (1965). I will attempt to show that Rome may be latent in the tradition, but that Roman conceptions of violence periodically emerge, and that Arendt's failure to come to terms with Benjamin leads her to misread the *Aeneid*. At stake are questions not only of justice, but also the model of identity the *Aeneid* sets for being European, and in turn for being American.

Law-Making and Law-Preserving Violence

In German, Benjamin's title is "Zur Kritik der Gewalt," and the standard English translation, "Critique of Violence," picks up only part of the resonances in *Gewalt. Cassell's Dictionary* lists "power, authority, dominion, sway…control…; might; force, violence" in its definition, and Hannah Arendt's differentiation among elements in a similar list in *On Violence* (1970, 43; cf. Derrida 2002, 234, 262) shows she also means *Gewalt*. My use of Benjamin's term already carries the assumption – one I think not ungrounded – that violence in the *Aeneid* operates within the workings of power. Benjamin opens his essay by stating that to critique violence means "expounding its relation to law and justice," but that since violence can never be an end, only a means, we would have to determine whether violence "in a given case, is a means to a just or an unjust end." The problem then becomes that the criterion needed would be not for violence as a principle, but for its use, and as a consequence "The question would remain open whether violence, as a principle, could be a moral means to just ends" (1978, 277).

The challenge then becomes how to critique violence itself. In our operating example, founding the Roman Empire appears in the *Aeneid* as a just, or at least fated, end, and the questions at the poem's close have to do with the use of violence toward that end. Benjamin attempts to discriminate between means themselves, "without regard for the ends they serve," and this leads him to question the distinction between "historically acknowledged, so-called sanctioned violence, and unsanctioned violence." This distinction belongs to the realm of positive law, which "sees violence as a product of history." Part of the issue at the end of the *Aeneid* is whether the violence there is sanctioned or unsanctioned, and who does the sanctioning: the poem's implied or real audience, the author, the gods, history itself? But the more important issue is what it means to make such an evaluation. Within a state what sanctions violence in the hands of individuals, according to Benjamin, is the law (1978, 277–80). But before there is a state in place, before the act of foundation or prefoundation that the *Aeneid* heralds, does "natural law" prevail where there is an assumption that people are justified in using violence so long as the end is just? Can Aeneas be faulted for killing Turnus before there is a state to make such violence illegal? Derrida (2002, 274) sums up the paradox: "On the one hand, it appears *easier* to criticize the violence that founds since it cannot be justified by any preexisting legality and so appears savage. But on the other hand…it is *more difficult*, more illegitimate to criticize this same founding violence since one cannot summon it to appear before the institution of any preexisting law: it does not recognize existing law in the moment it founds another."

This question brings up the relation of foundation to violence. I am not at all sure we can get back in our understanding to a moment of prefoundation, to a state of nature, whether in the *Aeneid* or even theoretically. There are two sources within the *Aeneid* for the history of early Italy, Evander and Latinus, and the stories they tell are contradictory. Evander tells Aeneas that the earliest inhabitants of the area were "indigenous Fauns and Nymphs" (8.314) as well as people from rocks and trees. The state of nature they represent is essentially subhuman and presocial. Latinus represents the Latins as a Saturnian people who still currently live in justice without laws. By contrast Evander's story of Saturnian foundation sounds strangely familiar. (See Casali's chapter in this volume on Evander's use of Greek models for early Italian history.) It came about through the violence of Jupiter, it resulted in Saturn's exile – an important parallel for Aeneas – and his giving of laws (8.319–22). The golden age that results differs significantly from other accounts of golden ages in that there are *already* laws. I think that the contradiction highlights the temptation to posit a prefoundational golden age in theory (Latinus' formulation), but reveals it to be hollow (Evander's). The golden age that Anchises announces Augustus will found (6.791–5) will similarly come about as a result of the violence of the civil wars, and there is no implication that the new Saturnian age will be lawless. At the very least, the contradiction between Latinus' and Evander's descriptions of Saturn's rule points to two different ways of constructing the theory (O'Hara 1994, 215–17; Adler 2003, 167–78).

Benjamin also finds the law always already in operation. He identifies a "law-making character" to violence, but cannot locate an origin for it. His evidence for law-making violence is that "even…in primitive conditions that know hardly the beginnings of constitutional relations, and even in cases where the victor has established himself in invulnerable possession, a peace ceremony is entirely necessary" (Benjamin 1978, 283; cf. Derrida 2002, 273–4). The treaty makes *de iure* a situation that violence has rendered *de facto*. Law follows on the violence, but there is no presumption of a situation before any violence whatsoever, such that there would not already be some law in place. All the issues of foundation and violence are already in place in Aeneas' prefoundation, which is not Rome's first foundation. Latinus and Evander already governed established states that participated in what later became Rome – Evander is actually called the founder of the Roman citadel (8.313) – so even Aeneas' prefoundation has multiple prefoundations.

Benjamin sees a duplicitous relationship between law-making and law-preserving violence. These are the two kinds of violence he envisions as a means, and the end in each case is the perpetuation of state power, which continually refounds itself in the act of defending itself against rival acts of violence that could potentially establish a new law (Fowler 1998, 164). That is the reason the figure of the "'great' criminal" is secretly admired by the public, because his violence threatens the preservation of the law itself and would lead, if successful, to a new order (Benjamin 1978, 281; cf. Derrida 2002, 268). This is perhaps also the reason why Turnus, so vilified by some as a treaty-breaker and a "rebel against the gods" (Stahl 1990, 177), elicits such admiration in some quarters. The pity felt for Turnus' youthful misguidedness masks a yearning for a credible threat to the order that would soon be established (Putnam 1995, 166; cf. Thomas 1998, 283).

The circular relation of law-making and law-preserving violence accounts, I think, for the series of images represented on Aeneas' shield leading up to the Battle of Actium. The categories of foundation, violence, law-making, and law preservation together unite what otherwise appear as disparate scenes from Roman history. Instances from Roman history anticipate the refoundation of Rome through civil war whose culmination in history and on the shield is Actium, and it is no accident that the final scene depicted is Augustus' triple triumph, the ritual that set an end to violence and paved the way for the first so-called "Augustan settlement."

I think all the instances of violence at the end of the *Aeneid* are similarly foundational. They give rise to a new order that will be the *imperium Romanum*. However, the two main instances of violence function in different ways that go beyond the merely historical violence of the shield. There is the death of Turnus, but there is also the violence done on the Trojan race in the reconciliation of Juno. The latter will require some new categories, but I think that Benjamin's double category of law-making and law-preserving violence applies well to the death of Turnus. Although the state has not yet been founded, hindsight – going by the name of fate – colors the actions of the poem so that any resistance to Rome's foundation appears as an attempt to overthrow the powers that be, even though they do not yet exist at the story level.

Within the category of legal violence, Turnus certainly threatens the attempt to establish a legal basis for peace between the Trojans and the Latins, and therefore violence against him is law-preserving. Someone has to pay for the breaking of the treaty that was so solemnly established at the beginning of book 12 and so quickly broken by the Italians. Since the treaty that was ratified depended on the resolution of conflict by a duel between Aeneas and Turnus, it makes sense for Turnus to pay for the treaty's dissolution with his life. The violence is at the same time law-making in that Turnus' death is necessary for the foundation of the new order. The law is a double reason for Turnus' death. Law-making and law-preserving violence reinforce each other.

Let us, however, consider more closely the categorization of Aeneas' violence against Turnus as law-preserving. This is only one aspect of it, and I think the multivalence of this violent act is what has given rise to the fierce debate between so-called optimists and pessimists about the death of Turnus. People can take such different views of Turnus' death because it is overdetermined. At issue is Turnus' status as a treaty breaker (W.R. Johnson 2004, 237 n.17). There are two agreements between the Trojans and the Latins, the first established informally at 7.266, but never enacted, the second a treaty formally ratified with sacrifice in book 12. After the first is broken, Aeneas exclaims, "what a penalty you will pay me, Turnus" (8.538). Aeneas here stays within the realm of legal violence: the treaty breaker will pay the penalty. When he actually kills Turnus in book 12, however, the nature of the penalty has changed. According to Aeneas' conception, Turnus is not killed as the enemy leader bearing the responsibility for the treaty's violation, but rather because he killed Pallas. Aeneas still speaks in terms of penalties, but in a way that exceeds the category of law-preserving violence: "Pallas sacrifices you with this wound, Pallas does, and he takes the penalty from your criminal blood" (12.948–9). Although an argument can and has been made that Turnus' killing of Pallas was criminal, and also that Aeneas is justified according to Roman standards of justice in taking revenge (Galinsky 1988; Stahl 1990, 205–9; Horsfall 1995b, 198–209), it needs to be recognized that this kind of violence is of a different order and exceeds the categories of law-making and law-preserving violence we have dealt with so far.

Furthermore, the reason for which Aeneas exacts a penalty from Turnus is not described as taking place within the legal sphere. It is a personal act of vengeance done in anger, and is therefore prelegal and heroic. After the Furies are converted to the Eumenides in Aeschylus' play of the same name, law courts will try cases of personal vengeance, but the Athenian solution depends on there being a society to sustain the court. There is no society yet between the Trojans and Latins such that a legal solution would be available, and even if there were, warfare operates according to a different set of rules. Benjamin uses anger as his transition out of the category of violence done within the confines of the law into a more mystical realm, and his new categories pertain to both Turnus' death and the divine decision to eradicate Troy (Morgan 1998, 186; Derrida 2002, 269).

Mythical Violence

Anger is Benjamin's everyday instance of violence that does not function "as a means to a preconceived end." It is rather expressive, "a manifestation." He calls his first category of violence outside that envisioned by legal theory "mythical violence," and he makes a leap from the anger of men to that of the gods: "Mythical violence in its archetypal form is a mere manifestation of the gods. Not a means to their ends, scarcely a manifestation of their will, but first of all a manifestation of their existence" (1978, 294). I find Benjamin's account of mythical violence inadequate on several counts. His examples are Niobe and Prometheus, where it is easy to confuse the manifestation of the gods' power with punishment, and questions of theodicy muddle the issue. Juno's pursuit of Aeneas is a much better example. If we turn our sights from narrative strategy, where Juno serves as a blocking figure, to theology, Juno's wrath is inexplicable. Certainly, she has various specific reasons that range from petty revenge against the Trojans for the judgment of Paris and Jupiter's rape of Ganymede to a more political desire to save Carthage from its fated destruction by Rome, but the poem opens with a rhetorical question that underscores the impenetrability of the divine. Unlike Homer, who calls on the Muse to identify the god who stirred up strife among the Achaeans (*Il.* 1.8), a question about information, Vergil ask the Muse a question with no answer: why a goddess would harass a man, namely Aeneas, renowned for what the Romans call *pietas*, duty (Feeney 1991, 130, 154): "Is anger so great in the heavenly spirits?" (*Aen.* 1.11). Juno's anger is disproportionate and misdirected. It is not even a test, as God tests Job. Aeneas was punished for no offense; on the contrary, part of his dutifulness (*pietas*) is reverence toward the gods (piety), and he does not deserve his suffering. Juno, though she knows full well that she cannot ultimately achieve her aim of saving Carthage, makes Aeneas suffer simply because she can (Heinze 1993, 148; Feeney 1991, 146). Her violence is immediate; it is not a means to an end; it has no purpose beyond the manifestation of her anger at fate, which she knows she cannot alter.

In order to understand Juno's anger, we have to take it as something beyond her character. Juno stands for the opposition to Rome that emerged from Carthage; her hatred finds expression in myth; she is allegorized as air in nature, and consequently has a strong connection with the storms that pursue Aeneas so relentlessly. But more than all these things, she is the personification of the destructive forces outside human control and understanding. The reason that Juno operates effectively as a character in an epic has to do precisely with the fact that as a goddess, she can unite disparate destructive forces. This method works in poetry, but it is rather strange to find a twentieth-century theorist putting forward categories of violence emanating from the gods without any of the allegorizing moves of the ancients.

I find Benjamin's category of mythical violence unsatisfying because his examples imply a distinction between human and divine violence, such that all mythical violence belongs to the gods, and this is not true, as his starting with anger as self-expression shows, even apart from whether or not we believe in the gods. Where he has a point is in showing that the immediate violence of expression, which does not have an end in view, is closely allied with law-making violence, which is mere means, in that both establish a new power. This opens up a hole in legal violence, which is supposed to countenance violence only as a means. Violence which is not a means has a way of sneaking in, even though it cannot, in Benjamin's view, be legally justified. I think that Aeneas' anger allows a violence that is not used as a means to an end to color his killing of Turnus, and overlays the more justified reason for killing Turnus as a law breaker. And this immediate violence is what the pessimists object to.

Divine Violence

The foundation of Rome, however, depends not only on the death of Turnus, but on the reconciliation of Juno. Here again we find overlapping kinds of violence. Before analyzing the types, it will be useful to step back to consider the underappreciated strangeness of the agreement bartered by Jupiter and Juno. We are blinded by our modern knowledge that Trojan culture was not active in forming Rome, and so accept its disappearance as a rationalization of a historical phenomenon (Horsfall 1989, 22; Stahl 1990, 194), but in narrative terms, the agreement is bizarre. Juno will cease obstructing the foundation of Rome in return for the destruction of the cultural identity of the victors. What? If Juno and Jupiter were arguing about the United States, the European colonists would be victorious, but we Americans would be speaking and dressing in Navaho or Cherokee (Horsfall 1989; Adler 2003, 197). Vergil's narrative, however, responds to a cultural strangeness. What need did the Romans have to create a foundation myth in which foreigners from the East, who had suffered defeat in the Trojan War, which Vergil represents as a conflict between Europe and Asia (7.224, 10.91), come and transform through their cultural assimilation a native culture that in historical terms was developing quite nicely into a world power anyway? You might think autochthony would have greater ideological resonance, but this idea has little appeal to Vergil (Momigliano 1984, 438, 442, 457; Grandazzi 1997, chs. 7–8, esp. 116–19; Dench 1995, 202). The people Evander calls indigenous have no society (8.314), but Vergil mentions many people who come from abroad and found settlements that will contribute to Rome. Autochthony lacks a moment of founding violence, as does the idea of a hospitable land subject to successive waves of colonization. Other narratives of early Rome, which all accept the role of Aeneas as founder of the race that would produce Romulus, do not represent an analogous moment of founding violence (Horsfall 1989, 12–24).

Juno sets her terms to Jupiter thus:

> When they settle a peace now with prosperous marriages – so be it – when they now join laws and treaties, may you not order the native Latins to change their name, nor to become Trojans or be called Teucrians, or order the men to change their tongue or alter their clothing. Let Latium be, let the Alban kings be through the ages, let the Roman progeny be powerful through Italian virtue: allow Troy to die, and die along with its name. (*Aen.* 12.821–8)

The question of cultural identity in Vergil is intimately tied up with the establishment of the law. With Juno's reconciliation, her mythical violence is transformed into law-making violence; it results in the fated establishment of a new world power. The agreement, however, comes at the price of yet another kind of violence: the destruction of Trojan culture. Difference in language and clothing is what marks the conquered peoples on the shield of Aeneas, and these are things the Trojans must give up, as if conquered. Juno effectively achieves a bloodless genocide under the name of peace and the establishment of the law. My tendentious formulation blends Benjamin's mythical violence with his last category, divine violence.

Divine violence is a complex term that Benjamin reaches for as an antidote to mythical violence. It comes from God with a capital "G," and for it he turns to the revolt of Korah in the Hebrew Bible (Numbers 16). What Benjamin is looking for is a way to critique violence itself, not just violence as a means. He nevertheless wants to preserve it as a vehicle for historical change. The Korah story is in fact political, since it is about rebels to Moses' power (Alter 2004, 762; Milgrom 1990, excursus 39). Since violence cannot be an end in itself within the legal sphere, Benjamin has to look for areas of immediate violence, and this is what the gods offer. Mythical violence as he defines it has immediacy, but ends up being compromised by its link to legal violence. It establishes a new law in its wake, and Benjamin wants to find a violence that inaugurates "a purer sphere." The Marxist in him is looking for a way to justify revolution, not some ordinary man-wrought, compromised political realignment, but something radical, that would found "a new historical epoch," something that turns out to be unknowable.

> If mythical violence is lawmaking, divine violence is law-destroying; if the former sets
> boundaries, the latter boundlessly destroys them; if mythical violence brings at once guilt
> and retribution, divine power only expiates; if the former threatens, the latter strikes; if
> the former is bloody, the latter is lethal without spilling blood. (Benjamin 1978, 297; cf.
> Alter 2004, 767; Milgrom 1990, 423)

While we can never know what the gods are or God is up to, we can do something
more modest, which is to see whether Vergil shares a similar conception to Benjamin.
Let us go over points of resemblance.

Juno's violence is bloodless. Her destruction of Troy, at least at this point, is not a
massacre, but rather the disappearance of Trojan culture without any need for spilling
blood. Juno is not interested in exterminating mere individual Trojan lives but in
establishing a superior culture. She is attempting to do something elevating, however
petty she may seem narratively.

The destruction of Troy is boundless. Troy is destroyed not only at her site; the destruction keeps Troy from popping up somewhere else. The name itself, a movable signifier,
will die. Juno does not bother with all the little Troys founded by Aeneas or others in
book 3 – they are pale shadows and will have no power. She destroys the heart of the
thing, if not the people (Horsfall 2000, on *Aen.* 7.295; 2003, on *Aen.* 11.306–7).

The violence of Jupiter and Juno is law destroying. They do not let the Latins and
Trojans revert to the treaty they worked out among themselves, but destroy it (cf.
Adler 2003, 167, 183). There is a fundamental difference between the terms of the
human treaty and that agreed on by the gods. For one, the gods agree on the annihi-
lation of the Eastern culture. By contrast, the terms set and ratified by Aeneas and
Latinus entail a more benign arrangement (as in Dion. Hal. 60.2), something Hannah
Arendt accepts as a model for working things out without violence. If Turnus wins,
Aeneas agrees to leave the territory, join with his ally Evander, and refrain from further warfare against the Latins. But if Aeneas wins, he will not impose his might on
the losers. Both races will remain *unconquered*.

> I will not order the Italians to obey the Teucrians nor do I seek rule for myself. The two
> races will join unconquered in eternal treaties with equal laws. I will contribute sacred
> things and my gods; let my father-in-law Latinus control warfare and formal sovereignty
> [*imperium*]. The Teucrians will build walls for me and Lavinia will give her name to the
> city. (12.189–94)

The humans let both races remain under the law, with a significant religious contribution from the Trojans; the gods eliminate the Trojans' cultural identity. The human
attempt to establish the law is a further casualty of divine violence.

Although Vergil does not use explicit language for expiation, Juno accepts what we
might call in loose terms the sacrifice of Trojan culture in exchange for her rage. The
Trojans give up their identity to appease the god, and the expiation works even though
their action is neither willing nor conscious. There is, however, a more explicit notional
sacrifice, and this is the life of Turnus.

The divine pact between Jupiter and Juno enables Aeneas on the human level
finally to go ahead and kill Turnus. Here is yet another way in which Turnus' death

is overdetermined. Vergil makes it clear that there is no need for Turnus to be killed as far as the establishment of the Roman race is concerned. Turnus concedes defeat publicly and pleads for mercy. Turnus' death would, in his own formulation, simply be a needless extension of violence, and Aeneas' famous hesitation shows that he has at least a theoretical point. The need for his death lies elsewhere. Turnus' death plays out contemporary concerns about vengeance and clemency, which were topical in the wake of civil war. Aeneas has a choice between the virtue of the sovereign, to show his power in his ability to suspend the law and grant reprieve, or to exact vengeance. Augustus himself made a transformation from pursuing vengeance for his posthumously adoptive father Julius Caesar's murder during the civil wars to sovereign clemency after he had won, and his dedication of a temple to Mars the Avenger many years later does not so much celebrate vengeance as a principle as hand it over to the gods. The founder of the race, however, was overwhelmed by rage described as divine; he drove his sword home, and the epic ends before we can see any transformation. His anger essentially removes what at the moment of hesitation appears as a choice. Aeneas' violence exceeds the legal realm, just as it exceeds the reach of reason. Benjamin states that divine violence does not demand sacrifice but accepts it (1978, 297). Aeneas speaks of Turnus' death as a sacrifice (Dyson 2001, 24). The final sentence of "Critique of Violence" is: "Divine violence, which is the sign and seal but never the means of sacred execution, may be called sovereign violence." Aeneas executes Turnus under the sign and seal of the sacred; he is the means of the sacred execution which sovereign violence accepts.

There are many problems here, but perhaps the most fundamental is that divine violence is unknowable. We may allegorize tsunamis as the work of Poseidon, but this is our attempt to come to an understanding beyond our capabilities of understanding. Rather than taking such attempts as truth, we should recognize them as acknowledgment of our own interpretive limits. And violence among men is no more or less than violence among men. It may operate within the law or partially exceed it, it may be law-making, law-preserving, or expressive, it may be political or personal, but it is visited upon men by men. The pessimistic interpretation of the *Aeneid* recognizes all the reasons that the optimists cite for justifying Aeneas' violence in cultural terms, but they still say no. This is because, while they might accept law-preserving violence, they are uncomfortable with law-making violence; immediate violence, furthermore, is an abomination – one which Hannah Arendt, for instance, does not recognize as a category (Arendt 1968; Haverkamp 2005, 998) – and divine violence appears as mystification. In "Force of Law," Derrida closes his critique of Benjamin by rejecting divine violence as an idea precisely because it could lead to dire human consequences: it could justify the "final solution" of the Nazis. Gas chambers, he points out, cause no bloodshed. As in the *Aeneid*, at issue is the attempted eradication of a race from the Near East, a race which under some representations calls down the anger of the gods or God. There are no bounds to the violence. Derrida says, "One is terrified at the idea of an interpretation that would make of the holocaust an expiation and an indecipherable signature of the just and violent anger of God" (Derrida 2002, 298).

Vergil and the Roman Exemplum

Derrida's discomfort with Benjamin's category of divine violence is especially poignant because of Benjamin's biography, and particularly the manner of his death (Arendt 1968, 170–1; Demetz, in Benjamin 1978, xiv–xv). Derrida is aware that Benjamin cannot have known in 1921, when "Critique of Violence" was written, nor even at his death in 1940 about the "final solution" (Derrida 2002, 260), but he is worried because the examples Benjamin uses to illustrate mythical violence come from Greek myth (Benjamin 1978, 294–5, 297), while that illustrating divine violence comes from the Hebrew Bible (Benjamin 1978, 297). Derrida is uncomfortable doing so, but he nevertheless tentatively suggests a generalization that mythical violence is a Greek and divine violence a Jewish idea (Derrida 2002, 259, 287–8, 291–2). There are both historical and moral problems with Derrida's partition. On his interpretation, it would be a Jewish tradition of divine violence that leads to the Holocaust, and the Jews would ultimately be responsible for the ideas that caused them harm. I think it is important to show that divine violence was already in operation as an idea within Europe "proper," and I hope to have been successful in showing its presence at the end of the *Aeneid*. We cannot displace responsibility for this destructive idea onto the Jews, an Eastern culture whose assimilation into Europe has been at the same time so partial and so complete.

What Derrida's scheme leaves out is the Roman. The Romans are often considered the mere inheritors of Greek culture, and it is symptomatic of scholarly blindness to Rome that Derrida overlooks the Ovidian source of Benjamin's version of the Niobe myth (Haverkamp 2005, 1002). But it is not a mere question of literary filiation. Rémy Brague in *Europe: la voie romaine* (1993) defines Europe as the culture where people care, or at one time cared, about Latin. Brague specifies Latin and not Rome. The language, with its literary heritage, has created a shared *culture*, while Rome was Eastern as well as Western, and eventually migrated to Byzantium. Brague has a sense that the reason we tend to overlook Rome in favor of the Greeks and the Hebrews as originators of European culture is the role Latin places in the transmission of these other cultures: the medium becomes transparent. Here he picks up T.S. Eliot's notion in *What is a Classic?* (1975, 130) that Greek and Latin are not "two systems of circulation, but one, for it is through Rome that our parentage in Greece must be traced." Both Ernst Robert Curtius and Eliot express a similar sense of Vergil, and of Rome, as central to Europe in the same period (Martindale 1997, 1–18).

> But [Aeneas] is a symbol of Rome; and as Aeneas is to Rome, so is ancient Rome to Europe. Thus Virgil acquires the centrality of the unique classic; he is at the centre of European civilization, in a position which no other poet can share or usurp. The Roman Empire and the Latin language were not any empire and any language, but an empire and a language with a unique destiny in relation to ourselves; and the poet in whom that Empire and that language came to consciousness and expression is a poet of unique destiny. (Eliot 1975, 128–9)

George Steiner (1990, 10) more recently took this idea further: "Above all, Virgil is European." He specifies that Vergil's concerns lie "at the roots of our European conditions." The statement is perhaps reversible: to be European means to inherit a legacy left by Vergil. Curtius and Eliot alike cling to Rome in a Eurocentric vision that is no longer politically relevant. The current expansion of the European Union is interesting, among other reasons, because it is dissolving anew the boundaries between what is and is not Europe. The debate over the inclusion of Turkey, the geographical home of Troy, is particularly ironic in light of the Roman foundation myth.

That Vergil should offer a model for being European depends first and foremost on the particular role he represents violence as playing in foundation, but furthermore in the interaction he establishes between literature and politics. The contingent historical orientation of the *Aeneid* lends it an inordinate power to represent Rome to posterity, as if it were a transparent window onto Roman history instead of a participant in the ideological construction of empire.

Arendt falls prey to the *Aeneid*'s seductions in her analysis of the American Revolution, and her use of the *Aeneid* is exemplary for its role in defining European – including American – models of foundation. Her dependence on a literary text in fact misleads her on a number of points. She wants to take the poem as a blueprint for the Roman Republic, while it is one, if anything, for the Empire. In *On Revolution* she devotes two chapters entitled "Foundation" to the American Revolution, and in the second spends considerable time on the use the Founders made of the Roman constitution. The particular aspect they imitated from Rome was to ground the constitution in neither some absolute, as the European monarchies had done, nor in the volatile will of the people, as the French Revolution would do, but rather in the very act of foundation itself as a new beginning. They innovated on the Roman model by not having the foundation be a refoundation, but rather a foundation from scratch. Arendt, however, turns to the *Aeneid* to support this idea without taking account of the fact that Vergil's foundation story is more about Augustus than the Republic. Although Augustus claims to restore the Republic after a period of civil war, one major constitutional change under his ascendancy is that *auctoritas*, previously located in the Senate, migrates to him, and along with it comes a large measure of sovereign power (Galinsky 1996, chs. 1–2).

By trying to make the *Aeneid* fit her understanding of what the Founders took from the Roman Republic in the framing of the American Constitution, Arendt whitewashes the *Aeneid* in several ways. First of all, Vergil does ground Roman power on an absolute. We can rationalize fate to some extent as history as it appears in hindsight, but Vergilian fate resides in the will of Jupiter. While fate does not correspond exactly to the Christian God which upheld European monarchies for so long, it is an innovation on Republican ways of grounding the state in that it lends divine sanction not only to the state, but also to the reigning Julian family. Arendt's presentation of Rome as a refoundation is also somewhat off. Here she is making a distinction between the American originary foundation and Rome, which continually needs refoundation, but she errs in making Rome a refoundation of Troy (1965, 208). With Juno's reconciliation, Vergil asserts emphatically that Rome is not a refoundation of Troy, and the numerous failed attempts to reestablish Troy in book 3 similarly attest to the impossibility of bringing back Troy. This is an idea Aeneas has to give up. Rome is only ever a refoundation of itself, and the connection to the East Arendt might wish to see as an instance of tolerance is broken. Arendt (1965, 209) furthermore goes out of her way to remove founding violence from the Roman foundation. She downplays the war between the Italians and the Trojans and presents it merely as a means to undo the previous defeat at Troy. This gets not only the Empire, but the Republic wrong. Rome inscribed violence in all its acts of foundation, from Romulus' murder of Remus, to Lucretia's suicide, to the execution of the Catilinarians, to the proscriptions of the triumvirate, and the multiple instances of civil war culminating in Augustus' rule (Arendt 1965, 209; cf. Bremmer and Horsfall 1987, 34–8; Cornell 1975, 27–31; Bannon 1997, 158–73). Founding violence is an element of continuity between Republic and Empire that Vergil understood. Arendt takes the treaty Aeneas establishes with Latinus in book 12 as the treaty that will hold, and emphasizes that both nations will join each other unconquered under equal laws. Her desire to take Rome as a healthy model for America leads her to overlook the fact that Juno explicitly rejects this treaty in favor of one where the winners will emerge as conquered. It is characteristic of Arendt to turn a blind eye to divine violence.

But it is precisely in a literary work that divine violence can be represented. We cannot see such things in life, but literature has no such constraints. Benjamin's instances of divine violence are literary. Arendt focuses on isolated parts of the *Aeneid* and neglects that Vergil's point is rather that all attempts to tame violence fail, and fail spectacularly. This is perhaps one of the reasons Rome is exemplary for Europe.

The question remains whether such violence belongs to Benjamin's category of divine violence. For Roman history we will, as Benjamin points out, never know, but the literature certainly represents it that way, and Augustus furthermore capitalized on the divinization of his adoptive father Julius Caesar in his attempt to avenge his murder. I am not at all sure Benjamin did not understand divine violence as emergent. The final page of the "Critique of Violence" (1978, 300) shows Benjamin altogether unsure:

> On the breaking of this cycle [the oscillation between law-making and law-preserving violence] maintained by mythical forms of law, on the suspension of law with all the forces on which it depends as they depend on it, finally therefore on the abolition of state power, a new historical epoch is founded. If the rule of myth is broken occasionally in the present age, the coming age is not so unimaginably remote that an attack on law is altogether futile. But if the existence of violence outside the law, as pure immediate violence, is assured, this furnishes the proof that revolutionary violence, the highest manifestation of unalloyed violence by man, is possible, and by what means.

Augustus' refoundation of the Roman state after the civil wars took place on the back of the suspension of the law, first during the second triumvirate, and then during the period between his victory at Actium (31 BCE) and the so-called first Augustan settlement (27 BCE). No matter how we regard his statement in the *Res gestae* that he handed back the state to the SPQR, he maintains his sovereign position in Carl Schmitt's definition: "The sovereign is he who decides on the state of exception" (1985, 5). Augustus is the one to decide and, in the relocation of sovereignty that his ability to decide indicates, a new historical epoch has been founded, as Benjamin describes it, on the suspension of the law. Revolutionary violence, which carries the characteristics of purity and immediacy of divine violence, is as close as we can get in

Benjamin to divine violence. I think it is not a coincidence that in the 1930s, Sir Ronald Syme chose to call the passage from Republic to Empire under Augustus *The Roman Revolution*. Derrida's generalization (2002, 269) that "all revolutionary discourses… justify the recourse to violence by alleging the founding, in progress or to come, of a new law, of a new state" could have been written of Augustus.

FURTHER READING

Essential for the reception of Vergil are Hardie (1993) for antiquity and Ziolkowski (1993) and Kallendorf (2007) for more recent periods. More on this topic can be found in Cox (1997) and the essays collected in Spence and Lowrie (2006); for Derrida and Latin, see Lowrie (2001). Some additional treatments of early legend and national identity are Perret (1942), Taylor (1955), Castagnoli (1982), Gruen (1992b), and Dench (2005). Hardt and Negri (2000) offer an overview of ideas about empire, but their account of Polybius is vitiated by an assumption that his description of the mixed Roman government pertained to the Empire rather than to the Republic. Those interested in tyranny should not miss Kojève (1963). The bibliography on Augustus and Actium as well as the end of the *Aeneid* is enormous: in addition to the pieces referred to explicitly above, worthy of note are, for the former, Tarn (1932), Carter (1970), and Gurval (1995) and, for the latter, West (1998) and Barnes (1999). For Arendt and Rome, see Taminiaux (2000) and Hammer (2002). A recent theorist who has worked on Rome, violence, and biopolitics is Giorgio Agamben in his *homo sacer* series, especially (1998) and (2005).

CHAPTER TWENTY EIGHT

Figuring the Founder
Vergil and the Challenge of Autocracy

Joy Connolly

We suffer not only from the living, but from the dead. Le mort saisit le vif!
Karl Marx, preface to *Capital*, vol. 1 (trans. Moore and Aveling 1967)

The wolf of Augustan autocracy arrived in the sheep's clothing of the traditional language of Republican refoundation. In exchange for his rule in what was now a permanent state of emergency, Augustus granted security (Tac. *Ann.* 1.1). His legitimization of autocracy exploited the ideology of self-restraint that had for centuries been the centerpiece of Republican virtue, an ideology Augustus pressed in two directions at once: he "gave back" the Republic to the Senate and people, restraining himself from accepting the powers and accouterments of monarchy (*RG* 1.34), and he transformed traditional senatorial competition for *gloria* into the gateway to civil war, by defining resistance to Caesar as war against the Republic (*RG* 1.2).

The Augustan consolidation shook Republican ideology to its core. Romans had long seen violence as a bulwark against tyranny – and even further, as a constitutive element in the Republic's formation and identity. Republican writers and their modern readers like Machiavelli and Montesquieu represent periodic eruptions of violence as necessary for the preservation of republican freedom and equality. It may occur outside the borders, as Sallust indicates in his diagnosis of Rome's social breakdown in the peace following the Punic Wars (*Jug.* 41), or in the body politic itself, as Livy suggests in his canonizing account of cyclical violence in early Republican history (Serres 1991, 89–103). This view makes civic sense of a history in which the founders of the Republic battle with the exiled Tarquins, the Senate executes Spurius Maelius and other would-be tyrants, and the *senatus consultum ultimum* is designed to suppress the brothers Gracchi (Lowrie 2007).

Through the first century BCE faith in the capacity of violence to dethrone tyranny persists, most visibly in Cicero's *De officiis* (1.34, 3.19, 3.83). With the tightening of Augustus' grip on autocratic power, this faith drained away, bringing to the surface a crisis in political subjectivity. Augustus admitted no lines of determination in custom or law and yet insisted on defining his rule as the latest permutation of tradition. To whom or what would Romans now attach themselves in this time of transformation? If both continuity and conflict were compromised, from what sources of authority, with what patterns of political identity and action were they to affirm themselves as free citizens within the new regime? Could one resist without self-destruction, assert oneself without killing oneself? What way forward might be discovered between assertion and abjection? Livy pointedly comments: "we can endure neither our own vices nor their remedy," since all has decayed into a "desire for death and destruction" (pref. 9, 12) – stressing that the violence he is about to narrate *ab urbe condita* no longer serves.

Vergil is often interpreted as a purveyor of the imperial melancholia Livy appears to exhibit here, and his strange confection of a hero, Aeneas, is taken as a response (critical or laudatory) of the *princeps*. To David Quint, in his influential study *Epic and Empire*, the *Aeneid* makes the experience of Aeneas the foundation of a Roman history "that culminated in world empire and in the rise to power of the new principate," a storyline that "correlates the historical fortune and eventual demise of epic with the political position of the early modern European aristocracy" (Quint 1993, 9–10). The choices that face Quint's Aeneas – especially his final choice of clemency or revenge as he stands over the body of Turnus – are the choices of Caesar or Augustus. If Aeneas seems ineffective or unfinished, "a shadow of a man" as Denys Page once called him (quoted in Porter 2004, 153), Quint claims it is because the Trojan leader is designed to reflect Augustus' careful styling of a community-oriented principate and himself as the literally self-less leader in contrast to the self-obsessed great men responsible for a century of civil war. "The political contradictions of the *Aeneid* are those of an ideology that preached both forgiveness and revenge" (Quint 1993, 81). While casting the epic as exclusively Augustan in its political concerns (whether pro- or anti- is irrelevant), Quint's reading establishes the leading female characters in the *Aeneid* as historical analogues to the figure depicted so prominently on the shield Vulcan forges for Aeneas, Cleopatra. Juno and Dido become archetypal of the obstacle/seducer of the (would-be) king – assuming a role in which the man's defeat of the woman, as Quint sees it, highlights the epic's generic affinities with romance.

If we abandon the assumption that Vergil is an Augustan melancholic, another context presents itself in which these figures may be placed: the cycle of Republican foundation. Women play two roles in this narrative. In the first, they are violated, usually by acts of rape that provide the proximal cause for cyclical violence: Mars' rape of Rhea Silvia, the Romans' rape of the Sabine women, Tarquin's rape of Lucretia, and the tyrannical decemvir Appius Claudius' attempted rape of Verginia (Joshel 2002; Matthes 2000, 23–50). (Niccolò Machiavelli, no stranger to Roman foundation myths, spoofs the motif in his Plautine comedy *La Mandragola*: he names his main character Lucrezia and transforms her "Tarquin" into the handsome young prince Callimaco, who manages by a trick to seduce her with her husband's consent.) Alternatively, women sustain the Republican foundation narrative by misdirection, diverting Roman men from their intentions and actions: this is Dido, Tanaquil – and Juno, who is conventionally interpreted as a blocking character, the obstacle to Aeneas' goal to reach

Italy. Whether female figures occupy the position of violation or misdirection, the cycle of refoundation clicks forward because these women are in the way. When they are forced to yield, the Republic is renewed, often over their dead bodies, while the male hero walks away, victorious.

I argue here that Vergil's *Aeneid* responds to the new challenge of political orientation created by civil war and its post-Actium consequences by inventing a new style of hero: a figure suspended between assertion and abjection, a figure commanded to obey who enacts obedience through delay, distraction, and the simple act of turning aside. Aeneas obeys Jupiter and the fates like the golden bough, which hesitates or delays as he plucks it free (*cunctantem*, 6.211). Daniel Selden perceptively emphasizes the "peculiar temporality that defines the subject in Vergil" who "abides for the present in the blank" that lies between words like *meminisse* and *iuvabit* (Selden 2006, 384–5). In the course of his wanderings, Aeneas unexpectedly emerges as the delay-causing double of the poem's primary force of delay, Juno – or not so unexpectedly, if we recall the place of reverence and honor Jupiter smilingly guarantees the goddess near the end of the epic (*nec gens ulla tuos aeque celebrabit honores*, 12.840). Back in book 1, in response to Venus' complaint, Jupiter described Juno in terms that implicitly make Aeneas her mortal double: both figures are "wearing down the sea, earth, and heaven," and both are gradually "turning their counsels toward the better" (*mare nunc terrasque metu caelumque fatigat / consilia in melius referet*, 1.280–1). Violence plays a notoriously complex role in the career of both figures. Not long after the reconciliation of Jupiter and Juno, in the most critically scrutinized scene in the epic, *pius* Aeneas murders his rival Turnus with vengeful fury. Though the calm smile Jupiter bestows on his wife suggests that Junonian violence is built into the founding narrative, that it is necessary to the Roman foundation, Aeneas' history and character earlier in the epic strain against that necessity. By turns isolated, melancholic, confused, and enraged, Aeneas both inaugurates the historical cycle of violence that constitutes Republican politics and invites a critical response to it. He is neither simply a Republican exemplum nor a kingly or imperial one; he is, rather, a figure of disconnected and resistant sensibility whose acts and words call into question the logic of exemplarity itself.

In an important essay on the interweaving of the themes of *eros* and war in Vergil, Michael Putnam commented briefly on the "interrelationship" between Juno and Aeneas, "polar opposites" at the poem's start who by its end "become equivalents… as Aeneas changes from passive to active, from sufferer of events to their apparent ruler, his enemy proves to be the hero's double, and initial, immediate distinctions between them yield, finally, [in the last scene] to a deep-seated affinity" (Putnam 1995, 45). His perceptive discussion sees the conflict between Aeneas and Juno as a power struggle of opposites where each element moves over time from a relation of separation to identification. I see what Putnam calls "affinity" as an interdependent relation of collusion which allows the *Aeneid* to broach questions of obedience and free agency made freshly urgent by Augustan rule. This interdependence incorporates but also transcends the kind of identification posited by Ernesto Laclau and Chantal Mouffe, who read antagonism as an interdependent relation in which "the presence of the Other prevents me from being myself," and in negating identity, shows that the maintenance of identity depends on a struggle whose essential interdependency ultimately collapses difference into meaninglessness (Laclau and Mouffe 1985, 125). Though interdependent, Aeneas and Juno are also crucially distinguished by their different relations to the finitude of mortality, which will be a major theme in my discussion.

The affinity of Juno and Aeneas unfolds through poetics, through the political dimensions of rhetorical figures like synecdoche and anacoluthon – aspects of ornament rhetoricians and philosophers have always painted as "feminine" when it suits them. Indeed, the gendered politics of Roman foundation maps onto the gendered politics of rhetoric, where according to *Howell's Devises*, "Women are Wordes, men are Deedes" (cited in Parker 1988, 22–3, 237). As this sixteenth-century proverb makes women and words the embodiment of passivity, the opposite of masculine action, it also equates women and words with displacement and misdirection, since words are construed throughout the rhetorical tradition as the replacement of, the preparatory step before, or that which distracts from action. Barbara Johnson draws attention to the subtle connection between misdirection and violence in her comments on a notorious CIA manual on psychological operations that ends with a list of rhetorical figures. If rhetoric has everything to do with covert operations, she asks, "are a politics of violence already encoded in rhetorical figures as such?" (B. Johnson 1987, 184). Figures of speech disclose what kind of Roman political self Aeneas is modeling – not an exemplum of Augustan autocracy (the *Aeneid*'s default political context in much current critical literature), but a figure who anticipates the cyclical violence and the eternally unfulfilled promise of Republican politics, whose repeated missteps and final lapse into *ira* acknowledge in advance the Republic's tragic fall.

Let me take a closer look at Aeneas and Juno. The goddess' role in the *Aeneid* is to block destiny, to oppose the law of Jupiter and the fates. At the beginning of the poem Vergil queries the ends of Juno's wrath with an apostrophe that underscores its own unanswerability: "are the rages of celestial spirits so great?" (*tantaene animis caelestibus irae?*, 1.11). Precisely because Juno understands that her plans must fail, "there are no bounds to her overwhelming desire to exact the greatest possible vengeance while she still has the chance to do so" (Heinze 1993, 148). Her antagonism extends beyond Jupiter's particular end, the founding of a new Troy; it is literally end-less, not only in the sense that it is unstoppable or eternal in a temporal sense, but also because it eludes the logic of closure itself. Near the end of book 12, Juno yields to Jupiter – on the condition that the new city, the proto-Rome, be founded on an act of cultural genocide:

> sit Latium, sint Albani per saecula reges,
> sit Romana potens Itala virtute propago:
> occidit, occideritque sinas cum nomine Troia.

> Let Latium be, let the Alban kings live through the centuries,
> let Rome be powerful with Italian strength:
> but Troy fell, let Troy fall with her name.
>
> (*Aen.* 12.826–8)

We know from Servius, from history, and from Dido's dying curse back in book 4 that Juno's antagonism will return when she favors Carthage in the Punic Wars. Denis

408

Feeney catalogues the passages in Vergil, in Ennius' *Annales* 51–4 Skutsch (= 60–5 Vahlen), and in Horace, *Ode* 3.3 where Juno's hatred for Troy remains unresolved, eternally incompatible within the world of the texts and with the historical reality of Roman religious practice (Feeney 1984, 185–92).

The endless quality of Juno's antagonism, her capacity to delay and defer events, makes her emblematic of the figure Renaissance rhetoricians called *dilatio*, that is, the spreading out, the open-endedness, that language creates in the world. *Dilatio* is specifically associated in the European rhetorical tradition with the way women like Juno and Dido use language as a prevention or substitution for male action (Parker 1988, 13). Indeed, it is characteristic of Juno to keep the field of action "open" precisely in and by her acts of speaking about the limits on her action. Her single-minded rage services an open-ended plot, and even her final reconciliation "lies beyond the poem's close" (Feeney 1984, 181). Jay Reed perceptively objects that Juno's rage is not exactly endless, since her beloved Carthage represents her chosen "end"; but as Charles Pazdernik points out, Vergil problematizes this end in his representation of the passage of time: Vergil's first reference to Carthage stresses its age and deadness: *urbs antiqua fuit* (1.12); further, from the perspective of the fates, Carthage historically enables Roman *gloria* and thus functions as its interdependent antagonist in Laclau and Mouffe's terms (Reed and Pazdernik, personal communications).

Juno is the first character to speak aloud in the *Aeneid*, voicing her antagonism to Aeneas and Jupiter's ends.

> **mene** incepto desistere victam
> **nec posse** Italia Teucrorum avertere regem?

> **Am I** to stand down from what I started, defeated –
> **am I not able** to turn the king of the Trojans away from Italy?
> (*Aen.* 1.37–8)

She speaks again in book 7, the "second beginning" of the epic, transcending the limits divine topography places on her action ("I shall move Acheron"), and anticipating the violent act with which the epic "ends," as Aeneas "founds" his blade in Turnus' breast (*hoc dicens ferrum adverso sub pectore condit / fervidus*, 12.950–1), thus beginning Roman history:

> heu stirpem invisam et fatis contraria nostris
> fata Phrygum!...
> ...optatoque **conduntur** Thybridis alveo
> securi pelagi atque mei...
> flectere si nequeo superos, Acheronta movebo.

> Alas, hated race, and standing in opposition to mine,
> the fates of the Phrygians!...
> **They are founded** on the longed-for shore of the Tiber,
> free of danger from the sea and from me...
> If I cannot sway the gods above, I shall move Acheron.
> (*Aen.* 7.293–4, 303–4, 312)

By a paradox, the problematization of the end and the valorization of the unrealized effort also figure a key assumption of Republican ideology: that the Republic is secured through its incapacity to realize itself (Pocock 1989, 94–101; on democracy, compare Butler 2000, 268). Whatever the Republic achieves, through external conquest or the successful negotiation of internal tensions, the *res publica* itself remains unachieved. Perfect realization would signify the end, above all the end of the foundational competition among the senatorial order and between the *ordines*. When Venus asks Jupiter what end he has given to Aeneas' suffering, and he answers that he will give *imperium sine fine*, "empire without end" (1.279), there is a sense in which he is granting Aeneas, and the Romans, no end at all, and that this sense of endlessness is a crucial element in Roman *virtus*. For realizing Rome is impossible: the desire for glory that underwrites Roman virtue always bears within itself the spur to vice and violence. Aeneas' famous *pietas* and its disintegration into *ira* in the final scene of the *Aeneid* are emblematic of the Republican notion of virtue and its decay. Virtue and vice are always close neighbors – a dynamic balance that, as I have argued elsewhere, Republican actors eternally remake in the cycle of their repeatedly refounded state (Connolly 2007, 208).

It is by this logic of endlessness that Aeneas' first speech echoes Juno's: he laments the limits placed on his will using the word *mene*, which he, like her, elides with a word that begins with "i" (in his case, the dramatically loaded word *Iliacis*), creating a combination that (as first noted by Levitan 1993, 14) may be a punning reference to the first word of the *Iliad*, *menis* or wrath:

> talia voce refert: "o terque quaterque beati,
> quis ante ora patrum Troiae sub moenibus altis
> contigit oppetere! o Danaum fortissime gentis
> Tydide! **mene** Iliacis occumbere campis
> **non potuisse** tuaque animam hanc effundere dextra,
> saevus ubi Aeacidae telo iacet Hector, ubi ingens
> Sarpedon, ubi tot Simois correpta sub undis
> **scuta virum galeasque et fortia corpora volvit!**"

> Such words he calls aloud: "O three and four times blessed
> were those who died before their fathers' eyes
> beneath the walls of Troy! O brave son of Tydides
> of the race of Danaans! **That I could not** lie on Trojan fields –
> nor pour out my life's breath by your right arm,
> where savage Hector lies thanks to the weapon of Achilles, where great
> Sarpedon lies, where Simois **rolls** under the waves **so many**
> **shields and helmets and brave bodies of men!**"
>
> (*Aen.* 1.94–101)

These passages are more than verbal echoes: they disclose two desires that Juno and Aeneas share. First, she does not want Rome to be founded; and he does not want Rome to be founded; he wants to obey, which is an important difference. As Ezra Pound cuttingly observed, quoting Yeats: "Ach, a hero, him a hero? Bigob, I t'ought he was a priest" (1934, 44; discussed by Farrell in this volume). If, as Mark Buchan has said (2007), Agamemnon is a hero who doesn't know what he wants, and Achilles is a hero who knows what he wants and wants what he knows, then Aeneas is a hero who doesn't want – what he doesn't know. In these passages, Juno assumes a position of open antagonism to Jupiter, whereas Aeneas seems unmindful of the god's will as he concentrates on his lost companions; but both set themselves apart from and against the law of the fates. Second, Juno wants Aeneas dead, along with the rest of the Trojans; and Aeneas wants to be dead along with the rest of the Trojans. Let us explore Aeneas' desire for death, the second point, which will lead us back to the first.

After Aeneas expresses his longing to have died at Troy in book 1, he elaborates this affinity with the dead in book 6, near the end of his journey through the underworld. When Anchises points out the Roman spirits lined up awaiting birth or rebirth in the world above, Aeneas speaks in what most readers, at this stage of the epic, now recognize as his characteristic mode of confused ignorance:

> o pater, anne aliquas ad caelum hinc ire putandum est
> sublimis animas iterumque ad tarda reverti
> corpora? quae lucis miseris tam dira cupido?

> O father, must we think that any souls go from here
> aloft to heaven, returned again to their sluggish
> bodies? Why this dreadful desire for the sunlight among these wretched men?
> (*Aen.* 6.719–21)

His second question, during which Aeneas seems to turn from his father to apostrophize the distant swarm of spirits, suggests that death delivers the self to freedom from the sluggish bodies up in the world above. Aeneas' encounter with the dead reminds him that the living community of which he is a part is a community filled with suffering and failure – a line of thought revived in Vergil's famous apostrophe to Nisus and Euryalus, the dead lovers who are called "the happy pair" (*fortunati ambo, Aen.* 9.446), and the many episodes in the poem that celebrate the tragic but lovely closure of young death.

What does Aeneas find among the dead? Jean-Luc Nancy diagnoses the idealization of death as a symptom of diseased politics. He suggests that the fantasy of glorious communal death, by salving profound anxieties in individuals about mortality and isolation, helps explain the fatal appeal of totalitarian ideology's promises of salvation. "This is why political or collective enterprises dominated by a will to absolute immanence have as their truth the truth of death," he writes; "immanence, communal fusion, contains no other logic than that of the suicide of the community that is governed by it" (Nancy 1991, 12). That is, in their suggestion that death constitutes the single shared experience of humanity, that which makes a "true" community, totalitarian ideologies end up valorizing death.

Isolated as he is – a point to which I shall return – Aeneas indeed appears to discover a meaningful community in death and the underworld. Upon his arrival in Carthage, when he sees the mural of his dead fellow Trojans fighting before the walls of Troy that decorates Juno's temple, Aeneas tells Achates that death creates a universal community of affective connection: "These are the tears of things, and things subject to death affect the mind" (4.462). Tellingly, Aeneas is not among his Trojan friends in this mural but is separated out, intermingled with the Achaeans in the larger "community" of the battlefield (Porter 2004, 144). The tears of things conclude the last conversation Aeneas and Anchises will ever have: in the underworld, when Anchises is about to turn away, Aeneas stops him with a question about the handsome Marcellus, whose future death prefigures many young men's deaths in the second half of the poem. Anchises addresses Marcellus with a tear-soaked apostrophe: *heu, miser-ande puer, si qua fata aspera rumpas – / tu Marcellus eris* ("Alas, unhappy boy, if you could only shatter the fates – you will be Marcellus," 6.882–3) – words Aeneas will reuse in his own apostrophes to two young Italians killed on the battlefield in Latium: Lausus at 10.825 and Pallas at 11.42.

A father who very rarely addresses his own son Iulus and who does not enjoy a single back and forth exchange of words with him in the entire poem, Aeneas finds paternal love apostrophizing on the battlefield, when he "groans miserably and extends his right hand" to the corpse of the young Lausus, whom he has just slaugh-tered, as "the image of paternal piety enters his mind" (*mentem patriae subiit pietatis imago*, 10.824). A few hundred lines earlier, Aeneas has learned of the death of his young ally Pallas. In one of the most surreally unsettling moments of the poem, Vergil derives a visualization of community from the act of killing:

> proxima quaeque metit gladio latumque per agmen
> ardens limitem agit ferro, te, Turne, superbum
> caede nova quaerens. Pallas, Evander in ipsis
> omnia sunt oculis, mensae quas advena primas
> tunc adiit, dextraeque datae.

> Whatever was nearby he harvested with his sword, and through the long line
> burning he drove a path with his weapon, you, Turnus, in your arrogance,
> with new slaughter, seeking you. Pallas, Evander, in his own eyes
> arise all these things – the first time he (a new arrival
> then) came to the table, and right hands were grasped.
>
> (*Aen.* 10.513–17)

Here, encapsulating Vergil's own pathetic apostrophe to Turnus (*te, Turne*), the slaughter of dehumanized victims, who are neutered (*proxima quaeque*) and then compared to harvested crops (*metit*), brings to Aeneas' eyes (*in ipsis oculis*) a vivid picture of the communities into which he has been welcomed: father and son, host and guest, ally and ally, and lover and beloved, since at that first welcoming meal Pallas had "seized Aeneas' right hand and holding on tight, crushed it" (*excepitque manu dextramque amplexus inhaesit*, 8.124). In this scene, when Mezentius clutches his dead son Lausus, just after he has fallen to Aeneas' sword (10.845), and when Hercules crushes Cacus to death (8.26), *inhaereo*'s clutch blurs the boundaries sepa-rating erotic and paternal love and violence (Putnam 1995, 33). The deaths of Nisus and Euryalus, Lausus, Camilla, and Pallas immediately summon a sympathetic com-munity of fellow soldiers who carry their bodies off the battlefield and redouble their efforts, surging together in a huge assembly of limbs and weapons (especially 11.831).

In the last book, when he exhorts Iulus, Aeneas evokes an exemplary community of the dead for his son to imitate, placing himself next to the dead Hector:

> disce, puer, virtutem ex me verumque laborem,
> fortunam ex aliis...
> sis memor et te animo repetentem exempla tuorum
> et pater Aeneas et avunculus excitet Hector.

> Learn, son, manly courage and true labor from me,
> and fortune from others...
> be mindful, and as you rehearse in your spirit the examples of your family,
> let both your father Aeneas and your uncle Hector urge you on.
> (Aen. 12.435–6, 439–40)

At first reading, Aeneas' comments in the underworld and his view of death as a site where a perfect community is formed might seem to confirm Jean-Luc Nancy's worst suspicions. Is Aeneas' affinity with the dead a perverted expression of his desire for a perfect community, which is also total submission to the law of mortality? Readers have often interpreted (and disdained) Aeneas as reverencing the sovereignty-governed economy of reason, goods, and ends, a reverence that explains his obedience to the father-figures Jupiter and Anchises. So James Porter calls Aeneas a Lacanian pervert, on the grounds that he is unconsciously acting out the desire for authority to be imposed on himself: he displays "complete subservience to a divine mission, the founding of Rome and its terrible imperium – in the guise of pious devotion. The pervert realizes his life-project in becoming the instrument of the jouissance of the Other, and that is the source of his piety" (Porter 2004, 138). But the Lacanian reinscription of resistance as submission defies answerability, does it not?

Aeneas' language is not easily classified. It works strange changes on traditional notions of Roman *pietas*, duty, and exemplarity:

> "...durate, et vosmet rebus servate secundis."
> talia voce refert curisque ingentibus aeger
> spem voltu simulat, premit altum corde dolorem.

> "...Endure, all of you, and preserve yourselves for a favorable future."
> He gave this speech, and sick with great cares, he feigned hope in his expression, and
> pressed the ache of grief deep down in his heart.
> (Aen. 1.207–9)

The act of dissembling following Aeneas' first speech to his men on the shores of Carthage makes us ask whether he believes in ends at all. For him, talk of goals and fulfillment is useful strategic rhetoric. These opening words establish his self-distancing from his destiny, a self-distancing enhanced by his repeated statements of ignorance and confusion about his mission, which together reveal his ambivalence toward, even an embryonic disavowal of, his fated role as the founder of community living a life defined by perfect obedience to the law of Jupiter and the fates.

In fact the figure of community in the *Aeneid* is not Aeneas but his rival Turnus, a man utterly defined by his connections and obligations, however warped they become under the influence of the underworld Fury Allecto. In his first description of Turnus, Vergil embeds him in family relations that are also erotic relations:

> filius huic fato divum prolesque virilis
> nulla fuit, primaque oriens erepta iuventa est.
> sola domum et tantas servabat filia sedes
> iam matura viro, iam plenis nubilis annis.
> multi illam magno e Latio totaque petebant
> Ausonia; petit ante alios pulcherrimus omnis
> Turnus, avis atavisque potens, quem regia coniunx
> adiungi generum miro properabat amore;
> sed variis portenta deum terroribus obstant.
> (*Aen.* 7.50–8)

A son, a manly heir, by the gods' fate
[Latinus] lacked, for his firstborn had been torn away still young.
All that preserved his house and his rule was a daughter
now ripe for a man, of full years to wed.
Many men from great Latium hoped for her, as did all
Ausonia; eager beyond all others was the beautiful
Turnus, powerful, from an ancient line, to whom the royal wife
rushed to be joined, wanting him as son-in-law, with surprisingly strong desire;
but with all kinds of terrors the portents of the gods stood in the way.

Turnus is figured here as a vital supplement fulfilling the needs of Latinus' family: he is life replacing death, filling the gap left by Latinus' dead son, a husband for the nubile Lavinia, "full ready" to marry (*plenis annis*), and a son-in-law for the ardent Amata. Turnus is also the one who vows himself up to his men (*devovi*, 11.442; *devovet*, 12.234). Though Turnus is no Drances, the cunning Italian rhetorician, he speaks easily and with effect to his men and to his family.

Aphasia is Aeneas' lot (Feeney 1983). Speech is crucial to Aeneas' acts as the founder of a new community, and this is especially true of the Roman community, where speech-making plays a central role in Roman conceptions of the *res publica*; it is a crucial element in the cyclical founding and refounding characteristic of Republican politics (Arendt 1965, 198–204). Cicero draws on the Greek rhetorical tradition of Isocrates in his founding narrative in which an eloquent man first establishes the state (*De inv.* 1–5). While Aeneas is capable at times of engaging in effective public speech, his characteristic figure of speech is not normally understood in terms of agency or effect: as we have already seen in Aeneas' battlefield speeches to dead men, it is apostrophe. The deflection expressed in the habitual turning aside of Aeneas' speech and the turning aside of those he attempts to speak with is the expressive figuration of the plot, which tracks Aeneas' turning aside, willing or no, from affective connections, notably Dido, which increase the burden of his traumatic losses back at Troy. Of course, his lifestory is also circular, cycling through repetition of Homer's *Iliad* and *Odyssey*.

In Homer, there is a great deal of conversation among the heroes and their families. In Vergil, the reverse is true. Of the 333 speeches in the *Aeneid*, nearly half (135) are single utterances which receive no reply in words. Aeneas' aphasic failures to converse are so common one perceptive reader calls them a "Vergilian type-scene" (Johnson 1986, 87; also Behr 2005). In Aeneas' speech to Venus in book 1, establishing a recurrent pattern through the poem, Aeneas speaks and his interlocutor turns away:

> ille ubi matrem
> agnovit tali fugientem est voce secutus:
> "quid natum totiens, crudelis tu quoque, falsis
> ludis imaginibus? cur dextrae iungere dextram
> non datur ac veras audire et reddere voces?"

> When he his mother
> recognized, he pursued her as she fled with this speech:
> "Why do you so often, so cruelly, mock your son
> with false images? Why is it not granted to join right hand with right hand
> and to hear and respond honest speech?"

(Aen. 1.405–9)

Elsewhere Aeneas' interlocutor turns away, runs away, or vanishes into thin air – or cannot respond because he lies on the battlefield, a corpse. Aeneas' face-to-face efforts to converse are transformed into apostrophe, the address or invocation of an absent person.

Apostrophe is more than a sign of Aeneas' tragic isolation. It bespeaks the difficulty he experiences eliciting recognition and acknowledgment from those closest to him. It is speech that by definition fails to reach its addressee; it is the rhetorical figure of Aeneas' incapacity for communication, which in light of his judgment of Hades speaks his disconnection from the community of the living. Apostrophe isolates Aeneas, over and against his fate to be the remedy for isolation, the hero who will generate the communal from the singular and from the exiled. He apostrophizes the dead Anchises: "here, best of fathers, you left me exhausted" (3.710–11); and Palinurus, "o Palinurus, too trustful of the tranquil sky and sea, you will lie naked on an unknown shore" (5.870–1); and the Tiber, Lausus, and Pallas, in lines we have already seen (8.537–40; 10.821–30; 11.42–6); and Dido in the underworld (6.472–3). Apostrophe is the figure of his repeated embrace of voids, when he tries but fails to embrace Creusa (2.790–4) and Anchises (5.740–2, 6.697–702). We recall Aeneas' first appearance in book 1, standing in isolation from his men on shipboard, his subsequent abandonment by his disguised mother, and his isolating concealment from others' view under the cover of Venus' misty cloak. These sightings are the visual complement of the moments when Aeneas is the one addressed by figures of pathos – notably Andromache, with her wretched tale of slavery in book 3, and Dido, in her final speech in book 4 – and he responds with silence (Johnson 1986, 92–9).

The Latin word for apostrophe is *aversio*, turning away. Quintilian defines it as "a diversion of our words to address some person other than the judge" (4.1.63; see Culler 2001, 135). Apostrophe cross-circuits the conditions of communication; it speaks past the situation of communicative rationality; it speaks right past the law. And here I turn back to Aeneas' affinity with Juno. In a poem all about motion (away from Troy, toward Italy and Rome) that is really about Juno's delay of motion, her turning aside of Aeneas, the prominence of apostrophe/*aversio* in Aeneas' speech patterns in turn maps his and the Trojans' movement onward in space as a movement sideways.

Now one might object that for all his failure to connect, for all his notorious expressions of uncertainty, reluctance, or ignorance, Aeneas does in fact fulfill his fate; he deserts Dido; he kills Turnus. Two points may be raised to meet this objection. First, in killing Turnus, Aeneas assumes a Juno-like wrath (Putnam 1995, 165–6). This may be interpreted as transgressive of the law, transgressive of Anchises' dictum that "Rome should spare the defeated and beat down the proud"; it is also transgressive in the personal, primitive quality of Aeneas' vengeance-taking, of his own treaty with the Italians (Lowrie 2005, 954–6). Second, when Aeneas kills Turnus, he does so in the self and voice of another, not himself; with the figure of apostrophe, for his naming of Pallas at first sounds like another apostrophe, he *turns aside* from his own action, which of course is also an act of founding (*condit*):

> "Pallas te hoc vulnere, Pallas
> immolat et poenam scelerato ex sanguine sumit."
> hoc dicens ferrum adverso sub pectore **condit**
> fervidus;

> "Pallas with this blow, Pallas
> sacrifices you and exacts his penalty from your criminal blood."
> Saying this, in the back-bent chest he **set fast** the blade,
> burning…
>
> (*Aen.* 12.948–51)

Aeneas' studied avowal that is also a disavowal of moral agency in this final scene caps his repeated refusal, at key points in the poem's second half, to play the part of self-celebratory moral exemplar for his people or for his son. In book 8, at the moment he accepts the path laid out by Jupiter back in book 1 (*ego poscor Olympo*), Aeneas acknowledges that his obedience means death for his Italian enemies. *Heu*, he says, echoing Juno's reference at the beginning of book 7 to the Trojans founding their new settlement on the Tiber, and turning it in an ominous direction:

> **heu** quanta miseris caedes Laurentibus instant!
> quas poenas mihi, Turne, dabis! quam multa sub undas
> **scuta virum galeasque et fortia corpora volves,**
> Thybri pater! poscant acies et foedera rumpant!

> **Alas**, what slaughter stands over these miserable Laurentians!
> What penalties, Turnus, you will pay to me! How many shields
> and helmets and brave bodies of men you will roll beneath your waves,
> father Tiber! Let them call their battlelines, let them break their treaties.
>
> (*Aen.* 8.537–40)

The new city will be founded on the corpses of Italians rolling in the waves. "Aeneas is now in the trap of History," Ralph Johnson writes of this passage, "he certainly feels this, and he almost manages to say it" (1986, 94). Aeneas' apostrophes, which stand for his broader identification with the world of the dead, undercut the logic and consistency of his other words and actions, compromising the heroic code he occasionally espouses.

Why does Aeneas, the founder of the Roman community, so often fail to communicate? Why does the exemplum of obedience to the law at so many points in the text so often wish for death? And why does he willfully commit murder at the end of the poem, invoking a law of vengeance whose primitive nature seems to stand at a distance from the vows and treaties Aeneas has earlier undertaken? Of Achilles Mark Buchan has written: "Behind…the system of ideal neutral laws that guarantee order is a traumatic voice that compels us to yield to the sense of these laws but that is itself senseless" (2004, 112). If the end of the *Aeneid* tells us anything, it is that Aeneas can act with the destructive fury embodied by Achilles in the *Iliad* and, in his own story, by Juno. These signs of turning away from his fates are signs that the transgressive violence Juno has practiced throughout the epic have been translated, the first *translatio imperii*, into the figure of its founder, Aeneas.

Celia Schultz has shown how important is the role of Juno Sospita in military and political affairs at Lanuvium and then at Rome, beyond the traditionally feminine areas of fertility and childbirth. For Schultz, Juno Sospita embodies Rome and more particularly Roman expansion itself, "usurpation and incorporation" (2007, 223). When Venus calls Juno's protégés the Tyrians "two-tongued" (*bilinguis*, 1.661), we see that Juno is the goddess of the Rome we know, the Rome of combined Italy and Troy, the polyglot imperialist Republican Rome, a Rome that shares Juno's own proclivity toward endless violence and revenge (Harris 1985, 164–75, 252–4). The Juno/Aeneas dyad, which stands for turning away and moving on, endlessness, the eternal suspension of fulfillment, is the expression of Rome's political identity on the global stage.

At the beginning of this essay, I asked: if the machine of Republican politics had become a tool of autocracy, where was a new account of political subjectivity, and especially an account of freedom, to be found? The old Republican order had incorporated into itself the belief that equality was maintained through struggle; now the element of struggle had been removed, and in the process, the impoverishment of the Republican order is revealed. According to Geoffrey Hartman, the most troublesome challenge for the historian is the tense balancing act of narrating the story of liberty while acknowledging the deadly power of tyranny. "What point of view can convey this twofold consciousness?" Hartman asks (1988, 33).

Vergil's response is to create a protagonist who consistently avoids heroic self-assertion without being for subjection. Until the final book, Aeneas cultivates a paradoxically non-assertive strength. In the final book, with his last act, the murder of Turnus, by resisting the lesson of exemplarity that his father Anchises had given him ("spare the defeated and cut down the proud"), he reclaims his singularity. But Vergil resists making this discovery of agency cause for celebration. The creation of community is made into a spectacle of willed violence, as Aeneas finally does something that he wants to do: he founds a community in death (*condit*, 12.950). When Aeneas' affinity

with Juno and with the dead, his self-distancing from his own fated ends, and his killing of Turnus call into question his self-restraint, indeed his self-sovereignty, this raises
a founding contradiction in Republican political thought – namely, that republics and
republican citizens are supposed to exist in balanced concord but are never fully complete: they exist in a constant process of renewal, eternally open-ended and unfinished. In refusing the kingly model of heroism, Aeneas reveals himself a Republican
hero not merely in his stoic adoption of responsibility, his rejection of his own desires
and loves, but in his embodiment of unfinalizability, his failure to connect.

But Aeneas' refusal to inhabit his own self and his own fated history also articulates
resistance. He does not quite become Juno. He imitates her in transgressing the law,
but in doing so he transforms the role of founder, of originary figure, of law maker.
He interrupts the myth, for his act recognizes the "irreducible desire that man is –"
precisely that which no political ideology can acknowledge (Nancy 1991, 16). If, in
exerting Juno's wrath on a helpless victim, Aeneas reinforces the end of faith in the
legitimizing power of violence, the end of faith characteristic of Augustan politics, he
also takes up a position of resistance to the law of the Father and the fates. He becomes
a figure of *dilatio*; he opens up the field of action. In sharing briefly in Juno's endless
fury, he figures the endless violence of Roman reality – the state Jupiter himself has
defined from the start as an *imperium sine fine*, an empire without end.

ACKNOWLEDGMENT

I would like to thank the members of my 2007 graduate seminar in Roman literature and
political thought, as well as Jill Frank, Don Herzog, Bonnie Honig, Miriam Leonard, Michèle
Lowrie, Elizabeth Wingrove, and the editors, for helpful comments on earlier versions of
this essay.

FURTHER READING

As a glance at any recent collection or companion reveals, the politics of the *Aeneid* has been
the central topic of debate in Vergilian studies for decades. Kennedy (1992) and Tarrant (1997)
provide an excellent overview of the question, while Barchiesi (2001) provides insight into the
deeper problem of authorial intentionality. The nature of Vergil's hero has also received close
attention: among much good work, Johnson (1976) eloquently reads Aeneas as Juno's victim,
while Reed (2007) perceptively explores the "shiftiness" of Vergil's hero. The seminal work of
Pocock (1989) reveals the persistence of anxiety about ends, perfectability, and finalizability in
Republican thought from Roman to early modern America and Europe. Conte (2007), carefully attentive to literary figures in Vergil, is best read in productive tension with contemporary
efforts to bring the techniques of poststructuralist deconstruction to bear in understanding the
shape of ethical expression in literature, such as Johnson (1986), the essays in Eldridge (1996),
and Armstrong (2000).

PART FIVE

Modern Reactions to the *Aeneid*

CHAPTER TWENTY NINE

Classic Vergil

Kenneth Haynes

To call the *Aeneid* a classic is to make a claim about its value, but from antiquity onwards the meaning of the claim and the grounds for it have shifted in complex ways. A basic problem is an enduring ambiguity in the notion of the classic: it means both excellent in its kind and representative of its kind, best of its class and characteristic of its class. It may be used either to evaluate or to describe; it may mean either excellent or representative, archetypal or typical, normative or normal. The ambiguity inheres in the claim to exemplary status, which may be a claim either that something is or that something should be an example. The entangled connection between the nature of the class to which a classic belongs and the source of its value has been evident since at least the second century when Aulus Gellius extended the application of *classicus* from Roman social classes to literary rank (*NA* 19.8.15: *classicus adsiduusque aliquis scriptor, non proletarius*; see Swain 2004, 35).

English, by means of the contrast between "classic" and "classical," has some resources to indicate the difference since the former can be used with an evaluative meaning (*OED*²: "Of the first class, of the highest rank or importance; approved as a model; standard, leading") and the latter with a more neutral, classificatory sense (*OED*²: "belonging to the literature or art of Greek and Roman antiquity"). Taking classic in the first sense of possessing intrinsic excellence, critics have argued about whether the *Aeneid* was a preeminent or inferior member of the category of epic; the poem has also been put forth as an instance of allegory and praised for its Platonic, Stoic, or Christian wisdom, or contrasted, sometimes invidiously, with Homeric allegory (for allegorical readings of Vergil in the Middle Ages and Renaissance, see Baswell 1995 and Allen 1970, 135–62). On the other hand, taking classic in its representative sense, readers have understood the *Aeneid* to express, represent, or embody Augustan Rome, and, so understood, it was natural to derive the *Aeneid*'s value, implicitly or explicitly, from the value of Rome or Roman civilization (or contrariwise to trace the faults of the epic to the sins of its people). The two perspectives, normative and representative, classic and classical, are distinct but not necessarily contradictory or even

422 *Kenneth Haynes*

in tension. In practice they tended to be combined or elided: the very words "classic" and "classical" have overlapped at times to the point of interchangeability in their historical usage, both senses falling within the semantic range of each word; in addition, an explicit distinction is unavailable in other languages, in which *classique* or *klassisch* and so on must do double duty for classic and classical. However, the difference in perspective matters: does the classic provide the supreme model of what to do, how to write, what to imitate, or is it rather something to read and understand on its own terms as the representative expression of a culture?

A major shift in emphasis from the normative to the representative took place in the late eighteenth and early nineteenth centuries as the older struggle between ancients and moderns was transformed into a new opposition between classic and Romantic. The subject of this essay is the fate of Vergil in the context and aftermath of this transformation. It will attend, for the most part, to three moments in this critical history. First, the editions by Christian Gottlob Heyne presented Vergil with constant and extensive reference to the particularities of Roman life and thought. The work was designed to assist readers to grasp the content of Vergil fully and comprehensively, rather than to show writers what to emulate. It formed a major part of the effort by German neohumanists (Winckelmann most famously) to provide a new understanding of and a new justification for antiquity. These efforts were followed, at the turn of the nineteenth century, by the far-ranging reevaluation of the ancient world by German Romantics, who would place a new premium on the autonomy, originality, and (in some cases) purity of a culture and therefore tended to depreciate and at times dismiss Vergil.

A second moment will then be marked by Sainte-Beuve's lectures on Vergil and his essays "Qu'est-ce qu'un classique?" (1850) and "De la tradition en littérature" (1858); these offered a self-consciously European defense of Latinity and Vergil, partly in response to German Romantic and nationalist enthusiasms. His invocation of Latinity constituted part of an argument about tradition, and the interlocking terms "culture," "classic," and "tradition" became a powerful triad preeminently supporting and supported by Vergil. This conservative position became reactionary among French nationalist writers toward the end of the century and in the early twentieth. Third, T.S. Eliot's essays on Vergil and Dante continued to invoke culture, tradition, and the classic; they drew on both international and nationalist strains of the argument to make the case for the enduring relevance of a European Latinity. With a few exceptions (notably the work of the philosopher Rémi Brague 2002), the terms of the position did not long outlast Eliot, and the question of the value of Rome was subsequently divorced from the question of the value of the *Aeneid*; a "representative" case for the *Aeneid* became harder to make.

The quarrel of ancients and moderns was not limited to the seventeenth and eighteenth centuries; it inherited and developed a central feature of Renaissance humanism, "le principe agonistique" (this has been recently described as the central principle of European culture since Petrarch, despite the constant flux in the specific identities of ancient and modern and in the terrain and stakes of the battle; see the introduction to Fumaroli 2001). In the strictest version of the two positions ("do not write French," "do not read Latin"), ancients and moderns did not quarrel at all, because they had nothing to say to each other; significant disagreement requires much tacit agreement. The major disputes involved questions about the possibility of progress and the degree of cultural remoteness. At first glance, the question of progress would seem to divide ancients from moderns, those who accepted the traditional authority of antiquity from those who believed in cultural progress, those for whom the classical was classic and those who would sever the two. However, the question was more complicated, and it further subdivided each of the camps themselves. Among the ancients, a narrative of regress or devolution was associated with those ancients who were partisans of Homer, who believed that Homer offered wisdom in all the sciences and a revelation of a primordial truth and that subsequent works could not attain this level of perfection. The allegorical reading of Homer which served to underwrite this belief endured into the eighteenth century, centuries longer than Vergilian allegory was viable.[1] (When readings of Homer became oriented toward myth, the vision of the unique achievement of Homeric epic nonetheless survived largely intact, along with the accompanying narrative of regress and rupture.)

However, this version of a fallen literature was not the only or even the main one among the ancients. Until the mid-eighteenth century, it was common for Vergil to be esteemed more highly than Homer (the critical context demanded a "winner" from the comparison, the correct exemplar of excellence, the single model to be imitated; for a discussion of the Homer–Vergil syncrisis in late antiquity and the early Renaissance, see Scaliger 1994–2003, 4: 32–5). The second book of Vida's *Ars poetica* (1527), and, even more influentially, the fifth book of Julius Scaliger's *Poetics* (1561), made the case for Vergil. Scaliger juxtaposed many passages from Homer and Vergil, inserting them into an implicitly progressive account that is unambivalent about Vergil's superiority (Scaliger 1994–2003, 4: 42–307 and Scaliger 1994, 11–154). This view continued to be shared by most critics in France, from Perrault to Rapin to Voltaire – that is, by both moderns and ancients, and then even after the dispute. Ancients and moderns therefore had more in common than was realized: both accepted a progressive account of culture, and both arrested it at privileged historical moments, the era of Augustus and that of Louis XIV respectively, between which a parallel was widely asserted. The high estimate of Vergil could therefore easily be shared by both sides, as Vergil could serve simultaneously as an ancient and a modern, classical and classic.

The second major point of contention between the sides was Homer, though even here there was some unacknowledged agreement between them, since the neoclassical arguments in favor of Vergil had supplied much of the ammunition of the moderns' attack on Homer (Levine 1991, 123). Perrault not only objected to Homer's violations of correct style but also, facing squarely the remoteness of the epic, found the heroes of the *Iliad* brutish and the gods embarrassing. Allegory had traditionally been used to rebut or mitigate criticism that objected to the coarseness of the Homeric world, but this was an increasingly limited resource in an age of neoclassical aesthetics. Late in the quarrel Mme Dacier, though she continued to appeal to allegory to defend the Homeric depictions of gods, acknowledged the unbridgeable differences between the behavior of a heroic age and that of the contemporary world. By mid-century – particularly after the work of Blackwell (1735) and Wood (1775) on Homer and with the wide success of the Ossianic poems – these differences were newly evaluated: the greatness of Homer was tied to the virtues and the culture of the primitive age he was believed to represent, as well as to his original, non-imitative genius.

This familiar story of Homer's role in the European discovery of the remoteness of its own cultural and historical past has been criticized. There is no sharp "before" and "after" in the eighteenth century: something like culture (even if not the word) had previously been invoked as part of an explanatory matrix; history as *magistra vitae* offering timeless lessons did not come to a sudden end, nor did critical history and a sense of historical relativism make a sudden appearance; and the primitive had previously been described and found attractive. After all, an awareness of historical difference, a sensitivity to anachronism, was necessarily present in humanism; the tension between the aesthetics of imitating ancient texts and the hermeneutics of reading them was present both before and after historicism; and cultural history was preceded by the *historia literaria*. Moreover, previous scholars had sought out primitive contexts for Homer.[2] Therefore, if we wish after all to speak of a major change of intellectual climate in the second half of the eighteenth century (as in a new significance attached to culture, national character, and historical explanation), it is necessary to emphasize that changes were not sharply introduced, and that a word or concept does not develop in isolation but in connection with the complex of ideas and motives in which new arguments are made to appeal to new audiences.

As an example in miniature, consider the phrase "the genius of language." The concept was a mainstay of Romantic nationalism and cultural relativism; nonetheless, appeals to the *ingenium linguae* were widely made in the sixteenth century; it attained a European popularity with the work of Bouhours in the seventeenth; and it played a major explanatory role in Condillac. But the mere fact of such antecedents cannot explain, for example, the powerful attractions of the new linguistic nationalism elaborated by Fichte and Humboldt, or the impact of the affinity posited between Greek and German. The kinds of arguments made by invoking culture and language changed, even when the constituent parts of those arguments have a more continuous history. The "genius of language" combined with the "genius of nation" to form a new complex of significance. The "genius of language," that is, was not only an idea but also a slogan and in the course of the nineteenth century functioned to assert national and racial identity.[3] The newly asserted inner connection among language, culture, and nation also meant that Rome and the *Aeneid* were to be linked together in new ways.

In the broad terms of the history of taste, Homer began to supplant Vergil in the second half of the eighteenth century, with the new primitivism inspired by Rousseau, Macpherson's Ossian, and others; the reaction against the politics of the Augustan eras of Louis XIV and Charles II (these are very broad terms, since those associations were hardly uniform); the development of a discourse on myth; a new vocabulary of nationhood and nationalism; and the like. A "cultural" Homer emerged in this context,[4] "cultural" first in the sense that understanding Homer was believed to be dependent upon understanding and valuing the primitive culture of the Homeric world. The semantic range of "culture," however, would become much larger; first in Germany and then elsewhere, it could be used as a word for a people's unique manner of thought and expression as evident in its literature, inherent in its language, and fulfilled in the autonomy of its nation. In such terms as these not only was Homer judged supreme but also, after the Napoleonic Wars, he could be used as a means to reject the *Aeneid* altogether; by an extreme version of the cultural argument, the *Aeneid* could be taken as a failed epic of a failed nation, a minatory example of what happens when a people's culture does not come to its natural expression but is distorted through imitation and political oppression.

Before such judgments could be made, a cultural Vergil, analogous to the new Homer, had to be established, and to a significant degree this was provided by the editions of Heyne, the first appearing in 1767–75, the second in 1788–9, and the third in 1803. Although Heyne preferred Homer[5] and indeed played a large role in the new German understanding of myth and of Homer's world, it was nonetheless his edition of Vergil that gained him international fame; Gibbon, for example, referred to him simply as the "last and best Editor of Vergil" (Gibbon 1966, 145). A generation after Heyne's death, Thomas Carlyle described Heyne's accomplishment: he was the first to read in ancient writers not only their language and their opinions, but also "their spirit and character, their way of life and thought" (Carlyle 1896–9, 1: 351 ("The Life of Heyne," 1828)); later he recalled the shock, "the revolution in my mind," provoked by Heyne's Vergil, which had introduced him, "for the first time, into an insight of Roman life and ways of thought" (Carlyle 1896–9, 4: 469 ("Inaugural Address at Edinburgh," 1866)). The reputation is justified, at least in part, for several reasons. Heyne took pains to distinguish not only Vergil's epic from Homer's but also the Augustan era from the Homeric, refusing to apply the standards of one to the other.[6] Attention to the specifics of the Roman world was the hallmark of the edition, which in its excursuses and notes was concerned above all with the mythology of the poem, its literary borrowings, and its realia; grammatical and rhetorical points were subordinate.

Studies in the historical background and literary context of Vergil, naturally, had long preceded Heyne.[7] His innovation lies in the neohumanist emphasis on the unity of the cultural background, and also, as Geoffrey Atherton recently argued, in how the edition intended readers to absorb information, in the guidance it offered toward reading the poem: the older *lectio stataria*, oriented to internalizing the style and rhetoric of the best models, was replaced by the *lectio cursoria*, a method for readers to comprehend the text in relation to the ancient world (Atherton 2006, 79–80; Carhart 2007b, 126). The new cultural Vergil, in other words, was accompanied by a new pedagogical Vergil. This is not surprising: the normative category of the classic implies a pedagogy, a canon of classics implies a curriculum, and when the classic was redescribed in relation to a totality of cultural particulars, a new pedagogy was needed to accompany it.

For the most part, it was only after Heyne's death that his edition was celebrated for its revelatory access to the culture, the spirit and ways of thought, of the Romans. His contemporaries praised another feature of it: its concern with the beauties of the poem, its detailed discussion of the poem's aesthetic merit (Heidenreich 2006, 144–5). This style of commentary we associate more readily with the notes to Dacier's or Pope's *Iliad*. Heyne's Vergil, that is, shares characteristics with both the older aesthetic commentary and the newer historical and cultural one, and to this extent Carlyle was anachronistic to represent Heyne's edition as revolutionarily modern. In this respect Heyne's work is like Winckelmann's, who likewise insisted that an ancient culture had to be seen as a unique whole that could be understood only in its historical context, but who likewise also praised and closely discussed its aesthetic accomplishments. Both Winckelmann and Heyne combined normative and representative views of antiquity; they merged in a new way the classic and the classical, without experiencing "the mismatch between beauty and history" in their works that is so apparent to us from our later perspective (Prettejohn 2005, 18–19). On the contrary, the great works of antiquity provided an opportunity to show the modern world how to join beauty and history: "to explain the cultural contexts of the poems, to judge their aesthetic merit, to teach others to do the same, and, most of all, to shape the soul of the modern through the beauty of the ancient" (Atherton 2006, 85).

The German reorientation toward Greece over Rome in the second half of the eighteenth century, underwritten both by an anti-French animus and by the social situation of the *Bildungsbürgertum* (see Williamson 2004, 7–8; Carhart 2007b, 127), was articulated by Winckelmann, Heyne, and others, and as a program for cultural research acquired institutional support above all in Göttingen (see further Burke 2008, 252–4; Butterfield 1955, 32–61; and Marino 1995). The preference for Greece varied in intensity and did not necessarily lead to a rejection of Vergil. Heyne's edition is an obvious example of how it was possible for the Philhellenist neohumanists to favor Homer but still register the value of Vergil, but it should also be recalled that Voss translated the *Aeneid* as well as the *Iliad* and *Odyssey*, and Herder, it has been argued, even with his increasing horror of the politics of Augustan Rome, refused "to draw the conclusion regarding Virgil that his position would seem to require" (Atherton 2006, 48). Likewise, while Goethe and Schiller preferred Greece to Rome, they both held Vergil in high regard. Goethe's cosmopolitanism left him receptive, in varying degrees, to the influence of Vergil throughout his career (see further Grumach 1949, 353–60 and Erxleben 1995). Schiller's case is more challenging: his Philhellenism is intense, yet so is his commitment to Vergil; he not only admires him but also provides a powerful theoretical justification for a literature that comes after an original and is conscious of its status as secondary; nonetheless, besides the translations from books 2 and 4, the *Aeneid* leaves relatively little trace in his oeuvre (see Jarislowsky 1928 and Oehlert 1995).

The Philhellenist and neohumanist position, which linked the artwork with its culture, merged a normative view of both with a historical one, and had room for both Vergil and Homer though preferring the latter, was unstable; its components were forced apart from several directions. If the value of the ancient world lies in its culture, and if culture forms an organic unity, on what grounds can one aspect of that culture be valued more highly than another? For F.A. Wolf, all the evidence concerning the ancient world (especially the Greek world) must be weighed, if the moderns were to learn how they themselves were to develop. This was a prime justification for *Altertumswissenschaft*, a name Wolf explicitly preferred to the "classical scholarship" of the British; he found the ambiguity of "classical" intolerable, since it refers both to "the authors of antiquity" and to "the most select models in antiquity" (Wolf 1831–5, 1: 11, quoted in Gildenhard 2003, 175; see further Grafton 1991, 216–17). Normative judgments were therefore to be referred to a culture, of which particular literary works are merely representative. This implicit hostility to aesthetic valuation of particular works would become more explicit in the course of the nineteenth century, as new sources of error were identified in subjectivity and literary and aesthetic judgments come to be opposed to objective statement.

The view that Vergil's epic was derivative, not merely secondary, and that its learned borrowings betrayed its natural power was developed by both Schlegels. A.W. Schlegel, who had written on Homer under Heyne's direction and assisted Heyne with the second edition of the Vergil, was grudging about the merits of the *Aeneid*, on the grounds that by borrowing materials Vergil thereby deprived them of their proper significance. Friedrich Schlegel, over the course of his career, became increasingly critical of the poem, which because of the deficiency of its "borrowed art" failed to revive and secure the native traditions of Italy and instead gave the Romans a "national poem" that was not commensurate with them (A.W. Schlegel 1989, 621–3 and 1964, 166; F. Schlegel 1958–, 6: 80; for discussion, see Atherton 2006, 17–21). Schelling found that the *Aeneid*'s single purpose was to flatter Augustus through a pompous language that appealed to the educated elite (Schelling 1989, 218). Barthold Niebuhr's search for a Roman Homer led him not only to posit a lost oral tradition of Roman heroic ballads but also to reject Vergil on the grounds that he was a lyricist who mistook both his poetic and his national vocation (Niebuhr 1846–8, 3: 130 and 132; see also Bridenthal 1972 and Rieks 1981, 735–6).

What motivated the strong sentiment against Vergil? In part it continued a strong eighteenth-century antipathy to the Roman Empire and a complementary feeling for Republican Rome (see Harrison 1967; Weinbrot 1978, 120–30; Turner 1989). The universal value of freedom was continually reiterated in the work of the German neohumanists and Romantics, and however varied the understanding of that freedom, it was in tension with Augustan Rome. Moreover, as the category of culture was taken to guarantee the connection between nationhood and literature, a learned poem drawing centrally on a literature in another language seemed to imply that it had betrayed the autonomy of its own people. In any event, since the *Aeneid* was understood to be representative of Augustan Rome, as that culture became increasingly despised, it was difficult to defend the value of the poem. The relationship between normative judgments about Rome and normative judgments about the *Aeneid* was placed under great strain.

Outside of Germany, an insistence on Vergil's unhappiness provided one way to establish the value of the *Aeneid* independently of the value of Rome. Chateaubriand, for example, underlined Vergil's "mélancolie," describing how he "cultiva ce germe de tristesse au milieu des bois" ("nursed this germ of sadness in the heart of the forest") and admiring him as "l'ami du solitaire, le compagnon des heures secrètes de la vie" ("the friend of the hermit, the companion of life's secret hours") (Chateaubriand 1836–40, 15: 46–7; Naylor 1930, 75–114; the appreciation for Vergil as a poet of nature had been well prepared by the eighteenth-century enthusiasm for the *Georgics*, see Chalker 1969). In mid-century Matthew Arnold likewise distanced Vergil from Rome, arguing that Vergil failed (as all Roman writers had failed) "to represent the epoch in which he lived, the mighty Roman world of his time…in all its fulness, in all its significance" and, having failed, expressed "the haunting, the irresistible self-dissatisfaction of his heart" in his final desire to destroy the poem; an "ineffable melancholy," "a sweet, a touching sadness" rests over the *Aeneid* (Arnold 1960, 34–6). Benjamin Constant, a generation before Arnold, had gone so far as to value Vergil's melancholy as a sign of resistance to Augustan Rome, even if this resistance did not take an active form.[8]

The melancholy Vergil, the poet of sensitive pathos, has usually been associated with Sainte-Beuve (see, for example, Williams 1987, 163), but this is misleading. Sainte-Beuve's continual stress was on "healthy" literature; he opposed the morbid sensitivity of the Romantics and strongly qualified the adjective "melancholy" before he applied it to Vergil.[9] Moreover, far from severing Vergil from Rome, Sainte-Beuve sought to reconnect and rehabilitate them. In his criticism, the *Aeneid* again becomes representative of Rome, the value of one infusing that of the other. The new valuation provides and depends on a new understanding of the relation of past and present.

The strong Romantic preference for Homer over Vergil – developed especially in Germany and in particular with the rise of strong national feelings after the Napoleonic invasions – was based on a view of the past as fundamentally discontinuous with the present. Vergil symbolized the discontinuity; he represented a barrier, a wrong turn, an obstacle between the remote past and the present. His epic, unlike Homer's, broke the promise of autonomous cultural expression, severed mythic origin from historical development. The movement from Homeric epic to Athenian democracy was exemplary for modern nationhood, and Vergil could provide no parallel; moreover, the speculative connection of Homer to Indo-European, of Greece to India, further excluded Augustan literature from the romance of origins. Sainte-Beuve influentially changed the terms of this contrast: rather than opposing Vergil and Homer, he rejoined them, by means of a newly energized defense of tradition. Against the Romantic effort to distance Greece from Rome, Sainte-Beuve insisted on the essential unity of what would eventually be called "Greco-Roman."

Vergil figures significantly in two of the most famous of Sainte-Beuve's *causeries de lundi*, "Qu'est-ce qu'un classique?" and "De la tradition en littérature et dans quel sens il la faut entendre," and was the subject of an aborted series of lectures delivered to hostile students at the Collège de France in 1855 and published subsequently as *Étude sur Virgile* in 1857. Sainte-Beuve reconfigures the meanings of the key terms "tradition" and "classic." In his thinking, the concept of tradition absorbs much of the work previously done by culture. He argues that tradition does not consist solely of memorable books but has passed "en bonne partie dans nos lois, dans nos institutions, dans notre éducation héréditaire et insensible, dans notre habitude et dans toutes nos origines" ("to a significant degree into our laws, our institutions, our hereditary and imperceptible upbringing, our settled habits, and all our origins"); it has penetrated and modified "le caractère même de cette nation gauloise" ("the very character of this Gallic nation") and "la trempe des esprits" ("the temper of minds") (Sainte-Beuve 1860–85, 15: 358; the passage and most of the following passages quoted from Sainte-Beuve are discussed by Prendergast 2007). In two important respects, however, his use of the term "tradition" modifies earlier nineteenth-century associations of "culture." First, while Sainte-Beuve accepts the role of the nation as a natural vehicle for culture, as is clear from his invocation of "cette nation gauloise," in his hands the equation is by no means exclusive; traditions are simultaneously national and international. (Sainte-Beuve, in contrast to many Romantic and post-Romantic intellectuals, was skeptical about nationalism, cultural provincialism, and self-validating origins; see Prendergast 2007, 41–2, 79, 125, 137.) Second, Sainte-Beuve's use of the term emphasizes the continuity of past with present. The past which Sainte-Beuve appeals to is international, mostly European, but the present custodianship of the past – a role that once fell to Rome – is now a primary though not exclusive responsibility of France, and moreover it is a major determinant of French identity. Instead of a willed renewal of a utopian past that had been disrupted by history, Sainte-Beuve seeks to guard tradition, a continuous past that is continuously under threat and which therefore imposes particular obligations upon the present.

Tradition in Sainte-Beuve's case means Latinity, which in his view is not in opposition to Greece but rather encompasses it. The Romans were the ones who realized the Greek dream of an "œuvre de constance, d'énergie durable et d'empire politique universel" ("work of steadfastness, durable energy, and universal political empire") (Sainte-Beuve 1860–85, 15: 364). Furthermore, Latinity means Vergil, "le poète de la Latinité tout entière" ("the poet of the whole of Latinity") (Sainte-Beuve 1883, 29); Sainte-Beuve therefore refuses to make a choice between Homer and Vergil and inveighs against all those, from Scaliger on, who chose one at the expense of the other (Sainte-Beuve 1883, 292). Aware that the French have too often been partisans of Vergil, he is at pains to praise Homer and to insist that each poet must be admired "dans son ordre et à son âge de civilisation" ("in his order and at his era of civilization") (297). In the essay on the classic, he acknowledges Homer's superiority and priority in relation to Vergil (Sainte-Beuve 1860–85, 15: 364); however, he is far from advocating a cultural or aesthetic relativism. Rather, by means of tradition he is introducing a new ground for ranking cultures and literary works: their proximity to us. Roman culture, in its language, literature, and social organization, and above all in Vergil, has a claim on us in the present not just through affinity and analogy but constitutively. While Homer may be on the summit of cultural achievement, Vergil is "sur la colline la plus en vue et de la pente la plus accessible" ("on the hill most to the fore and on the most accessible slope") (51–2). Vergil, that is, not only points back to Greece and is our means of access to it, but he also leads forward to France, to the *grand siècle* above all, but also to the nineteenth century, with its repeated assertions of imperial legitimacy, Gallic, rather than Frankish, identity, and exemplary urbanity (see Prendergrast 2007).

Vergil is the central figure of Latinity because of his status as classic. Sainte-Beuve explains that "l'idée de classique implique en soi quelque chose qui a suite et consistance, qui fait ensemble et tradition, qui se compose, se transmet et qui dure" ("the idea of the classic implies in itself something that has consequence and stability, that makes a cohesive tradition, that is self-composed and self-transmitted, and that endures") (Sainte-Beuve 1860–85, 3: 40). However, the classic, a work that has the power to shape a culture into a binding tradition, comes into being only under certain conditions, above all the presence of public calm and stability created by a strong political order. The claim, as a recent critic describes it, is "wish-fulfilment…rather than serious argument" (Prendergast 2007, 23), an intensely felt, not reasoned, response to the upheavals of 1848. As Sainte-Beuve was well aware, the Romans themselves did not subscribe to such a claim, nor did Vergil write under such conditions; the critic reconciled himself to the blatant contradiction by pointing to the greater robustness of the Romans and the mutual dependence of Vergil and Augustus (24, 148). While overt political uses of Vergil – from, say, Louis XIV to Enoch Powell[10] – have often been crass, the cultural Vergil, with varying degrees of self-awareness, has tended to mask its politics (for example by implying or desiderating the existence of a nation, or of Europe, when referring to a "culture," or authoritarianism by invoking "tradition," and the absence of disagreement by "health").

By the end of the nineteenth century, Sainte-Beuve's understanding of France, Vergil, and Latinity began to turn into something stridently nationalist, an urgent matter of blood and soil, a process that was greatly accelerated by World War I (Prendergast 2007, 291–308). Charles Maurras, Ferdinand Brunetière, and others emphasized the uniquely privileged relation between France and Latin antiquity; Ernest Seillière in 1907 derived from Vergil an imperial program of Latin power; and André Bellesort's study of 1920 used him as a cudgel with which to beat Germany (Prendergast 2007, 304–7). The study of Vergil by Bellesort's student Robert Brasillach, *Présence de Virgile* (1930), described by a friendly reviewer as "une sorte d'épopée d'Action française" ("a kind of epic of the *Action française*") (quoted in Ziolkowski 1993, 43 and Prendergast 2007, 306), emphasized the close connection between Vergil and France (he drew parallels, as Chateaubriand had done, between Vergil's style and Racine's) and above all celebrated Vergil's love for "sa terre charnelle" ("his carnal land") (Prendergast 2007, 306).

In the first half of the twentieth century, however, arguments about the cultural significance of Vergil were by no means limited to French reactionaries, nationalists, and Nazi sympathizers (Brasillach was executed in 1945, Maurras sentenced to life in prison). Vergil's bimillennium in 1930 prompted opportunistic celebrations of cultural heritage, political affiliation, and humanistic values in many nations, not only in Europe (surveyed by Ziolkowski 1993, 17–26 and cf. the chapter by Ronnick in this volume). Perhaps the most important restatement of Vergil's European, rather than national, significance was made by the German convert to Roman Catholicism Theodor Haecker, a philosopher, theologian, translator, and opponent of the Third Reich. Haecker's study *Vergil: Vater des Abendlands* ("Vergil: Father of the West," 1931) offers an unqualified equation of Vergil with Rome and of Rome with the West. The *Aeneid* is not merely representative of Roman culture; rather, "a single verse of the *Aeneid* contains all Rome" (Haecker 1934, 57–8); Rome, moreover, signifies reality itself, at least reality as experienced by Europeans (and soon for everyone else), who derive the very term from the Roman *res*, Vergil's "heart-word," and for whom, therefore – Haecker extends linguistic nationalism into linguistic Europeanism – reality is made of *res* and all the things without which *res* cannot subsist (97–8).

Vergil, along with Dante, was at the heart of T.S. Eliot's cultural criticism. Eliot's two essays on Vergil, *What is a Classic?* (1945) and "Virgil and the Christian World"

(1951), drew on both Haecker and Maurras, the former for his theological vision of Vergil's significance to the West and the latter for his understanding of classicism, especially "Mediterranean classicism," as a principle of order and intelligence (on Eliot and Haecker, see Reeves 1989, 96–116; Eliot's relation to Maurras (whom Eliot in 1948 called "une sorte de Virgile qui nous conduisait aux portes du temple" ("a kind of Vergil who would lead us to the doors of the temple"), in *Aspects de la France et du monde* (April 28), p. 6), has been much argued over; see Asher 1995, 55–65; Margolis 1972, 87–101; Schüller 2002, 65–132; Thompson 1997). In broad outline, Eliot's argument is like Sainte-Beuve's or Haecker's: Vergil is a classic because he is uniquely representative of Rome, and Rome is constitutive of the West. Vergil, for Eliot, was comprehensively representative of Rome, expressing "the maximum possible of the whole range of feeling which represents the character of the people who speak the language"; he is thus the "consciousness of Rome" (Eliot 1945, 27, 29). Rome, for its part, stands in unique relation to the West, possessing "an empire and a language with a unique destiny in relation to ourselves" (29); it is a precondition of our mutual intelligibility. The details of Eliot's essay are significantly different from his predecessors. His addition of Dante to the ranks of classic adds medieval Christendom to ancient Rome more seamlessly than Sainte-Beuve would allow, and Eliot does not make the *Aeneid* into the proto-Christian document which Haecker describes. Nonetheless, Eliot's criticism is the last major statement of the cultural Vergil, of the *Aeneid* as classic insofar as it is representative of Roman culture and insofar as Roman culture is central to our present and future identity.

"Classic" has two faces, the class and the member of the class, and further as a statement of value it points ambivalently in the two directions (is the value of a class secured by the value of its individual members or do they have their value imputed to them by virtue of their membership in the class?). At least two questions, then, always accompany the claim to classic status: the identity of the class to which the classic belongs and the source of the classic's value, the nature of its claim on the present and future. For roughly two centuries, from about 1750 to 1950, the class to which the *Aeneid* belonged was generally understood to be Roman culture, or the Roman world, a totality or inner unity of the particularly Roman ways of feeling and thought. This understanding of the *Aeneid* followed in the footsteps of the Homeric reception: Homer's intractable distance from the present led the quarrel of ancients and moderns to a dead end and in the mid-eighteenth century stimulated a new feeling for the remote past. However, the *Aeneid* followed the *Iliad* at a distance, and it was reduced to something like a second-class citizen when evaluated in these terms, which took it to be representative of a culture that was secondary to Greece. Over time, and in particular after the emergence of stark national feelings, it was further demoted, as imperial, as evidence of a failed nation, and as an instance of the borrowed learning of an elite rather than the anonymous expression of a people's culture. One way of defending Vergil in these circumstances was to break the connection between the *Aeneid* and Rome, for example by responding to Vergil as a nature poet, and later by underscoring a melancholy and more inwardly turned lyric Vergil, an emblem of unhappy modernity; another way was Sainte-Beuve's realignment of the *Aeneid* and Rome and, via the claims made by tradition, of Rome and the European present. After his death, Sainte-Beuve's argument was developed in nationalist directions as well as international ones. T.S. Eliot was influenced by both trends, but his depiction of Vergil as a classic placed the Roman solidly "at the centre of European civilisation" (Eliot 1945, 29).

In the second half of the twentieth century, Vergilian criticism was more skeptical that Vergil was "representative" or "expressive" of his age or of its values, although alternative descriptions of his relation to Augustan Rome ("resistant," "subversive") are in no less danger of misrepresenting or oversimplifying that relation. The solution whereby classic status was established, representatively, by taking a literary work as expressive of a culture, and normatively, by linking that culture to present values via tradition, ceased to enjoy general assent. However, even if the term "classic" is dropped, the questions that accompanied it in the past will remain: what is the relation of the *Aeneid* to its time, what relation should it have to future times?

NOTES

1   Allen (1970, 162) dates the termination of "the full-scale allegorization" of the *Aeneid* with Giovanni Fabrini's allegorical commentary (1588), an "Italian translation and augmentation" of Landino's interpretation. Murrin (1980, 173–96) explores the survival of Homeric allegorizing into the eighteenth century.
2   On the feeling for anachronism in the Renaissance, see Burke (1970, 1–6) and, for its rediscovery in a more acute form in the early nineteenth century, in reaction to the "philosophical history" of the Enlightenment, see ibid. (143–4). On the fortunes of history as *magistra vitae* see Koselleck (2004, 26–42); on the (pre)history of historical criticism, see Grafton (2007). On *historia literaria* and cultural history, see Carhart (2007a), Gierl (1992), and Grunert and Vollhardt (2007). The shift from "spirit" to "culture" as a means to express the character of society is noted by Kelley (2003, 21) and discussed by Carhart (2007b). An appreciation of the primitive nature of Homer's world is evident before the mid-eighteenth century in the work of Gian Vincenzo Gravina and Thomas Parnell; see Simonsuuri (1979, 87–8).
3   Schlaps (2004, 381). For the "genius of language" see further Christmann (1976, 1977), Stankiewicz (1981), and Trabant (2000). See also Gambarota (2006) on the relation of the "genius of language" to the "genius of nation"; Carhart (2007b, 100–4) discusses the new understanding of the relation between language and culture that emerged around 1780.
4   In the development of a historical understanding oriented toward the "culture" of a people, the new, eighteenth-century cultural Bible played as important a role as the new understanding of Homer; see further Sheehan (2005). (I have placed "culture" in quotation marks because the word did not have a significant circulation before the 1770s; see Carhart 2007b, 1–4, 296–7.)
5   See Heyne (1819, 2: 33): "delector ipse multo magis Homeri lectione quam Virgilii; regnat in Homericis heroibus naturalis habitus et affectus, animi impetus, iniuriae acceptae sensus, qualem et ipse habeo, desiderium reditus ad Lares, quale ipse sentiam; in Aeneide sunt consilia de novis sedibus in terra ignota parandis; nihil quod magnopere animum impellat et percutiat" ("I myself enjoy reading Homer much more than Vergil; in the Homeric

heroes a natural bearing and feeling holds sway, a passion of the soul, a sense of a wrong received, of the sort which I too have, a desire to return home, such as I feel; in the *Aeneid* plans for a new foundation in a foreign land are prepared; nothing that greatly excites or stirs the soul").

6   "Comparationes Virgilii et Homeri instituerunt multi...Sed piget videre viros doctos plerumque accedere ad eam rem studio in alterutrum poetam incensos, adeoque id agere, ut alterum deprimant, alterum immodicis laudibus extollant, facereque adeo eos utrumque sine subtili iudicio. Haerent porro in verbis et versibus singulis, nec summam carminis et partium concentum respiciunt, eoque animum ab eo avocant, quod in considerationem adduci debebat. Discrimen primarium statim ipsa temporum, quibus uterque vixit, et hominum, quibuscum vixerunt, et sermonis, quo usi sunt, diversitas inferre debuit" ("Many have made comparisons of Vergil and Homer...However, it is annoying to see learned men approach the subject excited by a zeal for one of the poets, and do so to such a degree that they sink one of them and extol the other with immoderate praise, and moreover do both without discriminating judgment. Then they get stuck in words and verses and do not see the height of the poem and the harmony of the parts, and they divert attention away from what needed to be brought into consideration. The unlikeness itself of the times in which either lived, and of the men with whom they lived, and of the language which they used ought to have established from the outset a fundamental distinction").

    See also 2: 34: "Cum itaque omnino Aeneidis alius ac diversus prorsus sit character quam Iliadis, quis non videt importunum esse, in Aeneide requirere ea, quae Iliadi sint propria" ("Because the character of the *Aeneid* is altogether different from and utterly unlike that of the *Iliad*, who does not see that it is inappropriate to demand in the *Aeneid* the things that are proper to the *Iliad*?"); 2: 14: "Alio ille aevo, ab heroica aetate nimis remoto, inter diversissimas hominum, rerum, temporum, locorum ac coeli rationes, opus suum erat aggressus" ("In a different time, very remote from the heroic age, among very different conditions of men, things, times, places, and climate, he [Vergil] had undertaken his work"); and 2: 10: "in alia rerum natura et ordine, alia cogitandi, sentiendi, et agendi via et ratione, aliis temporibus, inter alios homines" ("in a differently founded and ordered universe, with a different way and system of thinking, feeling and acting, in different times, among different men"). Heyne, nonetheless, remained committed, like Gottsched, to a deductive understanding of genre; see Heidenreich (2006, 127–8).

7   Allen (1970, 159) remarks on the emergence of the "historical, philological, and literary study of Virgil" as early as the sixteenth century, in the works of Campani, Leonberger, Maranta, Toscanella, and others.

8   Constant (1977, 856 and 859): Vergil and Horace "tournèrent toujours vers la liberté des regards de regret ou de désir et...ces désirs et ces regrets, dont l'expression leur échappait malgré eux, constituent ce qu'il y a de plus beau, de plus profond et de plus élevé dans leurs ouvrages" ("always turned toward liberty their gazes of regret or desire...these desires and these regrets, the expression of which escaped them in spite of themselves, constitute the most beautiful, profound, and lofty element in their works"). Moreover, "nous voyons Virgile se livrer à une melancolie habituelle" ("we see Vergil surrender himself to a habitual melancholy") ("De la littérature dans ses rapports avec la liberté," *Mélanges de littérature et de politique*, 1829).

9   Sainte-Beuve (1883, 36): "une mélancolie, non pas vague, mais naturelle et positive" ("a melancholy that is not hazy but natural and positive"); 100: Vergil "a la piété et la pitié, parfois une teinte de tristesse, de mélancolie presque, quoiqu'il faille prendre garde en cela de ne pas trop tirer Virgile à nous; la mélancolie...est déjà la maladie de la sensibilité: Virgile n'a encore cette sensibilité qu'à l'état naturel et sain, bien qu'avec une grande délicatesse"

("has piety and pity, sometimes a tincture of sadness, almost of melancholy, although it is necessary to be on guard in this not to draw Vergil too much to ourselves; melancholy… is the sickness of sensitivity; Vergil still only has that sensitivity in its natural and healthy state, although with a great delicacy").

10 On Powell's Birmingham ("Rivers of blood") speech of 1968 quoting Vergil and warning about the perils of immigration, see Schoen (1977, 93), Heffer (1998, 449–67), Huxley (1998), and Todd (1999); see also Wootten (2000).

FURTHER READING

For Heyne's Vergil, see Heidenreich (2006, 123–49) and Atherton (2006, 74–88); on Sainte-Beuve, tradition, the classic, and Vergil, see Prendergast (2007, 18–151). Both Atherton and Prendergast range more widely than their titles may suggest. On the quarrel of ancients and moderns, see Levine (1991) and the long introduction by Fumaroli (2001). On Eliot's *What is a Classic?*, see Kermode (Eliot 1975), and for the modernist Vergil generally, see Ziolkowsi (1993).

CHAPTER THIRTY

Vergil's Detractors

Joseph Farrell

Not long ago the first volume of the popular Harry Potter novels (Rowling 1997) was translated into "ancient Greek" (Wilson 2004). One reviewer praised the translation as "a delight to all Classicists, a boon to all teachers of Greek, and a possession for all time" and "in this reader's opinion, a complete success." He then went on to make some surprising points about J.K. Rowling's fiction itself:

> As for the worth of Rowling's opus, considered on its own merits…[h]er characters, themes, and incidents are all borrowed from a well-established tradition; she has created a successful pastiche which has caught the public mood, and has herself been turned into a cultural phenomenon and media event out of all proportion to her genius – in other words, there is no slander that can be leveled at her, which does not equally apply to Virgil. You who would defend the Mantuan, beware of denigrating the skills of a successful popularizer.

After briefly considering the sources of Rowling's inspiration and concluding that she is in her eclecticism less like Homer than like Vergil – "derivative, if you dislike it, tried and true, if you do, Virgilian in either case" – the reviewer admits that

> Rowling is more like Homer than Virgil in one important aspect. All of her books, setting aside the inadequately-edited fifth book, have the quality that Arnold noted in his essay on translating Homer: they are rapid, plain, and direct in expression. Unlike the Latin verse of the "wielder of the moldiest measure ever stated by the lips of man," Rowling's prose is never stilted, never cluttered up with purple patches; it never gets in the way of the story she sets out to tell. (Brennan 2005)

How did it come to pass that this reviewer, a classicist writing in a journal addressed mainly to other classicists, decided that the best way to convey his admiration for what is in essence a novelty item would be to denigrate the poet judged by Quintilian "second to Homer, but a lot closer to first place than to third," revered by Dante as "lo mio maestro e 'l mio autore," and considered by Eliot to have written "the classic of all Europe"?

There really is no accounting for taste, but it has to be said that, as a Vergil-basher, our reviewer finds himself in good company. On the one hand the *Aeneid* holds the most secure place of all Latin poems on any list of "great books." But among those works that in modern times make up "the literary canon," probably no work is criticized so often, so harshly, or on so many different grounds as is the *Aeneid*. The record of critical condescension and vituperation is remarkable. It is also in many ways instructive – not so much for opening readers' eyes to those passages in which, as a beloved teacher of mine once put it, "even Vergil nods," or even as a guide to the history of taste and the vagaries of literary history and criticism (though it is that as well). More than this, the complaints lodged by Vergil's detractors provide a valuable key that takes us deep into the heart of his distinctive aesthetics.

Ipsis inimicitiis gloriosus

If one simply tries to list Vergil's modern detractors, the sheer weight of critical authority is itself impressive. Samuel Johnson, Gotthold Ephraim Lessing, Samuel Taylor Coleridge, the entire Schlegel family, Matthew Arnold, Wilamowitz, Lukács, Housman, Ezra Pound, and Henry Miller are just some of the great names who have all gone on record to register their low opinion of the poet. Some manage to turn even Vergil's champions into detractors, as we shall see. And other apparent champions have done more damage than frank detractors. To this category belongs the aforementioned T.S. Eliot, whose own conception of Vergil is damaging enough in itself, but is all the more so because of the incredibly hostile reaction that it provoked from Robert Graves and perhaps also for the more measured demurral registered by W.H. Auden. Of course, it is a commonplace among Vergil's defenders to claim that adverse judgments are mainly the product of a Romantic overreaction to Vergilian formality, particularly as compared with the "original genius" of Homer; this is an important and complex factor (see the previous chapter in this volume by Haynes), but it is not the entire story. As my list of illustrious detractors shows, disparagement of Vergil transcends differences in critical perspective as well as of time and place. In addition, as the aforementioned parody of Tennyson's "stateliest measure" suggests, measured evaluation and even frank appreciation can come to sound like censure (or be turned into it). Accordingly, not only Tennyson, but other writers as well who arguably, and in some cases obviously, admire Vergil, such as Dante, Maffeo Vegio, or Robert Lowell, can also be read as detractors. And as the case of Eliot shows, there is the peculiar phenomenon that certain of Vergil's supporters, for reasons that have no intrinsic connection to the poetry itself, have been effective mainly in mustering adherents to the anti-Vergilian cause, a phenomenon that is difficult to parallel in the reception of any other poet. So it is not just the history of taste in general, but these particular factors, and several others, to which I would like to draw attention in this essay.

Self-Fulfilling Prophecy

Perhaps the main point I should make, though, is that the role of extraneous factors in explaining this strange tradition is decisive at every stage. We may begin with our ancient sources concerning Vergil's life, which are apparently very rich – richer than in the case of any other Roman poet. Scholars have, however, come to realize that almost every aspect of this tradition is suspect and that it has to be treated with extreme caution (Horsfall 1995b, 1–26; cf. Stok in this volume, as for much that follows). But this is a comparatively recent development, whereas for centuries the ancient *Vitae* were regarded as important, independent testimony about Vergil's work, so that the role they have played in conditioning reception of that work has been powerful.

One aspect of this tradition is the emphasis that it places on Vergil's repeated failures. The *Aeneid*, we are told, was not his first attempt at heroic epic. He had tried his hand at this genre in his youth with a historical subject, but found himself unable to handle the material (*VSD* 19). The "evidence" for this early failure is nothing but naïve inference drawn from the poetic manifesto pronounced by Tityrus in eclogue 6 – itself a very close paraphrase of Callimachus (fr. 1, 21–4 Pfeiffer) – which therefore gives it no biographical authority at all. Nevertheless, for thousands of years, readers believed that Vergil's career began with a failed attempt to write heroic epic. Failure stalks the *Georgics* as well. Often called Vergil's most perfect poem (Scaliger 1561; Montaigne 1993, 461; Dryden 1987, 153), and generally acknowledged to be the most ambitious work that he actually lived to complete, it has nevertheless been deplored because of its ending. Once again, the reason is a bit of ancient scholarship "informing" us that the poem originally ended with an encomium of Vergil's friend and fellow poet, Cornelius Gallus (Serv. *ad Ecl.* 10.1 and *ad Geo.* 4.1). The ending that we do have, an epyllion that combines the story of Aristaeus, inventor of the bugonia ritual, with that of Orpheus and Eurydice, is exquisitely beautiful and has been shown by contemporary critics to be an extraordinarily appropriate and successful conclusion to an intricate and subtle poem (e.g., Putnam 1979, 276–321). But it was once normal to find this dazzling composition disparaged even by Vergil's admirers as distinctly second-rate in comparison with the entirely hypothetical "original" ending. One by-product of supposedly "knowing" that ours is a second, and therefore second-rate, edition of the *Georgics* is the inference that Vergil borrowed material for his "new" ending from the *Aeneid*, which (it was supposed) he had already begun; this expedient, then, helpfully explained the close similarity between certain passages of the *Georgics* and the *Aeneid*. It also gave flat-footed critics an opportunity to decide whether a given passage was originally composed for one poem or the other; by corollary, such a passage must necessarily be "more at home" or "more successful" in its original context, less so in its transferred *sedes*. Therefore, the very same passage, even if successful in one poem, was a failure in the other. (For a sensitive and systematic exploration of these parallels see Briggs 1980.)

The Unfinished *Aeneid*

The ancient *Vitae* also tell us that Vergil died before he could finish the *Aeneid*, that he expected he would need three years before he could consider the job done, and that on his deathbed he was so dissatisfied with it that he wished to burn his unfinished poem (*VSD* 38). The story is a cornerstone of literary history. Ovid usurped it (*Tr.* 1.7). Hermann Broch wrote a long novelistic meditation on it (1945) that crystallized a tendency to focus on the poem's unfinished state and to associate this condition with the poet's own morbidity, derangement, and weighty sense of regret. But if we think carefully about this story, no one really knows what to make of it. The first question is whether the information is reliable; but even if it is, what does it mean? That in his death-throes Vergil had lost all perspective on his masterpiece? That he was such a perfectionist that he would rather destroy a poem that, though technically incomplete, was so highly finished that no other living poet and few if any from another time could have equaled it? That he wished to resolve at least some of the ambiguities that so many readers prize (see O'Hara in this volume, again, with reference to much that follows)? That he had not made up his mind how to resolve them? That he did in fact view the poem as seriously flawed in ways that we do not understand? We will never know. But the mere suggestion that he wished to destroy the poem raises doubts about it of a kind that attach themselves to no comparable masterpiece.

The fact is, however, that Vergil's masterpiece is indeed unfinished. It was once common for critics to wonder whether Vergil would have left the end of the poem – surely one of the most sublime passages and most effective conclusions in all literature – as we have it, or would have attached a more formal ending. Maffeo Vegio, whom I've mentioned, went so far as to compose a thirteenth book to tie up Vergil's loose ends (Putnam 2004). The *Aeneid* frankly attests its lack of the *ultima manus* in the considerable number of "half-lines" that it contains; and ancient testimony that the poet reduced the number of such gaps by composing "props" (in Latin *tibicines*) inevitably inspired critics to display their acumen by discerning which passages are marred by this stop-gap or otherwise bear witness to the poem's imperfect state.

For example, verbal repetition in the *Aeneid*, a poetic device that Vergil deploys with consummate tact and often to spectacular effect, was once viewed as a simple indicator of rough finish (Sparrow 1931; more reasonable is Moskalew 1982); the same was, and to some extent remains, true of half-lines – this despite the fact that some readers count certain of the half-lines among the most beautiful passages in the poem, and even speculate as to whether Vergil might have left them as they are, indeed could not himself bear to finish certain lines that seemed more perfect in their incomplete state. We cannot know this, of course, and must suppose that, had Vergil lived, he would have filled out the half-lines and revised the poem in certain other respects. Our ability to identify passages intended for significant revision is, however, extremely limited. Certainly the relative dearth or prevalence of half-lines tells us little: of all books, the one that contains the most half-lines (ten) is book 2, which is also one of the most admired in the poem.

Vergil's Language

To move on to a consideration of style, most readers have felt that, if nothing else, Vergil was able to turn a phrase. But Vergil's detractors frequently cite as faults the very traits that his champions most admire. We can bring this characteristic into focus by contrasting the attitude of Vergil's ancient detractors with those of their modern counterparts. It was in fact Vergil's language that incited his first critics, and that continues to annoy some today, though for very different reasons. The critics started to complain long before the *Aeneid*, when certain contemporaries pilloried Vergil for his weird Latinity. As is well known, we have the remains of a parody by one Numitorius called *Antibucolica* that mocked Vergil for using words like *tegmen* "covering" (*Ecl.* 1.1: normally used of skin, clothing, or body armor but applied by Vergil to a sheltering beech tree). Numitorius also objected to Vergil's use of the adjectival form *cuius, -a, -um* "whose" (*Ecl.* 3.1: a substandard back-formation based on *cuius*, the genitive of *quis*). On such evidence a certain M. Vipranius complained that Vergil indulged in *cacozelia*, a kind of wrong-headed striving for effect, in coining new words or abusing standard usage (*VSD* 44; Jocelyn 1979; Lyne 1989, 1–19). It is useful to be reminded that Vergil once made such an impression, and amusing that he is now both praised and blamed for quite the opposite effect. Tennyson, as was noted above, famously saluted Vergil as "wielder of the stateliest measure ever molded by the lips of man" (1987, 628–30). Strictly speaking, this concerns Vergil's meter, his "ocean-roll of rhythm" (16), but the poem also praises Vergil as "lord of language" (3) who gives his readers "all the chosen coin of fancy / flashing out from many a golden phrase" (4). If "stately" sums all this up, then Tennyson must have felt Vergil's stateliness to reside at least partly in his diction – the same diction that Vipranius deplored as too obviously *striving* for effect. Such striving is more or less the opposite of stateliness. It is one thing to offend guardians of language by straining (or enlarging) the capacity of the Latin *Dichtersprache*, and another to bore some modern critics with excessive stateliness. How is it that Vergil runs afoul of both parties?

The Curriculum Author *par excellence*

The explanation must have to do with the fact that the *Aeneid* was quickly adopted as a school text. Soon after it was made public it gained such authority that Vergil's poetic idiom, however eccentric it had once seemed, became a model for students, for later poets, and even for writers of prose. This was hardly a simple matter, and violence was done in the process to the poem and to our ability to respond to it directly. On the one hand, many words and phrases used first or in novel ways by Vergil were imitated by later writers, and so over time lost much of the impact that they had originally had. This is even more so for speakers of modern languages. For instance, when Juno incites Allecto to use her furial torches to set peaceable homes ablaze, she calls those torches *funereas* (7.337). The word hardly requires translation: these are "funereal" torches. But the reader will not automatically know that this is the earliest recorded appearance of the word, that Vergil (who has many occasions to speak of death) uses it only in two other passages (4.507, 11.143), and that even if it is used more commonly after Vergil, it is used only by poets (*OLD* s.v.). The familiarity of the English loan-word is thus very misleading, as is its tone. According to the *OED* s.v., "funereal" means "Of or pertaining to a funeral; appropriate to a funeral. Hence, gloomy, dark, dismal, melancholy, mournful," and it was apparently introduced in Pope's *Odyssey* (4.740), where it describes a feast. But (so the *OED*) it is most often used to describe a burial procession or, metaphorically, some other kind of ceremonial parade or, parodically, an inappropriately or comically slow march. It is, in effect, a near synonym of "stately." It is not impossible that Tennyson found words like *funereus* symptomatic of Vergilian "stateliness." But it is nothing of the kind: its form is in fact colloquial, though it apparently never sounded sufficiently normal to use in prose. The example is rather a good illustration of how Vergil's lexical experiments have come, over time, *and because of their very success*, to seem hackneyed or stodgy rather than daring.

On the other hand, some passages that are entirely straightforward in a lexical sense, but otherwise complex, have sometimes got quite seriously distorted. For instance: as the epic is just getting under way, the reader learns that Aeneas' difficulties are "the result of savage Juno's obsessive anger" (*saevae memorem Iunonis ob iram*, 1.4). The word *saevae* bothered ancient schoolteachers: why should the poet call the queen of the gods "savage"? The "solution" to this "problem" is a classic piece of obfuscation: "The ancients," Servius tells us (*ad loc.*), used *saevus* as a synonym of *magnus*; therefore, Vergil is saying not "*savage* Juno," but "*great* Juno." And he repeats the same general idea a number of times, for instance when Aeneas is called *saevus* (*Aen.* 12.107). But Vergil is saying nothing of the kind. Nowhere else in Latin have we the slightest indication that *saevus* can mean "great" or anything other than "savage." Servius of course is no more a detractor than Tennyson; but the passage illustrates clearly how institutional adoption distorted Vergil's language, homogenizing it both by treating his more daring lexical inventions as if they were standard Latin and by depriving "dangerous" ideas simply expressed of their natural force.

This process produced two collateral effects. In the first place, there is the schoolboy's simple resentment of the required subject. "I was compelled to learn about the wanderings of a certain Aeneas, oblivious of my own wanderings," complains Augustine (*Conf.* 1.13.20), "and I bore with dry eyes my own wretched self dying to you, O God." Such a passage goes well beyond its roots in schoolboy resentments, and the saint has been enlisted in the cause of Vergil's defenders (Haecker 1931; Espinosa Pólct 1932; Graves 1962), but his case is undeniably complex (as is shown by Wills' chapter in this volume). Not so that of a somewhat less repentant sinner, Henry Miller, for whom studying Vergil was sheer boredom and a distraction from more pleasant pastimes: "I am one individual who is going to be honest about Vergil and his fucking *rari nantes in gurgite vasto*. I say without blushing or stammering, without the least confusion, regret or remorse that recess in the toilet was worth a thousand Vergils, always was and always will be" (1936, 56–7; cf. Ziolkowski 1993, 192–3). For Miller, then, and no doubt for others as well, Vergil is the very embodiment of the compulsory subject.

But in addition to juvenile annoyance one encounters more mature perception that the *Aeneid* is bound to institutional forces, not accidentally but inextricably. Ovid, languishing in Tomis because of his lascivious *Ars amatoria* (as he would have us believe), complains to Augustus that "the happy author of **your** *Aeneid*" (*ille* **tuae** *felix Aeneidos auctor, Tr.* 2.533) also wrote about illicit love, and no part of the poem is more avidly read. The implication that Vergil received preferential treatment in high places is very clear. Ezra Pound in his tendentious translation of the passage where Propertius apparently hails the imminent appearance of the *Aeneid* imputes to it a similar attitude:

> Make way, ye Roman authors,
>   clear the street, O ye Greeks,
> For a much larger Iliad is in the course of construction
> (and to Imperial order)
> Clear the streets, O ye Greeks.
>
> (Pound 1956, 93–4)

Apropos of this passage, Michael Alexander (1998, 109) writes that "[t]o public schoolmasters turning out public servants, Aeneas was a more suitable model than any of Homer's heroes, and…Vergil a more convenient author." It is characteristic that Pound expresses this attitude by distorting Propertius' language towards a stilted officialese in an implied parody of Vergil's. For Robert Graves as well, Vergil is the consummate company man: "whenever a golden age of stable government, full churches, and expanding wealth dawns among the Western nations, Vergil always returns to supreme favour"; and it was always [negative qualities that] "first commended him to government circles, and have kept him in favour ever since" (1962, 13–14). On these grounds Graves opines that "few poets have brought such discredit as Vergil on their sacred calling" (1962, 35).

These observations take us beyond the immediate subject of Vergil's language; and, as I noted above, even most hostile critics have granted Vergil his eloquence. Quite a few, however, have granted him little else. Coleridge famously asked, "If you take from Vergil his language and metre, what do you leave him?" (1917, 8 May, 56). The spirit behind this question may be less dismissive than is commonly thought (O'Hara 1997, 241). Still, the inference usually drawn is that Vergil is all verbal artistry without much substance. Pound, once again, found a way of acknowledging Vergil's verbal mastery while at the same time damning it: Vergil "has a nice verbalism," he writes (1954, 215). Less snide, but perhaps more effective, is the sentence pronounced by Mark Van Doren: "Homer is a world; Virgil a style" (attributed by Mandelbaum 1971, ix).

Untranslatable Vergil

Another consequence of a preoccupation with Vergil's style is the belief that Vergil is "untranslatable" (see the following chapter in this volume by Braund). This may be another way of saying, with Pound, that "he has no story worth telling"

(1954, 215) – that his verbal mastery is unsupported by any comparable ability to construct a plot. But even admirers tend to admit that the *Aeneid* loses too much in translation. It may be telling that the most admired translations are in some ways the most distant stylistically from Vergil himself, the translations of Douglas and Dryden, and also the most distant chronologically from ourselves. (Pound, never missing a chance, proclaimed the Douglas translation "better than the original" because Douglas "had heard the sea" (1954, 35).) The last fifty years, a period when a spare, unelevated poetic style has been in favor, have seen many successful translations of Homer, beginning with Richmond Lattimore's still unsurpassed masterpieces (1951, 1967). Robert Fitzgerald (1961, 1974, 1983), Robert Fagles (1990, 1996, 2006), and Stanley Lombardo (1997, 2000, 2005) are among those who have tried follow their success with Homer by trying their hands at Vergil. Of these three, only Lombardo has served both poets equally well, and only he manages to tell Vergil's story precisely as a compelling story. Curiously, his versions are also the sparest in terms of style. Must the translator simply forget about Vergil's celebrated mastery of poetic language in order to produce an *Aeneid* that succeeds on other terms – for instance, as a good story?

A Style, But Not a Life

Not all of Vergil's detractors concern themselves with language. The majority grant him verbal mastery, but deny that he understands anything else about poetry, or about life. I have just mentioned the matter of plot, which speaks more directly to some basic human appetite than does beautiful language alone. The implication is that a poet who speaks well but cannot tell a story does not understand human nature. Related to this is the business of character. A common charge is that in Aeneas Vergil has created a failed character, one who is unheroic in two different ways. In the first place, as a man of action he does not measure up to Achilles or Odysseus. Pound insists on this point as well. Vergil has "no sense of personality," he complains; "His hero is a stick who would have contributed to *The New Statesman*" (1954, 215). As Bianca Tarozzi puts it, Pound regarded Vergil as "a sort of modest Victorian ecclesiastic" (1986, 491–2). She is thinking here of the well-known (and no doubt fabricated) story of the "plain sailor man [who] took a notion to study Latin" and, when given the *Aeneid* to read and asked what he thought of its hero, replied "Him a hero? Bigob, I t'ought he was a priest" (Pound 1934, 31). Georg Lukács made the same point in a different but equally vivid way: "The heroes of Virgil live the cool and limited existence of shadows, nourished by the blood of noble zeal, blood that has been sacrificed in the attempt to recall what has forever disappeared" (1971, 49).

One of the chief ways in which Aeneas famously does not measure up to characters like Achilles and Odysseus is in heroic egotism, in sublime disregard for anyone but the heroic self, a trait that both characters demonstrate abundantly in their dealings with women especially. But it is Aeneas and not they who is blamed for being, in Graves' words, "a cad to the last" (1962, 27). Samuel Johnson, echoing Dido, speaks of Aeneas' "perfidy" towards her, while the commentator Thomas Cooke (cited by Kallendorf in this volume) condemns Aeneas for both heroic failings, finding him too little the man of action but too much the womanizer, expressing the wish (while invoking the theme of the "unfinished *Aeneid*") that Vergil would have erased at least some of the hero's flaws if he had lived to revise the poem.

Sheer Cluelessness

Vergil's offenses, whether viewed in terms of literary artistry or understanding of human nature, have been seen as involving a lack of judgment or sense of propriety. Two examples will suffice.

A.E. Housman, himself of course an important minor poet and a major philologist, did not think much of Vergil's taste, at least in respect of proportion. "His besetting sin is the use of words too forcible for his thoughts, and the *moritura* of Aen. XII 55 makes me blush for him whenever I think of it." This opinion is cited by a biographer (Graves 1979, 202) to show that Housman had as instinctive a sense of Latin style as he did of English. In some respects this is true, but here Housman's opinion is conventional and misleading. Acting on his dislike of Vergilian excess, Housman proposed an emendation to the text of the *Aeneid* (1.395) that introduced an additional element of the very hyperbole that Housman himself found offensive. But as the previous quotation illustrates, Housman considered Vergil's taste defective in this respect, so that in "restoring" a bit of hyperbole that he supposed had got lost in the vagaries of textual transmission, he could honestly believe that he was reconstructing an accurate text. Perhaps as a way of softening the blow to Vergil's reputation, Housman drew on the commonplace of comparing him to Tennyson, noting that "between Tennyson and Virgil there is so much resemblance, perhaps in other respects but certainly in this habit of using language too grand for the occasion"; and he also made the excuse that "Virgil never meant them for our eyes," citing the *VSD* (24) on Vergil's use of temporary stopgaps (1972, 349–350). Housman's proposal was not widely accepted. But it found a defender in Philip Hardie, whose study of the *Aeneid* devoted a lengthy chapter (6) to "Hyperbole" not as a stylistic fault, but as an integral element of a coherent epic design (1986, 241–92; cf. 1987, 45–50). Thus in this curious turn of events, Housman the textual critic redeems Housman the literary critic.

A second instance of Vergil's "poor judgment" comes, once again, from the ancient biographies. After Augustus' persistent demands that Vergil recite some portion of his work in progress, the poet is supposed to have responded by reading passages from books 2, 4, and 6, but with such effect that the famous apostrophe (*tu Marcellus eris*, Aen. 6.883) to Augustus' nephew and son-in-law, Marcellus, who was recently deceased, caused the young man's mother, Augustus' sister Octavia, to faint (*VSD* 32). The episode is not presented in the spirit of criticizing Vergil: one version even represents Augustus as rewarding Vergil for the lines that caused Octavia's swoon (*Vita Donatiana aucta* 46–7). But the *Nachleben* of this anecdote has been more mixed. In Angelika Kauffmann's painting of the scene, one of Octavia's attendants glares at the poet almost as if he had struck her mistress (see Plate 7 and Winterer's chapter in this volume). Perhaps this is meant to indicate the servant's lack of literary sophistication: she takes Vergil's lines as a gauche failure that produces a disastrous effect. But it is far from clear that we are meant to understand that the lines are sublime while the servant does not. Vergil, for his part, looks completely abashed as if conscious of having given great offense; and Augustus, like everyone else in the painting, is concerned only for his sister. There is no hint of Vergil's eventual reward. The scene was represented in another medium by John Williams (1972), who represents Vergil's recollection of the event (in a letter to Horace) as follows:

> The sister of our friend Octavius [i.e., Augustus] still grieves for her son; time does not bring her that gradual diminution of pain, which is time's only gift; and I fear that my poor efforts to give her heart some solace may have had an effect I did not intend.

Vergil goes on to tell the story of how he read the Marcellus passage in the presence of a few of Augustus' intimates, and of what he saw when he looked at Octavia for her reaction:

> What I saw I cannot truly describe; her eyes blazed darkly, as if they burned deep in her skull, and her lips were drawn in the awful semblance of a grin that bared her teeth. It was a look, it seemed to me, almost of pure hatred. Then she gave a high toneless little scream, swayed sideways, and fell upon her couch in a dead faint.
>   We rushed to her; Octavius massaged her hands; she gradually revived, and the ladies took her away.
>   "I am sorry," I said at last. "If I had known – I only intended her some comfort."
> (Williams 1972, 174–5)

Once again, this entire strand of the tradition has nothing to do with the poem itself. It all follows from an episode in the biographies for which we have no independent evidence. It may well be a fiction. And, as I have noted, when read straightforwardly the story seems intended to illustrate both the power of Vergil's poetry and how much it was appreciated, at least by Augustus. But in reception the tale has taken on the character of a reproach to the poet.

Vergil and Homer

But for many and perhaps most Vergil-haters, the poet's ties to Augustus are a secondary consideration. In the preface to his *Aeneid* commentary, Servius (the opposite of a Vergil-hater, but he puts the matter conveniently) informs us that "Vergil's intention was two-fold: to imitate Homer and to praise Augustus through his ancestors." It is tempting to think that Servius put things deliberately in this order, so that mimesis precedes encomium. There have been times when Vergil was thought to have surpassed Homer (Scaliger 1561, on which see the remarks of Haynes in the previous chapter of this volume). But such moments have been rare. In essence, the highest praise ever accorded Vergil's Homeric agon is that of Domitius Afer, Quintilian's teacher, who said that Vergil is second to Homer, but closer to first place than to third (Quint. *Inst.* 10.1.86).

The general tendency, however, has been to dwell on the various qualities that distance Vergil from his poetic "father" in a way that proves to be quite misleading.

The key passage occurs in the life of Vergil ascribed to Donatus and deriving, ultimately, from Suetonius (*VSD* 43–6). "Vergil has never lacked for detractors," it begins. The life mentions Numitorius and Vipranius, who are discussed above, along with a book on Vergil called *Vitia* or "Faults" by a certain Herennius; another called *Furta* or "Thefts" by Perellius Faustus; a work entitled *Aeneidomastix* or "Scourge of the *Aeneid*" by Carvilius Pictor; and one in eight books entitled *Homoiotetes* or "Resemblances" by Q. Octavius Avitus. Each of these works has a different focus. Herennius' *Vitia* may have concerned itself with almost anything. Faustus' *Furta* is probably an important source of certain passages from earlier work of Latin literature that has been lost for the most part, but that survive in quotations only because Vergil imitates them. The same is true of Octavius' work, the title of which bespeaks a certain critical impartiality (although Donatus includes him among the *obtrectatores*) and also, one infers, an interest in Vergil's use of earlier Greek as well as Latin literature. No such impression of impartiality arises from Carvilius' title, which looks not only to Greek but to specifically Homeric criteria for damning the *Aeneid*.

But Donatus' (or Suetonius') perspective on the *obtrectatores* is instructive in a way that is seldom noted. "Vergil has never lacked for detractors," he writes, and then adds, "and no wonder: **for neither did Homer**" (*obtrectatores Vergilio numquam defuerunt, nec mirum; nam nec Homero quidem*, 43). This comparison of Vergil to Homer serves to introduce a number of works that also compared Vergil to Homer, to the Roman poet's disadvantage. But the more interesting point, which is not made explicit, is that ancient *Aeneid* criticism formed itself as much as possible on explicitly Homeric lines, no less than Vergil formed the *Aeneid* itself on Homeric lines. Today we remember Plato as Homer's most distinguished and most serious ancient critic. From the perspective of twenty-five centuries, however, Plato's objections to Homer, especially those that he registers in the *Republic*, are a bit embarrassing, linked as they are to an antidemocratic political economy and to mechanisms of thought-control such as state-sponsored censorship. But Plato's near-contemporary Zoilus composed a work called *Homeric Questions* – which became a standard title for works attacking or defending Homer – a work so harsh that it earned Zoilus the sobriquet "Homeromastix," or "Scourge of Homer." It is clearly Zoilus' *nom de plume* (or, as we could say in this case, *nom de guerre*) that Carvilius Pictor had in mind when he gave his book the title *Aeneidomastix*. We know little about the specific contents of this book, but it is an easy inference that Carvilius modeled his criticism of Vergil closely on traditional criticism of Homer, by Zoilus and others of his ilk. In fact, we find traces of this activity in the commentary of Servius, which is itself based on earlier commentaries that incorporated material from the works of Vergil's ancient detractors as well as his defenders. Servius is generally a dedicated defender of Vergil, which means that a number of his comments on particular passages take the form of rebuttals to hostile criticism of the poem. Many of these defenses probably go back to a work entitled *Against Vergil's Detractors* compiled by the first-century CE scholar Asconius Pedianus (mentioned in the *VSD* 46). What is really interesting, though, is that such criticism often has a history.

It is a remarkable fact that Vergil's imitation of Homer inspired Vergil's critics to imitate Homer's critics as well. What is more remarkable is the possibility that Vergil foresaw that this would happen and may actually have encouraged the process. His intentions are of course impossible to prove. Vergil did, however, devote a major episode of the *Aeneid*, the nocturnal escapade of Nisus and Euryalus in book 9, to the imitation of a Homeric episode, the "Doloneia" of *Iliad* 10, that Homer's ancient critics regarded as flawed. He did this despite knowing, in all probability, that critics held the "Doloneia" in low esteem. He might have designed his imitation in such a way as to take their criticisms into account and so to improve on Homer, as he arguably did elsewhere (Schlunk 1974; Schmit-Neuerberg 1999; and Hexter's chapter in this volume). Instead, he imitated Homer's faults; and these were duly noted by Vergil's own critics, who modeled their commentary on that of Homer's critics *in the corresponding episode*, in just the same way as Vergil's episode is modeled on Homer's (Casali 2004b). We cannot say with confidence that Vergil designed his imitation of Homer in such a way as to manipulate his critics so as to draw them into his plan. But we can say with certainty that this was the result.

Against such a critical background, the idea that Vergil was criticized simply because he imitated Homer seems incredibly banal; but of course he was criticized for this as well. Modern scholars owe a great debt to the early *obtrectatores*, whatever their motives: their work enabled Servius and his contemporary Macrobius to record Vergil's allusions to poems lost to us, about which we would otherwise have had no idea. They also give us some sense of how this extensively allusive poet was read in antiquity and of how the meaning of such rampant allusivity was debated. Modern Vergilians acknowledge the pervasiveness of Vergilian intertextuality, whether this aspect of Vergil's poetry is an important element in their own criticism or not. This makes it useful to be reminded that in ancient times as well there were readers who, for whatever reason, did not "get it." And beyond this, it is amusing as well as instructive to observe that ancient critics blamed Vergil for his excessive dependence on Homer, even as they copied their criticisms of Vergil right out of Homer's own critics. The intertextuality that pervades not only Vergil's relationship to Homer but that between Vergil's critics and Homer's critics as well is one of the remarkable features of the anti-Vergilian tradition. This is, of course, a dimension that the work of critics hostile to Homer simply lacked.

Vergil and Dante

There is an additional curious feature to this business of poetic influence, which is so often figured as a matter of "paternity" and "filiation." It is perhaps uniquely true of Vergil that he is found wanting both as a son and as a father himself. Allen Mandelbaum has commented perceptively on a number of bizarre "variations on the theme of Homer versus Virgil, using the father to club the son, coupled at times with some variations on the theme of Dante versus Virgil, using the son to club the father. Whichever way one turned the line of affiliation (Homer-Virgil-Dante) – toward parricide or filicide – the middleman Virgil lost" (1971, ix). Dante generally, and understandably, has a less direct effect upon classicists than does Homer. Nevertheless, anecdote attributes to one anonymous classicist the opinion that Vergil's greatest work was the *Divine Comedy* (Knauer 1964b, 62).

The Classic of All Europe

I have mentioned that denigration is so large a part of Vergilian criticism that anything other than extravagant praise can be taken for censure. We have seen, for instance, how the words of Propertius, Ovid, Tennyson, and others apparently in praise of Vergil have either been taken for criticism or else turned into it. It is equally true that extravagant praise, even when it is not directly inspired by Vergil's poetry, seems to invite extravagant censure. The most important such case involves none other than the greatest of Vergil's would-be champions, T.S. Eliot.

It was Eliot, as I noted at the beginning of this chapter, who praised the *Aeneid* as "the classic of all Europe." And yet, is it praise? Or if it is, then praise of what? It is curious how little Vergil, in the sense of Vergil's poetry, enters into the argument of Eliot's essay. Ziolkowski (1993, 119–34) shows very clearly just how slender Eliot's engagement with the text of the *Aeneid* really was, and how thoroughly he was concerned not with the *Aeneid* itself, but with the idea of the *Aeneid* – with what he took it to represent. His response was largely conditioned not by any deep familiarity with the poem but by a powerfully partisan critical discourse that had grown up around it, one having much more to do with the utility of Vergil as an emblem of the Risorgimento, with sentimental ideas about a contented, patriotic yeomanry upholding the various nation-states of a Europe somehow reunified under the banner of Christendom. And it was this perspective on the Vergil legend, rather than sympathetic analysis of the *Aeneid* itself, that led other men of letters to reply in terms of rebuke (Auden 1966) or even of contempt (Graves 1962) directed not so much at Eliot but at Vergil himself.

Conclusion

The purpose of this chapter has been not to defend Vergil against his detractors. There is no point in that, and no need. Rather, the purpose has been to show what can be learned from them. The interpretation of a poem must always be implicated in the history of its reception. But if a single lesson can be extracted from this survey, it is that lack of awareness can allow the history of reception not merely to inform, but to overwhelm a reader's response to a poem. This is perhaps especially true of a poem such as the *Aeneid*, for which the history of its reception is so overdetermined. This does not mean that we should not listen to Vergil's critics or keep their reactions to the poem in a box, where they can do no harm: far from it. Instead, their criticisms should send us back again and again with fresh appreciation to a text that, despite a remarkable history of critical hostility, remains a source of pleasure and of inspiration to those who take the time to know it.

FURTHER READING

The subject of Vergil's detractors is less often treated in Anglophone scholarship than in other traditions. Fundamental is Görler (1988) on the ancient *obtrectatores*, and, for some additional insight into the earliest period of reception, see Barchiesi (2004) (both of these in Italian). On the ancient *Vita* tradition see Horsfall (1995b) and Stok in this volume. On characteristics of Vergil's style see Lyne (1989) and, more briefly, O'Hara (1997). On the formation of ancient *Aeneid* criticism on a Homeric model see Schlunk (1974), Schmit-Neuerburg (1999) (in German), Casali (2004b), Hexter in this volume, and Farrell (2008). The shift in taste from preference for Vergil to preference for Homer in the early modern period is traced through the tradition of Vergilian commentary by Knauer (1964a, 62–106) (in German). Ziolkowski (1993) is a detailed and judicious survey of modern receptions, mainly from the late nineteenth century onwards, that pays due attention to the complex interrelationship between celebration and disparagement in all aspects of Vergil criticism.

CHAPTER THIRTY ONE

Mind the Gap
On Foreignizing Translations of the Aeneid

Susanna Morton Braund

The *Aeneid* has been translated into many languages, including Afrikaans, Bulgarian, Czech, Hebrew, Hungarian, Japanese, Polish, and Swedish; there will soon be an Arabic translation (Hoyle 2007). I present this list to provoke thoughts of the size of the gap between original and translation in terms of both language and culture: a gap that can be enormous. Some cultural traditions are comfortable with that kind of gap while others seek to elide it. Of course, elision can never be achieved – not even by the strategy imagined by Borges in his "Pierre Menard, Author of the Quixote," a pseudo-review about a fictional twentieth-century French writer whose effort to translate *Don Quixote* resulted in a recreation of it, line for line, in the original sixteenth-century Spanish (Borges 1939). Friedrich Schleiermacher set out the spectrum in his 1813 lecture *Ueber die verschiedenen Methoden des Uebersetzens* ("On the Different Methods of Translating"): "Either the translator leaves the author in peace, as much as possible, and moves the reader towards him; or he leaves the reader in peace, as much as possible, and moves the author towards him" (Schleiermacher 1977, 74; cf. Venuti 1995, 99–118). To use an image that is now common currency in translation studies, translations tend to "foreignize" or to "domesticate" their original texts (Venuti 1995; France 2000, 4). Lawrence Venuti has documented the tendency towards domestication in English-language translation from the seventeenth century onwards, a tendency that renders translators invisible and values fluency and transparency in translations (Venuti 1995, e.g. 38–42). His argument certainly applies to English translations of the *Aeneid*.

Dryden is explicit about his domesticating aspirations when he writes in the Dedication to his 1697 translation of the *Aeneid* (undoubtedly one of the most intelligent and sensitive essays on the poem, still relevant to every translator of Vergil), "I have endeavoured to make Virgil speak such English as he would himself have spoken, if he had been born in England, and in this present age." In this Dryden is echoing the words of Sir John Denham in 1656, in the preface to his translation of book 2 of the *Aeneid*, *The Destruction of Troy*: "if *Virgil* must needs speak English, it were fit he should speak not only as a man of this Nation, but as a man of this age" (Steiner 1975, 65, 72; see also the chapters by Power and Eastin in this volume). In this essay, I shall suggest that although such a project does a service to the Latin poet, it also does him a great disservice. After a frankly withering glance at what is possibly the nadir of domesticating translations in English, I shall examine three modern translations of the *Aeneid* which deliberately set out to foreground the alienness of the original poem, one in Russian, one in French, and one in English. Foreignizing translations such as these have often provoked controversy. It is my aim to explore debate around the foreignizing strategy by looking at the translators' apologiae, at the points of sensitivity in hostile and friendly criticism, and at the translations themselves. What emerges, in short, is a struggle about privileging form over content.

Dryden's translation can be counted the zenith of English domestications of the *Aeneid*, not least because it achieves status as a poem in its own right. A strong candidate for the nadir of domesticating translations might well be the 1956 Penguin Classics version by W.F. Jackson Knight. Knight's pedestrian prose so effectively eradicates the poetry of the Latin that students are sometimes led to believe that the work is a novel rather than an epic poem. Here is the opening, followed by the Latin text of *Aen.* 1.1–11:

> THIS is a tale of arms and of a man. Fated to be an exile, he was the first to sail from the land of Troy and reach Italy, at its Lavinian shore. He met many tribulations on his way both by land and on the ocean; high Heaven willed it, for Juno was ruthless and could not forget her anger. And he had also to endure great suffering in warfare. But at least he succeeded in founding his city, and installing the gods of his race in the Latin land: and that was the origin of the Latin nation, the Lords of Alba, and the proud battlements of Rome.
>
> I pray for inspiration, to tell how it all began, and how the Queen of Heaven sustained such outrage to her majesty that in her indignation she forced a man famed for his true-heartedness to tread that long path of adventure, and to face so many trials. It is hard to believe Gods in Heaven capable of such rancour.

> arma virumque cano, Troiae qui primus ab oris
> Italiam fato profugus Laviniaque venit
> litora – multum ille et terris iactatus et alto
> vi superum, saevae memorem Iunonis ob iram,
> multa quoque et bello passus, dum conderet urbem
> inferretque deos Latio, genus unde Latinum
> Albanique patres atque altae moenia Romae.
> Musa, mihi causas memora, quo numine laeso
> quidve dolens regina deum tot volvere casus
> insignem pietate virum, tot adire labores
> impulerit. tantaene animis caelestibus irae?

Knight oversimplifies with colloquialisms such as "This is a tale," "I pray for inspiration," and "It is hard to believe," which completely betray Vergil's laconic, almost lapidary style. This kind of domestication does a great disservice to the author – and the reader.

The characteristics of foreignization make a stark contrast. This essay is a study of three self-consciously foreignizing translations produced during the past century, along with the hostile reception given them by professional classicists. I shall come back to an English translation far superior to that of Knight later, but now I shall introduce the two non-English translations. The first is Valerii Briusov's into Russian, published in 1933, and the second is that of Pierre Klossowski into French, published in 1964. Both translations have been accused of inaccessibility or impenetrability, of sacrificing sense for sound, for syntax, or for both. Let us consider, then, what these translators thought they were about and why.

***

As a backdrop to Briusov's translation from the early twentieth century, which he began work on long before the Bolshevik Revolution of 1917 and was still incomplete at his death in 1924, a brief sketch of the reception of the *Aeneid* in Russia (following Chlodowski 1984–91) is in order. Given the hostility of the Russian Orthodox Church towards the Latin language, which one may style "Latinophobia" (Klyuchevskii 1908, 405, cited by Chlodowski 1984–91, 609), Vergil was not read until the second half of the seventeenth century, when Moscow identified itself as a "Third Rome," after Rome and Byzantium, of course (Wolf 1960; Lotman and Uspenskii 1984). As Peter the Great (1682–1725) imposed his vision of a Europeanized Russia at the start of the eighteenth century, Latin became indispensable and familiarity with Vergil among the educated grew. One signal example of this is the centrality of Vergil in Feofan Prokopovich's *De arte poetica* (1705), a treatise on poetry and rhetoric written in Latin; unsurprisingly, Prokopovich received important parts of his education outside Russia, in Poland and in Italy at the Jesuit Collegio Romano. Peter the Great's legacy was maintained by his daughter Elizabeth, the Augusta (r. 1741–61), and by Catherine the Great (r. 1762–96), who was a notable patron of the arts and a prolific author herself. As Carlo Testa points out (personal communication, 2008), in Western Europe "time was, by then, largely up for epic poems, as no less a writer than Voltaire discovered to his cost with his well-intentioned, but aesthetically outdated, *Henriade* (1723, 1728)." But, in Russia during the eighteenth century, epic emerged as the highest form of poetic achievement. Mikhail Lomonosov (1711–65), who towards the end of his life wrote a monumental but unfinished heroic poem, *Petr Velikii* ("Peter the Great"), seems to have been crucial in the ascendancy of Vergil, translating in blank verse many lines from the *Eclogues* and *Aeneid* in his vast *Ritorika* of 1747. But the first complete translation of Vergil's poems commenced only in 1770, with the publication of *Aeneid* 1–6 in alexandrine verse (i.e., rhymed iambic hexameters) by Vasilii Petrov (1736–99), just predating the appearance of the first complete Russian epic in 1779, Mikhail Kheraskov's (1733–1807) enormous (and allegedly tedious) *Rossiada* in twelve cantos, a classicizing treatment of the capture of Kazan in 1552 by Ivan the Terrible. Petrov's full translation of the *Aeneid* was published in St. Petersburg in 1786, complete with a lavish dedicatory preface praising Catherine the Great for her patronage and learning, in language inspired by Vergil's fourth eclogue. Petrov's translation is still highly regarded, but at the time its publication immediately stimulated a debate, with some praising his achievement of bringing the

Latin poem into the Russian heritage, while others criticized his style as pedantic and vilified his choice of alexandrines over the hexameter.

Choice of meter remained a central concern for nineteenth-century translators: alexandrines were condemned for their monotony and high value was set on the hexameter of the original. The next major figure in the story of the translation of the *Aeneid* into Russian is Vasilii Zhukovskii, founder of Russian Romanticism and a wide-ranging translator, who published his translation in hexameters of book 2 as "The Destruction of Troy" in 1822; it went into a third edition as soon as 1824. The same choice of meter informs the next landmark, the translation of the entire *Aeneid* (only the second complete translation, after Petrov) by I. Shershenevich, published serially in the literary periodical *Sovremennik* ("Contemporary") from 1851 on. Despite his avowed aim of simplicity and clarity, his translation was criticized as unnatural and affected in its phrasing. Several further translations appeared during the closing years of the nineteenth century. Bucking the hexametric trend was I. Sosneckii's 1878 translation of the *Aeneid* into anapaests, which is not regarded as successful. The famous lyric poet Afanasii Fet published his translation in 1888 and N. Kvashnin-Samarin his in 1893. But these seem to have enjoyed little more appreciation than the anapaestic translation by Sosneckii.

The twentieth century saw a major shift, as Russian poets turned away from classical and classicizing forms to formalist experiments. With one major exception. The poet and translator Valerii Briusov (1873–1924), a founder of Russian Symbolism and hence very influential at least until the 1910s, regarded the *Aeneid* as the acme of world literature, with only Pushkin coming close. He was a seasoned translator who started his poetic career by translating French Symbolist poetry (Verlaine, Maeterlinck, and Mallarmé). He went on to produce translations of Poe, Hugo, Racine, Molière, Byron, Goethe, and Wilde, as well as of Vergil and Ausonius and of some Armenian poetry. He helped establish Russian Symbolism by publishing three volumes of his own verse, entitled *Russian Symbolists: An Anthology (1894–95)*, under a number of pen names, and in 1904 became the editor of the influential literary magazine *Vesy* ("The Balance").

Briusov worked on his translation of the *Aeneid* for many years from 1895 onwards, trying different approaches and starting twice over from the beginning (Gasparov 1971). He was still working on it at his death in 1924 and had by then completed just the first seven books. His translation only appeared in 1933 after the publishers commissioned Sergei Solovyov to complete the project, presumably working from Briusov's drafts. It was reprinted in the series *Biblioteka antichnoi literatury* (Library of Ancient Literature) in 2000 and is one of the standard translations in Russia.

Briusov – clearly a product of the pre-Revolutionary era, even though he later supported the Bolshevik government and even held a position in the Soviet cultural ministry – seems to take the nineteenth-century concern with form to a new, higher, and, perhaps, unmatchable level, but with a switch away from the emphasis on metrics to other features. (In an early essay on lyric poetry, he identifies six crucial elements that a translator must attempt to render: style, imagery, meter and rhythm, the movement of the line, wordplay and soundplay.) He concedes that "to reproduce all these elements fully or exactly in a translation in verse form is inconceivable" (quoted by Gasparov 1997a, 124), which of course means that the translator's choice between them becomes critical. His translation of the *Aeneid* has three notable features: the word order, which is often astonishingly close to the Latin; the choice of vocabulary, which is very precise; and the sound effects, especially alliteration, widely regarded as one of his finest achievements. Yet, despite (or perhaps because of) its formal fidelity, Briusov's translation is difficult, strained, even tortuous to read because of his commitment to *bukvalizm* ("literalism"; *bukva* means "letter" of the alphabet). Here are the first eleven lines, with my interlinear translation, in which I use a hyphen where a single Russian word needs more words in English:

1 *arma virumque cano, Troiae qui primus ab oris*
   Брань и героя пою, с побережий Трои кто первый
   War and hero I-sing, from coasts of-Troy who first
   [acc.]   [acc.]

2 *Italiam fato profugus Laviniaque venit*
   Прибыл в Италию, Роком изгнан, и лавинийских граней
   came to Italy, by-fate expelled, and of-Lavinian borders

3 *litora – multum ille et terris iactatus et alto*
   К берегу, много по суше бросаем и по морю оный,
   to shore, much by land tossed and by sea that-one,
              [nom.]   [nom.]

4 *vi superum, saevae memorem Iunonis ob iram,*
   Силой всевышных под гневом злопамятным лютой Юноны,
   by-force of-most-high under anger unforgiving of-cruel Juno,
          [pl.]

5 *multa quoque et bello passus, dum conderet urbem*
   Много притом испытав   и в боях, прежде чем основал он
   much besides having-experienced also in battles, until founded he

6 *inferretque deos Latio, genus unde Latinum*
   Город и в Лаций богов перенес, род откуда латинов
   city and into Latium gods brought, race whence of-Latins
   [acc.]   [acc.][nom.]

7 *Albanique patres atque altae moenia Romae.*
   И Альбы-Лонги отцы   и твердыни возвышенной Ромы.
   and of-Alba-Longa fathers and stronghold of-lofty   Rome.
          [nom.]   [nom.]

8 *Musa, mihi causas memora, quo numine laeso*
   Муса! причины мне вспомни, какая   обида святыни
   Muse! Reasons to-me remind, what-kind-of offense of-sacredness
                    [nom.]   [nom.] [gen.]

9 *quidve dolens regina deum tot volvere casus*
   Иль что за скорбь побудила царицу богов – в стольких бедах
   or what-kind-of grief roused queen of-gods – in so-many troubles
                    [nom.]   [acc.]

10   *insignem pietate virum, tot adire labores*
     Мужа, кто славен своим благочестьем, томить и подвергнуть
     man, who [was] renowned by-his piety, to-torment and to-subject
     [acc.]

11   *impulerit. tantaene animis caelestibus irae?*
     Стольким трудам. Так безмерны ли душ небожительных гневы?
     [in] so-many toils. So limitless [= ?] [are] of-souls sky-dwelling angers?
                    [nom.]   [gen. pl.][gen.pl.]   [nom.]

The opening eleven lines do not offer much of an impression of Briusov's sound effects, but we can study the other two features, word order and vocabulary. In line 1, he retains the juxtaposition of *qui primus* in *kto pervyi*; in line 2 he captures the position in the middle of the line of *fato profugus*; in line 3 he gives the adverb *mnogo* the same position as *multum* and he separates *et terris…et alto* by the past participle; in line 4 he juxtaposes the adjectives for *saevae* and *memorem*; in line 5 *mnogo* has the same position as *multa*; in line 6 he sandwiches *otkuda*, the adverb that translates *unde*; in line 7 the word order is very close to the Latin, with "Rome" as the last word; in lines 8–9 he formulates the two questions like the Latin and links them with *il'*, which is exact for *-ve*; in line 11, he reserves "anger" for the last word. Departures from the Latin word order or syntax are astonishingly few: he gives *gorod*, his translation of *urbem* at the end of line 5, an emphatic position at the start of line 6 and he makes the accusative phrase *insignem pietate* (line 10) into a relative clause. He clearly keeps as close to the Latin word order as possible, exploiting the inflections of the Russian language to replicate the density of Vergil's Latin, even at the potential cost of straining the Russian. In other words, his method transmutes a complex Latin text into a complex Russian text, refusing to simplify Vergil for his readers.

In terms of vocabulary, Briusov is amazingly resourceful. In line 3, he uses an archaic Russian word, *onyi*, for *ille*, here employed in a pleonastic sense which according to Servius is also archaic; in line 4 he renders *superum* as "most high"; in line 8, *vspomni* (the root is "remember") is exact for *memora* and *svyatini* meaning "sacred thing" seems felicitous for *numine*; in lines 9–11 he maintains the repetition of *tot…tot* with *stol'kikh…stol'kim*; *bedakh* in line 9 is very close for *casus* and, like the Latin, plural; and line 11 has a clever rendering of *caelestibus* in *nebo-zhitel'nykh* = "sky-living." He does not repeat *virum* in lines 1 and 10, for a reason: *geroi* at line 1 in Russian denotes the subject of the story as much as his prowess; *muzh* at line 10 in a context such as this (as opposed to vernacular Russian where it is the usual word for "husband") is an archaic word that connects closely with the idea of masculinity inherent in *virum*. In short, Briusov was intent on reproducing the poetry – the structures, tropes, and sounds – of the Latin.

He makes his intentions clear in the six-page preface that precedes his translation ("O perevode 'Eneidy' russkimi stikhami" ("On the translation of the *Aeneid* into Russian verses"), Briusov 2000, 134–9). He starts by characterizing some of the Russian translations that had appeared during the preceding fifty-odd years as "conscientious" pieces of work, where "conscientious" is at least as damning a word in Russian as it can be in English. Noting that though some of them translate line for line and even word for word (*podstrochnik*), he asserts that they pay attention primarily to content and too little to form. Despite the palpable tension between preserving the content and conveying its aesthetic impact, he insists on the possibility of combining content and form by paying proper attention to "*how* everything is told in Vergil" (his emphasis). He asserts that in Vergil, the sound creates the image: "For every picture, for every image, for every idea Vergil finds an expression which with its own sounds strengthens, underlines, clarifies the sense of the word." Using musical imagery (melody, harmony, symphony), he praises Vergil as an "incomparable euphonist." According to Briusov, previous translators make everything too explicit and "arrange words in their correct grammatical order" without paying attention to the sound, whereas in Vergil "every syllable is weighed, every letter speaks." In short, Briusov is opposed to what we might term the dumbing down of Vergil's careful juxtapositions.

It is perhaps not surprising that Briusov views alliteration and assonance as crucial components in Vergil's sound, to the extent that he devotes almost two pages to examples from his predecessors where they fail to reflect Vergil's Latin and thus weaken or water down the original – another manifestation of dumbing down. The order and disposition of words within the line and the number of words compared with the Latin and their brevity or length are further criteria by which he finds his predecessors wanting. He does concede the impossibility of reproducing the original exactly in another language: translators have to be content with an approximation. He describes the kinds of choices he faced in his translation: to preserve the "music" while "sacrificing literal exactitude," to keep the arrangement of the words, to find a corresponding expression in Russian without concern for the sounds of the words, to alliterate with different sounds from the original – always trying to use "taste and smell." His aim is to enable people to read the Russian *Aeneid* not as a historical monument but as a poetic work worth studying in its own right.

Precisely this, his striving for formal fidelity, was criticized in an essay in 1966 by F.A. Petrovskii, an important classical scholar, translator of Lucretius and Martial, and editor of the complete works of Vergil in a volume, published in 1971, which contains the next translation of the *Aeneid* published in Russian, that of Sergei Osherov. The volume appeared in the highly prestigious series *Biblioteka vsemirnoi literatury* (Library of World Literature) and had an initial print run of 300,000. It was reissued in 1979 in the series *Biblioteka antichnoi literatury* (Library of Ancient Literature), with an introductory essay by M.L. Gasparov. Petrovskii criticized Briusov for producing a translation that was heavy, cerebral, complex, and "unintelligible," because on his view the translator's first duty is to convey the content. The most provocative thing Petrovskii says is that Briusov had no business elevating form to a level of importance it did not have for Vergil, a view that seems to miss something essential about Vergil. Petrovskii's view was surely driven at least in part by the persisting Stalinist ideological agenda: because the official aesthetic dogma of the Soviet Union under Stalin was "socialist realism," Briusov's "formalism" from an earlier era was inevitably frowned upon in the prevailing Soviet cultural environment. (On the relationship between preferred models of translation and cultural history see Friedberg 1997, 109–86 on the "pendulum-like movement from literalist to paraphrastic phases," an argument built on the essay by Gasparov 1971.) Friedberg predicts the reemergence of literalism in Russia in the foreseeable future (146) and links the shift away from literalism and formalism to the establishment in 1932 of the Writers' Union, with its brief of politicized literature following the principles of socialist realism (112–13).

Another Russian classical scholar, Mikhail Gasparov, fêted within Russia during his lifetime and after his death in 2005 as a leading thinker and writer (and subject of a panel at the meeting of the American Association of Teachers of Slavic and East European Languages in Philadelphia in 2006), and himself a translator of Greek and Latin authors including Aesop, Aristotle, Pindar, Euripides, Cicero, Horace, Ovid, Phaedrus, and Suetonius as well as many more recent European authors, has continued the debate since then in several articles on Briusov. Although Gasparov refrains from labeling literal or free translations as intrinsically good or bad, he is critical of the *bukvalizm* manifested in Briusov's *Aeneid* because it is such an extreme strategy, and he concurs with Petrovskii's verdict that the result is virtually unreadable. In his 1971 article "Briusov and Literalism (on Unpublished Materials for his Translation of the *Aeneid*)," he charts Briusov's "journey towards literalism" by studying seven drafts of Briusov's translation of the *Aeneid*, beginning as early as 1895; the last, which is more or less identical to the version published posthumously in 1933, is the fullest realization of Briusov's literalistic direction. Gasparov (1971) demonstrates Briusov's "journey towards literalism" (*put'...k bukvalizmu'*) (92) in his study of the seven drafts of Briusov's translation of the *Aeneid*, detecting six types of change, as follows: (1) elaboration of paraphrase, (2) elaboration of images, (3) elaboration of semantics, (4) elaboration of the grammatical forms of words, (5) elaboration of word order, and (6) elaboration of stress/accent. In a fascinating appendix to the article he prints the first twenty-four lines of *Aeneid* 2 along with Briusov's seven versions. Curiously, although he states that the last of these was the one used for the posthumous publication of the *Aeneid* in 1933, that is not true; none of these texts corresponds exactly to the printed version, although the last is closest.

Gasparov actually devised a method of measuring translations along a scale of precision versus latitude. This is made possible by the evidence of the interlinear translations sometimes used by Briusov and his contemporaries as an intermediary stage towards their polished products, as he explains in an article entitled "Briusov and Word-for-Word Translation" (Gasparov 1997b). His method is discussed by Barry Scherr (2008): Gasparov's "Index of Exactness" (*Pokazatel' tochnosti*) shows how many content words (nouns, verbs, adjectives, adverbs) of the interlinear translation are reproduced in the artistic version, while the "Index of Freedom" (*Pokazatel' vol'nosti*) indicates the percentage of significant words within the translation added by the translator, with no equivalents in the interlinear version. Not surprisingly, Briusov's later translations score high in "exactness" and low in "freedom."

Gasparov realizes that this is a deliberate choice on Briusov's part: "He wanted his *Aeneid* sounding strange and alien for the Russian reader" (1971, 103). This aim is entirely in keeping with the Russian formalist Viktor Shklovsky's principle of *otstranenie* ("making strange"): that the defamiliarization of a text or a procedure for a new generation of readers rejuvenates it and creates it anew (Shklovsky 2004, 16). In theory at least, this is something Gasparov approves of. According to Barry Scherr: "A fundamental principle for Gasparov appeared in the headline of an interview that he gave about translation: 'Don't Shield the Original from the Reader'" (Scherr 2008). It's just that Briusov goes too far in his *Aeneid*. Hence in a third discussion, entitled "Briusov-Translator: Journey to the Crossroads," Gasparov categorizes Briusov's translations with three labels: "fruitful failure," "unfruitful failure," and "unfruitful success" (Gasparov 1997a). (The absence of the category "fruitful success" is noticeable; it was probably prudent for Gasparov, in his still-Stalinist years, to deny that "fruitful success" could be achieved by the formalist Briusov.) He places Briusov's *Aeneid* in the first category. What he means is this: although Briusov failed in his aspiration of being Vergil's translator "for ever" (*navsegda*), his "titanic experiment" was not in vain, because of its influence on later translators who did not go to the same extreme. In an aside in his earlier essay on Briusov and literalism, Gasparov actually defends Briusov against Petrovskii's reproach that he "made no distinction in his translation between idioms of the Latin language and idioms of Vergil" by arguing that Briusov's *Aeneid* was "an ambassador to Russian culture not only of Vergil but of Latin culture in its entirety" (Gasparov 1971, 107). Paraphrasing Briusov's view that "the structure of a language corresponds to the worldview in the consciousness of a nation," Gasparov claims that "in striving to translate for the Russian individual the Latin worldview, Briusov…carries across into the Russian language the traits of the Latin language" (107–8). In other words, Briusov foreignizes.

***

Some of the same issues arise when we turn to the French translation of the *Aeneid* by Pierre Klossowski (1905–2001). As Briusov was in Russia, so Klossowski was a leading intellectual figure in twentieth-century France. Born in Paris to Polish émigrés, he moved in intellectual circles – his acquaintances included Rainer Maria Rilke, André Gide, Georges Bataille, and Walter Benjamin – and he wrote novels, philosophical essays, and translations that influenced French thought and aesthetics from the 1950s onwards. Carlo Testa (personal communication, 2008) suggests that Klossowski's passionate writing on Sade (Klossowski 1947) was not without a certain relevance to his theoretical *prises de position* on translation. Klossowski was a prolific translator throughout his life, translating among others Hölderlin, Nietzsche, Kafka, Heidegger, and Wittgenstein from the German, and Vergil, Suetonius, Tertullian, and Augustine from the Latin.

His translation of the *Aeneid*, published in 1964 by Editions Gallimard, one of the leading French publishers, provoked immediate controversy. His crime? That, as Fiona Cox writes, his translation "makes no attempt to familiarize Vergil or to make his work accessible" (1999, 119). Feeling that Vergil had been traduced by earlier translations – the claim on the cover was "Virgile non travesti" (according to his hostile critic Verdière, whose review is discussed below) – Klossowski's prime concern was to replicate the syntactical structure and word order of the Latin text, as becomes clear in the first eleven lines:

Les armes je célèbre et l'homme qui le premier des Troyennes rives
en Italie, par la fatalité fugitif, est venu au Lavinien

littoral; longtemps celui-là sur les terres jeté rejeté sur le flot
de toute la violence des suprêmes dieux, tant qu'à sévir persista Junon dans sa rancune,
durement eut aussi de la guerre à souffrir, devant qu'il ne fondât la ville   5
et n'importât ses dieux dans le Latium; d'où la race Latine
et les Albains nos pères, d'où enfin de l'altière cité les murs – Rome.

Muse, les causes? Dis-moi en quoi lésée sa divinité,
pourquoi la dolente reine des dieux précipitait de chute en chute
l'homme d'insigne piété, le poussait à connaître tant de tribulations.   10
Tant y aurait-il de colère dans les célestes esprits!

There is no need to retread the ground covered by Cox in her excellent study of Klossowski's translation in *Aeneas Takes the Metro* (1999, 119–31), but we should observe the lines of uneven length, strained word order including grammatical inversions and syntactical postponements (e.g., we wait a long time for "est venu"), archaisms (e.g., the construction "devant qu'il ne fondât"), and replications of Vergilian wordplay. I am also struck by the preponderance of vocabulary replicating the Latin roots (*armes, premier, fatalité, fugitif, venu, littoral, terres, jeté, violence, suprêmes, sévir, dieux, pères, altière, causes, lésée, dolente, reine, dieux, insigne, piété,* and *célestes*) as well as the names and other Latinate vocabulary (*précipitait, esprits*). There can be no doubt that Klossowski in an act of defamiliarizing or making strange (in Shklovsky's terms) has set out to strain the French language and to reach back towards its Latin origins. Cox is surely right when she remarks that "Klossowski's determination to follow Vergil's word play on so many occasions re-alerts readers, accustomed to the lulling ease of most modern translations, to the care and precision of Vergil's verse" (Cox 1999, 127).

   In fact, he is explicit about his aims in his brief preface (1964, XI–XII). The very first thing he mentions is "l'aspect disloqué de la syntaxe" (the dislocated appearance of the syntax): "la physionomie de chaque vers" (the physiognomy of each line of verse) consists of "la juxtaposition volontaire des mots" (the intentional juxtaposition of words), which should not therefore be treated "comme un arbitraire pêle-mêle" (as an arbitrary hotch-potch). The problem is that French does not retain Latin inflection, so that in conventional translations "tout de cette instrumentation incantatoire disparaît" (all this incantatory apparatus disappears), leaving one only with "le sens rationnel du discours" (the rational meaning of the text). He concludes: "C'est pourquoi nous avons voulu, avant toute autre chose, nous astreindre à la texture de l'original; suggérer le jeu des mots virgiliens; amener le lecteur à marcher pas à pas avec le poème; l'arrêter même, pour lui faire toucher un détail; et…lui faire sentir…le tracé de l'ensemble au travers de notre échafaudage malaisé" (That's why I wanted, more than anything else, to tie myself down to the texture of the original; to evoke the Vergilian wordplay; to lead the reader to walk in step with the poem; even to make him stop to have him touch a detail; and to make him feel the outline of the whole through my uneasy scaffolding).

   The French classicists – who had had a monopoly on translating the classics – hated Klossowski's translation. For example, Jean-Paul Brisson (now Professor Emeritus Paris-X-Nanterre) in *Virgile, son temps et le nôtre* (1966, 338; I owe this reference to Cox 1999, 119) calls this translation "un véritable contre-sens qui dénature profondément le texte de Virgile" (a real misunderstanding which profoundly distorts Vergil's text). Raoul Verdière, another classicist, is similarly disparaging in the only review in a scholarly journal that I have been able to locate, published in the Italian journal *Rivista di Studi Classici* (and not in a French journal, which I find odd; incidentally, the review is very overwritten). He too finds "misunderstandings" (*les contre-sens*) in Klossowski's translation, misunderstandings inherited from following earlier translations "blindly." Although he is aware that Klossowski intended to produce a literal translation and although he judges it free of the worst criticisms that tend to be leveled at such translations, he is more concerned to assert his academic superiority: "le philologue que je suis regrette que l'auteur ait négligé de nous dire sur quel texte il a établi sa traduction" (the philologist that I am regrets that the author has omitted to inform us which text he used as the basis for his translation). Since Klossowski's translation provides neither notes nor commentary, nor any introduction situating Vergil and his epic in context – nor, even, line numbers – it is clear that the scholar is being pedantically ridiculous in requiring a textual note; that is not the nature of the beast. Verdière proceeds to comment on the opening lines, criticizing Klossowski's translations of *arma, virum,* and *cano,* then calling "Lavinien littoral" (*Lavinia…litora*) an expression "rude à une oreille française sensible à la poésie" (crude to a French ear sensitive to poetry), saved not at all by the alliteration. He signs off the review: "*Traduttore, traditore…*C'est toujours vrai" (Translator, traitor…It's always true).

But how many people saw Verdière's dismissal of Klossowski, hidden away in an Italian classical journal, in comparison with numbers who read Michel Foucault's review in *L'Express* in August 1964 (Foucault 1964)? In a paragraph that particularly irritated Verdière, Klossowski in his preface calls Vergil's epic "un théâtre où ce sont les mots qui miment les gestes et l'état d'âme des personnages" (a theatre where it is the words that imitate the gestures and state of mind of the characters). He continues: "ce sont les mots qui prennent une attitude, non pas le corps; qui se tissent, non pas les vêtements; qui scintillent, non pas les armures; qui grondent, non pas l'orage; qui menancent, non pas Junon; qui rient, non pas Cythérée; qui saignent, non pas les plaies" (it is the words that adopt an attitude, not the body; that are woven, not the garments; that sparkle, not the armor; that growl, not the storm; that threaten, not Juno; that laugh, not Cytherea; that bleed, not the wounds). This provides Michel Foucault with the striking title of his review, "Les mots qui saignent."

Foucault seems to understand and appreciate Klossowski's aims. He asserts that the natural place for a translation is on the facing page and proceeds to construct the dynamics of translation as a horizontal movement: translations "font glisser les œuvres dans le plan uniforme des langues: … elles sont latérales" (slide works of literature into the general scheme of language, making them run alongside). By contrast "Pierre Klossovski [*sic*] vient de publier de 'L'Enéide' une traduction verticale," with the Latin "tombant à pic" (landing straight on) the French, not so much "juxta- mais supra-linéaire." It's clear that he admires the boldness (*hardiesse*) of Klossowski's word-for-word procedure, which emphasizes the difference between French and Latin, not the similarity. In other words, Foucault understands the foreignizing nature of this translation.

He goes on to distinguish two kinds of translation: the smooth (though he doesn't use that word) and the violent. Violent translations "hurl [*jeter*] one language against another": "elles prennent pour projectile le texte original et traitent la langue d'arrivée comme une cible" (they take the original text as a missile and treat the receiving language as a target), with the aim of using the original language to derail (*dérouter*) the receiving language. He uses vivid vocabulary to depict the kinds of violence that can be done to the French language: *hacher* (mangle), *éclater* (burst), *déchiqueter* (slash), *déchirer* (tear up). The effect of forcing the words back into their Vergilian positions, says Foucault, is to reconnect the French language with its own history, backwards through Montaigne and Ronsard, the *Roman de la Rose* and the *Chanson de Roland*, backwards through the Renaissance and the Middle Ages to its Late Latin foundations, in a kind of renewal or recreation. As the *Aeneid* is about foundations, so Klossowski's translation is about the foundations of the French language. In other words, the collision of words – Klossowski's "choc des mots" – is a deliberate tactic to emphasize the foreignness of a text that had become comfortably assimilated.

Klossowski's project as well as Foucault's review seem to be informed by Walter Benjamin's view that the best kind of translation can achieve a fusion of the two languages that strives towards a kind of pure speech in which content is sacrificed to form – not a communication of information but a new creation of "pure language" ("The Task of the Translator," first published in German in 1923; Harry Zohn's controversial 1968 translation appears in Venuti 2000). George Steiner explains and develops this rather mystical position: "A genuine translation evokes the shadowy yet unmistakable contours of the coherent design from which, after Babel, the jagged fragments of human speech broke off. Certain of Luther's versions of the Psalms, Hölderlin's recasting of Pindar's Third Pythian Ode, point by their strangeness of evocatory inference to the reality of an *Ur-Sprache* in which German and Hebrew or German and ancient Greek are somehow fused" (Steiner 1998, 67). In Schleiermacher's terms, I suppose that this would be the same as moving both author and reader away from their comfort zones and into a third realm that is foreign to both, but rewardingly, even transportingly, rather than puzzlingly or deterringly foreign. But the question that this strategy poses, even if it can be realized, is whether that is a step too far for readers who are unfamiliar with the original, who are not comfortable in both the languages.

***

Bearing in mind the hostility generated by foreignizing translations of the *Aeneid* in Russian and French, we turn now to translations in English. The tendency in English translation in general has been heavily towards domestication, with the concomitant erasure of the translator, since the mid-seventeenth century (Venuti 1995, 43–98). In the case of the *Aeneid*, the earliest translations actually exhibit a range of inventiveness that includes Gavin Douglas' translation into Scottish verse, written in 1513 and first printed in 1553; the Earl of Surrey's innovatory blank verse, i.e., unrhymed decasyllables (books 2 and 4, 1557); Thomas Phaer and Thomas Twyne's use of rhymed fourteeners (1584); and Richard Stanyhurst's dreadful quantitative hexameters (books

1–4, 1584). The seventeenth century saw the rise of the heroic couplet and with it a premium set upon fluency and transparency, ease and naturalness, as manifested in the translation of Sir John Denham (book 2, 1656) and then, of course, Dryden's complete Vergil of 1697 (Venuti 1995, 43–65 and Eastin's chapter in this volume). It is not until the Victorian era that we find a couple of translators attempting something different: the scholar John Conington uses Walter Scott's ballad meter (1866) in a new manifestation of domestication that received praise for its simplicity, while William Morris (1876) combines the fourteener with archaizing Anglo-Saxon vocabulary to produce the most alien effect since, perhaps, Gavin Douglas. In 1905 Robert Bridges began to revive the quantitative hexameter for his translation of book 6 (Bridges 1916; see Stanford 1978, 97), but since then translators have been notably less ambitious: they "turn their back upon archaic diction, poetic inversions, and metrical experiment, setting their sights more modestly on producing something that will render the sense unpretentiously for a modern audience suspicious of the high style and unfamiliar with classic niceties" (Robin Sowerby in France 2000, 510). In other words, more domestications: Rolfe Humphries (1951); C. Day Lewis (1952); Patric Dickinson (1961); Allen Mandelbaum (1971) and Robert Fitzgerald (1983); Edward McCrorie (1995). This tendency continues into the twenty-first century, in the translations by Stanley Lombardo (2005) and Robert Fagles (2006), the latter being explicit about trying "to find the middle ground (and not a no-man's-land, if I can help it) between the features of an ancient author and the expectations of a contemporary reader" (Fagles 2006, 390). The most recent translator, Frederick Ahl (2007), has a different creed.

In the very first paragraph of his "Translator's Note" (xlvi–lii), Ahl acknowledges the difficulty of translating the *Aeneid* into English and writes: "To translate it accurately, therefore, one must in some ways defamiliarize it, and thereby run the risk of outraging one's readers." There is no explicit mention of Russian formalist concepts, but Ahl's use of the word "defamiliarize" suggests his sympathies at least. His main diagnosis of the problem rings true: the fact that English "is so saturated with the Christian thought into which it was born that it is a poor vehicle for the pre-Christian philosophies of the *Aeneid*"; he might have said "pre-Christian ideology" or "pre-Christian world." His effort to find a mode that avoids triggering inappropriate associations determines his strategies in a number of areas.

He tells us that his choice in terms of diction and idiom is for the "informal" and "often colloquial," "as direct and Anglo-Saxon as possible," avoiding archaisms and only occasionally intensifying or borrowing words from beyond regular English. While Ahl's labels "informal" and "often colloquial" do not seem appropriate for Vergil's epic diction, and in fact often do not correspond to his practice, his preference for Anglo-Saxon roots over Latinate vocabulary is certainly commendable; Vergil's Latin, after all, was not full of Greek vocabulary but more redolent of the Latinity of Ennius and Lucretius. Uniquely among recent translators (although he does not comment on this) he retains the same number of lines as the Latin, which makes this translation exceptionally useful in the classroom, of course. Another area where he takes a similar stand – this time avowedly – is in using the same English word for certain important Latin words throughout his translation. The main instances are *felix, infelix,* and *pius/pietas,* which he renders as "fulfilled," "unfulfilled," and "righteous/righteousness" respectively. This consistency is to be applauded – it conveys the prominence of these leitmotifs – even if "righteousness" introduces distracting Christian concepts to *pietas.* Dryden astutely spotlights the difficulties in translating *pietas* accurately: "the word in Latin is more full than it can possibly be expressed in any modern language; for there it comprehends not only devotion to the gods, but filial love, and tender affection of all sorts" (Dryden 1975, xx; Harrison 1969). Ahl rightly draws attention to the way that the wider vocabulary of English tempts translators to draw distinctions that are not present in the Latin. He cites a telling example, namely the word *superbus,* which is often rendered "haughty" or "proud" depending upon whether the context is felt to be negative or positive; he makes an unassailable case for consistently translating *superbus* as "proud," "since pride can be virtue or vice in English."

There are two features of Ahl's translation that I predict will provoke controversy. One is his decision to write in meter, instead of the "free verse" characteristic of other recent translations, which is generally barely distinguishable from prose printed in short lines. Ahl uses a version of the hexameter, with the stress on the first syllable of each foot, which generates an interplay between dactyls and spondees reminiscent of the Latin. The other is his deliberate reproduction of Vergil's elaborate patterns of wordplay, including anagrams. This should come as no great surprise to anyone aware of Ahl's earlier work, above all his 1985 book *Metaformations* on soundplay and wordplay in Ovid. I shall confess that much of that book was a stretch for me, but my skepticism is in retreat now that I see Ahl's sensibilities devoted to translation. The example he cites in his "Translator's Note" is the incomplete line at *Aen.* 7.702, *pulsa palus,* which he unapologetically translates as "Loops in its pools": "The poet is describing the ripples in the surface of a lake (*palus*) caused by the sound of the cries of swans striking (*pulsa*) its surface. The impact of the sound destabilizes and rearranges the elements of the word *palus* itself, not just of the lake the word indicates." Ahl's approach is essentially like that of Klossowski when he asserts that it is the words themselves that mime the actions described in the text. Some will see this an overreading; yet there can be no doubt that Klossowksi and Ahl both succeed in drawing to the reader's attention special effects in Vergil's Latin. It is in such features that Ahl departs from his claim to "informal" English which is "as direct…as possible." Our study of the foreignizing translations in Russian and French along with the prefatory material by Briusov, Klossowski, and Ahl himself is good preparation for appreciating the first foreignizing translation in English for a long while.

> Arms and the man I sing of Troy, who first from its seashores,
> Italy-bound, fate's refugee, arrived at Lavinia's
> Coastlands. How he was battered about over land, over high deep
> Seas by the powers above! Savage Juno's anger remembered
> Him, and he suffered profoundly in war to establish a city,   5
> Settle his gods into Latium, making this land of the Latins
> Future home to the Elders of Alba and Rome's mighty ramparts.

Muse, let the memories spill through me. What divine will was wounded,
What deep hurt made the queen of the gods thrust a famously righteous
Man into so many spirals of chance to face so many labours?   10
Anger so great: can it really reside in the spirits of heaven?

The dislocations of conventional English word order abound, and yet this is still English, strained English in places, to be sure, such as the first line where Ahl deletes the comma traditionally printed after *cano* to make *Troiae* refer back to "arms and the man" as well as forwards to "seashores," but English nonetheless, and English that can be read aloud without difficulty. He has managed to replicate the Latin word order astonishingly closely, especially given the gulf between the inflected original and uninflected receiving language: he gives due prominence to *Italiam* with "Italy-bound," he renders the phrase *fato profugus* closely with "fate's refugee," and he reflects the significant echo of *Latio* in *Latinum* with his "Latium...Latins." He is sensitive to other effects in the Latin too. For example, he captures the repetition of *et...et* in "over...over," the echo of *memorem* ("remembered") in *memora* ("memories"), and the repetition *tot...tot* in "so many...so many." He makes Juno's anger the agent of remembering (*memorem... iram*), although in line 7, he neglects the agreement of *altae* with *Romae*. (He could have written "mighty Rome's ramparts," which would have had the added bonus of moving "Rome" closer to the end of the line, but at the cost of taking the metrical stress away from "Rome's," a sacrifice I assume he was unwilling to make.) Less serious is his moving "anger" to the front of line 11: unable to save it for the final word, the initial position is some compensation. His "spirals of chance" seems to me felicitous for the helplessness evoked by *volvere casus*, while he turns the problem posed by the ellipse of *sunt* in line 11 to advantage by using the alliteration of "really reside" to echo the assonance of *tantaene animis caelestibus*, likewise in the middle of the line. Particularly praiseworthy is his language for the divine apparatus: "powers above" accurately captures *superum* and "spirits of heaven" *animis caelestibus*, without importing any unnecessary baggage. And so he continues. Ahl seems to me to achieve his aim of defamiliarizing a text that has perhaps been too easily annexed into English literature, not least through the triumph represented by Dryden's version. In Ahl's own words, "I did not want to smooth out these differences" – nor does he.

Many of the features I have commented on here are features with parallels in the foreignizing Russian and French translations studied above. Yet it seems to me that Ahl's English is more readable than Briusov's Russian or Klossowski's French. Though to many, Ahl's translation will seem excessively foreignizing – and he, after all, anticipates a reaction of "outrage" – for me, the question remains as to whether Ahl's translation is actually foreignizing enough. On that, I expect the jury to be out for quite a while.

ACKNOWLEDGMENTS

A project like this cannot (and should not) be undertaken without help from experts in the fields into which I am now wandering. My warm thanks, therefore, to Fiona Cox, Valeriya Kozlovskaya, Ilya Kutik, Adam Morton, Barry Scherr, Carlo Testa, and Zara Martirosova

Torlone. I am also very grateful to audiences at UC Riverside, the University of Alberta, Stanford University, UBC, and Cumae at the 2006 Vergil Society conference, to members of my graduate seminars at Yale, Stanford, and UBC, and to Susan Atkey and other staff in the Koerner Library at UBC.

FURTHER READING

On English translations of Vergil see above all Burrow (1997b); Gransden (1996); and the entry "Virgil" by Robin Sowerby in France (2000, 507–12). Other studies include Conington (1872); Harrison (1967); Williams and Pattie (1982); Hill (1990); and Braund (2004).

On Vergil in French see Cox (1999). Chlodowski (1984–91) provides a starting place for Vergil in Russian.

On foreignizing in translation, a concept with a pedigree stretching back through Antoine Berman and Walter Benjamin to Friedrich Schleiermacher, see Venuti (1995, 108–12). Antoine Berman has a fascinating analysis of the ways in which the original can be deformed in translation that, even though his focus is the novel, has relevance for poetry too; see his 1985 essay "La traduction comme épreuve de l'étranger," translated by Venuti as "Translation and the Trials of the Foreign," in Venuti (2000, 284–97).

CHAPTER THIRTY TWO

Vergil's *Aeneid* and Contemporary Poetry

Karl Kirchwey

Introduction

The *Aeneid* feels much closer to our modern (or postmodern) sensibility than do Homer's epics. American poet Mark Strand remarks in an essay entitled "Some Observations on *Aeneid* Book VI" that "Epic does not allow much time for reflection" (2001, 66). Yet the stark and timeless fatalism of the *Iliad* and the *Odyssey*, which is part of what tends to make the heroes of these poems seem two-dimensional, gives way in Vergil's epic to a distinctive human vulnerability and self-consciousness, and to a tragic tension between heroic or epic vision and the limitations, not only of mortality, but also of human psychology and emotion. All the most famous tags from the poem confirm this: "A joy it will be, one day, perhaps, to remember even this" (1.239), says Aeneas to his men, in Robert Fagles' translation (2006); or, upon seeing himself depicted on the walls of Carthage, "Even here, the world is a world of tears / and the burdens of mortality touch the heart" (1.558–9, Fagles).When, near the end of the poem, Aeneas says to Ascanius-Iulus, "Learn courage from me, my son, true hardship too. / Learn good luck from others" (12.513–14, Fagles), there is audible a kind of resignation that goes beyond mere Odyssean endurance.

Vergil's poem includes, too, such a wealth of striking narrative incident that it ought to be irresistible to the contemporary imagination. To start with, there is the satisfaction of the full story of Troy's last hours, not provided by Homer, elaborated by Vergil in its horror (the fate of Laocoon and his sons) and its pathos (Aeneas' loss of Creusa in the city's dark streets). Indeed, the contemporary reader is bound to identify strongly with Vergil's account precisely because it is "belated": just as the Trojans, wherever they land, will have to inhabit, and thereby alter, a landscape already marked and crowded, both by indigenous tribes and by earlier Greek and Trojan settlement, so Vergil's story must, rather in the sense T.S. Eliot describes in his essay "Tradition and the Individual Talent," shoulder aside the existing Homeric narratives, exploit their interstices, and create a place for itself in the landscape of literature and posterity.

As Theodore Ziolkowski reminds us in his book *Virgil and the Moderns* (1993, 131), using the language of C.S. Lewis' *A Preface to Paradise* Lost (1942) that will provide the title of a later poem of Auden's, Vergil's poem is a "secondary epic." Aeneas, after all, even meets one of Odysseus' band, the survivor Achaemenides, in book 3, left behind in the Cyclops' cave. The past is unavoidable, to Aeneas, as it is to us moderns. The test of the heroic character lies not, as it does in Homer, in reflexive action, but in the extent to which the hero can live down the losses of the past in order to gain a future. Ziolkowski (1993, 131) further quotes C.M. Bowra's 1945 *From Virgil to Milton* that a literary epic like the *Aeneid* "flourishes not in the heyday of a nation or of a cause but in its last days or in its aftermath" (28). The tragic consciousness we feel in Aeneas, by this line of reasoning, derives from the age in which the poem itself was composed, and presumably requires us to see Augustan Rome as a falling-off from the days of the Republic.

Among the modernist pioneers, Ezra Pound, in his 1928 essay "How To Read" (see Pound 1954), provides a different perspective on the notion of "secondary epic." He distinguishes between "the inventors," "the masters," and "the diluters," in literature, and while admitting that they were "prolific," he places Vergil firmly in the third group (23–4), going so far as to declare, "I am chucking out Pindar, and Virgil, without the slightest compunction (28; for more on Pound and Vergil see the chapter by Farrell in this volume). Such a response may seem paradoxical, coming as it does from the author of the most bookish and hermetic of all modern epic poems, the *Cantos*. But it may also have set the tone for a general neglect of Vergil's *Aeneid* by poets coming after Pound. Eliot had more use for Vergil than did Pound, and while acknowledging, in his 1951 essay "Virgil and the Christian World," that the poet "made of Roman civilization in his poetry something better than it really was" (139–40), he found that Aeneas was "heroic as the original Displaced Person," a "foreshadow of Christian humility" (143). In this Eliot extends, presumably for his own Anglo-Catholic reasons, the famous proto-Christian reading (or misreading) of a passage in Vergil's fourth eclogue.

Incidents of great narrative and evocative power in Vergil's poem have not been explored by contemporary poets in their own work. Polydorus, the betrayed fugitive and son of Priam, buried under a bleeding grove of dogwood and myrtle spears, or the appalling and ambiguous prophecy of the Harpy Celaeno that the Trojans will be driven by hunger to gnaw their own platters (book 3; explained in book 7); the ship-burning insurrection staged by the weary Trojan women in book 5 at the instigation of Juno, or the irresistible sleep of Palinurus; the splendors and hope of the embassy to Latinus in book 7, to be undermined by the Fury Allecto possessing Lavinia's mother, and the sheer terror of Allecto's assault on Turnus; the impious anti-hero Mezentius; the graceful but conclusive transformation of Aeneas' last ships into dolphins by the Great Mother (in book 9), and the address by one of these, Cymodocea, to Aeneas in book 10; the nominally hybrid water-nymph Juturna, loyal to both her brother Turnus and to Juno; the treacherous rupture of the truce, in book 12, and the brilliant brief appearance of Camilla, an Amazon launched (as a baby) in a sleeve of bark, riding the cast of her father's own spear: all of these stories linger in memory as powerfully as any of Homer's, and invite contemporary poets to inhabit them for a while.

But indeed it seems that Homer, unlike Vergil, is never far from the imagination of contemporary poets. Whether in lyric, narrative, or dramatic form, poetic reimaginings of the Homeric myths are abundant. Perhaps the gaudiness of the slaughter (in the *Iliad*) and of Odysseus' pelagic detours (in the *Odyssey*) appeal to our visual culture, so accustomed to action movies and their violent changes. For when it comes to the Romans, it seems that it is Ovid, master of those "stories of changing forms," rather than Vergil, who has inspired the greatest contemporary poetic response. For all that we may feel, in the *Aeneid*, a vulnerability, a self-consciousness, and a sense of coming *after*, Rowena Fowler in her essay "'Purple Shining Lilies': Imagining the *Aeneid* in Contemporary Poetry" quotes Ziolkowski to the effect that "We do not live in Vergilian times" (2009, 3). Fowler suggests that the Ovidian taste for "shape-shifting, performance and disguise" (3) has been more congenial to our taste. As if both to confirm this and exemplify Ovidian technique, poets James Lasdun and Michael Hofmann gathered some forty contemporary poets' responses to different Ovidian myths in their *After Ovid: New Metamorphoses* (1994). These responses range from faithful translations to complete reimaginings.

Contemporary poets' original responses to the *Aeneid*, however, have been scattered and occasional, and certainly have not been assembled in an anthology. The only many-hands version of Vergil is the Penguin Classics volume *Virgil in English* (Gransden 1996), and this contains mostly translations, arranged in chronological order, by authors ranging from Chaucer to Seamus Heaney (whose Aeneas, in a translation of the search for the golden bough in book 6, sounds very much like Eliot's Tiresias when he says to the Cumaean Sibyl, "already I have foreseen and foresuffered all"). In her essay, Fowler discusses individual poems by mostly Anglo-Irish poets including Fleur Adcock, Eavan Boland, Medbh McGuckian, U.A. Fanthorpe, and Stevie Smith, as well as by Americans Rachel Hadas and Louise Glück. Fowler's discussion (15–18) of metaphors of flight and exile in the *Aeneid* as they apply in particular to contemporary poets' movement within Ireland (Seamus Heaney) or away from it (Paul Muldoon) is particularly helpful.

Overall, Fowler suggests that contemporary poetic taste may now be moving toward a greater appreciation of the *Aeneid*: "where the late twentieth century was often prejudiced against the unitary, preferring hybridity and collage, poems 'after Vergil' tend in the opposite direction: towards a kind of alert integration…attentive, reciprocal and, ultimately, conciliatory" (3). In his 1959 poem "Heroes," American poet Robert Creeley quotes the tag *hoc opus, hic labor est*, remarking "That was the Cumaean Sibyl speaking. / This is Robert Creeley, and Virgil / is dead now two thousand years," but in what is indeed a gesture of conciliation, concludes, "death also / can still propose the old labors." American poet Carl Phillips, himself a trained classicist, speaks at the end of a 2001 poem entitled "Roman Glass" of a "grand history that is / finally holy, there being always a holiness attached to that / which is absolute – even / should the subject prove, the entire time, to have been loss." And the attentiveness of which Fowler speaks is shown by American poet Frank Bidart, whose own work constitutes a kind of accumulating psychological epic, and who so positions his translation of the opening of Vergil's poem in his first book *Golden State* (1973) that Juno's unfathomable rage corresponds to the psychological trauma between child and unappeasable parent: "Muse, make me mindful of the causes, load upon me / knowledge of her sorrows."

One aspect of Vergil's epic that should make it resonate most strongly for contemporary readers and writers has perhaps, simultaneously, made them leery of it, and that is the poem's blending of mythic and historical time. The Homeric myths, despite modern advances in archaeology, anthropology, and history, continue to exist somehow *out of time*, but Vergil's explicit linking of the mythical material in his poem with the ascendancy of Rome under Augustus forces modern readers to consider myth *as* history, with all of the troubling imperial consequences this involves.

Ziolkowski (1993, 99–101) describes Robert Graves' 1962 "indictment of Vergil as a government toady" in response to T.S. Eliot's 1951 essay, and chronicles the "ambivalence" in attitude toward Vergil's epic wrought by the British experience of World War I. Graves' philippic is both learned and highly entertaining. He suggests that Vergil appeals to those living in "a golden age of stable government, full churches, and expanding wealth" (13) and identifies himself as having been once, like Eliot, "a young Romano-British imperialist," invited to subscribe to a vision of Rome as bound to "rule the world, to crush rival powers, and to impose a magnanimous peace upon the survivors" (14). The historical reality of Augustus' imperial program cannot but have distanced Vergil's poem from certain contemporary poets (Joseph Brodsky comes to mind, but also Czeslaw Milosz and Zbigniew Herbert) who have felt firsthand the tyranny of the state.

Modernism, as we have seen, presents a hung jury, when it comes to Vergil: Pound against, Eliot for. But in the work of seven poets from the past sixty years, all of them in relations of varying propinquity with modernism, the *Aeneid* has provided an invaluable touchstone by which to contemplate, not only the human relationship to time and its passage, but also the limitations of poetic vision itself. These responses have tended to focus on only three of the narrative moments in Vergil's poem: the romance between Dido and Aeneas; Aeneas in the underworld; and Aeneas' slaughter of Turnus. Critic Willard Spiegelman points out in his "Unforced Marches: A Virgilian Memoir" (2006) that the story of the two lovers clearly establishes "the struggle between passion and duty, pleasure and obligation, love and war" – something else which is not evident in Homer's warriors. Taken together, these responses do indeed suggest a growing willingness to put aside the *Aeneid*'s perceived limitations as propaganda or "secondary epic," and consider instead its depth of humanity. And they may achieve the "alert integration" to which Fowler refers by means of reconceiving Vergil's epic, as to its genre, considering it less as a narrative poem than as a series of fused lyrics.

Robert Lowell

Robert Lowell's poem "Falling Asleep Over the Aeneid," included in his 1951 volume *The Mills of the Kavanaughs*, is probably the single most powerful poetic meditation on Vergil's epic to have appeared in the last half-century. It is a dramatic monologue spoken by an old man, a New England Congregationalist in Concord, Massachusetts, who falls asleep at home one Sunday morning while rereading the *Aeneid* and misses church. Lowell thereby not only juxtaposes paganism and Christianity, but in narrative terms also exploits the imaginative possibilities of a sensibility dislocated or rearranged by the free association of dream. The poem is characterized throughout by a kind of barbaric splendor of detail to which the yellow buntings or yellow-shafted flickers singing in the old man's garden provide an overture: "The sun is blue and scarlet on my page, / And *yuck-a, yuck-a, yuck-a, yuck-a,* rage / The yellowhammers mating. Yellow fire / Blankets the captives dancing on their pyre" (1–4).

The modesty and obscurity of the old man's life are revised into the stuff of heroic legend as he imagines that he is Aeneas himself, speaking at the funeral of the Italian prince Pallas (in *Aeneid* 11). And the poem is not unaware of charismatic leaders after Aeneas, say in the twentieth century, as when the speaker declares, "I stand up and heil the thousand men." In a brilliant essay entitled "Robert Lowell's American Aeneas," scholar W.R. Johnson makes clear (2004, 230) the extent to which Lowell's choice of this episode in Vergil's poem – because of the Trojans' slaughter of captives it is a morally problematic episode, like the abandonment of Dido or the killing of Turnus – is perfectly appropriate to Lowell's own contradictory admiration of strong men and just wars, on the one hand, and his anti-militarism, on the other.

Readers of Lowell's *Imitations* (1961) will know that he is less interested in strict translation than he is in what he perceives as the *spirit* of the original, and part of the delight of this poem lies in Lowell's interweaving of details present in Vergil with inventions and interpolations of his own that successfully make the world of Aeneas alien and strange once again. Thus the dead Pallas' "face of snow," the "pall / stiff with its gold and purple" that Aeneas was given by Dido and gives, in turn, to Pallas, or the weeping horse Aethon: these details are in Vergil. But when Lowell speaks of the "gagged Italians, who must file by ones / Across the bitter river, when my thumb / Tightens into their wind-pipes," we recognize that, by having Aeneas personally strangle the prisoners, Lowell is heightening the moral ambiguity of the moment.

In a way that would please any trained psychologist, the old man's dream arises from details of the real world around him, including a bust of Augustus on the study shelf where the volumes of Vergil are kept, and the saber belonging to Lowell's cousin Charles Russell Lowell, who was killed in the Civil War. The old man exclaims, "My Uncle Charles appears. / Blue-capped and bird-like," and the uncle is thereby identified with the bird-priests of the Etruscans, just as Aeneas' war is made identical with the War Between the States. There are entirely surreal moments, too, as when Lowell's Aeneas declares, "I hold / The sword that Dido used. It tries to speak, / A bird with Dido's sworded breast. Its beak / Clangs and ejaculates the Punic word" (14–18), or when "Their headman's cow-horned death's-head bites its tongue, / And stiffens, as it eyes the hero slung / Inside his feathered hammock" (47–9). The verbal energy of such moments may not entirely excuse their narrative incoherence, however.

The Calvinist and Puritan certainty of predestination, the exaltation of the mid-nineteenth-century Great Revival, the fratricidal intensity of convictions during the Civil War: these qualities do not, in fact, seem foreign to the triumphalism inherent in the political program of Vergil's poem. But Dido's sword seems to ask, as if on behalf of both Aeneas and Lowell's old man, a question – "Who am I, and why?" – and then to answer its own question, in Pallas' voice, with a bleakness worthy of the Etruscan death-god Charun or the withered Cumaean Sibyl herself: "Brother, try, / O child of

Aphrodite, try to die: / To die is life." Lowell's Aeneas is aware of his mortal insignificance: "Our cost / is nothing to the lovers, whoring Mars / And Venus, father's lover." But also, mindful of what Anchises has told him about the future (book 6) and of what he has seen prefigured on the shield (book 8), Lowell's Aeneas can see beyond death into a historical future, that of Hannibal's march on Rome (218–211 BCE), which lies between him and the old man who is channeling his voice, as when he says of Ares,

> At the end of time
> He sets his spear, as my descendants climb
> The knees of Father Time, his beard of scalps,
> His scythe, the arc of steel that crowns the Alps.
> The elephants of Carthage hold those snows,
> Turms of Numidian horse unsling their bows,
> The flaming turkey-feathered arrows swarm
> Beyond the Alps... (61–8)

It was presumably the Native American tribes of Massachusetts who fletched their arrows with turkey feathers. And that phrase "beyond the Alps" will provide the title for the first poem in Lowell's ground-breaking volume *Life Studies* (1959), a poem connecting the cisalpine and the transalpine, the Old World and the New, by means of the "arc of steel" of a rail journey across the Alps. Or rather, *Life Studies* will be the volume in which Lowell yields up the mandarin Eurocentrism and stern Catholicism of his brilliant youth and turns to a more demotic and American subject matter. In "Falling Asleep Over the Aeneid" we might say that Lowell balances Pound's charges that Vergil is a "diluter," and Graves' subsequent formulation that he is an Augustan apologist, against Vergil's unique fusion of myth, religion, and history. But the balance between vision and mortality in Lowell's poem is troubled, and troubling.

The old man's dream ends when the Concord church service does – he is, as Keats would say, tolled back to his sole self by the church's bell, an auditory prompt like that of the yellowhammers' racket that led him into the dream in the first place – except that the yellowhammers now appear to be "stuffed" and "breathless," part of the furniture of his study. The old man's great-aunt is remembered declaring to him when he was a child reading Vergil on a Sunday morning eighty years before, "Boy, it's late / Vergil must keep the Sabbath." But Vergil *has*, precisely, kept the Sabbath. The tumult of the ancient epic poem has insinuated itself, momentarily but completely, into the life of a near-modern. Vergil's poem has asserted its ambiguous power, beyond the hermetic closure and infinite narcissism of all great art suggested by the last image of Lowell's poem, in which the old man's eyeglasses (but are they on his head or on the desk beside him?) mirror the scowling bust of Augustus. Having awoken, Lowell's old man feels a vertigo by which he is, briefly, identical with a hero (Aeneas) and a poet (Vergil) and an emperor (Augustus) who seemed to conquer time itself. Yet he is as "breathless" with his own mortality as are the stuffed birds, and the sword of his uncle's military valor becomes the cane by which he props himself up.

Allen Tate

"Falling Asleep Over the Aeneid" incidentally raises questions about destiny and two empires, one old (Rome) and one new (America). In several poems of the 1930s, Lowell's friend Allen Tate had explored this matter of parallel destinies. As Levi Robert Lind says in his essay "Aeneas Among the Poets," "The reader's eye is directed backward to the Vergilian story and forward to the American reality" (1980, 122). Furthermore, in his book *Allen Tate and the Augustinian Imagination*, Robert S. Dupree quotes an essay by Louise Cowan, "The *Pietas* of Southern Poetry," to the effect that the Southern writer can "find in *The Aeneid* a correlative for the Southern situation. Just as Aeneas and his men thought of themselves as Trojans all the more as they were forced to leave their burning homes, so the Southerners identified themselves in the instance of defeat" (1983, 137). Thus Tate not only parallels two empires, but finds a specific analogy of defeat between Troy and the American South in the wake of the Civil War.

Tate's poem "The Mediterranean" (1933) has as its epigraph the line from *Aeneid* 1 in which Venus pleads with Jove for her son, and asks, *Quem das finem, rex magne, laborum?* Fagles translates it "What end, great king, do you set to their ordeals?" (1.286). Tate, however, substitutes *dolorum* (pain) for *laborum* (labor). In her essay "Allen Tate's Use of Classical Literature," Lillian Feder (1972, 175) suggests that this substitution is accounted for by modern man's lack of a "heroic goal" that justifies labor, leaving instead only pain. Dupree (1983, 141) sees this as an imbalance between man's appetite and the suffering that should limit it and create a "proper sense of place," and Lind (1980, 122) reminds us of T.S. Eliot's imperative that the poet must have a "historical sense…a perception, not only of the pastness of the past, but of its presence" in order to understand his own "contemporaneity."

Dupree (1983, 139) confirms (from Tate) the autobiographical source of "The Mediterranean" as placing an American at a picnic in some Vergilian setting on the Mediterranean coast. The poem is spoken by one of Aeneas' "followers" (in chronological time), an American who is aware of the mythic dimension of Aeneas' original journey, declaring that "we went there out of time's monotone." The Mediterranean is already played out, for Tate's post-Reconstruction Southern speaker: "What prophecy of eaten plates could landless / Wanderers fulfill by the ancient sea?" (19–20). Tate's language is full of the paradox by which mythic exploits become old news, by which bravery and adventure lose the belief that first galvanizes them: "We for that time might taste the famous age / Eternal here yet hidden from our eyes / When lust of power undid its stuffless rage; / They, in a wineskin, bore earth's paradise" (21–4). Is the mythic time a simpler time, when earth's paradise can be contained in a wineskin? Aeneas' rage is "stuffless" because he is without the possessions of ruined Troy; such stufflessness is "undone" by the "lust of power" that characterized Rome's history, an age "eternal" in the marks it has left on story and landscape, yet hidden from the eyes of a later inhabitant without Aeneas' belief in the destiny the gods have outlined for him.

We might, in fact, call it *manifest* destiny, and the last two quatrains suggest that the human urge to explore and subdue must (but cannot) renew itself in subsequent ages: "What country shall we conquer, what fair land / Unman our conquest and locate our blood? / We've cracked the hemispheres with careless hand!" (29–31). Surely the carelessness of that hand is suggestive of American optimism and naïveté, and the poem's concluding movement is past Gibraltar and towards the New World: "Westward, westward, till the barbarous brine / Whelms us to the tired land where tasseling corn, / Fat beans, grapes sweeter than muscadine / Rot on the vine: in that land were we born" (33–6).

The sea, at least, retains its wild original restlessness, and is "barbarous"; but the weariness of Rome's decline and fall seems already to have infected the "tired" land of the New World and its inhabitants, so enervated they lack the strength to pick the American foods – corn, beans, Concord grapes – that should make the land the Eden any settler would seek. Indeed, the spiritual malaise suggested by the end of Tate's poem is not unlike the spooky quiet of a landscape in the grip of religious hysteria that Lowell will describe in his poem "After the Surprising Conversions," included in his first book *Lord Weary's Castle* (1946): "Sir, the bough / Cracks with the unpicked apples, and at dawn / The small-mouth bass breaks water, gorged with spawn." When Tate's speaker refers to "The green coast that you, thunder-tossed, would win" (14), one is reminded of the Dutch settler at the end of *The Great Gatsby* contemplating the green breast of the New World and "compelled into an aesthetic contemplation he neither understood nor desired."

During the same period Tate wrote what appears to be a matched set of poems, "Aeneas at Washington" and "Aeneas at New York." In the first of these, Aeneas speaks: as Dupree points out (1983, 143), the American in a Vergilian setting becomes Aeneas in an American setting, and as Lind observes (1980, 125–6), Aeneas is here a Confederate officer. Tate's Aeneas initially seems a passionless hero: "I bore me well, / A true gentleman, valorous in arms, / Disinterested and honourable" (5–7). Or perhaps Tate's Aeneas is being ironic. When he says of the fall of Troy, "That was a time when civilization / Run by the few fell to the many" (8–9), he is of course describing the evolution from oligarchy to representative democracy. Once again we hear the paradox of a mythic hero speaking, as it were, in historical time, as Aeneas itemizes what he was able to save from Troy: "a mind imperishable / If time is, a love of past things tenuous / As the hesitation of receding love" (14–16). But even that "receding love" is not without emotional power if we recall Creusa, left somewhere on the eastward horizon, below the stern of Aeneas' fleeing ships.

There follows a stanza of parenthesis that seems to read equally well whether spoken by the proto-imperial Roman, as Tate imagines him, or the shrewd American Tate might claim as his own forebear: "(To the reduction of uncitied littorals / We brought chiefly the vigor of prophecy, / Our hunger breeding calculation / And fixed triumphs)" (17–20). Prophecy – whether a confection of Venus and Jove or a thing called Manifest Destiny – seems suspect in its vigor. Hunger is a "lust of power" that works, by calculation, to achieve rigged results; these may or may not allay the "stuffless rage" that prompted the quest for them. In Tate's poem the "glowing fields of Troy" lie directly adjacent to the "thickening Blue Grass" of Kentucky, and there is only one heroic purpose, self-consuming in its anomie: "Now I demand little. The singular passion / Abides its object and consumes desire / In the circling shadow of its appetite" (27–9). Tate's Aeneas concludes his monologue knee-deep, not "in the salt marsh, heaving a cutlass" like Eliot's Gerontion, but in the reclaimed swamps of the District of Columbia, and there is despair in his voice: "Four thousand leagues from the ninth buried city / I thought of Troy, what we had built her for" (38–9). Tate therefore exploits and extends, for his own historical purposes, the tension in Vergil between heroic or epic vision and individual human feeling and mortality.

Eavan Boland

Robert Lowell speaks for Aeneas through an old man in Concord, Massachusetts, "birthplace of American patriotism and literature" (Lind 1980, 128). Allen Tate speaks for Aeneas by means of an American translated to a Mediterranean shore, or a Roman translated to the shores of the Potomac. It is contemporary Irish poet Eavan Boland, however, who entirely reimagines Aeneas' descent into the underworld so as to investigate both the power of language itself (as against experience and mutability) and the extent to which figurative language, in particular, is limited by the expectations of gender.

Boland's poem "The Journey" appeared, with a following "Envoi," as the second section of her 1987 book *The Journey and Other Poems*. It is useful to begin with the "Envoi" in order to understand Boland's perceptions of gender as they relate to writing. The second stanza reads, in a kind of challenge to the self: "My muse must be better than those of men / who made theirs in the image of their myth. / The work is half-finished and I have nothing / but the crudest measures to complete it with" (5–8). Presumably her discontent is with the male poet's female muse, a fantasy muse of idealized beauty. As in the work of Adrienne Rich, we are acutely aware of the isolation of the woman poet who would find a new way of seeing, and using, language itself: "What I have done I have done alone. / What I have seen is unverified. / I have the truth and I need the faith. / It is time I put my hand in her side" (25–8).

The Christ-figure into whose side this Doubting Thomas will put her hand (or does Eve put her hand into the side of the female Adam from which she sprang?) is in fact the poet Sappho. The narrative premise of Boland's poem "The Journey," akin to Lowell's, is that a woman writer, the speaker of the poem, falls asleep surrounded by her books (including a volume of Sappho's poems) and the domestic chaos of a household with small children in it. While asleep, or in a trance of poetic vision, she is accompanied to the underworld by Sappho. "The Journey" begins with an epigraph from *Aeneid* 6, the description of the wailing infant souls in the underworld: "the dark day had stolen them from their mothers' breasts and plunged them to a death before their time." It is perhaps the predictability of the pathos – that of the separation of mother and child by death – that makes the speaker of Boland's poem declare: " 'there has never / ...been a poem to an antibiotic: / never a word to compare with the odes on / the flower of the raw sloe for fever' " (1–4). A pragmatic and unmetaphorized poetry would address the antibiotic that might have kept the child out of the underworld in the first place: "'Depend on it, somewhere a poet is wasting / his sweet uncluttered metres on the obvious / emblem'" (7–9).

The male poet, it seems, is in love with metaphor. The problem here, though, is that for all that Boland's speaker, with a sharpness of eye worthy of Marianne Moore, is able to turn realistic details ("'the devious African-seeking tern / or the protein treasures of the sea-bed,'" 5–6) into poetry even someone who dislikes poetry would like, her metaphorical language is no less gorgeous and seductive: "'Instead of sulpha we shall have hyssop dipped / in the wild blood of the unblemished lamb'" (10–11). Thus the speaker's claim that "'every day the language gets less / for the task and we are less with the language'" (12–13) is indeed undercut by the power of her own poetic language. She wants to be anti-metaphorical, but cannot be.

After this outburst, Boland's speaker falls into her trance, still "listening out" (23), or outwardly aware; she is "ready to believe and still / unfevered" (26–7), or in a qualified state of myth-making. At this point she is met by Sappho, the "scholiast's nightingale" (40), and they make their descent, seeing immediately "women and children / and, in the way they were, the grace of love" (47–8). Mothers and children are together, it seems, not separated by death, though Sappho is clinical rather than metaphorical in explaining how they came to be there: "'Cholera, typhus, croup, diphtheria / …in those days racketed / in every backstreet and alley of old Europe'" (49–51). And Boland's speaker realizes that these "suckling darknesses" (55) after all make familiar "terrible pietàs" (40).

Interestingly, it is at this point that Sappho cautions Boland's woman poet, "'be careful. / Do not define these women by their work: / not as washerwomen trussed in dust and sweating… / nor as court ladies brailled in silk'" (57–9, 61). For all of their enslavement in female roles, "'these are women who went out like you / when dusk became a dark sweet with leaves, / recovering the day'" (65–7). Even without emblem or metaphor, there is a lyricism to life itself that Sappho will not have Boland's speaker discount: "'they too like you / stood boot deep in flowers once in summer / or saw winter come in with a single magpie / in a caul of haws'" (69–72). Boland's speaker begs to be these women's "witness," but is further cautioned by Sappho that her only capability will be that of memory, because the vision she has been given "'is beyond speech, / beyond song, only not beyond love'" (79–80). To this extent, Boland's poem moves beyond being any routine discourse on language and gender, and instead beautifully explores the ineffability of life itself.

The two women effect their Dantesque return to the upper world as Boland writes: "we emerged under the stars of heaven" (83). The Dantesque echo must be deliberate; in fact Fowler points out that often in contemporary poetry "Vergil is partly mediated via Dante" (7). And we might add that Dante provides a common ground between Pound and Eliot, in their divergent appraisals of Vergil. The lesson Sappho wishes to impart to her human interlocutor is that of "'the silences in which are our beginnings'" (87). Boland's speaker wakes and weeps as the Irish rain falls beyond her window and, in a domestic close not uncommon in Boland's poetry, her children continue to sleep safely. The action of one part of Vergil's narrative thus provides an armature on which Boland is able to build an original poem that questions several terms of that original narrative.

W.H. Auden

One of the fascinations of the *Aeneid* is that in it Vergil manages to make a seamless join between mythical and historical time. Yet in his poem "Secondary Epic" (1959), W.H. Auden takes Vergil to task for pretending to prophesy (of the period between Aeneas and Augustus, foretold by Anchises in the underworld, in book 6, and figured forth on Aeneas' shield, in book 8) without getting beyond prolepsis: for not exercising both his courage and his moral imagination by looking even farther ahead, beyond Augustus to the eventual end of the Roman Empire. Interestingly, "Secondary Epic" immediately follows Auden's "The Shield of Achilles" in the *Collected Shorter Poems, 1927–1957*. In the latter poem, Auden has his chance both to revise mythic history and to join it with contemporary history, and he does so in Orwellian terms bleakly faithful to the horrors of the twentieth century.

"No, Virgil, no," Auden begins "Secondary Epic," sounding like a scold, "Not even the first of the Romans can learn / His Roman history in the future tense, / Not even to serve your political turn; / Hindsight as foresight makes no sense" (1–5). Though Auden dismisses it as a rhetorical device, from the reader's point of view hindsight as foresight in fact makes considerable narrative sense. It must be as a historian, rather than as a writer, that Auden is criticizing Vergil. "Behind your verse so masterfully made," he writes, "We hear the weeping of a muse betrayed" (48–9). Calliope, muse of epic poetry, is well served by Vergil's poem; it must be Clio, the muse of history, who Auden feels is betrayed. And indeed, Ziolkowski (1993, 141) remarks that "Auden implicitly criticizes both the rewriting of history for political purposes and the suppression of evidence that would qualify the (ironic) course of history," concluding that Auden feels for Vergil "not the savage contempt of Robert Graves but an admiration qualified by irony."

Remembering the gates of horn and ivory through which true and false dreams pass, respectively, a reader less sophisticated than Auden might point out that, after all, Aeneas returns to the upper world through the gates of ivory, presumably because all he has seen prophesied in the underworld has not yet taken place and is therefore not "true." In his Introduction to the Fagles translation (2006, 32), Bernard Knox quotes the scholar G.P. Goold to the effect that "By making Aeneas leave by the gate of delusive dreams Virgil represents his vision of Rome's destiny as a dream which he is not to remember on his return to the real world....his hero has not been endowed with superhuman knowledge to confront the problems which face him."

Auden wants his *Aeneid* by way of Edward Gibbon, it seems, not limited to the glories of the Augustan Age and the *Pax Romana*. (In his biography *Later Auden*, Edward Mendelson suggests (1999, 370) that Auden intended an oblique parallel between the incomplete vision of the Romans and that of the framers of the twentieth-century *Pax Americana*.) As a modern, Auden is waiting for the other narrative shoe to drop, the shoe of irony and decay by which Octavian's imperial name echoes, infinitely diminished, in the name of the last Western emperor, Romulus Augustulus, who fell in 476 CE. And, since Vergil does not supply this narrative – for such would have required genuine prophecy rather than a revisionist history of Rome's past – Auden supplies it himself, in a fragment of italicized doggerel by a "decadent" and anonymous rhetorician: "Now Mainz appears and starry New Year's Eve / As two-horned Rhine throws off the Latin yoke / To bear the Vandal on his frozen back; / Lo! Danube, now congenial to the Goth…" (35–8).

Rosanna Warren

In her wonderful essay "The End of the *Aeneid*," however, poet and critic Rosanna Warren writes (2001, 117) that "cynicism and dread of empire" are the motivating forces behind "Secondary Epic." And of the four poems in Rosanna Warren's 2003 book *Departure* that have subjects drawn from the *Aeneid*, several explore the percep-tual and emotional discrepancies between ancient and modern (or mythical and his-torical) time. Her poem "Bonfires" takes its locus from the carnage and grief of book 11, and opens with a sentence in which the grammatical object ("light") is so long deferred that, like the heroic trajectory of Vergil's poem as a whole, it tends to disappear: "Dawn had brought, meanwhile – always / the story happens mean- / while, during nights of sorrow and sore muscles, days / on the mountains cutting pine, // ash, cedar, oak – / dawn had brought / light" (1–6). The reasons for war are lost to the soldier in moments of individual horror, just as the "program" of the epic poem is lost (usefully), for the reader, amid the architecture of individual incidents, so the soldier preparing the funeral pyre speaks not only to, but *as*, the modern reader: "To haul // one corpse, one foot, one line after another / onto the hacked logs – we / set stiff shoulders to stiffened limbs" (12–15).

Yeats writes that we achieve, if we do achieve, in little sedentary stitches as though we were making lace (1965, 104). The building of an empire or an epic is tiresome work. "Another tedious meanwhile is opening in the story" (31), Warren's speaker declares; but perhaps no story can redeem so much human waste and loss. The voice of the poem is both triumphant and appalled: "Roman epic is painted / in black fire on black ground. / When the rhythm holds, anything burns on those canted / lines" (21–4). Such a perspective is certainly in keeping with Warren's perceptive explora-tion, in her essay, of the darknesses of sacrifice implied by the end of Vergil's poem. Warren refers there to "the height of Vergil's art, an art which in its most stringent form consists in *not* saying; an art of the unspoken, perhaps of the unspeakable" (2001, 114).

Warren provides an ingenious frame for considering the whole of Vergil's poem in her innocuously titled "Poetry Reading," which takes up the historical moment when Vergil read aloud to Augustus and the emperor's sister Octavia from book 6 (a passage already discussed in several chapters of this volume; see also Plates 7 and 8). The setting evoked – "Down the long avenue / through silted shadow and pale leaking light / stalks the future" (4–6) – sounds more like the cave of the Cumaean Sibyl than the Auditorium of Maecenas. "It is a promise they hold in their hands," the poem begins: not only the text of the poem, but its prophecy of "power bounded / only by the edge of earth, the rim of heaven. / The arts of peace, the rule of law" (7–9). And yet, like the "meanwhiles" of "Bonfires," something erupts from the narrative itself to disturb Vergil's recital (to disturb the unspooling of Rome's destiny), as Octavia faints at the double vision in the underworld of the elder and younger Marcus Claudius Marcellus, the latter her lost son, Augustus' nephew, adopted son, son-in-law, and intended heir: "patrons and literati disband. / Servants clear away wine-cups, platters of cake" (19–20). After all, in telling this part of his prophecy, Anchises has said to Aeneas (in a Latin line providing the epigraph to Warren's poem), "Fill my arms with lilies." These are the lilies of grief. Individual suffering has once more given the lie to dynastic mythology, and it is for this reason, perhaps, that at the end of Warren's poem, "Aeneas climbs back into daylight / through the gate of false dreams" (22).

The tension between the epic program and the individualized narrative distractions on which all subsequent fiction came to depend is pointed up most effectively by Warren in a third Vergilian poem, called "Turnus," based on *Aeneid* 12. Warren's instinct, like Lowell's, is for a morally problematic moment of the poem, that of Aeneas' killing his wounded enemy. Scholar and critic Sarah Spence, in an essay entitled " 'A Curious Appearance in the Air,' " has identified in this poem what she calls a moment of "the irreducibility of lyric" (2003, 277), when the chronological narrative of epic is torn and the reader sees behind it the timelessness of the lyric moment. Warren's poem begins by discounting all heroic epithet: "Not lion, not wind, not fire, not sacrificial / bull, not in strength and sinew god- / like" (1–3). Turnus is no more than "a man alone" who with his wound has lost all that he was fighting for: "the ashen city, the girl with her eyes cast down, / away" (8–9). Aeneas' physical and narrative power are identical, in this moment, and make him like God, revising the course of history, as when Warren's speaker tenderly addresses Turnus: "And when you speak, and He seems inclined to hear, / it's the woods that reply, the shadowed hilltops near / and farther, and what they speak is a groan / for a lost world" (11–14).

But even Aeneas, in this vision, succumbs to the modern-seeming doctrine of "meanwhile." In Vergil, Turnus' first wound is not a mortal one; his humility almost moves Aeneas to spare him, in a moment of pity that Achilles would never have allowed himself. "Here's where you tear a hole in the poem" (17), Warren's speaker says to Turnus, because this is the moment at which the conventional epic or heroic fabric yields to the world of recognizably personal motivation: "We are trapped in meanings that circulate like blood" (21). In Vergil, this is the moment at which Aeneas catches sight of the dead Pallas' sword-belt, which Turnus is wearing as a trophy: and the rage and grief he feels over his lost friend propel his sword blade into Turnus' heart. Very nearly the last word in Vergil's poem is "outrage" (in Fagles' translation), applied to the message expressed by Turnus' dying groan: but Aeneas *has* committed a kind of narrative outrage, requiring the fillip of a purely personal (lyric) motivation to complete the arc of epic destiny. "And He who kills you," writes Warren, "is not / a myth, nor a city… / It was love He fought" (22–4). Not war, but love. Perhaps we understand that Achilles felt the same way about Patroclus; but Aeneas' wavering is what makes him recognizably human to us. The moral complexity of the end of Vergil's poem is formulated by Spence as a question: "Does the awareness that Jupiter's *pietas* is defined by, even acts in consort with, *furor*, in becoming a recognized entity, cast a shadow on *pietas* that deepens our sense of it?" (2003, 285).

Louise Glück

If Eurydice were an analysand with some legal training, a lot of attitude, and no fear, she would argue before the throne of Hades himself just as tenaciously as do the speakers in Louise Glück's poems. Suffering, for Glück, is a competitive sport, but not a spectator sport: her speakers are quite indifferent to whether or not they are heard. Her 1999 collection *Vita Nova* (the orthographical proximity to Dante's title is deliberate) contains several poems in which Vergilian characters dauntlessly set themselves athwart the epic machinery in a way that is recognizably Glück's. In the exquisite concluding aria (to a text by Nahum Tate), Henry Purcell's Dido sings, "Remember me, but forget my fate." In her poem "The Queen of Carthage," however, Glück's Dido seems to exclaim instead, "Forget me, but remember my fate." What obsesses Glück are the remorseless processes that govern the human heart: "Brutal to love, / more brutal to die. / And brutal beyond the reaches of justice / to die of love" (1–4). The deliberate flatness of Glück's voice has always been the most powerful foil to the emotional content of her poems, even when she ventriloquizes for Dido herself: "'Now the Queen of Carthage / will accept suffering as she accepted favor'" (20–1). And her ability to wring a bleak consolation from that suffering is miraculous: "'to be noticed by the Fates / is some distinction after all'" (22–3). Glück's Dido, in fact, has an almost scientific ability to distance herself from her suffering while making it as personal as anorexia: "'Or should one say, to have honored hunger, / since the Fates go by that name also'" (24–5). The Fates are a confection of old myth; hunger is a contemporary pathology.

Two other poems in Glück's book present Aeneas, first in the guise of paste-board hero, and second in the guise of afflicted modern. "Even the goddess of love / fights for her children" (1–2), Glück writes in "The Golden Bough" – "(but need not have done so)," we are tempted to add. "And beauty / ran in his veins: he had no need / for more of it" (11–13), she says of Aeneas, the son of Venus. Without discounting the effects on him of Creusa and Dido – "grief made more human a heart / that might otherwise have seemed immutable" (10–11), she writes – Glück achieves for her Aeneas a kind of emotional invulnerability by allowing him to recognize the fundamental paradox by which subjective judgments are transformed, by empire, into immutable law. All that is required is to steer clear of those fields in which resolution, boundary, and closure are impossible, so that her Aeneas "conceded to other visions / the worlds of art and science, those paths that lead / only to torment" (13–15). Glück does not *judge* Aeneas, for such emotional ruthlessness; she may rather admire him for it, though in the poem's last lines are audible a certain journalistic distaste: "Beauty ran in his veins: he had no need for more of it. / That and his taste for empire: / that much can be verified" (21–3).

It is characteristic of Glück, by the way (and in this case differentiates her from Boland), that she should explore both sides of gender. Occurring after "The Queen of Carthage" but before "The Golden Bough" in *Vita Nova*, her poem "Roman Study" portrays Aeneas in a mood of modern introspection. Glück's anachronism is also a characteristic device for her: "He felt at first / he should have been born / to

Aphrodite, not Venus, / that too little was left to do, / to accomplish, after the Greeks" (1–5). Perhaps the historical Romans felt this way, but Glück's poem chronicles the dawning, for Aeneas, of a contemporary self-consciousness, as he recognizes in himself "a new species of thought entirely, / more worldly, more ambitious / and politic, in what we now call / human terms" (15–18). Aeneas thinks his way, even to a "faint contempt for the Greeks," and it becomes "plain to him how much / still remained to be experienced, / and written down, a material world heretofore / hardly dignified" (27–30). Here is the world of Rosanna Warren's "meanwhiles" once again. And since not just the *destination* of thought but its *process* (its fundamental narcissism) are always of interest to Glück, her Aeneas turns, characteristically, on himself at the end of the poem: "And he recognized in exactly this reasoning / the scope and trajectory of his own / watchful nature" (31–3).

Mark Strand

The Spring 1999 issue of *Literary Imagination* contains an abecedary prose piece called "A Poet's Alphabet" by Mark Strand that amounts to a kind of *ars poetica* for him, one in which Vergil, too, figures. "S," says Strand, is for "Wallace Stevens" (it is also for "Strand"), about whom he writes, self-revealingly, "The rhetorical design of his poems points to explanation or annunciation" – that is to say that in Stevens, as in Strand, the syntax *suggests* a purpose. However, Strand continues, "there is no urgency that constructs 'nextness' – what comes next is a possibility, a choice, another invitation to imagine" (1999, 7). The apparent rhetorical purpose, in Stevens or Strand, is simultaneously countermanded by the deliberate obliquity of the subject. And this accounts for the dreamlike quality of so many of Strand's poems. In the "N" section, after invoking Neruda, whom he calls a "cosmetician of the ordinary," Strand writes, "Ah, nothing! About which anything can be said, and is. An absence that knows no bounds. The climax of inaction. It has been the central influence on my writing. It is the original sleep and the end of life" (1999, 5). To some extent it is true that Strand's poems are about "nothing" or about absence, giving them, beyond their air of comic paradox, a genuine tragedy about which we will have more to say in a moment. Yet they are not, as the critic Sven Birkerts has pointed out in another context about the poems of John Ashbery, finally *nihilistic*, in their self-referential and self-defeating qualities.

The "V" section of Strand's poem is dedicated to Vergil, but in order to understand it, we need to consider a sentence in the "D" section (not surprisingly dedicated to Dante): "death is the central concern of lyric poetry. Lyric poetry reminds us that we live in time. It tells us that we are mortal. It celebrates or recognizes moods, ideas, events only as they exist in passing. For what meaning would anything have outside of time?" (1–2). Strand finds his connection with Dante, not through epic (which Strand does not write), but through another D-word: "Death." In fact, in his "V" section, Strand seems to disregard Vergil as an epic poet (and the *Aeneid* as an epic poem) in order to recognize him as a contemporary: "All those exquisite passages of lament and exhaustion, of time passing and life lost, all that elegiac grace that seems to make of the *Aeneid* a long lyric, mark Vergil as the first great gardener in the landscape of grief" (8). Achilles, in the *Iliad*, also knows that he will die, but does not seem to feel the pinch of mutability. He knows death; he does not know the grief that goes along with it. But the heroes of the *Aeneid* do; and for all of its dreamlike unpredictability, its whimsical arbitrariness, Mark Strand's poetry does too.

At the end of the "V" section, Strand asserts, "I know only that any description of landscape has within it an elusiveness, an unobtainableness that goes beyond the seasonal cycles and what they mean, and that suggests something like the constant flourishing of a finality in which we are confronted with the limits of our feeling. We end up lamenting the loss of something we never possessed" (8). Landscape, for Strand, is important, not because of its particulars, but because it is infused with time, and therefore with grief.

A poem included in Strand's 1990 collection *The Continuous Life* is entitled "Cento Virgilianus" (in other words, "Virgilian Patchwork," but drawing of course on the late antique tradition of poetry composed, or re-composed, exclusively of literal quotations from Vergil (McGill 2005)) and illustrates this idea. The poem begins in the middle of the narrative action and is a monologue apparently spoken by one of Aeneas' crew: "And so, passing under the dome of the great sky, / Driven by storms and heavy seas, we came, / Wondering on what shore of the world / We were cast up" (1–4). No specific landscape, Punic or Italic, can be identified in Strand's poem; there are tombs and courtyards and a grassfire. It is a "patchwork." Memory is more specific: "At first, we didn't miss the towns we'd started from – / The houses painted pink and green, swans feeding / Among the river reeds" (11–13). But Strand's poem, like Glück's "Roman Study," is finally a chronicle of the ancient mind as it habituates itself to the modern, or of the mythic as it accustoms itself to the temporal and the historical. Glück's Aeneas realizes "how much / still remained to be experienced," and the anonymous speaker in Strand's "Cento Virgilianus" concludes, "So what if we'd hoped to find Apollo here, / Enthroned at last… / We'd come to a place / Where everything weeps for how the world goes" (15–18). *Lacrimae rerum*: it is the tears of a life in time that matter, the lesson to be learned beyond the particulars of geographical place.

Conclusion

Leaving aside the sheer narrative and imaginative power of many Vergilian moments as yet unexplored by contemporary poets, it is clear that the *Aeneid*, and in particular its eponymous hero, has provided poets from Allen Tate through Eavan Boland with a chance to understand their own modernity. In assuming the voice of Aeneas, they have engaged with the moral ambiguity of his search to found Rome, and the tension between lyric and narrative elements in poetry. For the poets of the mid-twentieth century (Tate, Auden, Lowell), Aeneas' quest epitomized questions of the relative power of the individual and the state; poets at the end of the century (Strand, Glück, Warren) have tended to find in Aeneas a model of the hermetic closure of the self, the radical instability of experience, and the impossibility of rendering it in language.

Indeed, it is possible that increasingly the *Aeneid* has come to be read not as an epic or narrative poem but as a lyric one. For all that a contemporary like English poet Christopher Logue has revealed the mandarin refinements of physical violence available in Homer's *Iliad*, it is Vergil's "secondary epic," dark with loss and poised between myth and history, that may yet speak most powerfully to writers in the third millennium.

FURTHER READING

In addition to those poems discussed in the essay, the sources for which are listed above, there are numerous other individual poems on themes from the *Aeneid*. Among the Americans, Rachel Hadas' first book, *Starting From Troy* (1975), opens with three Vergilian poems, "The Fall of Troy," "That Time, This Place," and "After the Cave" (the latter poem is discussed by Rowena Fowler). Edward Hirsch's "Sortes Virgilianae" appears in his *Earthly Measures* (1994). William Logan's poem "Camilla" appears in his first book, *Sad-Faced Men* (1982). John Peck's "Boat near the Capo Miseno" appears in his *Argura* (1993).

English poet John Heath-Stubbs' poem "Romulus" is included in his volume *The Immolation of Aleph* (1985). And Geoffrey Hill's poem "After Cumae" is included in his volume *For the Unfallen* (1959).

Bibliography

Abley, M., ed. (1985). *The Parting Light: Selected Writings of Samuel Palmer*. Manchester.

Adair, D. (1955). "A Note on Certain of Hamilton's Pseudonyms," *William and Mary Quarterly* 12: 282–97.

Adair, D. and Schutz, J.A., eds. (1966). *The Spur of Fame: Dialogues of John Adams and Benjamin Rush, 1805–1813*. San Marino.

Adams, J.N. (2003). *Bilingualism and the Latin Language*. Cambridge.

Adel, K. (1957). "Die Dramen des P. Johann Baptist Adolph, S.J.," in *Jahrbuch der Gesellschaft für Wiener Theaterforschung*, 8 (1952–3). Vienna: 5–89.

Adler, E. (2003). *Vergil's Empire: Political Thought in the Aeneid*. Lanham.

Aedo y Gallart, D. (1635). *Le Voyage du Prince Don Fernande Infant d'Espagne*. Antwerp.

Agamben, G. (1998). *Homo Sacer: Sovereign Power and Bare Life,* trans. Daniel Heller-Roazen. Stanford.

Agamben, G. (2005). *State of Exception,* trans. Kevin Attell. Chicago.

Agard, W.R. (1955). "Classics on the Midwest Frontier," *CJ* 51: 103–10.

Ahl, F. (1985). *Metaformations: Soundplay and Wordplay in Ovid and Other Classical Poets*. Ithaca.

Ahl, F. (1988). "Ars Est Caelare Artem (Art in Puns and Anagrams Engraved)," in *On Puns: The Foundation of Letters*, ed. J. Culler. Oxford: 17–43.

Ahl, F., trans. (2007). *Virgil: Aeneid*. Oxford.

Ailes, M., ed. (1998). *Reading Around the Epic: A Festschrift in Honour of Professor Wolfgang van Emden*. London.

Aldridge, A.O. (1967–8). "Thomas Paine and the Classics," *Eighteenth-Century Studies* 1: 370–80.

Alexander, M. (1998). *The Poetic Achievement of Ezra Pound*. Edinburgh.

Alföldi, A. (1965). *Early Rome and the Latins*. Ann Arbor.

Allen, D.C. (1970). *Mysteriously Meant: The Rediscovery of Pagan Symbolism and Allegorical Interpretation in the Renaissance*. Baltimore.

Alpers, S. (1971). *The Decoration of the Torre de la Parada*, in *Corpus Rubenianum Ludwig Burchard*, pt. 9. Brussels, London, and New York.

Alter, R. (2004). *The Five Books of Moses: A Translation with Commentary*. New York.

Aly, W. (1923). "Die Überlieferung von Vergils Leben," *PhW* 43: 645–8.

Ambaglio, D., ed. (1980). *L'opera storiografica di Ellanico di Lesbo*. Ricerche di storiografia antica 2. Pisa.

Ames, R.A. and Montgomery, H.C. (1934–5). "The Influence of Rome on the American Constitution," *CJ* 30: 19–27.

Ampolo, C., ed. (1988). *Plutarco: Le Vite di Teseo e di Romolo*. Milan.

Anceschi, G. (2007). "Il mondo cavalleresco di Nicolò dell'Abate," in *I luoghi di Nicolò dell'Abate. Pitture murali e interventi di restauro*, ed. A. Mazza. Studi boiardeschi, 52. Novara: 189–208.

Anderson, E. and Moss, A.A., Jr. (1999). *Dangerous Donations: Northern Philanthropy and Southern Black Education, 1902–1930*. Columbia.

Anderson, J. (1988). *The Education of Blacks in the South, 1860–1935*. Chapel Hill.

Anderson, W.D. (1965). "The Heritage of Rome: Religion, Philology, and the Classical," in *Matthew Arnold and the Classical Tradition*. Ann Arbor: 180–95.

Anderson, W.S. and Quartarone, L.N., eds. (2002). *Approaches to Teaching Vergil's Aeneid*. New York.

Andreae, B. (1988). *Laokoon und die Gründung Roms*. Kulturgeschichte der antiken Welt, 39. Mainz.

Andreae, B. (1991). *Laokoon und die Kunst von Pergamon. Die Hybris der Giganten*. Frankfurt am Main.

Andrisano, A.M. (2007). *Biblioteche del mondo antico. Dalla tradizione orale alla cultura dell'Impero*. Rome.

Anon. (1685). *Virgilius defensus, sive defensio Virgiliani Certaminis Aeneae cum Turno*. Liège.

Anon. (1744). "Advice to a Young Lady Just after Her Marriage," *American Magazine and Historical Chronicle* (December): 698–701.

Arendt, H. (1965). *On Revolution*, rev. 2nd ed. London and New York.

Arendt, H. (1968). *Men in Dark Times*. San Diego and New York.

Arendt, H. (1970). *On Violence*. San Diego, New York, London.

Ariosto, L. (1984). *Tutte le opere*, ed. C. Segre. Vol. 3: *Le Lettere*, ed. A. Stella. Milan.

Armstrong, D., Fish, J., Johnston, P.A., and Skinner, M.B., eds. (2004). *Vergil, Philodemus and the Augustans*. Austin.

Armstrong, I. (2000). *The Radical Aesthetic*. Oxford.

Arnold, M. (1960). "On the Modern Element in Literature," in *The Complete Prose Works of Matthew Arnold*. Vol. 1: *On The Classical Tradition*, ed. R.H. Super. Ann Arbor: 18–37.

Asher, K. (1995). *T.S. Eliot and Ideology*. Cambridge.

Assmann, J. and Gladigow, B., eds. (1995). *Text und Kommentar*. Beiträge zur Archäologie der literarischen Kommunikation, IV. Munich.

Athanassaki, L., Martin, R.P., and Miller, J.F., eds. (2009). *Apolline Politics and Poetics: An International Symposium, Delphi, July 4th–11th 2003*. Athens.

Atherton, G. (2006). *The Decline and Fall of Virgil in Eighteenth-Century Germany: The Repressed Muse*. Studies in German Literature, Linguistics, and Culture. Rochester.

Atkins, M. (1672). *Cataplus: or, Æneas his Descent to Hell. A Mock Poem, In Imitation of the Sixth Book of Virgil's Æneis, in English Burlesque*. London.

Aubrey, J. (1898). *"Brief Lives," chiefly of Contemporaries, set down by John Aubrey, between the Years 1669 & 1696*, ed. A. Clark, 2 vols. Oxford.

Auden, W.H. (1966). "Secondary Epic," in *Auden's Collected Shorter Poems, 1927–1957*. London: 296–7.

Augustine, St. (1993). *De Doctrina Christiana*, edited with an introduction, translation, and notes, by R.P.H. Green. Oxford.

Augustine, St. (1998). *The City of God*, trans. R.W. Dyson. Cambridge.

Auréas, H. (1961). *Un général de Napoléon: Miollis*. Paris.

Austin, R.G., ed. (1964). *P. Vergili Maronis Aeneidos Liber Secundus. Edited with a Commentary.* Oxford.

Austin, R.G., ed. (1971). *P. Vergili Maronis Aeneidos Liber Primus. Edited with a Commentary.* Oxford.

Austin, R.G., ed. (1977). *P. Vergili Maronis Aeneidos Liber Sextus. Edited with a Commentary.* Oxford.

Avery, S. (1989). *Up From Washington: William Pickens and the Negro Struggle for Equality, 1900–1954.* Newark.

Bailey, C. (1935). *Religion in Virgil.* Oxford.

Bailey, C. (1949). Review of Rose (1948). *CR* 63: 142.

Bailey, G.A. (2003). *Between Renaissance and Baroque: Jesuit Art in Rome, 1565–1610.* Toronto.

Bain, I., Chambers, D., and Wilton, A. (1977). *The Wood Engravings of William Blake for Thornton's "Virgil."* London.

Baker, D.J. (2001). "Historical Contexts: Britain and Europe," in *The Cambridge Companion to Spenser,* ed. A. Hadfield. Cambridge: 37–59.

Baldwin, B. (1983). *Suetonius.* Amsterdam.

Baldwin, B. (1993). "Half-Lines in Virgil: Old and New Ideas," *SO* 68: 144–51.

Balsamo, L. (2001). "How to Doctor a Bibliography: Antonio Possevino's Practice," in *Church, Censorship, and Culture in Early Modern Italy,* ed. G. Fragnito, trans. A. Belton. Cambridge: 50–78.

Bandera, C. (1981). "Sacrificial Levels in Virgil's *Aeneid,*" *Arethusa* 14: 217–39.

Bandiera, E. (1986). "La mitologia arcaica di Ascanio-Iulo." *Studi di Filologia e Letteratura, Università di Lecce.* Lecce: 15–61.

Banning, L. (1986). "Jeffersonian Ideology Revisited: Liberal and Classical Ideas in the New American Republic," *William and Mary Quarterly* 43: 3–19.

Bannon, C.J. (1997). *The Brothers of Romulus: Fraternal Pietas in Roman Law, Literature, and Society.* Princeton.

Barbantani, S. (2000). "*Aetia Romana. SH* fr. 957 (*PHamb.* 124 inv. 666 *verso*) e la leggenda della fondazione di Roma nel mondo greco," *SemRom* 3: 77–104.

Barchiesi, A. (1979). "La vendetta del silenzio. Uno schema esegetico antico e una pretesa correzione d'autore in Virgilio *Georgiche* 2, 225," *ASNP* 9: 527–37.

Barchiesi, A. (1984). *La traccia del modello. Effetti omerici nella narrazione virgiliana.* Pisa.

Barchiesi, A. (1994). "Immovable Delos: *Aeneid* 3.73–98 and the Hymns of Callimachus," *CQ* 44: 438–43.

Barchiesi, A. (1996). Review of Heinze (1993). *JRS* 86: 229–31.

Barchiesi, A. (2001). *Speaking Volumes: Narrative and Intertext in Ovid and Other Latin Poets,* ed. and trans. M. Fox and S. Marchesi. London.

Barchiesi, A. (2004). "Quando Virgilio era un moderno: una delle piu' antiche recite delle Georgiche, e il contesto di una spiritosaggine." *MD* (*Numero speciale in onore di Michael C.J. Putnam*) 52: 21–8.

Barchiesi, M., ed. (1962). *Nevio epico. Storia interpretazione edizione critica dei frammenti del primo epos latino.* Padua.

Barlaeus, C. (1643). *Faces augustae, sive poematia, quibus illustriores Nuptiae, à Nobili & Illustri viro, D. Jacobo Catsio, Eq. & Praepot. Holl. ac Frisiae Occidentalis Ord. Syndico, antehac Belgicis versibus conscriptae, Iam à Caspare Barlaeo & Cornelio Boyo Latino Carmine celebrantur.* Dordrecht.

Barkan, L. (1999). *Unearthing the Past: Archaeology and Aesthetics in the Making of Renaissance Culture.* New Haven.

Barnard, J. (1999). "Early Expectations of Dryden's Translation of Virgil (1697) on the Continent," *Review of English Studies*, n.s. 50: 196–203.

Barnard, J. (2000). "Dryden, Tonson, and the Patrons of the Works of Virgil (1697)," in *John Dryden: Tercentenary Essays*, ed. P. Hammond and D. Hopkins. Oxford: 174–239.

Barnes, J. (1997). "Roman Aristotle," in *Philosophia Togata II: Plato and Aristotle at Rome*, ed. J. Barnes and M. Griffin. Oxford: 1–69.

Barnes, W.R. (1999). "Seeing Things: Ancient Commentary on the *Iliad* at the End of the *Aeneid*," in *Amor:Roma: Love and Latin Literature*, ed. S. Braund and R. Mayer. Cambridge Philological Society, Suppl. Vol. 22. Cambridge: 60–70.

Barolini, T. (1984). *Dante's Poets: Textuality and Truth in the Comedy*. Princeton.

Baron, S.A. (2001). *The Reader Revealed*. Seattle and London.

Barratt, C.R. and Miles, E.G. (2004). *Gilbert Stuart*. New York and New Haven.

Bartoli, P.S., illus. (1780–2). *Picturae antiquissimi Virgiliani codicis Bibliothecae Vaticanae....* Rome.

Bartsch, A. (1803–21). *Le Peintre graveur*. Vienna.

Baschera, C., ed. (1999). *Gli scolii veronesi a Virgilio: Introduzione, edizione critica e indici*. Verona.

Basore, J.W., ed. and trans. (1932). *Seneca: Moral Essays*, vol. 2. Cambridge, MA.

Baswell, C. (1995). *Virgil in Medieval England: Figuring the Aeneid from the Twelfth Century to Chaucer*. Cambridge.

Bath, M. (1994). *Speaking Pictures: English Emblem Books and Renaissance Culture*. London.

Baumgartner, E. and Harf-Lancner, L., eds. (1997). *Entre fiction et histoire: Troie et Rome au Moyen-âge*. Paris.

Bayer, K. (1981). *Vitae Vergilianae/Vergil-Viten*, in *Virgil, Landleben*, ed. J. and M. Götte. 4th ed. Munich: 211–780.

Bayer, K. (2002). *Suetons Vergilvita. Versuch einer Rekonstruktion*. 2nd ed. Tübingen (Diss. Munich 1952).

Beard, M. (1990). "Priesthood in the Roman Republic," in *Pagan Priests: Religion and Power in the Ancient World*, ed. M. Beard and J. North. Ithaca: 19–48.

Beaune, C. (1991). *The Birth of an Ideology: Myths and Symbols of Nation in Late Medieval France*, trans. S.R. Huston, ed. F. Cheyette. Berkeley and London.

Beazley, J.D. (1963). *Attic Red-Figure Vase-Painters*. 2nd ed. Oxford.

Beck, H. and Walter, U. (2001). *Die frühen römischen Historiker*. Vol. 1: *Von Fabius Pictor bis Cn. Gellius*. Texte zur Forschung, 76. Darmstadt.

Behr, F.D. (2005). "The Narrator's Voice: A Narratological Reappraisal of Apostrophe in Vergil's *Aeneid*," *Arethusa* 38: 189–221.

Bellenger, S., ed. (2005). *Girodet 1767–1824: L'album de l'exposition*. Paris.

Benario, H.W. (1977). "The Classics in Southern Higher Education," *Southern Humanities Review* 11: 15–20.

Benario, H.W. and Briggs, W.W., Jr., eds. (1986). *Basil Lanneau Gildersleeve: An American Classicist*. Baltimore and London.

Benci, F., S.J. (1591). *Quinque Martyres, Libri Sex*. Venice.

Benesch, O. (1943). *Artistic and Intellectual Trends from Rubens to Daumier as Shown in Book Illustration*. Cambridge.

Benjamin, W. (1978). "Critique of Violence" (1921), in *Reflections: Essays, Aphorisms, Autobiographical Writings*, ed. P. Demetz, trans. E. Jephcott. New York: 277–300.

Benjamin, W. (1999). "Privileged Thinking: On Theodore Haecker's *Virgil*" (1932), in *Selected Writings*. Vol. 2: *1927–1934*, ed. M.W. Jennings, H. Eilend, and G. Smith, trans. R. Livingstone et al. Cambridge, MA: 569–75.

Benjamin, W. (2000). "The Task of the Translator" (English translation of "Die Aufgabe des Übersetzers," 1923), in *Illuminations*, ed. H. Arendt, trans. H. Zohn. New York, 1968: 69–82. Rpt. in Venuti, ed.: 15–23.

Benocci, C. and di Carpegna Falconieri, T. (2004). *Le Belle. Ritratti di dame del seicento e del settecento nelle residenze feudali del Lazio*. Rome.

Benoît de Saint-Maure (1998). *Le Roman de Troie. Extraits du manuscrit Milan, Bibliothèque Ambrosienne, D 55*, ed. and trans. E. Baumgartner and F. Vielliard. Paris.

Benson, C.D. (1980). *The History of Troy in Middle English Literature: Guido delle Colonne's Historia Destructionis Troiae in Medieval England*. Woodbridge, Suffolk and Totowa, NJ.

Berger, H. (1957). *The Allegorical Temper: Vision and Reality in Book II of Spenser's Faerie Queene*. New Haven and London.

Bergh, A.E. and Lipscomb, A.A., eds. (1903). *The Writings of Thomas Jefferson*. Washington, DC.

Beristáin y Souza, J.M. (1981). *Biblioteca Hispanoamericana Septentrional*, vol. 3 (facsimile of original publication, 1821). Mexico City.

Berman, A. (1985). "La traduction comme épreuve de l'étranger," *Texte*: 67–81. English translation in Venuti, ed., 2000: 284–97.

Bernard, J., ed. (1986). *Vergil at 2000: Commemorative Essays on the Poet and His Influence*. AMS Ars Poetica, 3. New York.

Berres, T. (1982). *Die Entstehung der Aeneis*. Wiesbaden.

Berres, T. (1993). "Vergil und Homer: Ein Beitrag zur Entmythologisierung des Verhältnisses," *Gymnasium* 100: 342–69.

Berrigan, J. (1968–9). "The Impact of the Classics upon the South," *CJ* 64: 18–20.

Berschin, W. (1980). *Griechisch-lateinisches Mittelalter: Von Hieronymus zu Nikolaus von Kues*. Berne and Munich.

Berschin, W. (1988). *Greek Letters and the Latin Middle Ages: From Jerome to Nicholas of Cusa*, trans. J. Frakes. Washington, DC.

Bertoni, G. (1919). *L'Orlando furioso e la Rinascenza a Ferrara*. Modena.

Bettini, M. (1976–7). "L'epitaffio di Virgilio, Silio Italico, e un modo di intendere la letteratura," *DArch* 9–10: 439–48.

Bettini, M. (2005). "Un'identità 'troppo compiuta.' Troiani, Latini, Romani e Iulii nell'*Eneide*," *MD* 55: 77–102.

Bews, J.P. (1984). "The Metamorphosis of Virgil in the *Tristia* of Ovid," *BICS* 31: 51–60.

Bialostocka, J. (1964). *Lessing, Laokoon. Suivi de lettres concernant l'antiquité et comment les anciens représentaient la mort*. Textes réunis et présentés par J. Jolanta Bialostocka, avec la collaboration de R. Robert Klein. Miroirs d'Art. Paris.

Bickerman, E.J. (1952). "*Origines gentium*," *CPh* 47: 65–81.

Bidart, F. (1990). *In the Western Night: Collected Poems, 1965–1990*. New York.

Bieber, M. (1942). *Laocoon: The Influence of the Group Since its Rediscovery*. New York.

Bigi, E., ed. (1982). Ariosto, *Orlando furioso*, 2 vols. Milan.

Bigi, E. (1984). "Ariosto," in *Enciclopedia Virgiliana*, ed. F. della Corte. Rome. Vol. 1: 314–17.

Bill, C.P. (1928). "Vergiliana," *CPh* 23: 65–8.

Binns, J.W., ed. (1973). *Ovid*. London.

Biondi, A. (1981). "La *Bibliotheca selecta* di Antonio Possevino: un progetto di egemonia culturale," in *La Ratio studiorum: Modelli culturali e pratiche educative dei Gesuiti in Italia tra Cinque e Seicento*, ed. G.P. Brizzi. Rome: 43–75.

Birt, T. (1882). *Das antike Buchwesen in seiner Verhältnis zur Literatur*. Berlin.

Bitzel, D. (1997). *Bernardo Zamagna. Navis Aëria: Eine Metamorphose des Lehrgedichts im Zeichen des technischen Fortschritts*, ed. and trans. D. Bitzel. Studien zur klassischen Philologie, 109. Frankfurt am Main.

Blackmore, R. (1695). *Prince Arthur: An Heroick Poem in Ten Books.* London.

Blackwell, T. (1735). *An Enquiry into the Life and Writings of Homer.* London.

Blessington, F.C. (1979). *Paradise Lost and the Classical Epic.* London.

Bloom, H. (1973). *The Anxiety of Influence: A Theory of Poetry.* New York.

Boiardo, M.M. (1989). *Orlando innamorato,* ed. and trans. C.S. Ross. Berkeley.

Boiardo, M.M. (1995). *Orlando innamorato,* ed. R. Bruscagli, 2 vols. Turin.

Boland, E. (1987). *The Journey and Other Poems.* Manchester.

Bond, D.F., ed. (1965). *The Spectator,* 5 vols. Oxford.

Bond, H.M. (1966). *The Education of the Negro in the American Social Order.* New York.

Bonifazi, N. (1984). *Lettere infideli. Ariosto, Giordani, Leopardi, Manzoni.* Rome.

Bono, B.J. (1984). *Literary Transvaluation: From Vergilian Epic to Shakespearean Tragicomedy.* Berkeley, Los Angeles, and London.

Borges, J.L. (1939). "Pierre Menard, autor del Quijote," *Sur* 56 (May). Rpt. in *El Jardín de senderos que se bifurcan* (Buenos Aires, 1941) and in *Ficciones* (Buenos Aires, 1944); trans. J.E. Irby, in *Labyrinths,* ed. D.A. Yates and J.E. Irby (New York, 1962); trans. A. Bonner in *Borges, a Reader,* ed. E.R. Monegal and A. Reid (New York, 1981).

Bossy, M.-A. (2006). "Roland's Migration from Anglo-Norman Epic to Royal French Chronicle History." Conference on Epic and History, Ancient and Medieval. Brown University, December 3.

Boswell, J. (1934). *The Life of Samuel Johnson,* ed. G.B. Hills and L. F. Powell. Vol. 4. Oxford.

Botein, S. (1978). "Cicero as Role Model for Early American Lawyers: A Case Study in Classical 'Influence,'" *CJ* 73: 313–21.

Bottkol, J.M. (1943). "Dryden's Latin Scholarship," *Modern Philology* 40: 241–54.

Boyarin, D. (1990). *Intertextuality and the Reading of Midrash.* Bloomington and Indianapolis.

Boyd, C.E. (1915). *Public Libraries and Literary Culture in Ancient Rome.* Chicago.

Boys, J., trans. (1661). *Æneas his Descent into Hell, as it is inimitably described by the Prince of Poets in the sixth of his Æneis.* London.

Bradford, M. (1977). "That Other Republic: Romanitas in Southern Literature," *Southern Humanities Review* 11: 4–13.

Brading, D.A. (1991). *The First America: The Spanish Monarchy, Creole Patriots, and the Liberal State, 1492–1867.* Cambridge.

Brading, D.A. (2001). *Mexican Phoenix. Our Lady of Guadalupe: Image and Tradition Across Five Centuries.* Cambridge.

Brading, D.A. (2005). "Prólogo," in Reyes (2005): 23.

Bradley, D.R. (1991). "Troy Revisited," *Hermes* 119: 232–46.

Brague, R. (1993). *Europe: la voie romaine,* 2nd ed. Paris.

Brague, R. (2002). *Eccentric Culture: A Theory of Western Civilization,* trans. S. Lester. South Bend.

Brant, I. (1941–61). *James Madison.* Indianapolis.

Brant, S., ed. (1502). *Publii Virgilii Maronis Opera.* Strasbourg.

Braun, L. (1999). "Lateinische Epik im Frankreich des 17. Jahrhunderts," *Neulateinisches Jahrbuch* 1: 9–20.

Braund, S. (2004). "Making Virgil Strange," *PVS* 25: 135–46.

Breed, B.W. (2000). "Imitations of Originality: Theocritus and Lucretius at the Start of the *Eclogues,*" *Vergilius* 46: 3–20.

Bremmer, J.N. and Horsfall, N.M., eds. (1987). *Roman Myth and Mythography,* BICS Suppl. 52. London.

Brennan, T. (2005). Review of Wilson (2004). *BMCR,* August 7.

Bridenthal, R. (1972). "Was There a Roman Homer? Niebuhr's Thesis and Its Critics," *History and Theory* 11: 193–213.

Bridges, R. (1916). *Ibant Obscuri: An Experiment in the Classical Hexameter*. Oxford.

Briggs, W.W., Jr. (1980). *Narrative and Simile from the Georgics in the Aeneid*. Leiden.

Brisson, J.-P. (1966). *Virgile, son temps et le nôtre*. Paris.

Briusov, V., trans. (2000). *Vergilii: Bukoliki, Georgiki, Eneida*. Moscow.

Broch, H. (1945). *The Death of Virgil*, trans. J. Starr Untermeyer. New York.

Brooks-Davies, D. (1985). *Pope's Dunciad and the Queen of the Night: A Study in Emotional Jacobitism*. Manchester.

Broome, E.C. (1903). "A Historical and Critical Discussion of College Admission Requirements," *Columbia University Contributions to Philosophy, Psychology, and Education* 11. New York.

Broughton, T.R.S. (1952). *The Magistrates of the Roman Republic*. Vol. 2: *99 BC–31 BC*. New York.

Brown, D.B. (2001). *Romanticism*. London.

Brown, D.B. (2005). "'To fancy what is lost to sight': Palmer and Literature," in *Samuel Palmer 1805–1881: Vision and Landscape*, by W. Vaughan, E.E. Barker, and C. Harrison. London.

Brown, P. (2000). *Augustine of Hippo: New Edition with an Epilogue*. Berkeley.

Brown, V. (1998). "*Vitae Vergilianae* in Unpublished Virgilian Commentaries (saec. XV and XVI)," in *Style and Tradition: Studies in Honor of Wendell Clausen*, ed. P. Knox and C. Foss. Beiträge zur Altertumskunde 92. Stuttgart and Leipzig: 174–98.

Brownlee, K. (1993). "Dante and the Classical Poets," in Jacoff, ed.: 100–19. 2nd ed. 2007: 141–60.

Bruce, D.D., Jr. (1980). "The Conservative Use of History in Early National Virginia," *Southern Studies* 19: 128–46.

Brucia, M. (2001). "The African-American Poet, Jupiter Hammon: A Home-Born Slave and his Classical Name," *IJCT* 7: 515–22.

Brugnoli, G. (1983). "Reges Albanorum," in *Atti del Convegno Virgiliano di Brindisi nel Bimillenario della morte (15–18 ottobre 1981)*. Perugia, 157–90.

Brugnoli, G. and Naumann, H. (1990). "*Vitae Vergilianae*," in *Enciclopedia Virgiliana*, ed. F. della Corte. Rome. Vol. 5*: 570–88.

Brugnoli, G. and Stok, F., eds. (1991). "Fontes ad vitam Vergilii pertinentes," in *Enciclopedia Virgiliana*, ed. F. della Corte. Rome. Vol. 5**: 427–539.

Brugnoli, G. and Stok, F., eds. (1997). *Vitae Vergilianae Antiquae*. Rome.

Brugnoli, G. and Stok, F. (2006). *Studi sulle Vitae Vergilianae*. Pisa.

Brummer, H.H. (1970). *The Statue Court in the Vatican Belvedere*. Stockholm Studies in the History of Art 20. Stockholm.

Buchan, M. (2004). *The Limits of Heroism: Homer and the Ethics of Reading*. Ann Arbor.

Buchan, M. (2007). "Homer, and the Origins of Greek Ignorance." Unpublished paper delivered at joint meeting of the Classical Association of the Canadian West and the Classical Association of the Pacific Northwest. March 27. Vancouver.

Buchheit, V. (1963). *Vergil über die Sendung Roms: Untersuchungen zum Bellum Poenicum und zur Aeneis*. Heidelberg.

Bullough, G. (1964). "Milton and Cats," in MacLure and Watt, eds.: 103–24.

Burckhardt, J. (1950). *Recollections of Rubens*, ed. H. Gerson, trans. M. Hottinger. London.

Burden, M., ed. (1998). *A Woman Scorn'd: Responses to the Dido Myth*. London.

Burke, P. (1970). *The Renaissance Sense of the Past*. New York.

Burke, P. (2008). "Paradigms Lost: From Göttingen to Berlin," *Common Knowledge* 14.2: 244–57.

Burkett, L. (1948). "Now Long Forgotten by Most Persons Town of Troy Still Stands in Macon," *Macon Telegraph*, April 11, 13a.

Burns, E. (1954). "The Philosophy of History of the Founding Fathers," *The Historian* 16: 142–61.

Burrow, C. (1993). *Epic Romance: Homer to Milton*. Oxford.

Burrow, C. (1997a). "Virgils, from Dante to Milton," in Martindale, ed.: 79–90.

Burrow, C. (1997b). "Virgil in English Translation," in Martindale, ed.: 21–37.

Burrow, C. (2008). "English Renaissance Readers and the *Appendix Vergiliana*," *PVS* 26: 1–16.

Bush, D. (1932). *Mythology and the Renaissance Tradition in English Poetry*. Minneapolis.

Bush, P.C. (1857). *Memoir of Anne Gorham Everett, with Extracts from Her Correspondence and Journal*. Boston.

Bussière, J. de, S.J. (1656–8). *Scanderbergus, poema. Accessit dissertatio de descriptionibus in poëmate epico*. Lyons.

Butler, J. (2000). "Dynamic Conclusions," in *Contingency, Hegemony, Universality: Contemporary Dialogues on the Left*, ed. J. Butler, E. Laclau, and S. Žižek. London and New York: 263–80.

Butler, S. (1967). *Hudibras*, ed. J. Wilders. Oxford.

Butterfield, H. (1955). *Man on His Past: The Study of the History of Historical Scholarship*. Cambridge.

Butterfield, L.H., ed. (1951). *The Letters of Benjamin Rush*. Princeton.

Butterfield, L.H., ed. (1963–73). *Adams Family Correspondence*. Cambridge, MA.

Cabani, M.C. (1995). *Gli amici amanti. Coppie eroiche e sortite notturne nell'epica italiana*. Naples.

Cabrera, F.J. (2004). *Monumenta Mexicana/Mexican Heritage*, trans. W. Cooper. Mexico City.

Cain, T. (1978). *Praise in The Faerie Queene*. Lincoln.

Cairns, D., ed. and trans. (1969). *The Memoirs of Hector Berlioz*. London.

Cairns, D. (1988). "Berlioz and Virgil," in Kemp, ed.: 76–88.

Cairns, D. (1999). *Berlioz*. Vol. 2: *Servitude and Greatness, 1832–1869*. London.

Cairns, F. (1989). *Virgil's Augustan Epic*. Cambridge.

Cairns, F. (1999). "Virgil *Eclogue* 1.1–2: A Literary Programme?," *HSCP* 99: 289–93.

Callu, J.-P. (1978). "'Impius Aeneas'? Echos Virgiliens du Bas-Empire," in Chevallier, ed.: 161–74.

Cameron, K. (1975). *Young Thoreau and the Classics, a Review: The Curriculum of the Concord Academy, Probabilities and Evidence*. Hartford.

Camps, W.A. (1969). *An Introduction to Virgil's Aeneid*. Oxford.

Capper, C. (1992). *Margaret Fuller: An American Romantic Life*. Vol. 1: *The Private Years*. New York.

Carhart, M.C. (2007a). "*Historia Literaria* and Cultural History from Mylaeus to Eichhorn," in *Momigliano and Antiquarianism: Foundations of the Modern Cultural Sciences*, ed. P.N. Miller. Toronto: 184–206.

Carhart, M.C. (2007b). *The Science of Culture in Enlightenment Germany*. Cambridge, MA.

Carlyle, T. (1896–9). *The Works of Thomas Carlyle*, 30 vols. London.

Carpenter, A. (2005). "Virgil Travesty in Restoration Ireland: Some Preliminary Notes on an Unexplored Literary Phenomenon," in Kenneally and Kenneally, eds.: 53–66.

Carsughi, R., S.J. (1709). *Ars Bene Scribendi/Studiosis Rhetoricae/Adolescentibus/Proposita olim in Collegio Romano/...Carmen Didascalicum*. Rome. www.uni-mannheim.de/mateo/desbillons/rainer.html.

Carter, J.M. (1970). *The Battle of Actium: The Rise and Triumph of Augustus Caesar*. London.

Casali, S. (1999). "*Facta Impia* (Virgil, *Aeneid* 4.596–9)," *CQ* 49: 224–37.

Casali, S. (2004a). "Terre mobili: la topografia di Azio in Virgilio (*Aen.* 3.274–289), in Ovidio (*Met.* 13.713–715) e in Servio," in Stok and Santini, eds.: 45–74.

Casali, S. (2004b). "Nisus and Euryalus: Exploiting the Contradictions in Virgil's Doloneia," *HCSP* 102: 319–54.

Casali, S. (2007a). "Killing the Father: Ennius, Naevius, and Virgil's Intertextual Imperialism," in *Ennius Perennis: The Annals and Beyond*, ed. W. Fitzgerald and E. Gowers. *Cambridge Classical Journal*, Suppl. 31. Cambridge: 103–28.

Casali, S. (2007b). "Correcting Aeneas' Voyage: Ovid's Commentary on *Aeneid* 3," *TAPhA* 137: 181–210.

Casali, S. (2008). "'Ecce dixit ἀμφιβολικῶς': allusioni 'irrazionali' alle varianti scartate della storia di Didone e Anna secondo Servio," in Casali and Stok, eds.: 7–37.

Casali, S. (2009a). "The Theophany of Apollo in Virgil *Aeneid* 9: Augustanism and Self-Reflexivity," in Athanassaki, Martin, and Miller, eds.: 299–327.

Casali, S. (2009b). "*Iasius pater*: Iasio, Dardano e i Penati nell'*Eneide*," in *οὐ πᾶν ἐφήμερον. Scritti in memoria di Roberto Pretagostini*. Rome: 77–91.

Casali, S. and Stok, F., eds. (2008). *Servio: stratificazioni esegetiche e modelli culturali/Servius: Exegetical Stratifications and Cultural Models*. Collection Latomus, vol. 317. Brussels.

Caskey, L.D. and Beazley, J.D. (1963). *Attic Vase Paintings in the Museum of Fine Arts, Boston*. Oxford.

Casson, L. (2001). *Libraries in the Ancient World*. New Haven.

Castagnoli, F. (1972). *Lavinium I. Topografia generale, fonti e storia delle ricerche*. Rome.

Castagnoli, F. (1982). "La leggenda di Enea nel Lazio," *StudRom* 30: 1–15.

Castagnoli, F. (1987a). "Lavinio," in *Enciclopedia Virgiliana*, ed. F. della Corte. Rome. Vol. 3: 149–53.

Castagnoli, F. (1987b). "Lupercale," in *Enciclopedia Virgiliana*, ed. F. della Corte. Rome. Vol. 3: 282–4.

Catalano, M. (1930–1). *Vita di Ludovico Ariosto*, 2 vols. Geneva.

Catterson, L. (2005). "Michelangelo's Laocoön?," *Artibus et Historiae* 52: 29–56.

Cavallo, G. (2002). *Libri, editori e pubblico nel mondo antico*. 3rd ed. Rome and Bari.

Cavallo, G. and Chartier, R., eds. (1999). *A History of Reading in the West*, trans. L.G. Cochrane. Amherst.

Cavallo, J.A. (2004). *The Romance Epics of Boiardo, Ariosto, and Tasso: From Public Duty to Private Pleasure*. Toronto.

Cerda, J.L. de la (1608–17). *P. Virgilii Maronis Bucolica et Georgica....* Frankfurt am Main, 1608. *Priores sex libri Aeneidos....* Lyons, 1612. *Posteriores sex libri Aeneidos....* Lyons, 1617.

Chalker, J. (1969). *The English Georgic: A Study in the Development of a Form*. Baltimore.

Chassignet, M. (1996). *L'Annalistique Romaine*. Vol. 1: *Les Annales des Pontifes et l'Annalistique Ancienne (Fragments)*. Collection Budé. Paris.

Chateaubriand, F.-R. (1836–40). *Œuvres complètes*, 36 vols. Paris.

Cheney, P. (1993). *Spenser's Famous Flight: A Renaissance Idea of a Literary Career*. Toronto.

Chevallier, R., ed. (1978). *Présence de Virgile*. Paris.

Child, L.M. (1883). *Letters of Lydia Maria Child with a Biographical Introduction by John G. Whittier and an Appendix by Wendell Phillips*. Boston.

Chinard, G., ed. (1928). *The Literary Bible of Thomas Jefferson: His Commonplace Book of Philosophers and Poets*. Rpt. New York, 1969.

Chinard, G. (1929–30). "Thomas Jefferson as a Classical Scholar," *Johns Hopkins Alumni Magazine* 18: 291–303.

Chinard, G. (1933). *Honest John Adams*. Boston.

Chinard, G. (1940). "Polybius and the American Constitution," *JHI* 1: 38–58.

Chiri, G. (1974). *L'Epica latina medioevale e la Chanson de Roland*. Geneva.

Chlodowski, R. (1984–91). "Russia," in *Enciclopedia Virgiliana*, ed. F. della Corte. Rome. Vol. 4: 608–17.

Christmann, H.H. (1976). "Bemerkungen zum Génie de la Langue," in *Lebendige Romania*, ed. A. Barrera-Vidal, E. Ruhe, and P. Schunck. Göppingen: 65–79.

Christmann, H.H. (1977). "Zu den Begriffen 'Génie de la Langue' und 'Analogie' in der Sprachwissenschaft des 16. bis 19. Jahrhunderts," *Beiträge zur Romanische Philologie* 16.1: 91–4.

Claassen, J.-M. (1999). *Displaced Persons: The Literature of Exile from Cicero to Boethius*. Madison.

Clapp, S.L.C. (1932–3). "The Subscription Enterprises of John Ogilby and Richard Blome," *Modern Philology* 30: 365–79.

Clark, W.S. (1955). *The Early Irish Stage: The Beginnings to 1720*. Oxford.

Clausen, W.V. (1987). *Virgil's Aeneid and the Tradition of Hellenistic Poetry*. Berkeley, Los Angeles, and London.

Clay, D. (1992). "Columbus' Senecan Prophecy," *AJP* 113: 617–20.

Cleary, M. (1990). *The Bulfinch Solution: Teaching the Ancient Classics in American Schools*. Salem.

Cleary, M. (2000). "Freeing 'Incarcerated Souls': Margaret Fuller, Women, and Classical Mythology," *New England Classical Journal* 27: 59–67.

Cleary, M. (2002). "'Vague, Irregular Notions': American Women and Classical Mythology, 1780–1855," *New England Classical Journal* 29: 222–35.

Coburn, K. and Harding, A.H., eds. (1973). *Notebooks of Samuel Taylor Coleridge*. Princeton.

Cohen, S.D. (1974). *A History of Colonial Education, 1607–1776*. New York.

Colbourn, H. (1957). "Thomas Jefferson's Use of the Past," *William and Mary Quarterly* 14: 56–70.

Coleridge, S.T. (1917). *Table Talk*. Oxford.

Collilieux, E. (1886). *Etude sur Dictys de Crète et Darès de Phrygie*. Grenoble.

Colonna, G. (1980). "Virgilio, Cortona e la leggenda etrusca di Dardano," *ArchClass* 32: 1–15.

Colonne, Guido delle (1974). *Historia Destructionis Troiae*, trans. M.E. Meek. Bloomington.

Commager, H. (1961). "Leadership in Eighteenth-Century America and Today," *Daedalus* 90: 652–73.

Commager, H. (1971). "The American Enlightenment and the Ancient World: A Study in Paradox," *Proceedings of the Massachusetts Historical Society* 83: 3–15.

Comparetti, D. (1997). *Vergil in the Middle Ages*, trans. E.F.M. Benecke, rev. ed. Princeton.

Conington, J., trans. (1866). *The Aeneid of Virgil*. London.

Conington, J. (1872). "The English Translators of Virgil," in *Miscellaneous Writings of John Conington*, ed. J.A. Symonds. London. Vol. 1: 137–97.

Conkin, P. (1974). *Self-Evident Truths*. Bloomington.

Conn, R. (2002). *The Politics of Philology: Alfonso Reyes and the Invention of the Latin American Literary Tradition*. Bucknell Studies in Latin American Literature and Theory. Cranbury, NJ.

Connolly, J. (2007). *The State of Speech: Rhetoric and Political Thought in Ancient Rome*. Princeton.

Conrad, S. (1976). *Perish the Thought: Intellectual Women in Romantic America, 1830–1860*. New York.

Constant, B. (1977). *Œuvres*, ed. A. Roulin. Paris.

Conte, G.B. (1986). *The Rhetoric of Imitation*. Ithaca.

Conte, G.B. (2007). *The Poetry of Pathos: Studies in Virgilian Epic*. Oxford.

Cooke, T., ed. (1741). *Publii Virgilii Maronis Bucolica, Georgica, et Aeneis.* London.

Cooper, W. (1993). *Classical Taste in America, 1800–1840.* New York.

Coppin, F. (1913). *Reminiscences of School Life and Hints on Teaching.* Philadelphia.

Corbier, M. (2006). *Donner à voir, donner à lire: Mémoire et communication dans la Rome ancienne.* Paris.

Cornell, T.J. (1975). "Aeneas and the Twins: The Development of the Roman Foundation Legend," *PCPS* 21: 1–32.

Costantini, C. (1998–2008). Transcription of anonymous biography, "La Giusta statera de' Porporati" (Bibliothèque Mazarine, MS. 1659 cc. 7v–10v), in *Fazione Urbana: Sbandamento e ricomposizione di una grande clientela a metà Seicento.* Online publication retrieved September 3, 2009 from quaderni.net (www.quaderni.net/WebFazione/gb.htm).

Courcelles, P. (1968). *Recherches sur les "Confessions" de Saint Augustin.* Paris.

Courtney, E. (1990). "Vergil's Sixth Eclogue," *QUCC*, n.s. 34: 99–112.

Cowley, A. (1973). *The Civil War*, ed. A. Pritchard. Toronto.

Cox, F. (1997). "Envoi: The Death of Vergil," in Martindale, ed.: 327–36.

Cox, F. (1999). *Aeneas Takes the Metro: The Presence of Virgil in Twentieth-Century French Literature.* Oxford.

Cramer, R. (1998). *Vergils Weltsicht: Optimismus und Pessimismus in Vergils Georgica.* Berlin.

Craven, W. (1963). "Horatio Greenough's Statue of Washington and Phidias's Olympian Zeus," *Art Quarterly* 26: 429–40.

Crawford, J. (1974). "The Classical Orator in Nineteenth-Century American Sculpture," *American Art Journal* 6: 56–72.

Crawford, J. (1979). "The Classical Tradition in American Sculpture: Structure and Surface," *American Art Journal* 11: 38–52.

Creeley, R. (1982). *The Collected Poems of Robert Creeley, 1945–1975.* Berkeley.

Cremin, L.A. (1970). *American Education: The Colonial Experience, 1607–1783.* New York.

Crouch, S. (1995). *The All American Skin Game, or The Decoy of Race.* New York.

[Crusca] (1905). *Vocabolario degli Accademici della Crusca*, 5th ed., 11 vols. Florence.

Cugusi, P. and Sblendorio Cugusi, M.T., eds. (2001). *Opere di Marco Porcio Catone Censore*, vol. 2. Turin.

Cullen, P. (1970). *Spenser, Marvell and Renaissance Pastoral.* Cambridge, MA.

Culler, J. (2001). *The Pursuit of Signs.* Ithaca.

Curtius, E.R. (1953). *European Literature and the Latin Middle Ages*, trans. W.R. Trask. New York. Rpt. Princeton, 1967.

Dainville, F. de, S.J. (1951). "Le *Ratio discendi et docendi* de Jouvancy," *Archivum Historicum Societatis Jesu* 20: 3–58.

Daly, P. (1998). *Literature in Light of the Emblem: Structural Parallels between the Emblem and Literature in the Sixteenth and Seventeenth Centuries.* Toronto.

D'Anna, G. (1961). *Ancora sul Problema della Composizione dell'Eneide.* Rome.

D'Anna, G. (1975). "Didone e Anna in Varrone e in Virgilio," *RAL* 30: 3–34.

D'Anna, G. (1976). *Problemi di letteratura latina arcaica.* Rome.

D'Anna, G., ed. (1992). *Anonimo: Origine del Popolo Romano.* Milan.

D'Arms, J. (1964). "Vergil's *Cunctantem* (*ramum*): *Aeneid* 6.211," *CJ* 59: 265–8.

Davies, M. (2004). "Some Neglected Aspects of Cacus," *Eranos* 102: 30–7.

Davies, P.V., trans. (1969). *Macrobius: The Saturnalia.* New York.

Davis, C.T. (1957). *Dante and the Idea of Rome.* Oxford.

Davis, P. (2001). "'But slaves we are': Dryden and Virgil. Translation and the 'Gyant Race,'" *Translation and Literature* 10: 110–27.

Davis, R. (1964). *Intellectual Life in Jefferson's Virginia, 1790–1830.* Chapel Hill.

Davis, R. (1973). *Literature and Society in Early Virginia, 1608–1840.* Baton Rouge.

Davis, R. (1978). *Intellectual Life in the Colonial South, 1585–1763,* 3 vols. Knoxville.

Day Lewis, C., trans. (1952). *The Aeneid of Virgil.* London.

de Selincourt, E., ed. (1935). *The Early Letters of William and Dorothy Wordsworth (1787–1805).* Oxford.

Dekel, E. (2005). "Vergil's Homer: The *Aeneid* and its Odyssean Lens," PhD Diss., University of California, Berkeley.

Delaborde, H. (1888). *Marc-Antoine Raimondi.* Paris.

Delattre, D. (2006). *La Villa des papyrus et les rouleaux d'Herculaneum. La Bibliothèque de Philodème.* Cahiers du CeDoPaL 4. Liège.

Della Corte, F., ed. (1984–91). *Enciclopedia Virgiliana.* Rome.

Dench, E. (1995). *From Barbarians to New Men: Greek, Roman, and Modern Perceptions of Peoples of the Central Apennines.* Oxford.

Dench, E. (2005). *Romulus' Asylum: Roman Identities from the Age of Alexander to the Age of Hadrian.* Oxford.

DeNeef, A.L. (1982). *Spenser and the Motives of Metaphor.* Durham, NC.

Derrida, J. (1992). *The Other Heading: Reflections on Today's Europe,* trans. P.-A. Brault and M.B. Naas. Bloomington.

Derrida, J. (2000). *Demeure: Fiction and Testimony,* trans. E. Rottenberg. Stanford.

Derrida, J. (2002). "Force of Law: The 'Mystical Foundation of Authority,'" in *Acts of Religion,* ed. G. Anidjar. London: 230–98. [First published in French and English 1990; complete French version 1994; complete English version 2001.]

Dethloff, H., ed. (1971). *Thomas Jefferson and American Democracy.* Lexington.

Dew, T.R. (1992). "Republicanism and Literature" (1836). Rpt. in O'Brien, ed.: 125–76.

Dickey, E. (2007). *Ancient Greek Scholarship: A Guide to Finding, Reading, and Understanding Scholia, Commentaries, Lexica, and Grammatical Treatises, from Their Beginnings to the Byzantine Period.* New York and Oxford.

Dickinson, P., trans. (1961). *The Aeneid of Vergil.* New York.

Dickinson, R.J. (1973). "The *Tristia*: Poetry in Exile," in Binns, ed.: 154–90.

Diederich, M.D. (1931). *Vergil in the Works of St. Ambrose.* Washington, DC.

di Matteo, A. (1989). "Spenser's Venus-Virgo: The Poetics and Interpretive History of a Dissembling Figure," *Spenser Studies* 10: 37–70.

Dindorf, G., ed. (1962). *Scholia Graeca in Homeri Odysseam* (rpt. of 1855). Amsterdam.

Dix, T.K. and Houston, G.W. (2006). "Public Libraries in the City of Rome from the Augustan Age to the Time of Diocletian," *MEFRA* 118: 671–717.

Doblhofer, E. (1987). *Exil und Emigration: Zum Erlebnis der Heimatferne in der römischen Literatur.* Darmstadt.

Donald, A. et al., eds. (1964–). *Diary of Charles Francis Adams.* Cambridge, MA.

Donatus, Aelius. (1996). *Life of Virgil,* trans. D. Scott Wilson-Okamura, rev. 2005, 2008. www.virgil.org/vitae/a-donatus.htm. July 23, 1997.

Donatus, T.C. (1905–6). *Interpretationes Vergilianae,* ed. H. Georgii. Leipzig.

Dorandi, T. (2000). *Le Stylet et la tablette: dans le secret des auteurs antiques.* Paris.

Draheim, J. (1993). "Vergil in Music," in *The Classical Heritage: Vergil,* ed. C. Kallendorf. New York and London: 317–44.

Dryden, J., trans. (1716). *The Works of Virgil...Translated into English Verse.* London.

Dryden, J., trans. (1803). *The Works of Virgil...Translated into English Verse.* London.

Dryden, J. (1942). *The Letters of John Dryden,* ed. C.E. Ward. Princeton.

Dryden, J. (1958). *The Poems of John Dryden,* ed. J. Kinsley. Oxford.

Dryden, J. (1975). "Dedication of the *Aeneis,*" in Steiner, ed.: 72–5.

Dryden, J. (1987). *The Works of John Dryden*. Vols. 5–6: *The Works of Virgil in English, 1697*, ed. W. Frost and V.A. Dearing. Berkeley.

Duberman, M. (1988). *Paul Robeson*. New York.

Dubois, E.T. (1955). "The *Eclogae* of René Rapin S.J.: Neo-Latin Bucolic Verse in the Virgilian Manner," *Classical Folia: Studies in the Christian Perpetuation of the Classics* 11: 3–15.

Dubois, E.T. (1979). "The Virgilian Tradition in Neo-Latin Poetry in France in the Seventeenth Century," in *Acta Conventus Neolatini Amstelodamensis. Proceedings of the Second International Congress of Neo-Latin Studies*, ed. P. Tuynman et al. Munich: 338–51.

DuBois, P. (2001). *Trojan Horses: Saving the Classics from Conservatives*. New York.

Dubrow, H. (1990). "The Arraignment of Paridell: Tudor Historiography in *The Faerie Queene* III.ix.," *SPh* 87: 312–27.

Dufallo, B. (2007). *The Ghosts of the Past: Latin Literature, the Dead, and Rome's Transition to a Principate*. Columbus, OH.

Duggan, J.J. et al. (2005). *La Chanson de Roland/The Song of Roland: The French Corpus*, 3 vols. Turnhout.

Dupree, R.S. (1983). *Allen Tate and the Augustinian Imagination: A Study of the Poetry*. Baton Rouge and London.

Durling, R.M., trans. (1996). *Dante's Inferno*. New York.

Durling, R.M., trans. (2003). *Dante's Purgatorio*. New York.

Durrill, W. (1999). "The Power of Ancient Words: Classical Teaching and Social Change at South Carolina College, 1804–1869," *Journal of Southern History* 65: 469–98.

Dury-Moyaers, G. (1981). *Enée et Lavinium. A propos des découvertes archéologiques récentes*. Brussels.

Dyson, J.T. (2001). *King of the Wood: The Sacrificial Victor in Virgil's Aeneid*. Norman.

Dyson, R.W., trans. (1998). *Augustine: The City of God*. Cambridge.

Eadie, J., ed. (1976). *Classical Traditions in Early America*. Ann Arbor.

Eck, W. (2007). *The Age of Augustus*, trans. D.L. Schneider. Malden, MA.

Eden, P.T. (1975). *A Commentary on Virgil, Aeneid VIII. Mnemosyne* Suppl. 35. Leiden.

Eder, W. (1990). "Augustus and the Power of Tradition: The Augustan Principate as Binding Link between Republic and Empire," in Raaflaub and Toher, eds.: 71–121.

Edmunds, L. (2001). *Intertextuality and the Reading of Roman Poetry*. Baltimore.

Edwards, C. (1996). *Writing Rome: Textual Approaches to the City*. Cambridge.

Edwards, H.S. (1906). "The Negro and the South," *Century Magazine* 72: 212–15.

Edwards, H.S. (1928). "The Tenth Generation," *Manufacturers Record*, Baltimore, February 2.

Edwards, M.W., ed. (1991). *The Iliad: A Commentary*. Vol. 5: *Books 17–20*. Cambridge.

Effe, B. (1975). "Zur Rezeption von Vergils Lehrdichtung in der karolingischen 'Renaissance' und im französischen Klassizismus. Walahfrid Strabo und René Rapin," *A&A* 21: 140–63.

Eisenhut, W., ed. (1973). *Dictys Cretensis, Ephemeridos Belli Troiani Libri*. Leipzig.

Eldridge, R., ed. (1996). *Beyond Representation: Philosophy and Poetic Imagination*. Cambridge.

Eliot, T.S. (1950). "Tradition and the Individual Talent," in *Selected Essays*. New York: 3–11.

Eliot, T.S. (1951). "Virgil and the Christian World," in *On Poetry and Poets*. New York, 1961.

Eliot, T.S. (1975a). *Selected Prose of T.S. Eliot*, ed. F. Kermode. San Diego.

Eliot, T.S. (1975b). "What is a Classic?" in *Selected Prose of T.S. Eliot*, ed. F. Kermode. San Diego.

Emerson, R.W., Channing, W., and Clarke, J.F. (1852). *Memoirs of Margaret Fuller Ossoli*, vol. 1. Boston.

Emmerich Gallery (1964). *Masterpieces of Greek Vase Painting. Catalogue of the André Emmerich Gallery, Inc*. New York.

Erbse, H. (1959). "Über Aristarchs Iliasausgaben," *Hermes* 87: 275–303.

Erbse, H. (1969–88). *Scholia Graeca in Homeri Iliadem (scholia vetera)*, 7 vols. Berlin.

Erskine, A. (2001). *Troy between Greece and Rome: Local Tradition and Imperial Power.* Oxford.

Erxleben, M. (1995). "Goethe und Vergil," in Irmscher, ed.: 131–41.

Espinosa Pólit, A. (1932). *Virgilio. El poeta y su misión providencial.* Quito.

Ettin, A.V. (1982). "The Georgics in *The Faerie Queene*," *Spenser Studies* 3: 57–72.

Ettlinger, L.D. (1961). "Exemplum Doloris: Reflections on the Laocoon Group," in *Essays in Honor of Erwin Panofsky*, ed. M. Meiss. New York: 121–6.

Evans, H.B. (1983). *Publica Carmina: Ovid's Books from Exile.* Lincoln.

Everson, J.E. (2001). *The Italian Romance Epic in the Age of Humanism: The Matter of Italy and the World of Rome.* Oxford.

Fagiolo, M., ed. (1981). *Virgilio nell'arte e nella cultura europea.* Rome.

Fagles, R., trans. (1990). *Homer: The Iliad.* Introduction and notes by B. Knox. New York.

Fagles, R., trans. (1996). *Homer: The Odyssey.* Introduction and notes by B. Knox. New York.

Fagles, R., trans. (2006). *Virgil: The Aeneid.* Introduction and notes by B. Knox. New York.

Fairclough, H.R. and Goold, G. (1999). *Virgil: Eclogues, Georgics, Aeneid.* Cambridge, MA.

Fairweather, J. (1974). "Fiction in the Biographies of Ancient Writers," *AncSoc* 5: 231–75.

Faivre d'Arcier, L. (2006). *Histoire et géographie d'un mythe.* Paris.

Fanshawe, R. (1997). *The Poems and Translations of Sir Richard Fanshawe*, ed. P. Davidson. Oxford.

"Farewell, J." (1689). *The Irish Hudibras, or Fingallian Prince, taken from the Sixth Book of Virgil's Æneids, and Adapted to the Present Times.* London.

Farnham, C. (1994). *The Education of the Southern Belle: Higher Education and Student Socialization in the Antebellum South.* New York.

Farrell, A.P., S.J. (1938). *The Jesuit Code of Liberal Education.* Milwaukee.

Farrell, A.P., S.J. (1970). *The Jesuit Ratio studiorum of 1599.* Translated into English, with an Introduction and Explanatory Notes. Washington, DC. www.bc.edu/bc_org/avp/ulib/digi/ratio/ratiohome.html.

Farrell, J. (1991). *Vergil's Georgics and the Traditions of Ancient Epic: The Art of Allusion in Literary History.* New York.

Farrell, J. (1997). "The Virgilian Intertext," in Martindale, ed.: 222–38.

Farrell, J. (2001). "The Vergilian Century," *Vergilius* 47: 11–28.

Farrell, J. (2005a). "The Origins and Essence of Roman Epic," in Foley, ed.: 417–28.

Farrell, J. (2005b). "Intention and Intertext," *Phoenix* 59: 98–111.

Farrell, J. (2008). "Servius and the Homeric Scholia," in Casali and Stok, eds.: 112–31.

Faugeres, M. (1793). *The Posthumous Works of Ann Eliza Bleecker, in Prose and Verse. To Which is Added, a Collection of Essays, Prose and Poetical.* New York.

Feder, L. (1972). "Allen Tate's Use of Classical Literature," in *Allen Tate and His Work: Critical Evaluations*, ed. R. Squires. Minneapolis.

Feeney, D.C. (1983). "The Taciturnity of Aeneas," *CQ* 33: 204–19.

Feeney, D.C. (1984). "The Reconciliations of Juno," *CQ* 33: 188–203.

Feeney, D.C. (1986). "History and Revelation in Vergil's Underworld," *PCPS* 32: 1–24.

Feeney, D.C. (1991). *The Gods in Epic: Poets and Critics of the Classical Tradition.* Cambridge.

Feeney, D.C. (1998). *Literature and Religion at Rome: Cultures, Contexts, and Beliefs.* Cambridge.

Feeney, D.C. (2005). "The Beginnings of a Literature in Latin," *JRS* 95: 226–40.

Feeney, D.C. and Nelis, D. (2005). "Two Virgilian Acrostics: *Certissima Signa?*," *CQ* 55: 644–6.

Feldherr, A. (1995). "Ships of State: *Aeneid* 5 and Augustan Circus Spectacle," *ClAnt* 14: 245–65.

Feldman, B. and Richardson, R., eds. (1972). *The Rise of Modern Mythology, 1680–1860.* Bloomington.

Ferrary, J.-L. (1988). *Philhellénisme et impérialisme.* Rome.

Fetterley, J. (1978). *The Resisting Reader: A Feminist Approach to American Fiction.* Bloomington and London.

Fichter, A. (1982). *Poets Historical: Dynastic Epic in the Renaissance.* New Haven and London.

Finley, G. (1999). *Angel in the Sun: Turner's Vision of History.* London and Ithaca.

Fiorentini, L. (2007). "Lirici greci nella bibliotheca di Virgilio: qualche appunto sulla presenza di Saffo, Alceo e Stesicoro nell'Eneide," in Andrisano, ed.: 127–45.

Fischer, H. (1887). *Lessings "Laokoon" und die Gesetze der bildenden Künst.* Berlin.

Fish, J. (2004). "Anger, Philodemus' Good King, and the Helen Episode of *Aeneid* 2.567–589: A New Proof of Authenticity from Herculaneum," in Armstrong et al., eds.: 111–38.

Fishbane, M., ed. (1993). *The Midrashic Imagination: Jewish Exegesis, Thought, and History.* Albany.

Fisher, P. (1998). *Wonder, the Rainbow, and the Aesthetics of Rare Experiences.* Cambridge, MA.

Fitzgerald, R., trans. (1961). *Homer: The Odyssey.* Garden City, NY.

Fitzgerald, R., trans. (1974). *Homer: The Iliad.* Garden City, NY.

Fitzgerald, R., trans. (1983). *Virgil: The Aeneid.* New York.

Fitzgerald, W. (2004). "*Fatalis Machina*: Berlioz's *Les Troyens*," *MD* (*Numero speciale in onore di Michael C.J. Putnam*) 52: 199–210.

Fletcher, K.F.F. (2006). "Vergil's Italian Diomedes," *AJP* 127: 219–59.

Foeller-Pituch, E. (1995). "Ambiguous Heritage: Classical Myths in the Works of Nineteenth-Century American Writers," *IJCT* 1: 98–108.

Foley, J.M., ed. (2005). *A Companion to Ancient Epic.* Oxford.

Fordyce, C.J., ed. (1977). *P. Vergili Maronis Aeneidos Libri VII–VIII, with a Commentary.* Oxford.

Foucault, M. (1964). "Les mots qui saignent," *L'Express*, August 29, 21–2.

Fowler, D. (1995). "Martial and the Book," *Ramus* 24: 31–58.

Fowler, D. (1998). "Opening the Gates of War: *Aeneid* 7.601–40," in Stahl, ed.: 155–74.

Fowler, D. (2000). *Roman Constructions: Readings in Postmodern Latin.* Oxford.

Fowler, P.G. (1997). "Lucretian Conclusions," in Roberts, Dunn, and Fowler, eds.: 112–38.

Fowler, R. (2009). "'Purple Shining Lilies': Imagining the *Aeneid* in Contemporary Poetry," in *Living Classics: Greece and Rome in Contemporary Poetry in English*, ed. S. Harrison. Oxford: 238–54.

Fox-Genovese, E. and Genovese, E. (2005). *The Mind of the Master Class: History and Faith in the Southern Slaveholders' Worldview.* Cambridge.

Fraade, S. (1991). *From Tradition to Commentary: Torah and its Interpretation in the Midrash Sifre to Deuteronomy.* Albany.

France, P., ed. (2000). *The Oxford Guide to Literature in English Translation.* Oxford.

Fränkel, H. (1932). "Griechische Bildung in altrömischen Epen," *Hermes* 67: 303–11.

Fraschetti, A. (1981). "Le sepolture rituali del foro Boario," in *Le délit religieux dans la cité antique (table ronde, Rome, 6–7 avril 1978).* Rome: 102–5.

Frazer, R.M. (1966). *The Trojan War.* Bloomington.

Frechulf (2002). *Frechulfi Lexoviensis episcopi opera omnia*, ed. M. Allen, 2 vols. Corpus Christianorum, Continuatio Mediaevalis 169–169A. Turnhout.

Frey, A. (1905). *Die Kunstform des Lessingschen Laokoon, mit Beiträgen zu einem Laokoonkommentar.* Stuttgart and Berlin.

Friedberg, M. (1997). *Literary Translation in Russia: A Cultural History.* University Park, PA.

Friedlaender, M. and Butterfield, L.H., eds. (1968). *Diary of Charles Francis Adams.* Vol. 4: *March 1831–December 1832.* Cambridge, MA.

Frier, B. (1979). *Libri Annales Pontificum Maximorum: The Origins of the Annalistic Tradition.* Rome.

Frings, I. (1998). "Mantua me genuit – Vergils Grabepigramm auf Stein und Pergament," *ZPE* 123: 89–100.

Frost, W. (1955). *Dryden and the Art of Translation.* New Haven.

Frost, W. (1988). *John Dryden: Dramatist, Satirist, Translator.* New York.

Fry, G., ed. (1998). *Récits inédits sur la guerre de Troie.* Paris.

Fumaroli, M., ed. (2001). *La Querelle des Anciens et des Modernes: XVIIe–XVIIIe siècles.* Paris.

Fumaroli, M. (2005). "Terror and Grace: Girodet, Poet of Painting," in Bellenger, ed.: 53–79.

Gabba, E. (1976). "Sulla valorizzazione politica della leggenda delle origini troiane di Roma," in Sordi, ed.: 84–101 [= E. Gabba, *Aspetti culturali dell'imperialismo romano.* Florence, 1993: 91–112].

Gaertner, T. (2004). "Die Ignatias des Laurentius Le Brun. Ein Jesuitenepos über den Ordensgruender Ignatius von Loyola," *Neulateinisches Jahrbuch* 6: 17–49.

Gaisser, J.H. (2002). "The Reception of Classical Texts in the Renaissance," in *The Italian Renaissance in the Twentieth Century,* ed. A.J. Grieco, M. Rocke, and F.G. Superbi. Florence: 387–400.

Gale, M. (2000). *Virgil on the Nature of Things: The Georgics, Lucretius and the Didactic Tradition.* Cambridge.

Gale, M., ed. (2004). *Latin Epic and Didactic Poetry.* Swansea.

Galinsky, G.K. (1969). *Aeneas, Sicily, and Rome.* Princeton.

Galinsky, G.K. (1988). "The Anger of Aeneas," *AJP* 109: 321–48.

Galinsky, G.K. (1992). "Aeneas at Rome and Lavinium," in Wilhelm and Jones, eds.: 93–108.

Galinsky, G.K. (1996). *Augustan Culture: An Interpretive Introduction.* Princeton.

Gall, D. and A. Wolkenhauer, eds. (2008). *Laokoon in Literatur und Kunst.* Schriften des Symposions "Laokoon in Literatur und Kunst" vom 30.11.2006, Universität Bonn. Beiträge zur Altertumskunde 254. New York and Berlin.

Galluzzi, T., S.J. (1621). *Virgilianae vindicationes et Commentarii tres de tragoedia, comoedia, elegia.* Rome.

Gambarota, P. (2006). "Syntax and Passions: Bouhours, Vico, and the Genius of the Nation," *Romantic Review* 97: 3–4, 285–307.

Ganducci, G.B., S.J. (1660). *Descriptiones poeticae ex probatioribus poetis Excerptae.* Parma.

Gantz, T. (1993). *Early Greek Myth: A Guide to Literary and Artistic Sources.* Baltimore and London.

Gardner, E.G. (1906). *The King of Court Poets: A Study of the Life, Work, and Time of Lodovico Ariosto.* New York.

Gasparov, M.L. (1971). "Briusov i bukvalizm (Po neizdannym materialam k perevodu 'Eneidy')," *Masterstvo Perevoda* 8: 88–128.

Gasparov, M.L. (1997a). "Briusov-perevodchik. Pyt' k pereput'yu'," *Izbrannye trudy,* vol. 2. Moscow. 121–9.

Gasparov, M.L. (1997b). "Briusov i podstrochnik," *Izbrannye trudy,* vol. 2. Moscow: 130–40.

Gay, J. (1974). *Poetry and Prose,* ed. V.A. Dearing and C.E. Beckwith, 2 vols. Oxford.

Geer, R.M. (1926). "Non-Suetonian Passages in the Life of Vergil Formerly Ascribed to Donatus," *TAPhA* 57: 107–15.

Geerlings, W. and Schulze, C., eds. (2002). *Der Kommentar in Antike und Mittelalter. Beiträge zu seiner Erforschung.* Clavis Commentariorum Antiquitatis et Medii Aevi, 2. Leiden.

Genovese, E. (2002). "The Gracchi and Their Mother in the Mind of American Slaveholders," *Journal of the Historical Society* 2: 455–82.

Gentili, V. (1988). "Spenser," in *Enciclopedia Virgiliana*, ed. F. della Corte. Rome. Vol. 4: 983–90.

Gevartius (Gevaerts, C.) (1641). *Pompa introitus honori Serenissimi Principis Ferdinandi Austriaci Hispaniarum Infantis.* Antwerp.

Giannettasio, N. (1685). *Piscatoria et nautica.* Naples.

Giannettasio, N. (1715–21). *Opera omnia poetica*, 3 vols. Naples.

Gianotti, G.F. (1979). "La metamorfosi di Omero," *Sigma* 12: 15–32.

Gibbon, E. (1770). *Critical Observations on the Sixth Book of the Aeneid.* London.

Gibbon, E. (1966). *Memoirs of My Life*, ed. G.A. Bonnard. New York.

Gierl, M. (1992). "Bestandsaufnahme im gelehrten Bereich: Zur Entwicklung der *Historia literaria* im 18. Jht," in *Denkhorizonte und Handlungsspielräume.* Göttingen: 53–80.

Gigante, M. (2004). "Vergil in the Shadow of Vesuvius," in Armstrong et al., eds.: 85–99.

Gigante, M. and Capasso, M. (1989). "Il ritorno di Virgilio a Ercolano," *SIFC* 7: 3–6.

Gildenhard, I. (2003). "*Philologia Perennis?* Classical Scholarship and Functional Differentiation," in *Out of Arcadia: Classics and Politics in Germany in the Age of Burckhardt, Nietzsche and Wilamowitz*, ed. I. Gildenhard and M. Ruehl. London: 161–203.

Gill, C. (2006). *The Structured Self in Hellenistic and Roman Thought.* Oxford.

Gillespie, N. (1972). *The Collapse of Orthodoxy: The Intellectual Ordeal of George Frederick Holmes.* Charlottesville.

Gillespie, S. (1992). "A Checklist of Restoration English Translations and Adaptations of Classical Greek and Latin Poetry, 1660–1700," *Translation and Literature* 1: 52–67.

Gilroy, P. (1993). *The Black Atlantic: Modernity and Double Consciousness.* Cambridge, MA.

Giraldi Cintio, G. (1864). *De' romanzi, delle comedie e delle tragedie ragionamenti*, 2 vols. in 1. Milan.

Giuliani, L. (1999). "Winckelmanns Laokoon. Von der befristeten Eigenmächtigkeit des Kommentars," in *Commentaries – Kommentare*, ed. G.W. Most. Aporemata 4. Göttingen: 296–322.

Glei, R. (2006). *Virgilius Cothurnatus – Vergil im Schauspielhaus: Drei lateinische Tragödien von Michael Maittaire.* Tübingen.

Glück, L. (1999). *Vita Nova.* New York.

Godi, M. (1967). *Una redazione poetica latina medievale della storia De Excidio Troiae.* Rome.

Goldberg, S. (2005). *Constructing Literature in the Roman Republic: Poetry and its Reception.* Cambridge.

Gombrich, E.H. (1956). *Art and Illusion.* Princeton.

Gombrich, E.H. (1957). "Laocoon," *PBA* 43: 133–56.

Gombrich, E.H. (1963). "The Style *All'Antica*: Imitation and Assimilation," *Acts of the XX International Congress of the History of Art.* Princeton.

Goold, G.P. (1970). "Servius and the Helen Episode," *HCSP* 74: 101–68. Rpt. in Harrison, ed., 1990: 60–126.

Goold, G.P. (1992). "The Voice of Virgil: The Pageant of Rome in *Aeneid* 6," in *Author and Audience in Latin Literature*, ed. T. Woodman and J. Powell. Cambridge: 110–23.

Görler, W. (1988). "Obtrectatores," in *Enciclopedia Virgiliana*, ed. F. della Corte. Rome. Vol. 3: 807–13.

Gorra, E. (1887). *Testi inediti di storia trojana.* Turin.

Goulet-Cazé, M.-O., ed. (2000). *Le Commentaire entre tradition et innovation. Actes du colloque international de l'institut des traditions textuelles (Paris et Villejuif, 22–25 septembre 1999).* Paris.

Govan, T. (1975). "Alexander Hamilton and Julius Caesar: A Note on the Use of Historical Evidence," *William and Mary Quarterly* 32: 475–80.

Graf, A. (1923). *Roma nella memoria e nelle immaginazioni del medio evo.* Turin.

Grafton, A. (1991). *Defenders of the Text: The Traditions of Scholarship in an Age of Science, 1450–1800.* Cambridge, MA.

Grafton, A. (2007). *What was History? The Art of History in Early Modern Europe.* Cambridge.

Grafton, A. and Jardine, L. (1986). *From Humanism to the Humanities: Education and the Liberal Arts in Fifteenth- and Sixteenth-Century Europe.* Cambridge, MA.

Grandazzi, A. (1997). *The Foundation of Rome: Myth and History,* trans. J.M. Todd. Ithaca.

Gransden, K.W., ed. (1976). *Virgil, Aeneid: Book VIII.* Cambridge.

Gransden, K.W., ed. (1996). *Virgil in English.* New York.

Grant, W.L. (1965). *Neo-Latin Literature and the Pastoral.* Chapel Hill.

Gratien, B. and Hanoune, R. (1997). *Lire l'écrit: Textes, archives et bibliothèques dans l'Antiquité.* Lille.

Graves, R. (1962). "The Virgil Cult," *Virginia Quarterly Review* 38: 13–35 [= "The Anti-Poet," *Oxford Addresses on Poetry.* London: 29–53].

Graves, R.P. (1979). *A.E. Housman: The Scholar-Poet.* London.

Grebe, S. (2004). "Augustus' Divine Authority and Vergil's *Aeneid,*" *Vergilius* 50: 35–62.

Green, R.P.H. (2006). *Latin Epics of the New Testament: Juvencus, Sedulius, Arator.* Oxford.

Greene, H., Hutchins, H.S., Jr., and Hutchins, B.E. (2004). *Slave Badges and the Slave Hire System, Charleston 1783–1865.* Jefferson, NC.

Greene, T.M. (1963). *The Descent from Heaven: A Study in Epic Continuity.* New Haven.

Greene, T.M. (1999). "The Natural Tears of Epic," in *Epic Traditions in the Contemporary World: The Poetics of Community,* ed. M. Beissinger, J. Tylus, and S. Wofford. Berkeley: 189–202.

Greenwood, E. (2009). "Review Essay: Re-rooting the Classical Tradition: New Directions in Black Classicism," *Classical Receptions Journal* 1.1:87–103.

Gregg, E.W., ed. (1982). *The Letters of Ellen Tucker Emerson,* vol. 1. Kent.

Gregg, G., ed. (1999). *Vital Remnants: America's Founding and the Western Tradition.* Wilmington.

Gregory, T. (2006). *From Many Gods to One: Divine Action in Renaissance Epic.* Chicago.

Grendler, P.F. (1989). *Schooling in Renaissance Italy: Literacy and Learning, 1300–1600.* Baltimore.

Grenfell, P.B., Hunt, A.S., and Goodspeed, E.J., eds. (1907). *The Tebtunis Papyri,* pt. II. London.

Grey, B. (1937). *The English Print.* London.

Gribbin, W. (1972). "Rollin's Histories and American Republicanism," *William and Mary Quarterly* 29: 611–22.

Griffin, J. (1985). *Latin Poets and Roman Life.* London.

Griffin, N.E. (1907). *Dares and Dictys.* Baltimore.

Griffith, M. (1990). "Contest and Contradiction in Early Greek Poetry," in *Cabinet of the Muses: Essays…in Honor of Thomas G. Rosenmeyer,* ed. M. Griffith and D. Mastronarde. Atlanta: 185–205.

Griffiths, A. (1998). *The Print in Stuart Britain: 1603–1689.* London.

Grilli, A. (1995). "Interrogativi su dove nacque Virgilio," *Paideia* 50: 207–13.

Griswold, A.W. (1971). "Jefferson's Agrarian Democracy," in *Thomas Jefferson and Agrarian Democracy,* ed. H.C. Dethloff. Lexington.

Gruen, E.S. (1992). *Culture and National Identity in Republican Rome*. Ithaca.

Grumach, E., ed. (1949). *Goethe und die Antike*, 2 vols. Berlin.

Grunert, F. and Vollhardt, F., eds. (2007). *Historia Literaria: Neuordnungen des Wissens im 17. und 18. Jahrhundert*. Berlin.

Guiniggi, V., S.J. (1626). *Allocutiones gymnasticae*. Rome; Venice, 1648.

Gummere, R. (1934). "John Adams, Togatus," *PhQ* 13: 203–210.

Gummere, R. (1955). "The Heritage of the Classics in Colonial North America," *PAPHS* 99: 68–78.

Gummere, R. (1956). "John Dickinson, Classical Penman of the Revolution," *CJ* 52: 81–8.

Gummere, R. (1957). "The Classical Politics of John Adams," *Boston Public Library Quarterly* 9: 167–82.

Gummere, R. (1962). "The Classical Ancestry of the United States Constitution," *American Quarterly* 14: 3–18.

Gummere, R. (1963). *The American Colonial Mind and the Classical Tradition: Essays in Comparative Culture*. Cambridge, MA.

Gummere, R. (1967). *Seven Wise Men of Colonial America*. Cambridge, MA.

Günther, H.-C. (1996). *Uberlegungen zur Entstehung von Vergils Aeneis*. Göttingen.

Gurval, R.A. (1995). *Actium and Augustus: The Politics and Emotions of Civil War*. Ann Arbor.

Hadas, R. (1975). *Starting From Troy*. Boston.

Haecker, T. (1931). *Vergil, Vater des Abendlands*. Leipzig.

Haecker, T. (1934). *Virgil, Father of the West*, trans. A.W. Wheen. London.

Hagendahl, H. (1958). *Latin Fathers and the Classics: A Study on the Apologists, Jerome and Other Christian Writers*. Göteborg.

Hagendahl, H. (1967). *Augustine and the Latin Classics*, 2 vols. Göteborg.

Hagstrum, J. (1958). *The Sister Arts*. Chicago.

Hale, J.K. (1995). "Paradise Lost, A Poem in Twelve Books – or Ten?," *PhQ* 74: 131–49.

Haley, J. (1895). *Afro-American Encyclopaedia*. Nashville.

Hall, E. (1989). *Inventing the Barbarian*. Oxford.

Hall, J.F. (1992). "The Original Ending of the Aeneas Tale: Cato and the Historiographical Tradition of Aeneas," *SyllClass* 3: 13–20.

Hamlin, T. (1944). *Greek Revival Architecture in America*. New York.

Hammer, D. (2002). *The Iliad as Politics: The Performance of Political Thought*. Norman.

Hammond, P. (1991). *John Dryden: A Literary Life*. New York.

Hammond, P. (1998). "Classical Texts: Translations and Transformations," in Zwicker, ed.: 143–61.

Hammond, P. (1999). *Dryden and the Traces of Classical Rome*. Oxford.

Hampe, R. (1972). *Sperlonga und Vergil*. Mainz.

Hannah, B. (2004). "Manufacturing Descent: Virgil's Genealogical Engineering," *Arethusa* 37: 141–64.

Hannah, B. (2007). "*Exegi Monumentum*: Architecture in Latin Epic," Diss., Cornell.

Hanoune, R. (1997). "L'architecture de la bibliothèque romaine," in Gratien and Hanoune, eds.: 109–17.

Hardie, C., ed. (1966). *Vitae Vergilianae Antiquae*. 2nd ed. Oxford.

Hardie, C. (1984). "Virgil in Dante," in Martindale, ed.: 37–69.

Hardie, P.R. (1986). *Virgil's Aeneid: Cosmos and Imperium*. Oxford.

Hardie, P.R. (1987). "Aeneas and the Omen of the Swans (Verg. *Aen.* 1.393–400)," *CPh* 82: 145–50.

Hardie, P.R. (1993). *The Epic Successors of Virgil: A Study in the Dynamics of a Tradition*. Cambridge.

Hardie, P.R., ed. (1994). *Virgil: Aeneid Book IX*. Cambridge.

Hardie, P.R. (1997). "Closure in Latin Epic," in Roberts, Dunn, and Fowler, eds.: 139–62.

Hardie, P.R. (1998). *Virgil*. Greece & Rome: New Surveys in the Classics, 28. Oxford.

Hardie, P.R. (1999). Review of Günther (1996). *CR* 49.1: 49–50.

Hardie, P.R. (2002). *Ovid's Poetics of Illusion*. Cambridge.

Hardie, P.R. (2004). "In the Steps of the Sibyl: Tradition and Desire in the Epic Underworld," *MD* (*Numero speciale in onore di Michael C.J. Putnam*) 52: 143–56.

Hardie, P.R. (2007). "Contrasts," in *Classical Constructions: Papers in Memory of Don Fowler, Classicist and Epicurean*, ed. S.J. Heyworth. Oxford: 141–73.

Hardison, O.B. (1962). *The Enduring Monument: A Study of the Idea of Praise in Renaissance Literary Theory and Practice*. Chapel Hill.

Hardt, M. and Negri, A. (2000). *Empire*. Cambridge, MA.

Harrington, J. (1658). *An Essay Upon Two of Virgil's Eclogues, and Two Books of his Æneis (If this be not enough) Towards the Translation of the Whole*. London.

Harrington, J. (1659). *Virgil's Æneis: The Third, Fourth, Fifth and Sixth Books*. London.

Harrington, J. (1977). *The Political Works of James Harrington*, ed. J.G.A. Pocock. Cambridge.

Harris, E. (1987). *Henry Purcell's Dido and Aeneas*. Oxford.

Harris, J. (1984). "Last of the Classical Republicans: An Interpretation of John C. Calhoun," *Civil War History* 30: 255–67.

Harris, S. (1989). "Transposing the Merton Thesis: Apostolic Spirituality and the Establishment of the Jesuit Scientific Tradition," *Science in Context* 3: 29–65.

Harris, W.V. (1985). *War and Imperialism in Republican Rome, 327–70 B.C.* Oxford.

Harrison, E.L. (1980). "The Structure of the *Aeneid*: Observations on the Links Between the Books," *ANRW* II.31.2, 359–93.

Harrison, E.L. (1985). "Foundation Prodigies in the *Aeneid*," *PLLS* 5: 131–64.

Harrison, S.J., ed. (1990). *Oxford Readings in Vergil's Aeneid*. Oxford.

Harrison, S.J. (1991). *Vergil Aeneid 10. With Introduction, Translation, and Commentary*. Oxford.

Harrison, T.W. (1967). "English Virgil: The *Aeneid* in the XVIII Century," *Philologica Pragensia* 10.1–2: 1–11, 80–91.

Harrison, T.W. (1969). "Dryden's *Aeneid*," in *Dryden's Mind and Art*, ed. B. King. Edinburgh: 143–67.

Harthan, J. (1997). *The History of the Illustrated Book: The Western Tradition*. London.

Hartley, H. (1889). *Classical Translations*. St. John.

Hartley, H. (1890). *Ta Tou Pragma Emou Biou, or Some Concerns of My Life*. Amherst, Nova Scotia.

Hartman, G. (1988). *Easy Pieces*. New York.

Hartman, G. and Budick, S., eds. (1986). *Midrash and Literature*. New Haven.

Haskell, Y.A. (2003). *Loyola's Bees: Ideology and Industry in Jesuit Latin Didactic Poetry*. Oxford.

Haskell, Y.A. and Ruys, J., eds. (2010). *Latinity and Alterity in the Early Modern Period*. Tempe.

Haslam, M. (1997). "Homeric Papyri and Transmission of the Text," in Morris and Powell, eds.: 55–100.

Havens, C.E. (1920). *Diary of a Little Girl in Old New York*. New York.

Haverkamp, A. (2005). "Anagrammatics of Violence: The Benjaminian Ground of *Homo Sacer*," *Cardozo Law Review* 26: 995–1003.

Hawkins, P. (1991). "Dido, Beatrice, and the Signs of Ancient Love," in Jacoff and Schnapp, eds.: 113–30.

Hawkins, P. (1999). *Dante's Testaments: Essays in Scriptural Imagination.* Stanford.

Hayes, K. (1996). *A Colonial Woman's Bookshelf.* Knoxville.

Hayley, W. (1782). *An Essay on Epic Poetry; in Five Epistles to the Revd. Mr. Mason, with Notes.* London.

Haynes, K. (2001). "Dryden: Classical or Neoclassical?," *Translation and Literature* 10: 67–77.

Heaney, S. (1991). *Seeing Things.* New York.

Heath, M. (1998). "Was Homer a Roman?," *PLLS* 10: 23–56.

Heath-Stubbs, J. (1985). *The Immolation of Aleph.* Manchester.

Heeren, M.W. and Brown, S.A., eds. (1988). *The Sacred Nectar of the Greeks: The Study of Greek in the West in the Early Middle Ages.* London.

Heffer, S. (1998). *Like the Roman: The Life of Enoch Powell.* London.

Heidenreich, M. (2006). *Christian Gottlob Heyne und die Alte Geschichte.* Munich.

Heinze, R. (1914). *Vergils epische Technik.* Leipzig.

Heinze, R. (1993). *Vergil's Epic Technique,* trans. H. and D. Harvey and F. Robertson, pref. A. Wlosok. Berkeley.

Helgerson, R. (1983). *Self-Crowned Laureates: Spenser, Jonson, Milton and the Literary System.* Berkeley, Los Angeles, and London.

Heller, W. (1998). " 'O Castita Bugiarda': Cavalli's *Didone* and the Question of Chastity," in Burden, ed.: 169–225.

Henderson, J. (1998). "Lucan: The Word at War," in *Fighting for Rome: Poets and Caesars, History and Civil War.* New York and Cambridge: 165–211.

Henderson, J. (2000). "The Camillus Factory: *per astra ad Ardeam,*" *Ramus* 29: 1–26.

Henderson, J.B. (1991). *Scripture, Canon, and Commentary: A Comparison of Confucian and Western Exegesis.* Princeton.

Henry, W.W., ed. (1969). *Patrick Henry: Life, Correspondence, and Speeches.* New York.

Herbst, J. (2004). "The Yale Report of 1828," *IJCT* 11: 213–31.

Herman, E. (2008). *Mistress of the Vatican: The True Story of Olimpia Maidalchini, the Secret Female Pope.* New York.

Hertl, M. and Hertl, R. (1968). *Laokoon. Ausdruck des Schmerzes durch zwei Jahrtausende.* Munich.

Hexter, R. (1986). *Ovid and Medieval Schooling: Studies in Medieval School Commentaries on Ovid's Ars Amatoria, Epistulae ex Ponto and Epistulae Heroidum.* Münchener Beiträge zur Mediävistik und Renaissance-Forschung, 38. Munich.

Hexter, R. (1988). "Medieval Articulations of Ovid's *Metamorphoses.* From Lactantian Segmentation to Arnulfian Allegory," *Mediaevalia: A Journal of Medieval Studies* 13: 63–82.

Hexter, R. (1989). "The *Allegari* of Pierre Bersuire: Interpretation and the *Reductorium morale,*" *Allegorica* 10: 49–82.

Hexter, R. (1990). "What Was The Trojan Horse Made Of? Interpreting Vergil's *Aeneid,*" *YJC* 3: 109–31.

Hexter, R. (1992). "Sidonian Dido," in Hexter and Selden, eds.: 332–84.

Hexter, R. (1993). *A Guide to the Odyssey: A Commentary on the English Translation of Robert Fitzgerald.* New York.

Hexter, R. (1997). "The Faith of Achates: Finding Aeneas' Other," Morrison Library Inaugural Address Series, 8. Berkeley.

Hexter, R. (1999). "Imitating Troy: A Reading of *Aeneid* 3," in Perkell, ed.: 64–79, 314–17.

Hexter, R. (2002). "Narrative and an Absolutely Fabulous Commentary on Ovid's *Heroides,*" in Lanham, ed.: 212–83.

Hexter, R. and Selden, D., eds. (1992). *Innovations of Antiquity*. New York.

Heyne, C.G., ed. (1819). *Publii Virgilii Maronis Quae Extant Omnia Opera*, 8 vols. Paris.

Heyne C.G. (1833). *P. Vergilius Maro varietate lectionis et perpetua adnotatione illustratus.* 4th ed. G.P.E. Wagner. Vol. 3: *Aeneid 7–12*. Leipzig and London.

Hibbard, H. (1965). *Bernini*. Baltimore.

Hiden, M. (1941). "Education and the Classics in the Life of Colonial Virginia," *Virginia Magazine of History and Biography* 49: 20–8.

Hill, C. (1977). *Milton and the English Revolution*. London.

Hill, D.E. (1990). "What Sort of Translation of Virgil Do We Need?," in *Greece & Rome Studies: Virgil*, ed. I. McAuslan and P. Walcot. Oxford: 180–8.

Hill, G. (1959). *For the Unfallen*. London.

Hiller, F. (1979). "Wieder einmal Laokoon," *MDAI(R)* 86: 271–95.

Himmelmann, N. (1991). "Laokoon," *AK* 34: 97–115.

Hind, A.M. (1952–64). *Engraving in England in the Sixteenth and Seventeenth Centuries*, vol. 3. Cambridge.

Hindman, S., ed. (1982). *The Early Illustrated Book: Essays in Honor of Lessing J. Rosenwald*. Washington, DC.

Hinds, S. (1985). "Booking the Return Trip: Ovid and *Tristia* I," *PCPS* 31: 13–32.

Hinds, S. (1998). *Allusion and Intertext: Dynamics of Appropriation in Roman Poetry*. Cambridge.

Hinds, S. (1999). "After Exile: Time and Teleology from *Metamorphoses* to *Ibis*," in *Ovidian Transformations: Essays on Ovid's Metamorphoses and Its Reception*, ed. P.R. Hardie, A. Barchiesi, and S. Hinds. Cambridge Philological Society Supplement 23: Cambridge: 48–67.

Hinz, B. (2001). "Laokoongruppe," in *Der Neue Pauly. Enzyklopädie der Antike. Rezeptions- und Wissenschaftsgeschichte*. Stuttgart and Weimar: Vol. 15/1, La–Ot: 9–19.

Hirsch, E. (1994). *Earthly Measures: Poems*. New York.

Hoeflich, M. (1997). *Roman and Civil Law and the Development of Anglo-American Jurisprudence in the Nineteenth Century*. Athens, GA.

Hofer, P. (1970). *Baroque Book Illustration: A Short Survey from the Collection in the Department of Graphic Arts, Harvard College Library*. Cambridge, MA.

Hoffman, R. (1978). "Classics in the Courts of the United States, 1790–1800," *American Journal of Legal History* 22: 55–84.

Hofmann, H. (1994). "*Adveniat tandem Typhis qui detegat orbes*: Columbus in Neo-Latin Epic Poetry (16th–18th Centuries)," in *The Classical Tradition and the Americas*, ed. W. Haase and M. Reinhold. Berlin and New York. Vol. 1: 420–656.

Hofmann, H., ed. (1999). *Latin Fiction: The Latin Novel in Context*. London.

Hofmann, H. (2001). "Von Africa über Bethlehem nach America: das Epos in der neulatein-ischen Literatur," in *Von Göttern und Menschen erzählen: Formkonstanzen und Funktionswandel vormoderner Epic*, ed. J. Rüpke. Stuttgart: 130–83.

Hofstadter, R. and Smith, W., eds. (1961). *American Higher Education: A Documentary History*. Chicago.

Holford-Strevens, L.A. (1979). "Nola, Vergil, and Paulinus," *CQ* 29: 391–3.

Hollander, R. (1983). *Il Virgilio dantesco: tragedia nella Commedia*. Florence.

Hollander, R. (1991). "Dante's Misreadings of the *Aeneid* in *Inferno* 20," in Jacoff and Schnapp, eds.: 77–93.

Hollander, R. (1993). "Le opere di Virgilio nella *Commedia* di Dante," in Iannucci, ed.: 247–343.

Hollis, A. (1996). "Virgil's Friend Varius Rufus," *PVS* 22: 19–33.

Holmes, P. (1935). *A Tercentenary History of the Boston Public Latin School, 1635–1935.* Cambridge, MA.

Honour, H. (1991). *Romanticism.* London.

Hopkins, D. (1986). *John Dryden.* Cambridge.

Horowitz, H. (1994). *The Power and Passion of M. Carey Thomas.* New York.

Horsfall, N. (1971). "Numanus Remulus: Ethnography and Propaganda in *Aen.*, ix, 598f.," *Latomus* 30: 1108–16. Rpt. in Harrison, ed., 1990: 305–15.

Horsfall, N. (1973). "Corythus: The Return of Aeneas in Virgil and his Sources," *JRS* 63: 68–79.

Horsfall, N. (1973–4). "Dido in the Light of History," *PVS* 13: 1–13.

Horsfall, N. (1974). "Virgil's Roman Chronography: A Reconsideration," *CQ* 24: 111–15.

Horsfall, N. (1979a). "Stesichorus at Bovillae?," *JHS* 99: 26–48.

Horsfall, N. (1979b). "Some Problems in the Aeneas Legend," *CQ* 29: 372–90.

Horsfall, N. (1981). "Virgil and the Conquest of the Chaos," *Antichthon* 15: 141–50.

Horsfall, N. (1984). Review of Small (1982). *CR* 34: 226–9.

Horsfall, N. (1985). "Enea: La leggenda di Enea," in *Enciclopedia Virgiliana*, ed. F. della Corte. Rome. Vol. 2: 221–9.

Horsfall, N. (1986). "The Aeneas-Legend and the *Aeneid*," *Vergilius* 32: 8–17.

Horsfall, N. (1987). "Corythus Re-Examined," in Bremmer and Horsfall, eds.: 89–104.

Horsfall, N. (1989). "Aeneas the Colonist," *Vergilius* 35: 8–27.

Horsfall, N. (1991a). *Virgilio: l'epopea in alambicco.* Naples.

Horsfall, N. (1991b). "Externi Duces," *RIFC* 119: 188–92.

Horsfall, N. (1993). "Empty Shelves on the Palatine," *G&R* 40: 58–67.

Horsfall, N. (1995a). "Rome without Spectacles," *G&R* 42: 49–56.

Horsfall, N., ed. (1995b). *A Companion to the Study of Virgil.* Leiden.

Horsfall, N. (1995c). "Virgil: His Life and Times," in Horsfall, ed.: 1–25.

Horsfall, N. (1995d). "Virgil's Impact at Rome: The Non-Literary Evidence," in Horsfall, ed.: 249–55.

Horsfall, N. (1997). Review of Günther (1996). *RFIC* 125: 468–72.

Horsfall, N., ed. (2000). *Virgil, Aeneid 7: A Commentary.* Leiden.

Horsfall, N., ed. (2003). *Virgil, Aeneid 11: A Commentary.* Leiden.

Horsfall, N. (2005). "Lycophron and the *Aeneid*, Again," *ICS*: 35–40.

Horsfall, N., ed. (2006a). *Virgil, Aeneid 3: A Commentary.* Leiden and Boston.

Horsfall, N. (2006b). "Fraud as Scholarship: The Helen-Episode and the *Appendix Vergiliana*," *ICS* 31: 1–27.

Horsfall, N., ed. (2008). *Virgil, Aeneid 2: A Commentary.* Leiden.

Housman, A.E. (1972). "A Note on Virgil," in *The Classical Papers of A.E. Housman*, ed. J. Diggle and F.R.D. Goodyear. Cambridge: 348–50.

Houston, G.W.(2009). "Papyrological Evidence for Book Collections and Libraries in the Roman Empire," in *Ancient Literacies: The Culture of Reading in Greece and Rome*, ed. W.A. Johnson and H.N. Parker. New York and Oxford: 233–67.

Howard, J. (2008). "Measuring the *Aeneid* on a Human Scale," *Chronicle of Higher Education*, May 16.

Howe, D. (1983). "Classical Education and Political Culture in Nineteenth-Century America," *Intellectual History Newsletter* 5: 9–14.

Howell, T. (1906). *Howell's Devises.* Oxford.

Hoyle, B. (2007). "How Pippi Longstocking and John Milton went Arabic." *The Times*, November 22. London. [Retrieved September 14, 2009 from http://entertainment.times-online.co.uk/tol/arts_and_entertainment/books/article2917627.ece]

Hughes, M.Y. (1929). *Virgil and Spenser*. New York and London.

Humphries, R., trans. (1951). *The Aeneid of Virgil*. New York.

Hunter, R. (1993). *The Argonautica of Apollonius: Literary Studies*. New York and Cambridge.

Hunter, R., ed. (1999). *Theocritus: A Selection*. Cambridge.

Hunter, R. (2006). *The Shadow of Callimachus: Studies in the Reception of Hellenistic Poetry at Rome*. Oxford.

Hurka, F. (2004). "Überlegungen zur Vita Vergiliana Probiana," *RhM* 147: 172–89.

Huskey, S. (2002). "Ovid and the Fall of Troy in *Tristia* 1.3," *Vergilius* 48: 88–104.

Hutchinson, E. (1980). "Antiquity and Mythology in *The Scarlet Letter*," *Arizona Quarterly* 36: 197–210.

Hutchinson, G.O. (2008). *Talking Books: Readings in Hellenistic and Roman Books of Poetry*. Oxford.

Huxley, H.H. (1998). "John Enoch Powell and Vergil, *Aeneid* 6.86–87," *Vergilius* 44: 24–7.

Iacopi, I. and Tedone, G. (2005–6). "Biblioteca e Porticus ad Apollinis," *MDAI(R)* 112: 351–78.

Iannucci, A., ed. (1993). *Dante e la "bella scola" della poesia: Autorità e sfida poetica*. Ravenna.

Iannucci, A. (1998). "Dante's Intertextual and Intratextual Strategies in the *Commedia*: The Limbo of the Children," in *Studies for Dante: Essays in Honor of Dante Della Terza*, ed. F. Fido, R.A. Syska-Lamparska, and P.D. Stewart. Florence: 61–88.

IJsewijn, J. (1990). *Companion to Neo-Latin Studies*, 2 vols. Vol. 2 with D. Sacré. 2nd, entirely rewritten edition. Leuven, 1998.

Indelli, G. (2004). "The Vocabulary of Anger in Philodemus' *De ira* and Vergil's *Aeneid*," in Armstrong et al., eds.: 103–10.

Inscoe, J. (1983). "Carolina Slave Names: An Index to Acculturation," *Journal of Southern History* 49: 527–54.

Irmscher, J., ed. (1995). *Vergil: Antike Weltliteratur in ihrer Entstehung und Nachwirkung*. Amsterdam.

Jackson, H.J. (2001). *Marginalia: Readers Writing in Books*. New Haven and London.

Jacoby, F., ed. (1923–). *Die Fragmente der griechischen Historiker*. Leiden.

Jacoff, R. (1991). "Intertextualities in Arcadia: *Purgatorio* 30.49–51," in Jacoff and Schnapp, eds.: 131–44.

Jacoff, R. (2002). "Dante's Vergil," in Anderson and Quartarone, eds.: 190–5.

Jacoff, R., ed. (2007). *The Cambridge Companion to Dante*, 2nd ed. Cambridge. [1st ed. 1993.]

Jacoff, R. and Schnapp, J., eds. (1991). *The Poetry of Allusion: Virgil and Ovid in Dante's Commedia*. Stanford.

Jahrbuch der Gesellschaft für Wiener Theaterforschung, 1952–1953 (1957). Vienna.

James, S.L. (1995). "Establishing Rome with the Sword: *Condere* in the *Aeneid*," *AJP* 116: 623–37.

Janko, R., ed. (2000). *Philodemus: On Poems, Book I*. Oxford.

Jarislowsky, J. (1928). *Schillers Übertragungen aus Vergil im Rahmen der deutschen Aeneis-Übersetzung des 18. Jahrhunderts*. Jena.

Javitch, D. (1991). *Proclaiming a Classic: The Canonization of Orlando Furioso*. Princeton.

Javitch, D. (1999). "The Grafting of Virgilian Epic in *Orlando furioso*," in *Renaissance Transactions: Ariosto and Tasso*, ed. V. Finucci. Durham, NC.

Jimoh, A.Y. (1988). "Double Consciousness, Modernism, and Womanist Themes in Gwendolyn Brooks's *The Anniad*," *Melus* 23: 167–86.

Jocelyn, H.D. (1979). "*Vergilius Cacozelus* (Donatus *Vita Vergili* 44)," *PLLS* 2: 67–142.

Jocelyn, H.D. (1990). "The Ancient Story of the Imperial Edition of the *Aeneid*," *Sileno* 16: 263–78.

Jocelyn, H.D. (1991). "Virgil and Aeneas' Supposed Italic Ancestry," *Sileno* 17: 77–100.

Johnson, B. (1987). *A World of Difference*. Baltimore and London.

Johnson, S. (2000). "Literary Imitation," *The Rambler*, 211 (May 14, 1751), in *Samuel Johnson: The Major Works*, ed. D.J. Greene. Oxford: 215–18.

Johnson, W.A. (2004). *Bookrolls and Scribes in Oxyrhynchus*. Toronto.

Johnson, W.R. (1976). *Darkness Visible: A Study of Vergil's Aeneid*. Berkeley and Los Angeles.

Johnson, W.R. (1986). "The Figure of Laertes: Reflections on the Character of Aeneas," in Bernard, ed.: 85–105.

Johnson, W.R. (1999). "*Dis aliter visum*: Self-Telling and Theodicy in *Aeneid* 2," in Perkell, ed.: 50–63.

Johnson, W.R. (2001). "Imaginary Romans: Vergil and the Illusion of National Identity," in Spence, ed.: 3–16.

Johnson, W.R. (2004). "Robert Lowell's American Aeneas," *MD* (*Numero speciale in onore di Michael C.J. Putnam*) 52: 227–39.

Johnston, P.A. (2004). "Piety in Vergil and Philodemus," in Armstrong et al., eds.: 159–73.

Joly, A. (1870). *Benoît de Saint-Maure et le Roman de Troie*. Paris.

Jones, C.P. (1999). *Kinship Diplomacy in the Ancient World*. Cambridge, MA.

Jones, H.M. (1974). *Revolution and Romanticism*. Cambridge, MA.

Jones, J.W., Jr. (1961). "Allegorical Interpretation in Servius," *CJ* 56: 217–26.

Joshel, S. (2002). "The Body Female and the Body Politic: Livy's Lucretia and Verginia," in McClure, ed.: 163–87.

Jouvancy, J. de, S.J. (1692). *Magistris scholarum inferiorum Societatis Jesu De ratione discendi et docendi….* Paris; rev. ed. Florence, 1703.

Jouvancy, J. de, S.J. (1892). *De la manière d'apprendre et d'enseigner, conformément au décret de la XIVe congrégation générale: ouvrage destiné aux maîtres de la Société de Jésus*, trans. H. Ferté. Paris.

Jung, M.-R. (1996). *La Légende de Troie en France au moyen âge*. Basle.

Jung, M.-R. (1997). "L'histoire grecque," in Baumgartner and Harf-Lancner, eds.: 185–207.

Kailuweit, T. (2005). *Dido – Didon – Didone. Eine kommentierte Bibliographie zum Dido-Mythos in Literatur und Musik*. Frankfurt am Main.

Kallendorf, C. (1989). *In Praise of Aeneas: Virgil and Epideictic Rhetoric in the Early Italian Renaissance*. Hanover and London.

Kallendorf, C. (1999). *Virgil and the Myth of Venice*. Oxford.

Kallendorf, C. (2001). "The *Aeneid* Transformed: Illustration as Interpretation from the Renaissance to the Present," in Spence, ed.: 121–48.

Kallendorf, C. (2002). "The Virgilian Title Page as Interpretive Frame; or, Through the Looking Glass," *Princeton University Library Chronicle* 64: 15–50.

Kallendorf, C. (2005). "Cristoforo Landino, Andrea Tordi, and the Reading Practices of Renaissance Humanism," in *Text, Interpretation, Vergleich: Festschrift für Manfred Lentzen*, ed. J. and E. Leeker. Berlin: 345–58.

Kallendorf, C. (2007). *The Other Virgil: "Pessimistic" Readings of the Aeneid in Early Modern Culture*. Oxford.

Kallendorf, C. (2008). "The Early Modern Roots of the 'Harvard' School of Virgilian Interpretation," in *Esegesi dimenticate di autori classici*, ed. C. Santini and F. Stok. Pisa: 99–112.

Kallendorf, C. (2009). *A Catalogue of the Junius Spencer Morgan Virgil Collection in the Princeton University Library*. New Castle, DE.

Kallendorf, C. (forthcoming). "Virgil in the Renaissance Classroom: From Toscanella's *Osservationi...sopra l'opere di Virgilio* to the *Exercitationes rhetoricae*," in *The Classics in the Medieval and Renaissance Classroom*, ed. J.F. Ruys, J. Ward, and M. Heyworth. Turnhout.

Karttunen, F. (1992). *An Analytical Dictionary of Nahuatl*. Norman.

Kaster, Robert A. (1988). *Guardians of Language: The Grammarian and Society in Late Antiquity*. Berkeley.

Kazhdan, A., Talbot, A.-M., et al., eds. (1991). *The Oxford Dictionary of Byzantium*. Oxford.

Keil, H., ed. (1855–80). *Grammatici Latini*. 8 vols. Leipzig.

Keith, M.S. (1899). "Final Preparation for College," in *Helen Keller Souvenir*, 2, 1892–9: *Commemorating the Harvard Final Examination for Admission to Radcliffe College, June 29–30, 1899*. Washington, DC.

Keller, H. (1903). *The Story of My Life*. New York.

Kelley, D.R. (2003). *Fortunes of History: Historical Inquiry from Herder to Huizinga*. New Haven.

Kelley, M. (1996). "Reading Women/Women Reading: The Making of Learned Women in Antebellum America," *Journal of American History* 83: 401–24.

Kelley, M. (2006). *Learning to Stand and Speak: Women, Education, and Public Life in America's Republic*. Chapel Hill.

Kemp, I., ed. (1988). *Hector Berlioz: Les Troyens*. Cambridge.

Kenneally, M. and Kenneally, R.R., eds. (2005). *From "English Literature" to "Literatures in English": International Perspectives. Festschrift in Honour of Wolfgang Zach*. Heidelberg.

Kennedy, D.F. (1992). "'Augustan' and 'Anti-Augustan': Reflections on Terms of Reference," in *Roman Poetry and Propaganda in the Age of Augustus*, ed. A. Powell. London: 26–58.

Kennedy, D.F. (1997). "Virgilian Epic," in Martindale, ed.: 145–54.

Kennedy, G.A., ed. (1989). *The Cambridge History of Literary Criticism*. Vol. 1: *Classical Criticism*. Cambridge.

Kenney, E.J. (1965). "The Poetry of Ovid's Exile," *PCPS* 11: 37–49.

Kenney, E.J. (1970). "That Incomparable Poem the 'Ille ego'?," *CR* n.s. 20.3: 290.

Kenney, E.J. and Clausen, W.V., eds. (1982). *The Cambridge History of Latin Literature*. Cambridge.

Kent, G. (1990). *A Life of Gwendolyn Brooks*. Lexington.

Ker, W.P., ed. (1961). *Essays of John Dryden*, 2 vols. New York.

Kerber, L. (1980). *Women of the Republic: Intellect and Ideology in Revolutionary America*. Chapel Hill.

Kermode, F. (1975). *The Classic: Literary Images of Permanence and Change*. New York.

Kimball, F., ed. (1916). *Thomas Jefferson, Architect*. Boston.

Kircher, A. (1650). *Obeliscus Pamphilius*. Rome.

Kircher, A. (1665). *Mundus Subterraneus, In XII libros digestos; quo divinum subterrestris mundi opificium, universae denique naturae majestas & divitiae summa rerum varietate exponuntur*. Amsterdam.

Kleberg, T. (1967). *Buchhandel und Verlagswesen in der Antike*, trans. E. Zunker. Darmstadt.

Klecker, E. (2002a). "Ein Missionar in Japan auf den Spuren des Aeneas: die *Paciecis* des Bartholomaeus Pereira S.J. (Coimbra, 1640)," in *De litteris Neolatinis in America Meridionali, Portugallia, Hispania, Italia cultis*, ed. D. Briesemeister and A. Schönberger. Frankfurt am Main: 99–112.

Klecker, E. (2002b). "Amor addidit alas: ein neulateinisches Epos über die Missionsreisen des H. Franz Xaver S.J.," in *Franz-Xaver – Patron der Missionen: Festschrift zum 450. Todestag*, ed. R. Haub and J. Oswald, S.J. Regensburg.

Klecker, E. (2003a). "Imperium Minervae: jesuitische Bildungspropaganda in der *Ignatias* des António Figueira Durão," in *Imperium Minervae: Studien zur brasilianischen, iberischen und mosambikanischen Literatur*, ed. D. Briesemeister and A. Schönberger. Frankfurt: 179–209.

Klecker, E. (2003b). "Mythos und Geschichte auf der Bühne der 'ludi Caesarei': Seneca und Vergil in Nicolaus Avancinis *Pietas Victrix*," in *Politische Mythen und nationale Identitäten im (Musik) Theater*, ed. P. Csobádi et al. Anif and Salzburg. Vol. 1: 151–72.

Klecker, E. (2007). "Kaiser Konstantin auf der Bühne des Jesuitentheaters," *Quaderni* [del Centro internazionale di studi sulla poesia greca e latina in età tardoantica e medievale] 3: 433–51.

Kleiner, D.E.E. (2005). *Cleopatra and Rome*. Harvard.

Kleinknecht, H. (1944). "Laokoon," *Hermes* 79: 66–111.

Klingner, F. (1967). *Virgil. Bucolica, Georgica, Aeneis*. Zurich and Stuttgart.

Kliuchevskii, V.O. (1908). *Kurs russkoi istorii, vol. 3*. Moscow.

Klonsky, M. (1980). *Blake's Dante: The Complete Illustrations to the Divine Comedy*. London.

Klossowski, P. (1947). *Sade mon prochain*. Paris.

Klossowski, P., trans. (1964). *Virgile. L'Enéide*. Paris.

Knauer, G.N. (1964a). *Die Aeneis und Homer: Studien zur poetischen Technik Vergils mit Listen der Homerzitate in der Aeneis*. Hypomnemata 7. Göttingen.

Knauer, G.N. (1964b). "Vergil's *Aeneid* and Homer," *GRBS* 5 (1964): 61–84. Rpt. in Harrison, ed. 1990: 390–412.

Knight, E.W. (1949–53). *A Documentary History of Education in the South before 1860*. Chapel Hill.

Knight, W.F.J. (1932). *Vergil's Troy*. Oxford.

Knight, W.F.J. (1956). *Virgil: The Aeneid*. Harmondsworth.

Koch, A. (1943). *The Philosophy of Thomas Jefferson*. New York.

Koch, A. and Peden, W., eds. (1946). *The Selected Writings of John and John Quincy Adams*. New York.

Kojève, A. (1963). "Tyranny and Wisdom," in *On Tyranny*, ed. L. Strauss. Ithaca: 143–88.

Korshak, Y. (1987). "The Liberty Cap as a Revolutionary Symbol in America and France," *Smithsonian Studies in American Art* 1: 52–69.

Koselleck, R. (2004). *Futures Past: On the Semantics of Historical Time*, trans. K. Tribe. New York.

Krier, T.M. (1986a). "The Mysteries of the Muses: Spenser's *Faerie Queene*, II.3, and the Epic Tradition of the Goddess Observed," *Spenser Studies* 7: 59–91.

Krier, T.M. (1986b). "'All suddeinly abasht she changed hew': Abashedness in *The Faerie Queene*," *Modern Philology* 84: 130–43.

Krier, T.M. (1990). *Gazing on Secret Sights: Spenser, Classical Imitation, and the Decorums of Vision*. Ithaca and London.

Kunze, C. (1996). "Zur Datierung des Laokoon und der Skyllagruppe aus Sperlonga," *JDAI* 111: 139–223.

Kunzle, D. (1973). *History of the Comic Strip*. Vol. 1: *The Early Comic Strip: Narrative Strips and Picture Stories in the European Broadsheet from c.1450–1825*. Berkeley.

Laclau, E. and Mouffe, C. (1985). *Hegemony and Socialist Strategy: Towards a Radical Democratic Politics*. London and New York.

Laird, A. (2002). "Juan Luis de la Cerda, Virgil, and the Predicament of Commentary," in *The Classical Commentary: Histories, Practices, Theory*, ed. C.S. Kraus and R.K. Gibson. Leiden: 171–203.

Laird, A. (2003). "Roman Epic Theatre? Reception, Performance and the Poet in Virgil's *Aeneid*," *PCPS* 49: 19–39.

Laird, A. (2006). *The Epic of America: An Introduction to Rafael Landívar and the Rusticatio Mexicana*. London.

Laird, A. (2007a). "The Virgin of Guadalupe and the Birth of Mexican Epic: Bernardo Ceinos de Riofrío's *Centonicum Virgilianum Monimentum*," in *Mexico 1680: Cultural and Intellectual Life in the "Barroco de Indias,"* ed. J. Andrews and A. Coroleu. Bristol: 199–220.

Laird, A. (2007b). "Latin America," in *A Companion to the Classical Tradition*, ed. C. Kallendorf. Oxford: 222–36.

Laird, A. (2010a). "Latin in Cuauhtémoc's Shadow: Humanism and the Politics of Language in Mexico after the Conquest," in Haskell and Ruys, eds.: 169–99.

Laird, A. (2010b). "The Cosmic Race and a Heap of Broken Images: Mexico's Classical Past and the Modern Creole Imagination," in *Classics and National Cultures*, ed. S. Stephens and P. Vasunia. Oxford.

Lamberton, R. (1986). *Homer the Theologian: Neoplatonist Allegorical Reading and the Growth of the Epic Tradition*. Berkeley and Los Angeles.

Lamberton, R. and Keaney, J.J., eds. (1992). *Homer's Ancient Readers: The Hermeneutics of Greek Epic's Earliest Exegetes*. Princeton.

Lang, B. (1995). "Homiletische Bibelkommentare der Kirchenväter," in Assmann and Gladigow, eds.: 199–218.

Lanham, C., ed. (2002). *Latin Grammar and Rhetoric: From Classical Theory to Medieval Practice*. London and New York.

Larabee, L.W., ed. (1959–). *The Papers of Benjamin Franklin*. New Haven.

La Rue, C. de, S.J. (1675). *P. Virgilii Maronis Opera, Interpretatione et Notis Illustravit, Carolus Ruaeus Societatis Jesu, Jussu Christianissimi Regis, ad Usum Serenissimi Delphini*. Paris.

Lasdun, J. and Hofmann, M. (1994). *After Ovid: New Metamorphoses*. London.

Laso de la Vega, L. (1998). *Huei Tlamahuiçoltica*, in *The Story of Guadalupe: Luis Laso de la Vega's Huei Tlamahuiçoltica of 1649*, ed. and trans. L. Sousa, S. Poole, and J. Lockhart. Los Angeles.

Lattimore, R., trans. (1951). *The Iliad of Homer*. Chicago.

Lattimore, R., trans. (1967). *The Odyssey of Homer*. New York.

Lauder, W. (1750). *An Essay on Milton's Use and Imitation of the Moderns, in his Paradise Lost*. London.

Leach, E.W. (1982). "Illustration as Interpretation in Brant's and Dryden's Editions of Vergil," in Hindman, ed.: 175–210.

Le Brun, L., S.J. (1655). *Eloquentia poetica…*. Paris.

Le Brun, L., S.J. (1661). *Virgilius Christianus…*. Paris.

Le Brun, L., S.J. (1667). *Novus apparatus Virgilii poeticus: Synonymorum, Epithetorum et Phrasium, seu Elegantiarum Poeticarum Thesaurum…Opus tum ex Virgilio, caeterisque Poetis antiquis, tum ex aliis, Gallis, Batavis, Scotis, Italis, etc*. Paris.

Lee, D. (1972). "Preface to Gwendolyn Brooks," in *Report From Part One*. Detroit.

Lefevere, A., ed. (1977). *Translating Literature: The German Tradition from Luther to Rosenzweig*. Assen.

Lefkowitz, M.R. (1981). *The Lives of the Greek Poets*. London.

Le Guin, U.K. (2008). *Lavinia*. Orlando.

Lehmann, K. (1965). *Thomas Jefferson: American Humanist*. Chicago.

Le Moyne, P. (1653). *Saint Louys, ou le héros chrestien…*. Paris.

León-Portilla, M. (2002). *Bernardino de Sahagún: First Anthropologist*, trans. M. Mixco. Norman.

Leonard, I. (1959). *Baroque Times in Old Mexico*. Ann Arbor.

Leonard, I. (1967). *Books of the Brave*. Cambridge, MA.

Le Plat du Temple, V.A.C. (1807–8). *Virgile en France, ou la nouvelle Enéide…*. Brussels.

Lessing, G.E. (1957). *Laocoon: An Essay upon the Limits of Painting and Poetry*, trans. E. Frothingham. New York.

Levine, J.M. (1991). *The Battle of the Books: History and Literature in the Augustan Age*. Ithaca.

Levitan, W. (1993). "'Give Up the Beginning?': Juno's Mindful Wrath (*Aeneid* 1.37)," *LCM* 18: 14.

Lewalski, B.K. (1985). *Paradise Lost and the Rhetoric of Literary Forms*. Princeton.

Liebeschuetz, J.H.W.G (1979). *Continuity and Change in Roman Religion*. Oxford.

Lightbown, R. (1978). "Foreword," in *Samuel Palmer, A Vision Recaptured: The Complete Etchings and the Paintings for Milton and for Virgil*. London.

Lima Leitão, A.J. de, trans. (1818–19). *As obras de Pùblio Virgìlio Maro....* Rio de Janeiro.

Lind, L.R. (1980). "Aeneas Among the Poets," *Rocky Mountain Review of Language and Literature* 34.2: 119–32.

Lindheim, N. (1999). "The Virgilian Design of *The Shepheardes Calender*," *Spenser Studies* 13: 1–22.

Lister, R., ed. (1974). *The Letters of Samuel Palmer*. Oxford.

Litto, F. (1966). "Addison's *Cato* in the Colonies," *William and Mary Quarterly* 23: 431–49.

Liversidge, M.J.H. (1997). "Virgil in Art," in Martindale, ed.: 91–103.

Livrea, E. (1973). *Apollonii Rhodii Argonauticon Liber IV*. Florence.

Llanos, B. de (1605). *Institutionum poeticarum liber*. Mexico City.

Lloyd-Jones, H., ed. (1996). *Sophocles: Fragments*. Cambridge, MA and London.

Logan, W. (1982). *Sad-Faced Men*. Boston.

Lombardo, S., trans. (1997). *Homer: Iliad*. Introduction by S. Murnaghan. Indianapolis.

Lombardo, S., trans. (2000). *Homer: Odyssey*. Introduction by S. Murnaghan. Indianapolis.

Lombardo, S., trans. (2005). *Virgil: Aeneid*. Introduction by W.R. Johnson. Indianapolis.

Looney, D. (1996). *Compromising the Classics: Romance Epic Narrative in the Italian Renaissance*. Detroit.

Looney, D. (2003). "Ariosto and the Classics," in *Ariosto Today: Contemporary Perspectives*, ed. D. Beecher, M. Ciavolella, and R. Fedi. Toronto: 18–31.

Looney, D., ed. and trans. (2010). *"My Muse will have a story to Paint": Selected Prose of Ludovico Ariosto*. Toronto.

López de Abilés, J. (1669). *Poeticum viridarium in honorem [...] Mariae eiusdem Dominae miraculosae mexicanae Imaginis de Guadalupae vocatae nominis litteris, transumptis, iconis, signis, circunstantilisque miris mirificae apparitionis, insitum, orantum variegatum, atque contextum*. Mexico City.

Lotman, I.M. and Uspenskii, B.A. (1984). "Echoes of the Notion of 'Moscow as the Third Rome' in Peter the Great's Ideology," in *The Semiotics of Russian Culture*, ed. A. Shukman, trans. N.F.C. Owen. Ann Arbor: 53–67.

Lounsbury, R. (1986). "Ludibria Rerum Mortalium: Charleston Intellectuals and their Classics," in Moltke-Hansen and O'Brien, eds.: 325–69.

Lowell, R. (2003). *Collected Poems*, ed. F. Bidart and D. Gewanter. New York.

Lowes, J.L. (1927). *The Road to Xanadu: A Study in the Ways of the Imagination*. Boston.

Lowrie, M. (2001). "Literature is a Latin Word," *Vergilius* 47: 29–38.

Lowrie, M. (2005). "Vergil and Founding Violence," *Cardozo Law Review* 25: 945–76.

Lowrie, M. (2007). "Sovereignty before the Law: Agamben and the Roman Republic," *Law and Humanities* 1: 31–55.

Lucarini, C.M. (2006). "Osservazioni sulle edizioni virgiliane di Vario e di Probo e sull'origine dell'*Anecdoton Parisinum*," *RAL* 153: 281–305.

Luck, G., ed. (1967). *P. Ovidius Naso: Tristia*. Vol. 1: *Text und Übersetzung*. Heidelberg.

Luck, G., ed. (1977). *P. Ovidius Naso: Tristia*. Vol. 2: *Kommentar*. Heidelberg.

Ludwig, W. (1982). "Neulateinische Lehrgedichte und Vergils *Georgica*," in *From Wolfram and Petrarch to Goethe and Grass: Studies in Literature in Honour of Leonard Forster*, ed. D.H. Green, L.P. Johnson, and D. Wuttke. Baden-Baden: 151–80.

Lührs, D. (1992). *Untersuchungen zu den Athetesen Aristarchs in der Ilias und zu ihrer Behandlung im Corpus der exegetischen Scholien.* Hildesheim.

Luiselli, B. (1978). "Il mito dell'origine Troiana dei Galli, dei Franchi e degli Scandinavi," *Romano Barbarico* 3: 89–121.

Lukács, G. (1971). *The Theory of the Novel: A Historico-Philosophical Essay on the Forms of Great Epic Literature,* trans. A. Bostock. Cambridge, MA.

Lupher, D.A. (2003). *Romans in a New World: Classical Models in Sixteenth-Century Spanish America.* Ann Arbor.

Lyne, R.O.A.M. (1987). *Further Voices in Vergil's Aeneid.* Oxford.

Lyne, R.O.A.M. (1989). *Words and the Poet: Characteristic Techniques of Style in Vergil's Aeneid.* Oxford.

Machacek, G. (1990). "Of Man's First Disobedience," *Milton Quarterly* 24: 111.

MacKendrick, P. (1976). "This Rich Source of Delight: The Classics and the Founding Fathers," *CJ* 72: 97–106.

MacLure, M. and Watt, F.W., eds. (1964). *Essays in English Literature from the Renaissance to the Victorian Age, Presented to A.S.P. Woodhouse.* Toronto.

Magi, F. (1960). *Il Ripristino del Laocoonte. MPAA* 3.9.1. Vatican City.

Magnuson, T. (1982). *Rome in the Age of Bernini: From the Election of Innocent X to the Death of Innocent XI.* New York.

Malkin, I. (1998). *The Returns of Odysseus: Colonization and Ethnicity.* Berkeley.

Mambelli, G. (1954). *Gli annali delle edizioni virgiliane.* Florence.

Mambrun, P. (1658). *Constantinus sive Idolatria debellata.* Paris.

Mambrun, P. (1661). *Opera poetica. Accessit Dissertatio de Epico Carmine.* La Flèche.

Mandelbaum, A. (1971). *The Aeneid of Virgil: A Verse Translation.* Berkeley.

Manganaro, G. (1974). "Una biblioteca storica nel ginnasio di Tauromenio e il Pap. Oxy. 1241," *PP* 29: 389–409.

Manni, E. (1963). "La fondazione di Roma secondo Antioco Alcimo Callia," *Kokalos* 8: 253–68.

Margolis, J.D. (1972). *T.S. Eliot's Intellectual Development, 1922–1939.* Chicago.

Mariano, A. (2010). "New World 'Ethiopians': Visions of Slavery and Mining in Early Modern Brazil," in Haskell and Ruys, eds.: 203–22.

Marino, L. (1995). *Praeceptores Germaniae: Göttingen 1770–1820.* Göttingen.

Mariotti, S. (2001). *Il Bellum Poenicum e l'arte di Nevio.* 3rd ed. Bologna.

Marolles, M., ed. (1649). *Les Œuvres de Virgile traduites en prose.* Paris.

Marrone, D. (2004). "Letture dai classici di Battista Mantovano," *Studi Umanistici Piceni* 24: 97–104.

Marshall, A.J. (1976). "Library Resources and Creative Writing at Rome," *Phoenix* 30: 252–64.

Martindale, C., ed. (1984). *Virgil and his Influence: Bimillennial Studies.* Bristol.

Martindale, C. (1993). *Redeeming the Text: Latin Poetry and the Hermeneutics of Reception.* Cambridge.

Martindale, C. (1996). Review of Watkins (1995). *CR* 46: 361–3.

Martindale, C., ed. (1997). *The Cambridge Companion to Virgil.* Cambridge.

Martindale, C. (2002). *John Milton and the Transformation of Ancient Epic,* 2nd ed. Bristol.

Marx, K. (1967). *Capital,* vol. 1, trans. S. Moore and E. Aveling. New York.

Masen, J., S.J. (1654). *Palaestra Eloquentiae ligatae....* Cologne.

Masen, J., S.J. (1771). *Sarcotis et Caroli V. Imp. Panegyris, Carmina.* London.

Mason, J. (1989). *The Poems of Phillis Wheatley. Revised and Enlarged Edition.* Chapel Hill.

Masters, J.M. (1992). *Poetry and Civil War in Lucan's Bellum Civile.* Cambridge.

Matthes, M.M. (2000). *The Rape of Lucretia and the Founding of Republics.* University Park, PA.

Maurach, G. (1992). "Der vergilische und der vatikanische Laokoon," *Gymnasium* 99: 227–47.

Mazhuga, V.I. (2003). "A quelle époque vivait le grammairien Phocas?," *RPh* 77: 67–77.

Mazzotta, G. (1979). *Dante, Poet of the Desert*. Princeton.

McCabe, R.A. (2002). *Spenser's Monstrous Regiment: Elizabethan Ireland and the Poetics of Difference*. Oxford.

McCabe, W.H., S.J. (1983). *An Introduction to the Jesuit Theater*, ed. L.J. Oldani. St. Louis.

McCaughey, R.A. (1974). *Josiah Quincy, 1772–1864: The Last Federalist*. Cambridge, MA.

McClure, L., ed. (2002). *Sexuality and Gender in the Classical World*. Oxford and Malden, MA.

McCrorie, E., trans. (1995). *The Aeneid, Virgil*. Ann Arbor.

McDonald, F. (1979). *Alexander Hamilton: A Biography*. New York.

McDonald, F. (1985). *Novus Ordo Seclorum*. Lawrence.

McDonald, M. (2001). *Sing Sorrow: Classics, History and Heroines in Opera*. Westport and London.

McElrath, J., Jr. and Robb, A. (1981). *The Complete Works of Anne Bradstreet*. Boston.

McGill, S. (2005). *Virgil Recomposed: The Mythological and Secular Centos in Antiquity*. American Philological Association American Classical Studies Series, 49. New York and Oxford.

McGregor, J.H. (1991). *The Shades of Aeneas: The Imitation of Vergil and the History of Paganism in Boccaccio's Filostrato, Filocolo, and Teseida*. Athens, GA.

McIver, K.A. (1998). "The Room and the View: A New Look at Giulio Boiardo's Private Apartments at Scandiano," in *Fortune and Romance: Boiardo in America*, ed. J.A. Cavallo and C. Ross. Tempe: 279–93.

McNeal, R. (1995). "Athens and Nineteenth-Century Panoramic Art," *IJCT* 1: 80–97.

Meade, R.D. (1957–69). *Patrick Henry*. Philadelphia.

Meckler, M., ed. (2006). *Classical Antiquity and the Politics of America: From George Washington to George W. Bush*. Waco.

Meister, F., ed. (1873). *Daretis Phrygii De excidio Troiae historia*. Leipzig.

Mendelson, E. (1999). *Later Auden*. New York.

Mendieta, G. de (1993). *Historia Ecclesiástica Indiana. Obra escrita a fines del siglo XVI* (1870), ed. J.G. Icazbalceta. Mexico City.

Merkle, S. (1996). "The Truth and Nothing but the Truth: Dictys and Dares," in Schmeling, ed.: 563–80.

Merkle, S. (1999). "News from the Past: Dictys and Dares on the Trojan War," in Hofmann, ed.: 155–66.

Meyen, J.A., ed. (1616). *Publii Virgilii Maronis Mantuani opera omnia....* Frankfurt.

Middlekauff, R. (1961). "A Persistent Tradition: The Classical Curriculum in Eighteenth-Century New England," *William and Mary Quarterly* 18: 54–67.

Middlekauff, R. (1963). *Ancients and Axioms: Secondary Education in Eighteenth-Century New England*. New Haven and London.

Miles, E. (1968). "The Whig Party and the Menace of Caesar," *Tennessee Historical Quarterly* 27: 361–79.

Miles, E. (1971). "The Old South and the Classical World," *North Carolina Historical Review* 48: 258–75.

Miles, E. (1974). "The Young American Nation and the Classical World," *JHI* 35: 259–74.

Milgrom, J., ed. (1990). *Numbers: The Traditional Hebrew Text with the New JPS Translation*. Philadelphia.

Miller, H. (1936). *Black Spring*. Paris.

Miller, J.F. (2000). "*Triumphus in Palatio*," *AJP* 121: 409–22.

Miller, J.F. (2009). *Apollo, Augustus, and the Poets*. Cambridge.

Milton, J. (1997). *Paradise Lost*, ed. A. Fowler, 2nd ed. London.

Mirsch, P., ed. (1882). "De M. Terenti Varronis Antiquitatum rerum humanarum libris XXV." *Leipziger Studien zur Classischen Philologie* 5: 1–144.

Moltke-Hansen, D., ed. (1979). *Art in the Lives of South Carolinians: Nineteenth-Century Chapters.* Charleston.

Moltke-Hansen, D. and O'Brien, M., eds. (1986). *Intellectual Life in Antebellum Charleston.* Knoxville.

Momigliano, A. (1984). "How to Reconcile Greeks and Trojans," in *Settimo contributo alla storia degli studi classici e del mondo antico.* Rome: 427–62.

Momigliano, A. (1989). "Come riconciliare greci e troiani," in *Roma arcaica.* Florence: 325–45. [Translation of Momigliano 1984.]

Monreal, R. (2005). "Vergils Vermächtnis: Die Gartenpraeteritio in den *Georgica* und Typen ihrer Rezeption im neulateinischen Lehrgedicht," *Humanistica Lovaniensia* 54: 1–47.

Monsigny, M. (1794). *Mythology. Or, A History of the Fabulous Deities of the Ancients: Designed to Facilitate the Study of History, Poetry, Painting, &c.* London.

Montaigne, M. de (1993). *The Essays of Michel de Montaigne*, trans. M.A. Screech. London.

Montgomery, H. (1936). "Washington the Stoic," *CJ* 31: 371–3.

Montgomery, H. (1960). "Addison's *Cato* and George Washington," *CJ* 55: 210–12.

Moore, E. (1969). *Studies in Dante. First Series: Scripture and Classical Authors in Dante* (1896). Oxford.

Mora-Lebrun, F. (1994). *L'Enéide médiévale et la naissance du roman.* Paris.

Morash, C. (2002). *A History of Irish Theatre, 1601–2000.* Cambridge.

Moreau, P., ed. (1648). *L'Enéide de Virgile traduite en vers François.* Paris.

Morford, M. (1978). "Early American School Editions of Ovid," *CJ* 78: 150–8.

Morgan, L. (1998). "Assimilation and Civil War: Hercules and Cacus: *Aeneid* 8," in Stahl, ed.: 175–98.

Morgan, L. (1999). *Patterns of Redemption in Virgil's Georgics.* Cambridge.

Morgan, T. (1998). *Literate Education in the Hellenistic and Roman Worlds.* Cambridge.

Moroney, S. (2001). "Latin, Greek, and the American Schoolboy: Ancient Language and Classical Determinism in the Early Republic," *CJ* 96: 295–307.

Morris, I. and Powell, B., eds. (1997). *A New Companion to Homer.* Leiden.

Morris, W., trans. (1876). *The Aeneids of Virgil.* London.

Mortier, R. (1940–4). *Les Textes de la Chanson de Roland*, 10 vols. Paris.

Mortimer, R. (1982). "Vergil in the Rosenwald Collection," in Hindman, ed.: 175–210.

Moses, W. (1998). *Afrotopia: The Roots of African American Popular History.* Cambridge.

Moskalew, W. (1982). *Formular Language and Poetic Design in the Aeneid.* Leiden.

Most, G.W., ed. (1999). *Commentaries – Kommentare.* Aporemata. Kritische Studien zur Philologiegeschichte, 4. Göttingen.

Mühmelt, M. (1965). *Griechische Grammatik in der Vergilerklärung.* Zetemata, 37. Munich.

Mullett, C. (1939). "Classical Influences on the American Revolution," *CJ* 35: 92–104.

Mullett, C. (1959). "Ancient Historians and 'Enlightened' Reviewers," *Review of Politics* 21: 550–65.

Munk Olsen, B. (1982). *L'Etude des auteurs classiques latins au XIe et XIIe siècles.* Paris.

Munk Olsen, B. (1991). *I classici nel canone scolastico altomedievale.* Spoleto.

Murgia, C.E. (1974). "The Donatian Life of Virgil, DS, and D," *CSCA* 7: 257–77.

Murgia, C.E. (2003). "The Date of the Helen Episode," *HSCP* 101: 405–26.

Murphy, J. (1974). "Rome at the Constitutional Convention," *CO* 51: 112–14.

Murphy, P.V. (2002). "The Jesuits and the Santa Casa di Loreto: Orazio Torsellini's *Lauretanae historiae libri quinque*," in *Spirit, Style, Story: Essays honoring John W. Padberg, S.J.*, ed. T.M. Lucas. Chicago: 327–64.

Murrin, M. (1980). *The Allegorical Epic: Essays in Its Rise and Decline*. Chicago.

Musti, D. (1984). "Arcadi," in *Enciclopedia Virgiliana*, ed. F. della Corte. Rome. Vol. 1: 270–2.

Musti, D. (1985). "Evandro," in *Enciclopedia Virgiliana*, ed. F. della Corte. Rome. Vol. 2: 437–45.

Mynors, R.A.B., ed. (1969 [= 1980]). *P. Vergili Maronis: Opera*. Oxford.

Nadal, J. (1594). *Evangelicae historiae imagines*. Antwerp.

Nagle, B.R. (1980). *The Poetics of Exile: Program and Polemic in the Tristia and Epistulae ex Ponto of Ovid*. Collection Latomus 170. Brussels.

Nagy, G. (1997). "Homeric Scholia," in Morris and Powell, eds.: 101–22.

Nagy, G. (2004). *Homer's Text and Language*. Champaign.

Nancy, J.-L. (1991). *The Inoperative Community*. Minneapolis.

Naumann, H. (1974). "Wert und Zusammenhang der jüngeren Vergil-Viten," *WS* 8: 116–23.

Naumann, H. (1976). "Gab es eine römische Dichter-Biographie?," *Sileno* 2: 35–50.

Naumann, H. (1981). "Suetonius' Life of Virgil: The Present State of the Question," *HSCP* 85: 185–7.

Naylor, L.H. (1930). *Chateaubriand and Virgil*. Baltimore.

Nelis, D.P. (1992). "Demodocus and the Song of Orpheus: Ap. Rhod. *Arg.* 1.496–511," *MH* 49: 153–70.

Nelis, D.P. (2001). *Vergil's Aeneid and the Argonautica of Apollonius Rhodius*, ARCA 39. Leeds.

Nelis, D.P. (2004). "From Didactic to Epic: *Georgics* 2.458–3.48," in Gale, ed.: 73–107.

Nelson, W. (1963). *The Poetry of Edmund Spenser*. New York.

Neuse, R. (1978). "Milton and Spenser: The Virgilian Triad Revisited," *English Literary Renaissance* 45: 606–39.

Nicholson, H.B. (1971). "Religion in Pre-Hispanic Central Mexico," in *Handbook of Middle American Indians*, ed. R. Wauchope. Vols. 10–11: *Archaeology of Northern Mesoamerica, Part I*, ed. G. Eckholm and I. Bernal. Austin: 395–446.

Nicholson, K. (1990). *Turner's Classical Landscapes: Myth and Meaning*. Princeton.

Nickau, K. (1977). *Untersuchungen zur textkritischen Methode des Zenodotos von Ephesos*. Berlin.

Nicolau d'Olwer, L. (1952). *Fray Bernadino de Sahagún 1499–1590*. Mexico City.

Niebuhr, B.G. (1846–8). *Vorträge über römische Geschichte an der Universität zu Bonn gehalten*, 3 vols. Berlin.

Nielson, K.P. (1983). "The *Tropaion* in the *Aeneid*," *Vergilius* 29: 27–33.

Nisbet, H.B. (1979). "Laokoon in Germany: The Reception of the Group since Winckelmann," *Oxford German Studies* 10: 22–63.

Nisbet, R.G.M. (1990). "*Aeneas Imperator*: Roman Generalship in an Epic Context," rpt. in Harrison, ed.: 378–89. [First published 1978–9 in *PVS* 18 (1978–80): 50–61.]

Nohrnberg, J. (1976). *The Analogy of The Faerie Queene*. Princeton.

Nolte, F.O. (1940). *Lessing's "Laokoon."* Lancaster.

Nora, P., ed. (1984–92). *Les Lieux de mémoire*, 3 vols. in 7 parts. Paris.

Norbrook, D. (1999). *Writing the English Republic: Poetry, Rhetoric, and Politics, 1627–1660*. Cambridge.

Nugent, S.G. (1999). "The Women of the *Aeneid*: Vanishing Bodies, Lingering Voices," in Perkell, ed.: 251–70.

Obbink, D., ed. (1995). *Philodemus and Poetry: Poetic Theory and Practice in Lucretius, Philodemus, and Horace*. Oxford.

Obbink, D. (2004). "Vergil's *De pietate*: From *Ehoiae* to Allegory in Vergil, Philodemus, and Ovid," in Armstrong et al., eds.: 175–209.

O'Brien, M. (1985). *A Character of Hugh Legaré*. Knoxville.

O'Brien, M., ed. (1992). *All Clever Men, Who Make Their Way: Critical Discourse in the Old South*. Athens, GA.

O'Brien, M. (2004). *Conjectures of Order: Intellectual Life and the American South, 1810–1860*. Chapel Hill.

O'Connell, M. (1977). *Mirror and Veil: The Historical Dimension of Spenser's Faerie Queene*. Chapel Hill.

Odermann, E. (1931). "Vergil und der Kupferstich," *Buch und Schrift* 5: 13–25.

Oechslin, W. (1974). "Il Laocoonte o del restauro delle statue antiche," *Paragone – Arte* 24: 287–329.

Oehlert, J. (1995). "Schillers Aeneis-Übertragung," in Irmscher, ed.: 143–8.

Ogg, D. (1963). *England in the Reign of Charles II*, 2nd ed. Oxford. [First ed. 1956.]

Ogilby, J., ed. (1649). *The Works of Publius Virgilius Maro*. London.

Ogilby, J., ed. (1654). *The Works of Publius Vergilius Maro. Translated, Adorn'd with Sculpture, and Illustrated with Annotations by John Ogilby*. London.

O'Hara, J.J. (1990). *Death and the Optimistic Prophecy in Vergil's Aeneid*. Princeton.

O'Hara, J.J. (1993). Review of Masters (1992). *CJ* 89: 83–6.

O'Hara, J.J. (1994). "They Might be Giants: Inconsistency and Indeterminacy in Vergil's War in Italy," *Colby Quarterly* 30: 206–32.

O'Hara, J.J. (1996). *True Names: Vergil and the Alexandrian Tradition of Etymological Wordplay*. Ann Arbor.

O'Hara, J.J. (1997). "Virgil's Style," in Martindale, ed.: 241–58.

O'Hara, J.J. (2005). "Trying Not to Cheat: Responses to Inconsistencies in Roman Epic." *TAPhA* 135: 15–33.

O'Hara, J.J. (2007). *Inconsistency in Roman Epic: Studies in Catullus, Lucretius, Vergil, Ovid and Lucan*. Cambridge.

O'Malley, J.W., S.J. (1993). *The First Jesuits*. Cambridge, MA.

Ong, W. (1959). "Latin Language Study as a Renaissance Puberty Rite," *SPh* 56: 103–24.

Osorio Romero, I. (1991). *El sueño criollo. José Antonio de Villerías y Roelas (1695–1728)*. Mexico.

Osthoff, H. (1954). "Vergils *Aeneis* in der Musik von Josquin des Prez bis Orlando di Lasso," *Archiv fur Musikwissenschaft* 11: 85–102.

Otis, B. (1964). *Virgil: A Study in Civilized Poetry*. Oxford.

Padoan, G. (1977). "Il limbo dantesco," in *Il pio Enea, l'empio Ulisse*. Ravenna: 103–24.

Page, T.E., ed. (1894–1900). *The Aeneid of Virgil*, 2 vols. London.

Palmer, A.H., ed. (1892). *The Life and Letters of Samuel Palmer*. London.

Panoussi, V. (2009). *Greek Tragedy in Vergil's Aeneid: Ritual, Empire, and Intertext*. Cambridge.

Papaioannou, S. (2003). "Founder, Civilizer and Leader: Vergil's Evander and his Role in the Origins of Rome," *Mnemosyne* 56: 680–702.

Papers of Thomas Jefferson, Retirement Series, Digital Library: www.monticello.org/papers/about.html. Accessed August 28, 2008.

Paratore, E. (2007³). *Una nuova ricostruzione del "De poetis" di Suetonio*. Urbino. [First ed. Rome, 1946; 2nd ed. Bari, 1950.]

Parker, P. (1987). *Literary Fat Ladies: Rhetoric, Gender, Property*. London.

Parnassus (1654). *Parnassus Societatis Iesu, hoc est poemata patrum societatis quae in Belgio, Gallia, Germania, Hispania, Polonia etc. vel hactenus excusa sunt, vel recens elucubrata nunc primum evulgantur....* Frankfurt.

Paschalis, M. (1997). *Virgil's Aeneid: Semantic Relations and Proper Names*. Oxford.

Pasquali, G. (1942). "Arte allusiva," *Italie che Scrive* 25: 185–7 [= *Pagine stravaganti II*. Florence, 1968: 275–82].

Pasquier, B. (1992). *Virgile illustré de la Renaissance à nos jours en France et en Italie*. Paris.

Pavano, A. (1996). "La quaestio daretiana," *Cassiodorus* 2: 305–21.

Pavlock, B. (1990). *Eros, Imitation, and the Epic Tradition*. Ithaca.

Payne, C. (1993). *Toil and Plenty: Images of Agricultural Landscape in England 1780–1890*. New Haven.

Pease, A.S., ed. (1935). *Publi Vergili Maronis: Aeneidos: Liber Quartus*. Cambridge, MA.

Peck, J. (1993). *Argura*. Manchester.

Peñalosa, J.A., ed. (1987). *Flor y canto de poesía Guadalupana, siglo XVII*. Mexico City.

Pereira, B., S.J. (1640). *Paciecis*. Coimbra.

Perkell, C., ed. (1999). *Reading Vergil's Aeneid: An Interpretive Guide*. Norman.

Perret, J. (1942). *Les Origines de la légende troyenne de Rome (231–81)*. Paris.

Perrin, P. (1664). *L'Enéide de Virgile fidelement traduite...*. Paris.

Perry, M. (1992). "Gwendolyn Brooks," in *Notable Black American Women*, ed. J.C. Smith. Detroit: 105–9.

Peter, H. (1914). *Historicorum Romanorum Reliquiae*. 2 vols. 2nd ed. Leipzig. Rpt. Stuttgart (1967).

Petrovskii, F.A. (1966). "Russkie perevody 'Eneidy' i zadachi novogo ee perevoda," in *Voprosy antichnoi' literatury i klassicheskoi' filologii*, ed. S. Sobolevskii and M.E. Grabar-Passek. Moscow: 293–306.

Petrucci Nardelli, F. (1991). *La lettera e l'immagine: le iniziali "parlanti" nella tipografia italiana (secc. xvi–xviii)*. Florence.

Pfeiffer, R., ed. (1949). *Callimachus*. Vol. 1. Oxford.

Pfeiffer, R. (1968). *A History of Classical Scholarship: From the Beginnings to the End of the Hellenistic Age*. Oxford.

Phillips, C. (2001). *The Tether*. New York.

Phillips, C. (2004). "Twist, Tact and Metaphysics," in *Coin of the Realm*. Saint Paul: 219–26.

Phillips, J. (1673). *Maronides, or, Virgil Travesty: being a new Paraphrase upon the Sixth Book of Virgils Æneids in Burlesque Verse*. London.

Pickens, W. (1930). *Abraham Lincoln, Man and Statesman*. Talladega.

Pickens, W. (2005). *Bursting Bonds*, ed. W.L. Andrews. South Bend.

Pidgin, C. (1907). *Theodosia, the First Gentlewoman of Her Time*. Boston.

Pierce, E.L., ed. (1878). *Memoir and Letters of Charles Sumner*. London.

Pietas Universitatis Oxoniensis in obitum serenissimæ Reginæ Annæ et gratulatio in augustissimi Regis Georgii inaugurationem (1714). Oxford.

Pigler, A. (1974). *Barockthemen*. Budapest.

Pigna, G.B. (1554). *I romanzi*. Venice.

Pinto, J.A. (1970). "Related Aspects of Roman Architectural Design." Unpublished honors thesis, Department of Fine Arts, Harvard College. Cambridge, MA.

Plüss, H.T. (1884). *Vergil und die epische Kunst*. Leipzig.

Pocock, J.G.A. (1989). *Politics, Language, and Time*. Chicago and London.

Polverini, L. (1984). "Darete," in *Enciclopedia Virgiliana*, ed. F. della Corte. Rome. Vol. 1: 1000.

Pomfret, J.E. (1932). "Student Interests at Brown University, 1789–1790," *New England Quarterly* 5: 135–47.

Pontano, G. (1902). *Ioannis Iouiani Pontani Carmina*, ed. B. Soldati. Florence.

Pontanus, J., S.J. (1594). *Poeticarum institutionum libri tres. Tyrocinium poeticum*. Ingolstadt.

Poole, S. (1995). *Our Lady of Guadalupe: The Origins and Sources of a Mexican National Symbol*. Tucson.

Pope, A. (2007). *The Dunciad (1728) and The Dunciad Variorum (1729)*, ed. V. Rumbold. London.

Porter, J. (2004). "Vergil's Voids," *Helios* 31: 127–56.

Porter, J.I. (1992). "Hermeneutic Lines and Circles: Aristarchus and Crates on the Exegesis of Homer," in *Homer's Ancient Readers: The Hermeneutics of Greek Epic's Earliest Exegetes*, ed. R. Lamberton and J.J. Keaney. Princeton: 67–114.

Porter, W. (1993). *Reading the Classics and Paradise Lost*. Lincoln.

Pöschl, V. (1962). *The Art of Vergil*, trans. G. Seligson. Ann Arbor.

Possevino, A., S.J. (1593). *Bibliotheca selecta qua agitur de ratione studiorum in historia, in disciplinis, in salute omnium procuranda*. Venice.

Pound, E. (1934). *An ABC of Reading*. London.

Pound, E. (1954). *Literary Essays of Ezra Pound*, ed. T.S. Eliot. London.

Pound, E. (1956). *Selected Poems*. New York.

Powell, J.U. (1925). *Collectanea Alexandrina*. Oxford.

Power, H. (2007). "'Teares break off my Verse': The Virgilian Incompleteness of Abraham Cowley's *The Civil War*," *Translation and Literature* 16: 141–59.

Pratt, K. (1998). "Reading Epic Through Romance," in Ailes, ed.: 101–27.

Preiss, B. (1992). *Die wissenschaftliche Beschäftigung mit der Laokoongruppe. Die Bedeutung Christian Gottlob Heynes für die Archäologie des 18. Jahrhunderts*. Bonn.

Prendergast, C. (2007). *The Classic: Sainte-Beuve and the Nineteenth-Century Culture Wars*. Oxford.

Prettejohn, E. (2005). *Beauty and Art 1750–2000*. Oxford.

Prizer, W. (1999). "'Une Virtu Molto Conveniente a Madonne': Isabella d'Este as a Musician," *Journal of Musicology* 17: 10–49.

Proudfoot, L. (1960). *Dryden's Aeneid and its Seventeenth-Century Predecessors*. Manchester.

Pucci, J. (1998). *The Full-Knowing Reader: Allusion and the Power of the Reader in the Western Literary Tradition*. New Haven.

Pugh, S. (2005). *Spenser and Ovid*. Aldershot.

Pugh, S. (2008). "Fanshawe's Critique of Caroline Pastoral: Allusion and Ambiguity in the 'Ode on the Proclamation,'" *Review of English Studies* 59 (240): 379–91.

Putnam, M.C.J. (1965). *The Poetry of the Aeneid: Four Studies in Imaginative Unity and Design*. Cambridge, MA and London. Rpt. Ithaca, 1988.

Putnam, M.C.J. (1979). *Virgil's Poem of the Earth: Studies in the Georgics*. Princeton.

Putnam, M.C.J. (1991). "Virgil's *Inferno*," in Jacoff and Schnapp, eds.: 94–112. Expanded version in Putnam 1995: 286–315.

Putnam, M.C.J. (1995). *Virgil's Aeneid: Interpretation and Influence*. Chapel Hill.

Putnam, M.C.J. (1998). *Virgil's Epic Designs: Ekphrasis in the Aeneid*. New Haven and London.

Putnam, M.C.J. (2001). "The Loom of Latin," *TAPhA* 131: 329–39.

Putnam, M.C.J. (2004). *Maffeo Vegio: Short Epics*. Cambridge, MA and London.

Putnam, M.C.J. (2005). "Virgil's *Aeneid*," in Foley, ed.: 452–75.

Putnam, M.C.J., trans. (forthcoming, 2011). *Imago Primi Saeculi Societatis Iesu a Provincia Flandro-Belgica Eiusdem Societatis Representata*.

Quint, D. (1985). "The Boat of Romance and Renaissance Epic," in *Romance: Generic Transformation from Chrétien de Troyes to Cervantes*, ed. and intro. K. Brownlee and M.S. Brownlee. Hanover, NH: 178–202.

Quint, D. (1989). "Repetition and Ideology in the *Aeneid*," *MD* 23: 9–54.

Quint, D. (1993). *Epic and Empire: Politics and Generic Form from Virgil to Milton*. Princeton.

Quint, D. (2003). "The Anatomy of Epic in Book 2 of *The Faerie Queene*," *Spenser Review* 34: 28–45.

Quint, D. (2004). "The Virgilian Coordinates of *Paradise Lost*," *MD* (*Numero speciale in onore di Michael C.J. Putnam*) 52: 177–97.

Quitslund, J.A. (2001). *Spenser's Supreme Fiction: Platonic Natural Philosophy and The Faerie Queene*. Toronto.

Raaflaub, K. and Toher, M., eds. (1990). *Between Republic and Empire: Interpretations of Augustus and his Principate*. Berkeley and Los Angeles.

Rabb, T.K. (1960). "Sebastian Brant and the First Illustrated Edition of Vergil," *Princeton Library Chronicle* 21: 187–99.

Rabel, R. (2007). "Odysseus Almost Makes It to Broadway: The *Ulysses Africanus* of Kurt Weill and Maxwell Anderson," *IJCT* 13: 550–70.

Rackham, H., ed. and trans. (1942). *Pliny: Natural History*. Vol. 2. Cambridge, MA.

Radice, B. (1963). *The Letters of the Younger Pliny*. London.

Radt, S., ed. (1999). *Tragicorum Graecorum Fragmenta*. Vol. 4: *Sophocles*. 2nd ed. Göttingen. [1st ed. 1977.]

Ragni, E. (1984). "Boiardo," in *Enciclopedia Virgiliana*, ed. F. della Corte. Rome. Vol. 5: 18–21.

Rahe, P. (1992). *Republics, Ancient and Modern: Classical Republicanism and the American Revolution*. Chapel Hill.

Rahn, H. (1958). "Ovids elegische Epistel," *A&A* 7: 105–20.

Rajna, P. (1975). *Le fonti dell'Orlando furioso*. Florence. [First published 1876, revised 1900.]

Rankine, P. (2006). *Ulysses in Black: Ralph Ellison, Classicism, and African American Literature*. Madison.

Rapin, R. (1659). *Eclogae sacrae et dissertatio de carmine pastorali*. Paris.

Rapin, R. (1664). *Comparaison des poèmes de Homère et de Virgile*. Paris.

Rapin, R. (1665). *Hortorum libri iv*. Paris.

Rapin, R. (1674). *Christus patiens*. Paris.

Rapin, R. (1970). *Les Réflexions sur la poétique de ce temps et sur les ouvrages des poètes anciens et modernes* (1674–5), ed. E. T. Dubois. Geneva.

Ratio studiorum (1599). *Ratio, Atque Institutio Studiorum Societatis Iesu Auctoritate Septimae Congregationis Generalis aucta*. Rome. www.bc.edu/bc_org/avp/ulib/digi/ratio/ratio-home.html.

Ratio studiorum (1616). *Ratio, Atque Institutio Studiorum Societatis Iesu Auctoritate Septimae Congregationis Generalis aucta*. Rome. www.uni-mannheim.de/mateo/camenaref/societasjesu.html#sj3.

Rawson, E. (1985). *Intellectual Life in the Late Roman Republic*. London.

Rebora, C., Staiti, P., Hirshler, E., and Stebbins, T., Jr. (1995). *John Singleton Copley in America*. New York.

Reed, J.D. (2006). "Virgil's Corythus and Roman Identity," *SIFC* 4: 183–97.

Reed, J.D. (2007). *Virgil's Gaze: Nation and Poetry in the Aeneid*. Princeton.

Reeves, G. (1989). *T.S. Eliot: A Virgilian Poet*. New York.

Reid, J.D., ed. (1993). *The Oxford Guide to Classical Mythology in the Arts, 1300–1990s*. Oxford.

Reinhold, M. (1975). *The Classick Pages: Classical Reading of Eighteenth-Century Americans*. University Park, PA.

Reinhold, M. (1984). "Vergil in the American Experience from Colonial Times to 1882," in *Classica Americana: The Greek and Roman Heritage in the United States*. Detroit: 221–49.

Rengakos, A. (1993). *Der Homertext und die hellenistischen Dichter*. Hermes Einzelschriften, 64. Wiesbaden.

Rexine, J. (1976). "The Boston Latin School Curriculum in the Seventeenth and Eighteenth Centuries," *CJ* 72: 261–66.

Reyes, A. (1930). "México en una nuez," in Reyes (1960), vol. 9: 45–8.

Reyes, A. (1931). "Discurso por Virgilio," in *Homenaje de México al poeta Virgilio*. Mexico City: 387–410.

Reyes, A. (1937). "Apéndice sobre Virgilio y América," in Reyes (1960), vol. 11: 178–81.

Reyes, A. (1960). *Obras Completas*. Mexico City.

Reyes, A. (2005). *América*, ed. C. Fuentes. Mexico City.

Richard, C.J. (1994). *The Founders and the Classics: Greece, Rome, and the American Enlightenment*. Cambridge, MA.

Richard, C.J. (2003). *Twelve Greeks and Romans Who Changed the World*. Lanham, MD.

Richardson, N.J. (1980). "Literary Criticism in the Exegetical Scholia to the *Iliad*," *CQ* 30: 265–87.

Richter, G. (1959). *A Handbook of Greek Art*. London.

Richter, S. (1992). *Laocoon's Body and the Aesthetics of Pain: Winckelmann, Lessing, Herder, Moritz, Goethe*. Detroit.

Ridder, A. (1902). *Catalogue des vases peints de la Bibliothèque Nationale*. Paris.

Rieks, R. (1981). "Vergils Dichtung als Zeugnis und Deutung der römischen Geschichte," *ANRW* II.31.2: 728–868.

Riese, A. (1894–1906). *Anthologia Latina*. 2nd ed. Leipzig.

Ring, B. (1993). *Girlhood Embroidery: American Samplers and Pictorial Needlework, 1650–1850*. New York.

Riofrío, B. de (1680). *Centonicum Virgilianum Monimentum*. Mexico City.

Risley, D.S. (1920). "Jacobite Wine Glasses: Some Rare Examples," *Burlington Magazine for Connoisseurs* 36 (207): 276–87.

Robathan, D. (1946). "John Adams and the Classics," *New England Quarterly* 19: 91–8.

Roberts, D., Dunn, F., and Fowler, D., eds. (1997). *Classical Closure: Reading the End in Greek and Latin Literature*. Princeton.

Roberts, J. (1994). *Athens on Trial: The Anti-Democratic Tradition in Western Thought*. Princeton.

Robeson, P. (1971). *Here I Stand*. Boston.

Robinson, P. (1985). *Opera and Ideas, from Mozart to Strauss*. Ithaca.

Roche, T.P. (1964). *The Kindly Flame: A Study of the Third and Fourth Books of Spenser's Faerie Queene*. Princeton.

Roe, A.S. (1953). *Blake's Illustrations to the Divine Comedy*. Princeton.

Roethlisberger, M. (1961). *Claude Lorrain: The Paintings*. New Haven.

Rolfe, J.C., ed. and trans. (1927). *Aulus Gellius: Attic Nights*. 3 vols. Cambridge, MA.

Rollo, D. (1998). *Historical Fabrication, Ethnic Fable and French Romance in Twelfth-Century England*. Lexington.

Romizi, A. (1896). *Le fonti latine del Orlando furioso*. Turin.

Ronconi, A. (1978). "Echi virgiliani nell'opera dantesca," in *Enciclopedia dantesca*, ed. U. Bosco. Rome. Vol. 5: 1044–9.

Ronnick, M. (1993). "A Classical Pun at Drayton Hall," *CML* 12: 167–9.

Ronnick, M. (1996). "'A Pick Instead of Greek and Latin': The Afro-American Quest for Useful Knowledge, 1880–1920," *Negro Educational Review* 47: 60–72.

Ronnick, M. (1998a). "Virgil's *Aeneid* and John Quincy Adams' Speech for the Amistad Blacks," *New England Quarterly* 71: 473–7.

Ronnick, M. (1998b). "Francis Williams: An Eighteenth-Century Tertium Quid," *Negro History Bulletin* 61: 19–29.

Ronnick, M. (2002). "George Morton Lightfoot (1868–1947)," *CO* 80: 22–3.

Ronnick, M., ed. (2005). *The Autobiography of William Sanders Scarborough: An American Journey from Slavery to Scholarship*. Foreword by H. L. Gates. Detroit.

Ronnick, M., ed. (2006). *The Works of William Sanders Scarborough: Black Classicist and Race Leader*. Foreword by H.L. Gates. New York.

Rooses, M. (1886–92). *L'Œuvre de P.P. Rubens*. Antwerp.

Roscher, W. (1897–8). *Ausführliches Lexikon der griechischen und römischen Mythologie*. Leipzig.

Rose, H.J. (1948). *Aeneas Pontifex*. London.

Rosenberg, A. (1905). *P.P. Rubens* [= *Klassiker der Kunst in Gesamtausgaben*, vol. 5]. Leipzig.

Rosenberg, J. (1943). "Rubens' Sketch for Wrath of Neptune," *Bulletin of the Fogg Art Museum* 10: 5–14.

Rosenmeyer, P.A. (1997). "Ovid's *Heroides* and *Tristia*: Voices from Exile," *Ramus* 26: 29–56.

Rosenthal, B.M. (1997). *The Rosenthal Collection of Printed Books with Manuscript Annotations*. New Haven.

Rouse, W.H.D. and Smith, M.F. (1992). *Lucretius, De Rerum Natura*. Cambridge, MA.

Rowland, I. (2001). "Th' United Sense of th' Universe: Athanasius Kircher in Piazza Navona," *Memoirs of the American Academy in Rome*, 46: 153–81.

Rowling, J.K. (1997). *Harry Potter and the Philosopher's Stone*. London.

Rubidge, B. (1998). "Catharsis through Admiration: Corneille, Le Moyne, and the Social Uses of Emotion," *Modern Philology* 95.3: 316–33.

Rudd, N. (2006). "Reception: Some Caveats," *Arion* 14: 13.

Ruden, S., trans. (2008). *Virgil: The Aeneid*. New Haven.

Rudolph, F. (1977). *Curriculum: A History of the American Undergraduate Course of Study since 1636*. San Francisco.

Runes, D., ed. (1947). *The Selected Writings of Benjamin Rush*. New York.

Rusk, R.L., ed. (1939). *The Letters of Ralph Waldo Emerson*. New York.

Russell, D.A., ed. and trans. (2002). *Quintilian: The Orator's Education*. 5 vols. Cambridge, MA.

Russo, J., Fernández-Galiano, M., and Heubeck, A. (1992). *A Commentary on Homer's Odyssey*. Vol. 3: *Books 17–24*. Oxford and New York.

Rutland, R.A. et al., eds. (1962–77). *The Papers of James Madison*. Chicago; (1977–) Charlottesville.

Ryan, C., trans. (1989). *The Banquet: Dante*. Saratoga, CA.

Sadurska, A. (1964). *Les Tables Iliaques*. Warsaw.

Sahagún, B. de (1950–82). *Florentine Codex* (Nahuatl text of *Historia General*), ed. and trans. A.J.O. Anderson and C.E. Dibble. Santa Fe.

Sahagún, B. de (1990). *Historia General de las Cosas de la Nueva España*, ed. J.C. Temprano, 2 vols. Madrid.

Sainte-Beuve, C.-A. (1860–85). *Causeries du lundi*, 15 vols. Paris.

Sainte-Beuve, C.-A. (1883). *Etude sur Virgile*. Paris.

Salles, C. (1992). *Lire à Rome*. Paris.

[Salviati, L.] (1588). *Lo 'nfarinato secondo ovvero dello 'nfarinato accademico della Crusca, risposta al libro intitolato Replica di Camillo Pellegrino ec. Nella qual risposta sono incorporate tutte le scritture, passate tra detto Pellegrino, e detti Accademici intorno all'Ariosto, e al Tasso in forma e ordine di dialogo*. Florence.

Sánchez, M. (1648). *Imagen de la Virgen María Madre de Dios de Guadalupe, milagrosamente aparecida en la Ciudad de México. Celebrada en su historia, con la profecía del capítulo doze del Apocalipsis*. Mexico City.

Sandys, G., trans. (1632). *Ovid's Metamorphosis Englished, Mythologized, and Represented in Figures*. London.

Sannazaro, I. (1988). *De partu Virginis* (1526), ed. C. Fantazzi and A. Perosa. Florence.

Santini, C., ed. (1995). *I frammenti di L. Cassio Emina: Introduzione, testo, traduzione e commento.* Testi e Studi di Cultura Classica 13. Pisa.

Scaffai, M. (2006). *La presenza di Omero nei commenti antichi a Virgilio.* Bologna.

Scafoglio, G. (2005). "Virgilio e Stesicoro: Una ricerca sulla *Tabula Iliaca Capitolina,*" *RhM* 148: 113–27.

Scaliger, J.C. (1561). *Poetices libri septem.* Lyon. Rpt. Stuttgart, 1964.

Scaliger, J.C. (1994). *La Poetique. Livre V: Le Critique,* trans. J. Chomarat. Geneva.

Scaliger, J.C. (1994–2003). *Poetices Libri Septem,* ed. L. Deitz and G. Vogt-Spira, 5 vols. Stuttgart and Bad Cannstatt.

Scarborough, W.S. (1881). *First Lessons in Greek.* New York.

Schaefer, G.H., ed. (1811). *Gregorii Corinthii et aliorum grammaticorum libri de dialectis linguae graecae.* Leipzig.

Schauer, M. (2007). *Aeneas dux in Vergils Aeneis. Eine literarische Fiktion in augusteischer Zeit.* Zetemata 128. Munich.

Scheid, J. (2003). *An Introduction to Roman Religion,* trans. J. Lloyd. Bloomington. [First published in French as *La Religion des Romains.* Paris, 1988.]

Schelkle, K.H. (1939). *Virgil in der Deutung Augustins.* Stuttgart.

Schelling, F.W.J. (1989). *The Philosophy of Art,* trans. D.W. Stott. Minneapolis.

Scherr, B.P. (2008). '"Don't Shield the Original from the Reader': Mikhail Gasparov on the Art of Translation," *Slavic and East European Journal* 52: 235–52.

Schiesaro, A. (1998). "Latin Literature and Greece," *Dialogos* 5: 144–9.

Schindler, C. (2001). "Nicolò Partenio Giannettasios *Nauticorum libri VIII:* Ein neulateinisches Lehrgedicht des 17. Jahrhunderts," *Neulateinisches Jahrbuch* 3: 145–76.

Schindler, C. (2003). "*Vitreas Crateris ad undas.* Le egloghe del pescatore di Nicolò Partenio Giannettasio (1648–1715)," *Studi Umanistici Piceni* 23: 293–304.

Schlaps, C. (2004). "The 'Genius of Language': Transformations of a Concept in the History of Linguistics," *Historiographia Linguistica* 31: 2–3, 367–88.

Schlegel, A.W. (1964). *Geschichte der klassischen Literatur,* ed. E. Lohner. *Kritische Schriften und Briefe,* vol. 3. Stuttgart.

Schlegel, A.W. (1989). *Vorlesungen über Ästhetik I (1798–1803),* ed. E. Behler. *Kritische Ausgabe der Vorlesungen,* vol. 1. Paderborn.

Schlegel, F. (1958–). *Kritische Friedrich-Schlegel-Ausgabe,* ed. E. Behler, 35 vols. Paderborn.

Schleiermacher, F. (1977). "On the Different Methods of Translating" [*Ueber die verschiedenen Methoden des Uebersetzens*] (1813), in Lefevere, ed.: 67–89.

Schleiner, W. (1976). "The Infant Hercules: Franklin's Design for a Medal Commemorating American Liberty," *Eighteenth Century Studies* 10: 235–44.

Schlunk, R. (1974). *The Homeric Scholia and the Aeneid: A Study of the Influence of Ancient Homeric Literary Criticism on Vergil.* Ann Arbor.

Schmeling, G., ed. (1996). *The Novel in the Ancient World.* Leiden.

Schmidt, G.P. (1936). "Intellectual Crosscurrents in American Colleges, 1825–1855," *American Historical Review* 42: 46–67.

Schmidt, W. (1983). *Vergil-Probleme.* Göppinger Akademische Beiträge 120. Göppingen.

Schmit-Neuerburg, T. (1999). *Vergils Aeneis und die antike Homerexegese, Untersuchungen zum Einfluss ethischer und kritischer Homerrezeption auf imitatio und aemulatio Vergils.* Untersuchungen zur antiken Literatur und Geschichte Band 56. Berlin and New York.

Schmitt, C. (1985). *Political Theology: Four Chapters on the Concept of Sovereignty,* trans. G. Schwab. Cambridge, MA. [First published 1922.]

Schnapp, J.T. (1986). *The Transfiguration of History at the Center of Dante's Paradise.* Princeton.

Schnapp, J.T. (1991). "'Sì pia l'ombra d'Anchise si porse'": *Paradiso* 15.25," in Jacoff and Schnapp, eds.: 145–56.

Schneider, B. (1982). *Vergil: Handschriften und Drucke der Herzog August Bibliothek*. Wolfenbüttel.

Schneider, B. (1983). " 'Virgilius pictus' – Sebastian Brants illustrierte Vergilausgabe und ihre Nachwirking: Ein Beitrag zur Vergilrezeption im deutschen Humanismus," *Wolfenbütteler Beiträge* 6: 202–62.

Schoen, D.E. (1977). *Enoch Powell and the Powellites*. New York.

Schröder, W.A., ed. (1971). *M. Porcius Cato, Das Erste Buch der Origines: Ausgabe und Erklärung der Fragmente*. Meisenheim am Glan.

Schüller, A. (2002). *A Life Composed: T.S. Eliot and the Morals of Modernism*. Münster.

Schultz, C. (2006). "Juno Sospita and Roman Insecurity in the Social War," *YCS* 33: 207–77.

Scodel, R. (1999). *Credible Impossibilities: Conventions and Strategies of Verisimilitude in Homer and Greek Tragedy*. Stuttgart.

Scodel, R. and Thomas, R. (1984). "Virgil and the Euphrates," *AJP* 105: 339.

Scott, S.C. (1987). "From Polydorus to Fradubio: The History of a *topos*," *Spenser Studies* 7: 27–57.

Scott, W. and Saintsbury, G., eds. (1892). *The Works of John Dryden*. Edinburgh.

Scudéry, M. de (1714). *The Female Orators: Or, the Courage and Constancy of Divers Famous Queens, and Illustrious Women, Set Forth in Their Eloquent Orations and Noble Resolutions. Worthy the Perusal and Imitation of the Female Sex*. London.

Scullard, H.H. (1959). *From the Gracchi to Nero*. London.

Sedley, D.N. (1998). *Lucretius and the Transformation of Greek Wisdom*. Cambridge.

Segal, C.P. (1965). "*Aeternum per saecula nomen*, The Golden Bough and the Tragedy of History: Part I," *Arion* 4: 617–57.

Selden, D. (2006). "Virgil and the Satanic *Cogito*," *Literary Imagination* 8.3 [= "The Aesthetics of Empire and the Reception of Virgil," ed. S. Spence and M. Lowrie]: 345–86.

Sellers, M. (1994). *American Republicanism: Roman Ideology in the United States Constitution*. New York.

Serres, M. (1991). *Rome: The Book of Foundations*. Stanford.

Sessions, W.A. (1980). "Spenser's Georgics," *English Literary Renaissance* 10: 202–38.

Settis, S. (1999). *Laocoonte. Fama e stile*. Rome.

Severyns, A. (1963). *Recherches sur la "Chrestomathie" de Proclos*. Vol. IV: *La "Vita Homeri" et les Sommaires du Cycle. Texte et Traduction*. Bibliothèque de la Faculté de philosophie et lettres de l'Université de Liège, vols. 169–70. Liège.

Seybold, E. (1951). *Thoreau: The Quest and the Classics*. New Haven.

Seznec, J. (1980). *La Survivance des dieux antiques*. Paris.

Shalev, E. (2003). "Ancient Masks, American Fathers: Classical Pseudonyms during the American Revolution and Early Republic," *Journal of the Early Republic* 25: 152–72.

Shalev, E. (2006). "Empire Transformed: Britain in the American Classical Imagination, 1758–1783," *Early American Studies* 4: 112–46.

Shalev, E. (2009). *Rome Reborn on Western Shores: Historical Imagination and the Creation of the United States*. Charlottesville.

Sheehan, J. (2005). *The Enlightenment Bible: Translation, Scholarship, Culture*. Princeton.

Sherberg, M. (1993). *Rinaldo: Character and Intertext in Ariosto and Tasso*. Saratoga, CA.

Shields, J. (1980). "Phillis Wheatley's Use of Classicism," *American Literature* 52: 97–111.

Shields, J. (2001). *The American Aeneas: Classical Origins of the American Self*. Knoxville.

Shklovsky, V. (2004). "Art as Technique," in *Literary Theory: An Anthology*, ed. J. Rivkin and M. Ryan, 2nd ed. Malden: 15–21.

Short, I., ed. (2005). "The Oxford Version," in Duggan et al., eds.

Sichtermann, H. (1957). *Laokoon*. Bremen.

Sigüenza y Góngora, C. de (1680). *Primavera Indiana*. Mexico City.

Simon, E. (1984). "Laokoon und die Geschichte der antiken Kunst," *AA* 99: 643–72.

Simon, E. (1992). "Laokoon," in *Lexicon Iconographicum Mythologiae Classicae*. Zurich and Munich. 6.1: 196–201.

Simonsuuri, K. (1979). *Homer's Original Genius: Eighteenth-Century Notions of the Early Greek Epic (1688–1798)*. Cambridge.

Singleton, C.S., trans. (1975). *Dante's Paradiso*. Princeton.

Sitterson, J.C., Jr. (1992). "Allusive and Elusive Meanings: Reading *Ariosto's* Vergilian Ending," *Renaissance Quarterly* 45: 1–19.

Skutsch, O. (1985). *The Annals of Quintus Ennius, Edited with Introduction and Commentary*. Oxford.

Small, J.P. (1982). *Cacus and Marsyas in Etrusco-Roman Legend*. Princeton.

Small, J.P. (1997). *Wax Tablets of the Mind*. London.

Smith, N. (1969). *Henry Stillwell Edwards*. Macon.

Smith, N. (1994). *Literature and Revolution in England, 1640–1660*. New Haven.

Smith, P.M. (1981). "Aineiadai as Patrons of Iliad XX and the Homeric Hymn to Aphrodite," *HSCP* 85: 17–58.

Snell, B. and Maehler, H., eds. (1970). *Bacchylidis Carmina Cum Fragmentis*. Leipzig.

Solmsen, F. (1986). "Aeneas Founded Rome with Odysseus," *HSCP* 90: 93–110.

Solomon, B. (1985). *In the Company of Educated Women: A History of Women and Higher Education in America*. New Haven.

Sommervogel, C. (1890–1909). *Bibliothèque de la Compagnie de Jésus. Première Partie: Bibliographie par les Pères Augustin et Aloys de Backer*, new ed. Brussels and Paris.

Sordi, M., ed. (1976). *I canali della propaganda nel mondo antico*. Milan.

Soubeille, G. (1982). "Le *Praedium Rusticum* de Jacques Vanière ou la fin d'une tradition virgilienne," *Pallas* 29: 79–97.

Soubeille, G. (1995). "Jacques Vanière (1664–1739). Le dernier Virgile toulousain," *Mémoires de l'Académie des Sciences, Inscriptions et Belles-Lettres de Toulouse* 157, ser. 17, vol. 5: 227–36.

Sowell, M.U., ed. (1991). *Dante and Ovid: Essays in Intertextuality*. Binghamton.

Spargo, J.W. (1934). *Virgil the Necromancer: Studies in Virgilian Legends*. Cambridge, MA.

Sparrow, J. (1931). *Half-Lines and Repetitions in Virgil*. Oxford.

Spence, J. (1966). *Observations, Anecdotes, and Characters of Books and Men, Collected from Conversation*, ed. J.M. Osborn, 2 vols. Oxford.

Spence, S., ed. (2001). *Poets and Critics Read Virgil*. New Haven and London.

Spence, S. (2003). "'A Curious Appearance in the Air': Lyric Irreducibility and the Cheshire Cat," in *Being There Together: Essays in Honor of Michael C.J. Putnam on the Occasion of His Seventieth Birthday*, ed. P. Thibodeau and H. Haskell. Afton: 275–86.

Spence, S. and Lowrie, M., eds. (2006). *The Aesthetics of Empire and the Reception of Vergil. Literary Imagination* 8.3.

Spiegel, G. (1993). *Romancing the Past: The Rise of Vernacular Prose Historiography in Thirteenth-Century France*. Berkeley and Los Angeles.

Spiegelman, W. (2006). "Unforced Marches: A Virgilian Memoir," *Parnassus: Poetry in Review* 30, 1 & 2: 81–106. Rpt. as ch. 1 in *Selected Literary Essays*. Oxford, 2008: 3–23.

Spivey, C. (1942). *A Tribute to the Negro Preacher*. Wilberforce, OH.

Stahl, H.-P. (1990). "The Death of Turnus," in Raaflaub and Toher, eds.: 174–211.

Stahl, H.-P., ed. (1998). *Vergil's Aeneid: Augustan Epic and Political Context*. London.

Stanford, D.E. (1978). *In the Classic Mode: The Achievement of Robert Bridges*. Newark, DE.

Stankiewicz, E. (1981). "The 'Genius' of Language in Sixteenth-Century Linguistics," in *Logos Semantikos: Studia Linguistica in Honorem Eugenio Coseriu*, ed. J. Trabant, 5 vols. Berlin and Madrid. Vol. 1: 177–89.

Stanton, E.C. (1993). *Eighty Years & More: 1815–1897 Reminiscences*. Boston.

Stanton, T. and Blatch, H.S., eds. (1922). *Elizabeth Cady Stanton as Revealed in Her Letters, Diary, and Reminiscences*, vol. 2. New York.

Starks, J.H., Jr. (1999). "*Fides Aeneia*: The Transference of Punic Stereotypes in the *Aeneid*." *CJ* 94: 255–83.

Starr, C. (1987). "The Circulation of Literary Texts in the Roman World," *CQ* 37: 213–23.

Starr, R.J. (1997). "Aeneas as the *Flamen Dialis*? Vergil's *Aeneid* and the Servian Exegetical Tradition," *Vergilius* 43: 63–70.

Stechow, W. (1968). *Rubens and the Classical Tradition*. Martin Classical Lectures, 22. Cambridge, MA.

Stefonio, B. (1998). *Crispus: tragoedia* (1620), ed. L. Strappini and L. Trenti. Rome.

Stein, P. (1966). "The Attraction of the Civil Law in Post-Revolutionary America," *Virginia Law Review* 52: 403–34.

Steiner, G. (1990). "Homer and Virgil and Broch." Review of Harrison (1990). *London Review of Books*, July 12: 10–11.

Steiner, G. (1998). *After Babel*, 3rd ed. Oxford.

Steiner, T.R., ed. (1975). *English Translation Theory, 1650–1800*. Assen.

Stephens, S.A. (2003). *Seeing Double: Intercultural Poetics in Ptolemaic Alexandria*. Berkeley.

Stockwell, L.T. (1968). *Dublin Theatres and Theatre Customs: 1637–1820*. New York.

Stok, F. (1994). "Virgil Between the Middle Ages and the Renaissance," *IJCT* 1.2: 15–22.

Stok, F. (2004). "Servio e la geopolitica della guerra italica," in Stok and Santini, eds.: 111–62.

Stok, F. (2008). "Sulpicius Apollinaris/Carthaginiensis: un' identità problematica," in *Incontri Triestini di Filologia Classica VII – 2007–2008*, ed. L. Cristante and I. Filip. Trieste: 201–18.

Stok, F. and Santini, C., eds. (2004). *Hinc Italae gentes. Geopolitica ed etnografia dell' Italia nel commento di Servio all'Eneide*. Pisa.

Story, R. (1975). "Harvard Students, the Boston Elite, and the New England Preparatory System, 1800–1870," *History of Education Quarterly* 15: 281–98.

Strahan, A. (1753). *The First Six Books of Virgil's Aeneid. Translated into Blank Verse*. London.

Strand, M. (1990). *The Continuous Life*. New York.

Strand, M. (1999). "A Poet's Alphabet," *Literary Imagination* 1: 1–9.

Strand, M. (2001). "Some Observations on *Aeneid* Book VI," in Spence, ed.: 64–75.

Straub, J. (1967). "Teaching in the Friends' Latin School in Philadelphia in the Eighteenth Century," *Pennsylvania Magazine of History and Biography* 91: 434–56.

Strunk, W. (1930). "Vergil in Music," *Musical Quarterly* 16: 482–97.

Styron, W. (1993). *The Confessions of Nat Turner*, 2nd ed. New York.

Suerbaum, W. (1981). "Von der Vita Vergiliana über die accessus Vergiliani zum Zauberer Vergilius. Probleme – Perspektiven – Analysen," *ANRW* II.31.2: 1156–262.

Suerbaum, W. (1983). "Vergil als Ehebrecher – L. Varius Rufus als Plagiator. Anekdoten um Plotia Hieria in der Vergil-Tradition," in *Festschrift für Robert Muth zum 65. Geburtstag am 1. Januar 1981 dargebracht von Freunden und Kollegen*, ed. P. Händel and W. Meid. Innsbruck: 507–29.

Suerbaum, W. (1992). "*Aeneis picturis narrata – Aeneis versibus picta*: Semiotische Überlegung zu Vergil-Illustrationen oder Visuelles Erzählen: Buchillustrationen zu Vergils *Aeneis*," *SIFC*, ser. 3, vol. 10: 271–334.

Suerbaum, W. (2008). *Handbuch der illustrierten Vergil-Ausgaben 1502–1840.* Hildesheim, Zürich, and New York.

Suzuki, M. (1987). "'Unfitly yokt together in one teeme': Vergil and Ovid in *Faerie Queene*, III.ix," *English Literary Renaissance* 17: 72–85.

Swain, S. (2004). "Bilingualism and Biculturalism in Antonine Rome: Apuleius, Fronto, and Gellius," in *The Worlds of Aulus Gellius*, ed. L. Holford-Strevens and A. Vardi. Oxford: 3–40.

Sweeney, G. (1975). *Melville's Use of Classical Mythology.* Amsterdam.

Syed, Y. (2005). *Vergil's Aeneid and the Roman Self: Subject and Nation in Literary Discourse.* Ann Arbor.

Syme, R. (1939). *The Roman Revolution.* Oxford.

Symonds, J.A. (1872). *Miscellaneous Writings of John Conington.* London. Vol. 1: 137–97.

Syrett, H.C., ed. (1961–79). *The Papers of Alexander Hamilton.* New York.

Taminiaux, J. (2000). "Athens and Rome," in *The Cambridge Companion to Hannah Arendt*, ed. D.R. Villa. Cambridge: 165–77.

Tanner, M. (1993). *The Last Descendant of Aeneas.* New Haven.

Taplin, O. (1992). *Homeric Soundings.* Oxford.

Tarn, W.W. (1932). "Antony's Legions," *CQ* 26: 75–81.

Tarozzi, B. (1986). "Virgilio nella cultura americana," in *La fortuna di Virgilio*, ed. M. Gigante. Naples: 475–505.

Tarrant, R.J. (1997). "Poetry and Power: Virgil's Poetry in Contemporary Context," in Martindale, ed.: 169–87.

Tarrant, R.J. (2004). "The Last Book of the *Aeneid.*" *SyllClass* 15: 103–29.

Tate, A. (1977). *Collected Poems, 1919–1976.* New York.

Taylor, M.E. (1955). "Primitivism in Virgil," *AJP* 76: 261–78.

Taylor, R.J., ed. (1977–). *The Papers of John Adams.* Cambridge, MA.

Tennyson, A. (1987). *The Poems of Tennyson*, ed. C. Ricks, 2nd ed. Harlow.

Thomas, R.F. (1982). *Lands and Peoples in Roman Poetry: The Ethnographical Tradition.* Cambridge Philological Society, Suppl. 7. Cambridge.

Thomas, R.F. (1988). "Turning Back the Clock." Review of Griffin (1985). *CPh* 83: 54–69.

Thomas, R.F. (1996). "Genre Through Intertextuality: Theocritus to Virgil and Propertius," in *Theocritus: Hellenistica Groningana*, vol. 2, ed. M.A. Harder, R.F. Regtuit, and G.C. Wakker. Hellenistica Groningana, vol. 2. Groningen: 227–44 [= *Reading Virgil and His Texts: Studies in Intertextuality.* Ann Arbor, 1999: 246–66].

Thomas, R.F. (1998). "The Isolation of Turnus: *Aeneid* Book 12," in Stahl, ed.: 271–302.

Thomas, R.F. (2001). *Virgil and the Augustan Reception.* Cambridge.

Thomas, R.F. (2004–5). "Torn between Jupiter and Saturn: Ideology, Rhetoric and Culture Wars in the *Aeneid*," *CJ* 100: 121–47.

Thomas, R.F. (2006). "Virgil, Robert Lowell, and 'the Punic Word,'" *MD* 56: 214–18.

Thompson, D.M. (1997). "Criticism and the Vichy Syndrome: Charles Maurras, T.S. Eliot, and the Forms of Historical Memory," PhD Diss., University of Chicago.

Todd, R. (1999). "John Enoch Powell and Vergil, *Aeneid* 6.86–87: A Supplementary Note," *Vergilius* 45: 73–6.

Toll, K. (1991). "The *Aeneid* as an Epic of National Identity: *Italiam laeto socii clamore salutant*," *Helios* 18: 3–14.

Toll, K. (1997). "Making Roman-ness and the *Aeneid*," *ClAnt* 16: 34–56.

Tolley, K. (1996). "Science for Ladies, Classics for Gentlemen: A Comparative Analysis of Scientific Subjects in the Curricula of Boys' and Girls' Secondary Schools in the United States, 1794–1850," *History of Education Quarterly* 36: 129–53.

Tomlinson, C. (2001). "Why Dryden's Translations Matter," *Translation and Literature* 10: 3–20.

Torquemada, J. de (1943–4). *Monarquía indiana*, 3 vols. Mexico (facsimile of 1723 ed.). [First published Seville, 1615.]

Toscanella, O. (1567). *Osservationi...sopra l'opere di Virgilio*. Venice.

Toscanella, O. (1574). *Bellezze del Furioso di m. Lodovico Ariosto*. Venice.

Toynbee, J.M.C. (1971). *Death and Burial in the Roman World*. Ithaca.

Toynbee, P. (1909). *Dante in English Literature, from Chaucer to Cary*. London.

Trabant, J. (2000). "Du génie aux gènes des langues," in *Et le génie des langues?*, ed. H. Meschonnic. Saint-Denis: 79–102.

Trapp, J.B. (1986a). "The Grave of Virgil," *Journal of the Warburg and Courtauld Institutes* 47: 1–31.

Trapp, J.B. (1986b). "Virgil and the Monuments," *PVS* 18: 1–17.

Turner, F.M. (1989). "Why the Greeks and not the Romans in Victorian Britain?," in *Rediscovering Hellenism: The Hellenic Inheritance and the English Imagination*, ed. G.W. Clarke. Cambridge: 61–81.

Tylus, J. (1988). "Spenser, Virgil, and the Politics of Poetic Labour," *English Literary History* 55: 53–77.

Uhl, A. (1998). *Servius als Sprachlehrer: Zur Sprachrichtigkeit in der exegetischen Praxis des spätantiken Grammatikerunterrichts*. Göttingen.

Unrue, D. (1995). "Edgar Allan Poe: The Romantic as Classicist," *IJCT* 1: 112–19.

Urofsky, M. (1965). "Reforms and Response: The Yale Report of 1828," *Higher Education Quarterly* 5: 53–67.

Vahlen, J., ed. (1903). *Ennianae Poesis Reliquiae*. 2nd ed. Leipzig.

Valette-Cagnac, E. (1997). *La Lecture à Rome*. Paris.

van der Valk, M. (1963–4). *Researches on the Text and Scholia of the Iliad*, 2 vols. Leiden.

Van Doren, M., ed. (1929). *A Correspondence of Aaron Burr and His Daughter Theodosia*. New York.

van Eerde, K. (1970). *Wenceslaus Hollar: Delineator of his Time*. Charlottesville.

van Eerde, K. (1976). *John Ogilby and the Taste of His Times*. Folkestone.

van Puyvelde, L. (1940). *Les Esquisses de Rubens*. Basle.

Van Sickle, J. (2000). "Virgil vs. Cicero, Lucretius, Theocritus, Callimachus, Plato and Homer: Two Programmatic Plots in the First *Bucolic*," *Vergilius* 46: 21–58.

Van Thiel, H. (1992). "Zenodot, Aristarch und andere," *ZPE* 90: 1–32.

Vance, W. (1989). *America's Rome*. New Haven.

Vanotti, G. (1995). *L'altro Enea. La testimonianza di Dionigi di Alicarnasso*. Rome.

Vaughan, W. (1991). *Romantic Art*. London.

Venuti, L. (1995). *The Translator's Invisibility*. London and New York.

Venuti, L., ed. (2000). *The Translation Studies Reader*. London and New York.

Verdière, R. (1964). Review of Klossowski (1964). *Rivista di Studi Classici* 12: 354–5.

[Vergil] (1586). *L'opere di Vergilio*. Venice.

[Vergil] (1811). *The Works of Virgil: Translated into English Prose, as Near the Original as the Different Idioms of the Latin and English Languages Will Allow: with the Latin Text and Order of Construction in the Same Page; and Critical, Historical, Geographical, and Classical Notes, in English, from the Best Commentators both Ancient and Modern Beside a Very Great Number of Notes Entirely New...For the Use of Schools, as Well as of Private Gentlemen: in Two Volumes*. New York. Stanford Special Collections and University Archives.

Vian, F., ed. (1969). *Quintus Smyrnaeus: La suite d'Homère*, vol. 3, books 10–14. Paris.

Videau-Delibes, A. (1991). *Les Tristes d'Ovide et l'élégie romaine: une politique de la rupture.* Paris.

Vittori, G.L. (1767). *Institutiones Philosophicae.* Rome.

von Blanckenhagen, P.H. (1969). "Laokoon, Sperlonga und Vergil," *AA* 84: 256–75.

von Franz, M.-L. (1943). *Die aesthetischen Anschauungen der Iliasscholien (im Codex Ven. B und Townleianus).* Zurich.

Walters, T. (2007). *African American Literature and the Classicist Tradition: Black Women Writers from Wheatley to Morrison.* New York.

Warner, J.C. (2005). *The Augustinian Epic, Petrarch to Milton.* Ann Arbor.

Warren R. (2001). "The End of the *Aeneid*," in Spence, ed.: 105–17.

Warren, R. (2003). *Departure: Poems.* New York.

Waswo, R. (1997). *The Founding Legend of Western Civilization.* Hanover, NH and London.

Watkins, J. (1993). ' "Neither of idle shewes, nor of false charmes aghast": Transformations of Virgilian Ekphrasis in Chaucer and Spenser," *Journal of Medieval and Renaissance Studies* 23: 345–63.

Watkins, J. (1995). *The Specter of Dido: Spenser and Virgilian Epic.* New Haven and London.

Webb, W.S. (1937). "Vergil in Spenser's Epic Theory," *English Literary History* 4: 62–84.

Weinberg, B. (1961). *A History of Literary Criticism in the Italian Renaissance,* 2 vols. Chicago.

Weinbrot, H.D. (1978). *Augustus Caesar in "Augustan" England: The Decline of a Classical Norm.* Princeton.

Weinfeld, M. (1993). *The Promise of the Land.* Berkeley.

Weinstock, S. (1971). *Divus Julius.* Oxford.

Weitenkampf, F. (1938). *The Illustrated Book.* Cambridge.

Wellbery, D.E. (1984). *Lessing's "Laocoon": Semiotics and Aesthetics in the Age of Reason.* Cambridge.

Wender, D., ed. and trans. (1980). *Roman Poetry from the Republic to the Silver Age.* Carbondale.

West, D., trans. (1991). *Virgil, The Aeneid: A New Prose Translation.* Harmondsworth.

West, D. (1998). "The End and the Meaning: *Aeneid* 12.291–842," in Stahl, ed.: 303–18.

West, M.L., ed. and trans. (2003). *Greek Epic Fragments from the Seventh to the Fifth Centuries BC.* Cambridge, MA.

West, S. (1983). "Notes on the Text of Lycophron," *CQ* 33: 114–35.

West, S. (1984). "Lycophron Italicised," *JHS* 104: 127–51.

White, A.D. (1905). *Autobiography of Andrew Dickson White,* vol. 1. New York.

White, P. (1996). "Martial and Pre-Publication Texts," *Echos du Monde Classique/Classical Views* 40 (n.s. 15): 397–412.

Whitman, C. (1958). *Homer and the Heroic Tradition.* Cambridge, MA.

Wiesen, D. (1980). "Herodotus and the Modern Debate over Race and Slavery," *AncW* 3: 3–16.

Wigodsky, M. (1972). *Vergil and Early Latin Poetry.* Wiesbaden.

Wilding, M. (1987). *Dragon's Teeth: Literature in the English Revolution.* Oxford.

Wilhelm, R.M. and Jones, H., eds. (1992). *The Two Worlds of the Poet: New Perspectives on Vergil. Festschrift for Alexander G. McKay.* Detroit.

Willcox, W.B. et al., eds. (1978). *The Papers of Benjamin Franklin.* Vol. 21: *January 1, 1774–March 22, 1775.* New Haven.

Williams, G. (1983). *Technique and Ideas in the Aeneid.* New Haven.

Williams, G.D. (1994). *Banished Voices: Readings in Ovid's Exile Poetry.* Cambridge.

Williams, G.D. (2002). "Ovid's Exile Poetry: *Tristia, Epistulae ex Ponto* and *Ibis*," in *The Cambridge Companion to Ovid*, ed. P. Hardie. Cambridge: 233–45.

Williams, G.D. and Walker, A.D., eds. (1997). "Ovid and Exile I," "Ovid and Exile II," *Ramus* 26, issues 1 and 2.

Williams, J. (1972). *Augustus: A Novel*. New York.

Williams, M.H. (2006). *The Monk and the Book: Jerome and the Making of Christian Scholarship*. Chicago.

Williams, R.D. (1960). *P. Vergili Maronis: Aeneidos Liber Quintus*. Oxford.

Williams, R.D. (1972). *The Aeneid of Virgil, Books 1–6*. New York.

Williams, R.D. (1987). *The Aeneid*. London.

Williams, R.D. and Pattie, T.S. (1982). *Virgil: His Poetry through the Ages*. London.

Williamson, G.S. (2004). *The Longing for Myth in Germany: Religion and Aesthetic Culture from Romanticism to Nietzsche*. Chicago.

Wills, G. (1984). *Cincinnatus: George Washington and the Enlightenment*. Garden City, NY.

Wills, G. (1992). *Lincoln at Gettysburg: The Words That Remade America*. New York.

Wills, J. (1996). *Repetition in Latin Poetry: Figures of Allusion*. Oxford.

Wilson, A., trans. (2004). *Harry Potter and the Philosopher's Stone*, by J.K. Rowling. Translated into ancient Greek. London.

Wilson, D. (1981). "The American Agricola: Jefferson's Agrarianism and the Classical Tradition," *South Atlantic Quarterly* 80: 339–54.

Wilson, D. (1991). "What Jefferson and Lincoln Read," *The Atlantic* 267: 51–62.

Wilson, N.G. (1967). "A Chapter in the History of Scholia," *CQ* 61: 244–56.

Wilson, N.G. (1983). "Scoliasti e commentatori," *SCO* 33: 83–112.

Wilton, A. and Mallord Turner, R. (1990). *Painting and Poetry: Turner's "Verse Book" and his Work of 1804–1812*. London.

Wiltse, C.M. (1944–51). *John C. Calhoun*. Indianapolis.

Wiltshire, S. (1967). "Thomas Jefferson and John Adams on the Classics," *Arion* 6: 116–32.

Wiltshire, S. (1973). "Sam Houston and the *Iliad*," *Tennessee Historical Quarterly* 32: 249–54.

Wiltshire, S., ed. (1977a). *The Usefulness of Classical Learning in the Eighteenth Century*. University Park, PA.

Wiltshire, S. (1977b). "Jefferson Calhoun and the Slavery Debate: The Classics and the Two Minds of the South," *Southern Humanities Review*. The Classical Tradition in the South. A Special Issue: 33–40.

Wiltshire, S. (1987). "Aristotle in America," *Humanities* 8: 8–11.

Wiltshire, S. (1992). *Greece, Rome, and the Bill of Rights*. Norman.

Winckelmann, J.J. (1913). *Kleine Schriften zur Geschichte der Kunst des Altertums*, ed. H. Uhde-Bernays. Leipzig.

Winckelmann, J.J. (1972). *Geschichte der Kunst des Altertums*. Darmstadt.

Winckelmann, J.J. (2006). *Geschichte der Kunst des Altertums. Katalog der antiken Denkmäler*, ed. A.H. Borbein, T.W. Gaethgens, J. Irmscher, and M. Kunze, rev. M.R. Hofter, A. Rügler, A.H. Borbein et al. Mainz.

Wind, E. (1968). *Pagan Mysteries in the Renaissance*, rev. and expanded ed. New York and London.

Winn, J. (1987). *John Dryden and his World*. New Haven.

Winner, M. (1974). "Zum Nachleben des Laokoon in der Renaissance," *JBerlM* 16: 83–121.

Winterbottom, M., ed. and trans. (1974). *Seneca the Elder: Declamations*, 2 vols. Cambridge, MA.

Winterer, C. (2001). "Victorian Antigone: Classicism and Women's Education in America, 1840–1890," *American Quarterly* 53: 70–93.

Winterer, C. (2002). *The Culture of Classicism: Ancient Greece and Rome in American Intellectual Life, 1780–1910.* Baltimore.

Winterer, C. (2005a). "From Royal to Republican: The Classical Image in Early America," *Journal of American History* 91: 1264–90.

Winterer, C. (2005b). "Venus on the Sofa: Women, Neoclassicism, and the Early American Republic," *Modern Intellectual History* 2: 1–32.

Winterer, C. (2006). "Classical Oratory and Fears of Demagoguery in the Antebellum Era," in Meckler, ed.: 41–53.

Winterer, C. (2007). *The Mirror of Antiquity: American Women and the Classical Tradition, 1750–1900.* Ithaca.

Wiseman, T.P. (1974). "Legendary Genealogies in Late-Republican Rome," *G&R* 21: 153–64 [= *Roman Studies: Literary and Historical.* Liverpool and Wolfeboro, 1987: 207–18].

Wish, H. (1949). "Aristotle, Plato, and the Mason-Dixon Line," *JHI* 10: 254–66.

Wolf, R.L. (1960). "The Three Romes: The Migration of an Ideology and the Making of an Autocrat," in *Myth and Mythmaking*, ed. H.A. Murray. New York: 174–98.

Wood, R. (1775). *Essay on the Original Genius and Writings of Homer with a Comparative View of the Ancient and Present State of the Troade.* London. [Privately published in 1767 and 1769.]

Woodbridge, K. (1970). *Landscape and Antiquity: Aspects of English Culture at Stourhead.* Oxford.

Woody, T. (1929). *A History of Women's Education in the United States*, vol. 1. New York.

Wootten, W. (2000). "Rhetoric and Violence in Geoffrey Hill's *Mercian Hymns* and the Speeches of Enoch Powell," *Cambridge Quarterly* 29.1: 1–15.

Wright, L. (1943–4). "Thomas Jefferson and the Classics," *PAPHS* 87: 223–33.

Wright, L.B. (1955). *Culture on the Moving Frontier.* Bloomington.

Yeats, W.B. (1965). *The Autobiography of William Butler Yeats.* New York.

Yost, M. (1976). "Classical Studies in American Colonial Schools, 1635–1776," *CO* 54: 40–3.

Zabughin, V. (1921–3). *Vergilio nel Rinascimento italiano da Dante a Torquato Tasso.* Bologna.

Zampese, C. (1994). *Or si fa rossa or pallida la luna. La cultura classica nell'Orlando Innamorato.* Lucca.

Zanker, P. (1974). *Klassizistische Statuen. Studien zur Veränderung des Kunstgeschmacks in der römischen Kaiserzeit.* Mainz.

Zanker, P. (1988). *The Power of Images in the Age of Augustus*, trans. A. Shapiro. Ann Arbor.

Zatti, S. (2006). *The Quest for Epic: From Ariosto to Tasso.* Toronto.

Zetzel, J.E.G. (1989). "*Romane memento*: Justice and Judgment in *Aeneid* 6," *TAPhA* 119: 263–84.

Zetzel, J.E.G. (1997). "Rome and its Traditions," in Martindale, ed.: 188–203.

Zetzel, J.E.G. (2000). Review of Zwierlein (1999). *Vergilius* 46: 181–91.

Zintzen, C. (1979). *Die Laokoonepisode bei Vergil.* Mainz.

Ziolkowski, J.M. (2004). "Between Text and Music: The Reception of Vergilian Speeches in Early Medieval Manuscripts," *MD* (*Numero speciale in onore di Michael C.J. Putnam*) 52: 107–26.

Ziolkowski, J.M. and Putnam, M.C.J. (2008). *The Virgilian Tradition: The First Fifteen Hundred Years.* New Haven and London.

Ziolkowski, T. (1993). *Virgil and the Moderns.* Princeton.

Zuccari, A. and Macioce, S. (2001). *Innocenzo X Pamphilj. Arte e Potere a Rome nell'Età Barocca*. Rome.

Zwicker, S.N. (1984). *Politics and Language in Dryden's Poetry: The Arts of Disguise*. Princeton.

Zwicker, S.N., ed. (1998). *The Cambridge Companion to English Literature, 1650–1740*. Cambridge.

Zwierlein, O. (1999). *Die Ovid- und Vergil-Revision in tiberischer Zeit*. Vol. 1: *Prolegomena*. Berlin and New York.

Index

Note: page numbers in italics denote illustrations

Riofrío, B.C. de   221, 223
Ripheus   150–1
Risorgimento   447
ritual   52–3, 56–8, 62–5
ritual meal   59–60
Rivista di Studi Classici   459
Roberts, M.D.M.   382
Robertson, D.   356
Robeson, P.   379, 384
Robinson, B.   379
Robinson, P.   352
Rojas, F. de: *Celestina*   239
Roland   141–4
Rollo, D.   146
Roma/amor   73
Roman College   203, 265, 451
Roman empire   67
romance
    epic poetry   158, 160, 164, 180–1
    models   177
    see also Romantics
Romans
    Augustine on   130–1
    and barbarians   160
    and Carthaginians   50, 66
    descended from Aeneas   40
    and Greeks   400
    identity   67, 71, 74, 78–9
    imperial expansion   409
    Jupiter   154–5
    and Trojans   66
    violence   404
    see also Rome
Romantics
    cultural relativism   424
    English/French painting   7
    Germany   427
    Homer/Vergil   428
    nationalism   429
    Nature   311
    Russia   452
    on Vergil   311–12, 436
Rome
    American Constitution   391
    book ownership/borrowing   15
    and Carthage   74, 407–8
    civil war   391
    cultural importance   258
    and Cybele, compared   75
    Dante   154–7
    and England, compared   191
    and Europe   391, 401

founding of   46–8, 416
and Moscow   451
public library   15
republicanism   413
Vulcan's shield   24
see also Romans
Romizi, A.   172
Romulus   44–7, 60, 70, 397
Romulus Augustulus   475–6
Roncevaux   143, 145
Ronnick, M.V.   7, 8, 377–8
Rosales, B.   222–4
Rosenberg, J.   277, 281
Rouse, W.H.D.   21
Rousseau, J.-J.   424
Rowe, G.C.   381
Rowland, I.   6–7, 269
Rowling, J.K.   435
Rubens, P.P.   7
    and Dryden   285–7
    marvelous   278
    *La Métamorphose d'Ovide
        figurée*   283
    Neptune   283
    Neptune Calming the Tempest   270,
        276–83, Plate 2
    Ovid as influence   282–5
    Thirty Years' War   261
    versions   280–1
Ruden, S.   375
Rufo, J.: *Austriada*   224
rumor   348
Rush, B.   358
Ruskin, J.   313
Russia
    Europeanized   451
    formalism   452, 455–7
    Romanticism   452
    socialist realism   456
    Symbolism   452
Russian Orthodox Church   451
Russo, J.   103
Rusticatio Mexicana (Landívar)   231–3
Rutulians   19, 34, 62–3, 70

Sacré, D.   215
sacrifice
    burial rites   62
    failed   61
    of humans   62–3, 327
    Iphigenia   327
    Laocoon   326

Vergil
  action-pictures 277
  allegory 421–3
  Appendix Vergiliana: *Ciris* 174;
    Culex 115, 174
  Augustan age 274–6
  biography: confiscation of land 118,
    120, 263–4; death of 97, 99, 101,
    111; exile 80–1; family 23, 113;
    modesty 115, 119; proposed
    retirement to Greece 97–9;
    self-consciousness 465;
    sexual preferences 108, 113,
    115, 119
  characters: *see individual names*
  as classic 429–30, 447
  criticism of: *cacozelia* 439
  cultural 425, 430
  and Dante 147–9, 318, 446–7
  epic poetry 437
  as historian-poet 312
  and Homer, compared 3, 114, 429,
    433n6, 441, 444–6
  Jesuits 203, 208–10, 213, 215
  library 3, 14, 18, 27–8
  Manuscripts: Codex Romanus 247;
    Codex Vaticanus 247
  prodigies 119
  Purgatory 153
  quoted 358
  rhetoric 126–7
  style 438; *cacozelia* 439; diction:
    funereus 439–40; hypallage 83;
    saevus 440; *superbus* 462; as
    untranslatable 441–2
  tomb of 311, 373
  will of 98, 108, 110–11, 117–18
  as wizard 345–6
  working methods 14, 25
  works *see individual entries*
  see also detractors
vernacular poetry 6, 158, 206
Vestals 350
Vesuvius, erupting 16
Vicars, J. 192–3
Vida, M.G.
  Christiad 204
  De arte poetica 203–4, 423
Viermännerkommentar 28
Villerías y Roelas, J.A. de 218, 223–4
  Aeneid as influence 224–8

De dialectis linguae Graecae 224
  Guadalupe 224–8, 231
  as influence 231
  Osorio Romero on 233
  Tonantzin 229
violence
  Aeneid 8, 57, 391–2, 394–5
  divine 396–400, 402
  Greek/Jewish 392
  Juno 397, 406, 408
  Jupiter 393
  law-destroying 398
  law-making/law-preserving 393–4
  mythical 395–7, 400, 402
  rape 405
  revolutionary 392, 401–3
  rhetoric 407
  Romans 404
  sanctioned/unsanctioned 392–3
  Spenser 174
  translation 460
  tyranny 404–5
Vipranius, M. 439, 445
Vipsanius Agrippa, M. 108, 114
Virgile en France (Le Plat) 236
Virgil's Tomb (Wright) 311
Visigoths 258
visual arts 6–7
visual culture 310
Vita Bernensis I 119
Vitruvius Pollio, Marcus 16
Vittori, G.L. 215
*Vocabolario degli Accademici della
  Crusca* 159
vocabulary 453–4, 461–2
Voltaire: *Henriade* 451
Voss, J.H. 426
Vulcan 24, 38, 66, 262–3, 405

Waddel, M. 356
Walters, T. 377
War of 1812 358
Warren, R. 9
  "Bonfires" 476–7
  Departure 476
  "The End of the *Aeneid*" 476
  "Poetry Reading" 476–7
  "Turnus" 477
Waterhouse, B. 368
Webster, D. 374
weeping: *see lacrimae rerum*

Printed and bound by CPI Group (UK) Ltd, Croydon, CR0 4YY